THE COLLECTED
WRITINGS OF
W.E.VINE

VOLUME 1

THE COLLECTED
WRITINGS OF
W.E.VINE

VOLUME 1

with Introduction by

F. F. BRUCE

THOMAS NELSON PUBLISHERS
Nashville ▪ Atlanta ▪ London ▪ Vancouver

Published in Nashville, Tennessee, by Thomas Nelson, Inc. and distributed in Canada by Nelson/ Word, Inc.

Library of Congress Cataloging-in-Publication Data

Vine, W. E. (William Edwy), 1873–1949.
  [Selections. 1996]
  Collected writings of W. E. Vine.
    p. cm.
  ISBN 0-7852-1159-4 (5-volume set)
      0-7852-1175-6 (Vol. 1)
  1. Bible—Criticism, Interpretation, etc. 2. Theology.
  I. Title.
BS511.2.V55 1996
220.6—dc20

96–8957
CIP

Printed in the United States of America.
1 2 3 4 5 — 00 99 98 97 96

"Qualified in Many Fields, Narrow in None"

Undoubtedly William Edwy Vine was qualified in many fields. As well as being a theologian and a man of outstanding academic intellect, he had a heart for all humanity that made him a master of communication.

Born in 1873, at the time when C. H. Spurgeon, D. L. Moody and F. B. Meyer were enjoying popularity on both sides of the Atlantic, Vine was brought up in a boarding school owned by and governed by his father as its headmaster. This factor was a major contribution to his interest in teaching. At the age of 17 he was a teacher at his father's school while attending the University College of Wales in preparation for his eventual London University degree, an M.A. in classics.

At the age of twenty-six he spent an Easter vacation at the home of a godly couple, Mr. and Mrs. Baxendale, where he met their daughter Phoebe; a few years later, they married. It was a marriage made in Heaven. They had five children: Helen, Christine, Edward (O.B.E.), Winifred, and Jeanette. During the time of their engagement, Vine's reputation as a clear Bible expositor was growing. It was not long before he accepted the joint headmastership of the school with his father. In 1904, after his father died, his brother Theodore then became joint headmaster with him.

It was during this time, in conjunction with Mr. C. F. Hogg, that he produced three classic works which are contained in this collection: Commentaries on 1 and 2 Thessalonians, followed by Galatians. These master works display the full scope of Vine's scholarship.

While Vine was teaching in the school, preparing for his M.A. and writing in-depth commentaries, he also developed a lifetime habit of teaching classes in New Testament Greek grammar. This laid the foundation for his all-time classic work, *An Expository Dictionary of New Testament Words,* and later, *An Expository Dictionary of Old Testament Words.* His Dictionaries are classics—copies are in excess of three million worldwide. They are available today in the best-selling *Vine's Complete Expository Dictionary of Old and New Testament Words* (published in a separate volume by Thomas Nelson Publishers)—proof that his scholarship and clarity of expression is as relevant as when first published.

"One who, in his less humble moments fancies himself to be something of a specialist in this field, must bear witness that the reading of the greater part of the *Expository Dictionary* in typescript and in proof before publication was for him a real education in New Testament usage."

Professor F. F. Bruce

A Bridge Builder between Missionaries Overseas and Local Churches at Home

When Vine was in his early thirties he felt God calling him to accept an invitation to share in the responsibility of a missionary work called "Echoes of Service," a project that is still very strong today. This is a missionary work which, at the time of Vine's appointment, formed a major link between 600 missionaries overseas and local autonomous independent churches known by many as "The Open Brethren." He continued in this work for forty years. At the time of his death the magazine's circulation had nearly doubled.

This responsibility inevitably meant tens of thousands of letters between local churches and the missionaries overseas. Many of the letters—beside being of a practical nature—involved answering theological questions. Because of the vastness of the work, the monthly magazine called "Echoes of Service" was used as one of the many means of linking overseas missionaries with the Christians and churches at home. This magazine gave news that would stimulate prayer and support for the missionaries as well as Bible teachings, which Vine contributed on a regular basis. Beside "Echoes of Service," he also wrote regular articles for other magazines. Many of his longer written works grew out of these articles, including his famous *Dictionaries*.

Besides the letter writing and the magazines, Vine also did much traveling, especially to annual missionary conferences held in key cities. He was well-suited to public teaching and stimulating missionary enterprises, as you can see in his practical, yet scriptural approach to missionary work in parts of this collection.

"For the theology of world-evangelization as for its practical consequences, 'The Divine Plan of Missions' will repay serious consideration."

Professor F. F. Bruce

A Bridge Builder between Theologians and Pastors and Bible Teachers

While Spurgeon, Moody, and Meyer were devotional preachers and teachers who appealed to the heart and conscience, the Bible was under attack by a new wave of critics influenced by the growth of scientific analysis. There were qualified theologians who were able to combat this criticism; however, many did not have Vine's "common touch." What was needed was a theologian who understood all the current academic issues but could communicate in a popular way. Vine was such a man.

As you read through this collection of his writings, you will become aware, time and time again, not only of the richness of his scholarship, but also of his ability to convey it without wasting words. When we remember that early this century many writers were

known for the amount of words they used and the weight of the books they produced, to have a writer who could be simple, direct, theologically sound, and yet practical, was most welcome.

"It is not every theologian who writes on Bible themes who answers questions with the accuracy, precision, and insight of Mr. Vine."

P. O. Ruoff

A Bridge Builder between Traditional Bible Translations and New Ones

Professor F. F. Bruce's article (included in this collection) introducing Vine as a theologian is worth reading carefully. It underscores that Vine was as familiar with the Greek manuscripts that formed the basis of the King James/Authorized Version (and the New King James Version) as he was with the manuscripts that made up the American Revised Version/Revised Version (and the New American Revised Version as well as the New International Version). This means that no matter which translation you use for personal study, you will find Vine's scholarship applicable.

"In short, Mr. Vine shows how great a service can be rendered to the Church by well-balanced, all-around scholarship when it is combined, as here, with reverent submission to the Word of God and spiritual insight into its meaning."

Professor F. F. Bruce

A Bridge Builder between this Century and the Next Millennium

To own this extensive library is to have tools that can only bring practical and spiritual insight both for new and mature Christians.

Expository Commentaries

Vine applies a "microscopic" approach to expository teaching—a word approach that takes into consideration every reference to that word in the Bible as well as its use in contemporary and classic Greek.

The value of these three books alone make this collection a must. They stand up with other great commentaries, such as J. Armitage Robinson on Ephesians, Lightfoot on Colossians, and Westcott on John's Gospel and Hebrews, to name but a few.

> "For the student of the English New Testament these three commentaries will long remains standard works."
> Professor F. F. Bruce

Vine's verse-by-verse exposition reveals a depth of understanding that commentaries many times their size fail to give. He explains the meaning of the key words in each verse and links them with the complete passage.

> "Here we have some of the most distinctive features of Mr. Vine's exegesis, which stamp him as a truly biblical theologian."
> Professor F. F. Bruce

Bible Doctrine

Few will offer such insight into Bible doctrines as W. E. Vine. Take his "Divine Inspiration of Scripture" and you will find your faith strengthened. "Christ's Eternal Sonship" will leave you in no doubt of the biblical teaching concerning the deity of Christ. Look at "The Twelve Mysteries of Scripture" and you will find numerous passages of God's Word being illuminated. Over and over, you will be surprised at the quality of writing as well as Vine's insight into divine truth.

> "His discussion of the subject was not confined to the purely intellectual plane, but revealed the author's insight into the true center of biblical authority and sufficiency."
> Professor F. F. Bruce

Analytical Outlines

Throughout the collection you will be pleased with the high standard of the analytical

outlines that Vine provides. These are skeletons to which you can add your own Bible studies, or you can use them to form the base for group studies or sermons.

Church, Missionary, and Practical Topics

The experience and challenging needs of Vine's work with "Echoes of Service" are reflected in the important practical books and articles that are part of this collection. Any person desiring to be, or already engaged in full-time Christian work, will be edified and challenged by Vine's practical writings.

> "He emphasized, too, that the New Testament has much to say about the methods as well as the aims of missionary work, and that its principles can be disregarded only to our loss."
> Professor F. F. Bruce

Prophetic Exposition

While many will agree with Vine's insight into the value and meaning of prophecy, this is a subject of varied interpretations. However, even if your own beliefs are different from Vine's, you will appreciate his openness to God's truth and his sense of excitement in seeing God's prophetic will revealed. He is not an extremist, but he conveys a genuine love for the prophetic teaching of Scripture.

> "He made many contributions to theological literature, over a long period of years; but theology for him was always exegetical theology, based on the application of grammar to the biblical text."
> Professor F. F. Bruce

A Bridge Builder between Mind and Heart

Concerning the man himself, I have come to know more of him through two of his daughters as well as from the local Christian church that he and his wife attended for so many years. Many of the members still remember the Vines, known for their hospitality, humor,

x   •   PUBLISHER'S PREFACE

hard work, and commitment to the Word of God and missionary enterprise. The writings of W. E. Vine come from the finest intellect in combination with a devoted missionary heart, truly a rare combination.

"The Scriptures' chief function is to bear witness of Christ, and the chief end of their study and exegesis is to increase our inward knowledge of Him, under the illumination of the Spirit of God. Nor would Mr. Vine, in all his study and writing, be content with any lower aim than this, for himself and his readers alike."

Professor F. F. Bruce

Robert Hicks

Bath, England
1996

CONTENTS

THE BIBLE
The Scriptures and How to Use Them

The Divine Inspiration of the Bible

COMMENTARY ON SELECTED BIBLE BOOKS
Isaiah: Prophecies, Promises, Warnings

The Leading Themes of the Gospel of John

John: His Record of Christ

Romans

W. E. Vine: The Theologian

By F. F. Bruce

1. Grammar and Lexicography

"What is theology," asked Martin Luther, "but grammar applied to the text?" If we bear that in mind, we shall not be surprised to find works on grammar and lexicography receiving pride of place in a review of theological writings. Luther's rhetorical question may be somewhat characteristically rough-and-ready; but what he meant is plain and true. True theology rests upon sound exegesis of the text of Scripture, and sound exegesis demands accurate grammatical study. To be sure, grammar alone will not make a man a theologian *(pectus facit theologum*)*; but theology without grammar is like a house built on sand. Since this is so, there can be no question of W. E. Vine's right to be enrolled among the theologians of our day. He made many contributions to theological literature, over a long period of years; but theology for him was always exegetical theology, based on the application of grammar to the Biblical text. His work was acclaimed by many competent judges outside the ecclesiastical circles in which he was best known, and it deserves to be more widely known than it is.

Mr. Vine was a well-equipped student in the ancient classics—the subject in which he received the degrees of B.A. with honors and subsequently M.A. from the University of London. His profession in earlier days was that of a schoolmaster—a profession in which habits of grammatical, textual and historical accuracy are specially fostered. And when he brought his classical equipment and his accurate habits of mind to bear upon the study of the Bible, the result was a long list of works to which many readers (the present writer among them) gladly acknowledge their indebtedness.

His desire to introduce others to some at least of the advantages which a competent acquaintance with New Testament Greek confers upon the student of the apostolic writings found practical expression in his *New Testament Greek Grammar: A Course of Self-help*. This little handbook gathered together a series of magazine articles which had served as a sort of correspondence school in elementary New Testament Greek. There is no subject which more devastatingly illustrates Pope's words that "a little learning is a dangerous thing"; but under Mr. Vine's guidance the novice in New Testament Greek was not encouraged to fancy that he knew more than he actually did. Soon after the book appeared, it was noticed by *The Expository Times* (May 1931) in these terms:

> An admirable introduction to the study of New Testament Greek . . . The course of lessons is well conceived and the directions are expressed in simple language. It is elementary but quite sufficient, and any intelligent person wishing to read the original with understanding could master the subject under this competent guide. There must be many Bible readers who would welcome such a book as this, and it can be unreservedly commended.

Two or three years ago a new and revised edition was produced by the same publishers (Pickering and Inglis), with an appreciative foreword by Professor Francis Davidson. The new edition has the advantage over the earlier one that the Greek words are provided with accents and therefore do not look so forlorn and unclothed as unaccented Greek words look in the eyes of some readers who care about such things!

But by far the greatest boon that Mr. Vine conferred upon the New Testament student

---

*"It is the heart that makes the theologian."

who wishes to ascertain as far as possible the sense of the original writings was his *magnum opus,* published by Oliphants in four volumes between 1939 and 1941, *An Expository Dictionary of New Testament Words.* This great work contained the quintessence of almost a lifetime's study of the language and text of the New Testament; and it is not too much to say that it goes far toward doing for the nonspecialist what is being done for the specialist by Kittel's monumental and yet unfinished *Theologisches Wörterbuch zum Neuen Testament.* Nor is it only the nonspecialist who would profit by the use of the *Expository Dictionary.* One who, in his less humble moments, fancies himself to be something of a specialist in this field, must bear witness that the reading of the greater part of the *Expository Dictionary* in typescript and in proof before publication was for him a real education in New Testament usage. The present writer's appreciation has already been expressed in detail in forewords to the last three volumes of the work, but once again the objective testimony of *The Expository Times* may be adduced. That periodical greeted Vol. I as follows in May 1939:

> It is obvious that much hard work has been expended, and the fruit is worthy. Mr. Vine's plan is to take a word occurring in the A.V. or R.V., indicate what is the Greek word so translated, and what a variety of Greek words may be involved, and give a careful explanation. The work may, therefore, be described as fundamentally an analytical concordance, but it is far more than that. For the class of nonacademic students of Scripture specially in view the work will be of great value; and even for those who can read the New Testament in the original its utility will not be small.

The following volumes were welcomed as fulfilling the promise of the first. Thus we read concerning Vol. II in the February 1940 issue of the same periodical:

> Mr. Vine is working well to scale, and this instalment bears out all that was said in our columns regarding its predecessor. Among the most important words here treated come "elect," "faith," "godliness," and "justification," and such are

critical tests. Mr. Vine's treatment is clear and truly illuminating, and strengthens our conviction that the work when completed will be a valuable possession for all who without a university standard of education have to teach the Scriptures.

In September 1940, it is noted that Vol. III "maintains the high standard of its predecessors"; and the same opinion is repeated when Vol. IV is welcomed in September 1941:

> The volume is worthy to rank with its predecessors for painstaking scholarship. The volume contains in addition "Addenda and Corrigenda" and a very full index. We are glad that the exigencies of our time did not prevent the completion of a remarkable work, which, as we have said before as each volume came under review, is fitted to be of great value to all students of the New Testament whether they have a knowledge of Greek or not.

In fact, the work is so indispensable a handbook to the study of the New Testament that many of us who have learned to use it regularly wonder how we ever got on without it. Mr. Vine revealed in it that he was not only a master of classical Greek, but also well acquainted with the more recent discoveries in nonliterary Hellenistic and general New Testament archaeology made accessible by such writers as Deissmann, Ramsay, Moulton and Milligan. Many of the entries in the *Dictionary* also reveal close study of Septuagint usage. But he knew that New Testament Greek is not completely explicable in terms of the Hellenistic vernacular or the translation-idiom of the Septuagint; and much of his treatment is more in line with that of such earlier masters as Lightfoot and Westcott. An example of this is his refusal to see no distinction between the two Greek verbs for "love" in John 21:15–17 *(agapao* and *phileo).*

In this above all his works, in short, Mr. Vine shows how great a service can be rendered to the Church by well-balanced, allround scholarship when it is combined, as here, with reverent submission to the Word of God and spiritual insight into its meaning.

2. Exegesis

As a classical scholar Mr. Vine's special competence was in the New Testament rather than in the Old. But the Semitic languages were no *terra incognita* for him; his copy of Mrs. A. S. Lewis's *Old Syriac Gospels*, which he presented to the present writer, bears traces of his study of that language; and he remarked a few years ago that he read his Hebrew Bible last thing at night, because he found that it helped him to sleep! In 1946 he made his principal contribution to Old Testament exegesis, a volume entitled *Isaiah: Prophecies, Promises, Warnings*. Here he did not go deeply into critical questions, although he indicated his belief in the unity of authorship of the book of Isaiah and listed sixteen features common to its earlier and later parts. His interpretation of the prophecies has a marked futurist element; for example, the tenth chapter of Isaiah refers not only to the Assyrian monarch reigning at the time but also "relates to the future time of 'the Day of the Lord.'" But the most valuable feature of the exposition is the way in which, at the end of each section, its moral and spiritual lessons are summed up and applied in a practical way to the conditions of the people of God today.

In the New Testament field, however, Mr. Vine was able to make the fullest use of his scholarly equipment. In a list of his contributions to New Testament exegesis it is easy to find omissions, because these contributions were so numerous. They include studies in the Fourth Gospel (an earlier one, *Leading Themes in the Gospel of John,* and a more recent one, *John: his Record of Christ*), a commentary on Romans (originally published in the early thirties in serial form by *The Bible Student* of Bangalore, India, and later—in 1947—by Oliphants), a commentary on 1 John, *Outlines of the Epistle of James,* and a work on *The Two Epistles of Timothy.* At his death he left in publishable form commentaries on Colossians and 1 Corinthians, and was contributing a similar commentary on Hebrews to *The Bible Student,* Bangalore, a new edition of his commentary on 1 John to *The Bible Expositor,* New Zealand, and notes on 1 Timothy to *Precious Seed.* It is to be hoped that all of these will yet appear in volume form for the profit of a wider circle of readers.

Mr. Vine's usual procedure in composing these commentaries was to give an introductory analysis of the complete book, then to print the text of the Revised Version clause by clause or phrase by phrase and add his notes on it, paying special attention to the words and their usage, and expounding more fully passages of theological significance. Among English versions he gave his exclusive preference to the Revised Version, which remains to this day the best translation for the accurate student of the English Bible. Mere quotation from his commentaries will give only a partial idea of his expository method; here, however, is his note on 1 John 2:2.

and He is the propitiation for our sins:— The pronoun "He" bears emphasis and we might render by "He Himself." The word *hilasmos* is used here and in 4:10 alone in the New Testament. It signifies expiation. In Numbers 5:8 the LXX has "the ram of the propitiation," and in Psalm 130:4, "With Thee is the propitiation" (*hilasmos,* in each place). It denotes the ground upon which God shows mercy to the guilty. Christ Himself, and He alone, is this, through His Death, in the shedding of His blood in sacrifice. Two things are thereby indicated: (1) the finished work of the Cross, (2) the value of the Living Person.

Not only was He the propitiator by offering Himself, He is in His own Person the propitiation. This is connected very closely with what has preceded. That He is the propitiation is what gives perfect effect to His advocacy, and thus the statement presents the abiding results of His atoning sacrifice for our sins. Cf. Heb. 2:17, R.V., "to make propitiation." Such phrases as "propitiating God" and "reconciling God" are foreign to the New Testament. God shows mercy through Christ, and man is the one to be reconciled, Romans 5:10; 2 Corinthians 5:18.

and not for ours only, but also for the whole world.—The little connecting word in the original, rendered "and," does not serve to add a new idea, so much as to counteract an erroneous teaching as to the application of the propitiation. The provision made by the sacrifice of Christ extends to the whole world, yet the actual effect is not universal. The whole world lies within the scope of the propitiation, no one being necessarily excluded from its benefits. The only exclusion is on the part of those who will not avail themselves of it. For the universality of the provision cf. 4:14, and John 1:20; 3:16. Nothing is served by the italicized addition in the A.V., "the sins of."

Here we have some of the most distinctive features of Mr. Vine's exegesis, which stamp him as a truly biblical theologian. In his treatment of *hilasmos* ("propitiation") and its cognates we see his wise refusal to understand the Greek words simply in the light of pagan classical usage (to which, indeed we owe the common idea of a sullen Deity who will be won over only by appeasement), but rather in the sense which they had acquired in the Septuagint as equivalents of the Hebrew terms in which God reveals Himself as taking the initiative in making His grace available for sinners. This interpretation of the terms has had wide currency since Professor C. H. Dodd published his commentary on Romans, but some of us had learned it from Mr. Vine before we sat at Professor Dodd's feet.

The two outstanding commentaries in which Mr. Vine had a hand, however, were those on Thessalonians (1914) and Galatians (1922) which he produced in collaboration with the late Mr. C. F. Hogg. These two teachers made an ideal combination. They were basically agreed in their interpretation of the great biblical doctrines, and when Mr. Hogg's theological penetration and command of felicitous and forceful English were united with Mr. Vine's special gifts, the result was hard to match, let alone to surpass. For the student of the English New Testament these two commentaries will long remain standard works.

3. Eschatology

Another literary enterprise in which Mr. Hogg collaborated with Mr. Vine was their volume on the Second Advent of Christ entitled *Touching the Coming of the Lord* (Oliphants, 1919). In it they showed their adhesion to that form of premillenarian interpretation which posits an interval between the resurrection-rapture of the Church (1 Thess. 4:16 f.; 1 Cor. 15:51 ff.) and the return of Christ to earth "with power and great glory" (Matt. 24:30),

and places in this interval the great tribulation of the end time. Mr. Vine had stated this thesis in an earlier work, *The Rapture and the Great Tribulation*. But their statement of the thesis deviated in several important respects from its usual statement, and these deviations were for the most part the result of better exegesis. For example, Mr. Vine was too good a Greek grammarian to suppose that "the blessed hope" of Titus 2:13 could be anything other than the "appearing of the glory of our great God and Savior Jesus Christ"—the two expressions being closely linked together under the regimen of a single definite article. Nor did they fall into the error of supposing that the Gospel to be proclaimed in that interval is different in essence from the Gospel as we know it. "The Gospel then, as now, will have for its center the once slain, now living, Lamb, and it will be made effective by the Holy Spirit, among both Jews and Gentiles" (*Touching the Coming of the Lord*). And mark the words "by the Holy Spirit," for the writers refused to identify the restraining power of 2 Thessalonians 2:6 f. with the Holy Spirit, interpreting it rather (as in their commentary on Thessalonians) of Gentile dominion—certainly an exegetically superior interpretation. But perhaps the most distinctive feature of *Touching the Coming* was their treatment of the word *parousia*. They insisted on the primary sense of "presence" and understood the word in its eschatological use to mean the presence of Christ with His raptured Church in the interval preceding His manifestation in glory. This manifestation—the *epiphany* of His *parousia,* as it is called in 2 Thessalonians 2:8—marked the end of the *parousia*. The *parousia* period they further identified with "the day of Christ" (Phil. 1:10; 2:16), "the day of Jesus Christ" (Phil. 1:6), "the day of the Lord Jesus" (1 Cor. 5:5; 2 Cor. 1:14), and "the day of our Lord Jesus Christ" (1 Cor. 1:8); but not with "the day of the Lord," which in their view was to begin where the *parousia* ended, at the manifestation of Christ in glory.

It may be questioned whether this interpretation of *parousia* does adequate justice to the sense which the word has in Hellenistic Greek. The writers did, indeed, appeal in support of their view to Cremer's lexicon; but Cremer wrote a good while before the study of vernacular papyri revolutionized our knowledge of the common Hellenistic speech. An amusing sequel to their appeal to Cremer materialized in 1937, when the Rev. Alexander Reese published his critique of Darbyist eschatology entitled *The Approaching Advent of Christ* (Marshall, Morgan and Scott Ltd.). Mr. Reese was also a premillenarian, but he represented the school which makes the rapture of the Church and the manifestation of Christ in glory practically simultaneous. In reference to the treatment of *parousia* in *Touching the Coming,* he accused the two authors of reading their Cremer "on the skew" and completely misunderstanding his account of the word. "When teachers misread the Lexicon," he added, "how can we trust their reading of the N.T., which it explains?" In the author's reply to Mr. Reese—*The Church and the Tribulation,* to which Mr. Hogg and Mr. Vine separately contributed a section apiece Mr. Hogg suggests that the reader can safely be left to judge whether Mr. Vine "is incompetent to read a lexicon," and justifies the turning of Mr. Reese's question back upon himself. But, as one might suspect, the real fault in this small matter lies with Cremer, whose style is not free from obscurity and ambiguity. When two intelligent students understand a writer in quite contrary senses, the fault is likely to be the writer's, and it is certainly so in this case.

But the main defect of Mr. Reese's criticism of Hogg and Vine lay in his lumping them together with the Darbyist school. As independent students and interpreters of Scripture, they cannot properly be classed as belonging to this or any other particular school. If in one distinctive feature they came to the same conclusion as Darby and his disciples, they disagreed with them in many other matters which are equally distinctive of the Darbyist school, and they could by no means be described as conventional dispensationalists.

One further remark in *Touching the Coming* has been thought by many readers to merit fuller development. In the chapter on "The Judgment Seat of Christ," Colossians 3:25 is quoted, and the following comment made on the words, "shall receive again the wrong that he hath done" (R.V. margin):

It may be difficult for us to conceive how God will fulfill this word to those who are already in bodies of glory, partakers of the joy of the redeemed in salvation consummated in spirit, soul and body. Yet we may be assured that the operation of this law is not to be suspended even in their case. He that "knoweth how to deliver the godly out of temptation, and to keep the unrighteous under punishment unto the day of judgment" (2 Pet. 2:9), knows also how to direct and to use the working of His law of sowing and reaping in the case of His children also. The attempt to alleviate the text of some of its weight by suggesting that the law operates only in this life, fails, for there is nothing in the text or context to lead the reader to think other than that while the sowing is here, the reaping is hereafter.

One line of interpretation which did *not* appeal to them in this connection was that which envisages the rapture of the Church as partial and the first resurrection as selective, so that unworthy Christians may "receive again the wrong" that they have done by exclusion from the millennial blessedness and by consignment for that period to the "outer darkness." This view was specially propounded by G. H. Pember, who on one occasion, as Mr. Vine mentioned in a letter some years ago, "wanted to encourage me to advocate the views he had put forth, but I could not do so, and feel that they are contrary to Scripture."

Another contribution by Mr. Vine to Biblical eschatology was *The Roman Empire in the Light of Prophecy,* a popular work which appeared with slightly varying titles in several editions (the latest is dated 1936). Here Mr. Vine stated the futurist interpretation of the fourth kingdom of the book of Daniel which identifies that kingdom with the Roman Empire and looks for its yet future revival within roughly the same frontiers as it had in the first century A.D. After an outline of the rise of the Roman Empire and its decline and fall in west and east, the book goes on to give an exposition of the relevant passages in Daniel and Revelation from which the future revival of that Empire is deduced, and considers what features in world affairs in the present century do in fact point to such a development. This was written before the revolutionary events of the Second World War and its aftermath. Many of these events—notably the recent emergence of the state of Israel (the first independent Jewish state since 63 B.C.)—will necessitate the revision of a good deal of futurist literature.

An interesting sequel to the publication of this book may be stated in Mr. Vine's own words (quoted from a letter):

> As to my book *The Roman Empire*, not long after this was published I had a letter from a Mr. N . . . , evidently an earnest believer, whom however I have not known personally, asking if I had a book on the subject. He said he was personally acquainted with Signor Mussolini and had often had conversations with him. I replied saying that I was sending him (Mr. N . . .) a copy of my book. This he acknowledged and asked if he might show it to Mussolini and if I had any objection to its being translated into Italian. I told him that he might feel perfectly free to make whatever use of it he liked. I understand that he had some conversation with Signor Mussolini on the subject, and that the latter was interested to hear that the Bible foreshadowed what he himself has at heart as to the resuscitation of the Roman Empire.

Alas for Mussolini's imperial ambitions! It was in the year in which this letter was written (1940) that he took the plunge which involved himself and his regime in ruin. And alas for those theorists who (less disciplined in mind than Mr. Vine) envisaged Mussolini as a subject of Biblical prophecy—except insofar as he, in common with many another of the same character, exemplifies the truth of the prediction made concerning another dictator: "Yet he shall come to his end, and none shall help him!"

4. Church Doctrine and Practice

Another branch of biblical theology to which Mr. Vine paid special attention was the doctrine of the Church. Here, as elsewhere, his theology was based on exegesis. "The only way to attain unto the knowledge of the true notion of the Church," as Bishop Pearson wrote nearly three hundred years ago in his *Exposition of the Creed*, "is to search into the

New Testament, and from the places there which mention it, to conclude what is the nature of it." This was Mr. Vine's procedure. And his searching of the New Testament usage of the word *ekklesia* led him to the conclusion that in its distinctively Christian sense it is used with two applications:

> (a) to the whole company of the redeemed throughout the present era, the company of which Christ said, "I will build My Church," Matthew 16:18, and which is further described as "the Church which is His body," Ephesians 1:22; 5:23; (b) in the singular number (e.g. Matt. 18:17, R.V. marg., "congregation"), to a company consisting of believers, with reference to the place in which they are accustomed to meet together, and in the plural, with reference to churches in a district.*

That is to say, the word as used in the New Testament with a Christian connotation refers either to the whole company of God's elect throughout the Christian age, or to any local congregation of Christians. There are, of course, other views on the matter, and Mr. Vine was aware of these and readily produced his reasons for dissenting from them. As for his conception of the Church Universal, there are many who would broaden his definition to embrace the whole company of God's elect not of the present age only but of every age—who would trace the history of the Church Universal back to Abraham, if not indeed back to Abel. What happened in New Testament days, of course, marked a new beginning; but the new beginning was not divorced from what went before. The believers on the first Christian pentecost were not only the nucleus of the people of God of New Testament times; they were also the remnant of the people of God of Old Testament times. And there is significance in the fact that the word *ekklesia*, which was so quickly used to denote the people of God in New Testament times, was taken over from the Septuagint, where it is used to denote the people of God in Old Testament times, both in the universal and in the local sense.

---

*Expository Dictionary, vol. I.

But Mr. Vine was specially emphatic in denying that the New Testament countenances the common use of the term Church to denote the aggregate of Christians on earth at any particular time.

> The view that the term "the Church" is also used to comprise all the saints in the world at any given time is not borne out by the teaching of Christ and His apostles. Such believers could not be spoken of as either "a body" or "the body" of Christ. At the inception of the present period only a small fraction of the Church, the Body of Christ, was actually in existence; since then those who have fallen asleep do not cease to form part of the complete corporate company. The use of the phrase "the Church on earth" is a contravention of the teaching of Scripture on this subject.*

While most of the New Testament occurrences of *ekklesia* are definitely assignable to one or other of the two senses indicated above, there are a few which make one pause; and it may be as difficult to assert dogmatically that these do not denote "the Church on earth" as it would be to assert that they do.

But these questions are largely theoretical. The practical implications of the New Testament doctrine of the Church emerge in relation to the local congregation—"the Church Universal in its local manifestation." And here Mr. Vine excelled in his insistence on the importance of the local church, as one who was acquainted with this matter in practice as well as in doctrine. He rightly insisted on the administrative independence of each local church as "a foundation truth taught in all the passages that deal with the subject in the New Testament," and he appreciated the necessity of wise government and godly order in the local church in order that it might most effectively discharge the functions entrusted to it by the Lord. His latest contribution to the subject was a chapter on "Discipline in the Church" which he wrote for the symposium entitled *The Church,* edited by Mr. J. B. Watson (Pickering & Inglis, 1949). His chief work in this field was the volume *The Church and the Churches,* published about twenty years ago on the basis of a series of articles which had previously appeared from his pen in the missionary periodical *Echoes of Service.*

The mention of *Echoes of Service* (of which he was an Editor for so many years) reminds us of his interest in another sphere of Church activity—the spread of the Gospel throughout the world. A careful study of this subject in the light of Scripture appeared in 1927 in his book *The Divine Plan of Missions* (similarly based on articles which he had contributed to *Echoes of Service*). The proper aim of the preaching of the Gospel, in any land whatsoever, he saw to be not only the conversion of men and women but their incorporation into independent churches, administered by their own elders according to the Scriptural order, responsible not to a mission or home church or central board of control but to Christ alone. He emphasized, too, that the New Testament has much to say about the methods as well as the aims of missionary work, and that its principles can be disregarded only to our loss. "To adopt expedients of human devising in order to meet any contingency, is to tamper with the Divine arrangements and mar God's handiwork." For the theology of world-evangelization as for its practical consequences, *The Divine Plan of Missions* will repay serious consideration.

5. General Theology

An experienced exegete of Scripture is well equipped to deal with any branch of theology, and in addition to those branches already dealt with, there were several to which Mr. Vine made valuable contributions. A volume on *The Divine Inspiration of the Bible,* published in 1923, set out the lines of study and argument which had led, in the author's own words, to "a strong confirmation of his faith in the integrity, authenticity, and Divine and plenary inspiration of the writings which comprise the Bible." His discussion of the subject was not confined to the purely intellectual plane, but revealed the author's insight into the true center of Biblical authority and sufficiency.

The Church and the Tribulation.

The Scriptures have proved themselves sufficient, not only to meet the deepest spiritual need on account of sin, but to provide adequately for the formation of character and for efficiency in every form of Christian service, to direct the life not simply into philanthropic effort for the sake of mere philanthropy, but into that far higher form of service to our fellowmen which is rendered in pure devotion to Christ. It is the revelation of Christ in the Scriptures which draws the soul into personal attachment to Him, and thereby to an understanding of, and sympathy with, His heart of compassion for mankind.

Mr. Vine's work on *The Gospel of the Bible* (1929), surveyed the main aspects of soteriology: the Person presented, Sin, Christ the Propitiation, the Cross of Christ, the Vicarious Sacrifice of Christ, Redemption, the Resurrection of Christ, Justification by Faith, Repentance, Righteousness, the Holy Spirit and the New Birth, Sanctification, and the Second Advent. (A helpful appendix dealt with the Atonement and bodily sickness, in the light of teaching current then as now in certain evangelical circles). One reviewer dismissed the work with the remark that the Gospel was no longer preached in these terms—a double-edged criticism, had he only stayed to think! The expression "the simple Gospel" too often reveals marvelously superficial thinking about those things which the angels desire to look into. The present writer remembers Mr. C. F. Hogg remarking once that some people's idea of the Gospel could be summed up in the words "Come to Jesus or you'll go to hell." But the scope of the true Gospel displayed in this work of Mr. Vine's was calculated to give the thoughtful reader high, worthy and worshiping thoughts of the divine wisdom revealed in the way of salvation.

The Twelve Mysteries of Scripture was the title of a volume which brought together a number of studies by Mr. Vine in some of the key passages of the New Testament, dealing with the mysteries of (1) the faith (1 Tim. 3:9); (2) the Godhead of Christ (Col. 2:2, 9); (3) godliness (1 Tim. 3:16); (4) the Gospel (Eph. 3:4, 6; Col. 1:27); (5) the Kingdom of God (Matt. 13:11; Luke 8:10); (6) the seven stars and lampstands (Rev. 1:20); (7) the transformation of the bodies of the saints (1 Cor. 15:51); (8) Israel's hardening (Rom. 11:25); (9) Babylon (Rev. 17:5); (10) lawlessness (2 Thess. 2:7); (11) God's purposes in judgment (Rev. 10:7); (12) God's will (Eph. 1:9). In all these instances, the word *mystery* "denotes that which, being outside the range of unassisted natural apprehension, can be made known only by divine revelation, and is made known in a manner and at a time appointed by God, and to those only who are illumined by His Spirit."

A number of other studies in Christian doctrine by Mr. Vine appeared in article and pamphlet form; some of these, along with others by Mr. Hogg, were published in a volume entitled *The Good Deposit*. But in conclusion we may notice his studies in Christology—an earlier book entitled *The First and the Last* and a later one on *Christ's Eternal Sonship*. With regard to the title of the latter work, it might have been objected to by one who was a biblical rather than a systematic or historical theologian, that the title "Eternal Son" is not applied to our Lord in the Bible. (In fact, about the time when this book appeared, one generally evangelical community had formally given up belief in the eternity of Christ's Sonship, though not in His eternal being as a person of the Godhead.) But Mr. Vine was a master of words, not a slave of words.

It is true that the word "eternal" is not used in Scripture in connection with the Sonship of Christ, but that affords no proof that the relationship did not exist in the eternal past. Phraseology that is endorsed by the general teaching of Scripture is sound, and the Scriptures give abundant evidence that the relationship was eterna.

On the other hand, he did not care to use the expression "eternal generation," first coined by Origen to convey the relation subsisting between the Divine Father and the Divine Son. But his objection was not that the expression is not found in Scripture, but rather that the idea conveyed by the expression is not warranted by Scripture. Theological terms and formulae which "may be proved by most certain warrants of holy Scripture" are unexceptionable and may indeed be positively valuable, but Mr. Vine did not rank "eternal generation" in this category.

The phrase "eternal generation" finds nothing to correspond to it in Scripture. It does not serve to explain the doctrine of the eternal relationships in the Godhead. Human limitations prevent a full comprehension of the eternal. Yet God has in grace conveyed the facts relating to Himself in language the phraseology of which we can understand, though the facts themselves lie beyond the range of human conception.

The question then arises how we are to understand the adjective "only-begotten" (Gk. *monogenes*) applied to Christ as the Son of God, and in what sense New Testament writers saw fulfilled in Him the divine allocution of Psalm 2:7: "Thou art my Son; this day have I begotten thee" (where "this day" is patristically interpreted as "the day of eternity"). Mr. Vine's study of both these questions is worth our attention. From a comparison of the Septuagint and New Testament occurrences of *monogenes* he concludes rightly that the idea of generation, though etymologically present in the word, is actually otiose; in its general usage in the Greek Bible it "signifies both uniqueness and endearment"; and "in addition to the thought of uniqueness and endearment, the term when coupled with the word 'Son' conveys the idea of complete representation, the Son manifesting in full expression the characteristics of the Father."

As for the words of Psalm 2:7, it is frequently inferred from their quotation in Acts 13:33 that "this day" means the day of our Lord's resurrection—an idea supported by the reading of the A.V.: "in that he hath raised up Jesus again." But the word "again"—which, as Mr. Vine points out, "has nothing corresponding to it in the original" and was added "by way of interpretation"—is rightly omitted from the R.V. Mr. Vine understood the words "he raised up Jesus" here in the same sense as the raising up of David in verse 22 and the raising up of a prophet like unto Moses in Acts 3:22; 7:37. The matter of resurrection does

not appear in Acts 13 until it is explicitly introduced in verse 34. What verse 33 means, therefore, by speaking of the raising up of Jesus is that "God raised Him up in the midst of the nation in the same sense as in the other passages just quoted." What then is the point of time denoted by "this day" when Ps. 2:7 is quoted as being fulfilled in Christ's being so raised up? His incarnation, Mr. Vine held; although a strong case could be made out for the day of His baptism, when part at least of Psalm 2:7 was included in the words then addressed to Him from heaven, and when He was raised up publicly as Israel's promised King, anointed with the Holy Spirit and with power. But whether we think of "this day have I begotten thee" as pointing to His incarnation or baptism, or even resurrection (in the light of Rom. 1:4), it is plainly indicated that His Divine Sonship was not then initiated, but simply proclaimed.

The Scriptures' chief function is to bear witness of Christ, and the chief end of their study and exegesis is to increase our inward knowledge of Him, under the illumination of the Spirit of God. Nor would Mr. Vine, in all his study and writing, be content with any lower aim than this, for himself and his readers alike. The words with which he concluded the preface to the last volume of his *Expository Dictionary* amply express the spirit in which he sought to carry out all his work:

In any work in which we engage as servants of Christ, His word ever applies, "When ye shall have done all the things that are commanded you, say 'We are unprofitable servants; we have done that which it was our duty to do'" (Luke 17:10). So with the reminders given by the apostle Paul, "it is required in stewards that a man be found faithful . . . and what hast that that thou didst not receive?" (1 Cor. 4:2, 7). We ever have reason for humbling ourselves before God, for none of us knows yet as he ought to know, and at the Judgment Seat of Christ "the fire itself shall prove each man's work of what sort it is."

F. F. Bruce

THE BIBLE

The Scriptures and
How to Use Them

· LIST OF ABBREVIATIONS ·

The undernoted abbreviations are used in the Notes.

A.V.	Authorized Version
chh.	chapters
ca., circa	about the year
cp.	compare
ct.	contrast
e.g.	for example
Eng.	English
et al.	and other passages
Gk.	Greek
Heb.	Hebrew
i.e.	that is
in orig.	in the original
lit.	literally
LXX.	the Septuagint, a translation of the Old Testament from Hebrew into Greek, made between 250 and 150 B.C.
marg.	margin
MS., MSS.	manuscript(s)
N.T.	New Testament
O.T.	Old Testament
R.V.	Revised Version
vv.	Verses
viz.	namely

|| at the end of a paragraph or note indicates that all the New Testament occurrences of the Greek word under consideration are mentioned in it.

The Scriptures and How to Use Them

The vitality of the Bible is its most evident characteristic. It has survived alike the indifference of some ages and the active opposition and the hostile criticism of others. It is necessary always to bear in mind the fundamental laws of the Universe in which we live, and among these not the least important is that there is no effect without adequate cause. What then is the sufficient cause of the survival of the Bible through the vicissitudes of the millenniums of its existence? The cause is not to be found in its literary value, though that is high. Nor in any sanctity clothing it in mystery, for it is open to all to read "in their own tongues" as well as in the languages in which it was originally written.

The vitality of the Bible is capable of but one explanation. It is of Divine origin. Only God could thus hold the mirror to the soul of man, only God could thus plumb the depths of human personality, and only God could thus meet every human need. Hence its searchings which lay bare the inmost heart of the reader and its promises which bring with them peace, courage and victory. In some way not readily defined, but not at all to be evaded, when men read the Bible they are constrained to say very much what the posse of constables sent to arrest the Lord Jesus said of Him, "Never book speaks as does this Book."

There is a condition, however, for only to the diligent does it yield its treasures. If the Scriptures are indeed God-breathed (not "inspired" but "God-inspired" is the word the apostle Paul used in the famous passage in his letter to Timothy), whatever else the term may mean, at least it means that they were written with care, that they are an accurate record of the message of God to men. It follows then that they must be read with care, that the reader who begrudges pains in his reading stands to lose and to be led astray. For while the way of Salvation is set forth with the simplicity appropriate to such a theme, this is not the sole content of the Bible, which has for its object also "that the man of God may be complete, furnished completely unto every good work" (2 Tim. 3:15–17).

To render some help to those who desire to use the Bible intelligently, and with a good conscience, is the purpose of the following pages (C.F.H.).

The Voice of God

The Scriptures are the voice of God to the soul of man. He who reads them to listen to that voice finds what the apostle Paul said to Timothy confirmed in his own experience, that they are "profitable for teaching, for reproof, for correction, for instruction which is in righteousness" (2 Tim. 3:16); profitable for teaching, since he learns the will of God; profitable for reproof, since what is wrong in his life is revealed and acknowledged; profitable for correction, since his ways are "directed to the keeping of God's statutes"; profitable for instruction in righteousness, since by the understanding gained from the Scriptures he not only "cleanses his way" but learns to "hate every false way" and to "walk in the way of righteousness." Obedience to the Word of God begets increasing delight in it. This is implied by the writer of Psalm 119, when he says, "My soul hath observed Thy testimonies; and I love them exceedingly" (v. 167). To him who thus obeys their voice the Scriptures are a constant subject of happy meditation. His soul is fed by them, and they become "sweet to his taste" and produce spiritual growth. They become his counselor in all circumstances and upon all occasions: his guide in difficulties, giving light to his path; his comfort in adversity, giving him patience and hope; his weapon in spiritual warfare, giving him victory over his adversaries. Storing them in his memory, and so "laying them up in his heart," he proves them to be a power against sin and temptation.

Witness Bearing

This private use of the Word of God is, however, inseparable from another. For the light shines into our own souls that it may shine out to others. Every Christian is called to bear witness to the truth. To this end we are exhorted to be "seen as lights in the world, holding forth the Word of Life," and by a godly life to "adorn the doctrine of God our Savior in all things." The right use of the Scriptures in this respect produces a new translation of them, not into a written language, but into deeds and words and ways, a translation "known and read of all men."

Next in importance to the private reading of the Scriptures as the voice of God to the individual soul is the prayerful and methodical study of them. The subject of Bible study, however, is too comprehensive for our present pages, and must be reserved for separate treatment. We proceed to consider the use of the Scriptures for the purposes of imparting instruction. And firstly as to public reading, which should be an effective means to this end.

Public Reading

The public reading of the Word of God was ordered for Israel from the earliest times of their existence as a nation in Canaan. Moses had given command that at the end of every seven years, at the Feast of Tabernacles, the priests should "read the Law before all Israel in their hearing" (Deut. 31:10–13). After his earliest conquests in Canaan Joshua similarly read "all the words of the Law" to assembled Israel, omitting "not a word of all that Moses had commanded" (Josh. 10:3, 4). Again, Nehemiah records of Ezra that on the completion of the rebuilding of the walls of Jerusalem he read the Law to all the people, and, of the Levites, that "they read in the book, in the Law of God, distinctly; and they gave the sense" (Neh. 8:1–8). In later times the Law was read regularly in the synagogues. The New Testament also gives abundant evidence that public reading obtained in the gatherings of the earliest Christian churches. To such ministry Paul referred in his injunction to Timothy, "Till I come give heed to reading," intending thereby in public, for he couples with it exhortation and teaching, 1 Timothy 4:13, and similarly John, in the introduction to the Apocalypse, "Blessed is he that readeth, and they that hear" (Rev. 1:3).

There is no gathering of Christians in which the reading of Scripture is out of place. In the home the daily assembling of the household for the purpose is of the utmost importance. God is honored, and the family derives incalculable benefit. The recognition of this leads many to gather the household twice in the day to hear the Word. A family without Scripture reading is like a ship without chart and compass. In a prayer meeting the reading of a suitable portion is a valuable help, where the nature and purpose of the meeting and the appropriate length of time available for prayer are duly considered. Again, where Bible addresses form one of the special objects of a meeting, the reading of the Word should have prominence. There is a tendency to overestimate the value of an address in comparison with the reading which introduces it. It is, however, of paramount importance that the company present should hear God's voice directly from His Word; important and necessary as the service of exposition is, it is yet subsidiary to this. Of a certain servant of God the remark was made that to hear him read a chapter from the Bible was a sermon in itself.

There is perhaps nothing in public ministry demanding more care and attention than the reading of Scripture. It is required in a reader that he should endeavor to enter intelligently into the meaning and force of what he is reading, in order that he may read earnestly, for in the reading of Scripture earnestness is but the handmaid of reverence. Soulless reading fails to impress the hearer. The greater the reader's discernment of the divine meaning of the Word the more intelligent and earnest his utterance. Accordingly the measure of his spirituality is the measure of the spiritual effect produced.

In addition to this the force of the words can be properly conveyed only (1) when they are rightly pronounced and distinctly articulated, (2) when emphasis is given to the particular word or words which require it, (3) when the reading is characterized by that deliberateness of utterance which, without being drawled, is sufficiently slow for the hearer to grasp the sense, and (4) when the necessary pauses are duly observed, pauses not only grammatical but rhetorical, as, for example, after the subject of a sentence when it consists of more than one word, or after an emphatic word. Other points are important, such as the attitude of the body and the proper modulation of the voice. Good reading has been described as "like the conversation of an earnest person thinking to himself aloud." This being so, the voice will be natural and yet expressive, and the reading will be as much like speaking and as little like reading as possible.

The Teacher: His Responsibilities

One of the offices of the Spirit of God is to guide the Christian into all the truth contained in His Word. This implies the need of supernatural guidance to understand its teachings, and forbids anyone to attempt to expound the Scriptures save those who are themselves taught of the Spirit.

The mere unaided intelligence is incapable of understanding or rightly expounding the oracles of God. That which has been "given by inspiration of God" requires spiritual life and understanding in him who handles it. "The natural man receiveth not the things of the Spirit of God: for they are foolishness unto him; and he cannot know them, because they are spiritually judged" (1 Cor. 2:14).

The Bible lifts its voice against any attempt to add to it or take from it: "Ye shall not add unto the Word which I command you, neither shall ye diminish from it" (Deut. 4:2). "Add thou not unto His words, lest He reprove thee, and thou be found a liar" (Prov. 30:6). The word of Jeremiah, too, is ever to be remembered in dealing with the Holy Scriptures in the way of exposition, "He that hath My Word, let him speak My Word faithfully" (Jer. 23:28). James found it necessary to warn his brethren against being "many teachers," "knowing," he says, "that we shall receive the heavier judgment" (James 3:1). Timothy, who was enjoined by Paul to "give heed to reading, to exhortation, to teaching," to "be diligent in these things," and give himself wholly to them, was also exhorted to "give diligence to present himself approved unto God, a workman that needeth not to be ashamed, handling aright the word of truth" (1 Tim. 4:13, 15; 2 Tim. 2:15).

To the question put by Philip to the eunuch, "Understandest thou what thou readest?" (Acts 8:30), the responding question, "How can I, except someone shall guide me?" expresses generally the needs of the seeker after truth; and though the author of the Word oftentimes communicates directly the meaning of some portion of it to the inquiring soul, He ordinarily employs human instrumentality, as He did for the Ethiopian in the desert of Gaza. Human instruments, however, require divine preparation, and the character of this we now briefly indicate.

The Teacher: His Qualifications

Granted the enjoyment of the first indispensable possession, spiritual life in Christ through the new birth, the requisite qualifications of one who engages in exposition of the Word of God may be comprehended under the following three headings: (1) *Subjection to the Word;* (2) *Sense of its sacredness;* (3) *Soundness of judgment.*

Subjection to the Word of God

"If any man willeth to do His will, he shall know of the teaching" (John 7:17). In these words the Lord laid down an all-important condition, applicable to that acquirement of the knowledge of Scripture which is essential for the teacher of its doctrines. The knowledge that results in obedience leads to increased power to apprehend the meaning of the truths of Scripture. A subject will begets an understanding heart. One cannot yield submission to God's Word without gaining an increased understanding of it. The understanding which is necessary in order to teach it is in direct proportion to our conformity to the will of God revealed in it. "If ye abide in My Word, then are ye truly My disciples; and ye shall know the truth" (John 8:31, 32). A disciple is, literally, a learner. That anyone is a teacher presupposes that he has first been a learner. Discipleship of Christ, however, involves the practice of what has been taught by Him, and that is what is implied by "abiding in His Word." For the learner, precept must come before practice; for the teacher, practice before precept.

This, then, is the progressive order inevitable for one who is to unfold the meaning of holy writ—subjection of heart, conformity of life, increase of understanding, capacity for teaching. So it was with the apostles whom the risen Lord was about to commission to go forth to preach and teach. His work of tender grace and loving patience in molding their wills to His own was completed. There was not one of them of divided heart toward Him. Then it was that He "opened their mind, that they might understand the Scriptures" (Luke 24:45). That was evidently a special preparation for their work. Loyalty of the heart to Him, and minds enlightened by Him, this, with the Holy Spirit's power, rendered their ministry effective. Preparation for all right exposition of God's Word must be of this character.

Sense of Its Sacredness

The Word of God is a hallowed shrine, and one who enters its precincts must bear in mind that it is holy ground—holy, because its "Architect and Maker is God." God Himself is there. There, too, He has enshrined His Son. The description "the Holy Scriptures," as used by Paul in writing to Timothy (2 Tim. 3:15), was evidently that by which the Law, the Prophets and the Psalms were known at that time. By the word "Holy" they were distinguished from other writings. And what is there stated of the writings of the Old Testament was intended to be equally applicable to those of the New, for in the succeeding verse the apostle refers, with special emphasis, to the New Testament Scriptures, though of course embracing in his statement the whole, both Old and New.

What God has said as to the character of His Word is calculated to make us weigh well the responsibility attached to handling it. "The words of the Lord are pure words; as silver tried in a furnace on the earth, purified seven times" (Ps. 12:6). How great the need, then, of a heart which has first experienced the effects of their purity and learned to stand in awe of their holiness! He who has not learned to tremble at God's Word is not fit to expound its truths. Simple mental apprehension of the meaning of Scripture is imperfect machinery for giving instruction in it. Where the mind is darkened spiritually, educational training is unavailing in this respect. For there are two sides to the sacredness of Scripture; it is both holy itself, and is intended to make men holy. The power of the Word to affect the heart

and mold the life is the great reason why we are bidden to "take heed" to it; and the very passage which thus warns us also declares of the words of the prophets that in uttering them they were "borne along" by the Holy Ghost, not putting their private interpretation upon what God revealed to them (2 Pet. 1:19–21.). By implication, therefore, private interpretation on the part of others is forbidden. The holy regard begotten by the realization that we are dealing with the Word of God will debar us from ascribing to any portion a meaning which is not supported by the rest of Scripture, and from receiving teaching from any man without examining it ourselves in the light of that Word. The believer is to "prove all [teachings]" and to "hold fast that which is good" (1 Thess. 5:21).

Soundness of Judgment

No other book has been written the words of which may be made to bear so many meanings as the words of the Bible. This is owing both to the fact that its purpose is to convey spiritual truth, and to the figurative nature of much of its language. The limitations of our minds necessitate the employment of things material for instruction in things spiritual. But the very variety of the forms of figurative expression, the different senses in which the same expression is used for embodying various spiritual ideas, and the spiritual teaching underlying many of the statements of historical fact, present dangers for the teacher. He needs to guard against the bias of opinions which he may have derived from others, and his imagination and fancy require due restraint, lest he should attribute to a passage of Scripture a meaning not intended by its author.

Now the soundness of judgment which is necessary for this is to be derived only from communion with God, and is therefore largely the outcome of the subjection to His Word and the regard for its sacredness which we have been considering. The discretion which enables one to judge what is truth and what is error comes by constant and prayerful meditation in and study of the Word of God in its entirety. This it is, too, which guards the teacher against giving prominence to any doctrine at the expense of other teachings of Scripture. He learns also to discern what is figurative and what is literal, what historical facts have an allegorical meaning and what is written to convey spiritual instruction simply and directly. Vivid conception is not without its value, but, apart from the restraining influences to which reference has been made, it leads a teacher to imagine in the narratives of Scripture circumstances unwarranted by the facts stated, or to spiritualize these historical records to the beclouding of the truths embodied in them. Fanciful exposition is not glorifying to God; His people are not thereby built up on their holy faith.

Guided by a sanctified judgment the faithful teacher of God's Word, while not refusing any legitimate aid to the study of its pages, will turn to the Word itself for the light it throws upon its own teachings.

The Teacher: His Guiding Principles

Right exposition of the Word of God is based upon the recognition of certain broad principles, the most important of which may now be enunciated and illustrated.

The Scriptures Present an Essential and All-pervading Unity

To enter at length upon this subject would be beyond the scope of these pages; we refer to it briefly to indicate its importance for the teacher. Variety of theme and treatment is a marked characteristic of Scripture, but it is a variety blended into harmony. God's Word, like His works, presents unity in diversity. The consideration of a particular subject therefore demands due regard to the various aspects in which it is found in different parts of the Book. To take, for instance, the gospel, its promises are given in the Old Testament, the person Who constitutes its subject is revealed in the gospels, the record of its testimony is given in the Acts, and the exposition of its nature in the Epistles. Recognition of the unity of Scripture will keep before us that balance of truth which involves the due consideration of widely different yet closely associated subjects, such as divine sovereignty and human responsibility, or, again, the necessity of faith without works, and of works as the evidence of faith.

This unity is especially to be borne in mind when comparing the contents of the New Testament and those of the Old. This is illustrated by the revelation of the character of God. One of the early errors of the present era was that of Marcion, in the second century, who declared that the Old Testament reveals the righteousness and holiness of God while the New Testament reveals His goodness and mercy. The truth is that Scripture throughout reveals God as infinitely merciful in His justice and infinitely just in His mercy. That greater prominence is given to one side of God's character in one part of Scripture than in another is obvious, but in considering such subjects we must keep before us that blending of truth which is revealed in the whole.

Men often speak of the discrepancies of Scripture. Careful study shows that as a rule these are only apparent. It must be recognized that in some cases, as, for instance, of numbers or the order of events, it is not easy to see how certain statements can be harmonized, but the man of faith will rest assured that even in these cases further light from God would remove all difficulty. And it is often found that what at first sight seemed discrepancies, so far from marring the unity of Scripture, afford, when they are really understood, striking instances of it, and thus add their quota to the proof of the genuineness of the books in which they occur. An instance occurs in the Lord's explanation of the parable of the sower. Matthew's Gospel describes the one who brings forth fruit as "he that heareth the Word and *understandeth* it" (Matt. 13:23); the corresponding word in Mark's Gospel is *"accept"* (Mark 4:20); the word given by Luke is *"hold fast"* (Luke 8:15). How comes it that three different words are given for the Lord's single utterance? Apart from other considerations, the language spoken by Christ was not that used in the Gospels, the writers of which represented in the Greek tongue what the Lord spoke in the Aramaic. This at once accounts for variety of rendering, for of this the word used was doubtless capable. The point for the careful expositor is the harmony contained in this variety, the progression of thought which is evidenced in the three words. To bear fruit one must first understand the Word, then receive it, and then hold it fast. Thus while one idea pervades the whole, the different expressions convey additional teaching to that of the facts of the parable itself. Possibly one word might have sufficed to represent that used by the Lord; but the Spirit of God had other purposes in view, and chose to use the three distinct words for the purposes of imparting instruction in their variety. Thus so far from discrepancy there is harmony.

Since almost all themes of Scripture are treated of by more than one of its writers, and most themes by a large number, it is important in taking up a subject to study all that Scripture reveals concerning it, so as to have a well-proportioned view of the truth.

Revelation in Scripture Is Progressive

Associated with the unity of the Word of God is the continuity and progressive character of His communications therein recorded. Since to Him Who "inhabits eternity," to Whom therefore the future is as real as the present, the whole plan of His dealings was known from the beginning, it was in full view of all subsequent revelations that the earliest were given. Each revelation contains the germ of those that follow it, and by them accordingly receives its explanation. No better example is afforded than the sublimely comprehensive declaration given immediately after the Fall, "I will put enmity between thee and the woman, and between thy seed and her seed: it shall bruise thy head, and thou shalt bruise his heel" (Gen. 3:15). In that primal prediction lay the foreshadowing of the conflict between the kingdoms of light and darkness with which later revelations of the Scripture are concerned, and which received its great fulfillment in the cross of Christ.

If, however, the earlier revelations were capable of development, in none was there essential defeat. Though incomplete, according to the providential arrangement of God, each was, like His own character, perfect in itself. Each admitted of expansion, but not of rectification. The manifestation of a new method in His dealings with men does not indicate inherent imperfection in any of the methods that preceded it. Whatever limitations characterized the earlier, they were limitations imposed by God Himself, according to His foreknowledge of the conditions of humanity at the time, and with a view to those dealings which were

to follow. This is well illustrated by the case of the Law given at Mount Sinai. In writing to the Galatians, Paul refers to it as "weak and beggarly rudiments" (Gal. 4:9). This does not indicate any defect in the Law itself, which is thus described only by way of contrast with the succeeding revelation of the gospel. In itself, "the Law is holy, and the commandment holy, and righteous, and good" (Rom. 7:12). It was given in view of the gospel age which was to follow it, and was itself instrumental in the fulfillment of the promises given in the age which preceded it. Nor when the gospel was declared was the Law repudiated. "What the Law could not do, in that it was weak through the flesh, God, sending His own Son in the likeness of sinful flesh, and as an offering for sin, condemned sin in the flesh; that the ordinance of the Law might be fulfilled in us" (Rom. 8:3, 4). Here, then, we have both continuity and progression. A recognition of the progressive character of revelation helps us to obtain that perspective of the ways of God with men which forms the basis of the true exegesis of Scripture.

Scripture Interprets Itself

The unity of the Scriptures and the progressive nature of their revelations sufficiently establish the divine origin of the Bible. For it is not possible to show that any two of the nearly fifty writers agreed together that their statements should not be found at variance. To the contrary, indeed, the discrepancies already mentioned testify. Moreover, the books were written at intervals through a period of over fifteen hundred years.

The divine origin of the Bible, however, involves a divinely-established relationship of thought in the writers. The obvious conclusion from which is that this Book is self-explanatory. And such is found to be the case. Truths and topics are interwoven throughout the volume; and in such a way as to demand that those who would know the mind of God concerning any part of the Scriptures should search the whole of them. In this connection no little significance attaches to that useful array of references which fills the margin of many editions of the Book, both testifying to its uniqueness and giving evidence that the people of God have been guided to look to His

Word itself for illumination upon all its passages.

The light of Scripture is usually thrown upon a passage in one or more of three ways: *(a)* by the context, *(b)* by the scope of the book in which it occurs, and *(c)* by some parallel passage or passages.

Text and Context

(a) What is generally understood as the context is that which immediately precedes and follows a Scripture. This definition, though largely true, is, however, inadequate. The word "context" means "what is woven together," and in this sense is not inappropriate, as having to do with the web, so to speak, of a written discourse. The context, indeed, embraces the whole series of statements or arguments connected with the passage in view. Unless this is taken into consideration, the meaning directly intended by God, which is of course the main thing in exposition, is likely to be missed.

When, for instance, the apostle Paul says "Ye are fallen away from grace" (Gal. 5:4), the statement, if detached from its connection, might be made to imply that it is possible for one who has been saved by grace to lose his salvation. The context, immediate and more remote, shows that the apostle is remonstrating with those who were being led by false teachers to seek justification by the Law as well as by faith in Christ, and that he is protesting in vivid language that any who did so were putting themselves into a position incompatible with the grace brought to them by the gospel. Again, the statement "Nothing is unclean of itself: save that to him that accounteth anything to be unclean, to him it is unclean" (Rom. 14:14), might, if isolated from its setting, be perversely used as a license for carnality. The context shows that the writer is treating, not of practices which, by the universal witness of the human conscience, as well as by express declarations of Scripture, are known to be wrong, but of meats and drinks and the observance of days, concerning which convictions may vary.

The context will frequently determine whether words have a literal or a figurative meaning. The statement of Christ, "He that eateth Me, even he shall live by Me" (John 6:57), was not intended to be understood literally. The more immediate context makes clear that He was speaking figuratively. For, firstly, the Lord had already shown the spiritual import of His words in His statement, "He that believeth on Me hath eternal life" (v. 47). Secondly, He subsequently said, "The words that I have spoken unto you are spirit, and are life" (v. 63). Thirdly, the larger context shows that He was speaking to the Jews with increasing obscureness of utterance because of their persistent unbelief and hardness of heart.

Scope

(b) The scope (literally, "what is in view") of a book denotes the writer's aim, his design, general or particular, according as the whole or a section of his writing is under consideration. Clearly, if the meaning of a passage is to be obtained from this source, the book in which it occurs should be read through. Diligent perusal of the whole is indispensable for an understanding of the parts. A point that may of itself seem obscure often becomes clear in the light of the entire record. Sometimes the scope is directly mentioned. Here we may note that the scope of the Old Testament is briefly given us by the apostle Peter under three headings, (1) "the grace that should come unto you" (lit., "the grace unto you"), (2) "the sufferings of Christ" (lit., "the sufferings unto Christ"), (3) "the glories that should follow them" (1 Pet. 1:10, 11). Of much of the Old Testament the true exposition cannot be given save in view of these three themes. Again, the design of the Gospel of John is declared in the words, "these [things] are written that ye may believe that Jesus is the Christ, the Son of God; and that believing ye may have life in His Name" (John 20:31).

Parallel Passages

(c) A third means of obtaining light upon a portion is by the study of parallel passages. These may be classed, firstly, as verbal. In this respect the help of a really good concordance is invaluable, especially one which shows readily, not only all the places where

the same English word occurs, but also all those containing the same word in the original.

Verbal Parallels

A word or phrase used somewhat obscurely in one place may be clearly explained by the connection in which it occurs elsewhere. Thus, on comparing the word rendered in 1 Corinthians 15:20 "are asleep" (lit., "have fallen asleep") with Daniel 12:2, it becomes clear that, since the physically dead are there described as "them that sleep in the dust of the earth," the passage in 1 Corinthians refers, not to the soul or spirit, but to the body, to which alone the words "in the dust" are applicable; and so with other occurrences of the word in a like connection in the New Testament.

To take another example; when it is suggested that since the word rendered "chosen" (R.V. "appointed") in 2 Corinthians 8:19 literally denotes "to extend the hand," and that therefore the churches may have made choice of a man by vote, we are safeguarded against the idea by noticing that the same word (extended by a prefix, which, however, does not affect the meaning so far as the word itself goes) is used in Acts 10:41 of a choice made by God Himself.

Again, the study of all, or some of, the occurrences of a word often provides us with a complete view of a subject, so far as the Word of God gives it to us, light being frequently thrown on each occurrence by the others. Thus the word rendered "first-born" is used of Christ five times in the New Testament, in reference to (a) creation (Col. 1:15), (b) His resurrection (Col. 1:18, Rev. 1:5), (c) His future position among His glorified saints (Rom. 8:29), (d) His manifested glory in the earth (Heb. 1:6, R.V.). Each of these passages therefore has an important connection with the rest.

Again, the same word may be used in different senses or connections, and in such cases the context or the scope generally serves to give the true meaning. Thus the word "works," in Romans 3:27, 28 and Galatians 3:10, signifies observance of the law of God in contrast with faith. In James 2:24 it signifies obedience to God's commands as resulting from, and in attestation of, faith.

Verbal parallels include quotations, and these invariably direct attention to the Scriptures whence they are taken.

Doctrinal Parallels

Parallel passages may further be classified as doctrinal. There are, for instance, three passages which speak of the provision and administration of spiritual gifts in the Church. Romans 12 represents them as derived from God, (v. 3); Ephesians 4 as from Christ (vv. 7, 11); 1 Corinthians 12 as from the Holy Spirit (vv. 4, 11). The combined teaching of these passages thus reveals the activities of the three Persons of the Godhead on behalf of and in the Church.

Historical Parallels

Associated with doctrinal parallels are the historical, for the historical records are themselves doctrinal, (2 Tim. 3:16). Historical facts in the Old Testament are interpreted in their illustrative and typical import by fact and doctrines recorded in the New. Again, parallels in the Old Testament, such as those of the books of Kings and Chronicles, and corresponding records of the prophets, and parallels in the New Testament, such as those in the Gospels, mutually supplement and explain one another. There is nothing superfluous in the Word of God. What may seem to be repetition will be found, it may be in the light of a future age, to have had its divinely appointed purpose to fulfill in the declaration of the ways of God with men and of His sovereign will for them.

A Scripture the meaning of which is obscure is to be explained by that which is clear. That there are passages in Scripture which are "hard to be understood" is the testimony of one of the writers, 2 Peter 3:16, and is but consistent with the supernatural origin of the Book. One subject at least is everywhere expressed in the clearest terms, in language plain even to "wayfaring men." That subject is "the Way of Salvation." What, however, is not so clear, must be explained by means of, and in harmony with, those Scriptures the meaning of which is obvious. What is incidentally mentioned is to be viewed in the light of what is more fully revealed. On the other hand, what is not plain is not to be used to obscure what is clear. Sometimes the difficulty of a Scripture may be due to its brevity, a fuller expression, or an explanation, not having been demanded, perhaps, by the subject with which the writer was dealing. We read, for instance, that "the hour cometh, in which all that are in the tombs shall hear His voice (the voice of the Son of God) and shall come forth; they that have done good, unto the resurrection of life; and they that have done ill, unto the resurrection of judgment" (John 5:28, 29).

Two questions arise here: first, whether these resurrections will take place simultaneously; and second, whether life will be granted solely upon the condition of good works. Now the Lord did not say that all would be raised at the same time, nor would it be right to read that into His words. On this point Scripture is elsewhere perfectly clear. The word "hour" does not always signify a portion of a single day. The Lord's use of the word here is made clear by His similar expression in verse 25, where it denotes an extended period (cp. Rev. 3:10). Then in reference to the first resurrection we are explicitly told in Revelation 20:5 that the "rest of the dead lived not until the thousand years should be finished" (the past tense being prophetically used of what is yet future). Again, we may not gather from the words of Christ referred to above that He is speaking of good works from a merely human standpoint, i.e., apart from the new birth. His brief utterance is to be explained in harmony with His explicit statements to Nicodemus, that no one can see the kingdom of God who is not born again, and that eternal life is granted only to him who believes on the Son of God. Other Scriptures also make it plain that in the Divine estimate the doing of good depends on union with Christ by faith.

The significance of a revelation is not always to be measured by the apprehension of the writer. Concerning the great theme of salvation, the prophetic writers of the Old Testament "sought and searched diligently, . . . searching what time or what manner of time the Spirit of Christ which was in them did point unto, when it testified beforehand the sufferings of Christ, and the glories that should follow them" (1 Pet. 1:10, 11). This clearly shows that, in this matter at least, to these writers the significance of their statements was not always fully revealed. The same apostle says that "no prophecy ever came by the will of man: but men spake from God, being moved (or "borne along") by the Holy Ghost" (2 Pet. 1:21). We must not, however, suppose from this that the prophets, in some ecstatic condition, put on record words to which they attached no meaning. What they wrote was the expression of what was supernaturally communicated to their minds, though in many cases it went far beyond their comprehension.

Certain prophecies can receive their full interpretation only in the light of further revelation or of subsequent events. This alone explains why a particular revelation was not fully apprehended by the prophet to whom it was given. None but those who deny the fact of divine inspiration in the Scriptural sense of the term (see 2 Tim. 3:16; 2 Pet. 1:21) would suppose that Isaiah, for instance, in chapter 53 of his prophecies, was referring to some person contemporaneous with the period in which he lived. That the Servant of Jehovah of Whom he was writing, and Whose advent was still future, was the promised Messiah, was probably made known to him, but not so the exact application of his prophecy and the circumstances attending its accomplishment. In writing the sixteenth Psalm, David, foreseeing the fulfillment of God's promises, "spake of the resurrection of the Christ" (Acts 2:25–31). That does not indicate, however, that David understood the language of his Messianic Psalms as it is given to us to understand them in the light of the accomplished facts. Though the opening words of Psalm 22 may be read as a forcible description of the sorrows of the writer, we recognize that above and beyond the personal experiences of the Psalmist, and above and beyond his limited knowledge of the details of the fulfillment of God's promise, the Holy Spirit was directing his language with a precision unknown to him, and in such a way that its interpretation could be given only by a later and fuller revelation. And so with other prophets.

It is evident, therefore, that we are not to measure the meaning of a revelation by the apprehension of the writer to whom and through whom it was communicated. What the Holy Spirit intended to teach we learn by means of His completed work, the full canon of Holy Writ.

The true explanation of a Scripture never contradicts what is elsewhere revealed on the same subject. That God is omniscient and immutable is known to be a foundation truth of Scripture; with Him "can be no variation, neither shadow that is cast by turning" (James 1:17). Such words, therefore, as "it repented the Lord that He had made man on the earth, and it grieved Him at His heart" (Gen. 6:6) are not to be explained as if God had reversed His decisions, and His eternal counsels had altered. "God is not a man that He should repent" (1 Sam. 15:29). All His dealings are in exact accord with His predetermined and unalterable plans. The change is in man, not in God. Inconstancy and perverseness in man lead, by reason of the very immutability of God, to a change in His dealings with him. But both man's inconstancy and the consequent change in God's dealings were foreknown to him. The alteration is in His method, not in His nature. In this sense, then, is to be understood the word "repent" when used of God (Gen. 6:6, 1 Sam. 15:11, Joel 2:13, etc.). Jeremiah makes it clear that its use in this respect is different from its use in reference to man, and is in complete accord with the facts of God's essential immutability, and with His universal providence (see Jer. 18:7-10). Moreover, in thus speaking of Himself, and in order to make known His ways to us, the infinite God has but condescended to the limitations of our finite minds.

Every doctrine is to be taught consistently with every other, and with the whole tenor of Scripture regarding it. When the Lord, speaking of His death, said, "I, if I be lifted up from the earth, will draw all men unto Myself," the Jews protested, objecting that the Law said that "the Christ abideth forever" (John 12:32-34). That was true, but it was not the whole truth. Their mistake was due to a defective apprehension of the teaching of Scripture concerning the Messiah. One truth was being pressed to the exclusion of another. Their objection was based upon such statements as those of Isaiah, "of the increase of His government there shall be no end" (9:7), and of Daniel, "His dominion is an everlasting dominion" (7:14). They had not considered, however, that the same prophets had foretold that the Messiah would be "cut off" (Is. 53:8, Dan. 9:26).

Their error is not without its lessons. It is possible to lay such stress upon the doctrine of election, for example, that the responsibility of preaching the gospel to the perishing is underestimated or even set aside. Again, the great truth of justification by faith may not be treated as if it implied freedom from the necessity of works of righteousness on the part of him who has been justified. Each doctrine has its place and importance. Each is to be recognized and received. One must not be weakened or neglected in the interest of another. Attention devoted to a statement of any particular doctrine, without the consideration of all that Scripture teaches about it, leads to erroneous views. Undue stress upon one element of truth to the neglect of others has been largely responsible for heresy and sectarianism.

Are we called to the holy and solemn yet blessed work of teaching the Word of God, let us give ourselves to our teaching, Romans 12:7, continually seeking grace from God that we may never do so apart from the guidance of "the Spirit of truth," of Whom our Lord and Master has said, "He shall guide you into all the truth." Let us heed the injunction of the apostle Peter, that he who speaks is to speak "as it were oracles of God: . . . that in all things God may be glorified through Jesus Christ, Whose is the glory and the dominion forever and ever. Amen."

The Divine Inspiration
of the Bible

· PREFACE ·

I gladly accede to the request of my dear friend the author of this book, that I should write a few introductory words.

I have carefully read what he has written, and while his aim has not been to produce anything that is new upon the important subject with which it deals, one is thankful to have in a portable form this help to the understanding of the truth of inspiration.

It is satisfactory to find that he views inspiration as attaching not to the oral expressions before they were recorded, still less to any subsequent oral or written rendering of the autographs, but to the autographs themselves. To quote the words of the late Dr. H. C. C. Moule in connection with the Gospels: "This record God has given His Son. Such faith leaves unanswered and without the least anxiety very many questions on which strictly literary investigation may quite legitimately enter. It does not tell of itself in what language, Aramaic or Greek, the words were actually uttered. It does not even assure me that precisely those syllables, no less, no more, nor otherwise in any detail, came as sounds from His lips, but it does assure me that in the record as it stands we have a report revised by the ever blessed Speaker." Yes, it is the Scriptures, the writings, as originally given and (insofar as is the case) as presented to us in the resultant texts that are God-breathed. To lose certainty here is to be exposed to every wind of doctrine. But having settled this question in our hearts, then we can go on and say that by whatever media that Word reaches men, whether in the original autographs or in faithful copies or in the resultant texts, or in a faithful translation, it is in reality God's own voice to our souls. In connection with the remarks of the author on the wondrous "how" of inspiration, I may further quote Dr. Moule: "He who chose the writers of the Holy Scriptures, many men, scattered over many ages, used them each in his surroundings and in his character, yet so as to harmonize them all in the Book which, while many, is one. He used them with the sovereign skill of Deity. And that skillful use meant that He used their whole being which He had made, and their whole circumstances, which He had ordered. They were indeed His amanuenses; nay, I fear not to say they were His pens. But He is such that He can manipulate as His facile implement no mere piece of mechanism which, however subtle and powerful, is mechanism still and can never truly cause anything; He can take a human personality, made in His own image, pregnant, formative, causative, in all its living thought, sensibility and will, and can throw it freely upon its task of thinking and expression—and behold, the product will be His; His matter, His thought, His exposition, His Word, 'living and abiding forever.' "

May God bless this effort to reaffirm the truth!

Bath, *5th October,* 1923.   W. R. LEWIS.

The subject of the following pages is one upon which the writer has been asked to give addresses on various occasions during several years. While the effect has been to deepen his conviction as to his inability to handle so profound a subject at all adequately, he has ventured to hope that the presentation, in a simple form, of what he believes to be the truth may prove of service to some of the household of the faith in these days of apostasy from it. The pretentious claims made by Higher Critics, based upon the means of arousing a still more careful spirit of inquiry on the part of many whom they call "traditionalists" into the internal evidences of Holy Scripture as to the character of its Inspiration. In the writer's own case the result has been a strong confirmation of his faith in the integrity, authenticity, and divine and plenary Inspiration of the writings which comprise the Bible. There are many eminent scholars today who have weighed the Higher Critical theories in the balances and have found them wanting, and this, not because of the influence of their own preconceived ideas, or a blind adherence to traditional views, but as the result of a careful and unbiased sifting of the evidences. Present-day theorists of the Higher Critical schools have become traditionalists after their own order. No matter how thoroughly recent discovery and scholarship disprove one after another the statements and suppositions advanced by the Higher Critics of former generations, these are still put forward by their successors.

The following pages have not been written, however, with the aim of attacking the critical position; they constitute an earnest attempt to set forth the result of careful study, in the hope that God may use them for His glory in the spiritual profit of the reader. Invaluable help has been rendered in the course of the preparation of the book by two of the author's colleagues in editorial and expository work, to whom he is greatly indebted, Mr. W. R. Lewis, of Bath, and Mr. C. F. Hogg, of London, each of whom kindly went through the MSS, making useful suggestions.

CHAPTER ONE

Preliminary Considerations

To discuss the subject of Inspiration at all exhaustively would necessitate the devotion of more space than we can give to the connected subject of divine revelation. It is true that the question whether we have a revelation from God lies behind any discussion regarding divine inspiration. But this involves a consideration of the various ways in which God has revealed Himself. There is, for instance, the revelation He has given of His power and His Godhead through nature. Then there are the various means intimated in the Bible through which He has made personal communications to man. This brings in the question whether the Bible consists of a revelation of the mind of God. But the following pages have not been written with a view to proving this, nor shall we here discuss the contingent problem of the relationship of Inspiration to Revelation. There are, however, not a few Christians, who, while believing in the fact of the divine inspiration of the Bible, are yet in some amount of perplexity as to what this means, and to what extent it is true. That such may receive some help from these chapters is the writer's earnest desire. The subject is one of the utmost importance today when the views of what is known as Modernism are being advanced on every hand. The Bible has been the most widely and thoroughly discussed Book in the world, and this is true to a greater extent today perhaps than at any time in the past. The activities of the Higher Critics have had this beneficial effect, that devout students of Scripture have been led thereby to consider more carefully the authenticity, integrity, and divine authority of the books which compose the Volume, and to examine more thoroughly the whole question of the Inspiration of its contents.

It will be necessary to notice some of the theories which have been advanced in regard to the subject, bearing in mind that inspiration is impossible of explanation by any theory. Inspiration is a doctrine taught in Scripture, whatever theories may be held about it. The supernatural acts of God do not admit of human analysis. It is no more possible to describe exactly how the divine action described by the word "God-breathed" took place than it is to explain any other miracle recorded in the Bible. The appeal of the Word of God is to faith. "By faith we understand that the worlds have been framed by the Word of God, so that what is seen hath not been made out of things which do appear" (Heb. 11:3, R.V.). The faith that accepts that fact accepts likewise the claims and evidences of Scripture that it is divinely inspired. The fact of inspiration may be proved by evidence and received as an ascertained part of the faith, the mode of inspiration lies outside the range of discovery. The process is undefinable, the result is clear. The operations of the Spirit can be registered only by their effects.

But while faith is the ground for the acceptance of the doctrine of the divine inspiration of Scripture, it is possible to see that there is really no conflict between faith and what may reasonably be expected from God. Mere evidences never equal in cogency the experience of faith, yet faith does not necessarily render a man unreasonable, and it is useful to inquire into the subject with a view to removing any difficulty which may be perplexing the heart of a believer.

We are told that the Bible does not need to be defended, that it will defend itself. Needless to say, in maintaining the divine and complete inspiration of the Bible we are not trying to defend it from attack; we agree that there is no necessity for this. The fact is that the foundations of the faith are being shaken in the hearts of numbers of Christians today, and it is with the desire to counteract this and to strengthen their faith that we seek to set forth what the Bible reveals concerning its divine origin and accuracy. We are told that our loyalty is due to a Person, Christ, rather than to a book. But this is no matter for comparison. Loyalty to Christ must indeed be paramount in our lives, and loyalty to the Bible in no way detracts from it. The Book itself leads us to loyalty to Christ.

Some Theories

The theories which have been advanced regarding the subject may be examined according as they have given undue prominence either to the divine element or to the human in the production of Scripture.* There is, on the one hand, the mechanical or organic theory. It virtually rules out the human element. According to this theory the Spirit of God used the writers as mere reporters to record messages word for word as by dictation; they were simply penmen, machines employed, as a typist might be employed, to express the divine mind apart from the cooperation of their own faculties, the Holy Spirit acting not so much through them as upon them. Such a notion is void of support from Scripture itself and finds few, if any, advocates today. It was, indeed, so prejudicial to the cause of truth as to produce a reaction in the other direction, *viz.*, a denial of the supernatural element altogether. This reaction has developed especially along the lines of what is called Higher Criticism. Without going into its most advanced forms we may notice the more moderate views as expressed in recent literature. According to these the Bible is simply "a fragmentary remains of a literature to which no special quality of divineness attaches. It is said to contain 'many contradictions and inconsistencies.'" The view is taken that "Special religious interests affected the minds of many of the writers in dealing with early material, and they felt justified in modifying the narrative for their own purposes. . . . Myths and legends are related as though they were actual occurrences." While it is admitted that there was "a Divine element in the creation of Scripture," yet the truth may have "been more or less distorted in expression, without losing its Divine quality."†

Again, as to the Gospel records concerning Christ, we are told that "we are far from having any proof . . . or any guarantee that the events of His life are related with absolute accurance. . . . There is reason to believe that reverent imagination has been at work on traditional material . . . It is no longer possible to insist on the literal accuracy of the Gospel narratives."‡

These statements represent the views of what may be termed the less extreme Higher Critics of the present time. As with the mechanical theory first mentioned so with this purely humanistic theory, we shall find that both have to be rejected on the ground of the Scripture evidences to be considered later. Those who advocate the latter seem to regard the Bible as revealing a search for God on the part of religiously-minded people among the Jews, rather than as the authoritative record of God's revelation of Himself to men. Thus in the first section of Principal E. Griffith Jones' introductory article in *Peake's Commentary* we meet with the statements that the Bible "registers on the one side the progressive outreach of the soul in the various stages and moods of its search for God"; and again, "It reveals man to himself as a seeker after God"; and again, "studying the Bible is only another way of studying life itself."

This is not the account the Bible has to give of itself. Its own testimony shows that it is a record of God's search after man, and not man's search after God.

A Via Media

In rejecting the mechanical theory we are not shut up to the views of the Higher Critics. It is quite possible to believe in the divine inspiration of the words of the Bible without holding that the writers of Scripture were like mere typists taking down what was dictated to them.

Professor Westcott well sums up the two views as follows: "It is easy to state the fatal objections which a candid reader of Scripture

---

*The term "Scripture" is to be understood in these pages as that which consists of the recognized canons of the Old and New Testaments.

†Principal E. Griffith Jones in *Peake's Commentary*, pp. 4–9.

‡*Ibid.*, p. 15.

must feel to both these views; and in general sense it is not less easy to show how the partial forms of truth in virtue of which they gained acceptance may be harmoniously combined. The purely organic theory of inspiration rests on no Scriptural authority, and, if we except a few ambiguous metaphors, is supported by no historical testimony. It is at variance with the whole form and fashion of the Bible, and is destructive of all that is holiest in man, and the highest in religion, which seeks the coordinate elevation of all our faculties and not the destruction of any one of them. If we look exclusively at the objective side of inspiration, the prophet becomes a mere soulless machine, mechanically answering the force which moves it, the pen and not the penman of the Holy Spirit."

As to the other view he writes, "If we regard inspiration only subjectively we lose all sense of a fresh and living connection of the prophet with God. He remains indeed a man, but he is nothing more. He appears only to develop naturally a germ of truth which lies within him, and to draw no new supplies of grace and wisdom from without. He may deduce, interpret, combine truth, but in the absence of a creative power he is deficient in that which an instinct of our being declares to be the essential attribute of the highest teacher. Such a theory removes all that is divine in our faith, and destroys the title-deeds of the Church's inheritance. It is opposed to the universal tenor of Scripture and tradition, and leaves our wants unsatisfied and our doubts unanswered by God. If it be true, man is after all alone in the world, abandoned to the blind issues of fate or reason or circumstance. His teachers are merely his fellow men, and their words claim his hearing only so far as they find a response in a heart already influenced by personal and social life. And who then shall answer him that their promises are more than the echoes of his own cravings; and that the ready acceptance which their doctrine has found is anything but a natural result of its correspondence to the wants and wishes of men? Happily, however, we are not confined to the two extreme theories: the elements of

truth of which they are respectively based are opposite indeed, but not contrary. If we combine the outward and the inward—God and man—the moving power and the living instrument—we have a great and noble doctrine to which our inmost nature bears its witness."*

A Distinction in the Use of the Term

In view of the loose use of the word, it is needful to distinguish between the term inspiration as applied to secular writers and the use of the term in Scripture.

"The inspiration which gives its distinctive quality to Scripture, as claimed for its writings by the Lord Jesus, by prophets and apostles, and often by the books themselves, is not of a kind that can properly be paralleled by human genius, or even by the ordinary illumination of Christians. It is sometimes said: 'Isaiah was inspired as Shakespeare, Burns, Scott or Carlyle was; Paul was inspired as Luther or Mazzini was.' But could any of these gifted men have prefaced their utterances, as the prophets did, with a 'Thus saith the Lord'; could it be said of the greatest of them what is said of New Testament apostles and prophets, that a Church was founded on their witness? . . . The Spirit is given to all Christians, but in diversity of measures, and with specific gifts. And what ordinary Christian will feel that he could use language about himself like the above."†

The difference then lies in this, that the writers of the Bible were "men who spake from God, being moved by the Holy Spirit," and, as to their writings, they are "God-breathed." This could never be predicated of other authors or their writings. Further, since it is the Scriptures themselves that are God-breathed, inspiration attaches in their case to the writings and not merely to the ideas expressed. True, the sentiments were given by God, but in the communication of the thoughts of God the phraseology employed cannot be divorced from the sentiments expressed. Whether a vocabulary is essential to thought

*"Introduction to the Study of the Gospels," by B. F. Westcott, D.D., pp. 6, 7.
†"Revelation and Inspiration," by Prof. Jas. Orr, p. 204.

process or not, the writings of Scripture, in order to be understood by us, involve the use of a human vocabulary, and the writings, in order to carry authority, need to be "God-breathed."

Divine and Human

Divine inspiration then in no way sets aside human authorship. The surrounding, the calling, the experience and the faculties of the various writers, all have a part in the form and substance of what they wrote. Their character as well as their style comes out in their narratives and records. The Spirit of God, making use of those qualities, so operated in the writers that the words they use are truly their own, yet at the same time they are God-breathed. It is this that imparts divine authority and accuracy to their words. No matter what the character of the subject matter may be, whether given by divine revelation, or whether the authors made use of their own knowledge of facts, or of written material at their disposal, all was, according to the apostle's testimony, under the control of the Holy Spirit. The divine influence, working in and through men, chosen for the purpose, and producing the words of Holy Writ, embraced every part of the Book, for, as we shall see, the whole is so interrelated that it stands or falls together.

The attentive reader will be forced to the conclusion that God raised His human agents into cooperation with Himself not excluding the natural factor, but developing and expanding their faculties. The language was in a very real sense their own, yet it was that which God willed that they should use, and that which was fitted for His purpose. The reader cannot but be struck with the fact that there is an absence of studied attempt at mere eloquence. All is exquisitely natural in its mode, though divine in its subject matter. Such a result, produced by that combined naturalness and grandeur and dignity which characterizes the Scriptures, can hardly have been effected otherwise than by the work of the Spirit of God.

Again, there is no trace of toilsome effort after some special style. Each writer retains his own natural style. Peter, for instance, is seen to be ardent and impetuous; John is seen to be full of love and zeal. It is just this fact which makes the whole Book so human, and calculated to meet the differing needs of the human heart. Yet this very fact bears evidence of being divinely ordered, for the characteristic forms of expression which individualize the writers were the means divinely chosen for the conveyance of truth. The divine control is evidenced in the fact that their feelings are strongly and suggestively suppressed when we might naturally have expected to find the strongest expression of emotion. There is no outburst of sympathy when they are recording the agony in the Garden, and the horrors of the trial and of the Cross, no manifestation of exuberant feelings in the record of the Resurrection. Any ordinary writer would have added words to express his own ideas and emotions, but of this there is a complete absence.

That the divine and human are combined in the Scripture records, that is to say, that they were neither mere machinists nor solely responsible for what they wrote, is clear both from the statements in the Bible and from the character of its contents. Thus while Paul speaks of the Scriptures as "Scriptures of the prophets," he says at the same time that they were given according to revelation, and according to the command of the eternal God (Rom. 16:25, 26; cp. Acts 3:20, 21). On the other hand, while the words are said to come from God, sometimes the human author alone is named (see Rom. 4:6; 10:5; Heb. 7:14, etc.).

This union of the divine and human, "the moving power and the living instrument," gives us a Bible "competent to calm our doubts, and able to speak to our weakness. It then becomes not an utterance in a strange tongue, but in the words of wisdom and knowledge. It is authoritative, for it is the voice of God; it is intelligible, for it is in the language of men. . . . Even when they speak most emphatically the words of the Lord, they speak still as men living among men; and the eternal truths which they declare receive the coloring of the minds through which they pass. Nor can it be said that it is easy to eliminate the variable quantity in each case; for the distinguishing peculiarities of the several writers are not confined to marked features, but extend also to a multitude of subtle differences which are only felt after careful study. Everywhere there are traces of a personality not destroyed but even quickened by the action of the Divine power—of an individual consciousness not suspended but employed at every stage of the heavenly commission."*

The Inspiration of the Words

This view, that the divine power acted on man's faculties in accordance with natural laws, is known as the dynamical view of inspiration. It does not by any means deny the fact that the words of Scripture were arranged by the operation of the Spirit of God, but maintains that "God, who gave the message, chose and prepared His messengers, and by His almighty power, using the faculties of the messengers, produced statements of absolute truthfulness. In combining His divine power in perfect union with the exercise of man's faculties, God was surely able to effect results accurate in every detail in spite of the natural fallibility. The divine ray, while using the human medium through which it passed, yet retained its own purity. . . . To suppose that words and cases are convertible, that tenses have no absolute meaning, that forms of expression are accidental, is to abjure the fundamental principles on which all intercourse between men is based. A disbelief in the exactness of language is the prelude to all philosophical skepticism. And it will probably be found that the tendency of mind which discredits the fullest teaching of words leads, however little we may see it, to the disparagement of all outward revelation."†

Limitation of Writers' Conception

Though the writers of Scripture wrote their statements intelligently, i.e., in language which was their own, yet frequently their conception of the meaning and application of what they wrote was narrower than the scope of their writings. The writers shared in the limitations of the readers in this respect. They themselves were cognizant of their limitations, although they were conscious of the divine authority of their messages. It was indeed the divine authority given them that made them realize that their writings covered a far wider range of meaning than could be measured by their own apprehension. To this the Scripture itself bears witness. For, firstly, we are told that they searched into their own records to examine the details of what the Spirit of Christ was testifying through them; and, secondly, it was revealed to them that they were ministering not merely to the men of their own time but to God's people of the present age. "The prophets sought and searched diligently, who prophesied of the grace that should come unto you; searching what time or what manner of time the Spirit of Christ which was in them did point unto, when it testified beforehand the sufferings of Christ, and the glories that should follow them. To whom it was revealed, that not unto themselves, but unto you, did they minister these things, which now have been announced unto you" (1 Pet. 1:10, 11). Similarly when Daniel was receiving divine messages which he records in his prophecies he says, "I heard, but I understood not." The words were intelligible as such, but their divine meaning was "shut up and sealed" for the time (Dan. 12:8, 9).

It is contrary to evidence to suppose that the meaning of the Old Testament Scriptures was confined to the experiences of the writers and applicable only to the circumstances of the people of their own generation. Were that the case, no exposition would now be necessary, nor any present operation of the Spirit of God in unfolding the Scriptures to us.

How the New Testament reveals the wider scope of teaching lying latent in Old Testament records is strikingly illustrated in such passages as Hebrews 7:1–17, where the Genesis narrative of Melchizedek receives a new light, and again in Galatians 4:21–31, where the record concerning Abraham and his sons is shown to convey a wide range of spiritual truth.

The Letter and the Spirit

Attempts have been made to distinguish between the letter and the spirit, as if inspiration

---

*Westcott. "Introduction to the Study of the Gospels," p. 13.
†Westcott, *ibid*. p. 40.

merely attached to the spirit, of the written records and passages. This is due to a mistaken idea concerning the words of the apostle Paul, when he contrasts "the newness of the Spirit" with "the oldness of the letter" (Rom. 7:6), and speaks of himself as a minister "not of the letter, but of the Spirit," and says that "the letter killeth, but the Spirit giveth life" (2 Cor. 3:6). The "letter" here does not stand for the words, either apart from the literal meaning, or with any other meaning than what they were prima facie intended to convey; it denotes the law of Moses, the old Covenant, which if not obeyed by man would kill him. It is in contrast, not with the spirit or the significance of a message, but with the Spirit who gives life through the gospel. These verses then have really no bearing upon the subject now before us, *viz.*, the question whether inspiration attaches not only to the thought but to the words by which the thought is expressed. It is very clear that it attaches to both. Just as in the interpretation of human documents the actual letter of the document is all important in arriving at the intention designed to be conveyed by the expression used, and the meaning of the words used is the question rather than what the writer may have intended to say. Words are signs with a definite value. Defect in the signs involves defect in the meaning conveyed. The inspiration of its words, and the words themselves must be taken to express its real intention.

"The essence of inspiration does not lie in the form alone, or in the spirit alone, but in the combination of both. If the form alone is the result of direct inspiration, it follows that Scripture contains a revelation of pure physical truth, which is contrary to experience; if, on the other hand, the action of Inspiration be limited to the spiritual element, it follows that this must be separable from the form, which has been shown to be impossible."*

The theory that the conceptions were of God, the language of man, that the subject matter was provided by the Holy Spirit, while the language was left to the unaided selection of the writers, is as fallacious as the theory that the words were merely dictated by the Spirit apart from the mental abilities of the writers.

Had the operation of God ruled out the circumstances of a writer's upbringing or his individual temperament or style, the whole Volume could have been reduced to a uniformity of style which is obviously not the case. On the other hand, while the character of the writers and their style stand out distinctly in their writings, there is not a particle of evidence that the truth has, as the critics say, taken on the color of the writers' temperament and individuality to such an extent that their writings have become "distorted in expression." Such an idea is not only unfounded, it also puts an imaginary limitation upon the power of God.

Errors Are Suppositional

We shall be told that the errors exist. That, however, has never yet been irrefutably substantiated. Abundant efforts have been made to find and expose the errors, but no one has been able actually to prove their existence. Mere assertions, however oft repeated, that certain passages or utterances are erroneous, do not make them so. In innumerable passages where error was supposed to exist incontestable proof has been given that there is no mistake or discrepancy at all. In numerous cases in which certain passages of Scripture are said to contain discrepancies, the criticism is due to superficiality of thought or to failure to weigh the evidences impartially failure, for instance, to take into account the circumstances which lie behind the records of certain discourses or events, or to examine with sufficient care the condition relating to the original writings and the extant manuscripts.

The existence of difficulties, or of apparent contradictions and inconsistencies, should only lead us the more carefully to examine the evidences. The carelessness of copyists, for instance, has given currency to a number of false readings, but in most cases it has been found possible to trace the actual original at least within the range of practical certainty.

The day has not yet arrived when any critic has been able to point to any single passage

---

*Westcott. "Introduction to the Study of the Gospels," p. 37.

and show irrefutably that a single word of the original Scriptures, as they appear in the resultant text, was a mistake. The fact that writers of Scripture when writing on the same subject have not stated things exactly in the same way serves to prove that there was no collusion on the part of writers as to their records. The writers of the Gospels, for instance, have never laid themselves open to the charge of fraud by mutually agreeing to represent certain facts in any particular way. Whatever differences there are in the records only serve as a twofold witness, firstly to that of the individuality of the authors, and secondly, to the design of the Holy Spirit in providing us with a wider scope of teaching, and a perfect fabric of truth.

There is a supposition that, as the Bible was written to guide men to salvation and teach them doctrine, divine inspiration did not ensure that the writings should be immune from error on other points, such as historical inaccuracies and scientific mistakes. But, if so, where is the line to be drawn? If this were the case, inasmuch as there are many passages which are not immediately devoted to Christian doctrine, it would be impossible to determine the inspiration of these with any certainty. Who would decide as to the elimination of such passages? The amount eliminated would depend entirely on the standard adopted in each case. No dependence could be placed upon the critics, for not only are they at variance among themselves, but the "assured results" arrived at by one generation are contradicted by the next. If the excisions were freely made, the Bible would become no Bible. If, on the other hand, they were limited to such things as lists of names and similar details, the amount would be so small and trifling that the theory would be stultified. Is it to be supposed that writers, writing for their own nation, or for the Church, books which were actually received and used without complaint or criticism, should have stumbled like ignorant men over dates and names and quotations? Had mistakes of this sort occurred, the writings would at once have been regarded as inaccurate, and would have met with incredulity. But such is known not to have been the case. The supposed inaccuracies have at least been so sufficiently explained as to render any special theory of inspiration framed to meet them a gratuitous exercise of ingenuity.

The Original Texts

In speaking of these supposed inaccuracies we are of course referring to the original autographs and not to translations. Considerations of the subject of inspiration must be based upon the originals as now represented in the ascertained texts, always bearing in mind that extant manuscripts are copies of copies of the originals. For the purpose of giving a written revelation to mankind, God chose the Hebrew and Greek languages, and to a small extent the Chaldaic, in which latter a portion of the book of Daniel was written. Though the autographs themselves do not exist, yet the evidence goes to show that the resultant text arrived at by the collation of the best manuscripts practically represents the originals.

The importance of most of the variations in the manuscript readings has been greatly exaggerated. Westcott and Hort tell us that the "proportion of words virtually accepted on all hands as raised above doubt is very great, not less, on a rough computation, than seven-eighths of the whole." As to the remaining eighth, the variations here are "formed in great part by changes of order and other comparative trivialities." These writers further tell us that "the amount of what can in any sense be called substantial variation . . . can hardly form more than a thousandth part of the entire text." There is no doctrine in Scripture which would be affected if all the various readings were allowed or if all the disputed words, or those about which there is any doubt, were omitted.

The Importance of the Autographs

Because God has not been pleased to preserve the actual originals for us the doctrine of the inspiration of the originals is in no way affected. We need not be surprised that God so ordered that the originals should not be preserved. Dr. Westcott's words are forceful in this connection. In concluding his prefatory chapter to his Introduction to the Study of the Gospels, he says:

"We have no reason to conclude from our knowledge of the whole character of God's dealings that He might be expected to preserve ever inviolate what He has once given. The world which was at first good is now full of evil; man who was at first blessed has fallen under the curse of sin; and such contingencies seem to be involved necessarily in the idea of a finite existence. But a redemption has been wrought for both; and so, too, on the historical side of our religion an uncorrupted Bible lies before us if we patiently and candidly search for it, and a true personal interpretation may be gained by sincere and faithful study. . . . Variations may exist on the one side, and ambiguities on the other, which disappear when brought before the scrutiny of the spiritual judgment . . ."*

We are told that belief in the inerrancy of the autograph originals is only of practical value if we can decide as to which of the variations accord with the originals, and that where a difference of judgment still remains such belief is impossible. But there is no doubt at all as regards the great bulk of Scripture.

Translations

Further, it is said that even if certainty were possible it would be of no value to the majority of Bible readers who have to go by translations, and that inspiration attaches equally to translations as to the originals. Those who are confined to the use of good translations rightly value them, but they also appreciate the fact that the translations are only of value as they faithfully represent the originals. If we regard translations as of equal value with the original text, then we make room for almost every possible form of error. For translation work is open to anyone who has knowledge of Hebrew or Greek, and it is possible to suit the translation to fit wrong doctrine, a practice unfortunately exemplified in some translations.

Again, it is urged that in insisting upon a perfect original there is a danger of losing sight of the Holy Spirit's work in our hearts. We are always indeed exposed to this danger, but it is certainly not produced nor increased by the belief that the Bible as it came from God by the operation of the Holy Spirit through His human instruments was inerrant. That belief cannot detrimentally affect our appreciation of, and response to, the Spirit's work within us.

Accuracy Ensured

If a public speaker or writer exercises the greatest care in selecting his words, so that through their medium his thoughts may be conveyed in the clearest manner possible, how much more is it to be supposed that the Spirit of God, in causing to be put on record divine thoughts and purposes, would see to it that the minds of the men whom He used should be so under His control that they would express correctly, and in the most suitable manner, the words to be used for the purpose. In the case of the Bible, moreover, we have something more than records of great importance from the human point of view; we have nothing less than the permanent expression of the testimony of God to mankind, and the revelation of His counsels for the guidance and support of those who desire to obey Him. Here we have something that was calculated not simply to affect man's mind, or to provide him with mere human instruction, but to mold his life and shape his eternal destiny. It is therefore unreasonable to imagine that with these vital issues at stake God would permit His human instruments, prepared by Him for the purpose of communicating His mind, to convey wrong impressions, or to mislead the mind of the reader by carelessness of thought or expression, or by irrelevant utterance. If it is admitted that God spoke to His people by the Scriptures, the admission demands that He spoke accurately. The accuracy must be assumed till proof is given to the contrary.

Writers and Readers— A Distinction

It is sometimes urged that the Holy Spirit empowered the writers, and that He also guides the believing reader, and that therefore the influence is the same in each case. But the

---

*Ibid., page 43.

Holy Spirit was more than merely an inspiring influence over the writers, He imparted a power to the words which makes them permanently living and effective. The transactions between God and the reader are one thing; the fact that what he is reading is due to a work essentially perfect in its inception is another. Denial of the perfections of that initial work of God strikes at the very foundations of the faith.

CHAPTER TWO

Evidences in Scripture

The Testimony of Christ

Introductory

The most important of Scripture evidences is the testimony of our Lord as given in the Gospels. We will examine somewhat in chronological order His use of the Old Testament. His first recorded reference to it is in His conflict with Satan in the wilderness. He meets the attack of His adversary by a thrice repeated "It is written," each time quoting from the book of Deuteronomy (Matt. 4:4, 7, 10). The narrative makes clear that both Christ and the tempter regarded the declarations of Scripture as providing an irrefutable reply to any challenge or suggestion. There is no question on the part of either of an appeal from that authority. The devil showed his realization of its irresistible force by adopting it as his own weapon. Our Lord's "It is written" carries with it, then, His witness to the divinely authoritative character of the words of Scripture. Of this more later.

Part I—His Application of the Old Testament to Himself

We follow Him into the synagogue at Nazareth. The roll of the prophet Isaiah is handed to Him. He finds the passage beginning, "The Spirit of the Lord is upon Me" (Is. 61:1). Having read the passage, He closes the roll, gives it to the attendant, sits down and begins His discourse to the congregation with the words, "This day is this Scripture fulfilled in your ears," This is the first illustration of an important feature which characterizes His use of the Old Testament throughout the course of His ministry, namely, that He represents Himself as fulfilling in His own Person the scheme of the former Covenant. Let us trace His teaching in this respect from this first instance in the Nazareth synagogue to the forty days' period after His resurrection, and observe what bearing it has on the subject of Inspiration.

In His public discourses He applies the prophecy of Malachi 3:1 to John the Baptist as being the messenger who was to prepare His way (Matt. 11:10; cp. Matt. 11:14 and 17:12, and Mal. 4:5). Again, He makes Jonah's experiences a prefiguration of His burial and resurrection (Matt. 12:40; cp. 16:4). His method of teaching the people He claims to be a fulfillment of Isaiah's prophecy (Matt. 13:14 and Is. 6:9, 10). He tells the Jews who oppose Him that whereas they search the Scriptures, thinking that therein they have eternal life, the Scriptures really bear witness to Himself and that eternal life is only to be obtained by coming to Him for it (John 5:39); that Moses wrote of Him, and if they really believed Moses they would believe Him; and, further, that failure to grasp the truth of the Mosaic teachings must involve failure to believe the words of the One of whom he wrote (John 5:46, 47). The two are inseparable. The old embodies the new, the new unfolds the old. Again, as the Living Bread from Heaven, He is the reality of which the manna given by God to their fathers under the leadership of Moses was a figure (John 6:32, 33, and 49, 51). Isaiah's prophecy, "All thy children shall be taught of the Lord" (Is. 54:13), finds its center, Christ declares, in Himself: "Everyone," He says, "that hath heard from the Father, and hath learned, cometh unto Me" (John 6:45). Again, "Abraham," He says, "rejoiced to see My day; he saw it, and was glad" (8:56).

Further, against their charge of blasphemy in His having made Himself God, He appeals to Psalm 82:6, as follows: "Is it not written in your law, I said, Ye are gods. If He called them gods, unto whom the Word of God came (and the Scripture cannot be broken), say ye of Him whom the Father sanctified, and sent into the world, Thou blasphemest; because I said, I am the Son of God" (John 10:34–36). True,

His appeal here to the Old Testament is of a different character, yet He is basing His vindication of His claims upon a Scripture the authority of which they might perhaps have been tempted to question. It contained a mention of "gods." Just here, then, He declares "the Scripture cannot be broken."

As He drives the money changers and dove vendors from the temple, He gives as the authority for His action the words of Isaiah 56:7 (Matt. 21:12). When appealed to by the chief priests and scribes in their remonstrance against the adoration given Him by the children in the temple, He expresses His appreciation of their praise by quoting Psalm 8, asking the objectors, "Did ye never read, Out of the mouths of babes and sucklings Thou hast perfected praise" (Matt. 21:16). What a significance attaches to His "Did ye never read"! The words are there in the Scripture for them to accept. Both for His hearers as well as for Himself they are the absolute and final court of appeal. Again, Psalm 118, which speaks of the stone which the builders rejected as having become the head of the corner, He applies to the rejection of Himself by the chief priests and elders and to God's vindication of His claims (Matt. 21:42). In His discussion with the Pharisees concerning the Christ, though He does not state directly that He was Himself both David's Son and David's Lord, yet He does so by implication, applying to Himself the words of Psalm 110:1, "The Lord said unto my Lord, Sit Thou on My right hand till I put Thine enemies under Thy feet" (Matt. 21:41–45).

We pass now to the circumstances connected with the Cross. On the night of His betrayal He tells His disciples that the hatred of the Jews is a fulfillment of the words recorded in Psalm 69:4; that the words of Psalm 41:9 are to be fulfilled in the case of the traitor (John 13:18); and even in His prayer He makes known that the doom of the traitor is the fulfillment of Scripture (John 17:12). Again, He tells them that the words of Isaiah 53:12, "And He was reckoned with the transgressors" are to be fulfilled in Himself (Luke 22:37). He declares that His death is the fulfillment of the prophecy of Zechariah 13:7 (Matt. 26:31). When Judas and his company come to capture Him, He tells Peter that, though He had only to pray His Father, and angels would come to His deliverance, in that case, "How should the Scriptures be fulfilled." To His captors He states that what they were doing was taking place that the Scriptures might be fulfilled (Matt. 26:54, 56).

We follow Him to the cross. There we hear Him still taking the Old Testament as fulfilled in His own case. In the hours of His crucifixion His "I thirst," is spoken "that the Scriptures might be accomplished" (John 19:28). In His other utterances on the cross He uses the opening and closing words of Psalm 22, "My God, My God, why hast Thou forsaken Me" (Matt. 27:46), and "It is finished" (John 19:30), and the words of Psalm 31:5, "Into Thine hand I commend My spirit" (Luke 23:46).

This use of the Old Testament is more fully illustrated than ever after His resurrection. Now more than previously He shows Himself to be the great theme of the Scriptures. In His conversation with the two disciples on the road to Emmaus, "beginning from Moses and from all the prophets" He interprets to them "in all the Scriptures the things concerning Himself" (Luke 24:27). This outstanding characteristic of His teaching, while illustrated first in the Gospel narratives in Luke's record of the discourse in the synagogue at Nazareth, finds its most comprehensive instance at the close of that Gospel, where, reminding the disciples of what He had previously taught them, He says, "All things must needs be fulfilled, which are written in the law of Moses, and the prophets, and the Psalms concerning Me." He then opened their mind that they might understand the Scriptures, and said, "Thus it is written, that the Christ should suffer and rise again from the dead the third day: and that repentance and remission of sins should be preached in His Name to all the nations, beginning from Jerusalem" (Luke 24:44–47). His "Thus it is written" carries with it the tacit understanding that His hearers, alike with Himself, regard the words as of divine authority.

Here, then, He reviews the Old Testament in its full extent in this respect. Gathering up in His own Person all parts of the sacred Volume, Law, Psalms, Prophets (a known and recognized collection), each of which He had referred to separately on previous occasions in the same way, He puts His own imprimatur upon each as being divinely inspired.

In thus representing Himself as the fulfillment of Old Testament Scripture, Christ not only establishes its divine authority, He also indicates its relationship with the new age of grace which He came to introduce. Perhaps the most striking evidence of this is His statement in the Sermon on the Mount, "Think not that I came to destroy the law or the prophets: I came not to destroy, but to fulfill. For verily I say unto you, Till heaven and earth pass away, one jot or one tittle shall in no wise pass away from the law, till all things be accomplished" (Matt. 5:17, 18). He uses the same language to assert the permanency of His own teaching; He says, "Heaven and earth shall pass away, but My words shall not pass away" (Matt. 24:35). Thus He links together the words of the Old Testament and His own sayings, and stamps them alike as imperishable and divine.

Part II—His Testimony to Old Testament Historicity

We may view our Lord's testimony to the inspiration of Old Testament Scripture in another way. He was constantly giving His endorsement to the historicity and divine authority of Old Testament narratives, apart from the principle we have been considering. He obviously views as authoritative several passages which have been considered by higher critics as uninspired or even legendary. The Gospel narratives make clear that both Christ and those whom He was addressing invariably regarded the historical records as authentic. Let us examine these allusions.

Besides His references mentioned above, to Jonah's being three days and three nights in the belly of the great fish, to the provision of the manna in the wilderness, and to Abraham and Moses, He speaks of the following circumstances as facts, the historicity of which He Himself confirmed, and His hearers, both disciples and opponents, accepted without question.

This list is suggestive in more ways than one. The authority of the Lord's opinions as to the validity of Old Testament passages is set in contrast in several cases to Higher Critical views. On this see below.

	Recorded in	New Testament
The creation of man	Gen. 5:2	Matt. 19:4
The murder of Abel	Gen. 4	Matt. 23:35
The times of Noah	Gen. 7	Matt. 24:37
The Flood	Gen. 7	Luke 17:27
The days of Lot	Gen. 13	Luke 17:28
The destruction of Sodom	Gen. 19	Luke 17:29
The Word of God to Moses	Ex. 3:6	Matt. 22:32
The rite of circumcision	Gen. 17:10	John 7:22
The giving of the Law	Ex. 20	John 7:19
The commandments of the Law	Ex. 20:12–16	Matt. 19:18
The ceremonial law *re* leprosy	Lev. 14	Mark 1:44
The lifting up of the serpent of brass	Num. 21:9	John 3:14
The profanation of the Temple by the priests	see Num. 28:9, 10; 1 Chr. 9:30–32	Matt. 12:5
David's eating of the shewbread	1 Sam. 21	Matt. 12:3
The glory of Solomon	1 Kin. 10	Matt. 6:29
The Queen of Sheba's visit to Solomon	1 Kin. 10	Matt. 12:42
The famine in the days of Elijah	1 Kin. 17	Luke 4:25
The sending of Elijah to a widow in Sidon	1 Kin. 17	Luke 4:25
The healing of Naaman by Elisha	2 Kin. 5	Luke 4:27
The stoning of Zechariah	2 Chr. 24:21	Matt. 23:35
Daniel's prophecy of the abomination of desolation	Dan. 9:27, etc.	Matt. 24:15
Jonah's message to Nineveh	Jon. 3:5	Matt. 12:41

Again, the list, coupled with His other references to the Old Testament, shows how His mind was stored with the Holy Scriptures. It was His habit to use them on all occasions, and to base His arguments upon them.

We notice that the validity of the Lord's argument on the subject of divorce and of His command, "What therefore God hath joined together let no man put asunder," He makes to depend upon the assumption that the account of the creation of man and woman given in Genesis 2 is authoritative (Matt. 19:3-6).

Again, He speaks of Exodus as part of "the book of Moses" (Mark 12:26), and bases His teaching on the resurrection upon words recorded therein as being spoken by God to Moses. Further, He speaks of the Law as having been given by Moses and as being the commandment of God (Mark 7:9, 10). Both parts of the book of Isaiah are referred to by Him as coming under Isaiah's authorship. He quotes from the twenty-ninth chapter as being the words of Isaiah (Mark 7:6), and it is as from "the roll of the prophet Isaiah" that He quotes the words of the sixty-first chapter (Luke 4:17). He not only ascribes Psalm 110 to the authorship of David, but says that he wrote it by the Spirit of God (Matt. 22:43, R.V.).

"I am perfectly aware," wrote the late Bishop Moule, "that now, our Lord's own interpretation of that Psalm, involving as it does His assertion of its Davidic authorship, is treated as quite open to criticism and disproof. One such scholar does not hesitate to say, that if the majority of modern experts are right as to the non-Davidic authorship, and he seems to think that they are, 'our Lord's argument breaks down.' Such utterances must surely open the way toward conceptions of His whole teaching which make for the ruin of faith. For the question is not whether our Redeemer consented to submit to limits in His conscious human knowledge . . . it is whether He consented to that sort of limitation which alone, in respect of imperfection of knowledge, is the real peril of a teacher, and which is his fatal peril—the ignorance of his own ignorance, and a consequent claim to teach where he does not know. In human schools the betrayal of that sort of ignorance is a deathblow to confidence, not only in some special utterance, but in the teacher, for it strikes at his claim not to knowledge so much as to wisdom, to balance and insight of thought."*

Again, our Lord speaking from Psalm 82 lays down the general principle that the Scripture cannot be broken, thereby marking as of permanent authority the whole of what was known as the Scripture, i.e., the volume of the Old Testament, the contents of which were well defined and accepted as the Word of God (John 10:35).

Did He in so doing merely, as is now so often argued, adopt consciously and of purpose the current erroneous views of His age? This is a more serious question even than whether He really knew and was ignorant of His ignorance. That is fatal to His claim to be in some sense the only teacher (Matt. 23:8), but this is to suggest that He accommodated His language to current notions knowing them to be false. It other words, the one gives me an imperfect Christ, the other an untrustworthy one. To quote the concluding words of Dr. Moule in the above quoted paragraph, "I venture to say that recent drifts of speculation show how rapidly the conception of a fallible Christ develops toward that of a wholly imperfect and untrustworthy Christ.

"The evidence of the Gospels is undeniable that He believed in the Old Testament as the inspired record of God's revelation, in the historicity of its narratives, in its Messianic utterances as pointing to Himself and based His teaching upon its words and history. Was it Christ who was wrong in this, or is it criticism so far as criticism denies these things? . . . The error lies in supposing that the only way of being assured of the truth of the revelation by God in the Scripture is by modern critical study. Christ went with unerring certainty to the very heart of the Old Testament. He not only penetrated to its truth, but intuitively perceived the inner connection of truth and history. Essential truth to Him implies historical truth. Revelation with Him was historical. Hence the confidence with which he uses the

---

*"Messages from the Epistle to the Hebrews," by H. C. G. Moule, D.D., p. 27.

Old Testament Scriptures and continually appeals to them as the Word of God."*

Part III—His Testimony to the Divine Inspiration of the Words

A judge, in dealing with a case before him, construes not the sentiments but the words of the statute bearing upon the case. So with the Scriptures as Christ used and spoke of them. With Him the actual words that are written are all-important, for only as they are rightly understood can the ideas which they enshrine be really grasped and find their practical application. The Lord views the Scriptures not so much as bearing the impress of the personality of the writers, nor as representing merely the conditions under which they wrote, but as being the words of God. We have proof of this in the fact that He treats Scripture as an entity, all the parts of which have equal authority. In His abundant use of the Old Testament He mentions only four of the writers by name as authors—Moses, David, Isaiah, and Daniel; and in each case there is either a plain statement or an intimation that the writers are not the source of the authority of their utterances. In the other cases, of which there are about thirty, they bear no reference to the human authorship; the Scriptures are simply viewed either as the law, or as having the quality of law, the appeal being to what is written. Never does Christ once allude to the inspiration of the authors. Nor yet does He ever hint that there was such a thing as misconception or error on their part. Considering that He Himself was so inseparably associated with the Scriptures, and that He spoke of Himself as a witness to the truth, He could not in faithfulness have omitted to notice an error in the Old Testament had there been one there.

Now as to the four writers above mentioned. When questioned by the Pharisees and scribes, the Lord replies that Moses said, "Honor thy father and mother" (Mark 7:10), but He refers to these words as "The commandment of God" (v. 9). Clearly their divine authorship is independent of the name Moses. So again Mark reports Him as saying, "Have ye not read in the book of Moses . . . how,

etc.?" (Mark 12:26), but in the corresponding passage in Matthew, in quoting the same words, the writer quotes Him as saying, "Have ye not read that which was spoken unto you by God?" and here there is no mention of the authorship of Moses (Matt. 22:31).†

Again in quoting from Isaiah, while the Lord does mention His name in the quotations in Matthew 12:17–21, and 15:7–9, yet elsewhere in quoting from the same writer He simply says, "Is it not written, My house shall be called a house of prayer for all the nations?" (Mark 11:17; cp., 12:37).

So with regard to David; in one place, where it is obviously necessary to mention the writer, Christ says, "David himself said in the Holy Spirit" (Mark 12:36); He is not mentioning David merely as the authority for the statement, it is essential to His argument that He should name him. But quoting from another Psalm he says, "Is it not written in your law, I said, Ye are gods? If He called them gods unto whom the Word of God came (and the Scripture cannot be broken) . . ." (John 10:34, 35; cp. John 15:25). Not only is the Divine authority of the quotation independent of the writer, but obviously the Lord looked upon the Psalms as of an equally binding character with that of the law.

In regard to Daniel, the Lord referred to the "abomination of desolation" as "that which was spoken of by Daniel the prophet." Thus He places Daniel's words in the category of prophecy, and thereby marks them as divinely inspired.

Whenever Christ or His disciples allude to the Scriptures they do so in language implying in the strongest possible manner their divine authority and inspiration. Such phrases as "It is written," "The Scripture saith," and such statements as "The Scripture cannot be broken," "David in the Spirit calleth Him Lord," provide clear evidence of this. The uniform way in which they speak of the Old Testament is entirely incompatible with any other idea. He claims this authority not only for the statements of Scripture, but for each word and each part of a word. He says, "Think not that I came to destroy the law or the prophets; I

---

*Orr in "Revelation and Inspiration," p. 154.
†For the differences in the Gospel records see pp. 25 and 86–97.

came not to destroy, but to fulfill. For verily I say unto you, Till heaven and earth pass away, one jot or one tittle shall in no wise pass away from the law, till all things be accomplished" (Matt. 5:17, 18).

2 Timothy 3:16

The divine inspiration of the written words of the Bible is stated plainly by the apostle Paul in his second Epistle to Timothy (3:16). The Authorized Version reads, "All Scripture is given by inspiration of God, and is profitable for doctrine, for reproof, for correction, for instruction in righteousness." The Revised Version reads, "Every Scripture inspired of God is also profitable for teaching, for reproof, for correction, for instruction which is in righteousness."

There is really no essential difference between these two versions. In the matter of translation the Revised Version rendering is equally possible with that of the Authorized Version. Each bears testimony to the fact that the Scriptures are God-breathed. A recent writer justly remarks, "It would be too absurd to think that Paul meant to speak of a line which nobody could see, and which nobody could draw, running straight or crooked up and down inside the Bible, so that some of it was inspired and useful, and some of it was useless, being uninspired. The Revised Version only gives additional emphasis to the fact that in those sacred writings with which Timothy had been familiar since he was a babe, every Scripture, being inspired, was also profitable."*

We may go further than this and say that the apostle was intimating to Timothy that not only were the Old Testament Scriptures God-breathed, but that others were being written (which now form part of the New Testament) which were equally inspired, and that these latter must be similarly regarded by Timothy as profitable, etc. Probably all Paul's Epistles had been written by that time as well as other books of the New Testament. We may note too that in 1 Timothy 5:18 Paul quotes as Scripture the words spoken by the Lord, as recorded in Luke 10:7, "The laborer is worthy of his hire."

This passage in 2 Timothy testifies, then, to the divine origin, authority, and profitableness of every part of Scripture, its sufficiency for all spiritual requirements, and its finality in doctrine.

Concerning his own utterances, whether oral or written, Paul declares that what he taught was the word of God and not the word of man (1 Thess. 2:13). Elsewhere he states that his ministry is "in words which the Spirit teacheth," a direct claim to the divine inspiration of his language (1 Cor. 2:13).

Scripture Ascribed to God

A great proportion of the Scriptures is definitely stated to consist of the words of God. To take illustrative cases, practically the whole of the first chapter of Genesis is covered by the repeated statement "God said" (Gen. 1:3, 6, 9, 11, 14, 20, 24, 26, 29). So with large portions of other chapters. Other phrases are, "The Lord God said . . ." (chaps. 6:3; 7:1; 9:1; 12:1; 26:2; 31:3, etc.); see also Exodus *passim;* "God spake, . . . saying . . ." (chaps. 8:15; 46:2, etc.). "The Lord spake saying, . . ." (Ex. 6:10, etc.). In the Pentateuch alone the list extends to nearly 700. In the historical books there is a similar list of considerably over 400. On turning to the writings of the prophets we find the declaration "Thus saith the Lord God" and similar phrases occurring some 150 times in Isaiah alone, and recurring characteristically throughout the whole of the prophetic books of the Old Testament. Again and again the prophets aver "The Word of the Lord came unto me saying, . . ." This and like statements are found almost 350 times in Ezekiel.

If the amount of subject matter which is recorded in the Old Testament under one or other of the above mentioned declarations as being the utterances of God were put together, the proportion of the Volume would be startling. Cumulatively it stamps the whole book with a Divine impress.

The way in which the writers speak of the Scriptures as the work of the Spirit of God indicates clearly that in their view the words

*G. C. M. Douglas, D.D., in Vol. 1 of the "New Biblical Guide." It is generally acknowledged among competent scholars that the Revised Version rendering is legitimate from the grammatical point of view.

were inspired. For instance, David says, "The Spirit of the Lord spake by me, and His word was upon my tongue" (2 Sam. 23:2). Mark narrates how the Lord, quoting from Psalm 110, declared that the words were uttered by David "in the Holy Spirit" (Mark 12:36). Peter testifies that in Psalm 41 the Holy Spirit spake by the mouth of David (Acts 1:16). The writer of the Epistle to the Hebrews ascribes the words of the 95th Psalm to the Holy Spirit (Heb. 3), and so with the words of Jeremiah 31:33, 34 (Heb. 10:15).

Similar testimony is given in such statements as the following: "The words of the Lord are pure words; as silver tried in a furnace on the earth, purified seven times" (Ps. 12:6); "Every word of God is tried" (Prov. 30:5). Compare Psalm 19:7–11.

Again, when the Lord was preparing the apostles for the testimony they were to give after He had gone, He assured them that it would be given to them what they were to speak. "Whatsoever shall be given you . . . that speak ye: for it is not ye that speak, but the Holy Ghost" (Mark 13:11; cp. Matt. 10:19, and see Luke 12:12 and John 16:12, 15). This was made good in the case of the apostle Paul, for he tells the Corinthian church that Christ speaks in him (2 Cor. 13:3), and again he declares that in ministering the things of God he speaks, "not in words which man's wisdom teacheth, but which the Holy Spirit teacheth" (1 Cor. 2:13). Obviously he is referring not merely to his ministry in general, but to the words which he uttered, as being the outcome of the immediate operation of the Spirit of God. It is plain, too, that the Lord promised more than that divine communications should be made to the apostles which they would be able to interpret to their hearers; the very words were to be given them, and this would hold good both for their oral and their written testimony.

2 Peter 1:20, 21

The apostle Peter states that "no prophecy of Scripture is of private interpretation. For no prophecy ever came by the will of man; but men spake from God, being moved by the Holy Ghost" (2 Pet. 1:20, 21). Without going at length here into the nature of prophecy as a means of divine revelation, it must not be forgotten that the Scripture use of the term covers a far wider ground than prediction. Prediction is only one form of prophecy.

It is essential to the character of prophetic Scripture as such that it should not only be derived from prophetic authorship, but should be told in the name of the Lord. The writers being men prepared of God for the purpose, it was only on this ground that any man could say, "Thus saith the Lord," or "Hear ye the word of the Lord." As Professor Orr says, "Taking the extensive prophetic literature of the Old Testament, it will not be denied that this claims to be produced under direct divine inspiration. The prophets . . . , called and equipped for their special work by God, receiving their messages from His hand, delivering them under the solemn sanction of a 'Thus saith the Lord,' accrediting them with supernatural prediction, speak and write with an authority which cannot be taken from them. Their writings, accordingly, answer in the highest degree to the test of inspiration."*

Prophetic Utterances

The mission of the prophet, then, was to speak in the name of the Lord. The message consisted in uttering the mind of God. "With the idea of a prophet there was this necessarily attached, that he spoke, not his own words, but those which he had directly received" (Gesenius' Hebrew Lexicon, sub voc.). Thus when Moses argued his inability to reason with Pharaoh God said, "Aaron thy brother shall be thy prophet" (Ex. 7:1), that is to say, Aaron would utter the word of God on Moses' behalf. The nature of prophecy in this respect applies to all the prophets of Scripture whether in the period covered by the Old Testament or in apostolic times.

The passage quoted above from Peter's second Epistle consists of an initial declaration followed by three explanatory statements. "No prophecy is of private interpretation." This is explained, firstly, by the statement that "no prophecy ever came by the will of man." That

*"Revelation and Inspiration," p. 190.

prophecy was not of private interpretation means, then, that it did not originate in the will of the prophet. On the contrary, secondly, it was given by God; "men spake from God." Then as to the divine action in and through the prophets, "they were moved (lit. borne along) by the Holy Ghost." Accordingly, not only did prophecy not originate in the will of the prophet, but neither did he put his own construction upon the message he was to communicate. Both origin and control lay with God. The prophets did not obtain a general sense of what they were to say, mastering their subject and expressing it at their will; their statements were so under divine influence that the forms of expression which their communications took were the outcome of the action of the Holy Ghost.

Exemplified in Balaam's Case

In this connection the case of Balaam is instructive. Despite his desires to the contrary, the Lord compelled him to declare messages exactly as he gave them. Balaam himself said, "I cannot go beyond the word of the Lord my God, to do less or more" (Num. 22:18), and again, later, "Have I now any power at all to speak anything? the word that God putteth in my mouth, that shall I speak" (22:38). On the next occasion it says, "The Lord put a word in Balaam's mouth, and said, . . ." (23:5). Again, replying to Balak's remonstrance he says, "Must I not take heed to speak that which the Lord putteth in my mouth?" (23:12). The next record is that "the Lord put a word in his mouth, and said, . . ." (v. 16). Finally, when Balak's anger is kindled because of his utterances, Balaam says, "If Balak would give me his house full of silver and gold, I cannot go beyond the word of the Lord, to do either good or bad of mine own mind; but what the Lord speaketh that will I speak" (24:13).

All this shows clearly that the Spirit of God determined, in the case of a prophet, not only the form of his prophecy but the very words. Even if Scripture were silent on the point it would be a perfectly reasonable conclusion that what was thus true of the spoken proph-

ecy was likewise true of the written Scriptures. The statement of the apostle Peter quoted above is authoritative on the subject.

The language of their messages was thus inspired, and if this was true in the case of the spoken words, it was at least equally possible in the case of written words. That it was so with the former is indicated in several passages of Scripture. For instance, concerning the prophesying of the seventy elders with Moses, the narrative states that "When the Spirit rested upon them they prophesied, but they did so no more" (Num. 11:25). That is, the Spirit was speaking by them. They were not simply interpreting a divine message imparted to them. While they were under the power of the Spirit their words were not their own as on ordinary occasions; they were the words of God. Their utterances were not the outcome of their own volition. Not that the prophets were carried into an ecstatic condition of mind, rendering them incapable of entering intelligently into the meaning of their words. They did not speak apart from their understanding though they did not comprehend fully the purpose or complete application of their message.

Predictive Prophecy

As to predictive prophecy, the accuracy of Bible predictions affords a striking evidence of its divine inspiration. Many attempts have been made to eliminate as far as possible this predictive element.* The whole character of these predictions, however, and especially in regard to Messianic prophecy, presents such "marvelous unity, self-consistency and comprehensiveness" as bears witness against all such efforts. The words of Professor Flint in this respect are worth quoting: "This broad, general fact—this vast and strange correlation of correspondence—cannot be in the least affected by questions of the 'higher criticism' as to the authorship, time, origination and mode of composition of the various books of the Old Testament. . . . Answer all these questions in the way which the boldest and most rationalistic criticism of Germany or Holland ventures to suggest; accept in every properly

*See "Bible Predictions and the Critics," by the writer. Also Prof. Orr, "The Problem of the Old Testament," p. 455.

critical question the conclusions of the most advanced critical schools, and what will follow? Merely this, that those who do so will have, in various respects, to alter their views as to the manner and method in which the ideal of the Messiah's person, work, and kingdom was, point by point, line by line, evolved and elaborated. There will not, however, be a single Messianic word or sentence, not a single line or feature the fewer in the Old Testament."

New Testament Quotations

A reader of the New Testament cannot fail to be struck with the manner in which the writers and speakers introduce their quotations from the Old Testament. The phrase "It is written" occurs about eighty times, and a careful perusal of the various passages shows what importance attaches to the actual words of the Scriptures quoted. The regular appeal is not to the sentiments expressed, but to the words. This we have seen in the preceding section. Concerning the characteristic "It is written," Urquhart well says, "This mode of quotation has special force. Judges refer in this way to the statute book; and executors naturally use it in interpreting the will or the deed whose terms they are legally bound to execute. *They go by what is written*. They have regard to the words. Their one aim is to understand and to apply these written or printed words in all their strictness. They themselves interpolate nothing; they allow no one to interpolate anything. There may be different interpretations of a clause or of a word; but they test all the interpretations by what is written. The statute or the deed is supreme; its lightest word is highest law. And there is nothing little, or mean, or irrational in all this. No man possessed of common sense would dream of making it a reproach to them. He would never think of hurling at them such epithets as 'literalists,' 'worshipers of the letter,' 'deifiers of a book,' etc. He would not counsel them to abandon the literal interpretation; nor would he give to each judge and to each executor power to act according to his own notions. The safety of the State, confidence in contract, and the very existence of worldwide trade and commerce, depend upon absolute loyalty to the letter of that which is written."

Another mode of introducing quotations in the New Testament writings, bearing testimony to the verbal accuracy of Old Testament Scripture, is the use of the phrase "The Scripture saith" or "the Scripture hath said." These, like the other phrases, show that in the view of the writers their actual words were stamped with divine authority. Paul goes so far as to personify Scripture, as, for instance, when he says, "The Scripture foreseeing that God would justify the Gentiles by faith, preached the gospel beforehand unto Abraham" (Gal. 3:8), and again, "The Scripture hath shut up all things under sin" (v. 22). For other evidences of the importance attaching to the words of the Old Testament the reader may be referred, by way of illustration, to the quotations in Matthew 1:22, 23; 2:15; 8:17; 12:17; 13:14; 15:7; 21:4.*

James 2:23

There is in this connection a unique testimony given by James in his Epistle. In showing that works are the essential counterpart of faith in the matter of justification, he illustrates his point by relating how Abraham offered up Isaac upon the altar. In this act he says that "the Scripture was fulfilled which saith, And Abraham believed God, and it was reckoned unto him for righteousness." When Abraham offered Isaac, the Scripture in Genesis 15, recording the fact of this faith, now manifesting itself in works, had not been written. How then could the act be the fulfillment of a Scripture, the writing of which was future to the event? The Scripture apparently was regarded by James as an ever-present thing in the mind of God, foreknown and foreordained in the divine design, and therefore certain of being recorded in course of time. Just as conversely, we meet with statements to the effect that God is now speaking by the Scripture, though in point of fact the record has long ago been made. Such a statement as James makes would be impossible in connection with any historical record apart from divine inspiration.

---

*For the arbitrary way in which Higher Critics treat these passages, see the author's "Bible Predictions and the Critics."

Obviously the event must have occurred before the writing which records it, as in ordinary histories. But James states that the event fulfilled the Scripture, a circumstance which involves supernatural action in the record.

Old Testament Testimonies

Turning now especially to the Old Testament testimonies to the inspiration of its words, we may take the following:

Deuteronomy 18:18–20

In the divine instructions to Israel concerning the prophets who were to be raised up for them, God said, "I will raise them up a prophet from among their brethren, like unto thee; and I will put My words in his mouth, and he shall speak unto them all that I shall command him. And it shall come to pass, that whosoever will not hearken unto My words which he shall speak in My name, I will require it of him. But the prophet, which shall speak a word presumptuously in My name, which I have not commanded him to speak, or that shall speak in the name of other gods, that same prophet shall die" (Deut. 18:18–20). It will be observed that the Lord speaks of "the words" not as so many statements, but as the separate words which constitute the statements. The utterances were to be given word for word. Obviously a prophet had the power of uttering fresh communications carrying with them the authority of divine law, and which, if put on record, would become part of Holy Scripture.* The authority of the written Word is unquestionable with Israel. It was always accepted among the Jews that the appeal to that Word was final.

Deuteronomy 29:1

There is a remarkable passage in the twenty-ninth chapter of Deuteronomy which relates to the instructions given by Moses to Israel at the end of their journeyings. Speaking of these instructions the narrative says, "These are the words of the covenant which the Lord commanded Moses to make with the children of Israel in the land of Moab" (chap. 29:1). What is here mentioned covers practically the entire book of Deuteronomy, which accordingly consists almost throughout of words given by God to Moses for Israel.

Deuteronomy 31 and 32

We may compare the similar testimony in the words of the Lord to Moses concerning his song recorded in chapter 32. The commandment regarding it is, "Now therefore write ye this song for you, and teach thou it the children of Israel: and put it in their mouths, that this song may be a witness for Me against the children of Israel" (chap. 31:19). "And Moses spake in the ears of all the assembly of Israel *the words* of this song, until they were finished" (v. 30). This song therefore was not merely an expression of Moses' own sentiments. Both the theme and the words of the theme were given him direct from God.

Joshua

Again, the book of Joshua opens with the words of the Lord to him regarding the book of the Law as written by Moses. He was to meditate therein day and night that he might observe to do "according to all that is written therein" (Josh. 1:1, 8). Again, before Joshua dies, he exhorts the people "to keep and to do all that is written in the book of the Law of Moses" (chap. 23:6). There was to be absolute compliance with its minutest detail. The nation was taught that this book of the Law was given by God, and that it consisted of His words. It was for them a safe and absolute guide, and if it could be conceived of as having contained an error in the slightest particular they could not have been expected to show the reverence it demanded and in which they held it. The greatest possible confirmation as to its verbal accuracy is the statement of Christ: "Verily I say unto you, Till heaven and earth pass away, one jot (i.e., the smallest Hebrew letter) or one tittle (i.e., the smallest part of a letter) shall in no wise pass away from the Law, till all things be accomplished" (Matt. 5:18); and again, "It is easier for heaven and earth to pass away, than for one tittle of the Law to fall" (Luke 16:17).

---

*For the nature of prophecy see under section 2 Peter 1:20, 21.

1 Chronicles 15:13

To take another example, in the instructions given in the Law concerning the ark there is a passage which is suggestive as to the importance of verbal details. When David was making final arrangements to bring up the ark of the Lord to its place in Jerusalem, he reminded the priests and the Levites of the mistake they had made on the former occasion, and said, "The Lord our God made a breach upon us, for that we sought Him not according to the ordinance" (1 Chr. 15:13). This has reference not to one of the Ten Commandments, but to one point in the ceremonial laws relating to the ark.

2 Samuel 23:2

In speaking of the way in which he received and communicated divine messages, David says, "The Spirit of the Lord spake by me (lit., 'in me'), and His word was upon my tongue" (2 Sam. 23:2). This latter statement makes clear that the Spirit of God was actually selecting the words that were to be spoken. But this was not only true of the immediate prophecy to which he was referring, it was, for instance, also true of the details given him by divine revelation concerning the building of the house of the Lord. In giving Solomon his son the instruction about this, the historian says that David had the pattern given him by the Spirit (1 Chr. 28:12). Still more specific is David's own word concerning every detail, both of the temple and its equipment. After going minutely into the particulars, he said, "All this have I been made to understand in writing from the hand of the Lord, even all the works of this pattern" (v. 19). This statement is important as indicating the method by which the wording was divinely arranged. The particulars were given him from God to the minutest detail, and must have been entirely void of inaccuracy. Now if this was so in the special instance of the temple, it was, to say the least, possible in all other cases in which men wrote by divine inspiration. If the words relating to the building of the temple were God-breathed, why should it be thought impossible or unlikely that the same thing is true of the other writings of Scripture?

Ezra 7:11

There is, again, a passage in the book of Ezra which lays stress upon the words of the commandments. Ezra himself is called "the scribe *of the words* of the commandments of the Lord, and of His statutes to Israel." The commandments were recorded not merely as conveying the will of God in a general way, but as coming word for word from Himself. Suggestive also in this connection is the fact that on the day when the people gathered under Ezra in Jerusalem to hear the Law, those who read it "read in the book, in the Law of God distinctly; and they gave the sense, so that they understood the reading" (Neh. 8:8).

Jeremiah 36

A striking passage in Jeremiah which illustrates the divine inspiration of the words of Scripture is the narrative which tells of the roll of the book which the prophet was commissioned to write. "This word came unto Jeremiah from the Lord, saying, Take thee a roll of a book, and write therein *all the words that I have spoken* against Israel, and against Judah, and against all the nations, from the day I spake unto thee, from the days of Josiah even unto this day." The prophet uses Baruch as his amanuensis: "Baruch wrote from the mouth of Jeremiah *all the words of the Lord, which he had spoken unto him,* upon a roll of a book. And Jeremiah commanded Baruch, saying, 'I am shut up; I cannot go unto the house of the Lord: therefore go thou, and read in the roll, which thou hast written from my mouth, *the words of the Lord* in the ears of the people . . .' And Baruch, the son of Neriah, did according to all that Jeremiah the prophet commanded him, reading in the book *the words of the Lord* in the Lord's house" (Jer. 36:2–8).

Nothing could be clearer than this, as confirmation of what has been said above, that while the faculties and intelligent cooperation of a prophet were not ruled out, yet the words he was to record were arranged for by God. In confirmation of this, in verse 10, what has been spoken of as "the words of the Lord" are said to be "the words of Jeremiah." And, further still, there follows in the same chapter the statement by Baruch as to how the writing was produced. In reply to the question asked by the princes, "How didst thou write all these words at his mouth?" he says, "He pronounced all these words unto me with his mouth, and I wrote them with ink in the book" (vv. 17, 18). Thus emphasis throughout the whole passage is laid upon the words. Moreover, this does not refer to what the prophet had just written, it consists of all the prophecies uttered by him up to that time concerning Israel and other nations (see v. 3).

This is substantiated by what Jeremiah says at the very beginning of his prophecies. In stating how the word of the Lord came to him at the first, making known to him that he was to be His messenger, he states that the Lord said to him: "Behold, *I have put My words in thy mouth;* see, I have this day set thee over the nations and over the kingdoms, to pluck up and to break down, and to destroy and to overthrow; to build, and to plant" (chap. 1:9, 10).

After the king had burned the roll, "the word of the Lord came to Jeremiah, saying, Take again another roll, and write in it all the former words that were in the first roll, which Jehoiakim the king of Judah hath burned. . . . Then took Jeremiah another roll, and gave it to Baruch the scribe, the son of Neriah; who wrote therein from the mouth of Jeremiah all the words of the book which Jehoiakim king of Judah had burned in the fire, and there were added besides unto them many like words" (vv. 27–32). Clearly there was to be no deviation in phraseology from the former record; the records of the burnt roll were to be repeated verbatim, though other words were added. The Spirit of God who had been the author in the first case came to the prophet's aid in the rewriting. In view of Peter's testimony that "men spake from God, being moved by the Holy Spirit," we are safe in taking this example of Jeremiah's case as illustrative of the other writings of Scripture.

Zechariah 7:12

Again, when God is speaking to the prophet Zechariah concerning his former messages to the nations He speaks of the Law and "the words which the Lord of Hosts had sent by His Spirit by the hand of the former prophets" (Zech. 7:12). Thus the messages of the prophets were verbally inspired. Compare with this the exhortation of the apostle Peter that his readers "should remember the words which were spoken of before by the holy prophets, and the commandment of the Lord and Savior through your apostles" (2 Pet. 3:2). Jude similarly lays stress upon the words spoken by the apostles (Jude 17).

Other General Evidences

Among many of the evidences of the importance of each word of Scripture there are those passages which show how much depends on a single word or even part of a word. For instance, the importance of a whole argument in Paul's Epistle to the Galatians depends upon the fact that the word "seed" is in the singular and not the plural (Gal. 3:16). "It is true that the use of 'seeds' would have been unnatural and meaningless, in Hebrew and Greek as in English, but had it been the intention of God to refer only to the natural descendants of Abraham, another word could have been chosen, one with a plural in ordinary use, such, e.g., as 'children.' But all such words were passed over in favor of one that could be used only in the singular. Was this accidental? No, the apostle declares, it was designed, the seed intended was Messiah."*

The Size of the Bible

Books of false religions are bulky. They contain much superfluous material from which their readers may extract some items of value or profit. Not so the Bible! Its historical records give the clearest witness to the divine skill in their selection. What the apostle John says at the end of his Gospel as to the other signs done by the Lord which are not written in the book, and as to the enormous number of books which would be required if they were to be recorded, is only an instance of what may be applied to the whole Volume. When he says, "These are written that ye may believe," he is writing what is true of the other parts of Scripture. This is borne out by Paul's statement that all Scripture is profitable for teaching, for reproof, for correction, for instruction

*"The Epistle to the Galatians," by C. F. Hogg and W. E. Vine, Volume 2, p. 136.

which is in righteousness. Had the Scriptures contained erroneous matter they would have been far more bulky than is the case. To suppose that any part of the Book can be dispensed with only shows how little the spiritual importance of the contents has been considered.

Concordances

One of the most significant testimonies to the Inspiration of the words of Scripture is the existence of concordances to the Old and New Testaments in languages in which they were written. The careful use of such concordances for the purpose of studying the phraseology of the Bible reveals a significant precision in the employment of the same words by different writers and in the appropriate use of synonyms. Instances might be multiplied almost indefinitely.

As C. H. Waller says in his article on "Inspiration" in the Imperial Bible Dictionary, "Even when the use of a concordance is limited to the investigation of the language of a single writer, the reasoning of modern expositors implies an exactness and precision in the employment of words, which we do not expect from ordinary human writings. Else why are concordances to classical writers so seldom seen?" The study of the phraseology of Scripture by means of concordances is ever yielding to the devout student some fresh gem of divine truth. Such studies have, since the use of concordances came in, covered practically the whole field of the Sacred Volume, and the results achieved bear striking witness to the divine inspiration of the words of the Book.

Most striking too is the avoidance throughout the whole of the New Testament Greek of certain forms of verbs which might have been confused, not only by the identity between these and the forms of other verbs, but by the association of somewhat similar meanings conveyed by them. Cases of these are well-known to students of the Greek Testament.*

Synonyms

In scarcely any department of Bible study do the divine wisdom, and the accuracy of the writers, in the selection of words become so manifest as in that of the synonyms of Scripture. It becomes abundantly clear with careful study that the choice and position of words and phrases are not mere matters of linguistic refinement, but of divine control on the one hand, and deep spiritual exercise on the other, and all in view of the extreme importance of the subject matter from the spiritual point of view. To this Archbishop Trench strikingly draws attention in the introduction to his work on "The Synonyms of the New Testament." He says: "If by such investigations as these we become aware of delicate variations in an author's meaning, which otherwise we might have missed, where is it so desirable that we should miss nothing, that we should not lose the intention of the writer, as in those words which are the vehicles of the very mind of God Himself? If thus the intellectual riches of the student are increased, can this anywhere be of so great importance as there, where the intellectual may, if rightly used, prove spiritual riches as well? If it encourage thoughtful meditation on the exact force of words, both as they are in themselves, and in their relation to other words, or in any way unveil to us their marvel and their mystery, this can nowhere else have a worth in the least approaching that which it acquires when the words with which we have to do are, to those who receive them aright, words of eternal life." There is plenty of scope for investigation with respect to Bible synonyms, and it is a realm of truth which amply repays closest investigation, while also constantly impressing the mind with the fact that the words of Scripture are God-breathed.

The Closing Pronouncement

The reader will find other evidences from Scripture in the chapter which deals with objections. We will close this chapter with a ref-

---

*E.g., the avoidance by all the writers of the forms of *eimi*, to go, which are identical with those of *eimi*, to be; the avoidance of the imperfect of *archomai*, to begin, which is the same as that of *archomai*, to come; and the avoidance of certain forms of *ageirō*, to awaken; which might have led to confusion of ideas regarding the resurrection.

erence to the words of the Lord Himself recorded at the termination of the Apocalypse. The testimony to the divine authority of every word of that book is most explicit and solemn: "I testify," says the Lord, "unto every man that heareth the words of the prophecy of this book, If any man shall add unto them, God shall add unto him the plagues which are written in this book: and if any man shall take away from the words of the book of this prophecy, God shall take away his part from the tree of life, and out of the holy city, which are written in this book" (vv. 18, 19). The warning is given against an attempt to add to, or take away from, not the topics or subject matter, but the words, and if the words are thus sacred in that book they are equally so in the rest of the Volume. This is borne out by the similar warnings given in connection with the Mosaic Law (Deut. 4:2), and again at the close of the book of Proverbs, where the writer says, "Add thou not unto His words, lest He reprove thee, and thou be found a liar" (Prov. 30:6).

The foregoing evidences are but a selection out of a very large number. Among other evidences there are, for instance, the organic unity which characterizes the whole Book in all its great fundamental truths, the progress and development of its doctrine, the accuracy of its predictions, the searching tests which its pages from beginning to end apply to the human heart. To deal with these evidences and others of a similar character would expand this chapter unduly.

CHAPTER THREE

Some Objections

The objections which have been raised against the divine inspiration and accuracy of the Scripture are almost innumerable. They have served the purpose of turning the attention more carefully to the Word of God with a view to weighing the evidences. The result has been to vindicate it at the points at which it has been attacked. It would be obviously beyond the scope of this chapter to meet such objections exhaustively. We can deal only with those which are usually put forward.

Inaccuracy to Be Expected!

We are told that accuracy must not be expected in those subjects of Scripture which lie within the range of human knowledge, and that it is unreasonable to consider those parts as inspired which the writers were competent to write without the aid of inspiration, such parts for instance as a genealogy, a catalogue of names, or even those events which a writer himself saw or recorded as the result of diligent research, as in the case of Luke's Gospel, of which he says that he traced the course of all things accurately from the first (Luke 1:3).

According to this the writers were left to their unaided skill and memory in such matters, for in these complete accuracy is hardly called for, and therefore only in matters relating to spiritual truth are we to expect the Book to be infallible. If this is so, then we have a book which may be our guide in the things which lie beyond natural investigation, but it may mislead us in things material. But what confidence could we place in such a book as that? No teacher whose instructions were of that kind would hold his place as a teacher long. How could a book which erred in matters of which we could judge be reliable in those things of which we could not form a judgment? The fact is that the advancement of knowledge has but served to verify the historical and scientific statements of Scripture in the past, and

it is only reasonable to expect that further knowledge will verify them in the future. It is opinion, or inference drawn from facts, not the knowledge of the facts themselves, which is so frequently found contradictory to Scripture. Conjecture is mistaken for certainty, and discovery is too often assumed before the fact. Again and again, when the Bible has been assumed to be erroneous, it has turned out that the error was in the assumption and that the Scripture was accurate. Modern investigations are making these perpetually renewed suppositions ludicrous. That writers of Scripture upon occasion used other writings, or wrote of circumstances which they had seen with their eyes, provides no argument against the Inspiration of those parts of their work. "Inspiration is seen in the use made of these materials, not in the providing of them." There is no reason why the Holy Spirit should not have directed them to make use of material. Why should not quotations, or transcribed records, be inspired in the quoting? The Spirit of God could inspire transcriptions as such equally with what was given by direct divine revelation. What is meant by the inspiration of Scripture is that its words are words of God. The subject matter may differ in kind, but there is no difference in degree of Inspiration. There are of course degrees of importance in the moral or spiritual significance of the subject matter, but the words cannot be more or less God-breathed; they all equally come from Him.

Supposing that an ordinary writer incorporates into his writing information which he has gathered from another source; in weaving this material into his own work he makes it part of his own book. How much more, then, when the Spirit of God is the controlling agent! Every part of what the writer records is the Holy Spirit's message. If I send a messenger to give a message, however it is composed, it is my message, and the messenger has to deliver it as mine. Whether the message I send is mine or not does not depend upon the character of the subject matter. So with the records of Scripture. They are the messages of the Spirit of God, conveyed, indeed, not mechanically as my servant might convey mine, but by the direct action of the Holy Spirit upon the spirit of the messenger, the personality and character of the latter being employed in the process. It is folly therefore to divide the Scriptures, treating those which are moral or spiritual as inspired, while those parts which consist of genealogy or facts of history which the writer could have given by himself are to be considered uninspired or inspired to a lesser degree. There is indeed a difference between divine revelation of truth regarding a matter which the writer could not have known without a special communication from God, and the knowledge of facts acquired from human sources. But the records of both the one and the other in the Scriptures are equally inspired. Revelation is not the same as Inspiration. Revelation has to do with communications from God to the writer or speaker whose words are recorded, while Inspiration has to do with the words themselves as recorded. Many men received revelations who did not pen Scripture. We do not know that Luke ever received a divine revelation, and yet his writings were divinely inspired. If any part of Scripture is not inspired, it is void of absolute authority. It cannot be used in proof of anything. If the inspiration supplied to the writers did not guard against inaccuracies, then the Bible becomes an uncertain book, useless for the objects for which it claims to have been written, objects which, however, have been entirely fulfilled.

History and Doctrine

Again, we have to remember that the historical portions of Scripture bear the divine impress equally with the others. No writer records them as mere histories. A selection of events is made in a way which marks divine control. Events are recorded, not as a writer would narrate them if he had been merely an eyewitness, nor as if he had simply consulted human sources with a view to write history, but as a messenger from God viewing events as from the point of view of the divine estimate or revealing the divine judgment upon them, and thus conveying spiritual truth. It is this which makes the Bible unique in its historical records.

History and doctrine are inseparably interwoven in Scripture. This is specially evidenced both in our Lord's teaching and in the Epistles of the New Testament. For instance, in the Epistles to the Romans and Galatians events recorded in the Old Testament in connection with patriarchs and with the people of Israel not only are incorporated into the teaching, but their spiritual significance forms an essential element in the truth set forth. For numerous instances see the Epistle to the Hebrews, *passim.**

"Scripture history differs from profane history in this, that while God is ever the Disposer of the affairs of men, see Daniel 4:17, the latter cannot take account of His hand, since the only sources of the information of profane history are human; it records events as seen from below. But the writers of Scripture history are directly concerned with the interpositions of God; guided by the Spirit of inspiration, they not only record events, they also record the part that God Himself took in these events, and this could only become known to them by revelation; Scripture history records events as seen from above. There are thus two possible conceptions of the origin of the Bible. Either men wrote of God and His ways what they were able to discover for themselves, which is the naturalistic view, or God revealed Himself and His ways to men and inspired the records they made, which is the Bible's own account of itself. The Scripture histories are thus seen to be representative in character, embodying spiritual principles, which principles are always in operation, indeed, though they are not always recognized."†

The Holy Spirit is not a reporter. He has given not a mechanical account of the doings of a Person called Jesus of Nazareth, but a

---

*See also "The Gospel of the Glory," Volume 4.
†"A Commentary on the Epistle to the Galatians," by C. F. Hogg and W. E. Vine, Volume 2, p. 136.

spiritual revelation of the Person and work of the One who is King of the Jews, Jehovah's Servant, the Son of Man, the Only Begotten of the Father. Each Gospel contains only a selection connected with its particular view of the subject. It is very evident that these accounts are not the outcome of mere memory. Take, for instance, the appearances of the Lord after His resurrection. We know that He was seen of the disciples forty days, and that there were several distinct appearances of the risen Savior (1 Cor. 15). Yet Matthew must have remembered more than the one interview recorded in chapter twenty-eight, and John more than the three he records. They simply gave, under the control of the Spirit, what was suitable to the special aim of the Gospel. How many things John witnessed which he does not relate! The fact is that the Spirit of God preserved in each Gospel the design of each and guided in the selection inserted in each.

Is the apostle John writing less by inspiration of God when he states that he was at the Cross as an eyewitness than when he puts on record the teachings of the Lord? Does inspiration come and go, appear here and there, simply according to the varying character of the subject matter? If so, who is to be the judge as to what part is inspired and what is not? All such theories, if accepted, would make the Book worthless as a divine revelation.

The Objection Applied to Quotations

Take again the quotations in the New Testament from the Old. Writers no doubt had access to the Old and could quote word for word. But some of the quotations vary considerably from the passages quoted. They manifest all manner of variations. So the writers are charged with ignorance of Hebrew or Greek, or with a capricious memory and so on. On the contrary, the wording of the quotations in the New Testament gives abundant evidence of the work of the Spirit of God. Under His guidance writers are led to enlarge the scope of the passage quoted, or interpret in quoting, adapting the passage to the subject in hand, in order that the spiritual needs of God's peo-

ple may for all time be met by a complete and permanent revelation.

As an illustration of the principle of adaptation referred to, we may take Paul's quotations in Romans 10:6–8 from Deuteronomy 30:11–14. In doing so we are not suggesting that there is any real difficulty regarding the question of Inspiration. On the contrary, alterations of this sort strengthen the evidence of the Inspiration of the words of Scripture.

The passage in Deuteronomy is considerably altered. A part is omitted which would not serve the apostle's purpose. The wording of what he does use is changed, and he gives an interpretation which has a gospel application in what Moses uttered as concerning the law. The words of Moses are, "For this commandment which I command thee this day, it is not too hard for thee, neither is it far off. It is not in heaven, that thou shouldest say, Who shall go up for us to heaven, and bring it unto us, and make us to hear it, that we may do it? Neither is it beyond the sea, that thou shouldest say, Who shall go over the sea for us, and bring it unto us, and make us to hear it, that we may do it? But the word is very nigh unto thee, in thy mouth, and in thy heart, that thou mayest do it" (Deut. 30:11–14). Apart from the New Testament the reader of this passage might never have suspected that there was anything there referring to faith in Christ, yet that is the testimony of the apostle. Paul follows the Septuagint to some extent, but he changes "Who shall go over the sea" to "Who shall descend into the abyss," which is neither the Hebrew nor the Greek version.

There is, however, an indication that these words of Moses embraced in the scope of their meaning truth relative to the Christian faith. He says, "Neither with you only do I make this covenant and this oath; but . . . also with him that is not here with us this day" (Deut. 29:14, 15). The Targum explains this latter as meaning "with every generation, with every race unto the world's end." This idea is confirmed in Peter's message on the day of Pentecost, "For to you is the promise, and to your children, and to all that are afar of, even as many as the Lord our God shall call unto Him." Further, the word of this second covenant in Deuteronomy 29, 30 contained no mention of ceremonial rites or observances. When circumcision is referred to it is circumcision of the heart (chap. 30:6). In changing the word "sea" to "abyss" Paul simply passes from the literal sense to give the spiritual scope of the passage, and the fact that Christ had accomplished His redemptive work on the Cross and had ascended to Heaven accounts for the change.

We have taken this quotation in Romans as illustrative of many others. No New Testament writer gives the meaning of the Old Testament Scriptures merely by way of accommodation or as the result of mere study. It is under the Spirit's guidance that he perceives the significance of a message and records it. Cp. Hebrews 2:13 and Isaiah 8:8 for instance.

Defects in Mosaic Laws

To turn to another class of quotations, the Inspiration of parts of the Mosaic Law is denied on the ground that Christ in His teaching corrected errors and defects in that Law, as, for instance, when He said repeatedly in the Sermon on the Mount, "Ye have heard that it was said to them of old time, . . . etc., . . . But I say unto you, . . . etc." (Matt. 5:21, 22, 27, 28, 33, 34, etc.). But where is there a suggestion in a word of His teaching that in giving it He was implying the existence of a single defect in the Law? On the contrary, He precedes all these remarks by saying, "Think not that I came to destroy the Law or the prophets: I came not to destroy, but to fulfill. For verily I say unto you, Till heaven and earth pass away, one jot or one tittle shall in no wise pass away from the Law, till all things be accomplished. Whosoever therefore shall break one of these least commandments and shall teach men so, shall be called least in the kingdom of heaven: but whosoever shall do and teach them, he shall be called great in the kingdom of heaven" (Matt. 5:17–19).

Accommodating Quotations

It has been contended that writers of the New Testament make use of the Old Testament in order to accommodate the latter to the circumstances about which they were writing, or to suit the prejudices of the age in which they lived. Modern criticism, for instance, which, as we have stated, gives evidence of an effort to eliminate the supernatural character of Old Testament predictions, supposes that Matthew, who constantly refers in his Gospel to prophecy as having been fulfilled, was merely making use of the Old Testament in an arbitrary manner, and that really the Scripture he quotes did not refer to circumstances in the life and death of Christ as he states they did. For example, when Matthew states that the sojourn of Joseph and Mary to Egypt took place that the prophecy might be fulfilled "Out of Egypt have I called my son," a Higher Critical Commentator remarks, "It looks as if Matthew made the incident fit the quotation."* If that were so, Matthew, instead of writing by divine inspiration, was under a misapprehension. The critic overlooks the fact that to accommodate Old Testament prophecies to incidents, in such a way as to carry conviction of the fulfillment of prophecy to those who were not easily to be convinced, would be far more incredible than that the incident should be the fulfillment of prophecy.

As to the passage in Matthew 2:15, there are many evidences in the New Testament that Christ takes up the history of Israel afresh ideally in His own Person, and embodied in Himself the fulfillment of much which that history foreshadowed. For instance, Israel is described in Isaiah 5:1–7 as the Vine brought out of Egypt, and Christ describes Himself as the true Vine (John 15:1). In Isaiah 41:8, 9, Israel is the servant of Jehovah; in chapter 42 Messiah is so described. So again, while Israel is spoken of as God's Son (Ex. 4:22, 23), in the New Testament the Son is Christ. In each case Christ is the "true," the real, Vine, Servant, Son.

Everything goes to show that Matthew found in the past history of Israel, as referred to by Hosea, a prophetic import which had its fulfillment in the sojourn of Christ as a child in Egypt. There is certainly nothing in Matthew's use of the passage from Hosea, nor in any other of his quotations, that is inconsistent with divine inspiration. To consider him as having made an incident fit the quotation is an unwarranted assumption.

---

*Peake's "Commentary on the Bible," p. 702.

If we were to look at the matter from the purely naturalistic point of view we might see in Matthew's quotation nothing more than that he found certain words in Hosea and appropriated them to Christ. But we cannot both accept the evidences of Scripture and adopt the naturalistic view.

The suggestion has been made that Matthew, finding certain words in Hosea, appropriated them to this use in the Gospel. We must judge of this in the light of the testimony of Scripture. Hosea himself was no doubt thinking of the historical event of the deliverance of Israel from Egypt. Now Scripture shows that in many cases the history of Israel was prophetically illustrative of future events. Paul states that certain things happened to Israel by way of example and were written for our admonition (1 Cor. 10:1–11). He shows again that there is far more in the history of the sons of Abraham than what would be gathered by the reader from the record in Genesis (Gal. 4:21–31). The writer of the Epistle to the Hebrews makes clear that the history of Melchizedek foreshadowed details of the priesthood of Christ, and conveyed teachings far beyond the mere statements of fact in the Genesis narrative. These are only a few of many instances showing that in the conception of the writers of the New Testament there was a wider range of meaning in Old Testament narratives than what could have been apprehended by the Old Testament writers themselves. At the same time there are intimations in the Old Testament that the writers, at all events in some cases, had this wider significance in view. Thus the writer of Psalm 78 says, "I will open my mouth in a parable; I will utter dark sayings of old: which we have heard and known, and our fathers have told us." Now what the Psalmist writes about consists of a simple narrative of events which took place in the history of Israel from the time of the Exodus till the reign of David, and he describes this history as "a parable" and speaks of himself as uttering dark sayings. This suggests that there was something more than history in what he was about to narrate.

To this must be added Peter's statement that Old Testament prophets searched into their own writings regarding events of the future which formed the subject of their testimony (1 Pet. 1:10–12).

Quotations from the Septuagint

The subject of the use of the Septuagint by the New Testament writers is deeply interesting, and while it is impossible within the limits of the present book to treat the subject at all fully, yet it calls for some mention. This Greek translation of the Hebrew Bible, made between 250 and 150 B.C. in Alexandria, is evidently of very variable quality; it was plainly not intended to be literal. Few, if any, would now be found to hold that the Septuagint translation was made by Divine Inspiration; yet there are numerous quotations from it in the New Testament. The question therefore arises whether such quotations are inspired.

There are many quotations in which the Hebrew, Septuagint, and the New Testament agree. There is a larger number of quotations where the Septuagint quoted is not in agreement with the Hebrew. Such, for instance, is the case in Hebrews 1:6, where the quotation "let all the angels of God worship Him" is quoted word for word from the LXX of Deuteronomy 32:43, but this is entirely absent from the Hebrew text of that passage. Again, Matthew 19:5, "For this cause shall a man leave his father and mother, and shall cleave to his wife; and the twain shall become one flesh," is from the LXX of Genesis 2:24, not from the Hebrew.

There are a still larger number of cases where the New Testament differs both from the Hebrew and the Septuagint. Thus Romans 11:8, "God gave them a spirit of stupor," is neither from the Hebrew nor from the LXX of Isaiah 29:10, each of which has "the Lord hath poured upon you the spirit of slumber." Again, Ephesians 4:8, "When He ascended on high, He led captivity captive, and gave gifts unto men," is from neither the Hebrew nor the Greek of Psalm 68:18.

There are some cases where the Hebrew is partly followed and partly the LXX and partly neither. This is the case, for instance, in Matthew 12:17–21, which chiefly follows the Hebrew of Isaiah 42:1–3, but departs from both Hebrew and LXX in the clause "Till He send forth judgment unto victory," and finishes by following the LXX.

There are a few where the Septuagint has been altered in quoting, in accordance with the Hebrew, as for instance in 2 Timothy 2:19, where the words "The Lord knoweth them that are His" are from the LXX of Numbers 16:5, but the title "God" is changed to "the Lord" as in the Hebrew. In some cases the Hebrew has been followed and not the LXX, as in Matthew 2:15, from the Hebrew of Hosea 11:1 (the LXX has "out of Egypt did I call his children"), and John 19:37, from Hebrew of Zechariah 12:10, with the exception of "Him" for "Me" (i.e. interpreting the Hebrew).

Sometimes one New Testament writer adopts the Hebrew and another the Greek. Matthew closely follows the Hebrew in Matthew 8:17, "Himself took our infirmities, and bear our diseases," from Isaiah 53:4, 5. Peter in 1 Peter 2:24 follows the LXX. This provides an instance of the use of the same passage to cast light upon different aspects of the same subject. These facts show with what variety of method the quotations have been made.

Evidently the Septuagint was used by the New Testament writers only to a limited extent.

Taking a purely naturalistic view, it will surely be conceded that a writer is at liberty to select his version in handling the subject before him, or even to adapt a quotation to his own purpose. The translation adopted by a writer would be used to convey his sense of the meaning of the passage, and so would to all intents and purposes be his translation. What would be legitimate for an ordinary writer may certainly be expected no less in the case of one who was writing by Divine Inspiration. Quotations in this way would express the mind of God as to the meaning and bearing of an Old Testament Scripture. The quality of inspiration would attach to it in virtue of its being a part of the New Testament Scriptures. It is significant that New Testament writers like Paul who naturally as Jews looked upon the words of the Old Testament with the utmost regard for even the letter of the text, and would ordinarily have copied the original with extreme care, should have made such alterations as occur in the New Testament. The writer of the Epistle to the Hebrews, for instance, writing as he did to those who were of Jewish nationality, might be expected to guard against a possible prejudice by adhering closely to the Hebrew text in his quotations. He not infrequently deviates from both the Hebrew and the LXX. As an instance we may take Hebrews 10:30, where the quotation, "Vengeance belongeth unto Me, I will recompense" is neither altogether from the Hebrew nor from the LXX of Deut. 32:35. Paul himself intimated that he was governed not merely by his own discretion, but by the Spirit of God, with the result that he uses, as he says, "words which the Spirit teacheth, comparing spiritual things with spiritual" (1 Cor. 2:13).

The whole subject of the quotations of the New Testament repays careful investigation. The student of Scripture will find many a treasure of Divine truth in this respect if he has regard to the progressive character of revelation, to the different character of successive eras, and to the unity of the teaching on any given subject throughout the Volume. For instance, the quotation "A body hast thou prepared Me" (Heb. 10:5) is taken from the LXX of Psalm 40:6. The Hebrew reads "ears hast thou digged for Me," as in the margin of the Revised Version, but the LXX has "a body didst Thou prepare for Me," and in this form the passage is quoted in Hebrews 10:5. "The thought is the same in either case, though it is differently expressed, for whereas in the Hebrew text the part is put for the whole, i.e., if there is an ear there is, of course, a body of which that ear forms a part, in the Greek translation and in the New Testament quotation, the whole is put for the part, i.e., if there is a body it must, of course, include an ear as part thereof."*

Supposed Contradictory Records

When objection is made to belief in the accuracy and Inspiration of certain records owing to the apparent discrepancy between the statements of writers who record the same events, as in the instances of the Gospels, the fact is often overlooked that the writers are not using the same language as that in which the words were actually spoken. For instance, the balance of evidence is in favor of the belief that Christ spoke in Aramaic; the Gospel

*The Epistle to the Galatians, by C. F. Hogg and W. E. Vine, Volume 2, p. 136.

writers recorded His words in Greek. The written words were inspired, and it is quite reasonable to suppose that the Holy Spirit, a law to Himself in the direction of what should be written, should design to present variations in the records, causing one writer to translate one way and another another, so as to provide a wider scope of teaching, for the sake of instructing the people of God. This would equally apply if the original utterances were in Greek. For after all it is the report of what was said or done that is inspired, and not necessarily the words as they were first spoken.

Take for example the title on the Cross. It was written in three languages, but has been recorded for us in one alone. Being in three languages the words could not have been the same in each case. The Greek translations in the Gospels doubtless faithfully represent the originals, and it is the Gospel records that are inspired. The report is given in words divinely arranged.

That there should be any difficulties of this sort in Scripture is no indication of faults on the part of the writers. It is remarkable that differences of record which relate minute particulars seem to cause greater perplexity in some minds than the gravest doubts on matter of doctrine in general. In almost every case the so-called discrepancies vanish on careful consideration. The writers are entitled to our confidence as to the accuracy of every word they wrote till it can be proved clearly that they have, any one of them, made a single mistake.

The Gospels

The Gospels are to be viewed as four testimonies in one Gospel; as Origen said, "The Gospel writers are four, but the Gospel is one." And it is consistent with this that the four books have been called the Gospel according to Matthew, the Gospel according to Mark, etc. There is a variety characterized by harmony. The four writers have again and again been charged with inconsistency and discrepancy, the charge only serves to make us consider the evidences. The so-called discrepancies vanish when the circumstances recorded are duly examined. To quote the words of Dean Burgon, "A single word of explanation, the discovery of one minute circum-

stance, . . . serves to remove the difficulty which before seemed insurmountable; . . . when this has been done the entire consistency of the account becomes apparent, while the harmony which is established is even of the most beautiful character." Let us recall the fact, too, that variations in the records only show that there was no collusion on the part of the Gospel writers; they could not have agreed together to write the same things about the subjects which they handle. The difference in their accounts shows the individuality of their work. The harmony reveals the operation of the Spirit of God in each of them. Moreover, the effects of the Spirit's work are manifest in the very variations in detail, both in the circumstances narrated and in the phraseology employed. As to any apparent inaccuracies, as the above-mentioned writer says, "it must be admitted that any possible solution of a difficulty, however improbable it may seem, any possible explanation of the story of a competent witness, is enough logically and morally to exempt that man from the imputation of an incorrect statement."

The Healing of the Centurion's Servant

There are considerable differences, for instance, between the accounts by Matthew and by Luke of the healing of the centurion's servant. Matthew says that the centurion himself came to Christ; Luke that he sent some elders of the Jews asking Him to come, that Jesus went with the elders, and that when He was not far from the house the centurion sent friends to him. See Matthew 8:5–13 and Luke 7:1–10. There is not necessarily any discrepancy at all. We may well suppose that what Matthew records as to the personal application of the centurion took place after the two companies of messengers had come as mentioned by Luke. In that case what took place would be as follows. First the elders of the Jews came. As a result of their appeal Christ went some distance with them. Then came the centurion's friends with their message, which he had commissioned them to take. There is no difficulty in supposing that the centurion eventually decided to come himself. Such a step is what anyone might make up his mind to take. He would naturally say the same thing as what he had told his friends to say. So Matthew's narrative simply follows on after what Luke states. Then comes the Lord's reply, which Matthew gives more fully than Luke, and without any discrepancy. There is complete harmony also in the closing detail. The Lord says to the centurion, "Go thy way; as thou hast believed, so be it done unto thee" (Matt. 8:13). The servants, returning home, find the servant healed (Luke 7:10).

Blind Bartimaeus

Another case is the account of the healing of blind Bartimaeus. The charge of discrepancy is made in view of the fact that Matthew mentions two blind men, whereas Mark and Luke mention one, and that Matthew and Mark speak of the incident as having taken place when Christ was coming out of Jericho, while Luke seems to indicate that it was when He was drawing near to the city. There is little difficulty about the former of these differences, for it is quite consistent with the actual facts that two men should be healed but that the second and third writers should tell of one of these only. As to the exact locality of the healing, it is futile to impute inaccuracy to any one of the Gospel writers on this ground, seeing that the full details are not given in any one case. Were all the circumstances known each writer would no doubt be found perfectly accurate. For one thing, Luke's narrative does not make it necessary to suppose that the blind man was on the side of the town where Christ was entering. It may be objected that the narrative continues with the record of Christ's entering into the house of Zacchaeus, and that therefore the healing of the blind man must have taken place before. But this objection cannot stand, for it is not at all necessary to suppose from the first verse of the nineteenth chapter that Luke was narrating things in exact chronological order. In writing the narrative of Zacchaeus he was possibly reverting to an incident which had taken place while Christ was in Jericho. Moreover, it is a well-known feature in Luke's Gospel that he narrates details of this sort without exact chronology.

He frequently has an eye to the moral or spiritual association of incidents, which causes him to group events in this way rather than to observe the strict order of their occurrence.

There is a striking contrast between the two sections at the end of chapter 18 which the writer seems to set off one against the other. In the section verses 31–34 there is the spiritual blindness of the disciples; then comes the incident of the physical blindness of the beggar by the wayside, suggesting that Luke was guided by the Spirit of God so to record the events as to bring to the notice of the diligent inquirer the means whereby spiritually blind people may receive their sight.

He makes it clear, too, that he is connecting the story of Zacchaeus with the parable of the pounds, for he says that as the people heard what Christ said to Zacchaeus, He spoke the parable of the pounds because they thought that the Kingdom of God was immediately to appear (v. 11). It is noticeable, too, that Christ's going up to Jerusalem is mentioned immediately after He had told them the parable (v. 28).

Further, the way in which Luke begins the Zacchaeus narrative makes it quite natural to suppose that he was reverting to something that had taken place while Christ was in the city before He healed the blind man. Literally the first verse of chapter nineteen reads "and after having entered, He was passing through Jericho," a way of putting it which may be easily connected, not with the healing of the blind man, but with the initial statement of 18:35, when Christ was coming to the city. Every detail of the three records could be easily accounted for in some such way. The veracity of the writers at least remains unimpaired.

In reading the Gospel of Luke a great deal is missed if we do not observe that the object of the writer is not the mere sequence of events, but the grouping of the teachings of the Lord as well as His works and His ways.

The Divine Utterance at Christ's Baptism

To take another instance, difficulty is found in the matter of the words spoken by God the Father out of Heaven when Christ was baptized. Matthew's record of the words is somewhat different from those of Mark and Luke, and the difficulty seems to lie in this, that each narrative is said to be inspired, and yet two variants of the same utterance are put on record. There is really no difficulty at all, however. Mark and Luke give the actual words, "Thou art My beloved Son, in Thee I am well pleased" (Mark 1:11; Luke 3:22). Matthew gives the import of the declaration rather than the actual words, thus laying emphasis on the fact, while the other writers emphasize the words. Instead of inaccuracy we can observe the work of the Spirit of God in causing Matthew to state the fact in a way appropriate to the character of his Gospel, which sets forth in a special manner the dignity of Christ as the King of Israel. Moreover, the utterances recorded in the Gospel, being in Greek, are translations of the actual utterance, a fact which allows of both variation in form and of Inspiration in the variation.

The Parable of the Wicked Husbandmen

Another difficulty is in the difference between Matthew's record of the parable of the wicked husbandmen and those of Mark and Luke. Mark and Luke make the Lord answer His own question as to what the Lord of the vineyard will do (Mark 12:9 and Luke 20:15, 16). Matthew makes His hearers give the answer (Matt. 21:41). The two passages taken together are consistent with the probable facts. It is quite natural to suppose that after the Lord's question had been answered by His hearers He Himself repeated the answer. Such an occurrence is not infrequent in open-air testimony.

Jeremiah or Zechariah?

Matthew is charged with inaccuracy because in reference to the death of Judas and the price paid for the potter's field he gives as a statement of Jeremiah the prophet what is supposed to be a quotation from Zechariah because the words are something like the words Zechariah wrote (Matt. 27:9, cp. Zech. 11:12, 13). Now in the first place there is considerable difference between the words which Matthew writes and the actual words of Zechariah. It is a curious course of procedure to suppose that Matthew is quoting Zechariah if he is not actually doing so, and then to charge him with lapse of memory or some such mistake because he attributes the statement to Jeremiah. If Matthew had said, "Then was fulfilled that which was spoken by Zechariah the prophet,"

a charge of inaccuracy might have been made against him, but he does not say so. It is quite reasonable to suppose that Jeremiah uttered this prophecy orally, and that when Matthew says that it was spoken by him he is simply quoting nonrecorded but well-known words of Jeremiah. Paul quotes words of the Lord Jesus which are not previously written in the Bible (Acts 20:35), and Jude quotes a prophecy of Enoch which is not recorded elsewhere. As to whether Zechariah was himself quoting Jeremiah, that is another matter. Zechariah himself does say, "Should ye not hear the words which the Lord had cried by the former prophets?" (chap. 7:7). The later prophet indeed expressed himself more than once in language like that of the former. Moreover, it was commonly held among the Jews that the spirit of Jeremiah rested upon Zechariah, but apart from all this the so-called inaccuracy is purely imaginary. Certainly there is nothing in this passage that need puzzle anybody very long.

Jairus's Daughter

As another illustration of the unreasonableness of some of the accusations of inconsistency in the records of Scripture, we may take the case of the apparent discrepancies between the records of Matthew and Mark of what Jairus said about his daughter. Matthew reports that he said, "My daughter is even now dead" (chap. 9:18); Mark that he said, "She is at the point of death" (chap. 5:23). Apart from an endeavor to find something wrong in the Scriptures, the charge of discrepancy could scarcely have been made here. The difference in the accounts serves to show how true to life they are. It is a natural conclusion that Jairus, under stress of his emotions at a time like that, would break out into more than one statement, and people would forgive him if he were not accurate and precise in every statement he made about his daughter.

It is reasonable to suppose that Matthew and Mark were recording what he said at different moments under the excitement of the occasion.

The Genealogies of Christ in Matthew and Luke

Objections are raised against the differences in the genealogy of our Lord as recorded in the Gospels of Matthew and Luke. There is no real inconsistency between the two, however. The genealogy in Matthew is traced through one line of descent and that in Luke through another. It is not at all improbable that the genealogy given by Luke was really Mary's. Jesus was supposed to be, as Luke states, the son of Joseph, and so if Heli was the father of Mary, as seems likely, he would be regarded as the father of both Joseph and Mary. This genealogy traces the ancestry through Nathan to David. In Matthew the line is traced downwards through Solomon. Matthew states distinctly that "Jacob begat Joseph, the husband of Mary, of whom was born Jesus" (Matt. 1:16).

The two genealogies are consistent respectively with the special characteristic which each writer has in view in presenting the Lord Jesus. The genealogy given by Matthew is appropriate to the presentation of Christ as the King. Luke's is appropriate to the presentation of Him as Son of man. Matthew gives His royal genealogy; Luke gives that which emphasizes His humanity.

Then, again, there are certain omissions in the line of descent recorded by Matthew. The writer evidently has in view the division of the genealogy into three sets of fourteen generations. The center one of the three is reduced to fourteen by the purposive omission of certain details, and it is suggestive that the following are omitted, namely, Ahaziah, Joash, and Amaziah, who were descendants of Ahab of the third and fourth generation, and Jehoiakim who committed the trespass of burning the roll of Scripture (Jer. 36:28). Matthew is marking off prophetic periods of time instead of giving all the details of a genealogical list. There are three uses of the word "generation" in Scripture: (1) to denote the production of offspring; (2) to denote a nation as to its moral character, (3) to denote a period of prophetic time. It is the last of these that Matthew apparently has in view.

Variations in the Records of the Parable of the Sower

As another instance of variations in the similar records by the Synoptists in which not only is the discrepancy merely apparent, but which, on the contrary, gives evidence of the divine

inspiration of the very wording in each case, we may take the parable of the sower. Matthew describes the one who brings forth fruit as "he that heareth the word, and understandeth it" (Matt. 13:23). The word in Mark's Gospel corresponding to "understandeth" is "accept" (Mark 4:20), while that used by Luke is "hold fast" (Luke 8:15). The difference between the Aramaic in which the Lord spoke and the Greek of the Gospel records at once accounts, to some extent, for the variety of rendering. A little consideration, however, shows that, while the writers could not have agreed together as to the variety of expression, the Spirit of God, knowing beforehand that the writings would be bound together to form part of the Volume committed to the Church, so ordered that there would be harmony and progression of thought in the three words used. In order to bear fruit one must first understand the word, then accept it, and then hold it fast. Accordingly, while one idea pervades the whole, and the words give each a translation of what the Lord Himself said, the different expressions convey additional teaching to that of the facts of the parable itself. No doubt one word might have sufficed to translate that used by the Lord, but the Spirit of God had other purposes in view, and so ordered the three different translations for the sake of imparting instruction in their variety. Moreover, when we recall the purpose which Matthew had in view, the special class of people for whom he was immediately writing, we see the appropriateness of the thought to which he gave expression. Here, then, is a good illustration of the careful selection of words by a Master Mind working through three different human agents, it being impossible for the writers to consult one with another as to the choice of their phraseology.

Other Instances

We might compile a number of instances like this. To take another, in reporting the departure of Christ from Capernaum in the early morning, Mark records His having said to the disciples, as a reason for His departure, "To this end came I forth" (Mark 1:38); Luke records Him as saying "therefore was I sent" (Luke 4:43). The critic may point to this as a discrepancy, yet he has to show that the Lord did not say both things to the disciples. It is quite probable that He did, judging from the records of His utterances in general. There is nothing necessarily inconsistent in the narratives. Both are in accordance with probable facts, but they give together a variety of teaching, which is valuable to those who have the Gospels side by side in one volume. For other instances see the records concerning the wineskins, Mark 2:19, Matthew 9:15, Luke 5:34; the leaven of the Pharisees, Mark 8:15, Matthew 16:6; Peter's denial, Matthew 26:34, Mark 14:30, Luke 22:34, John 13:38. In each case we have gained by the variety. The reports, so far from being given word for word, may have been purposely abbreviated or rearranged. In each case they are consistent and accurate, as divinely inspired translations of what was said. Variations of this kind are often found to be appropriate to that particular aspect of our Lord's life and ministry which the Gospel writers were respectively guided to present.

Are Some of Paul's Utterances Uninspired?

The divine inspiration of certain passages in Paul's Epistles is denied in view of statements he makes which are supposed to assert the contrary. For instance, it is asked, if Paul's writings are inspired throughout, how is it he can say in his first Epistle to the Corinthians, "But this I say by way of permission, not of command" (1 Cor. 7:6), and again, "I think that I also have the Spirit of God" (v. 40), whereas in the 10th verse he definitely states that it is not he who gives charge, but the Lord? Is he not making a distinction here, it is urged, between his own thoughts which may not have been inspired and those which were directly received from the Lord?

As to the 6th verse, the difference between his giving advice and receiving permission from God does not affect the Inspiration of his words. His statements in both verses, 6 and 10, are inspired. They are what the Holy Spirit gave him to write. In the first case his statement is inspired, that he is declaring something by way of permission, not of command; in the second case he is recalling what was well-known to be the command of the Lord in

forbidding the wife to depart from her husband. He was simply repeating the command that what God had joined together no man was to put asunder. He was not making any such distinction as that he merely gave his own thoughts in the one instance and expressed the Lord's mind in the other.

In regard to verse 40, anyone who understands the use of the word *dokeō*, "I think," will know that the apostle is not suggesting for a moment that he has any doubt about the truth of what he is saying, but that he is expressing the certainty that he has the Spirit of God. The same word is used to express an emphatic asseveration, just as when we say "I should think not indeed," giving the hearer to understand that there is no doubt in our mind. The apostle uses the word in the same way in 1 Corinthians 4:9.

We may compare his words in the second Epistle, "Herein I give my judgment" (2 Cor. 8:10). There he is exhorting the Church to contribute to the needs of poor saints. In regard to the matter of his message, the words themselves are as much inspired as any other part of the Epistle. The Holy Spirit was causing him to express himself that way as being the best mode of giving his exhortation. The fact that he was pronouncing his own judgment instead of giving a command from the Lord in no way affects the Inspiration of His words. His words are authoritative in either case. Concerning the instructions which he gave without having received a revelation or command from the Lord, he says, "So ordain I in all the churches" (1 Cor. 7:17 with v. 10). In giving his judgment upon such matters he was not instituting anything contrary to his Divinely given authority.

If a father were about to leave his children for a considerable time, he might gather them round him before doing so and give them instructions as to what they were to do during his absence. Those might be given in two ways, some by way of commandments to be obeyed, others as advice as to how he would desire them to act in certain circumstances which were likely to arise. His children would be expected to accept both command and instruction as authoritative and to act accordingly. So with the apostle's instructions, there is a difference in the mode of conveyance, but the same Spirit of God inspires his language, and the converts would accept the command he gave as from the Lord, and the judgment he himself gave, as divinely authoritative in each case.

Moral Difficulties

The difficulties which confront the reader in the matter of what are known as the imprecatory Psalms have occasioned much misgiving in regard to the Inspiration of these passages. The same is the case with the instructions given to the people of Israel to destroy the Canaanites. If such passages are considered merely as the outcome of human vindictiveness, and if the narratives of Israel's treatment of other nations are regarded simply as national zeal for the acquisition of territory, or as lust for conquest, in other words, if the history is viewed from a purely naturalistic point of view, then the objection is valid and the possibility of Inspiration is ruled out.

Another light, however, is thrown upon these passages if they are considered in their relationship to the whole scheme of divine revelation as contained in the Scriptures. The problem has, for instance, to be viewed in connection with the broader subjects of the attitude of God toward evil, and His dealings with regard to the people of Israel.

The divine revelation given to Abraham, hundreds of years before Israel entered Canaan, concerning the character of the Canaanitish nations, gives a clue. What Scripture itself reveals of their condition shows that for such a period to elapse before the divine judgment fell upon them through the instrumentality of Israel was after all only an example of the longsuffering of God.

"God permits men to go far in wickedness, because He is longsuffering and gives time for repentance, as in the days of Noah (1 Pet. 3:20, cp. 2 Pet. 3:9, Rom. 2:4). On the other hand, God permits the evil things He sees in a man, or in a nation, to grow and develop until they become manifest to other eyes than His own, that thus the righteousness of His judgments, when they do come, may be put beyond dispute (see Ps. 89:2, 14). Gabriel ascribed this reason for the delay of the divine

retribution (Dan. 8:23); and the Lord warned the leaders of Israel itself that they were pursuing the same infatuated course that involved their fathers in disaster and exile" (Matt. 23:32).*

The reason given why Abraham's descendants were not to come into the land of promise was that the iniquity of the Amorites was not yet full. There is an intimation in this of the abominable character of that people. Yet God would extend His mercy toward them until their condition was such that to withhold the execution of divine judgment was no longer possible. At the date of the Israelitic conquests the iniquity of the Canaanites had reached such a climax that their destruction became necessary, not only retributively but preventatively. For similar reasons destruction had fallen upon Sodom and Gomorrah in the period in which the revelation was given to Abraham. In such cases destruction is in the interests of humanity.

Concerning these moral difficulties, Professor Orr writes as follows: "In facing this problem, our first duty is to beware of solutions which are not really, or only very partially, such. We do not solve the problem by denying that these lower forms of morality were, for that age and stage of development, really wrong, or did involve elements of evil." Again, he rightly takes exception to the arguments based on evolutionary theories by which it is attempted to show "that there are numerous intermediate grades between no morality and the highest morality; that the moral idea is only gradually developed, and that, till it is developed, such practices as slavery, polygamy, unchastity, mercilessness in war, etc., are not really sinful; that there can be no wrong, therefore, in recognizing and sanctioning them." This, he rightly says, "like the whole evolutionary conception of a necessary development of humanity through evil, is a dangerous line of defense; it is, moreover, repugnant to the genuine Christian point of view. Jesus did not, e.g., regard the Mosaic Law of divorce as *per se* right even for the Jews. It was given them, He said, for the hardness of their hearts, and He re-

---

*"The Epistles to the Thessalonians," by C. F. Hogg and W. E. Vine, Volume 3, p. 15.

ferred them back to the purer primitive idea of marriage."*

On the other hand, to take the critical view, and put the passages containing these moral difficulties down to the mistaken notions and feelings of the writers, or to consider the narratives as merely legendary, provides us with no help whatever. While these suppositions may remove an imputation against the character of God, they are after all only a denial of the reality of the revelation. There has been a tendency, too, to exaggerate the difficulties and to lower the character of Old Testament morality, as when Israel is charged with being devoid of human feelings toward others than their fellow-nationals, and that they were governed purely by considerations of expediency. Such accusations are not borne out by the history of the Old Testament.

"The sword of the Israelite is, after all, only a more acute form of the problem that meets us in the providential employment, in even more horrible forms, of the sword of the Assyrian, the Chaldean, or Roman, to inflict the judgment threatened of God on Israel itself. Yet only a little reflection is needed to show that, if the world is to be upheld, governed, and judged at all, it is only in some such way that even the Holiest can govern and judge it. As Paul says, in repelling the objection that God is unrighteous in taking vengeance for sins which He has overruled for His own glory: 'God forbid; for then how shall God judge the world?'"

Professor Orr points out,† that at whatever point revelation begins, it takes man up at the stage at which it finds him. The nation of Israel at the time of the Exodus was in a more rudimentary state than in later periods of its history, but the revelation God gave to it was both compatible with Divine righteousness and suitable to the conditions of the nation at the time. Again, revelation, while dealing with circumstances as they exist at the time, leads on to something further, which is to be unfolded according to the divine counsels. This accounts for the vast difference between the revelations given by Christ and His apostles in

relation to the Gospel and the Church, and those of the preceding age in connection with Israel. "Revelation, without parting with anything of its reality or authority, is, in the truest sense, an organic process—a growing from less to more, with adaptation at every point to the state of development of its recipients—a light shining often in a dark place, but still shining more and more unto the perfect day. Its higher stages criticize, if we may so speak, its lower; shed off temporary elements; disengage principles from the imperfect forms in which they are embodied, and give them more perfect expression; yet unfailingly conserve, and take up into the new form, every element of permanent value in the old. Prophecy does not let fall one element that was of permanent value in the law; Christianity conserves every jot and tittle of the spiritual content of both law and prophets."‡ As to the imprecatory Psalms, obviously the language of vengeance and retribution is impossible for Church use, nor is there a shadow of evidence that such was the divine intention. It is due to a most unhappy confusion that such Psalms should have been appointed for the worship of the Christian Church. The arrangements of divine providence in connection with Israel under the Law are quite distinct from those relating to the Church in the present age. Paul's argument in the Epistle to the Romans that God is not unrighteous in visiting with wrath (Rom. 3:5, 6) has a bearing on the subject. If it is consistent with the character of God that He executes punishment on the ungodly, it cannot be inconsistent for those who live in a period when divine retribution is being meted out to use such language as is in keeping with it. The present era is not an age of vengeance, and therefore the use of imprecatory Psalms is wholly out of place now. But it was not so in the age prior to the Gospel, nor again will it be so in the time spoken of by the apostle Paul as that of "wrath to come" (1 Thess. 1:10).

It must be borne in mind, too, that Christ Himself upon occasion used language similar to that of the Psalms in question. As Arch-

---

*"The Problem of the Old Testament," by Prof. J. Orr, p. 467.
†"The Problem of the Old Testament," by Prof. J. Orr, p. 465.
‡"The Problem of the Old Testament," by Prof. J. Orr, p. 476.

bishop Alexander has said, "It may be plausible to deny, not without bitter indignation, the Messianic application of the 110th Psalm, or the subjectively Messianic character of the 69th or 109th Psalm, on the ground that imprecation can never issue from those gentle lips; that themes of carnage have nothing in common with the Messiah of the New Testament. Yet, after all, who uttered the sentence, 'Those mine enemies, who would not that I should reign over them, bring hither, and slay before Me'? Who is to say, 'Depart from Me ye cursed,' 'Depart from Me all ye workers of iniquity,' in the words of the 6th Psalm?

"No passage in the Psalms has given more offense than that which comes at the close of the 137th Psalm:

"'O daughter of Babylon, that art to be destroyed; happy shall he be, that rewardeth thee as thou hast served us. Happy shall he be, that taketh and dasheth thy little ones against the rock.'

"From the point of view of the Psalmist this language has a tone of distress in it, as if he longed to say something else. There is certainly no vindictive spirit, there is almost a lament that the daughter of Babylon should have brought such a fate upon herself. For the attentive student, the doom of Babylon hangs in the air of prophecy. We close the Psalter for a time, and after many days, as we draw near to the end of the whole volume of revelation, we are startled by a new echo of the words of the old 137th Psalm, 'Babylon the great is fallen, is fallen. Reward her even as she rewarded you; and double unto her according to her works.'"*

Dr. Alexander rightly says concerning the solemn utterances of Christ, "These passages. . . are correlatives of the doctrine of retribution. They are spoken, if we conceive rightly, by One who expresses, as far as human language can, the doom which is the sure decree of the Governor of the world. Unless it is wrong and incredible that God should punish terribly, it is not wrong or incredible that His Son should give warning of it in the most vivid and impressive way." In similar manner the apostle Paul, speaking of the Second Advent, describes it as a time when the Lord Jesus shall be revealed from Heaven "in flaming fire, rendering vengeance to them that know not God, and to them that obey not the Gospel" (2 Thess. 1:8), and that "it is a righteous thing for God to recompense affliction to them that afflict" (v. 6).

Wherever this kind of sentiment is expressed by the writers of Scripture, the underlying motive is not vindictiveness against personal enemies, but antagonism against the enemies of God, enemies upon whom a divine sentence of wrath has been passed.

The Bible Unscientific

The objection is raised that the Bible contains statements contrary to the facts of natural science. In the first place, the Bible was not written as a handbook on geology or astronomy; its language is suited to the minds of ordinary people. It was the Son of God who said, "When the sun was up, they were scorched." Is He who knew all about these things, which He Himself had fashioned, to be accused of inaccuracy for speaking thus? That Scripture is not precisely technical does not disprove its accuracy or veracity. When the Astronomer Royal speaks of the sun's rising and setting, no one accuses him of unscientific language. He is speaking in everyday speech and describing subjects just as they appear. So with the Scriptures. But while the Bible was not written in order to teach science, neither was it written so as to mislead us in science. Evidences abound that the language is wonderfully scientific when the Bible touches upon scientific matters. Never yet has it been inarguably proved that the Bible contains any statement that contradicts the known facts of science.

The Bible Unhistorical

We are told that there are statements in the Scripture contrary to historical facts, and that these cannot be verbally inspired. Not a single case of this, however, has been irrefutably proved. The supposed cases have been greatly diminished in number under the processes of

---

*"The Witness of the Psalms to Christ," by Dr. W. Alexander, pp. 48–50.

modern research. The increase of discovery only tends to confirm the accuracy of the Bible. As to the fact that uninspired history is found to disagree with Bible history, the results of research make it safer to rely on the Scripture records, or at least to wait for further light. There are instances of minor details of discrepancy in extant manuscripts which clearly indicate errors on the part of copyists. Possession of the originals would no doubt remove these difficulties. A critic must be hard put to it for a point of attack if he seeks to impugn the veracity of the Word of God on this ground.

Some Records Incredible

Some of the statements of Scripture are said to be incredible. It so happens that the chief cases usually referred to, such, for instance, as the temptation of man, the utterance of Balaam's ass, the swallowing of Jonah, are those which Christ and His apostles speak of as facts to serve. Were they likely to relate fables as facts to serve their own ends? There were plenty of hostile critics in their times who would have been the first to hold them up to scorn if it had been possible to find a means of proving their inconsistency or unreliability.

Some Details Said to Be Trifling

Some of the details of Scripture are considered as too trifling to be inspired. No valid proof, however, has yet been produced to show that anything in the Bible is insignificant. The smallest details in the records are found on careful study to contain a deep significance, either in the matter of doctrine or in substantiating the authenticity of the writings, or in some other way. The apostle Paul's words will be found to be accurate that "every Scripture . . . is profitable for reproof, for correction, for instruction which is in righteousness."

How Can Wrong Utterances Be Inspired?

Another objection, that the Bible records sentiments which are foolish and inconsistent with its teachings, is due to an illogical conception of what Inspiration really is. The mistaken utterances of Job's friends, the falsehoods told by Peter in his denial of the Lord, the speech of the town clerk in Ephesus, the oration of Tertullus, and many similar statements were certainly not inspired in the lips of those who made them, but the records of their words by the writers of Scripture are inspired, and that these records are faithful and accurate has not been disproved.

The Grammar of the Apocalypse

Exception is taken to the Inspiration of the language of the Apocalypse on the ground of its deviations from conformity to grammatical rules. Now while adherence to the laws of grammar may not be regarded as a mark of Inspiration, yet it may be pointed out that there are evidences of a design in such deviations. That John knew the grammar of the language in which he was writing is clear from the fact of his general adherence to grammatical laws. The special character of his subject matter led him upon occasion to run counter to them. Moreover, he is not alone in this. Paul, as we shall see, does the same thing. Some of the instances in the Apocalypse may be put down to the errors of copyists. Where the text is obviously an accurate copy of the original, the departure from grammatical law is purposive. Take the first case, in chapter 1:4. The nominative case follows the preposition, *apo,* instead of the genitive, because "Him which is, and which was, and which is to come," is an appellation of God. In the next sentence the preposition is made to govern its normal case. This is accordingly not a case of a slip or carelessness or even lack of scholarship, whatever may be said of the writer's qualifications in this latter respect. The remark about the divine appellation in verse 4 applies still more strikingly in verse 5, where the titles "Jesus Christ" are in the genitive case, according to rule, but the titles which follow, "The Faithful Witness," "The Firstborn," "The Ruler," instead of following in apposition are in the nominative. They need not have been, grammatically, nor can they be said to be proper names (which are sometimes indeclinable). The nominative is purposely adhered to in order to lend dignity to the description.

We might multiply instances, but these

must be left to the student to consider. In some places the majesty of the symbolism, which is one of the chief features of the book, is accountable for the deviations, but in every case there is an explanation, and it well repays the careful student of the Greek Testament to go into them. They will afford striking evidence of the divine inspiration of the phraseology. Moreover, solecisms neither affect the veracity of the writer, nor indeed do they affect Divine Inspiration at all.

Examples in Paul's Epistles

There are two examples in Paul's Epistles of departure from grammatical law with the obvious design of bringing out a point of doctrine. The simple rule that the verb agrees with its subject in number and person is ignored in two passages. When the apostle says, "Now our God and Father Himself, and our Lord Jesus direct our way unto you" (1 Thess. 3:11), he puts the verb "direct" into the singular number, although grammatically the subject is plural. This gives a striking evidence of the unity of the two Persons of the Father and the Son in the Godhead. The other instance is in 2 Thessalonians 2:16, 17, where he says, "Now our Lord Jesus Christ Himself; and God our Father . . . comfort (singular number) your hearts and stablish you." The verb "stablish" is again in the singular. As in the Apocalypse, these breaches of grammatical law are designed.

There are other difficulties in Scripture which have been brought forward from time to time by critics, such as the alleged errors in the book of Daniel. These, and other similar objections, have been capably dealt with in recent years by competent writers, and to take them up adequately in these pages would extend the work beyond its designed limits. One of the most cogent articles on the book of Daniel is given in the report of the meeting of the Victoria Institute held in the Central Hall, Westminster, on 23rd May, 1921. The scholarly handling of the subject in D. St. Clair Tisdall's paper read on that occasion, and in the discussion which followed, explodes the higher critical view, and goes far to confirm the early date and authenticity of the book of Daniel.

CHAPTER FOUR

The Effects

Since the Scriptures are "God-breathed," they are "profitable for teaching, for reproof, for correction, for instruction which is in righteousness" (2 Tim. 3:16). This has been abundantly confirmed in human experience. Those who have been known as men of God have lived under the power and guidance of the Scriptures. The frequent testimony of such men is that instruction and help have been derived from every part of the sacred Volume. Each page has yielded its store of enrichment to the soul in the way stated by the apostle. The Bible has not only been the means of working the radical change of regeneration in the heart of mankind, it has enabled men to live holy lives.

Prayerful meditation in the Scriptures has been the key to real prosperity, a prosperity that reaches beyond the bounds of this life and extends into the ages to come. Joshua's Bible consisted of the Pentateuch. The command given him by the Lord to meditate in the Book of the Law day and night was accompanied by the promise, "For then thou shalt make thy way prosperous, and then thou shalt have good success," (Josh. 1:8). So the Psalmist later on described the success attending the life of him who delights in the Law of the Lord, and constantly meditates therein: "He shall be like a tree planted by the stream of water, that bringeth forth its fruit in its season; whose leaf also doth not wither, and whatsoever he doeth shall prosper" (Ps. 1:3). The heart that is directed by the Word of God into obedience to His will, inevitably finds increasing delight in pondering its pages. That is what the writer of Psalm 119 expresses when he says, "My soul hath observed Thy testimonies; and I love them exceedingly" (v. 167). His soul is nourished by the Scriptures, and he finds them sweet to his taste. They become his counselor in all circumstances, and his weapon in spiritual warfare, giving him victory over adverse powers.

The contents of the Bible have proved their divine inspiration by their power to probe the conscience, to penetrate to the inmost depths of the soul, to appeal from every page to the heart of man. "The Word of God is living, and active, and sharper than any two-edged sword, and piercing even to the dividing of soul and spirit, of both joints and marrow, and quick to discern the thoughts and intents of the heart" (Heb. 4:12). It is "living" because it is the voice of the living God; it is "active" because it affects the whole being, regenerating the heart and regulating the life. "Other books inform, and some reform, this one Book transforms." It "pierces to the dividing asunder of soul and spirit," the soul by which a man influences his fellowmen, and the spirit by which he holds communion with God. The teachings of this Book reveal the character of "the thoughts and intents of the heart" in each respect, and by its light we know whether our influence over others, in the sphere of the soul, is for good or for evil; and whether, in the sphere of the spirit, our thoughts, motives, and aspirations are Godward or selfward. In measure as the Scriptures enter our hearts and pierce them as with a two-edged sword, in measure as they affect our nature and character, so shall we be constrained to give due weight to the other elements in the contents of the Book, and to attribute to it divine inspiration in the fullest degree. "The vitality of the Bible is capable of but one explanation. It is of divine origin. Only God would thus hold the mirror to the soul of man, only God could thus plumb the depths of human personality, and only God could thus meet every human need. Hence its searchings which lay bare the inmost heart of the reader, and its promises which bring with them peace, courage, and victory. In some way not readily defined, but not at all to be evaded, when men read the Bible they are constrained to say very much what the posse of constables sent to arrest the Lord Jesus said of Him, 'Never book speaks as does this Book.'"*

There is a divine authority about all the Scriptures which reveals itself not only subjectively, in the evident consciousness of that authority on the part of the writers, but also objectively, in the heart of the reader. It speaks with an authority upon which the feebleness of the soul can implicitly rest. No want is left unsatisfied, no sorrow remains unsoothed, no perplexing circumstance continues unilluminated. Here we find the means of pardon for sin, of reconciliation with God, of the impartation of eternal life, a life the pulsations of which beat with the heart of God Himself a life of divine sonship, with all the infinite inheritance of glory which that sonship, that coheirship with the Son of God, brings with it. The revelations of Scripture depend for their effects not upon the power of the human understanding of the writers; the contents of the Book are instinct with the Spirit of God, by whose almighty strength the weakness of the human soul is sustained and the waywardness of human affections directed through its teachings.

The Scriptures have proved themselves sufficient, not only to meet the deepest spiritual need on account of sin, but to provide adequately for the formation of character and for efficiency in every form of Christian service, to direct the life not simply into philanthropic effort for the sake of mere philanthropy, but into that far higher form of service to our fellowmen which is rendered in pure devotion to Christ. It is the revelation of Christ in the Scriptures which draws the soul both into personal attachment to Him, and thereby to an understanding of, and sympathy with, His heart of compassion for mankind.

All this objective reality remains as characteristic of the Bible independently of human belief or disbelief, and accordingly the result involved in rejecting the Scriptures is incalculable. Infidelity and skepticism cannot destroy the truth, but may undermine belief in it. They derive their strength from the corruption of human nature. The very character of the Scriptures makes a demand upon our faith. We are so constituted that we may either accept or reject the testimony. Our power to will is after all a gift of our Creator. He has not seen fit to compel affection by such a manifestation of irresistible proof as would have rendered disbelief impossible. Had that been the case the moral character of faith would have been nullified, for faith would have been a necessity and not a choice. Skepticism, however, provides nothing satisfactory in place of what it takes away. It affords us vague abstractions, extravagant assumptions of independence, a cloud of words and phrases, but nothing to sustain the soul in its yearning and its needs. The conscience-stricken man finds nothing to dispel his trouble, no remedy for his malady. His only source of solid comfort is to be found in the revelation in the Scriptures of the divine provision for his needs in and through Christ.

But while the Scripture satisfies the higher aspirations of the soul, showing us the means of our approach to God through Christ, it stands in uncompromising contradiction to all our lower impulses and appetites, and not only so, it denounces all that belongs to our unregenerate nature. It demands that we deal drastically and peremptorily with the fleshly affections which characterized our former selves, and even with those things which appeal to the natural mind as innocent as they are fascinating. It demands the subordination of all that we naturally hold dear to the will of a Person whom we have not seen, and to the hope of an inheritance which lies beyond this life. True the demand comes to the believer not by way of despotic and arbitrary law, but as the irresistible claim of a Savior's love expressed in His atoning sacrifice and in the attractive appeal of the Gospel, which draws us to the heart of the living Christ Himself. But yet the demand is there, pressed upon us by the Spirit of God, antagonistic to the flesh and all that really militates against our present spiritual good and our future reward.

It need occasion no surprise, therefore, that this Book is arrayed against the vices, vanities, and worldliness of mankind, that it rouses the antagonism of those whose life is characterized by these things.

But, further, the Bible aims its blows at human pride and wisdom. Its line of teaching

---

*C. F. Hogg in the Foreword to "The Scriptures and How to Use Them," by the present writer, p.5.

But, further, the Bible aims its blows at human pride and wisdom. Its line of teaching does not satisfy the merely intellectual inquirer whether he approaches it from the scientific, or historical, or literary, or even theological point of view. Being the voice of God to those who are sin-stricken, its first lesson is a sense of sinfulness and an acknowledgment of entire need and dependence. The fundamental doctrine that runs through the Volume, namely, that of the atoning sacrifice of the Son of God, is set in utter opposition to all self-trust, and is calculated to keep alive within the believer the spirit of complete self-renunciation. The Book holds out the highest reward to the meek and lowly and trustful. It leads the one who desires to obey its teaching, not only into a life of humility and subjection to the will of God, but also to wage an unremitting warfare against all that would interfere with the allegiance of the soul to its Redeemer, directing the heart into a fixed determination to do and to suffer, not in the spirit of mere heroism, but for the sake of Christ Jesus Himself.

The Bible yields nothing to natural curiosity. It is no wonder that the person who looks into its pages with a view to studying literature or history or any other form of human knowledge finds himself faced with what to his natural mind are inconsistencies, discrepancies, contradictions, and statements impossible of acceptance.

The teaching of the Cross, which forms the center of all its doctrines, runs counter to all natural inclinations. Human nature has rebelled against it, and hence the gigantic efforts which have been made to destroy the Book. Yet in the face of almost every form of opposition it stands today in its impregnable position, winning the souls and molding the lives of millions. Its circulation goes on with ever-increasing rapidity, and its triumphs not only over the souls of men, but in the life and history of nations, are amazing. Those who have found, by means of its teachings, deliverance from the penalty and domination of sin, and the enjoyment of spiritual life in unending union with the risen Christ, learn to sing with the seer of old, "Unto Him that loveth us, and loosed us from our sins by His blood, and who made us to be a kingdom, to be priests unto His God and Father, to Him be the glory and dominion forever and ever. Amen."

COMMENTARY
ON SELECTED
BIBLE BOOKS

Isaiah: Prophecies, Promises, Warnings

PREFACE

This work is the outcome of the preparation of notes written on behalf of many of the Lord's servants abroad during a course of several years. The many expressions of appreciation received have encouraged the writer to produce the volume.

The notes have a twofold aim: firstly, to seek to unfold the Scriptures, secondly, to bring to bear upon the lives of believers the practical effects of the warnings, promises and prophecies of the book of Isaiah, since "all Scripture is profitable for teaching, for reproof, for correction, for instruction which is in righteousness: that the man of God (a description of every faithful believer) may be complete, furnished completely unto every good work" (2 Tim. 3:16, 17). Introductory chapters on the life and times of Isaiah have been purposely omitted.

The writer unhesitatingly maintains the view that there was only one human author, the prophet Isaiah, of the sixty-six chapters of the book. Evidences of this unity are noted from time to time in the course of the commentary, and in the appendix, which gives a number of instances in which the same characteristic phraseology is used in both parts of the book.

Bath.   W.E.V.

The name Isaiah signifies "Jehovah's salvation." His call came in 756 B.C. in Uzziah's reign. There were three periods of his ministry: (1) in the reigns of Uzziah and Jotham; (2) from the beginning of the reign of Ahaz to that of Hezekiah; (3) from Hezekiah to the fifteenth year of his reign. After this he lived till the beginning of the reign of Manasseh. Tradition says that he was then sawn asunder (cp. Heb. 11:37).

As with Amos in Israel so with Isaiah in Judah, they were called to declare that the time of God's longsuffering was coming to an end. His prophecies consist of two parts, (I) Chapters 1—39, (II) Chapters 40—66; but these are closely connected with (I).

The book may also be divided into three parts, (I) *Prophetic,* of Israel and Gentile nations, especially Assyria (chapters 1—35); (II) *Historic,* relating to the reign of Hezekiah (chapters 36—39); (III) *Messianic,* especially regarding the deliverance of a remnant in Israel (chapters 40—66). Part I has four main sections: *(a)* prophecies concerning Judah and Israel (chapters 1—12), *(b)* prophecies against Gentile nations (chapters 13—23), *(c)* concerning Divine judgments and deliverances and concerning woes (chapters 24—33), *(d)* the future of Gentile nations and Israel (chapters 34, 35). Part II has two main sections: *(a)* concerning the Assyrian Invasion and Hezekiah's distress and deliverance (chapters 36, 37), *(b)* concerning the Chaldeans and Hezekiah's sickness and sin (chapters 38, 39). Part III has three main sections: *(a)* concerning Israel and the Gentiles and Divine deliverance (chapters 40—48), *(b)* concerning Jehovah's Servant, His sufferings and glory (chapters 49—57), *(c)* concerning the godly and ungodly in Israel and the contrasted issues of their ways and doings (chapters 58—66).

The book has been the subject of much expenditure of Higher Critical and Modernistic energy in recent times. One of the underlying principles in this kind of teaching is the denial of the predictive element in the book. The various suppositions of the exponents of these theories have tended only to confirm the faith of those who maintain the view of the unity of the whole book as being the work of the one human author writing what is given him by inspiration of God. Deny the predictive element and the only conclusion resulting is the disunity of the book and the composition of certain parts by different writers; a conclusion derogatory to the Person of the Holy Spirit as being the Divine Author through whom the book is "God-breathed."

Part Ia
Prophecies Concerning
Judah and Israel
Chapters 1—12

Chapter 1

The prophet begins with the mention of his subject and the time of his writing. The subject is Judah and Jerusalem and it is to be noticed that this twofold theme is prominent in chapters 40—66 as much as in 1—39, and that it involves a constant reference throughout the book to the whole nation of Israel.

He invokes the heavens and the earth to be witnesses to what the Lord has spoken, just as Moses did in Deuteronomy 32:1, and, as also did Moses, he proceeds to declare the grievous ways of God's people. God had acted toward Israel as a Father, nourishing (R.V. marg., "exalting," i.e., making them great, as in natural growth) and bringing them up, and they had fallen away from Him (v. 3). Israel was His wayward son (Ex. 4:22, 23; cp. Deut. 14:1; 32:20).

What He had done for them as a nation He has done for us individually and spiritually. The record of their apostasy is written "for our admonition" (1 Cor. 10:11). How we need therefore to take heed lest we grieve Him, as they did, and suffer eternal loss!

In *verse 3* the Lord declares that the way His people have behaved is worse than that of the brutes. **"The ox knoweth his owner, and the ass his master's** (a plural in the original, not of number, but expressive of fullness of authority, as in Ex. 21:29) **crib: but Israel doth not know, My people doth not consider,"** *i.e.,* that the Lord was their Owner and Master, that they belonged to Him and were dependent upon Him for all they required.

This twofold relationship with God is ours and needs to be kept in mind at all times, in all our ways and service.

In *verse 4* Isaiah speaks, breaking out into stern denunciation and lamenting over Israel as sinful, guilt-laden, a race of evildoers, a family corrupt in their ways. Their guilt was threefold. Each description is set in contrast to what God had designed them to be. They are *(a)* a **"sinful nation";** the Lord had said "ye shall be unto Me . . . a holy nation" (Ex. 19:6); *(b)* **"a people laden with iniquity";** God had chosen them to be "a peculiar people unto Himself (a people for His own possession) (Deut. 14:2); *(c)* **"a seed of evildoers";** God had made them the "seed of Abraham" (Is. 41:8, of Isaac, Gen. 21:12, of Jacob, Is. 45:19); *(d)* **"children that deal corruptly";** the Lord had declared to them "ye are the children of the Lord, your God" (Deut. 14:1).

All this is again admonitory for us upon whom the very "height of the ages" has come. The description given concerning us in 1 Peter 2:9 is similar to that given to Israel as God's people just mentioned: "Ye are an elect race, a royal priesthood (as in Ex. 19:6), a holy nation, a people for God's own possession, that ye may shew forth the excellencies of Him who called you out of darkness into His marvelous light." We should therefore take heed lest we fall as they did, lest there be in any of us "an evil heart of unbelief in departing from the living God."

The fourfold description is followed by a threefold declaration of the way in which Israel had acted toward God; they had become evil in heart, in speech, in act: *(a)* they had **"forsaken the Lord,"** their *heart* had turned away from Him; *(b)* they had **"despised the Holy One of Israel"** (the word signifies to mock, to scorn), they had sinned in *speech,* and that against the Holy One of Israel (a title which is especially connected with Isaiah's prophecies, see also 5:19, 24; 10:20; 12:6; 29:19; 30:11, 12, 15; 31:1; 37:23; 41:14, 16, 20, etc., and finally, 60:9); as the Holy One He was Israel's Sanctifier, and they should have sanctified themselves in response; He had said "ye shall be holy: for I the Lord your God, am holy" (Lev. 19:2); *(c)* they were **"estranged"** and had **"gone backward,"** they were guilty in *act;* they chose their own way instead of His.

This is followed in *verse 5,* by the remonstrance: **"Why will ye be still stricken, that ye revolt more and more?"** (or rather, "revolting continually"). Why reap the consequences of persistent rebellion, adding iniquity unto iniquity?

How fearfully the spirit of rebellion had permeated the nation is vividly portrayed in *verses 5 and 6:* **"the whole** [or rather "every"] **head is sick, and the whole heart faint."** The head represents the outward controlling power, the heart the inward emotions. The whole condition was a divine judgment. They were like a diseased body throughout. If the head and the heart are unsound the entire body is affected. From the sole of the foot to the head there was nothing sound, but **"wounds, bruises, and festering sores."**

The wounds needed binding up; the bruises needed mollifying with oil; the sores required closing (or pressing) so as to cleanse them and quicken their healing. The remedies are mentioned in almost the opposite order to that of the evils (thus forming a sort of chiasm, or reverse order, for the purpose of vividness or emphasis).

At *verse 7* Isaiah passes from metaphors to direct language, which recalls, no doubt purposively, the punishments threatened in Leviticus 26:33; Deuteronomy 28:49-52; 29:22, 23. These things had come upon them. The land had been unprecedently productive under Uzziah (2 Chr. 26:10), but now wickedness was prevalent to such a degree that in 9:18 it is described as burning like a fire.

In *verse 8* the phrase **"the daughter of Zion"** depicts Zion as a daughter, not a mother; it means "Zion the daughter" (see Zech. 2:10 and cp. Jer. 46:19; 48:18). It is expressive of the tenderness with which the Lord had regarded the relation which He had

established between Jerusalem (as representing His people) and Himself.

Her diminished population and desolate state were **"as a cottage** [a mere hut] **in a vineyard, as a lodge** [or rather, a booth or hammock for a gardenkeeper to use to scare animals away, and so corresponding to a scarecrow] **in a garden of cucumbers, as a besieged city,"** a picture of isolation and difficulty.

Only a remnant was left. There always has been, and there will be in the coming time of Jacob's trouble, "a very small remnant." Were it not so, says the prophet, **"we should have been as Sodom, we should have been like unto Gomorrah"** *(v. 9).*

We should take heed lest what was literally true of Israel becomes spiritually true of us, lest we be diminished, not it may be in numbers but in spiritual power and fruitfulness. If we yield to sin in our own hearts and lives, we are bound to make way for the enemy against us collectively as the Lord's people.

In Revelation 11:8 Jerusalem is described as Sodom. Isaiah now addresses the authorities and people as **"rulers of Sodom"** and **"people of Gomorrah"** *(v. 10).*

Ezekiel 16:49 shows that the sins of Sodom were pride, lust, luxury and cruelty, and now rulers and people under them in Jerusalem were guilty of the same sins. But there was something additional. Over all the abominations there was a garb of religion, a perfunctory discharge of certain details of the law. They presented their offerings to God, but of what value were they in His sight? They were simply trampling His courts *(v. 12).* Their observance of the appointed days and feasts was hateful: **"I cannot away with iniquity and the solemn meeting,"** He says *(v. 13,* R.V.); in other words, "I cannot bear ungodliness and gatherings at festivals."

Mere external religion is ever a cloak to cover iniquity. The Lord exposed all that in His strong denunciations in Matthew 23. The guilty combination in Judaism has largely developed in Christendom. The conscience of a believer may become so seared that a person can practice religion while yet living in sin.

The Lord warns His people in *verse 15* that, if they stretch out their hands to Him, He has to hide His eyes from them. If they make ever so many prayers He does not hear, for their hands are full of blood. God listens to those who lift up holy hands (1 Tim. 2:8 and see Ps. 24:4, 5). The word "blood" is plural, which points, not merely to murder, but to acts of violence akin to murder, and to bribes which purchased the ruin of widows and orphans (cp. Mic. 3:9–11). They are therefore called upon to wash and cleanse themselves, and put away the evil of their doings in His sight, to **"cease to do evil and learn to do well, and seek judgment, relieve the oppressed, judge the fatherless, plead for the widow"** *(vv. 16, 17)*. Let them learn the first principles of well-doing. God has a special care for widows and orphans (Ex. 22:22–24; Deut. 10:18; Ps. 68:5; James 1:27).

If they would do this and turn from their evil ways, there was mercy for them, both in the removal of their sins and in the prospect of eating the good of the land. The message of *verse 18* invites them to realize both the graciousness of His appeal and the justice of His demands: **"Come now** [or Come, I pray you], **and let us reason together** [as if challenging them to a trial], **saith the Lord: though your sins be as scarlet, they shall be as white as snow; though they be red like crimson, they shall be as wool."** The scarlet may suggest the deep-dyed character of sin. There would seem to be a reference to Numbers 19:2, 6, 9, where scarlet was burnt in the sacrifice, and thus there is an intimation as to the atoning efficacy of the blood of Christ. The glaring character of sin is certainly in view, and for the whiteness of snow see Psalm 51:7. Some regard the scarlet and white as emblematic of the relation of fire to light, i.e., of the wrath of God against sin to His pardoning grace.

"If ye be willing and obedient, ye shall eat the good of the land" *(v. 19)*.

The offer of justifying grace is designed to lead to repentance, not to be repented of. True repentance leads to willingness and obedience, to listen to the voice of God and do His will. This leads to spiritual blessing. What was the good of the land for Israel is to us the provision made for us in Christ as the nourishing and sustaining power of our life by the Holy Spirit. Refusal must bring judgment *(v. 20)*.

The lamentation which follows bewails the apostate state of the nation. The once faithful wife (pictured as a strong citadel) had become a harlot. Judgment had given place to violence and murder. The pure silver of righteousness had become dross, an amalgam of formal religion and vileness. The wine of divinely imparted wisdom (Prov. 9:5) was diluted with the water of mere tradition. The princes, forsaking righteous judgment and the cause of the widow, had become lawless *(vv. 21–23)*.

There was One who acted as the righteous judge, **"the Lord, Jehovah of hosts, the mighty One of Israel."** This last title is used here only. He was mighty to deal with these adversaries and to restore the nation *(v. 24)*. Promises are therefore given to Zion: **"I will turn My hand upon thee"**; His strong hand would be outstretched to redeem from iniquity, to smelt out the dross and take away the tin (or lead) *(v. 25)*.

Righteous judges and counselors would be installed as in the earliest days, e.g., of the reigns of David and Solomon. The day is approaching when Zion shall be called **"The city of righteousness, the faithful city"** (or "citadel"), a different word from that rendered "city" in the preceding clause (cp. 60:14). The names express the nature. These glorious characteristics will result from the great basic acts of God in redeeming Zion with judgment and her converts (those who have looked on Him Whom they pierced and turned to Him in repentance) with righteousness *(vv. 26, 27)*.

It will be all God's doing. God's justifying grace in Christ leads to righteousness and steadfastness in the lives of the justified. These are the evidences of genuine conversion.

In contrast to these converts who will enjoy the Millennial Kingdom, those who have followed the Antichrist will be destroyed together and consumed *(v. 28)*.

In *verse 29* the "oaks" which they have desired represent the mighty ones of earth, the Man of Sin and the leaders under him. The "gardens" which they have chosen symbolize the pleasures and glories of the world *(v. 29)*. They themselves will be as a fading oak and a waterless garden *(v. 30)*. They forsake "the Fountain of living waters" (Jer. 2:13). To choose anything but the will and way of God results only in loss and shame.

The close of this first chapter *(v. 31)* points on to the close of the whole book and speaks of the time of the end. The strong man is a phrase suggestive of the two great "beasts" of Revelation 13, the final Gentile world ruler and his colleague (perhaps a Jew). He shall be **"as tow, and his work** [R.V.] **as a spark"**; his sin will kindle the fire of the punishment that will fall upon him; **"they shall both burn together, none shall quench them"** (see Rev. 19:20).

Chapter 2

The opening word of this chapter resumes what Isaiah stated at the beginning of his prophecies *(1:1)*, but now introduces the subject of chapters two to five. In 1:1 he spoke of seeing a vision, now he speaks of seeing a word. This marks the communication as supernatural. When men speak to one another they hear; God's word was seen. This suggests two things; firstly, the word of God is "living," its energizing effect is to impart a revelation impossible to the merely natural mind; therefore, secondly, it involves a mind prepared and qualified to behold intelligently what God has to reveal.

The seeing of the word will lead to a vision of the Lord's glory in chapter six. In chapter one divine justice deals with rejected mercy; in 2:5 divine mercy restores holiness. Accordingly the prophecy opens, not with denunciation of sin (that is to be renewed at v. 6), but with the promise of blessing **"in the last days."**

"It shall come to pass" does not begin a quotation from Micah 4:1–3. It is a direct revelation to Isaiah. What is now in view is the glory of the Millennial Kingdom. **"The mountain of the Lord's House shall be established in the top of the mountains, and shall be exalted above the hills"** *(v. 2)*. The temple will apparently have a loftier site than formerly. There may be also an indication of the domination exercised therefrom over all other earthly powers (cp. Ps. 76:4, 5). **"All nations shall flow unto it,"** a metaphor from the peaceful flowing of a river, in contrast to the tossings of the sea of national strife and upheaval. The builders of Babel who sought to establish a world center found their scheme brought to confusion under divine judgment, and were scattered abroad. Mount Zion and the Lord's House will become a gath-

ering center for the nations in their recognition of His power and His claims.

There will be a mutual agreement and decision among many (not all, it would seem) of the nations to go up to Mount Zion, **"to the House of the God of Jacob,"** with a genuine desire to be taught His ways and to walk in His paths: **"for out of Zion shall go forth the law, and the word of the Lord from Jerusalem"** *(v. 3)*. Genesis 22:14 will be fulfilled (see also chap. 51:4; Mic. 4:2; Zech. 8:3).

"He shall judge among [i.e., between] **the nations"** *(v. 4)*. He will administer justice regarding international questions and difficulties, which now so often give rise to war. He will **"rebuke** [*or reprove*] **many peoples,"** rectifying their mistaken and selfish ideas, with the result that, after the tremendous clash of arms at Armageddon (Har-magedon) at the close of the great tribulation (the time of Jacob's trouble), the manufacture of weapons of war will cease and agriculture shall flourish. No longer will they learn war.

In *verse 5* the glorious future prospect assured to Israel stirs up Isaiah to plead with his people to return to God immediately, and to walk **"in the light of the Lord."** Hence the renewal of the lamentation for their deplorable apostasy. *Verse 6* should begin with "For" (not "Therefore"): **"For Thou hast forsaken Thy people, the house of Jacob"** (not here the noble title of "Israel"). They were filled with customs and ways from the east (cp. Num. 23:7) and had adopted from the Philistines the arts of divination, and had joined hands with the sons of strangers (that is the meaning of **"please themselves"**).

That gold and silver and horses and chariots *(v. 7)* filled the land was a complete ignoring of the command given in Deuteronomy 17:16, 17. Solomon had erred in this respect, and from the throne downwards the nation thereby became permeated with idolatry under the influence of pagan peoples; high and low engaged in it; the mean man bowed down to what his hands had made, and the great man degraded himself *(vv. 8, 9)*. Hence the intercessor was now compelled to plead against his people that they might not be forgiven (cp. Hos. 1:6).

The answer is given. Judgment is impending. They had forsaken the Rock (Deut. 32:4;

Is. 17:10; 26:4; 30:29); they must therefore flee to the natural rock and hide in the dust of the earth, from before the terror of the Lord and **"the glory of His majesty"** *(v. 10).* Pride must be humbled. They had bowed down to idols; now their haughtiness must be bowed down, that the Lord alone might be exalted *(v. 11).*

Where God is not given His rightful place everything falls into ruin.

The passage from here to the end of the chapter passes from immediate circumstances to the end of Gentile dominion and to the judgments which must fall upon the nations at the time of the Second Advent, preliminarily to the setting up of the Millennial Kingdom.

The period is described as **"the day of the Lord."** The word "day," when used in this way, in the Old Testament and the New Testament, has the twofold significance of time and judgment. The natural day brings into light that which has been in darkness. The present period is called "man's day" (1 Cor. 4:3, A.V. and R.V. margins, for the text "man's judgment"), for now man passes his benighted and often perverted judgment upon things. There have been days of the Lord in His judicial dealings with Israel in the past, especially by victory over the foes (Jer. 46:10; Ezek. 13:5; 30:3).

Here, however, as in Joel 2:31 and Malachi 4:5, the period indicated is yet future. It will see the complete overthrow of gentile power (Is. 13:9-11; 34; Dan. 2:34, 44; Obad. 15) and the deliverance of the Jews.

In *verse 13* the cedars of Lebanon and the oaks of Bashan, illustrative of natural glory and power, are symbolic of military leaders of the nations gathered finally against the Jews.

In *verse 14* the mountains and hills, likewise emblematic of natural power, symbolize the mighty kingdoms of the nations. All that they have accomplished, in their pride and independence of God, both by way of strongholds on land *(v. 15),* and in traffic and commerce by sea *(v. 16),* is to be brought to nought. The self-exaltation of man must yield place to the exaltation of God alone *(v. 17).*

Idolatry will be stopped *(v. 18),* and men who gloried in their prowess and strength will flee to underground shelters, to **"the holes of the rocks, and into the caves of the earth, for fear of the Lord, and for the**

glory of His majesty, when He ariseth to shake terribly the earth" *(vv. 19, 20;* see 13:9-13; Joel 2:30, 31; 3:16; Hag. 2:6, 7; Matt. 24:29, 30; Rev. 6:12-17; 16:18-20).

Pagans, convinced of the futility and delusions of their idols, will hide them in the haunts of moles and bats, as if disgusted with them under their revulsion of feeling, and under the terror of Divine judgments. They themselves will flee to the cavities and crevices (the real meaning of the word rendered "tops") of the rocks—not that these will afford protection from the wrath of God.

Verse 22 exposes the impotency of the Antichrist, the Man of Sin, the leader of the great confederacy of the nations, the would-be conqueror of the world, the determined destroyer of the Jewish people, the man upon whom the nations had set their hopes of world-organization and prosperity, the man who "set himself forth as God" (2 Thess. 2:3, 4). His **"breath is in his nostrils: for wherein is he to be accounted of?"**—an exposure of his human frailty in face of the almighty power of the true God. For his doom see Deuteronomy 32:42, R.V.; 2 Thessalonians 2:8; Revelation 19:19.

Chapter 3

Judgment must begin at the House of God. Israel would suffer almost immediately at the hand of the Chaldeans, and the chapter gives warning of this. The people had provoked the Lord. Cruelty and oppression were practiced by their rulers *(vv. 14, 15)* and godless gaiety and luxury characterized the ways of the **"daughters of Zion"** *(vv. 16-23).* In the future the nations cannot be blessed till divine judgment has been wrought upon God's earthly people in "the time of Jacob's trouble"; and upon their Gentile aggressors.

The opening verses give a testimony to the effects of national sins. The divine titles **"the Lord, Jehovah of hosts"** combine the supreme and absolute authority and power of God as Ruler and Judge. "Stay" and "staff" are different forms of the same Hebrew word, and denote every sort of support. The removal must produce famine conditions, natural and spiritual, and not only so, it would mean the removal of every kind of national leader and official, every counselor and guide, as well as every skilled laborer (vv. 2, 3). The nation would be stripped of all organization and power. Inexperienced youths and babes (lit., childish things, or puerilities) would govern (v. 4).

Utter confusion must result. Men would ask for help from one another, but all would be helpless, unable to provide remedies or sustenance, or to rule (vv. 6, 7). A few faithful men would remain, and acknowledge that the whole situation was the result of iniquity and provocation of the Lord (v. 8). In *verse 9* **"the shew of their countenance"** means their glaring effrontery (cp. Hos. 5:5; 7:10). They openly avow their sin, as the people of Sodom did. But like them they must bring retribution upon themselves (cp. Amos 5:10–20).

Amidst it all there is a word for the godly by way of a contrasting parallel: **"Say ye to the righteous, that it shall be well with him** [lit., "it is good," the same phrase as in Gen. 1:4, 10, 18, etc.]; **for they shall eat the fruit of their doings."** "Whatsoever a man soweth, that shall he also reap." What seems so terrible for the godly will be found to be for their eternal good. The apparent prosperity of the wicked will eventuate in his own destruction: **"the reward of his hands shall be given him"** (vv. 10, 11).

Verses 12 to 16 describe further the degraded condition of the people. Mere youths, with all their inexperience, governed them with oppression, and women ruled over them, as had Maachah (1 Kin. 15:13) and Athaliah (2 Kin. 11:1, 13). These leaders did nothing but mislead; they destroyed (lit., "swallow up," cp. Job 39:24) the paths appointed for Israel, obliterating and hiding them. Therefore Jehovah would interpose to judge the peoples (the word is plural in *v. 13*), the nations in general and especially the rulers of His own nation, dealing with them for crushing His people and "grinding the face" of the suffering, a vivid metaphor, not found elsewhere, taken from the action of the millstone and describing unmerciful severity.

The general worldliness found its great expression in the ways and doings of the females, in their luxurious style of dress, and adornment, adopted partly by imitating the priestly vestments and partly from idolatry. Dire retribution must ensue. The "scab" (v. 17) is a word connected with leprosy. The word rendered "discover" is used in Psalm 137:7 of razing a city. The men (civilians) would fall by the sword and the mighty men (lit., "might," i.e., the entire military body) would perish in war. The gates, places where worshipers thronged and ceremonies were held, would become scenes of mourning, and the city being "desolate" or purged (the word is rendered "be free" in Num. 5:19, 28, in connection with the water of jealousy), would sit upon the ground, a phrase expressive of utter humiliation, used in 47:1 and Job 2:13.

When worldliness comes into a church, the Lord has to administer rebuke and chastening and takes an outside place (Rev. 3:19, 20). Let the individual backslider repent with earnest zeal, and the Lord's desire to re-enter will be fulfilled.

Chapter 4

The first verse of this chapter probably belongs to the end of the preceding chapter, and continues the effects of the Divine judgments upon the proud, godless daughters of Zion. The prevailing conditions would be reversed. Whereas the young women had each gloried in being an attraction to suitors, the time of humbling was coming when seven women would make suit to the same man, whoever he might be, saying **"We will eat our own bread, and wear our own clothes** [renouncing the claim established by the law for provision of food and clothing by the husband, Ex. 21:10]; **only let us be called by thy name; to take away our reproach,"** i.e., the reproach of being single. The number seven is here suggestive of the fullness of Divine judgments.

But mercy rejoices against judgment, and the second verse introduces a passage dealing with eventual restoration. "In that day" marks the yet future part of the long period of God's dealings with His earthly people. When the sinners in Zion have been removed, a remnant will be brought forth in the glory of their fidelity. "The escaped of Israel" will constitute the reigning earthly power under the King of Kings.

It is He Who is called in *verse 2* **"the Branch of Jehovah,"** and **"the fruit of the** earth." This twofold description combines His Deity and His humanity. He will be revealed as **"beautiful and glorious,"** lit. "for beauty (ornament) and glory," the same two words as describe the priestly robes in Exodus 28:2, 40. He will be a Melchizedek priest. With the phrase "the fruit of the earth" compare the statement "our Lord sprang out of Judah" (Heb. 7:14). He will be **"excellent and comely,"** or "majesty and splendor" (cp. 28:5). "Except a grain of wheat," He said, "fall into the earth and die, it abideth by itself alone; but if it die, it beareth much fruit" (John 12:24, R.V.). Accordingly here it says that He will, in all this glory, be **"for them that are escaped of Israel."**

Just as Christ, when He comes to receive the dead saints and change the living, will be "our Deliverer from the coming wrath" (as the rendering should be in 1 Thess. 1:10), i.e., the wrath of God upon the world at the end of this age, so when He comes in glory with the angels and the Church He will be "the Deliverer" of the godly remnant in Israel (the same phrase and title in Rom. 11:26), not from wrath but from their foes.

Then those who are **"left in Zion,"** those who are **"written among the living in Jerusalem"** (cp. Luke 10:20; Phil. 4:3; Heb. 12:23; Rev. 17:8), will be called "holy" *(v. 3)*, Israel's primary and real vocation (Ex. 19:6).

This is our vocation too; it involves a life of complete separation to God, an identification with His character (1 Pet. 1:16). Let us therefore who are written among the living "cleanse ourselves from all defilement of the flesh and spirit, perfecting holiness in the fear of the Lord."

The people failed to obey the command **"Wash you, make you clean"** (1:16). In the coming day the Lord will Himself **"wash away the filth of the daughters of Zion"** and purge **"the blood of Jerusalem,"** and that **"by the Spirit** [or blast] **of judgment, and by the spirit of burning"** *(v. 4)*. This will be the baptism of fire, foretold by John the Baptist (Matt. 3:11).

In the wilderness the Lord provided for the journeying of the people a pillar of cloud and fire. In the coming Millennium there will be, not a pillar, but a **"canopy"** of cloud by day and fire by night **"over the whole habitation"** and upon the festal assemblies of the people. The figure is that of a wedding canopy carried above the bridegroom. **"Upon all the glory shall be a covering** [not "a defense"]," *(v. 5)*. The term gives an intimation of the Lord's joy over His redeemed people, as the rejoicing of a bridegroom over his bride. There is likewise a suggestion of the close association of the Church in its Heavenly position with the restored earthly nation.

"And there shall be a tabernacle [or rather, a pavilion] **for a place of refuge, and for a covert from storm and from rain"** *(v. 6)*. Nature will continue its activities during the Millennial age. The most glorious feature of the whole scene will be the conjoint existence of the restored and glorious Jerusalem on earth, "the city of the Great King," and the Heavenly Jerusalem, consisting of all the glorified saints, and described figuratively in Revelation 21:10 to 22:5, the great City-Bride, the wife of the Lamb, the "Light-Giver" of which is Christ Himself.

Chapter 5

Isaiah is now led to adopt a new mode of appeal to Israel. He is in the closest fellowship with Jehovah, Who gives him a song to record concerning His vineyard. It is **"a song of My Beloved"** (not addressed to Him). The vineyard belongs to Jehovah, and there is an intimation that His Well Beloved is Christ.

The vineyard is **"the house of Israel,"** and the vine is **"the men of Judah, His pleasant plant** (lit. the plant of His pleasures)." God had done everything for His people that they might be blessed in glorifying His Name and fulfilling His will. He had fenced His vineyard *(v. 2)*. He had given Israel His Law, separating them from all other nations. He had gathered out the stones, dealing with the Canaanites, who rendered the land barren. He had planted **"the choicest vine"** (the word is found elsewhere only in Gen. 49:11 and Jer. 2:21, rendered "noble"). He had built a tower, the central city of Jerusalem, where He would place His Name (cp. Prov. 18:10), a tower from which His appointed priests and prophets could watch against spiritual foes. He had hewed out a wine vat to receive the juice of the grapes, symbolic of the temple, where the offerings, worship and praise would be rendered to Him by the operation of His Holy Spirit.

For all this fruit the Lord "looked," waiting patiently for the prosperous outcome of His dealings. There appeared instead the small bitter berries of the wild vine (v. 2).

Let the inhabitants of Jerusalem and the men of Judah judge the matter, taking the circumstances into careful consideration. Let them have regard to what Jehovah had wrought for them, and what they had done in their rebellion against Him and the dishonor done to His Name (vv. 3, 4). Divine retribution was impending and inevitable. The hedge must be removed and eaten up (devoted to grazing). The fence must be broken down and be trodden upon by the Gentiles (v. 5). The whole must be laid waste. Pruning and hoeing would be futile. Rainless clouds would produce barrenness. What might have been so fruitful must yield briers and thorns, the very emblems of stunted growth.

The Lord's doctrine "drops as the rain" and His speech "distill as the dew"; but where there is no heart to receive it, how can there be anything but unproductiveness and blights? (v. 6).

Verse 7 also interprets the metaphor of the wild grapes. God **"looked for judgment, but behold oppression; for righteousness, but behold a cry."** It has been pointed out that the fact that the Hebrew pair of contrasting words have a certain similarity of sound, gives an intimation that as the wild grapes have a certain resemblance to the good, so in mere outward appearance the evildoers seemed religious, while actually they were full of iniquity (cp. Matt. 23:28).

The lesson from this passage is clear. It is possible to become so familiar with the routine of religious exercises that, while outwardly conformed to what has been learnt from Scripture, real heart devotion to Christ Himself has waned; the first love has been lost, and with it true spiritual power. The declension may open the way for grosser forms of evil, and the Lord has to stand at the door and knock, waiting for a response from any who really desire to enjoy communion with Him, and real conformity to His will and way.

This parable of the vineyard is followed by six denunciatory woes. In much the same way the Lord in dealing with the leaders of the people followed His parable of the vineyard, in Matthew 21:33 to 41, by a sevenfold series of "woes" in 23:13 to 36.

The first "woe" uttered by Isaiah, is against covetousness and greed (v. 8). There were those who added house to house and field to field, aiming at monopolies, and violating the law of property laid down in Numbers 36:7. Desolation and scarcity must follow (vv. 9, 10). The land was the Lord's, not theirs.

Failure to realize that all that we are and have belong to Christ leads to such misuse of what has been entrusted to us, that we seek to serve our own ends thereby and bring the disaster upon ourselves of spiritual barrenness and want.

The second woe is against self-indulgence and pleasure seeking (vv. 11, 12; with v. 12 cp. Amos 6:4, 5). They heeded not the work of the Lord and were blind to the operation of His hands. Hence captivity without knowledge. The phrase rendered **"for lack of knowledge"** (v. 13, R.V.) may mean "without knowing it," i.e., without discerning the reason for, and the meaning of, the Lord's dealings. As a result their glory (the high and mighty in the nation) would become "men of starvation," and the multitude (the riotous mass of the people) would be men parched with thirst.

Self-indulgence dulls the spiritual sense by which we understand the ways of the Lord.

But a further consequence would ensue. Death follows famine. The foe would be cruel. Sheol (the underworld) would open wide its jaws, and the glory (the men of note) and their multitude (the people in general), with all the pomp and godless rejoicing, would descend into it. The mean man would be brought down and the mighty humbled (the order is chiasmic, or inverse, in contrast to that in v. 14). The eyes of the lofty, open to anything but the Lord, would be humbled (v. 15; cp. 2:9, 11, 17).

When men are persistently blind to God's dealings in grace and longsuffering, He manifests Himself in righteous retributive judgment. So it was with Israel and its captivity. So it will be with the world at the end of this age. Jehovah of Hosts will be (lit., will show Himself) **"exalted in judgment,"** and God the Holy One will be **"sanctified** [lit., will sanctify Himself] **in righteousness"** (v. 16). He will compel recognition of His attributes and claims. Jew and Gentile alike will be made to give Him the glory which is His alone (cp. Phil. 2:9–11).

And as to the land that remained after the nation had gone into captivity, it would be occupied by foreign nomad shepherds; lambs would feed **"as in their pasture"** (v. 17, R.V.). and the places left waste by the removal of the nation, would be eaten by strangers. For centuries Arabs have literally fulfilled this, and Jerusalem has been given up to Islam.

The third woe (vv. 18, 19) is against daring presumption and defiance against God. They **"draw iniquity with cords of vanity** [not pride, but lying and seductive teaching], **and sin as it were with a cart rope."** The figure is that of beasts of burden roped to a wagon. Iniquity was the burden they dragged by their vain delusions, and sin the wagon to which they were roped. However presumptuously they might glory in their ungodliness, it would bring the inevitable punishment. The description is sarcastic. Vaunting themselves in their evil in word and deed they failed all the time to apprehend the retribution it was bringing upon them.

They scoffed at God's Word and derided His Name. **"They say, Let Him make speed, and hasten His work, that we may see it** [i.e., let Him fulfill what He has foretold, let us see whether He can actually carry it out]; **and let the counsel of the Holy One of Israel draw nigh and come, that we may know it** (i.e., experience its fulfillment)!" This way of taking God's Name in vain was a gibe at Isaiah's use of it (1:4; 5:24; 30:10, 11). Such taunts were the very height of defiance. They would be repeated at the Cross, and will be repeated by the Antichrist (see also 2 Pet. 3:3, 4).

The fourth woe (v. 20) denounces those who subvert moral principles. They **"call evil good, and good evil."** They put **"darkness for light, and light for darkness"**; **"bitter for sweet, and sweet for bitter."** Evil loves darkness and delights in sin, the bitter thing. To forsake the Lord is evil (Jer. 2:19); they pronounce it good. It is good to draw nigh to God (Ps. 73:28); they declare it to be evil. Thus they flagrantly contradicted the very precepts and revealed will of the Lord.

The fifth woe (v. 21) denounces the pride and self-complacency of those who are **"wise in their own eyes, and prudent in their own sight"** (in contradiction to Prov. 3:7). This condition is closely connected with those mentioned under the two preceding woes. It is the natural concomitant of the rejection of God's Word and the subversion of morals.

The sixth woe (vv. 22, 23) denounces those who pervert justice and use their administrative powers to enrich themselves by bribes and to indulge in drunken debauchery. The prophet is again sarcastic. They are "mighty," i.e., men of renown, in their twofold criminality.

The divine judgment upon all this is likened to a fire (lit., a tongue of fire, a phrase here only in the O.T.) devouring stubble, a flame consuming chaff (or rather, dry grass sinking down in flame). All that they gloried in would be as moldy rottenness and vanishing dust (v. 24). They despised Jehovah's law and scornfully rejected **"the word** [the speech, as in Deut. 32:2] **of the Holy One of Israel."** Hence the righteous and irrevocable anger of the Lord and the stretching forth of His hand in wrath. The hills would tremble by the marching of hostile armies, and the carcasses of the people would be like street sweepings (v. 25).

What is foretold in verses 26–30 came to pass in the invasions of Nebuchadnezzar, the first of which took place in 589 B.C. God is described as lifting up **"an ensign to the nations from far,"** i.e., planting a banner to summon them to Jerusalem as His military rendezvous, to fight His battles against His apostate people. How great the change from the time when He Himself was their banner (Jehovah-nissi) against their first foe after the overthrow of Pharaoh and his hosts (Ex. 17:15)! Secondly, that He would **"hiss unto them** [the Chaldeans] **from the end of the earth"** presents the figure of a bee-keeper enticing the bees, by hissing, to leave their hives and settle on the ground.

The foe would roar over it (v. 30), i.e., over Judah and Jerusalem, and God's nation would look to the earth and see only darkness and tribulation, and in the heavens the darkness of night instead of light.

The general description given in these verses points not only to the Chaldean invasions but to those by subsequent powers, reaching a climax in the Roman conquest and eventual destruction of the city and the scattering of the people.

This fifth chapter thus has three parts: (1) Jehovah's planting and care of His vineyard, and His disappointment in its failure *(vv. 1–7)*, (2) the actual transgressions of both rulers and people, denounced under the six woes *(vv. 8–23)*, (3) the judgments which would fall upon them *(vv. 26–30)*.

All has its warnings against departure from the Word of God, and against the adoption of evil practices, the inevitable result of such departure. So it has been in the history of Christendom. All must meet with divine retribution at the hands of the nations. For this see Revelation 17:16–18.

God in His grace has left nothing undone to enable us to be fruitful for His glory, by His Spirit and His Word. Once we turn from this we not only become unfruitful but open our hearts to many forms of evil, and "judgment must begin at the House of God."

Chapter 6

This chapter is closely connected with chapter five. The sad condition of things described in that chapter existed in Uzziah's reign, and now in the year of his death (a jubilee year, which began on the evening of the Day of Atonement—that was the fourteenth jubilee since Israel occupied Canaan) Isaiah is given a vision of the Lord's glory, in contrast to the nation's shame. The glory was about to depart from the earthly Temple. It has never returned nationally since. In this connection it is significant that shortly after Uzziah's death Rome was founded, the power that was destined to consummate the devastation of Jerusalem and the scattering of the Jews.

The vision was of **"the Lord** [Adonai, sovereign or absolute Lord] **sitting upon a throne, high and lifted up"** *(v. 1)*. The apostle John makes it known that the glory seen by the prophet was that of Christ Himself (John 12:41). "High and lifted up" almost certainly refers to the Throne. Some would regard it as descriptive of the Lord. The word rendered "train" means the hem or fringe of His robe, as in Exodus 28:33, 34. His garment consists of light (Ps. 104) and fills the heavenly temple, just as the cloud filled the tabernacle (Ex. 40:35).

That the seraphim stood "above" *(v. 2)* signifies that they were in attendance (not in a superior position). They differ from the cherubim. They are the fiery guardians of the holiness of the Lord, and are possessed of certain human features. With two wings they covered their faces, in awe that dared not gaze at the glory. With two they covered their feet, in acknowledgment of the lowliness of their glorious service. With twain they were flying, or hovering. The verbs are in the imperfect tense, describing what they were doing continually.

"One cried unto another" *(v. 3)*. This suggests that their utterances were antiphonal, though not in song. There is no record in Scripture of angels singing. The worship offered is thus expressed: **"Holy, holy, holy, is Jehovah of hosts: the whole earth is full of His glory"** (or rather, His glory is the fullness of the whole earth). Possibly the first part was said by the seraphim on one side, the second part by those on the other.

As to the threefold utterance of the word "holy," three is the number of unity expanded or developed. There is more than mere emphasis here. What is suggested is probably the realization of the character of the Tri-unity, the Three in the one Godhead, their attribute in its purity and perfection, rather than three different modes of Their dealings.

The determinate counsel of God is not only that the earth "shall be filled with His glory" (Num. 14:21) but that "the earth shall be filled with the knowledge of the glory of the Lord" (Is. 11:9 and Hab. 2:14). His glory stands for His character and actings, and all this is to be manifested and is to receive worldwide recognition and acknowledgment (Jer. 31:34; cp. Phil. 2:11).

"And the foundations of the thresholds [R.V.] **were moved at the voice of him** [a collective pronoun, signifying "them," the company of the seraphim] **that cried, and the house was filled with smoke"** *(v. 4)*. The smoke, the outcome of the worship of the seraphim, arose from the altar of incense. It was therefore connected with the fire on the altar *(v. 6)* and was indicative of the acceptance of Isaiah himself *(v. 7)* and the preparation for his testimony *(v. 8)*. This completes the vision of the glory of the Lord as set in contrast to the dishonor done to Him by the ways and doings of His people.

The effect upon Isaiah was to bring him down before the Lord in the realization of his own natural state and in acknowledgment of his identification with his nation in their evil condition *(v. 5)*.

So should it ever be with us. The more we apprehend the facts and character of the atoning sacrifice of Christ and the glories of His Person the more deeply we realize our own sinfulness. The nearer we are to the Lord the greater the sense of our utter unworthiness. Further, in this our own rightful attitude before Him we learn to identify ourselves with the condition of those fellow members of the Body of Christ who have proved unfaithful and lapsed into evil ways, and to confess their sins, as ours. Only so can we really be prepared to give an effectual testimony. It is one thing to condemn the saints, it is quite another to take upon ourselves the confession of their sins as ours. It is that which causes the Holy Spirit to use us for real blessing amidst them.

The fire on the altar of incense did for Isaiah all that was necessary. The vision of the glory caused him to exclaim, **"Woe is me! for I am undone** [or, cut off], **because I am a man of unclean lips, and I dwell in the midst of a people of unclean lips: for mine eyes have seen the King, Jehovah of hosts"** *(v. 5)*. Uzziah had been cut off, and had to cover his lip and cry "Unclean, unclean" (Lev. 13:45). Now Isaiah feels himself in the like condition spiritually. No man could see God without suffering death (Ex. 33:20). His vision of the glory had reduced him, in his own estimate, to the level of his guilty and defiled nation.

For such a contrite heart there was immediate mercy (see 57:15). A seraph became a ministering spirit, in the vision. He brought in his hand a burning coal taken from the incense altar by the tongs of the sanctuary *(v. 6)*. A seraph could not touch the sacrifice or that which arose from it, he brought the effects of it. With the coals he touched the prophet's mouth, that member the uncleanness of which he had deplored (cp. Jer. 1:9). His iniquity was removed, and his sin expiated *(v. 7)*.

The whole vision and the divine dealings were the appointed preparation for the solemn testimony he was to deliver. This was not the beginning of his witness, the occasion was a special one. If we are to engage in any particular service for the Lord, we can render it effectively only as we freshly appropriate to ourselves the efficacy of the atoning sacrifice of Christ for the cleansing of our hearts from sin. For each occasion we must come to the Throne by way of the Cross. We must come to the Mercy-Seat (Christ Himself) "that we may obtain mercy."

All was now clear for the prophet to deliver his solemn message. He hears the voice of the Lord *(Adonai,* as twice elsewhere in this chapter, *vv. 1 and 11,* the supreme Ruler and Judge), saying **"Whom shall I send, and who will go for us?"** *(v. 8)*. The plural is suggestive of the Tri-unity of Persons in the Godhead. This was not a question of mere deliberation, it was directed to the heart of Isaiah himself, whom the Lord had already prepared for the purpose. The response was immediate. Isaiah was standing in unhindered communion with his Master. **"Here am I; send me,"** he says. There was no questioning or reasoning. No burden would be too cumbersome, if the Lord committed it to him.

There is no task laid upon us by the Lord which we shall not have power from Him to fulfill, when everything that would hinder our communion with Him has been removed.

Nothing could be more solemn than the message he was commissioned to give: **"Go, and tell this people, Hear ye indeed** [or hear ye still], **but understand not; and see ye indeed, but perceive not"** *(v. 9)*. They were "this people," not "My people" (cp., e.g., Ex. 32:9, 21, 31; Num. 11:11–14), and thus frequently in subsequent chapters of Isaiah. They were "a people of unclean lips."

The message was not only for immediate purposes, it pointed on to the time when Christ Himself, in the days of His flesh, pronounced this very doom upon the apostate nation (Matt. 13:14, 15).

The commands in *verse 10,* to make the heart of the people fat, to make their ears heavy, and to shut their eyes, involved the punitive measures which God Himself would carry out. Isaiah's message would be God's own instrument in doing it. Prophets were often said to do themselves by their messages what God actually did through them (see, e.g., Jer. 1:10; 31:28; Ezek. 43:3; Hos. 6:5).

What follows is in the inverse order of what has just preceded; **"lest they see with their eyes, and hear with their ears, and understand with their heart."** This inverted parallelism is called Chiasm, from the shape of the Greek letter Chi (X). It lends vigor and emphasis in the handling of a subject. For a simple example see Matthew 12:22.

The people had so persistently perverted their ways that they had gone beyond the possibility of conversion and healing. A man may so harden himself in evil as to render his condition irremediable, and this by God's retributive judgment upon him.

The prophet, while willing and obedient, was so weighed down by the nature of his message, that he cried, **"Lord, how long?"** For Isaiah knew that He would not cast off His people forever (cp. Ex. 32:9–14). The Lord responds by foretelling the wasted, depopulated condition of the cities, the uninhabited state of the houses, the utter desolation of the land, the removal of the people far away, and a multitude of forsaken places in the very heart of the country *(vv. 11, 12)*.

There is always a "remnant" of faithful ones in the nation and God shows His mercy to it in and through such. Accordingly He now says, **"But in it shall be a tenth, and it shall again be eaten up."** Even so this remnant will come through a time of trouble. It will be "eaten" (or "burnt"), i.e., by a purifying fire (see Mal. 3:3). This was the case with those who returned from captivity by the decree of Cyrus, as recorded in the books of Ezra and Nehemiah. So in the coming day, in "the time of Jacob's trouble" under the Antichrist (Jer. 30:7).

It will be **"as a terebinth and as an oak, whose stock remaineth, when they are felled** [or when the branches are cut off and only a stump remains]; **so the holy seed is the stock thereof"** *(v. 13)*. The stump has life in it after the cutting off of the branches; it can shoot out into verdure again. All this describes, in a twofold application, the circumstances of the remnant both after the return from captivity and hereafter in the great tribulation. The nation, consisting of the remnant, will, under the hand of their Messiah-Deliverer, revive and be glorified (see 11:1).

Chapter 7

After the death of Uzziah (6:1) and during the reign of Jotham, Isaiah was given no written prophecy to record. Jotham, probably exercised by his father's death, sought to be conformed to God's Law. Evil went on in the nation (2 Chr. 27:2), and Ahaz broke out into open defiance of God. And now a new series of prophecies is committed to His messenger.

The kings of Syria and Israel combined to invade Judah and attack Jerusalem, but were frustrated. The northern tribes were at least as guilty as Judah. In *verse 2* Ephraim stands for Israel (as distinct from Judah), for Ephraim was the paramount tribe of Israel and was a rival to Judah. A second expedition was planned by the allies, and the house of David was moved that is to say, trembled with fear, **"as trees are moved with the wind."**

Isaiah was therefore commanded to take his son Shear-jashub and to go to meet Ahaz at the end of the aqueduct of the upper pool, at the road of the fuller's field *(v. 3)*. This would be on the west of Jerusalem, and the king was probably carrying out operations to prevent the foe from a water supply while yet retaining its use for the city.

Shear-jashub means "the remnant shall return (or turn)." This forms a continuation of the message given in 6:13, marking the unity of the distinct prophecies. The name was designed to be to Ahaz both an inducement to him to turn to God himself, and a warning that, if he refused to do so, he would have no part in the restoration of that part of the nation described as the remnant.

God in His longsuffering was showing Ahaz mercy in spite of his iniquity. He promises him that the northern confederacy will be overthrown, and Ephraim would be broken in pieces *(vv. 4–9)*. Yet let him beware lest, persisting in his unbelief, he would be excluded from the promised blessing: **"If ye will not believe, surely ye shall not be established,"** or, to bring out the similarity of the expressions in the two clauses, "If ye are not firm in faith, ye shall not be made firm in fact."

This warning serves to remind us, positively, of the power of faith. Faith is encouraged and strengthened by difficulties. Faith faces what to the natural mind are impossibilities, and, resting on the promises of God, relies upon Him to fulfill His counsel concerning them and to turn the obstacles to account for His glory.

Ahaz did the opposite. He was no true child of Abraham. When the Lord invited him to ask a sign from Him, as a pledge of the fulfillment of His word, seeking it whether from below **"the depth"** (an allusive remonstrance against his resort to necromancy), or from heaven **("the height above"),** he replied, **"I will not ask, neither will I tempt the Lord"** *(vv. 11, 12).*

This was self will under the guise of piety, and received the Lord's rebuke through Isaiah, **"And he said** [addressing Ahaz], **Hear ye now, O house of David** (the royal line of privilege and honor, now represented by this degenerate king); **is it a small thing for you to weary men** [i.e., Isaiah, himself and others with him, who mourned over the rebellious attitude of the king], **but will he weary my God also?"** *(v. 13).* Would he make it impossible for God to grant the mercy of repentance and restoration?

As Ahaz refused to ask for a sign, the Lord would give one of His own choosing, and a sign the range of which would extend to circumstances far beyond those of the time of Ahaz, and would bring to a culmination the prophecies and promises relating to "the house of David." Ahaz and men of that sort would have no share in the blessings and glories of the fulfillment of the sign: **"behold, a** [Heb., the] **virgin shall conceive, and bear a son** [the present tenses in the Hebrew vividly convey the future event in its certainty, as if it were already accomplished], **and shall call His Name Immanuel"** *(v. 14).*

"Behold," in Isaiah, always introduces something relating to future circumstances. The choice of the word *almah* is significant, as distinct from *bethulah* (a maiden living with her parents and whose marriage was not impending); it denotes one who is mature and ready for marriage. The various conditions relating to the prophecy are such that the only possible fulfillment is that recorded in Matthew 1:22, 23 and Luke 1:31–35. An outstanding feature of Old Testament prophecies is that they connect events chronologically separated. Conditions more immediately relating to Assyria were developed under subsequent powers successively, culminating in the Roman,

under which Immanuel was born. The circumstances depicted by Isaiah as prevailing in the land continued up to and in Immanuel's day.

This sign would be **"in the depth,"** for Immanuel (God with us, or, as in the order in the original, with us is God) would be one condescending to become man, and to go down into the depths of vicarious judgment and death. It would be also **"in the height,"** for Immanuel would be "very God" (see v. 11 and 8:10).

"Butter and honey shall He eat when He knoweth to refuse the evil, and choose the good" *(v. 15,* R.V.). This is indicative of impoverishment. Thickened milk and honey were the food of desert wanderers. They were, of course, not the only articles of food; but instead of abundance of provisions there would be comparative scarcity. Such was the condition at the birth and in the childhood of Christ. There was no luxury in the home in Nazareth. "He became poor." The R.V. correctly gives the time indication, that, namely, of the days of his childhood.

This rendering is confirmed by the context in *verse 16.* Before the period of the early lifetime of Immanuel, He the only One who alone perfectly knew to refuse evil and choose good, the land, instead of being full of oliveyards, cornfields and vineyards, would be reduced to comparative poverty.

The desolation began in the time of Ahaz. The two kings of Syria and Israel, of whom Ahaz was afraid, were overpowered by the Assyrians. Their attack upon Judah followed *(v. 17),* and though recovery was granted in Hezekiah's reign, it was only temporary. The Egyptians **("the fly")** and the Assyrians **("the bee")** jointly devastated the land, fulfilling *verses 18 and 19.* The King of Assyria is spoken of as a hired razor *(v. 20).* Ahaz had determined to hire him for help. God would hire him (the sarcasm is noteworthy) for destruction. Judah would be shaved in a manner bringing the utmost shame. The head, the hair of the feet, the beard would be shorn, indicating respectively the removal of kingly authority, national independence and the priesthood.

Again the Nazirite had to shave his head, were he defiled (Num. 6:9). Israel as a Nazirite nation, set apart to God, had become defiled. The leper had to shave all his hair (Lev. 14:9). Israel had become leprous. The Levite, after contact with the dead, had to be completely shaved (Num. 8:7). Levitical service must be made to cease. But not forever. "God did not cast off (i.e., irremediably) His people whom He foreknew."

Yet as a result of the destruction wrought by national foes, there would be poverty; instead of abundance of milk, just the thickened milk, or curd, and wild honey; instead of a flourishing vineyard, **"briers and thorns."** As for the hills formerly digged with the mattock (the verb in the first clause of v. 25 should be rendered in the past tense), men would go there apprehensive of briars and thorns, not for agricultural purposes, but with arrows and bows. Oxen would roam about wherever they could, and lesser cattle would tread down any growth *(vv. 21–25).*

Where a company of God's people departs from the right ways of the Lord, fruitless and noxious products are sure to develop, and there will be spiritual barrenness instead of fertility that glorifies God. Bows and arrows suggest strife, instead of "the whole armor of God" that wards off and defeats the spiritual foe.

Chapter 8

Warnings concerning Assyria are now given by means of a significant undertaking enjoined upon Isaiah. He was commanded to take a great tablet, or slab (not a parchment roll), and write on it **"with a man's pen"** (i.e., in common or popular characters, for all to read without difficulty) **"for in Maher-shalal-hash-baz,"** i.e., plunder speedeth, booty hasteth *(v. 1).* This was confirmed by the granting of a second son to the prophet (for the eldest see 7:3) to whom he was bidden to give the same name as on the tablet.

Moreover, since the fulfillment of the prophecy would arouse the people to the fact that God had spoken through him by the mysterious name, the Lord himself says **"I will take** [as the R.V. rightly renders it] **unto Me faithful witnesses to record, Uriah the priest, and Zechariah the son of Jeberechiah"** (see 2 Kin. 16:10 and 2 Chr. 29:1 and 13). These would tell the people how Isaiah had long before foretold, by his inscription and

by the name of his son, what had now come to pass *(vv. 2, 3).*

Before the child, i.e., Isaiah's, not Immanuel, had learned to say in baby language **"my father, my mother,"** the king of Assyria, Tiglath-Pileser, would have despoiled the capitals of Syria and the northern Israelitic ally *(v. 4).* His prophecy was not designed to be, nor was it actually, a comfort to Ahaz, for the success of the Assyrian King would be only the steppingstone to his attack upon Judah, and that is confirmed in verses 5–8. The nation, both Israel and Judah ("this people"), refused the softly-flowing waters of Shiloah ("that which is sent"), Divinely provided at Zion and Moriah and symbolic of God's promises concerning the throne and lineage of David, and rejoiced in setting their hopes upon earthly powers, Israel and its ruler Remaliah's son, of Samaria, rejoicing in its alliance with Rezin, King of Syria, and Judah relying upon Assyria *(v. 6).*

Both Israel and Judah, and Syria with them would therefore suffer at the hands of the King of Assyria, symbolically depicted as the rushing overflowing waters of the eastern river, in contrast to the waters of Shiloah *(v. 7).* But Judah, would reach only to the neck—a dangerous height, but kept under Divine restraint, inasmuch as Immanuel would eventually come to Judah, and the land is His possession. Hence the sudden address to him, **"Thy land, O Immanuel"** *(v. 8).*

God did through Isaiah what He has done ever since, and will do, through His completed Word, confirming the truth of its prophecies by their fulfillment in the course of human events. We may not read Scripture in the light of events, but we can see, as Judah did in Isaiah's day, the veracity and power of the Divine revelations in their fulfillment.

In *verse 9,* in view of the glory of Immanuel, the prophecy points on to the final gathering of the nations under the Antichrist against the Jews in "the war of Har-mageddon" and the utter overthrow of their confederate effort to annihilate them: **"Associate yourselves, O ye peoples"** (plural R.V.). Another version gives the meaning "Disquiet yourselves," i.e., "raise the war cry." Let them gird themselves for the attempt. Three times their doom is pronounced, **"Ye shall be broken in pieces."**

Their counsel will be brought to naught. Their propaganda will fail of realization. The scene and the circumstances are the same as those in Psalm 2:1-5; Joel 3:2; Zechariah 14:1-3; Revelation 19:15-21.

In this *10th verse* of Isaiah 8 the nations are bidden to speak the word, i.e., "utter your sentence." It will not stand. The secret of the overflow lies in the great Name Immanuel.

Verses 11 and 12 continue the remonstrance against the reliance upon Assyria instead of upon God. Isaiah declares that Jehovah had spoken to him, overpowering him with His hand (see margin), instructing him not to walk in the way of his people. The command in verse 12 is addressed to Isaiah and the few with him who feared God and dissociated themselves from the apostasy of the time. The true meaning of the verse is unfolded if the accurate rendering "A conspiracy" is substituted for "A confederacy." The reference here is not to the alliance between Pekah and Rezin. Isaiah and his associates were being accused of a conspiracy against Ahaz and Judah under him, because of the prophet's denunciation of the alliance with Assyria. This kind of calumny was what prophets had to endure whenever they opposed an appeal by God's people for the help of Gentile aid (Amos 7:10).

While, then, Isaiah was comforting the faithful with the promises concerning Immanuel, he was to warn them against the popular idea, and against sharing in fears of the people. "Call ye not conspiracy all that this people calls conspiracy. What they fear, fear ye not, nor regard it as dreadful": this seems the true rendering of the verse. *Verse 13* sets a positive command in direct contrast: **"Sanctify Jehovah of hosts Himself, and let Him be your fear, and let Him be your dread."**

To sanctify the Lord is so to live that He has absolute authority and control over the heart and will, over every activity of the life, to walk in His fear, dreading to displease Him. This is the due response to His redeeming grace and love in Christ. "Sanctify in your hearts Christ as Lord" (1 Pet. 3:15, R.V.; see Is. 29:23 and contrast Num. 20:12).

The effect of the fulfillment of this is that the Lord becomes "a sanctuary" to us *(v. 14)*. Just as the Temple was designed to be to Israel the center of their spiritual life, their joy in worship and praise, a place of holiness and peace as well as a defense, so Christ Himself is to the believer. "We live in Him." Our life is "hid with Christ in God."

To unbelieving Israel He has become **"a stone of stumbling . . . a rock of offense . . . for a gin and for a snare."** They have been "broken" on the stone and "taken" in the snare *(v. 15)*. That was the case with Judah and Israel in Isaiah's day in their attitude toward Jehovah. So Christ became to them and still is (Rom. 9:33; 1 Pet. 2:8), till the veil is removed from their heart.

In *verse 16* the testimony refers to what has preceded, concerning both Immanuel and the future condition of Israel. It was to be secured and kept for the godly remnant then and in the coming generation. The law, which the people had cast away (5:24), was similarly to be sealed among the faithful disciples, those who humbly sought to know and follow it (possibly this verse is Isaiah's prayer instead of the continuation of God's word to him, and in that case his disciples are "the children" given him by the Lord, *v. 18*). Amidst the darkness of the people from whom God hid his face, Isaiah determines the more steadfastly to wait upon (or for) God and look for Him.

There is a helpful lesson for us in this. Conditions of declension from God and refusal to listen to His Word will be the means, if we abide faithful and stand in His counsels, of directing our hearts the more steadfastly to wait upon Him, that our expectation may be from Him. The backsliding state of some who once gave hopes of being blessed and made fruitful through our ministry, tends to depress the spirit. In these circumstances, and amidst difficulties of whatever nature, the Spirit of God would draw us nearer to Him, that we may ever find our resources in His power still to glorify His Name through us.

The prophet finds comfort and assurance in the children the Lord had given Him *(v. 18)*, Shear-jashub and Maher-shalal-hash-baz were **"for signs and wonders in Israel from Jehovah of hosts, which dwelleth in Mount Zion."** The one was a sign that "a remnant would return," the other that "plunder would speed and booty would haste." The *sign* was a token or pledge by word and deed portending the fulfillment of an event; the *wonder* was an indication of the divinely supernatural source and cause of it. Thus the two children were tokens of redemption for Israel through judgment.

The first part of this verse is quoted in Hebrews 2:13, where the Spirit of God (who is a law to Himself in the matter of quotations from the O.T.) applies it to the spiritual children of God in relationship to Christ. Isaiah's natural children were symbolically representative of believers, who likewise are to be a testimony in the world.

Instead of accepting the signs and messages given by God, the people made application to those who had "familiar spirits," i.e., to spiritist mediums, as Saul did at Endor, and indulged in the arts of necromancy and wizardry *(v. 19)*. The Lord's remonstrance is twofold; **"should not a people seek unto their God? On behalf of the living should they seek unto the dead?"** This is the folly of Spiritism. The disastrous character of it is that its dupes, both the mediums and the applicants, put themselves into the delusive and destructive power of evil spirits.

Before every great crisis in human affairs there has been an outburst of spiritism. So it was in Judah and Israel just before the captivity. So it was at the time of Christ's Incarnation and atoning Death. So it is today. God has provided all that is requisite for our guidance and spiritual needs in the Scriptures of truth (2 Tim. 3:16, 17).

So it was in the nation of Israel, ere even the Old Testament was completed: **"To the law** [i.e., the teaching, *thorah*] **and to the testimony! if they speak not according to this word, surely there is no morning for them"** *(v. 20)* or "they are a people for whom no morning dawns"; they abide in perpetual darkness. **"And they shall pass through it** [or rather, "they, the rebellious nation, shall go about therein," i.e., in the darkness], **hardly bestead** [i.e., hard pressed or hardened] **and hungry."** Then, instead of repenting, they would fret themselves, curse the king and curse God (or rather cursed by the king and by God), and would "look upward," turning their face in despair toward heaven, to see if light would come from thence, and look downward to the earth, to find relief therefrom: and behold, distress and darkness, the gloom of anguish, and into thick darkness they shall be driven away, i.e., cast out of Immanuel's land.

Chapter 9

The "Nevertheless" marks an immediate connection with the close of chapter 8, and a contrast to the judicial darkness there foretold. God had provided (and would provide) a light if the rebellious nation would receive it. Here again the prophecy passes from the immediately subsequent calamities of invasion to the shining light of the Incarnate Christ amidst the people, and especially in Galilee.

That district, the region of Zebulon and Naphtali, was to suffer from the invasions of the Syrians and then the Assyrians. Yet in contrast to that **"former time"** of contempt, **"in the latter time"** God would "make it [the region] glorious" (see the R.V.). **"The people that walk** [the tense is prophetic present] **in darkness see a great light: they that dwell in the land of the shadow of death, upon them a light shines"** *(v. 2)*. The fulfillment of this is described in Matthew 4:12 to 25, where the Evangelist writer quotes this passage. How the Light shone in Cana of Galilee is recorded in John 2:1–11.

From this point to the end of *verse 7* the prophecy stretches across another interval and passes to the overthrow of the Antichrist, the oppressor, and the establishment of the Messiah's kingdom of peace and righteousness.

Verse 3 is correctly rendered in the R.V. There is no word "not" (see the A.V. margin). **"Thou hast multiplied the nation, Thou hast increased their joy: they joy before Thee according to the joy in harvest, as men rejoice when they divide the spoil."** This has never been fulfilled in the nation yet. Only a remnant returned from the captivity. The very opposite of these conditions has prevailed under successive Gentile domination. At the close of the coming great tribulation, when the Lord comes in Person to deliver His earthly people, they will joy over blessings granted and destruction averted. The Millennium will see a vast increase in the nation's population.

They will joy before the Lord. That ever should be the character of our joy—not mere exuberance of natural feeling, not merely joy in mercy and prosperity, in deliverance and supply, but joy before the Lord, a joy that exults in Him, His power and presence.

In *verse 4* the past tense looks upon the future event as an assured accomplishment. The pronoun "his," thrice in the verse, refers to Israel. The Lord will break **"the yoke of his burden,"** i.e., the burden inflicted upon it by the oppressor; **"the staff of his shoulder,"** i.e., the stout stick of the yoke burdening and chafing the shoulder; and **"the rod of his oppressor,"** the scepter of the imperial tyrant, the emblem of tyranny. The **"day of Midian"** was the time of Gideon's victory (Judg. 6 and 7). God saved the nation, not by its military power or prowess, but by His own choice of a small company and by means far otherwise than that of human might, so that they could not boast in their own strength (Judg. 7:2). So in the coming day, it will be all the Lord's personal act, for the nation will be in its extremity of weakness.

The lesson for us is clear. What we seek to accomplish by our own devices and in our own strength, only plays into the hands of our spiritual foe. It is when we are weak that we are strong (2 Cor. 12:10). Compare what is recorded of Ahaz himself in 2 Chronicles 28:21. His self-efforts "helped him not."

Verse 5 points directly to the war of Harmagedon (Rev. 16:14, R.V.). That climax will see **"all the armor of the armed man in the tumult"** (Joel 3:9–14; Zech. 14:13), **"the garments rolled in blood"** (Is. 63:3; Rev. 14:20), **"burning,"** and **"fuel of fire"** (Is. 66:15, 16; Joel 2:30).

But all this victory, deliverance and joy is based upon the Birth of Christ. *Verse 6* is an expansion of the meaning of "Immanuel" in 7:14. There He was spoken of as a sign, here He is a gift: **"For unto us a child is born"**; He is partaker with **"the children"** of flesh and blood (Heb. 2:14); **"unto us a son is given,"** One who grows up into Manhood, qualified to exercise the power and reveal His nature and character now to be mentioned: **"and the government shall be upon His shoulder: and His Name shall be called** [cp. 7:14] **Wonderful, Counsellor, The mighty God, The everlasting Father, The Prince of Peace."**

For the first of these titles compare Judges 13:18 (R.V. and A.V. margin); for the second, see Isaiah 11:2; and for the two together, 25:1. These two are not to be combined into one phrase as if the first was an adjective de-

scribing the Counsellor as wonderful: each is a noun. Contrast 28:29, where the phrase is different.

In the next title, "The mighty God," "God" is *El,* the last syllable of Immanuel, and again the deity of Christ is declared. El is contrasted with man in 31:3 and Hosea 11:9. "Mighty" is used of God in Deuteronomy 10:17 and elsewhere. "The everlasting Father" is, lit., "The Father of eternity." There is a twofold revelation in this: (1) He inhabits and possesses eternity (57:15); (2) He is loving, tender, compassionate, an all-wise Instructor, Trainer and Provider.

The title "The Prince of Peace" comprehends His actings in respect of each of the four preceding titles. His eternity and His provision of peace are combined in 57:15–19. He is a Prince who will in Person completely subdue every opposing foe, banish every disturbing element and thus bring peace to His people and to the nations. This the angels heralded at His Birth (Luke 2:14).

To the extension of His government and to peace there will be no limit *(v. 7).* He will Himself establish **"the throne of David,"** in fulfillment of 2 Samuel 7:16, ordering and establishing it with judgment and righteousness unending. **"The zeal** [or rather, the jealousy] **of Jehovah of hosts shall perform this."** His jealousy has two objects. It is a fire of indignation against all who maltreat His chosen earthly people, and a fire that burns with such a love for them and zeal for their welfare that it must consume all unfaithfulness in their midst (cp. Song 8:6, 7, and see Deut. 4:24; 5:9; 6:15).

The jealousy of the apostle Paul concerning the church at Corinth was but the expression of the Lord's own jealousy on their behalf. "I am jealous," he says, "over you with a jealousy of God: for I espoused you to one Husband, that I might present you as a pure virgin to Christ" (2 Cor. 11:2). The cup of jealousy had been put into the hand of that church in the first Epistle. She had drunk it and had cleared herself (2 Cor. 7:11; see Num. 5:11–21). What the Lord does with a local church He does with the individual members of the church, and in the coming day He will similarly deal with Israel.

The promises of *verses 6, 7* are now followed in *verses 8—10:4* by further denunciations of evil and warnings of impending judgments (just as the promise in 7:14 had been followed). The nation had to be reminded again and again that such was its condition that evil and consequent trouble and darkness would reach a climax before the promised blessing and light could be given. Though Ephraim is especially mentioned the passage deals with the whole nation, as is clear from *verse 9*. Ephraim was guilty of persistent hardness of heart. In spite of the utter failure of their alliance with Syria, which broke down under the attacks of the Assyrian, Tiglath-Pileser, there was no repentance. In their pride and stout-heartedness they said, **"The bricks are fallen down, but we will build with hewn stones: the sycomores are cut down, but we will replace them with cedars"** *(v. 10).*

For this cause fresh adversaries were raised up (Philistines against Judah and Syrians against the other tribes); the Lord's indignation was continued, and His hand was still stretched out in judgment (not in pleading with them, as some would interpret it), *verses 11, 12.*

In *verses 13 to 16* the prophet gives a second exposure of the causes of, and necessity for, the Divine judgments. In spite of these they refuse to turn and seek the Lord. Those who were chiefly responsible were the elders and men of prominent position ("the ancient and honorable"); they are described as the "head." Then there were the false prophets, teaching lies. These were the "tail" (i.e., the wagging tail of a dog), delighting in their guileful flatteries. The former were the palm branch, waving aloft; the latter were the "rush," down in the marshy ground. Each must be **"cut off . . . in one day."** In *verse 16* they are directly called "the leaders," and the people that follow them are destroyed (lit., "swallowed up").

Such was the evil that the Lord could have no joy in their young men (those who should have become powerful to maintain the spiritual vitality of the nation), and the fatherless and the widows (ordinarily the special objects of divine compassion, Deut. 10:18) would obtain no mercy. All were profligate, evildoers and blasphemers. Hence a second time Isaiah has to say that the Lord's anger was not turned away, but His hand is still stretched out in judgment *(v. 17).*

And now a third time warnings of Divine vengeance are given. Wickedness, whether in an individual or a nation, brings its own retribution. It becomes a burning fire consuming the evildoers themselves. As thorns and thickets are ready for the burning, so hardened sinners are ripe for judgment *(v. 18).*

The land would be "darkness" (the word here means turned like coal into fuel for the fire). With the civil war (see *v. 21*) there would be cruelty, famine, and self-destruction *(v. 20).* And a third time the solemn declaration is uttered that the Lord's anger continues and His hand is still stretched out in judgment. The whole circumstances, and all that led up to these calamities, are described in Nehemiah, chapter 9.

We need to beware of despising our higher privileges, of turning away from the right ways of the Lord, and, in a spirit of self-satisfaction, of rejecting God's commandments, "which if a man do, he shall live in them" (Neh. 9:29).

Chapter 10

The first four verses of this chapter are a continuation of chapter nine. Evil is again denounced, fresh sins are exposed, and warning of impending judgment is given. Injustice, robbery of the poor, the fatherless, the widows, will bring the day of visitation and desolation. There will be no one to whom to flee for help. His presence in their midst had been their "glory" *(v. 3).* Now it would "fly away as a bird" (Hos. 9:11). They would suffer desolation, shame and captivity *(v. 3).*

The presence of the Lord in the midst of His people is their highest glory, their greatest privilege. It is the secret of blessing, of power in testimony, of strength against the spiritual foe. At the same time His presence is intensely solemn. It is designed to enable us to live in His fear, not the fear that shrinks from Him, but the fear that shrinks from grieving the Holy Spirit. Failure to apprehend this leads to spiritual declension, resulting either in a mere form of godliness without the power, or in manifest ungodliness. So it was in Israel.

Verses 5 to 19 give a striking example of how God has used gentile nations to chastise His earthly people, permitting these nations to attain to a high degree of domination. They on their part have prided themselves on what they consider to be their own attainments, and on this account have brought upon themselves the retributive judgments of the Lord.

That was the case with Assyria, **"the rod of His anger,"** against His **"hypocritical nation," "the people of His wrath."** *Verses 7 to 11 and 13 and 14* recount his self-glorying and pride, his determination to found a universal empire. So it has been with recent tyrants and their schemes. So it will be with the Man of Sin, who will achieve a greater measure of success than all his predecessors. What an axe or rod is in relation to him who handles it, so is a mere man to Almighty God Who uses him. A stick unused is virtually **"not wood"** *(v. 15).*

When therefore the Lord had accomplished **"His whole work upon mount Zion and on Jerusalem,"** purging out its abominations, He punished **"the stout heart of the king of Assyria, and the glory of his high looks"** (cp. Hab. 1:11). This likewise applies to the final events of the present age.

The Divine titles in *verse 16* are significant. "The Lord" (Ha-Adon) is used by Isaiah always in connection with the power exerted judicially and penally. *Adonai Sabaoth,* "the Lord of hosts," is used here only, and indicates His absolute Sovereignty.

The fat men of Assyria would be made lean. Under its boasted glory God, as **"the light of Israel"** *(v. 17),* and **"His Holy One"** would be a consuming fire, making a bonfire of the mighty ones as of briars and thorns (just as with Israel, 9:18). The armed forces, **"the glory of his forest and of his fruitful field,"** would be consumed **"from the soul even to the flesh,"** i.e., internally, externally, and therefore "utterly," the whole army being demolished. In *verse 19* the fewness of **"his forest"** depicts the scattered remnants of the army that march against Jerusalem, so few that a boy could easily count them.

On the other hand, the remnant of Israel (Shear-jashub, 7:3) would no more rely upon the Gentile power, the Assyrian, that smote them, but upon God *(vv. 20, 21;* see 2 Chr. 30:6).

Verse 22 makes clear that here again (as often in O.T. prophecy) the passage points not merely to the immediate fulfillment, as in the case of the Assyrian invasion, but looks on to later circumstances. For the apostle Paul in Romans 9:27 applies verses 22, 23 to the yet future time, when Israel, passing through the great tribulation, will be reduced in number to a mere remnant, the nucleus of the redeemed nation at the inception of the Millennium. This will be the issue of **"the consumption decreed,"** i.e., the judgments of "the time of Jacob's trouble," executed **"with righteousness"** in the midst of the land. Accordingly the prophecy relates to the future time of "the Day of the Lord."

The remainder of the chapter is occupied with a prediction of the actual details of the Assyrian invasion and the overthrow of the invader. On which account God's people were not to be afraid of him. The rod must be used, but the smiter must himself be smitten. So it was with Egypt *(vv. 24, 26).* Assyria and Egypt are coupled again in 52:4.

In *verse 27* the statement **"the yoke shall be destroyed because of the anointing"** is understood in two ways. The English Version points to the anointing of the kings and priests in Jerusalem as those who were consecrated to God, on account of which God would destroy the foe. The mention of the yoke and the neck, however (metaphors from the wooden yoke on the ox), suggests that the neck of the bullock is so fat that the yoke will not go round it. So Israel would grow strong and assert its freedom. Accordingly the rendering will be, "the yoke shall be destroyed by reason of the fat" (cp. Deut. 32:15). The whole scene foreshadows the doom of the Antichrist.

Chapter 11

This chapter introduces a striking contrast to the close of chapter ten, a contrast between a proud cedar of Lebanon and a twig out of a hewn-down stock, a shoot from its roots. The former was symbolic both of the Assyrian and his final antitype the Antichrist, the latter is descriptive of the Christ, His lowly birth, His growth under the delighted eyes of Jehovah, and eventually of His mighty power to overthrow the very Antichrist and rule in righteousness and peace.

"And there shall come forth a shoot [or a twig] out of the stem [the stock or stump] of Jesse, and a Branch [a shoot] out of his roots shall bear fruit" (v. 1, R.V.). The house of David had become so degenerate that it resembled the stump of a tree that had been felled. There would, however, grow out of it a twig which would take the place of the whole trunk. To confirm this promise another figure is used. Springing up from the earth-covered roots there would arise a green shoot (*netzer*, from *natzer*, to shine or blossom, and hence the word "Nazarene," Matt. 2:23) which would develop and bear fruit (cp. Phil. 2:7–9).

Verse 2 gives a glorious description of Christ's perfect character and virtues. "The Spirit of Jehovah shall rest upon Him," expressive of the complete and complacent delight of the Father in Him, and of the abiding nature of His virtues (cp. John 1:32, 33). The statement contains a mention of the Three Persons of the Trinity. The Spirit of Jehovah is the Holy Spirit, operating in the fullness of the Divine powers (cp. Col. 2:9).

Following this are six spirits in three pairs. The first, "the spirit of wisdom and understanding," relates to powers of mind: wisdom discerns the nature of things, understanding discerns their differences. The second, "the spirit of counsel and might," relates to practical activity: counsel is the ability to adopt right conclusions, might is the power exercised in carrying them out. The third pair, "the spirit of knowledge and of the fear of the Lord," relates to fellowship with Jehovah; knowledge is here a knowledge of Jehovah (both details of this pair go with "of Jehovah"); Christ Himself said "ye have not known Him [*ginōskō*, i.e., ye have not begun to know Him], but I know Him [*oida*, i.e., I know Him intuitively and fully]," (John 8:5); the fear is that which, enjoying the presence of the Lord, refrains, therefore, from displeasing Him. Christ said "I do always the things that are pleasing to Him" (John 8:29).

These seven correspond to the seven-lighted lamp stand, with its main shaft and the three pairs of branches from its sides (Ex. 25:31, 32; see also Rev. 1:4; 4:5; 5:6).

These powers and virtues would "make Him of quick understanding [*rewach*, scent] in the fear of the Lord" (v. 3), i.e., quick to appreciate as fragrance "all that is of the fear of the Lord," or, as it is otherwise rendered, "the fear of the Lord shall be fragrance to Him." Accordingly He will not judge by mere appearance, nor will He pass sentence on mere hearsay, but by reason of His possession of the Spirit of Jehovah He will judge the poor with righteousness, and pass sentence equitably on behalf of the meek, the humble, those who cannot undertake their own cause.

Before peace is established, He will "smite the earth with the rod of His mouth, and with the breath of His lips shall He slay the wicked" (v. 4), i.e., the Antichrist. This prophecy is expanded in 34:1–10 and 63:16 (where see notes), a testimony to the unity of the book of Isaiah. The rod of the Lord's mouth and the breath of His lips are elsewhere described as "the voice of the Lord" (cp. 2 Thess. 2:8).

The rest of this chapter depicts Millennial conditions. The new era which Christ will introduce will see the exercise of "righteousness as the girdle of His loins, and faithfulness as the girdle of His reins" (the same word as that rendered "loins" in 5:27, and denoting the hips), emblematic of the energetic activity of His powers and attributes in fulfilling the Divine will.

Verses 6 to 9 are not to be regarded as symbolic. The actual fulfillment of the conditions in the animal world will be the natural outcome of the presence and authority of Christ. In *verse 8* the cockatrice is probably the adder (see Jer. 8:17, R.V. marg.). In *verse 9* the "holy mountain" stands for the land, with Zion as its governmental center. The phrase "as the waters cover the sea" signifies the covering of the bed of the ocean by its waters, a symbol of the depth and fullness of the experimental knowledge of Jehovah.

Verse 10 describes again the lowliness and exaltation of Christ. He Who had been in obscurity as the sprout from the root of Jesse, figurative of His lowly birth, will "stand for an ensign of the peoples" (plural), a banner, summoning them, not to war, but to Himself as the benign Ruler, exercising His authority in righteousness and peace. To Him the nations will seek, and His resting place, the seat of His authority, "shall be glorious," lit., "shall be glory." So it was with the Shekinah glory in the Tabernacle (Num. 10:33; cp. 2 Chr. 6:41 and Ps. 132:8, 14).

Then will the Lord gather "a second time" the scattered remnant of Israel (vv. 11, 12). There was a gathering of His people at the return from captivity in the time of Ezra. True, the Lord delivered Israel from Egypt under Moses, but that was not the gathering of a remnant. There will be peace and unity in the nation (v. 13) and they will subdue surrounding foes (vv. 14, 15).

There will be geographical changes, making for the welfare of Israel. The sea between Egypt and Arabia will be destroyed (lit., "be under a ban"), and the river Euphrates will be smitten into seven shallow brooks. From Egypt to Assyria there will be a highway for traffic (v. 16; cp. Zech. 10:11).

Chapter 12

This foretells the redeemed nation's song of praise at the inception of the Millennial reign of their Messiah-Deliverer, after His overthrow of their Antichristian foes. The song will be the earthly counterpart of the heavenly doxology sung as preliminary to the judgments preceding and issuing in the overthrow (Rev. 5:9, 10, 12, 13; 15:3, 4), and as an immediate counterpart to the doxology in Revelation 19:6, 7.

The Lord's righteous anger in His retributive dealings with His people, culminating in their great tribulation, will be followed by the mercy by which He becomes their strength, their song and their salvation (v. 2; cp. Ex. 15:2). The double title **"Jah Jehovah"** is found only here and in 26:4.

The promise follows that with joy (rapturous joy) they shall **"draw water out of the wells of salvation"** (v. 3), all found in Him Whom they once rejected, "the waters of Shiloah" (8:6), and Who invites the thirsty to come to Him and drink (John 7:37).

They will call upon themselves to declare His doings among the peoples (the Gentiles), glorifying Him in the proclamation to them that **"His Name is exalted"** (v. 4). All the earth must know of His **"excellent things,"** His "manifested Majesty." For God has determined that the salvation of Israel shall mean the bringing of salvation to the Gentiles, and this by reason of the fact yet to be fulfilled, **"great is the Holy One of Israel in the midst of thee"** (v. 6).

It is the presence of the Lord in the midst that here and now satisfies the desires of His people, produces their worship, provides the power of their testimony. His realized presence is the gladsome dominating factor in their assembling. Where this is lost sight of all is mere routine, though there may be enthusiasm for a cause, and resounding jubilation.

CHAPTER TWO

Part Ib
Prophecies Against Gentile Nations
Chapters 13—23

Chapter 13

Chapters thirteen to twenty-three consist of oracles concerning surrounding Gentile nations. These come appropriately after the great subject of Messianic prophecies in chapters seven to twelve. It had been foretold therein that the authority of the Messiah will be exercised over all the kingdoms of the world, and consolatory messages had been given concerning the ultimate blessing and glory of Israel. Accordingly the doom of these Gentile powers one after another is predicted.

First comes Babylon. For the Chaldean rule would succeed the already doomed Assyrian. It must, however, be borne in mind that many of the utterances go beyond the more immediate judgment upon that power.

Verses 2 to 5 are descriptive of the Medes, who are mentioned in verse 17, and of the Persians; *verse 4* speaks of kingdoms (plural). These combined powers are called **"My consecrated ones,"** i.e., those chosen by God for the fulfillment of His counsels against Babylon *(v. 3)*. That they "rejoice in His highness," or excellency, does not necessarily imply a consciousness on their part that they are acting for God's glory. Yet the Persians regarded the destruction of idols as part of their vocation, and Cyrus the Persian did rejoice in the recognition of God and the fulfillment of His mind (cp. 44:28; 45:1, and see Ezra 1:1–4). The Medo-Persian powers were to be **"the weapons of His indignation, to destroy the whole land"** (i.e., Chaldea).

From *verse 6 to verse 13* the prophecy passes from the doom of Babylon to the future judgments of God upon the whole world at the end of this age, in the time of the coming "Day of the Lord." This is indicated by the mention of "the world" (*tebel*, not *eretz*, land)

in *verse 11*. In *verse 9* "the land" should be "the earth." With this passage the following should be compared: 34:1–8; Joel 2:31; 3:15; Matthew 24:29; Mark 13:24; Luke 32:35.

Verse 12 foretells the reduction of the world's population at the time of the end, as the Lord Himself has foretold in Matthew 24:22.

Verse 14, if rightly translated, returns to the destruction of Babylon, as the rest of the chapter makes clear: **"And it shall come to pass** [the "it" is not a pronoun, referring to the earth], **as with a gazelle which is scared, and as a flock without gatherers, they shall turn every one to his own people, and flee every one to his own land."** That is to say, all foreigners would escape from the city, which attracted them as being the market of the world. The Medes, under Darius, began a work of destruction. Alexander the Great purposed rebuilding it, but his early death prevented it. In 20 B.C., Strabo described the site as a "a vast desolation."

And yet *verses 19 to 22* have never had a complete fulfillment. Its destruction has never been like that of Sodom and Gomorrah. Here again the principle of expanded prophecy in a twofold fulfillment is exemplified. The key to the question as to whether Babylon is yet to be a fresh center and to receive its complete destruction, is provided at the beginning of chapter fourteen, which begins with the word "For," i.e., as an explanation of what has preceded. Chapter fourteen introduces the day of Israel's deliverance and Millennial blessing, and it is in the day that the Lord gives them rest from sorrow and fear and bondage, that they will rejoice in the destruction of Babylon and utter their taunt against the city's oppressor.

There would be little or no point in Israel's glorious note of triumph over the destruction that took place over two thousand years ago. See, too, the prophecy of Zechariah 5:11. It is not at all unlikely that part of the coming Antichristian policy of defiance of God, will be the resuscitation of the great city, and that the prophecy of this passage in Isaiah will then have its complete fulfillment (see also Rev. 18).

Chapter 14

As we have pointed out, the explanatory word "For," which continues the subject of the preceding chapter, introduces a reason for the overthrow of the Gentile oppressor. This illustrates the following principles of the divine dealings with God's chosen people Israel: (a) the self-will and rebellion of His people causes Him to use Gentile powers to chastise them: (b) the arrogance and outrageous cruelty of these Gentile nations in the permitted exercise of their power, brings His judgments upon them, when the chastisement of Israel has accomplished its purpose: (c) His covenant mercy in the fulfillment of His promises to the "fathers" means the eventual restoration of Israel: (d) this in turn makes them instrumental in blessing to Gentile nations.

Verse 1 tells of Jehovah's purposes for Israel in a fourfold way: mercy, choice, establishment, influence. Verse 2 shows that those who remain of their former oppressors, after the divine judgment upon them, will become servants and handmaids to Israel.

At the same time the nation, in its rest from sorrow, bondage and affliction, will rejoice over the destruction of Babylon and its king, with a note of taunting triumph (for the fact of this immediately preceding overthrow of the revived city, see notes at the end of chapter 13), verses 3–6.

In verse 8 the statement as to the fir (or rather, the cypress) trees and cedars, is to be taken literally. The Chaldeans had cut down large parts of the forests to make use of the timber for a great variety of purposes.

Another circumstance is now predicted concerning the final overthrow of Babylon. The spirits of the slain potentates and people of the city are seen entering Sheol, the region of departed spirits, here the lost. Those who are there already address them at their arrival. Sheol is the Hebrew word in verse 9 (wrongly

translated "Hell" and "the grave"); it is not Gehenna, but what the corresponding Greek word in the New Testament calls Hades. **"Sheol from beneath is moved** [or violently disquieted] **for** [i.e., on account of] **thee: it stirreth up the dead** [the *rephaim*, the spirits of those who had been mighty among men, the giants] **for thee, even all the chief ones** [the leaders, lit., he-goats, i.e., leading goats among herds] **of the earth; it hath raised up** [raiseth up] **from their thrones** [a word which retrospectively contemplates their position when on earth] **all the kings of the nations."**

This passage demonstrates the fact of the conscious state of the souls of the dead in Hades, their power to exchange thoughts, and their vivid recollection of their past circumstances on earth. There is no Scripture to support the supposition of the unconsciousness of the soul.

"All they shall speak and say unto thee, Art thou also become weak as we? art thou become like unto us?" This is all the spirits in Sheol have to say to the newcomers. Verse 11 resumes the triumphant taunt of redeemed Israel as from verse 4. Babylon's pomp is cast down to the grave (not Sheol here). The "viols" refer to the instruments of music, as in Daniel 3:5. The statements **"the worm is spread under thee, and the worms cover thee,"** are sarcastically figurative allusions to the luxurious cushions and pillows on which the inhabitants of Babylon lay and to the gorgeous rugs and coverlets under which they rested. All were now maggoteaten.

In verse 12 Lucifer, lit., "light-bringer," is primarily symbolic of the fallen monarch of Babylon. The language which describes him is used of Satan (Luke 10:18; Rev. 12:8, 9), who spiritually energized the founder of Babylon, Satan's great seat, from which the world has been corrupted. Pride was Satan's sin and caused his downfall, so with Babylon (v. 13), the boasting purpose of the king who was to defy God in heaven and rule over the utmost limits of the earth "(the north")), and to rival His power (v. 14). Yet Babylon's doom is Sheol, and the sides (or corner) of the pit (in contrast to the sides of the north), verse 15.

In verse 16 **"they that see thee"** are not the spirits in Sheol, but people on earth, astonished at the downfall of the tyrant. *Verse 18* is the prediction of Isaiah, introducing the retribution foretold by Jehovah Himself *(vv. 22–25)*. First there is a contrast. Other kings **"lie in glory,"** i.e., have an honorable burial. But Babylon's monarch, Belshazzar, lies cast away from (not "out of") his prepared sepulcher. Other corpses of those slain in the battle, their bloodstained raiment gathered in heaps, are thrown into holes filled up with stones and earth. But his carcass lies unburied, trodden under foot, for he had destroyed his land, and slain his people. His dynasty would perish, without renown, an example of the doom of all evildoers *(vv. 20–22)*.

Afterwards, the bittern (or the hedgehog) in place of inhabitants, and marshland in place of palaces! And the city swept away with the besom of destruction!

In *verse 24* the scene passes back to the doom of Assyria (presenting a contrast to that of Babylon), to be followed by that of other foes of Israel (for the order see Jer. 1:18, 19). All this is introduced by a general declaration of the unthwartable purpose of Jehovah of hosts. "Man proposes, but God disposes" (see 46:10; Ps. 33:11; Prov. 21:30; Acts 2:23; 4:28; Eph. 1:11; Heb. 6:17).

The breaking of the yoke of Assyria is mentioned as a sample of the similar purposes of God concerning all the nations of the earth *(vv. 26, 27)*. Not an event can take place out of the line of God's predetermined counsels.

Verse 28, recording the death of Ahaz, is to be taken with what follows, not with what has preceded. This burden (or oracle) refers to the doom of Philistia (R.V., for A.V., Palestina). Upon the death of Ahaz, Hezekiah ascended the throne. He it was who utterly defeated the Philistines (2 Kin. 18:8).

In *verse 29* the rod is the scepter of David. That had been broken by all that had taken place in and against Judah, and over this the Philistines gloated. The cockatrice (or basilisk) is Hezekiah. The closing phrase is, lit., "a fiery flying one." This points on to the benign government of the Messiah, when the poor and the needy will be satisfied *(v. 30)*. *Verse 31* likewise points to the time of the end (see Dan. 11:40–42).

In *verse 32* the word rendered "nation" is plural, and the question is, "What answer do the messengers of the nations bring?" Are not these Jews, who will declare the mighty acts of Jehovah? The answer is that **"The LORD hath founded Zion."** All the foes in the long history of their efforts to destroy it will have been foiled in their attempts, and Zion will be the peaceful refuge of His people.

Chapters 15, 16

These chapters contain the Divine oracle concerning Moab, Isaiah mourns over its doom. For fuller details of this see Jeremiah 48, which ends with a promise of eventual restoration in the Millennial day. Accordingly the prophet's heart is roused to pity, unlike his pronouncements concerning Assyria and Babylon. Moab's pride procured its punishment *(15:6)*.

In *15:5* Zoar, a fortress in the south, is described as **"an heifer** [or ox] **of three years old,"** i.e., an ox in the fullness of its powers (cp. Jer. 46:20; 50:11). To this unconquered stronghold Moab's fugitives would flee from the northern foe.

In *16:1* **"the ruler of the land"** is the occupant of the throne of David, to whom the tribute of lambs is to be paid by Moab, here represented by Selah (or Petra). This tribute had been sent to Samaria (2 Kin. 3:4); now the lambs must be sent to Jerusalem and this will be the case, by way of Gentile tribute, when Christ comes to deliver Israel (see *v. 5*).

The exhortation to Moab to be a refuge for the outcasts of Israel, that is to say, the godly remnant, is deeply significant prophetically. The time indicated is that of the future great tribulation, "the time of Jacob's trouble." At the end of the warfare of Har-Magedon, the king of the north will pass through Palestine, "the glorious land," on his way to conquer Egypt, but Edom, Moab and Ammon will "be delivered" (Dan. 11:41, R.V.). Satan will have instigated the Antichrist to lead the armies of the Roman power to endeavor to exterminate the Jewish people, and particularly the godly remnant. These will have fled to the mountains of Moab from Jerusalem, fulfilling the Lord's word in Matthew 24:16 to flee from Jerusalem to the mountains. They are to be guarded and nourished there for three and a half years *(Rev. 12:14, with v. 6)*. The serpent will cause a flood, perhaps symbolic of a military expedition, to rush forth, with the endeavor to destroy them (v. 15), but the earth (probably the desert region between Palestine and the mountains) will swallow up the army. The sandy nature of the district could easily be made to accomplish this.

The very nature of the deep rocky gorges in that region of the mountains, enormous depths where kings of ancient times have had their palaces, as, e.g., at Petra, will afford a complete refuge to the thousands of this remnant of Jews, appointed to form the very nucleus of the race when Christ comes in glory at His Second Advent, to set up His Kingdom on earth (cp. Jer. 48:47). This explains the decree, "Let Mine outcasts dwell with thee, Moab; be thou a covert to them from the face of the spoiler," the Antichrist (Is. 16:4). The fact that David put his father and mother in Moab to safeguard them from Saul, was a typical foreshadowing of this (1 Sam. 22:3). The Antichrist oppressors will be consumed. The throne will be established in mercy, and One will sit thereon, **"judging, and seeking judgment** [or rather, zealous for right] **and hasting** [or practicing] **righteousness"** (v. 5).

Thus, as so constantly, the prophecy looks on from the near fulfillment to the final accomplishment at the end of this age and the establishment of Messiah's Kingdom.

Verses 6 to 14 revert to the impending doom of Moab, as a result of his pride, wrath and lying. "Pride goeth before destruction, and an haughty spirit before a fall" (Prov. 16:18). At the end of *verse 10* God speaks in fellowship with Isaiah, who thereupon resumes his lamentations.

Moab's prayers to his idols would be unavailing. Judgment would come in three years, **"as the years of a hireling,"** i.e., exactly at the time predicted; for a hireling does not exceed his period of labor, and his employer will not allow him to leave earlier.

Chapter 17

This chapter gives a brief oracle concerning Damascus, and proceeds with judgment upon Israel, and especially Ephraim, because it had allied itself with Damascus against Judah. Only a remnant would be left (vv. 4–6); this would

turn steadfastly to God (v. 7), and abandon idolatry (v. 8).

Forgetfulness of God brings barrenness; there may be much labor and activity in the spirit of self-reliance, but it produces no real fruit (vv. 9–11). Let us never be unmindful of the true Source of our strength, **"the Rock,"** Christ Jesus lest we bring upon ourselves **"grief"** and **"desperate sorrow"** (v. 11), the sorrow not of contrition but of remorse.

Again, consistently with the prophetic principle the oracle points, in *verses 12–14,* to the time yet future, when the nations, rushing like mighty waters, gather together "against the Lord and against His Anointed" (Ps. 2:2), only to be driven like chaff, and like "the whirling dust before the storm" (v. 13, R.V.; cp. Joel 3:11, 12; Zech. 9:14; 14:2, 3; Ps. 46:2).

Chapter 18

The beginning of this chapter seems best understood with reference to the fact that Assyria was threatening the nations. The word rendered "Woe" is the same word as that rendered "Ho" in 55:1, and is expressive of a summons to hear the word of God. Many interpretations have been suggested of the phrase **"shadowing with wings."** The most probable seems to be that indicating protection. The land is mentioned as beyond or outside the rivers of Ethiopia, and therefore may be regarded as a region outside the activities of the lands overrun by the powers that had attacked or would attack Israel and the surrounding nations.

The idea of protecting care is confirmed by the command to the outside nation to go as swift messengers to Israel. Israel is **"scattered and peeled"** (other suggested renderings do not appeal as suitable). Israel was terrible to the Canaanites. Israel is **"meted out"** by God's decrees and dealings of righteousness, and **"trodden down"** under divine judgments. Israel's land was destined to be temporarily spoiled (or divided) by nations famed for their rivers, e.g., the Nile, the Euphrates, and even the Tiber, the "rivers" standing for the oppressing Gentile powers.

The outside nations were to go with messages to Israel. They will take part in gathering the scattered outcasts of God's people, as

Isaiah's prophecies declare, e.g., 11:12, which speaks of the same ensign as here in *verse 3*.

Verse 4 intimates that for the time being He will wait while, under His control, circumstances are developing until the actual time of His intervention, the time figuratively described as "harvest," before which the bud appears and the sour or unripe grape. In due course the Lord would do His pruning upon the foes of Israel and cut down their branches, for fowls and beasts to dwell among them. So it happened in the case of Sennacherib.

So it has been, and will be, in every crisis of the strife of nations, and especially when efforts have been put forth to crush God's chosen people. The passage gives us lessons of confident patience to await God's time of direct interposition for deliverance, assured that in all our experiences everything is under His absolute control. "The bud may have a bitter taste, But sweet will be the flower." Trials and difficulties are sent to cast us upon God in simple and unwavering dependence upon Him.

The nations outside Ethiopia (a comprehensive term) were to wait till God acts and will present Israel itself as an offering to Jehovah of hosts, a beautiful description of the combined act of Gentile nations in helping to assemble the people of Israel at the beginning of the Millennial period. This is confirmed by the closing sentence of the chapter, and the tremendous significance of the event is indicated by the repetition in *verse 7* of the facts concerning Israel.

Chapters 19, 20

These give the oracle concerning Egypt. Jehovah **"rideth upon a swift [or light] cloud,"** that is to say, He is about to display His judicial dealings. Civil war would ruin the nation *(v. 2)*. Idolatry and spiritism were rampant among the Egyptians, but the futility of all this would become evident. The cruel lord, the fierce king *(v. 4)* was probably not a foreign invader, such as Sargon or Nebuchadnezzar, but an Egyptian monarch himself, as, e.g., Pharaoh Necho.

There were to be further calamities, in connection with the sea and the Nile, i.e., the commerce carried on in regard to them. The various characteristic occupations would come to grief *(vv. 5–10)*. The princes of Zoan (an ancient capital of Egypt), advisers and wise men would all be of no avail. So with Noph, or Memphis, a renowned city near Cairo. God can judicially impart a perverse spirit of self-will to rulers, to their own doom *(v. 14)*. Hardness of heart would give place to timidity and fear *(v. 16)*.

The rest of the nineteenth chapter points, as in other prophecies, first to a more immediate fulfillment and then to the yet future time of the Millennial Kingdom. There are five paragraphs each beginning with **"In that day."** The day consists of a period extending from the impending judgments upon Egypt to the end of the present age and the Second Advent of Christ.

Firstly, Judah was about to be the divine instrument of judgment *(vv. 16, 17)*. Secondly, the attitude of Egypt toward Israel would be changed. There would come a time when the language spoken in Canaan would be the language spoken in Egypt, to a limited extent ("five cities"). This was fulfilled when in the empire founded by Alexander the Great the Hellenistic Greek language became the common tongue in Canaan and elsewhere and was adopted in Egypt (where the Septuagint Version was produced). **"The city of destruction"** (lit., the city Ir-ha-heres) probably indicates the destruction of idolatry *(v. 18)*. That took place, after the successive invasions of the Assyrians, Chaldeans, Persians and Greeks.

Thirdly, there would come a time when an altar would be erected to the Lord in the midst of the land, and **"a pillar"** at the border. The Jewish religion actually spread in Egypt *(v. 21)*. Synagogues were built, and one especially at Heliopolis, and later on a church was erected at Alexandria. Subsequently Egypt was smitten *(v. 22)* by the power of Islam. Islam will not prevail permanently. There will be healing.

Fourthly, we are directed to the change to take place at the beginning of the Millennial reign of Christ. A road will run from Egypt to Assyria. Both nations, whose separate aim had been the conquest of the world, will unite to serve the Lord.

Fifthly, Israel will be the intermediary in the Assyrian-Egyptian combine. Instead of being subdued by each, as formerly, God's people will reach their destined height of power and glory; they will be **"a blessing in the midst of the earth,"** and will be God's own inheritance (cp. Acts 2:39 and 3:25, 26).

In chapter 20 we are taken back to the conquest of Egypt by Assyria. As Philistia was allied with Egypt, Tartan, Sennacherib's chief of command, subdued that country (represented by Ashdod) on the way *(v. 1)*. Isaiah himself was appointed as a sign of the impending overthrow of Egypt and Ethiopia. The coastland ("isle" in *v. 6* stands for all Palestine).

Chapter 21

Three oracles are pronounced in this chapter, concerning Babylon, Edom and Arabia. **"The desert of the sea"** *(v. 1)* is Babylon (cp. Jer. 50:38; 51:13, 36, 55). It was soon to be conquered by the Medes (Elam, *v. 2*, is Media), who would come upon it with violence and rapidity, like the storms which in Chaldea spring up from the south. Isaiah was overcome with emotion at the prospect *(vv. 3, 4)*. He was deprived of the pleasure of rest at night in realizing the horror of the destruction.

The Babylonians would be indulging in luxury and debauchery when the calamity fell upon them *(v. 5)*. So it came to pass, as described in Daniel 5. The prophet was to employ a watchman, (in *v. 11* he is himself the watchman; cp. Hab. 2:1, 2).

The watchman is one who stands in God's counsels, knows what is coming and looks out for the event. So now, he who learns from the completed Scriptures what God has foretold, discerning His purposes, not by speculative interpretation, but by comparing Scripture with Scripture, and accepting what is therein made plain, is able to warn and exhort others. He stands upon the watchtower *(v. 7)* in fellowship with God.

What the watchman saw was a procession of chariots, driving in pairs (R.V.). Contemplating the vision carefully, he discerned the impending calamity, and cried **"as a lion"** (R.V.). He beheld "a troop [or cavalcade] of men, horsemen in pairs" *(v. 9)*.

In *verse 10* the **"threshing, and child of my threshing-floor"** is figurative of crushing oppression (41:15; Mic. 4:12, 13), and of Divine judgment (Jer. 51:33), and this reference is to God's use of Babylon as an instrument of chastisement upon His people Israel.

In *verse 11* Dumah is Edom. Dumah means "silence" (i.e., of death). Isaiah, the watchman, received an inquiry, earnest in its repetition, **"How far on is it in the night?"** the reply is to the effect that while the morning is coming, night will yet envelop it. If they wish to inquire, let them do so, but the one thing necessary is that they should turn to God in repentance.

For Israel and the world the morning is coming, the dawn of the Millennial day; but there must come the Day of the Lord in judgment, and Israel must pass through the night of the great tribulation.

As to Arabia *(vv. 13–17)*, the caravans of the Dedanites must pass the night in the forest (or wilderness). The inhabitants of Arabian Tema must bring (margin) them water and bread. In *verse 16* Kedar stands for the Arabian tribes. First the Assyrians and then the Chaldeans would subdue Arabia (see Jer. 49:28–33). The time was predicted precisely: for the phrase **"according to the years of an hireling,"** see on 16:14.

Chapter 22

The valley of vision, concerning which this oracle is uttered, is not Samaria (as suggested by some) but Jerusalem. Though not exactly situated in a valley, yet there are mountains round about it (Ps. 125:2), and God had chosen it as a place shut in, so to speak, from the world, a place where He would give, through his prophets, visions of His will and purposes. Man's cities are spiritually and morally deserts.

Judgments were about to fall on Jerusalem, through Gentile powers, but the chapter is not confined to events of the then near future. Much of the opening verses will be fulfilled when the nations are gathered together against the city at the end of this age. There will be **"a day of trouble, and of treading down, and of perplexity"** *(v. 5)* such as Jerusalem has never experienced.

Elam and Kir *(v. 6)* were strategic places in Assyria, and the passage primarily refers to the Assyrian invasion. *Verses 8 to 11* describe what was done in Hezekiah's time (2 Kin. 20:12–21; 2 Chr. 32:2–7, 30). While God blessed Hezekiah's efforts, he did some scheming; but the people were in such a state of apostasy from God that He could not purge their iniquity (v. 14). They had no idea of looking to their Maker (v. 11), and when he called for mourning and repentance, they indulged in feasting and entire carelessness as to the judgments, impending, even though they were aware of their doom (vv. 12, 13).

The lesson of the passage, verses 8 to 11, is of the utmost importance. Whatever we attempt by our own efforts is futile and disastrous unless directed by God and wrought by His power. Evil can never be averted by means adopted by our natural wisdom. Forgetfulness of God leads to reliance upon human resources and means, and ends in disappointment and misery.

In verses 15 to 19 we learn facts about Shebna additional to those in chapters 36 and 37 and 2 Kings 19. He was a sort of vizier, or chamberlain, over the king's household, with charge of his treasury. The word "this" (v. 15) expresses divine contempt. His arrogance led him to hew out a sepulcher for himself, hollowed out in the rocks of the city, copying the high and mighty of earth. His doom of captivity would prevent him from lying there. Jehovah would turn (lit., coil) him violently, and toss him like a ball into a land far and wide. The state carriages which he had provided for himself would go too, and become the shame of Hezekiah's house. In captivity he would meet his death. So is he who "layeth up treasure for himself and is not rich toward God" (Luke 12:21).

His place would be filled by Eliakim, who would have a still more honorable and extensive position. What is said of him in verses 22 to 24 marks him as a type of Christ, of whom what is mentioned in verse 22 is spoken by Christ Himself in Revelation 3:7, while Shebna, whose doom is repeated in verse 25, foreshadows the Antichrist. As Eliakim replaced Shebna, so will Christ replace the Man of Sin.

Eliakim's family would be benefited by his position, as metaphorically described in verses 23, 24, a foreshadowing of the effect of Christ's coming glory upon those who, spiritually, being born of God, are related to Christ.

Chapter 23

The oracle concerning Tyre is the last of the series concerning the nations. Babylon represented imperial power. Tyre stood for commercial power. Its influence, with that of the older city Sidon, here spoken of as a mother in relation to Tyre, (vv. 4 and 12) exercised a more potent effect in this respect than any other nation. Tarshish was in the west of the Mediterranean, and perhaps stood here for the whole of that sea.

In verse 3 Sihor is the Hebrew name for Siris, the upper Nile (here called "the river"), the region of which was a grain mart for the nations. Egypt and Tyre are associated in verse 5. In verse 9 Tyre is made an example of a divine purpose concerning all potentates who glory in their prowess and their attainments of power and domination. Jehovah of hosts will **"stain the pride of all glory, and bring into contempt all the honorable** [the chief men] **of the earth."**

In verse 10 Tarshish is set free. Just as the Nile overflows its banks, so the people can now enjoy liberty and be independent of the mother city. It can exercise no more restraining girdle (see margin) of authority. Let the Sidonians escape to Cyprus (Chittim); they will have no rest there (v. 12). The Chaldeans, who succeeded the Assyrians (v. 13), would desolate Tyre and bring it to ruin (Ezek. 29:17, 18). During the seventy years of Chaldean supremacy (Jer. 25:9, 11; 29:10) it would be forgotten. **"The days of one king"** marks a fixed period. After this the Lord would permit the restoration. Not that Tyre would turn to God. She could renew her melodies and, like a harlot, attract nations again to herself by her traffic and enterprise (v. 17).

Verse 18 received a fulfillment in that Tyre and Sidon assisted in the building of the temple after the captivity (Ezra 3:7).

CHAPTER THREE

Part Ic
Divine Judgments and Deliverances
Chapters 24—33

Chapter 24

This chapter, following the account of the dealings of God with the individual nations one after another, takes into view the whole scene, all the nations, including Israel, as destined to come under the judgments of the Lord at the end of this age.

The separate nations, reviewed in chapters 13 to 23, display differing conditions of the world's alienation from God, influenced and directed by the hosts of spiritual wickedness in the heavenlies. All must meet the divine retribution in the coming Day of the Lord. Babylon represents systematized corruption and oppression in all the earth; Assyria, antagonism against God's people; Philistia, constant and closer hostility; Moab, human pride; Damascus, the ally of apostasy; Dumah, self-reliance; Jerusalem, mere profession; Tyre, worldly glory.

All that is represented in the world by these characteristics must hereafter experience the judgments foretold in the opening verses. Everything is to be overturned *(v. 1)*. In *verse 4* the earth and the world are broadly synonymous; speaking generally the distinction may lie in this, that *the earth* is that especially in which God's governmental dealings have been manifested, *the world* is the same scene presenting man's condition in its alienation from God. The rendering "earth" sometimes should be "land," with reference to the land of Israel. This is apparently the case in *verse 5*. The inhabitants of the world have not broken the covenant of Genesis 9:16. That covenant was virtually a Divine promise, God alone undertaking the fulfillment. Israel it was who broke the Covenant of God's Law (see Deut. 31:16–20; Jer. 11:10). And as to the future, the agreement which the apostate nation (the

godly remnant excluded) will make with the Man of Sin, will absolutely fulfill all that is stated in verse 5. The judgments which follow will depopulate the earth, so that "few men will be left" *(v. 6)* fulfilling the Lord's word that "except the Lord shortened the days no flesh would be saved." For the elect's sake He will do so. This depopulation is figuratively described in *verse 13*.

Verses 14, 15 and the first part of *16* describe the exultation and praise after the judgments upon the Antichrist and his worshipers have been executed. Israel is delivered and peace brought to the diminished nations. The words for "sing" and "cry aloud" in *verse 14* are the same as those used of Zion in 12:6.

In the latter part of *verse 16* Isaiah mourns over all that is to happen to his people, especially in "the great tribulation," resulting from two cases of treachery, first the treachery of Israel in turning from God to make a covenant with the Antichrist, and secondly the treachery of the Antichrist in breaking that covenant and endeavoring to exterminate the Jews.

The final judgments upon the nations under the Satanic rule of the Beast and the False Prophet (Rev. 13) are foretold in the rest of the chapter, the consummation being the Personal intervention of Christ at the Second Advent *(v. 23)*.

Chapter 25

This and most of chapter 26 consist of the song of praise which will rise from the godly remnant after "the great tribulation," the nucleus of redeemed Israel. There is first a praiseful recognition of God's faithfulness in view of His relation to His earthly people *(v. 1)*, and of His overthrow of the hostile city of the nations, a reference probably to Rome (v. 3), while verse 2 points to Babylon. All the proud organizations of man are doomed. God will be a stronghold to the poor and needy in the perils and distress of the times of the Antichrist (v. 4). The Gentile peoples which remain will come to mount Zion to share the festal provision Jehovah will make for Israel (v. 6). The veil that has blinded the nations under Satanic delusions, will there be cast away (v. 7). Death will be "swallowed up in victory"; the quotation of this in 1 Corinthians 15:54 shows that resurrection is in view. These who have been slaughtered by the Antichrist and his agents during the great tribulation will be raised to share the reign of Christ. Tears will be wiped away, and the "rebuke" (i.e., the shame) of Israel will be removed (v. 8). The godly remnant will celebrate their deliverance (v. 9). Moab with its pride and plunder will be utterly humbled (vv. 10–12).

Chapter 26

The first eighteen verses of this chapter consist of the song of the delivered remnant in Israel as they enter upon Millennial peace and blessedness. The whole land is called the land of Judah, in view of the concentration of power and domination in Jerusalem. The strong city is set in contrast to "the city of the nations" (25:3). Israel, redeemed and converted to their Messiah, is **"the righteous nation"** (vv. 1, 2).

Verse 3 primarily applies to the members of the redeemed nation. They in their great deliverance will realize the assurance, **"Thou will keep him in perfect peace** [lit., peace, peace], **whose mind is stayed on Thee** [or firmly established in Thee]: **because he trusteth in Thee."**

This is to be enjoyed at all times by those who, instead of being overcome by difficulties or by yielding to the pressure of spiritual foes and human antagonism, put their trust in the Lord, staying their mind upon Him. The peace possessed is not the outcome of mere self-determination, it is ministered by the keeping power of the Lord Himself. It is that peace which essentially characterized Christ, and of which He said, "Peace I leave with you, My peace [lit., the peace which is Mine] I give unto you."

The experience of this leads the possessor to utter the exhortation, **"Trust ye in the Lord forever: for in the Lord JEHOVAH is the rock of ages"** (v. 4; cp. 17:10; 30:29, margin: Deut. 32:4, 15).

Verse 5 provides a reason for trusting Him and a proof of His strength, and verse 6 tells how He will impart it to His people. Verse 7 is a further comment on verse 4.

God makes smooth the path of His people. Not only so, He imparts His character to them. He is upright; so are they. This is not mere moral rectitude, it is fellowship with Him.

This is confirmed in verse 8. Israel will have learned to wait for God in the way of His judgments. God rewards the patience of those who, discerning His counsels and purposes, await His time. Their desire is not simply for deliverance, but for the honor of His Name, that is to say, His character, and toward the remembrance of what He has done in the past.

Verse 9 continues the song of the redeemed remnant. In the night of their tribulation they had desired Him. They had learned to seek Him early, that is, earnestly. This is ever the response of the trusting soul in times of affliction.

In the coming judgments of the Day of the Lord the nations that are left will learn righteousness. Yet there will be many who refuse to do so (v. 10), and will retain their animosity against the Jews (v. 11). The Lord will deal with them in person, and fire will devour the adversaries. The bestowment of peace upon His people will be the consummation of His mercies in accomplishing all their works for them (the same word "for" as in the preceding clause), verse 12.

In verse 13 they review the various tyrants who have oppressed them throughout "the times of the Gentiles," but the intervention of Christ on their behalf will call forth their praise in ascribing the glory to His Name. While the enemies are overthrown God's people will be increased. The R.V. gives the correct rendering of the end of verse 15: **"Thou hast enlarged all the borders of the land"**; (cp. 54:2, 3). The land allotted to Israel in the Millennium will be extended.

Verses 16 to 18 depict the agonies and supplications of the godly in Israel during their time of trouble under the Antichrist, in the realization and acknowledgment of their utter helplessness to deliver themselves or others. *Verse 19* gives the divine promise of the revival of the nation. The word rendered **"My dead body"** is used in a collective sense (some would therefore render it "my dead bodies"). Israel will, so to speak, be brought to life, as from the dead.

At the close of the pouring out of the wrath of God upon the nations under the Antichrist (Rev. 6 to 16) during the great tribulation, the Lord is coming forth in person to visit the iniquity of the inhabitants of the earth upon them *(v. 21)* for the fulfillment of which see especially Revelation 19:11–21. A place of refuge will be provided for the godly remnant, who will form the nucleus of the redeemed nation *(v. 20)*.

Chapter 27

In *verse 1* the leviathans (there are two, R.V.), the swift serpent and the crooked, or winding, serpent, and the dragon are doubtless symbolic both of the great world powers at the end of this age and of the evil one who will instigate them; he is spoken of both as the serpent and the dragon (Gen. 3:1; Rev. 20:2, 10), the latter of which foretells his punishment. The passages in Isaiah and Revelation are parallel as to the course of events: Revelation 19 corresponds to Isaiah 26:21, and Revelation 20 to Isaiah 27:1.

For the third time a prophetic song hymns the happiness of redeemed Israel *(vv. 2–5)*. There are four, but the first (ch. 5) was of a different character. Here Jehovah rejoices over His people. They are a vineyard of red (or fiery) vine (some manuscripts have "pleasant" cp. Amos 5:11), constantly kept and watered by Him. "Wrath have I none," He says. That will be a thing of the past for them. If enemies rise up against them again, they will be but thorns and thistles for the burning. Nay, let the would-be foe take the wise alternative, and take hold of His strength for protection, and make peace with Him.

On the contrary, Israel is to take root, blossom, bud, and **"fill the face of the world with fruit,"** thus becoming "the riches of the Gentiles" (Rom. 11:12), *verse 6*.

This, spiritually, is the Lord's purpose and desire for believers during the present period till the Church is complete (John 15:1–16). Filling the earth with fruit is suggestive of the effects of missionary service in all nations.

The Lord had to smite His people, but not as He smote their foes *(v. 7)*. How he smote Israel is now described *(vv. 8–11)* and all with a view to their restoration. His covenant promises remain unalterable. How God has, and will have, chastised His people is described in *verse 8*, R.V.: **"In measure** [i.e., not in fullness of wrath, but by indignation tempered by forbearance] **when Thou sendest her away, Thou doest contend with her: He hath removed her with His rough blast in the day of the east wind."** He sifted His chosen people among the nations. He blew violently upon them, sifting them but not destroying them; and all this with a view to purging their iniquity *(v. 9)*. The fruit of God's dealings is that the stones of idol altars are made like chalk stones broken in pieces. The images of Astarte and the sun images will never be set up again. These are suggestive of everything substituted for God.

As it is the punishment which causes the sin of Israel to cease, the prophet now gives, as a warning, details of the nature of the punishment *(vv. 10, 11)*. Jerusalem, once so populous, would be left like a wilderness; animals would browse off the bits of foliage growing among the ruins, and their women would gather sticks for their fires, since the hostile armies, having accomplished their aim, would have left.

Yet mercy will rejoice against judgment, and Israel, repentant, shall be gathered. Just as in the year of jubilee, the trumpet sounded on the evening of the Day of Atonement, and every man returned to his own possession (Lev. 25), so will scattered Israel return to worship at Jerusalem when the Lord gives His signal among the nations *(v. 13;* cp. 11:12).

Chapter 28

This chapter introduces a fresh series of "woes." There were six in chapter five. There are six now from this chapter to chapter thirty-three. The first five are pronounced against Israel and especially Judah and Jerusalem. The sixth is against Assyria.

The chapter may be divided into three parts, (1) verses 1–13; (2) verses 14–22; (3) verses 23–29.

In the first section there is a record of the grievous condition of the leading men in Israel at that time.

In the first verses of the chapter Samaria is denounced. It is called (1) **"the crown of pride,"** in which the intoxicated Ephraim has gloried, (2) **"a fading flower"** (cp. 1:30; 40:7, 8). The **"fat valley"** (R.V.) refers to the situation of the town. The people were given to luxury and self-indulgence. All must meet the judgments of the Lord *(vv. 2–4)*, the Assyrian, **"the mighty and strong one,"** being the instrument. Samaria would be to him **"as a firstripe fig"** (R.V.), ripe in June instead of August, easily plucked and immediately swallowed.

This throws light upon the incident of the fig tree recorded in Matthew 21 and Mark 11. After the figs are gathered and stored away in August or September, there is still sap in the tree, which puts forth a second crop of figs through the winter. This begins to ripen in the spring, but does not come to anything. You can eat the figs, but they are not worth storing.

Now Palestine lay between Assyria and Egypt, and armies passing from either side must traverse it, hence the reference to the overflowing scourge. God's people were tempted to go to one or the other for help, but the Lord constantly warned them against this, and to trust in Him. That is the great teaching of the first thirteen verses of this chapter.

It has its lessons for us. The Lord teaches us to avoid seeking help from man and to trust in Him alone. On the other hand we are to guard against the spirit of selfish ease and luxury which characterized Israel of old.

In *verse 5* the residue of His people are the faithful in Judah, and to them Jehovah would be **"a crown of glory"** (in contrast to the crown of pride of Samaria), a spirit of judgment to those who acted justly in their seat of judgment, and a strength against the foe *(v. 6)*.

This holds good for those who walk in the fear of the Lord, in a day of widespread declension, as at the present time. Righteousness and strength are their portion from the Lord.

We need to see to it that we deal righteously with our fellows, and are overcomers by the power of the Holy Spirit.

Judah as a whole had gone astray *(vv. 7, 8)* and must receive retribution, and this is confirmed in *verses 9–15*. The questions asked in *verse 9* are a remonstrance against the self-satisfied, self-righteous, ungodly people of Judah, and especially their priests and prophets (they were like the scribes and Pharisees of a later date). Instead of being so superior in knowledge and attainment, as they imagined they were, in reality they were like tiny children, who must be taught the very elements of knowledge. Just as with children, precept must be upon precept, line upon line, here a little and there a little. The retributive side comes out in *verse 11,* in the incomprehensible way God would speak to them. Their sneers at His prophet made it impossible for them to receive the truth He would speak to them by the Assyrians, people of "another tongue" (cp. 29:9–12 and see Jer. 6:10). The Lord had offered them rest and refreshing, and the means of giving rest to the weary, but they would not hear. Therefore they must suffer the retribution appointed *(v. 13)*.

The second section *(vv. 14–22)* gives the foreign policy of the leaders of the people. They thought that their predecessors did not know how to deal with Egypt and Assyria. They themselves had done better than that, and made treaties with both, and boasted that they had hoodwinked them. Their name for Egypt was Death and for Assyria, Hell. God again gives them warning, offering them wise counsel, but showing them to what their ways will lead. The third section *(vv. 23–29)* deals with the faithful in the nation. They would be strongly criticized for lack of patriotism, then when instead of peace foreign troops are in the country accompanying famine, the faithful will not have a better time.

Whatever the circumstances are, those who fear God and trust in Him will never have an easy time of it, but there is an end to the trial and God never goes beyond what is necessary, and so promises instruction and guidance if we will be faithful to Him and rely upon Him whatever may happen.

But the rulers of Jerusalem had gone further in their defiance of God. They scornfully imagined that they need have no fear of death and Hades. As for the Assyrians they proposed a secret alliance with Egypt, boasting in their false attitude toward God and His messengers *(vv. 14, 15)*.

In contrast to this the Lord again points to the future deliverance to be wrought by Christ, and to the glories of His person and work *(v. 16)*. He is to be in Zion a foundation stone, tried (lit., a stone of proof), not only proved Himself but able to bear up and sustain those who trust in Him, a cornerstone of the building. The last statement has also been rendered "shall hasten it to," or, again, "will not have to move." However it might be translated it presents Christ as the sure confidence of the believer. Judgment and righteousness will be the plumbline to test everything, instead of injustice and iniquity. The lies and the hiding place referred to in *verse 15* will be swept away *(v. 17)*.

In *verse 18* the covenant with death and agreement with Hades, while referring to the immediate circumstances, also point to the future agreement of the nation as a whole with the Antichrist. The ungodly in Israel who have entered into this covenant will meet their merited doom. The infliction of the scourge will be constant, and, whereas the rulers and people refused to listen to Isaiah's message, in the coming time the nation will understand the truth only to their own vexation *(v. 19)*.

They thought that in getting help from Egypt they would prepare a comfortable bed and a nice coverlet for their rest from danger. But they would find to their dismay that their preparations would be futile, the bed too short, the coverlet too narrow *(v. 20)*.

So is it ever with any of God's people. Reliance upon the world will only beget shame, misery and disaster. It is faith that triumphs. Christ is a "sure foundation" for us upon which to build our hope. "Blessed are all they that wait for Him." "He that believeth shall not make haste."

The Lord would have to act against His people as He had acted in past days against their foes at Perazim and Gibeon *(v. 21)*. Let them turn from their mockery lest their fetters be strengthened. The time would come, and yet will, when a "consumption," a destructive judgment, would fall upon the whole earth *(v. 22;* cp. 26:21).

The third section *(vv. 23–29)* contains God's appeal to the faithful ones suffering for their loyalty to Him. It conveys His promise and His covenant. He uses the illustration of the husbandman, somewhat as the apostle Paul does in 1 Corinthians 3:9. God does not go on plowing indefinitely, nor does He indefinitely exercise discipline. He has gracious purposes for all, and there is an end to the time of trial.

In the figurative questions and statements in *verses 24 to 28* Israel is the Lord's farm land and threshing floor. His chastisements and punishments are the harrow and plowshare. But He does not continue the use of these indefinitely, any more than the farmer continues plowing. There is the resultant sowing and reaping. Again, Israel is His threshing, the corn of His floor (see 21:10).

The husks of iniquity must be separated from the wheat of the persons dealt with. This is not a never-ending process either in God's dealings or in the farmer's occupation. The Lord of hosts, who as Creator provides the farmer with the instinct and discretion necessary for his work, knows how to act in His perfect wisdom in dealing with His people. He will not destroy them. They remain His own possession. He chastens us "for our profit, that we may be partakers of His holiness," and His chastening yields "peaceable fruit unto them that have been exercised thereby, even the fruit of righteousness" (Heb. 12:10, 11).

Chapter 29

At the beginning of the last chapter Samaria was symbolized as a fading crown of flowers. Now the woe-judgment is pronounced against Jerusalem, symbolized as the hearth (i.e., altar) of God. Ariel may have its other meaning of "lion of God," but in 31:9 the Lord is stated to have His fire and furnace (or hearth) there. Moreover in Ezekiel 43:15, 16, Ariel is the altar-hearth of God (R.V. margin).

Let them continue their formal religion, their round of feasts and sacrifices *(v. 1)*. Judgment must come, and Ariel would become a veritable altar-hearth of slaughter and fiery indignation *(v. 2)*. National foes would reduce them to utter weakness *(vv. 3, 4)*. Yet deliverance is assured. All nations that rise against Zion must be brought to nought under the mighty hand of God *(vv. 5–8)*.

Verses 9 to 16 contain a remonstrance against the condition of God's people, and a description of the inevitable and terrible judgments to be inflicted upon them because of their apostasy, luxury and hardness of heart. In *verse 9* the prophet judicially bids them carry on in their perverseness: **"Tarry ye** [i.e., do as Lot did when he lingered in the doomed city] **and wonder, take your pleasure** [or, as in the margin, blind yourselves]. **and be blind."** That is, "go on in your heedless ways."

The waywardness of the rulers, seers and people had brought upon them spiritual slumber and blindness. The revealed will of God had become like a sealed book or letter, so that even one who could understand writing could not open it, and when it was unsealed and handed to an illiterate man to read he had to refuse owing to his inability to make out the words *(vv. 10–12)*.

Mere lip worship and external conformity while the heart was alienated, and all this the effects of "the precept of men," must result in the loss of the wisdom of the wise and the hiding of the understanding of the intelligent *(vv. 13, 14)*. The same state of things prevailed when Christ was on earth (Matt. 15:3; Mark 7:6).

How far into the dark the backslider can go is revealed in *verse 15*. *Verse 16* really begins with an exclamation of sorrow: **"Alas for your perversity!"** They had in their ideas turned upside down the relation between the creature and the Creator: **"Shall the potter be counted as clay, that the thing made should say of him that made it, He made me not, or the thing framed say of Him that framed it, He hath no understanding?"** (R.V.). They thought they had no need of Jehovah, they could manage for themselves, as if a pot should inform its maker and owner that it could itself do all that was required of it. Such is the preposterous attitude of all who seek to act independently of God.

But God would expose their folly. He Himself would turn things upside down (the paragraph begins at *v. 17*, not 18; 18 explains 17). The Lebanon forest would be changed into a fruitful field, and the fruitful field would be regarded as a forest. The deaf would hear the words of the book, in contrast to the sinners mentioned in *verses 11, 12*, and the blind would see out of obscurity and darkness.

This and what follows bear reference to the coming Millennial reign of Christ. The meek will joy in Jehovah, the poor will rejoice in Christ, "the Holy One of Israel."

So it is now. It is the meek and the poor, those among believers who are conscious of spiritual need, who have the greatest joy in the Lord. For the Holy Spirit ministers the fullness of Christ especially to such (see Is. 61:1; Zeph. 3:12; Matt. 5:3–5).

In the day to come **"the terrible one,"** the Man of Sin, will have been brought to nought, the scoffer destroyed, plotters of evil cut off, those who act unrighteously and pervert justice *(vv. 19–21)*.

Jehovah's covenant relationship with Abraham as his Redeemer is made the basis of the blessings promised to the seed of Jacob *(v. 22)*. His house, freed from shame and terror, will rejoice in being surrounded by their redeemed children, and "sanctify" (i.e., pay due and reverent regard to) the Name of Jehovah and Christ as "the Holy One of Jacob" and, unlike the rebels against whom Isaiah was protesting, will **"fear the God of Israel."** Instead of erring in spirit they will come to understanding and instead of murmuring they will rejoice in receiving instruction.

Chapter 30

Woe is now pronounced against Judah for seeking help from Egypt against Assyria. This the northern kingdom of Israel had done with disastrous results. In *verse 1* the phrase rendered **"that cover with a covering"** may also be translated "that weave an alliance" (some would render it "that form a molten image"; this seems less suitable). The counsel was contrary to that of the Spirit of God. It was adding sin to the sin of their hardness of heart, their self-will and apostasy from God. The effect would be shame and reproach *(v. 5)*.

In *verse 6* Isaiah utters an oracle (R.V. margin) concerning **"the beasts of the south"** not the beasts that are going southward, as in the end of the verse, but the beasts that are native to Egypt, such as the hippopotamus; there too are the lioness and lion, the viper and the flying serpent. Just as all these are dangerous and troublesome, so would the rulers of Egypt prove to be. To bring treasures on camels and asses so as to secure the help of the country from which God had long before delivered His people, would procure no help at all. **"For Egypt helpeth in vain, and to no purpose: therefore have I called her Rahab that sitteth still"** (*v. 7,* R.V.). Rahab signifies "arrogance." Proud aloofness prevented help from that quarter.

The next verse shows that this warning against going to Egypt for help was intended not merely for God's people in Isaiah's day, but for all in every period. It was to be written on a tablet and inscribed in a book **"that it may be for the time to come, for ever and ever."** To seek help and counsel from the Egypt world instead of from God can result only in disaster.

Verses 9 to 11 reveal the utter perverseness of the nation in their rejection of the testimony of the prophets of God and their determination to do without the Lord Himself. They preferred oppression (or fraud) and iniquity, the effect of which would be like that of a falling breach in a towering wall *(v. 13).* They would be broken in pieces like a potter's vessel (the destruction which Gentiles will yet experience, Ps. 2).

Mercy was offered to those who would return to the Lord and find rest. But they refused and would flee to Egypt on swift steeds *(v. 16).* For this they would flee from their enemies, one of whom would chase a thousand, and five chasing them all, till they became like a single pine on a mountain top and a single banner on a hill *(v. 17).*

In *verse 18* the "therefore" gives the key to the true meaning. The Lord has been foretelling the judgments that must come upon these guilty people. For this reason the eventual blessing of the nation is delayed. He will **"wait"** (i.e., will delay) until the right time comes for Him to be gracious, in the exercise of His restoring mercy; He will **"be exalted"** (i.e., will withdraw himself on high), in His dealings in judgment, so that, when this has fulfilled His purpose, and not till then, He may show His mercy. The time has not come even yet. Israel has hindered its own deliverance and salvation.

"For Jehovah is a God of judgment." This forms a connecting link between what

has just been set forth as to His necessary chastisements upon the backsliding, and what is now to be said as to the assured mercy for those, who, walking in fellowship with Him, abide His time. In both cases He is righteous, both in chastising and in showing mercy. He always has, and will have, until the day of deliverance, a remnant of godly ones. "Blessed are all they that wait for Him."

The people will dwell safely, will weep no more, and will receive the answer to their supplication. During the preceding time of adversity they will be supplied with bread, and with water in their affliction *(v. 20).* This is the true meaning of the first part of this verse. It contains the promises of mercy. The bread and water are not symbolic of adversity, they represent the promised supplies of need during the affliction. Moreover guidance and instruction will be imparted by God-sent teachers *(vv. 20, 21).* For the people will, in the spirit of repentance, purge themselves from their iniquities *(v. 22).*

All this is in harmony with other Scriptures which speak of the circumstances of the great tribulation and those who turn to Him therein and wait for the promised Deliverer. When He comes, *verses 23 to 26,* with their description of Millennial fruitfulness and glory, will be fulfilled.

Verses 27 to 32 foretell the outpouring of the wrath of God upon the gathered enemies. And, as in so many other passages, while the immediate foe was the Assyrian, the prophecy points on to the coming power of his antitype, the Antichrist. The very fact of the assurances of Millennial glory, which will follow, is sufficient to confirm this. The word rendered "people" in *verse 28,* A.V., is plural, and is the same as that rendered "nations" just before. God will put a bridle in their jaws, causing them to err under the deceptive Satanic power of the Man of Sin.

The godly in Israel will have a song in that night of tribulation, rejoicing in the prospect of the coming day. It will be an earnest of the "Songs of Ascents" when they come to Jerusalem, to the mountain of Jehovah, **"to the mighty One** [the Rock] **of Israel"** *(v. 29).*

. *Verses 30 to 32* depict the scene of the warfare of Armageddon. Tophet *(v. 33)* denotes, not the burning, but the aborted. It is the place in the valley of Hinnom, where cruel and abominable sacrifices were offered to Moloch. There at the center of the battle line of 200 miles (1,600 furlongs, Rev. 14:20) of the gathered armies of the Antichrist, the breath of Jehovah will kindle the fire of His wrath, and Israel will be delivered (see 63:1–6; Ps. 2:1–6; Joel 2:11; 3:9–16; 2 Thess. 2:8; Rev. 19:11–21; Deut. 32:42, R.V.).

Chapter 31

Again Isaiah denounced the evil of seeking help from Egypt instead of seeking the Lord. The scheme is wise in the eyes of apostate Israel; yet Jehovah is wise (v. 2), and will vindicate His wisdom in His judgment both upon the Egyptians and upon those who have sought their assistance (v. 3). **"He will arise against the house of the evildoers and against the help of them that work iniquity"** (that is, the help afforded by the Egyptians to the evildoers of Israel).

In *verse 3* the prophet speaks of the Egyptians as creatures of dust, in contrast to God, and their horses as mere flesh in contrast to spiritual power.

A message of the assurance of deliverance is given in *verses 4–9*. The comparison of his interposition is that of lions roaring on their prey, a comparison of attack. In *verse 5* it is that of hovering or fluttering birds, a comparison of protection and deliverance. Hence there is a call in *verse 6* to turn in repentance to God, for the day is coming when never again will Israel be guilty of idolatry. Let the repentant therefore anticipate this. The Assyrian is to be utterly defeated (v. 8), for God's fire is in Zion and His furnace in Jerusalem, again an anticipation of the destruction of the Antichrist.

Chapter 32

The first five verses of this chapter depict the issue of the deliverance, and foretell (1) the personal, Millennial reign of Christ, (2) the authority of those who rule under Him, (3) the protecting power of Christ as the One Who combines in Himself the prerogatives of Deity with the sympathy and compassion of humanity, (4) His protecting care, (5) His full supply of need, (6) His comfort

for the weary, (7) the happy condition of the redeemed people with their clear vision, their attentive listening, their possession of knowledge and their ready testimony (vv. 1–4).

Until then there will be vile men practicing deceit and cruelty. The word rendered "churl" signifies a crafty one.

Now follows a warning appeal, which is really a continuation of the fourth woe. It consists of a rousing remonstrance against the flippant self-security of the women in Jerusalem. Their carnal ease is doomed. Levity will give place to lamentation. Instead of luxurious dwellings, there will be weeds and briars, and instead of palaces desolation (vv. 9–14). So it was when king and people were carried away into captivity.

From this point Isaiah looks right on again to Millennial conditions, and identifies himself with his people in their redeemed state. The Holy Spirit will yet be poured upon the nation, and there will be abundance of righteousness, peace and fruitfulness. What was then valued as a fruit garden will become more glorious. Even the uncultivated districts will be as full of verdure as a forest. Righteous judgment will be universal (v. 16). There will then be what the world has ever failed to establish, peace and safety (vv. 17, 18), but before this happy condition can obtain, there must be judgments upon the oppressor. The forest, in verse 19, represents the Antichristian foes, and the city their organized hostility.

While the closing verse gives a word of comfort to the godly in the nation who will live to see these times of blessedness, and will till the ground, free from all anxiety, it also gives a message of spiritual comfort to those who in the present time scatter the seeds of the Word of Life, and labor in doctrine.

Chapter 33

In chapters twenty-eight to thirty-two five woes were pronounced against Israel and Judah. The sixth woe is now uttered against Assyria, and again the prophecy looks on from Isaiah's own time to the yet future and final overthrow of the Antichristian powers and the day of Zion's deliverance (vv. 20–24), all being introductory to a fuller development of this twofold theme in chapter thirty-four.

Primarily the time is that of the fourteenth year of Hezekiah. The Assyrian has actually entered the land and God's judgments are visiting **"the sinners in Zion"** *(v. 14)*.

But the Assyrian must be brought low. There is to be retribution, point for point *(v. 1)*, and Isaiah, after the denunciatory woe, intercedes for his people in their time of trouble *(v. 2)*. The divine response is sure, not only in Hezekiah's day, but at the close of "man's day," the time of the great tribulation. The gathered peoples (plural, *v. 3*) are to be scattered. Their plunder will be seized and destroyed, as it were, before caterpillars and locusts.

Verses 5 and 6 form an interlude looking on to the establishment of the Millennial Kingdom. No preceding period of deliverance has filled this picture. The Lord will be **"filled with judgment and righteousness."** He will Himself, as its "wisdom and knowledge," be the stability (i.e., security) of its times, its strength (or wealth) of salvation (so the clauses are probably to be rendered). Judah's treasure will be the fear of the Lord (a striking contrast to Hezekiah's dealings as recorded in 2 Kin. 18:13-16).

The next verses describe Israel's pitiable state, not merely under the Assyrian, but under the Antichrist. There is his breaking of the covenant made with them (as in Dan. 9:27), the despair of the mighty ones among the Jews and their ambassadors, and the desolation of the land.

Yet the Lord will arise, the schemes of the enemy will be rendered futile, and the Gentile nations ("peoples") will be consumed *(vv. 10-12)*.

The nations "far off," those not actually gathered at Armageddon, the Gentiles that remain after the worldwide judgments of the day of God's wrath, are to hear what He has done, and those that are near are to acknowledge His might *(v. 13)*.

As for the Jews, there are "the sinners," "the hypocrites." They will not escape the judgments. There is no partiality with God *(v. 14)*. There is the godly remnant; they shall dwell on high, they shall be protected and nourished *(vv. 15, 16)*. They will see their King-Messiah **"in His beauty"**; they will behold **"the land of far distances"** (a greatly extended Israelitic territory), *verse 17*. That is the reward of refusing to see evil *(v. 15)*.

They will muse on the terror they experienced during their great tribulation. The "scribe" (the political secretary) will be no more. The "receiver" (the Chancellor of the Exchequer) will be no more. "He that counted the towers" (the military commander) will be no more. The mighty foe with their foreign tongue will pass away *(vv. 18, 19)*.

Zion will be seen in its glory, peaceful, permanent, prosperous, and all will center in Him who is their Deliverer, the Bestower of peace and prosperity incalculable, the Judge, the Lawgiver, the King, the Savior *(vv. 20-22)*.

Verse 23 speaks of the weakness and inability of the people themselves, pictured whether as unable to guide the ship of state, or, what is more probable, arrange their tent as their dwelling place, with the necessary cord, tent pole and canvas. Yet it will be given them to divide the booty of the enemy, and the lame will take the prey *(v. 23)*. Sickness, physical and spiritual, will be things of the past. The inhabitants "shall have their sins forgiven" *(v. 24)*.

God teaches us, as He will teach them, the impossibility of delivering ourselves by our own strength. He sends us weakness that out of weakness we may be made strong. Jacob had to learn this. Made physically lame, he proved more than ever the almighty power of the Lord. Paul learned to glory in his infirmities, that the power of Christ might rest upon him ("spread a tabernacle" over him), 2 Corinthians 12:9. In our trials and difficulties we are made to know the love of Christ in a way impossible without them. "In all these things we are more than conquerors through Him that loved us" (Rom. 8:35-37).

CHAPTER FOUR

Part Id
The Future of Gentile
Nations and Israel
Chapters 34, 35

Chapter 34

This and the next chapter are an expansion of the two subjects of chapter thirty-three, namely, the judgments of the Day of the Lord, and the subsequent Millennial blessedness of Israel and their land.

Under the satanic power of the Beast and the False Prophet the armies of the nations will be gathered in one great effort to annihilate the Jews (see Rev. 19:19-21), a passage which describes in detail what is here foretold in 34:1-3. With *verses 4-7* compare Revelation 6:13, 14. In *verse 6* Idumea (i.e., Edom, always figurative of the natural state of man in his antagonism against God) is particularly mentioned as the great scene of the divine intervention.

Bozrah is a central stronghold of the country. It will be the culminating locality of the warfare of Armageddon (see 63:1 and notes there). The judgments of this "day of the Lord's vengeance" will extend over 200 miles, the 1,600 furlongs of Revelation 14:20, and the district of Bozrah will, it would seem, be the southernmost limit of the conflict. For there the King of the North, having gone to subdue Egypt, will be returning northward with a view to the destruction of Jerusalem and the Jews, because of tidings which will trouble him from the north. He will not reach Jerusalem, and that by reason of the personal intervention of Christ (Dan. 11:43, 44). He will pitch his military headquarters (not "palace," v. 45) in this Idumean region, and there will meet his doom at the Lord's hand, as will also the Antichrist further north of Jerusalem itself.

The figurative language of *verses 6 and 7* describes the mighty leaders of these Gentile powers. "The times of the Gentiles" will have come to an end. **"It is the day of the Lord's vengeance, the year of recompence in the controversy of Zion"** (v. 8), i.e., to assert the rights of God's King. With *verses 9, 10* compare Revelation 18:18 and 19:3.

As for the land of Edom, it will be eternally barren, overgrown with nettles and thorns, and the habitation of wild beasts and birds of prey (vv. 11-17). The description is symbolic of the futility of the flesh and of all human schemes. Just as the creative power of the Lord assigns to animals their relation, condition and region ("no one of these shall fail, none shall want her mate"), so in fulfillment of His prophetic word, each fulfillment will answer to the prophecy which has predicted it. His Spirit carries out the twofold design. He it is who governs the creatures and He it is who accomplished the fiat of His unthwartable Word, detail for detail.

Chapter 35

The Millennial conditions of peace and prosperity foretold in this chapter and the definite contrasts with what is predicted in chapter thirty-four, make clear that the judgments of the wrath of God foretold in that chapter are those to be carried out at the close of the present age. The overthrow of the antichristian powers by the Second Advent of Christ will be followed by what set forth. In contrast to the barren condition of Edom, the land of Palestine will **"blossom as the rose"** (v. 1). **"The glory of the Lord, the excellency of our God"** will be manifested (cp. 40:5). Weak hands are to be strong to work; tottering knees are to be confirmed. Fear will geance of God upon the foe will be healed. The lame will leap, the dumb will sing *(vv. 3–5)*. The woeful conditions of distress in the great tribulation will yield place to all that makes for the glory of God in the happiness of His redeemed.

The wilderness, the desert, the parched ground, the thirsty land, will all become fertile, for nature itself will reap the benefits of the removal of antagonistic powers, spiritual and human, and of the presence of the glory of the Lord and His people, earthly and heavenly *(v. 7)*.

The very means of intercourse and communication will be consecrated to God. Both the highway and the ordinary road will be holy. The walk of life will be **"The way of holiness."** No unclean person will traverse it. It will be for those who have fellowship with God, those in whose heart are "the high ways to Zion" (Ps. 84:5, R.V.). Even the simple folk will not go astray *(v. 8)*.

The nature of the ravenous beasts will be changed. The lion will eat straw like the ox. There will be nothing to mar the peace of the redeemed *(v. 9)*. The whole passage closes with a promise, which is repeated in 51:11, the assurance marking both parts of the book with the same message of comfort: **"And the ransomed of the Lord shall return, and come to Zion with songs, and everlasting joy upon their heads; they shall obtain joy and gladness, and sorrow and sighing shall flee away."**

CHAPTER FIVE

Part II
The Assyrians, Chaldeans, and Hezekiah
Chapters 36—39

Chapter 36

$\mathbf{A}$ new section of the prophecies begins here. These and the two following chapters are suitably introduced in their historical setting. For the circumstances of Hezekiah's reign, mentioned in 2 Chronicles 32:32 as a part of the "vision" of Isaiah, are a fulfillment of what Isaiah had predicted nearly thirty years before (8:5–10), and had alluded to subsequently (see 10:12–19, 33, 34; 14:24, 25; 30:28–31; 31:8).

The two chapters, dealing with the invasion and overthrow of the Assyrian, form, therefore, the historical consummation of chapters seven to thirty-five.

Chapters thirty-eight and thirty-nine, on the other hand, with the account of Hezekiah's sickness, recovery and failure, form the historical basis of chapters forty to sixty-six. Chapters thirty-six and thirty-seven are retrospective. Chapters thirty-eight and thirty-nine are prospective. The four are clearly in their divinely appointed setting in the whole book. The fact that the whole passage is found in 2 Kings 18:13 to 20:19 provides no argument for the supposition that two or more authors compiled the book. The internal evidence is to the contrary. There are indications that these chapters form the original of the narrative in 2 Kings.

However that may be, the facts remain that chapters thirty-six and thirty-seven record the judgments which began to descend upon the nation because of their persistent rejection of God's testimonies and their defiant rebellion against Him, judgments of which the prophet had warned them. On the other hand, while in Hezekiah's reign national corruption had been checked, and there was a measure of restoration, yet the very failure on the part of the king after the mercy of his recovery, provided evidence that Judah would have to be subjected to the disasters of the Captivity.

But, prospectively, all this only serves to call forth the assurance that God would not permanently cast away His people. Hence the opening of the latter part of the book, beginning with chapter forty, a great part of which is an extension of the promised blessings in chapter thirty-five and certain preceding passages. The whole book demonstrates God's pleasure in causing mercy to rejoice against judgment.

CHAPTER SIX

Part III
Introductory Note on Chapters 40 to 46

The latter half of Isaiah consists of three divisions, *(a)* chapters forty to forty-eight, *(b)* chapters forty-nine to fifty-seven, *(c)* chapters fifty-eight to sixty-six. The subject of the whole is twofold, the call to repentance and the promise of eventual deliverance. In connection with the former, each division closes with a solemn warning as to the state of the wicked: *(a)* "There is no peace, saith the Lord, unto the wicked," 48:22; *(b)* "There is no peace, saith my God, to the wicked," 57:21; *(c)* "their worm shall not die, neither shall their fire be quenched; and they shall be an abhorring to all flesh," 66:24. In division *(a)* the contrast is between Jehovah and idols, and between Israel and the Gentiles, in *(b)* between the sufferings of the Servant of Jehovah and His future glory, in *(c)* between the hypocrites and the rebellious and the faithful and persecuted.

Other divisions have been suggested. The above seems the most likely. To all the themes in this latter portion of Isaiah the first thirty-nine chapters lead up.

CHAPTER SEVEN

Part IIIa
Israel, Gentiles, and
Divine Deliverance
Chapters 40—48

Chapter 40

In chapter forty the promise of deliverance opens with the consolatory message **"Comfort ye, comfort ye My people, saith your God,"** and that and what follows to the end of *verse 11* form a prologue to the rest of the book. The word rendered "comfort" lit. means to cause to breathe again, and thus is expressive not only of consolation but of enduring power, as a result of reviving and relief. The repetition is indicative of urgency.

The phrase "saith your God" and other similar phrases are found in both parts of the book (1:11; 33:10; 40:1, 25; 41:21; 66:9). It here not only indicates the unthwartable decree of God, but makes clear that the comfort to be bestowed is conditioned by relationship to Him.

The command is repeated more emphatically: **"Speak ye comfortably to** [Heb., "Speak ye to the heart of"] **Jerusalem."** The city stands for the people. The Lord desires not only to minister comfort to us but to win our heart while doing so.

Three reasons for the comfort are given: (1) **"that her warfare is accomplished"**; the word primarily denotes military service, then feudal service, and hence any wretched and miserable state (see Job 7:1, R.V. and margin); (2) **"that her iniquity is pardoned"**; the verb signifies to receive satisfaction by the payment of a debt; hence to pay off the debt of sin by enduring punishment. This points to the sacrifice of Calvary; the justice of God has been satisfied by atonement made; (3) **"that (R.V.) she hath received of the Lord's hand double for all her sins"**; this last states more fully the substance of the previous two.

Various ideas have been suggested as to the significance of "double"; the meaning most in keeping with the context is that punishment has been meted out in full measure (cp. Jer. 16:18), not more nor less than had been deserved. The mercy of God shines out in the words "for all"; nothing is left requiring punishment. God delights in the restoration of His people, on the ground that expiation has been accomplished. The meaning of liberation, by handing the counterpart or double of a bond, does not seem to be so appropriate to the scope of the passage.

Everything that hindered a right condition before God having been dealt with and removed, as in *verse 3*, the way is now opened for the blessing kept in store. A voice cries **"Prepare ye in the wilderness the way of the Lord, make straight in the desert a highway for our God."** It is like a king's courier appointed to see that his way is put in good condition. Of old God had led the way through "the wilderness from Egypt to Canaan. Now Israel has been in the wilderness of the peoples," the Gentile nations (Ezek. 20:34, 35); there she will have passed through her great tribulation, and everything is prepared for Millennial deliverance, glory and blessing. Every valley is to be exalted (those who have been cast down and oppressed in the valley of humiliation are to be encouraged); every mountain and hill is to be made low (the self-righteous and presumptuous are to be humiliated); the crooked is to be made straight (doublemindedness is to give way to simplicity); the rough places are to be made plain (the ruggedness of pride is to be reduced to submission); the glory of the Lord is to be revealed, and all flesh shall see it together *(v. 5).* This is called in 2 Thessalonians 2:8 "the manifestation of His Coming" (lit., the epiphany, or shining forth, of His Parousia). "Behold He cometh with the clouds; and every eye shall see Him, and they which pierced Him; and all the tribes of the earth shall mourn over Him" (Rev. 1:7). Nothing can hinder it, **"for the mouth of the Lord hath spoken it."**

How often, just when things seem to be at their darkest, and opposition and difficulty have risen to their highest height, this provides the occasion for the intervention of God! Faith has stood the test and receives its victorious reward.

Now another voice is heard, saying **"Cry"**; and yet another **"one said, What shall I cry?"** The answering message declares the perishable nature of man and the imperishable nature of the Word of God. His word is one with Himself. What He says that He is. Hence, as He is everlasting, so His word shall stand forever *(v. 8).* Since Christ is the Word of God, this is all true of Him, and is especially declared in His reply to the Jews in John 8:25, R.V., that He was what He had spoken to them from the beginning (or completely, altogether). His teaching was the expression of His nature and character.

So then the oppressors of Israel will fade and die as the grass, under the retributive judgments of God.

What follows in *verses 9 and 10* is really addressed to Zion and Jerusalem, which again stand for the inhabitants thereof, and the A.V. and R.V. margin are almost certainly right, **"O Zion that tellest** [bringest] **good tidings . . . O Jerusalem, that . . ."** (52:7 and 62:11 are in a different connection). The announcement of the immediately impending Advent of the Messiah will go forth from Zion; it will be known that such Scriptures as Zechariah 14:3, 4 are about to be fulfilled. Hence a threefold "Behold": first the proclamation **"Behold, your God"** (the comma should be observed), and then the two assurances, **"Behold, the Lord God will come as a mighty One, and His arm shall rule for Him; behold, His reward is with Him, and His recompense before Him,"** the recompense being twofold in character, both of retribution for the enemies of His people, and for the compensation of the faithful.

All this is judicial; now follows that which is consolatory. The figures of the Victor and the Judge are succeeded by that of the Shepherd: **"He shall feed** [or rather, "tend"] **His flock like a shepherd"** (John 10:4-16), a sweet word of affectionate consolation for those who have been scattered among the Gentiles and have passed through fiery trial. **"He shall gather the lambs in His arm, and carry them in His bosom";** they could not keep pace with the flock; **"and shall gently lead those that give suck";** for the mother sheep require special care (cp. Gen. 33:13). This is how the Lord will bring about the issues from "the time of Jacob's trouble." Not a member of the godly remnant in Israel, with their varied spiritual conditions, will go unattended by their great Shepherd.

This verse provides lessons for those to whom, as undershepherds, is committed the present day care of the spiritual flock (1 Pet. 5:2-4). How much discernment and devotion are requisite in order to follow the example of the Good Shepherd, concerning the three conditions here mentioned of those who form the flock! The Lord teaches us the need of dealing in tender compassion and grace with those committed to our care.

This verse closes the prologue to the remainder of the book. Having shown who it is who is about to interpose for the redemption and comfort of His people, the prophet will now testify as to the incomparable attributes of their Creator-God, who will undertake for them. They must be awakened to a consciousness of His infinite greatness, His character and power. And as idolatry has been an outstanding transgression of Israel, leading to the sufferings they have received from the Gentile nations, these attributes are set in contrast both to the condition of nations *(vv. 15–17)* and to the nature of idols and their makers *(vv. 18–20).* All this leads up to a renewal of consolatory assurances *(vv. 29–31).*

Two comprehensive and challenging questions (what appears as a third is really part of the second) are asked, the first *(a)* concerning His omnipotence, the second *(b)* concerning His omniscience:

(a) **"Who hath measured the waters in the hollow of his hand** [how very small are the contents possible to a human hand!], **and meted out heaven** ["the heavens"]

with the span [the verb signifies to prove, weigh, measure out, and so to regulate—see "directed" in *verse 13*, contrast the width and ability of a human span], **and comprehended the dust of the earth in a measure** [how small is human capacity, which measures with the third part of an ephah!], **and weighed the mountains in scales, and the hills in a balance"** (how little can man weigh, whether in a steelyard or in a pair of balances! did man adjust the equilibrium of the earth?).

The questions are a magnificent way of bringing home the puny activities and power of mere man compared with the mighty Creator.

(b) The second series of questions relates to His omniscience, a fact which forecloses all instruction from others: **"Who hath directed** [or "regulated"; the same word as is rendered "meted out" in *v. 12*] **the spirit of the Lord** [that is, who provided Him a standard by which to act], **or being His counselor hath taught Him? With whom took He counsel, and who instructed Him** [or "made Him understand"—see margin] **and taught Him in** [or "concerning"] **the path of judgment, and taught Him knowledge, and shewed to Him the way of understanding** [or "made known to Him prudent counsels"]?" *verse 14*.

All this combines the faculties of knowledge, wisdom and understanding. The questions resemble, and have the same object as, those which the Lord asked Job (chaps. 40 and 41), whom He converted by the argument from design. Here He uses the argument of analogy. Let Israel then consider the nature of their Redeemer and turn away from imaginary and futile sources of help.

From His attributes as Creator the thoughts are now directed to His absolute control as Governor of the nations, a control which never causes Him any difficulty or presents Him with any problem. **"Behold, the nations are as a drop of a bucket** [i.e., a drop hanging on a bucket: does the drop cause the carrier any burden?], **and are counted as the small dust of the balance** [the merest speck of dust or sand! how much does that make a scale descend?]: **behold, He taketh up the isles as a very little thing** [or as in the R.V. margin, "the isles are as the fine dust that is lifted up" i.e., by a puff of wind], *verse 15*.

Further, whatever can be offered to God in worship and sacrifice must ever be far short of the glory of His Being. **"Lebanon is not sufficient to burn"** (i.e., to provide wood for the fire of an offering), nor could its pastures provide an adequate supply of sacrificial beasts. The privileged Jew would ever come short in this respect. And as for the Gentiles, sacrificial offerings are not in the question. The nations are **"as nothing before Him; they are counted to Him less than nothing** [their moral corruption renders them worse than if they were nonexistent] **and vanity"** *(tohu,* a waste or chaos—the same word as in Gen. 1:2, R.V., "waste," and Is. 45:18, R.V.), *verse 17*.

This being so with man, much greater are the insignificance and worthlessness of an idol. Let Israel beware! **"To whom then will ye liken God? or what likeness will ye compare unto him?"** *(v. 18).* Accordingly there follows the first of a series of passages characterized by withering sarcasm poured upon the infatuation of idol framers and worshipers, and aimed at Israel. Here the idol makers are especially in view, both the rich man who can afford one made of metals and adorned with gold and silver, and the poor man who applies for the fashioning of a wooden one *(vv. 19, 20).*

Four questions follow in *verse 21*, addressed to Israel. They are in the *(a), (b), (b), (a),* or chiasmic, order: *(a)* "known," *(b)* "heard," *(b)* "told you," *(a)* "understood"—a strong method of appeal or instruction.

(a) Failure to recognize and acknowledge God from the evidences of creation *(vv. 22 to 26)* prevents the reception of the knowledge of His will, *(b)* by preaching, and *(b)* by teaching, through *(a)* the darkening of the understanding. So had it been with Israel. They had become like the Gentiles (see Rom. 1:20 to 32).

Let us ever beware lest the wonders of nature fail to produce in us the adoration of its Maker.

So now there follow statements of God's position, power and authority, and the prophet passes alternately from the physical universe to the inhabitants of the world: **"It is He that sitteth** [here of sitting enthroned] **upon** [or "above"] **the circle of the earth** [the vault which arches over the earth]." That is His position relatively to creation. Now for the puny diminutiveness of the inhabitants of the earth: they are **"as grasshoppers"** (i.e., in His sight; cp. Num. 13:33). Next, again, as to creation *(v. 22):* **"that stretcheth out** [lit., "has stretched out"] **the heavens as a curtain** [a thin, transparent fabric; margin, "gauze"], **and spreadeth** [lit., "has spread out"] **them out as a tent to dwell it."** Further, again, as to earth-dwellers, and especially their rulers: **"that bringeth princes to nothing; He maketh the judges of the earth as vanity"**—two classes of authorities, the former those who possess the highest distinction and greatest influence; the latter those who exercise the chief judicial and administrative power. The former are made to be as though they were nonexistent; the latter are made a desolation (a *tohu:* see *v. 17*). See 1 Corinthians 2:6.

The R.V. marginal rendering of what follows depicts more accurately the suddenness with which the naturally promising great men of the earth just mentioned are brought to nought under the mighty hand of God: **"Scarce** [scarcely] **are they planted, scarce are they sown, scarce hath their stock taken root in the earth, when He bloweth upon them, and they wither, and the whirlwind taketh them away as stubble"** (*v. 24*, R.V. margin). The breath of the Lord consumes them (cp. 11:4; 2 Thess. 2:8, R.V., and Rev. 2:16); the forces of nature, which are His, blast them.

As in *verse 18,* where the prophet challengingly declared the incomparableness of God, after recording the insignificance of the nations, so here, recalling this challenge, God, after the demonstration of the finiteness of the inhabitants and the evanescence of their governors, Himself says, **"To whom then will ye liken Me, that I should be equal to him? saith the Holy One"** (*v. 25*). This is a change in the distinction; it is not now between His illimitableness and their insignificance, but between His essential and absolute holiness and the self-degradation of His corrupt and idolatrous people. Alas, the folly of making and worshiping any but their true and living God!

This is pointedly followed by a third mention of the incomparable power of God as Creator. The first *(v. 12)* was given as a challenging question; the second *(vv. 21, 22)* as a number of appealing reminders of what they had been

taught to recognize; the third is given as a command: **"Lift up your eyes on high, and see who hath created these** [or "see: who hath created these?"], **that bringeth out their host by number,"** causing them to come forth, so to speak, night after night, as a general brings out his armored host to the field: **"He calleth them all by name: by** [or rather, "because of"] **the greatness of His might, and for that He is strong in power, not one is lacking."** Not one is absent from the muster-roll *(v. 26)*.

Omnipotence alone is requisite for the whole constant, glorious and orderly procedure. The heavenly host exists and moves, not simply by natural laws. The Son of God is Himself the sustaining Center, Upholder and Controller of all: "all things have been created through Him, and unto Him: and He is before all things, and in Him all things consist" (i.e., hold together), Colossians 1:16, 17. He upholds "all things by the word of His power" (Heb. 1:3).

While what has just preceded is retrospectively a protest against idolatry in the nation, it is also introductory to a message of comfort to the remnant of the godly who are cast down and despairing. Hence they are addressed in the words "O Jacob" as well as "O Israel," to remind them of the covenant made with their ancestor. They thought that the Lord had abandoned them in His wrath, having grown weary of them: **"Why sayest thou, O Jacob, and speakest, O Israel, my way is hid from the Lord, and my judgment is passed away from** [or "overlooked by"] **my God?"** *(v. 27)*. Their way was one of great suffering and their judgment, their right, was withheld by their oppressors. This is prophetic of what they will yet experience in "the time of Jacob's trouble" at the hands of the Antichrist. They thought, as some of them will no doubt yet think, that God had entirely forgone the judicial vindication of His people.

The baselessness of such despair is met by a double question, recalling the same questions as in verse 21: **"Hast thou not known? hast thou not heard? the everlasting God, the Lord, the Creator of the ends of the earth, fainteth not, neither is weary; there is no searching of His understanding"** *(v. 28)*.

Any of us who are tempted to despondency because of the pressure of adverse circumstances should lay hold of the facts which we have accepted by faith, as well as gather from our experiences of God's merciful dealings with us, that He, the Creator of all things, is "the same yesterday and today, *yea*, and forever," and therefore has the same power at our disposal as He manifested in His creative acts. He never suffers from overexertion; and since His understanding is infinite, He knows all about us. Our most trying experiences, whether from without or within, are not only known to Him, but are under His absolute control. He appoints the time for His interposition and our deliverance.

So far from becoming faint, **"He giveth power to the faint; and to him that hath no might He increaseth strength** [or giveth strength abundantly]," *verse 29*. What we need is faith to open our hearts to receive the strength He is ever ready to impart while we are undergoing the trial. That is His way of making our trials blessings. He aims at making us realize our utter incapability, so that we may take hold of His strength instead of despairing under the affliction.

The strongest can never be sure of freedom from weariness, and an obstacle placed in their path may easily make them stumble: **"Even the youths shall faint and be weary, and the young men shall utterly fall: but they that wait upon the Lord shall renew their strength** [margin, change, i.e., gain fresh]; **they shall mount up with wings as eagles; they shall run, and not be weary; they shall walk** [or go forward], **and not faint"** *(vv. 30, 31).* To wait upon the Lord is not simply a matter of patience, or even of longing, it means trust and the confidence which characterizes our hope. To experience this is to go from strength to strength, drawing continually from the resources of His power. To mount up with wings is to rise above difficulties, to fly above the mists and darkness of earth into the clear sunshine of God's presence. Would that we more readily entered into this delightful experience. We shall do so, if Christ is a reality to us.

Some suggest that the meaning is that of putting forth fresh feathers, as birds do after moulting, but the rendering in our Versions seems better. The eagle is characterized by three things: rapidity of flight, power of scent, keenness of vision. So our mounting up is not only a matter of rising above difficulties, it involves a joyous and quick discernment of the will and way of God for us and the keen vision of Himself by faith.

But then we are very much on the earth, and hence the metaphor of running and walking: "I will run the way of Thy commandments, when Thou shalt enlarge my heart" (Ps. 119:32). "I will walk at liberty; for I have sought Thy precepts" *(v. 45).* Running is suggestive of energetic effort, but what is also needed is the steady progress in the Christian path in the enjoyment of quiet communion with God.

Chapter 41

At the beginning of chapter forty-one the Lord speaks to the Gentile nations. Let them try to contend with Him *(v. 1).* The fact that He declares beforehand the raising up of a conqueror from the east is but a sign that God Himself is the supreme Controller of the world's affairs *(vv. 2–4).* The idolatry of the nations will eventually bring Divine judgments upon them, and Israel, as God's chosen people, will become His instruments in chastising them *(vv. 5–16).* There follows another challenge to the Gentiles. Let them show their ability to foretell the future, as God does. They and their objects of worship shall be brought to naught *(vv. 21–29).*

The opening challenge by the Lord to the Gentile nations is issued as follows: **"Keep silence before Me, O islands** [standing for great nations at the extremities of the continents]; **and let the peoples** [Gentiles, not Israel, as one might gather from the A.V., "people"] **renew their strength** [i.e., get fresh strength: they need it from their point of view if they are to contend with God; compare and contrast 40:31]; **let them come near; then let them speak** [that is, let them make a reply after hearing the evidence]: **let us come near together to judgment."** The nations are called, not to a tribunal for God to pass a verdict of condemnation upon them, but to a tribunal of reason, to hear facts and draw conclusions.

God Himself opens the contest by way of challenging questions followed by statements of fact. The person in view is Cyrus, the raisng up of whom is prophetically foretold in the past tense, which regards a future event as just as certain of accomplishment as if it had already taken place. But there is not only the power thus to predict the future with certainty (that is God's prerogative alone), but the power to raise up a man for the accomplishment of the Divine purposes. This is the meaning of *verses 2, 3:* **"Who hath raised up one from the east** [in v. 25 he is said to be raised up from the **north,** and both become true of Cyrus, for he was connected both with Persia in the east and Media to the north], **whom He calleth in righteousness to His foot** [see, however, the R.V. margin]. **He giveth nations before him, and maketh him rule over kings"**: what follows describes his conquests that were to be.

The challenge is then uttered in another way: **"Who hath wrought and done it, calling the generations from the beginning?"** *(v. 4).* That is to say, who is the Author, and whose is the authority, through whom such an event derives its origin and progress? Jehovah provides His own answers: **"I the Lord, the first, and with the last, I am He."** That He is "the first" means that He is preexistent to all history and that all things are under His control; He brings in one generation after another; that He is "with the last" means that He brings all things to their appointed end; hence the isles will be made to see and fear, and the ends of the earth will tremble. **"They drew near, and came"** *(v. 5).* That is, they would come to meet the threatening danger. So they would in regard to Cyrus. So they will at the end of this age.

And what lies behind these futile efforts? **"They helped every one his neighbor; and** *every one* **said to his brother, Be of good courage"** *(v. 6).* Accordingly they resorted to their idolatry. **"So the carpenter encouraged the goldsmith, and he that smootheth with the hammer him that smiteth the anvil, saying of the soldering, It is good: and he fastened it with nails, that it should not be moved."** With what scorn the description of this is given, in contrast to the statements concerning the attributes and controlling authority of God!

The Lord now continues His message of consolation to Israel, addressing them by the same twofold names as in 40:27, but now in the opposite order; for now it is not a message to the weak and faint, but a reminder of His electing grace and the promise of restoration and deliverance, though further on the former order will be resumed *(v. 14).*

He reminds them that they are His own by choice, and children of promise. They are **"The seed of Abraham My friend."** Their earliest history is a guarantee of irrevocable blessing. Three times Abraham is called the friend of God: in 2 Chronicles 20:7, in the prayer of Jehoshaphat; here, in the Divine confirmation of this; and in James 2:23, which combines God's dealings with Abraham with this passage in Isaiah. The word rendered "friend" denotes one who is loving and beloved, an object of desire, and one who enjoys the utmost intimacy. So the Lord reminds His people of what they owe to the faith of their ancestor. **"Thou,"** He says, speaking of Israel, **"whom I have taken hold of from the ends of the earth, and called thee from the corners thereof."** The R.V. is right in the rendering "taken hold of," and the meaning seems to be not so much that of strengthening as that of attaching firmly to oneself. From the point of view of Palestine, Ur of the Chaldeans was sufficiently remote to be called the ends and corners of the earth. God called Abraham from thence with a view to the rise of his seed as a nation, which was preexistent in His counsels.

God's calling is always effectual. We may remind ourselves of this in our own experience in connection with the sphere of service allotted to us. If it has not been a matter simply of our choice and decision, it is ours by reason of His plan and appointment and the directing power of the Holy Spirit.

The Lord now speaks of Israel as His servant, here first in Isaiah, and this is frequently repeated, down to the 6th verse of chapter 49. He says here **"Thou art My servant, I have chosen thee and not cast thee away** (or despised thee)," *verse 9.* So the servant character of Israel is the outcome of an act of pure grace and not through any merit on their part, as is intimated by the hint that He might reasonably have despised them and cast them away. But further, the nation had become, in spite of its waywardness and transgressions, the servant of Jehovah in the fulfillment of His purposes thus far, and it is destined to act in this capacity in full measure hereafter.

Accordingly His people have good reason to abstain from fearfulness and dismay. Hence the Lord says to them, as He still says to us, **"Fear thou not, for I am with thee; be not dismayed, for I am thy God: I will strengthen thee; yea, I will help thee; yea, I will uphold thee with the right hand of My righteousness"** *(v. 10)*.

Three reasons are given by the Lord for freedom from fear and dismay: (1) His presence: "for I am with thee"; (2) His relationship: "I am thy God"; (3) His assurances, and these are threefold, *(a)* of power: "I will strengthen thee," fortifying in weakness, difficulty and opposition; the word combines also the meaning of taking hold of; *(b)* of assistance: "yea, I will help thee," giving guidance, direction and protection; *(c)* of support: "yea, I will uphold thee with the right hand of My righteousness," suggestive of His faithfulness in the fulfillment of His promises; the Hebrew word for the right hand is associated with the idea of power and success, and suggests prosperity. The "yea" is cumulative, it gathers up what precedes and thus imparts added assurance to what follows.

Let us not fail to take to ourselves the comfort of these promises, whether by regarding them as applicable only to Israel, or by a self-complacent state of soul, which unfits us for the ever needed comfort and power for acting as the servants of the Lord in the realization of our own demerit and helplessness.

Israel, as the people of God, have ever had numerous and mighty foes, and their persecuting power and antagonism grow and will grow more intense as the end of this age draw near. The comforting promises which have just preceded lead now to the assurance of the overthrow of their enemies and the repeated guarantee of help.

In *verses 11 and 12,* four descriptions of the enemy are given: (1) All that **"are incensed"** against His people (indicative of the fierce heat of their satanically instigated antagonism) are to be ashamed and confounded; (2) **"they that strive with thee"** (lit., "the men of thy conflict"); (3) **"them that contend with thee"** ("the men of thy feuds"); (4) **"they that war against thee"** ("the men of thy warfare"). Every sort of foe is included in the doom. They are to perish, and are to become **"as nothing,"** as a nonentity.

Verse 13 follows with the comforting assurance, **"For I the Lord thy God will hold thy right hand, saying unto thee, Fear not; I will help thee."** Not only is there the promise of the overwhelming defeat of all their foes, but likewise the promise of protection and strength. Not only is there to be deliverance, but Israel itself is to be taken up and used for the accomplishment of God's purposes. The assurance of help is repeated from verse 10.

Our right hand is that with which we do our work, it is the emblem of our activities. That God will hold that, indicates that we can do nothing apart from Him and that it is His will for us to realize that the power we require to do anything of value must be His.

In *verse 14* the "Fear not" is repeated as an introduction to the promise that Israel is to have power over those who have opposed them. The twofold address presents different aspects of their state. Firstly, **"thou worm Jacob,"** suggesting a helpless and prostrate condition, as of a struggling creature of the dust (cp. Job 25:6), the object of contempt and disgust. With that condition their Messiah has identified Himself in His sufferings at Calvary, by very reason of which He will be their Redeemer (Ps. 22:6); secondly, **"Ye men of Israel"**; the Hebrew word is suggestive of a diminished condition, as in the A.V. margin, "men few in number" (the same word as in Gen. 34:30; Deut. 4:27); this they will be after their great tribulation.

The Lord brings us down that He may lift us up. For the third time He says, **"I will help thee,"** and guarantees it, first by His Name Jehovah, and then by the pledge **"and thy Redeemer is the Holy One of Israel"** (R.V.). He appends, so to speak, His signature to His declaration. Jehovah is the unoriginated, self-existent, ever-existent One, and again and again He announces His title as the ground of the assurance of His redemptive work (see, e.g., 43:14; 44:6, 24; 48:17; 49:26; 54:5, 8; 60:16; Jer. 50:34; cp. Is. 29:22; 51:11; 62:12; Jer. 31:11). In each place the word rendered "Redeemer" is the verb corresponding to the noun *goel,* a kinsman-redeemer avenger. The redemption is ever based upon His gracious fulfillment of the obligation of a kinsman (Lev.

25:48, 49), in becoming incarnate with a view to His atoning sacrifice.

Verses 15 and 16 vividly depict the nation as the Lord's instrument in bringing their enemies to nought. Israel will be a sharp, new threshing roller with two-edged knives, like an instrument that cuts up the straw for fodder, and separates the grain from the chaff. The mountains and hills (figurative of proud and powerful foes) will be threshed to powder, and scattered and destroyed, as chaff is blown by the wind. The Lord's irresistible whirlwind will abolish the last remnant of them.

The nation will have learnt to glory, not in their own prowess and might, they will **"rejoice in the Lord,"** and **"glory in the Holy One of Israel."** But Jehovah, looking into the assured future, thinks compassionately of **"the poor and needy,"** pining away through thirst (there is no "when" in the original), not only the exiles in Babylon, but all such among His people in their privations and sufferings at all times. The Lord promises to have regard to them and to answer their prayer. He will **"open rivers on the bare heights, and fountains in the midst of the valleys."** He will **"make the wilderness a pool of water, and the dry land springs of water."**

While all this depicts a change from the homeless condition of Israel to the abundant blessing they will receive in the Millennium cp. 35:6, 7, a passage which confirms the fact that Isaiah wrote both parts of this book), yet these promises clearly convey a spiritual significance. For the allusion is to the water supernaturally provided in the wilderness journeys from Egypt, and this is applied spiritually in 1 Corinthians 10:4 (cp. John 4:14; 7:37–39, and see Rev. 22:17).

Verse 19 goes on to describe figuratively the manifold provision of refreshment and comfort for the nation in the coming day. This fullness is indicated in the mention of the seven trees which the Lord says He will plant in the wilderness, which will be turned into a veritable paradise. Beautiful branches will be provided for the Feast of Tabernacles. The trees are all fragrant as well as durable, and again this twofold character is figurative of the spiritual fragrance and permanency of the Spirit-given communion to be enjoyed.

Moreover, this planting and plenteousness will be manifest not as the outcome of mere natural production. The people will realize in a fourfold way that all this is to be the effect of the operation of "the hand of the Lord" and of His creative power. They will **"see, and know, and consider, and understand together"** *(v. 20)*.

The progress of idea in these four verbs is noticeable and significant. They describe what should be the result of our meditations in the Scriptures, and of His dealings with us.

At the beginning of chapter 41 the Lord declared the fact of His Deity by His absolute power to raise up a potentate to subdue nations, and to overrule the rise and course of generations. Now He declares His Deity on the ground that He alone has knowledge of, and predicts, the future. Formerly He issued His challenge to idolaters; now His challenge is to the idols themselves, the gods of the nations. Jehovah and His people (for He is **"the King of Jacob"**) are on one side, the idolatrous Gentiles are on the other. Let their gods come forward, produce their **"strong reasons"** (i.e., their proofs) and thus establish their deity if they can *(v. 21)*.

And, in addition, says the Challenger, **"Yea, do good, or do evil** [i.e., express yourselves in one way or another, that is to say, show some sign of life], **that we may be dismayed** [or rather, as in the R.V. margin, may look one upon another, i.e., look one another in the face so as to measure ourselves in the contest; cp. 2 Kin. 14:8, 11], **and behold it together** [i.e., see what the result of the contest will be]," *verse 23*.

Will the idols now speak to prove their deity? Of course they cannot. Hence the withering scorn Divinely poured upon them and their makers: **"Behold, ye are of nothing, and your work** [or doing] **of nought: an abomination is he that chooseth you"** *(v. 24)*.

The Lord again makes clear that power and authority alone belong to Him in the supreme disposal of national affairs. Accordingly the prophecy about Cyrus is resumed. This great potentate, a follower of the religion of Zarathustra, or Zoroaster, would be taught to recognize and call upon the name of Jehovah. He would **"come upon rulers as upon mortar, and as the potter treadeth** [or kneadeth] **clay"** *(v. 25)*. The Lord in foretelling this declares again His omniscience and continues

His challenge. No one else could do it, nor indeed could any of the heathen deities give any utterance at all; **"there is none that heareth your words"** *(v. 26)*. Had they been able to do so, their divine power would have been acknowledged.

Verse 27 should be read as in the R.V.: **"I first will say unto Zion . . ."** His alone is the prerogative to give the primary promise of blessing to His people. All others can only repeat what He has already said. And with what manifest delight in His people's lasting God He promises to give evangelists to Jerusalem (cp. 40:1, 2, 9)! In the words **"Behold, behold them,"** He calls upon Zion to see how His promises have been fulfilled (looking on to the future time of the fulfillment).

Verse 28 brings the contest to its foreseen issue. The idols and their devotees are silent; there is no counselor to answer a word. The matter closes with a declaration of the Lord's contempt and wrath, and the last verse might be rendered closely to the original thus: "Look at them all! Vanity! Their productions are nothingness; wind and desolation are their molten images."

The judicial procedure ends at verse 25; verses 25–29 review the evidence and the verdict.

Chapter 42

The way is now open for the first great revelation and prophecy, in this second part of the book, concerning Christ. All the promises of restoration and its consequent blessing are shown to center in Him. Later on His sacrificial Death will be before us. Now we are to see the delight of God the Father in Him, and what great things will be accomplished by Him. We are given a view of His life and character in the days of His flesh, His tenderness as well as His power, and of the great deliverance He will accomplish hereafter.

The light of the glory of His Person puts Cyrus into the shade for the time being, though more remains to be said about the latter afterwards. But it is Christ who now comes into view as the Blesser of Israel and the Savior of Gentiles.

It is Christ whom the Lord calls His Servant in *verse 1:* **"Behold My Servant, whom I**

uphold; My chosen, in whom My soul delighteth." The quotation in Matthew 12:18 speaks of Him as "My Beloved," giving the other meaning of the Hebrew word, and harmonizing with the declaration of the Father in 3:17. He assumed His Servant character for the fulfillment of His Father's will on earth (Phil. 2:7). He was "chosen" in the eternal counsels of God in the past, for the purposes of propitiation.

The demonstration of the delight of the Father in Him was the coming of the Holy Spirit upon Him, in fulfillment of this prophecy (Matt. 3:16; Mark 1:10; Luke 3:22; John 1:32, 33). This statement, **"I have put My Spirit upon Him,"** is the center one of three great declarations in Isaiah concerning the Holy Spirit in connection with Christ. The first is in 11:2, which speaks of His Incarnation. The second, here, points to His baptism. The last is in 61:1, pointing to the beginning of His public ministry.

From this the prophecy momentarily leaps forward to the effects of Christ's Second Advent, in His Millennial reign: **"He shall bring forth** [or "cause to go forth"] **judgment to the Gentiles."** The mode of the fulfillment was given in detail by the prophet in 2:1–4.

In regard to the apparent contradiction in the statement **"He shall not cry"** *(v. 2)*, and that in verse 13, **"He shall cry,"** the verbs rendered "cry" are different. The first has to do with His people, the second with His enemies. The first indicates His gentleness and tenderness and the absence of self-advertising, noisy demonstration; the second is His voice as a Conqueror, "the voice of the Lord," by which the foes of God are to be overthrown at the end of this age.

Next comes *(in vv. 3, 4)* a series of promises in chiasmic (or a, b, b, a) order (see note on 40:21). First there is the bruised reed, which He will not break; then the smoking, or dimly burning, flax, which He will not quench. In *verse 4*, in the statement **"He shall not fail,"** the word "fail" signifies to burn dimly, and, in the next, **"nor be discouraged,"** the word "discouraged" signifies to be bruised or broken. So the last and first go together; so do the second and third. He will not bruise the broken reed, nor will He Himself be bruised. He neither will quench the dimly burning torch, nor will He Himself burn dimly. Thus He causes His tried ones to share His glory.

These "precious promises" have much encouragement for us in His loving care for us now. If we sometimes feel like the broken reed, fit only for crushing, or feel that our light is but a poor flickering thing, let us bear in mind His desires toward us, and present ourselves to Him for His gracious renewing and His restoring power.

Having called upon the hearers to contemplate His Servant, Jehovah now addresses Him Himself, but this is introduced by a description of His Almighty power *(v. 5)*. Speaking of Himself by His title **GOD THE LORD,** titles of omnipotence and eternity, He declares that He is the Creator (or Arranger) of the heavens, and of the earth and its products, and the Giver of life and spirit to its inhabitants. This tremendous utterance is made the basis of an assurance and promise, and of a revelation of His purposes. The assurance is as to the call He has given; the promises are: (1) **"I will hold Thine hand,"** (2) **"will keep Thee,"** (3) **"will give Thee for a covenant of the people, for a light of the Gentiles."** The purposes are: (1) **"to open the blind eyes,"** (2) **"to bring out the prisoners from the dungeon,"** (3) **"and them that sit in darkness out of the prison house."**

All this will be made true in regard to the Person of the Lord Jesus Christ, concerning Israel, in a day to come.

Yet what a comfort it all is to us in its secondary application to ourselves as servants of God! We are justified in applying verses 6 and 7 to ourselves by the fact that the Lord Jesus uses similar language to His apostle as recorded in Acts 26:18. He who has called us in righteousness will still hold our hand, and will keep us, making us ministers of His Gospel, enabling us to bring light and liberty to those who are in spiritual darkness and captivity.

The Lord now makes the solemn affirmation **"I am Jehovah; that is My Name,"** recalling His twice repeated Name in *verses 5 and 6*. That was the Name by which He revealed Himself to Moses, as a pledge that He would fulfill His word in regard to the commission given to him. By this title He declared (1) His self-existence, Exodus 3:14; (2) the assurance of the everlasting and unchangeable nature of His character, verse 15; (3) His

power to redeem, 6:2–6; (4) His authority as the One who, having redeemed, claims obedience to His commands, 20:2. That His Name is the guarantee of the fulfillment of His word, is the clear intimation here in Isaiah 42:8.

How sure and steadfast is His word! What an incentive it provides for faith to lay hold of His promises, even in the darkest hour and amidst the most perplexing and distressing circumstances!

To this declaration He adds the authoritative assurance, **"My glory will I not give to another, neither My praise unto graven images."** This is a ratification of the significance of His Name. His glory is the manifestation of His nature, attributes and power (cp. John 1:14; 2:11). "My glory . . . My praise!" The revelation of His glory is designed to draw forth the praise of those to whom He reveals it. His glory and praise are incommunicable. They will not be yielded to another. All idol-devotees shall acknowledge the fact. Let them recognize now the essential difference between His glory and power and the impotence of their gods. This is the great point of the twofold utterance in *verse 9;* firstly, **"Behold, the former things are come to pass,"**— that which had been predicted, as foreordained to take place up to that time, had already been fulfilled; secondly, **"and new things do I declare; before they spring forth I tell you of them."** The new things are those which have just been foretold in verses 1–7, as well as others which are to follow. All this is one great indication of the significance of His title "Jehovah," a title the prerogatives of which belong to the Lord Jesus Christ equally with the Father (see John 12:41).

This 42nd chapter presents some striking contrasts. There is, for instance, the promise of the opening of the eyes of the blind *(v. 7);* on the other hand, there is the blindness of the Lord's Servant in having his eyes closed to all that is not consistent with His will *(v. 19)*. This contrast calls for a special consideration. The whole paragraph *(vv. 10–17)* is Millennial in its aspect, and contains some of the "new things" to which reference was made in *verse 9*. The first of these is the "new song" mentioned in *verse 10,* the song of praise from nations that had long been lying in spiritual darkness, and from the lips that before had sung songs of vanity and vileness, and mournful dirges in celebration of their pagan gods.

The mention of the isles in *verses 10 and 12* suggests the uttermost parts of the earth. In *verse 11* Kedar, a stronghold of Arabia, represents the Arabs in general (cp. Ps. 120:5). The name was that of Ishmael's second son (Gen. 25:13). So again, in the same verse Sela (meaning a rock), R.V., is the same as *Petra* (the corresponding Greek word). It originally belonged to Edom, then to Moab, but afterwards was occupied by the Arab prince Aretas. The "wilderness," in the same verse, is the Arabian desert.

In the coming Day the Arabs will no longer be followers of the False Prophet. The Lord will overthrow the rule of Islam, together with the ten-kingdomed dominion of the Beast. Christ will **"go forth as a mighty Man; He shall stir up jealousy** [or zeal] **like a Man of war; He shall cry, He shall shout aloud"** *(v. 13)*. The cry which He will raise against His foes is referred to in Joel 3:16 (cp. Is. 63:1, and Jer. 25:30, and, for the same scene, Rev. 19:11–21).

At the *14th verse* the Lord Himself again speaks, as in the earlier part of the chapter. Confirming now the effect of His victorious shout, He says, **"I have long time holden My peace,"** indicating the longsuffering, which is so significant in these days wherein the Gospel of His grace is permitted to go forth to all nations in spite of the antagonism of His foes and "the falling away" foretold in 2 Thessalonians 2:3.

There is another striking contrast in the latter part of the chapter, concerning His people's blindness. On the one side are those who are deprived of sight because of their sin and its consequent retribution. There is, however, a gracious promise for them and then an appeal to them to open their eyes. There are ways of which they are ignorant, paths that they know not. They walk in darkness with its accompanying misery and hopelessness. The Lord will yet expel all this from them and will lead them into His own paths of righteousness and peace, making darkness light before them and crooked places straight *(v. 16)*. But the Lord cannot rest content with present deafness and blindness. His people are called upon to hear and to look, that they may know His voice and see His ways.

On the other hand, and in direct contrast, come questions that contain their own answer, as to blindness and deafness with which God is well pleased. This is the blindness of one who stands in His counsels and acts as His servant, one who enjoys constant communion with Him and is blind to all that would detract from this. **"Who is blind but My servant? or deaf as My messenger that I send? who is blind as he that is at peace with Me, and blind as the Lord's servant? Thou seest many things, but thou observest not; his ears are open, but he heareth not"** *(vv. 19, 20)*.

This is true of the excellencies of Christ as Jehovah's Servant. It gives a cogent and instructive message to us who by grace have been called into His service. How many things come into our experience which obscure our vision of the Lord Himself, which would make us deaf to His voice, things to which our fleshly nature is all too ready to respond! In how many ways are we tempted to forgetfulness of the fact that we are here simply to do the will of Him who has called and sent us! To act according to our own will brings grievous sorrow to our hearts. Be it ours to listen to His voice and to be deaf to all that is contrary to it, to walk as those who "look not at the things which are seen, but at the things which are not seen," whose eyes are open to behold the glory of the Lord and are blind to that which would dim the vision.

After the record of this faithful blindness, the reproof given to Israel is resumed from verse 18. They saw many things but observed not; their ears were opened but they heard not. They would not walk in His ways, neither were they obedient to His Law. Even when the judgment of God fell upon them, they laid it not to heart *(vv. 24, 25)*. *Verse 21* again interposes a record of the counsels of the Lord, and now in regard to the Law, **"It pleased the Lord, for His righteousness' sake, to magnify the law and make it honorable."** The inherent character of the Law is set in contrast to the ways of His people to whom He gave it.

There is also an indication of the way in which God has exhibited His glory in all His dispensational dealings in connection with the Law, and particularly in its complete fulfillment in the perfect character and life of the Lord

Jesus. To this Psalm 40 bears the predictive testimony, "I delight to do Thy will, O My God; yea, Thy Law is within My Heart." His perfect obedience is succinctly described in Philippians 2, in the statement, "He humbled Himself, becoming obedient even unto death" (R.V.), that is to say, obedient from the beginning of the days of His flesh until the climax of His obedience was reached on the Cross.

In the Person of His Son Jehovah magnified the Law both by His life and by His death, to which the life was preliminary, as showing that He was the only One who could make expiation for sin. God thus magnified the Law "for His righteousness' sake." Christ Himself is spoken of as "Jesus Christ the Righteous," and His work on the Cross is described in Romans 5:18 as "one act of righteousness" (R.V.), in contrast to Adam's one trespass. The Law put all men under condemnation. The death of Christ brings "justification of life." Thus the Lord has demonstrated His unswerving righteousness in providing the ground upon which righteousness is reckoned to the sinner through faith. The Law has been made honorable, i.e., glorious, so that it might be "established" (Rom. 3:31), and might be fulfilled, not as a means of life, but by those who have life. This is the essence of the Gospel we are commissioned to preach, and in the fellowship of this glorious ministry, we are "ambassadors on behalf of Christ."

At *verse 23,* the beginning of the last paragraph of the chapter, the last of the series of appealing questions is made: **"Who is there among you that will give ear to this? that will hearken and hear for the time to come?"** The question relates to what has preceded, and immediately to the deplorable state of Israel, who as a nation were yet in their hardened condition, **"robbed and spoiled"** *(v. 22)* and given up to suffer at the hands of Gentile nations, a suffering yet to be intensified at the close of the "times of the Gentiles" *(vv. 24, 25).* The appeal is, again, to godly ones in the nation, amidst which the Lord has never ceased to possess a remnant of those who fear His Name and wait for the consolation of Israel, those who are ready to give ear to the voice of God.

It is possible for a believer to be robbed and spoiled, possible so to yield the inner springs of his being to the outer influences of the world, that, like Samson of old, he loses the consciousness of the Lord's approval and is robbed of his spiritual power. An irretrievable loss! For though he may be restored, the loss of a reward consequent upon the period of backsliding will be eternal. To be taken captive by our spiritual foe is to be **"snared in holes"** and **"hid in prison houses"** *(v. 22).* There are many such places in the world for the one who turns from the will and way of the Lord.

On the contrary, there are those whose ears are opened to hear the voice of God and will **"hearken and hear for the time to come"** *(v. 23).* The scriptures are constantly pointing God's people to events determined for the future by His unthwartable counsels. Such parts of Scripture are generally termed prophecy, and this is by some counted as too deep for consideration, and as having very little practical effect upon the daily life and work of the believer. The very opposite is the case. The assembly at Thessalonica was not many months old when the apostle reminded them how often, when he was with them in his pioneering work, he instructed them about the Man of Sin and the Day of the Lord and other matters of the future (2 Thess. 2:5). Such instruction would not only guide their thoughts but prove a barrier against the influences of the world. Today, then, the Lord appeals to us to hearken "for the time to come," that is, to know His mind as to what is coming on the world and as to our eternal destiny, so that our lives may be conformed to His will.

The saddest feature of the peoples's state, next to the fact that they had so grievously sinned against their God, was, that, in the judgment that retributively fell upon them in their being given up "for a spoil" and to the cruelty of "the robbers" *(v. 24),* they failed to discern that all this was the Lord's doing. He it was who had kindled the fire of human persecution and tyranny. A preferable rendering for "the fury of His anger and the strength of battle," is "the heat of His wrath and the violence of war" (or, as in the Septuagint, "the war that prevailed against them"). It had set His people **"on fire round about,"** yet they **"knew not"**: it burned them, yet they **"laid it not to heart."**

These things are written that we may not fail to discern the gracious purposes, the wisdom, the love, that lie behind the chastening hand of the Lord. If we strive not against sin with the utmost resistance, we shall forget the exhortation "which reasoneth with us as with sons." Let us, on the contrary, bow in the subjection that apprehends the motive and meaning of His dealings with us, realizing that what He does is "for our profit, that we may be partakers of His holiness." This is the very acme of blessedness, and the means of power in our service! Thus shall His ways with us produce "peaceable fruit . . . even the fruit of righteousness" (Heb. 12:4–11).

Chapter 43

In the 43rd chapter the Lord turns from His lament over the blinded, hardened, unrepentant state of Israel to unfold His covenanted dealings of mercy, past, present and future, and bases all both upon His creative power and His redeeming grace. Doubly precious are God's irrevocable assurances and promises in this passage, to us who stand in the fulfillment of Christ's atoning sacrifice, His Person being ministered to us by His Holy Spirit.

The change from righteous indignation to loving consolation and comforting promises and assurances is deeply significant. It is designed to demonstrate that restoration could not be accomplished by any meritorious efforts on the part of His erring people. Their dire need must be met by Divine grace.

The love of God is not sentimental, it is never exercised at the expense of His holiness, it never compromises His justice. The love that chastises antedates the chastisement.

So when the Lord says, **"I have loved thee"** *(v. 4)*, He is recalling a love that was in exercise long before the apostasy and rebellion that inevitably called forth His righteous retribution. His love was in evidence (1) in His creative and formative acts: **"the Lord that created thee,"** a supernatural act involved in His predetermined counsel, **"and He that formed thee,"** a supernatural process, similarly predetermined and witnessed in His dealing with the patriarchs and the offspring of Jacob; (2) in His redeeming power: **"I have redeemed thee"**; how constantly He reminds them that nothing but His immediate

strength gave them deliverance from Egypt! (3) in His call of them: **"I have called thee by thy name, thou are Mine."**

To call by name, in Scripture phraseology, is not simply to give a name to anyone, it conveys a tenderness that delights in the possession of the called: "He calleth His own sheep by name, and leadeth them out" (John 10:3). Hence the addition "thou are Mine." In 48:12 He speaks of them as "My called."

Creation, redemption, calling—these three, are all fulfilled for each one of us—"created in Christ Jesus," redeemed "through His blood," called "through His grace."

In *verse 1* the "fear not" is based upon the past facts of God's mercy; the repetition in *verse 5* is based upon the fact and comfort of His presence.

When circumstances tend to cause anxiety, and the threatening attitude of things might give rise to natural apprehensions, it is good, not only to recall the gracious dealings of our God, but to hear His reminders of what He has wrought on our behalf in the past, of His inalienable presence with us, and the unthwartable fulfillment of His promises, as in the present passage.

The first promise assures us that when we pass **"through the waters"** the Lord will be with us, and **"through the rivers, they will not overflow"** us (reminders of the Red Sea and the Jordan). Spiritually He has brought us out of Egypt and into Canaan, and His assurances that He will never leave us nor forsake us holds good amidst all that would overwhelm us.

The next promise assures us of preservation when we walk **"through the fire."** If water speaks of danger that springs from circumstances, fire speaks of that which arises from persecution, as in the case of the three youths in Nebuchadnezzar's furnace. Both forms enter in one way or another into the lives of God's people, but it is the design of the Lord to banish fear from our hearts, and to strengthen our faith, by all that is contained in the assurance **"I am the Lord thy God,"** titles which tell first of the majesty and grandeur of His infinite Being, and then of His almighty power *(v. 3)*.

The statement **"I have given Egypt as thy ransom, Ethiopia and Seba for thee"** is in the perfect tense, putting facts which were in the near future in Isaiah's time as already completed in the unalterable purposes of God. To Him, the timeless One, future events, alike with those in the past, are as real as those in the present. It was after the return of the Jews from captivity that God rewarded Cyrus the Persian monarch for liberating them, by permitting him and his son Cambyses to possess Egypt and the neighboring kingdoms. Seba was the large district between the White and the Blue Nile, contiguous to Ethiopia. The possession of these lands was not merely a gift, it was a ransom price (a *kopher,* or covering), the people on whose behalf payment was made being covered by it.

This remarkable prediction, which had its fulfillment in the reign of the Persian monarchs, was but the beginning of similar events that have followed and are yet to follow. This is declared in *verse 4,* where the Lord says **"I will give men for thee, and peoples for thy life"** (R.V.), words which point not only to already accomplished facts but to the establishment of the Millennial Kingdom, as the next verses show. But all this is based upon divine grace. In spite of all the failure of Israel the Lord regards them as precious in His sight, and honorable, and declares His immutable love for them.

Here we may see a comparison and a contrast in regard to ourselves. He views us as precious in His sight because we are "accepted in the Beloved"; the love which He has for us is of the same degree as the love which He has for His Son (John 17:23). The contrast lies in this, that, whereas earthly nations are given for Israel's life, the life which God gives us is to be devoted to the blessing of every nation in the work of the Gospel.

The assurances in *verses 5 and 6* are of peculiar interest in these times when the question of the Jews is occupying the attention of the world. What is taking place is surely preparatory to the fulfillment of the promises of God when Gentile nations in general (here represented by "the north" and "the south") will be compelled to restore His "sons and daughters." The phrase in *verse 7,* **"every one that is called by My Name,"** resumes the comforting message in verse 1. Identification in character with Himself, and possession by Him for the display of His glory and grace, are the two chief thoughts suggested.

The three statements at the end of verse 7 form a progress to a climax:

1. **"I have created him for My glory";** that expresses the thought of His power in bringing the nation into being;

2. **"I have formed him";** that points to the process of His transforming grace by which the one created is made to reflect His glory;

3. **"Yea, I have made him";** this points to the completion of the divine act. The verb rendered "I have made" signifies more than simply to make, it conveys the thought of bringing a work to perfection.

All this is true for every one of us, and expresses the wonders of God's counsels and power, and the riches of His grace. He who has (1) created us anew in Christ, (2) is transforming us by the operating power of His Holy Spirit, and (3) will perfect that which concerns us, at the coming of the Lord.

In *verse 8* the command, **"Bring forth the blind people that have eyes, and the deaf that have ears,"** is not issued with regard to bringing Israel out of captivity, but is a general summons to assemble to the place appointed for the vindication of the being, character, authority and decisions of God. The command is thus to be distinguished from the promise, "I will bring," in verse 5. God will indeed first restore His earthly people to their land, but after this the summons is both to His people and then to all the nations to attend for the purpose mentioned. Israel, no longer in blindness and deafness, are to have eyes to see and ears to hear, as was intimated in 42:18, 19, but *verse 9* states that the Gentile peoples (the word is plural and does not refer to Israel) are to be assembled.

Before the Gentiles can be enriched in Millennial fullness, they must be made to acknowledge the facts relating to the true God, in contrast to their idolatry, superstition, man-worship and rejection of the Divine claims. The challenge is issued to the nations to bring their witnesses, that they may be justified. But there will be no such possibility. The only alternative is **"let them hear, and say, It is truth."**

In *verse 10* the Lord declares that Israel are His "witnesses, and His servant whom He has chosen" (cp. 44:8). The nation has always been a witness to His existence, but will be

His combined witness and servant in a special way when restored.

Meanwhile He has taken us up in His sovereign grace and has made us His witnesses and servants, that we may declare His saving grace to the ends of the earth.

There is a special significance in the identification of Israel as God's servant with the Lord Jesus as similarly mentioned in chapter 42:1. They could never be His servant apart from their Messiah, and it is only as we realize our identification with Christ that we can be owned as His witnesses and fulfill our service worthily of Him.

God's challenge to the nations is to "bring" their witnesses that they may justify their acknowledgment of those who are no gods (v. 9). The A.V. "bring forth" does not adequately express the meaning. It is a case of bringing witnesses to a court of judgment. The Gentiles would do so only to be condemned. In contrast to this Jehovah makes the twofold declaration concerning His earthly people, **"Ye are My witnesses"** (vv. 10 and 12).

Connected with the first of these is their witness to the unoriginated and self-sustained nature of His Being. **"I am He"** is a declaration that He is God exclusively and eternally in the past and future. Since His Being has no beginning and no end, the idea that there could be any other being apart from His, possessed of the attributes of Deity, is self-contradictory: **"Before Me there was no God formed, neither shall there be after Me."** How futile, therefore, are the efforts of the heathen to demonstrate that the objects of their worship are true gods! And not only so, but how utterly doomed to failure will be the attempt of the Man of Sin to compel the combined nations under him to venerate him as God! The doom of that blasphemous arrogance will be sealed by the Son of God Himself.

The second declaration, that His earthly people are His witnesses, is put into connection with the facts, not only that He is the one and only God, the great Jehovah, but that He alone is the "Savior" (v. 11), and that, besides this, there is none that can deliver out of His hand (v. 13). He is not only the Eternal One but He is the Almighty One. **"I will work,"** He says, **"and who shall reverse it?"** (R.V. margin; A.V. "turn it back"). Not only can no

one hinder Him, but no one can change what He has established.

Since all this is so with regard to His earthly national witnesses, let us take courage and renew our strength, as those whom He has called to be His witnesses through the Gospel.

The *14th verse* begins a new section, extending to 44:5, the subjects being Avenging, Deliverance, and the Outpouring of the Spirit. The first of these has to do with the execution of divine judgments upon the Chaldeans, called down upon them by their maltreatment of God's people. For their sake, i.e., for the purpose of releasing them, He has **"sent to Babylon,"** that is to say, has sent there the agents of His judgments (cp. 13:3). The Chaldeans would be driven **"as fugitives . . . in the ships of their rejoicing"** (R.V.), thus overthrowing all their proud commercial enterprises. Ancient history makes known that they navigated both the Euphrates and the Persian Gulf, using vessels built by Phoenicians, both for commerce and war. The vessels of their navy, in which the Babylonians gloried, would be degraded into becoming the means of an escape.

In view of the deliverance of Israel, God gives them (in v. 15) a fourfold reminder concerning Himself: (1) He is Jehovah (the ever and self-existent One), the Name of His covenant relationship with His people and His "memorial unto all generations" (Ex. 3:15; Hos. 12:5); (2) **"your Holy One,"** a title here set in contrast both to their unholy departure from Him and to the unholy character of their pagan captors; (3) **"the Creator of Israel,"** the One who, having brought this nation into being, having formed them for His praise, and therefore sustaining them through all their grievous circumstances and vicissitudes, would not allow them to be in permanent rejection and bondage; (4) **"your King,"** a title set in contrast both to the deplorable condition of the kings of Judah and Israel, and to the eastern despot who had temporarily been permitted to reign over them, through their rejection of God's sovereign claims upon them.

The Lord assures them now that it is He who **"maketh a way in the sea and a path in the mighty waters"** (v. 16).

While this holds good for Israel, it is likewise true in the experiences of all His saints.

The waters of the nations "roar and are troubled," yet God has a path for His people through all this, a path not only of deliverance but of gospel witness, which will go on its way until its appointed end.

Verse 17 affords a reminder (appropriate to the present times) of the overruling power of God in regard to the armies of the nations. Whatever the hearts of potentates may devise, it is the Lord who **"bringeth forth the chariot and horse, the army and the power."** The calamities of war are "His judgments." By these means He designs to turn the hearts of men to repentance. He also has His national purposes to fulfill, and the day will come when the enemies of His earthly people will **"lie down together,"** and will be **"quenched as flax"** (i.e., as a wick).

Verse 18 is a command not to call to mind the former things. That does not mean that we are not to remember God's past mercies. These we are indeed to keep in memory. But here the subject is confined to what He is about to do *(v. 19).* He will **"do a new thing; now it shall spring forth"** (lit., "even now it sprouts up"). Contrasts 42:9, where a distinction was drawn between the former things which had to come to pass and new things which God was declaring. It was there said of the latter that they "were not yet sprouting up." His future mercies are brought before us as if they were already beginning. He will make a way in the wilderness, and rivers in the desert.

Let us apply these promises to our own experiences, and gather together the four phrases, designed for our comfort in times of trial and difficulty; (1) **"through the waters"**—they are themselves a means of giving us to experience the presence of the Lord, *verse 2;* (2) **"through the fire"**—we are assured of preservation, *verse 2;* (3) **"in the sea," and "in the mighty waters,"** *verse 16*—here God provides a way; troublesome conditions are a means of giving us to realize the guidance of God; (4) **"in the wilderness" and "in the desert,"** *verse 19*—guidance and refreshment are our portion there. If the waters speak of overwhelming trials, the wilderness and the desert speak of the condition of the world around us, with which if we are unduly occupied we shall suffer spiritual depression. But God has a way amidst

such conditions, a path of fellowship with Him, a path of joy and fruitfulness.

God promises to do **"a new thing."** The whole earth is to be blessed when God's earthly people enjoy the blessings of His redemptive work. This subject is continued in *verses 20 and 21.* The termination of the sufferings of Israel will involve the termination of the sufferings of creation. Because God will give waters in the wilderness and rivers in the desert for His people, **"the beasts of the field,"** He says, **"shall honor Me, the jackals and ostriches"** (see the R.V. and A.V. marg). Contrast what is said of these animals in 13:21, 22. God's care for animals (about which the Lord Himself spoke when on earth) has already been stated in 11:6–9; 30:23, 24; 35:7 (see also 65:25).

But these blessings are not to be granted merely for the welfare of the animal world and of humanity. The paramount object is the honor of God Himself. The animals, in their unconscious enjoyment of Millennial bliss, will thereby give "honor" to God, and as to Israel, He speaks thus: **"My people, My chosen, the people which I formed for Myself, that they might set forth My praise"** (R.V., *v. 21*). What a change from their present condition! How greatly the Lord Himself must look forward to the coming day!

This purpose is exactly what is designed for us in this present period, whom God has called "out of darkness into His marvelous light," that we may "show forth His praises" (1 Pet. 2:9; R.V. "excellencies," or, what is more commonly the meaning of the word, "virtues," as the A.V. margin). Virtue is moral excellence. When used of God it is more comprehensive, and stands for all His attributes, His power, His grace, and all that has been exhibited in the Person of His Son. The conduct of our life and our whole activity are to be devoted to this highest of all objects.

There can scarcely be found any more striking contrast in the Old Testament than that between the remonstrance uttered by God in *verses 22–24* and the grace and mercy that follow in *verses 25, 26.* The former part records the iniquities of Israel both negative and positive, five negative and three positive. Instead of calling upon the Lord they had become weary of Him. Instead of presenting their offerings to Him they have "made Him to serve with their sins and wearied Him with their iniquities."

The phrase **"thou hast made Me to serve"** is very significant. The verb thus rendered denotes to impose servile labor upon a person. *Verse 23* says that God had imposed no such servile labor upon them, but their sins weighed heavily upon Him, as a burden does upon a servant.

Our minds instinctively turn to the Cross. At what a cost the Lord undertook the burden of human guilt! We shall never know how heavily it weighed upon God the Father to spare not His own Son but deliver Him up for us.

In the light of this we can the better understand the contrast in *verse 25;* **"I, even I, am He that blotteth out thy transgressions for Mine own sake, and I will not remember thy sins."** This is love manifested, not at the expense of divine holiness and justice, but on the very ground of it.

"For Mine own sake"—that expresses the free grace by which our sins are removed, for there is nothing in the sinner which merits it. By the sovereign act of God's grace in the death of Christ His justice dealt with sin; His grace and love blot it out.

When the Lord calls upon Israel in *verse 26,* saying **"Put Me in remembrance; let us plead together; set thou forth thy cause, that thou mayest be justified,"** He is summoning them to remind Him, if they can, of any merit on their part whereby they might be justified. He had just stated that He, and He alone, could and would blot out their transgressions and clear them of guilt, and further that, such had been their guilt, He would do it not for their sakes but for His own. Acquittal must be by grace alone. If they think otherwise let them state their case (as in a court of justice) and set forth their cause, as against His.

Immediately He shows the impossibility of their success. Their first father had sinned, their teachers had transgressed against Him. They were **sinners** from the beginning and throughout their history, and, in view of their persistent impenitence, judgment was inevitable: **"I will profane,"** He says, **"the princes of the sanctuary, and I will make Jacob a curse and Israel a reviling"** *(v. 28).*

So verse 25 is not simply a sweet promise; it is part of an argument. It anticipates what is set forth in Romans in regard to the Gospel, namely, that man has no merit, that justification is by grace, and that it is conditional upon repentance and faith (though there is, of course, a distinction between God's dealings with Israel and those now relating to the Gospel). These O.T. foreshadowings deepen our understanding of the ways of God with men.

Chapter 44

The unbounded grace of God is marvelously demonstrated in the opening part of this chapter. Reproof and remonstrance in chapter 43 are immediately followed by assurance and promise, based upon His predetermined counsel and creative acts regarding the nation. In wrath He remembers mercy.

The Lord recalled His gracious utterances at the beginning of chapter 43, with the added fact that Israel is His "chosen." In the two passages He uses the same three words as in the record of His creation of man, "created" (Gen. 1:27), "made" ("make," Gen. 1:16), "formed" (Gen 2:7), but now with reference to the birth of the nation. All this makes His purpose and His pledge to Jacob unalterable, despite the gross apostasy of His people. He even calls them "Jeshurun" (a Hebrew word meaning "upright"; the Sept. translates it "beloved"), an appellation previously assigned through Moses (Deut. 32:15; 33:5, 26), and anticipative of Israel's future condition of righteousness *(vv. 1, 3).*

Divine delight breathes through the promises that follow: the thirsty are to be satisfied, the seed of Jacob to be blessed by the outpouring of the Spirit, with resulting national and spiritual fertility *(vv. 3, 4).* The time is near. Grace will triumph.

This was written for our present comfort too. Let us walk as God's Jeshurun and "be filled with the Spirit."

Verse 5 is a prediction of the effects upon Gentiles of Israel's restoration. The threefold statement is to be read in the light of Psalm 87:4, 5, where Rahab (i.e., Egypt), Babylon, Philistia, Tyre and Ethiopia are mentioned as coming in for the privilege of knowing God, and one and another are to be noted as having been born in Zion.

Among the Gentiles in Millennial blessing one will declare himself as belonging to Jehovah; another will "call himself by" (or rather, "will solemnly name") the name of Jacob, i.e., will make it the object of a solemn exclamation; another will declare in handwriting (not, as in the margin, "write on his hand") "unto Jehovah," witnessing that he belongs to Jehovah alone; he will add the name of Israel as a name of high honor, a twofold joyous attestation. As Romans 11:12 says, "the fullness of Israel" will be still more "the riches of the Gentiles," than even is the case with the present effects of the gospel.

There is a striking parallel between this verse in Isaiah and the results of the gospel we preach. Just as in the coming day a Gentile will own that he belongs to Jehovah, so the convert today learns to acknowledge that he is the Lord's possession (1 Cor. 3:23; Gal. 3:29); so also does he name "the Name of the Lord" (2 Tim. 2:29, R.V.: cp. 1 Pet. 4:16, R.V.).

In *verse 6* the Lord renews for the third time His pledge of redemption, by His title of Redeemer (see 41:14; 43:14), and introduces another remonstrance against the evil and folly of idolatry by a series of further declarations concerning Himself: He says **"I am the first, and I am the last."** This title, claimed by God three times in Isaiah, here, in 41:4 and 48:12, and by Christ three times, in Revelation 1:17; 2:8; 22:13, indicates Their oneness in the Godhead, Their eternal preexistence and Their absolute supremacy. It predicates that all creatures animate and inanimate owe their existence to Them, and that the beginning, course and issue of all circumstances are under Their supreme control. Israel may therefore rest assured that all the divine promises and pledges will be fulfilled by Him who is their "King," their "Redeemer, Jehovah of Hosts."

He who has redeemed us by His blood is "the First and the Last" in all our circumstances and experiences. He who gave us being, who was the Beginner of our new life in Christ, will be with us as the Fulfiller of His purposes in and through us now and forever. In the commencement, the course and the completion of any circumstance in our life, as, for instance, in the case of our special service

for Him, He is "the First and the Last." He was the Beginner of our service, as the One who called us to it, and, when it is finished, the completion will be His by His Holy Spirit. Has He not said "I will never leave thee nor forsake thee"? Well may we rely upon His grace and power and love.

In *verses 7 and 8* the Lord repeats to a large extent what He said in 41:22, 23 and 43:9, 10. Here again He issues His challenge as to who can proclaim (that is the meaning of the word "call," see the R.V. margin) and declare things as He does, setting them all in order. This He Himself has done since He appointed **"the ancient people."** He has raised up prophets among them, making known **"the things that are coming."** Note the two predictive phrases, (1) **"the things that are coming,"** that is, future things, (2) things **"that shall come to pass,"** that is, things that are approaching, which are more immediately at hand. What other nation could produce prophets like that? What other nation had been so dealt with by God? Let the gods and the prophets of Gentile peoples declare such things. The prophecies uttered by Jehovah reach back to the beginning of human history. In the two preceding passages the challenge was as to the possibility of declaring or unfolding former things (what scorn this pours upon the philosophies of skeptics and propagandists of mere scientific theories!). Here stress is upon matters of the future, not upon former things.

Seeing that none of the heathen gods could answer such challenges, well might Israel be freed from fear and be confident that God, beside whom there is no other (*v. 6*), would, and will, certainly accomplish what He has foretold; and since this is made good in the history of His people, they, in contrast to the prognosticators of the nations, are His witnesses. The utmost ferocity and antagonism of Satan and his hosts, and of all human foes, can never prevent Israel from being His witnesses, witnesses to His own Being and the unthwartable character of His counsels. **"Is there a God beside Me?"** He says, **"yea, there is no Rock; I know not any."** The R.V. rightly has "Rock" (see the A.V. margin), and this is appropriate to the comforting exhortation, "Fear ye not, neither be afraid," appropriate also to the declaration of His own character.

The Rock is representative of immovability, strength and protection. Let us whom He has raised up to be His witnesses take comfort in this. Things around us are in a state of upheaval and uncertainty. The earth (i.e., its inhabitants) is changing, and the mountains of many governments are falling into the seas of revolution and disturbance. Let us, therefore, renew our confidence in our God and take courage to bear witness boldly and steadfastly for Him.

Verses 9 to 20 contain the most striking of all the divine remonstrances against the makers of idols. In contrast to Israel as God's witnesses, the idols are **"their own witnesses"** (*v. 9*, R.V.). From that point onward withering scorn is poured upon the blindness and grotesque folly of the framers thereof. All this was a remonstrance against Israel, who had turned from their own Maker to fall into the degradation of the heathen about them.

In *verse 21* the Lord calls upon His people to bear these things in mind, basing His admonition upon the facts that they owed their very existence as a nation to His supernatural operation, and that as His people they were His "servant"—a direct contrast to the idolatrous slaves to the stock of a tree.

And now the yearning heart of the Lord breaks forth in accents of infinite grace. His people would not be forgotten of Him. He had blotted out as a thick cloud their transgressions and as a cloud their sins. Let them return to Him, in view of the fact that He had redeemed them (*v. 22*).

There is a striking element of gospel grace in this, grace that manifests itself even before conversion. But what is set immediately before us is God's gracious desire toward us as His servants, in order that fellowship with Him may be constantly maintained, for the joy of His own heart, and for the efficiency of our witness for Him and of the service we render.

In the assurance of *verse 22*, the word rendered **"I have blotted out"** is used of blotting out (*a*) a name, whether from a book or otherwise, Exodus 32:32, 33; Deuteronomy 9:14; 29:20; 2 Kings 14:27; Psalm 69:28; 109:13; (*b*) curses, with the water of bitterness, Numbers 5:23; (*c*) the remembrance of a people, Deuteronomy 25:19; (*d*) sin or sins,

Nehemiah 4:5; Psalm 51:1, 9; 109:14; Jeremiah 18:23; Isaiah 43:25, and here.

As to (*d*), whatever the particular metaphor may be, whether of a stain or a debt from a ledger, or, as in this verse, accompanied by the simile of the removal of a dense mist (**"a thick cloud"**) or any such element ("a cloud"), transgression and sin are vividly depicted as separating man from God and preventing that holy and blessed intercourse which delights His heart and that of His redeemed. Only the cleansing of His wind (Job 37:21) and the sunshine of His grace can dispel the cloud. All removal of guilt has been made possible actually and only by the blood of Christ, whose sacrifice underlies the descriptive language of the assurance here given.

Here the subject is that of restoration, the renewal of communion: **"return unto Me."** Here the reason assigned is that of His redeeming mercy; in 43:25 the reason for the blotting out was **"for Mine own sake,"** the vindication of His attributes and character.

Verses 21 and 22 contain most cheering assurances of past redemption, a promise of remembrance in the future, and an invitation to return to fellowship with God in the present. And now, in view of the glorious and assured issues of all this, the whole creation is called upon to exult and **"break forth into singing"** (*v. 23*). "The creation itself also shall be delivered from the bondage of corruption into the liberty of the glory of the children of God" (Rom. 8:21, R.V.); i.e., liberty will be characteristic of the glory, and creation will have full scope for the exercise of the powers imparted to it by God.

Here the essence of the glory to be enjoyed by the nations lies in this, that Jehovah **"will glorify Himself"** in Israel (R.V.). For Israel's Redeemer, who formed His earthly people from their earliest existence, is He **"that maketh all things; that stretcheth forth** (or "extendeth," the same word as in 40:22, where the figure is that of stretching a curtain) **the heavens alone; that spreadeth abroad** [the same word as in Ps. 136:6, "spread forth," R.V., and Is. 42:5] **the earth by Himself** (*v. 24*).

Verse 25 refers to the Chaldean soothsayers (cp. 47:9). It reminds us, too, of 1 Corinthians 1:20. *Verse 26* is strikingly paralleled in 1 Corinthians 1:21, 22. God turns worldly wisdom into foolishness, and **"confirmeth the word of His servant and performeth the counsel of His messengers."**

Let us, to whom is committed the message of the gospel, take fresh courage in this. Amidst religious superstition and varied antagonism, we know that "His word will not return unto Him void." Be it ours to preach "Christ, and Him crucified" faithfully, perseveringly and devotedly. He will confirm the word "with signs following."

As to the primary application of the phrase "His servant" *(v. 26)*, that Israel is in view seems clear from verse 21, but now as represented (according to the confirmatory statement which follows) by "His messengers." That is to say, Israel here stands for the faithful prophets, the Lord's spokesmen in the nation. His promises given through them would be fulfilled, of the restoration from captivity, the rebuilding of Jerusalem and the temple, under the decree of Cyrus, and of the drying up of "the deep" and "the rivers" of Babylon (literally accomplished by Cyrus, in respect of the Euphrates, and figuratively portending the destruction of the power of Babylon), *v. 27*.

Rightly we who are messengers of the Gospel may apply to ourselves and our ministry the truth of the words "that confirmeth the word of His servant, and performeth the counsel of His messengers." So it was with the first heralds of the Gospel, "the Lord working with them, and confirming the word by the signs that followed" (Mark 16:20). Our work is essentially the Lord's; it is ours only in a secondary sense. The word spoken is to be derived from Him. His servant is His mouthpiece. The counsel we take is imparted by Him if our fellowship is really with Him and with His Son Jesus Christ. "It is God which worketh in you both to will (according to His "counsel") and to work (according to His "word") for His good pleasure" (Phil. 2:13, R.V.).

Chapter 45

The forty-fifth chapter begins with a second word from the Lord as to Cyrus. The first, at the end of chapter forty-four, was an utterance about him; now the Lord addresses him personally. The titles assigned to him and the provision made for him are unique. Such things were never said of or to another Gentile monarch. He is called the Lord's "anointed" as well as "My shepherd." Jehovah had called him by his name, and surnamed him; the former refers to his actual name (a Persian designation of the sun: cp. vv. 6, 7); the surnaming refers to the two titles now given him as already mentioned.

By his conquests nations would be subdued and made to recognize the Person and claims of Jehovah *(v. 6)*. Before him the doors would be opened. The Lord would go before him, making the **"rugged places plain"** (cp. 40:4). He would be given the treasures of darkness (his conquest made him immensely rich; he obtained over £126,000,000 worth). And all this because he was the deliverer of Israel, releasing the Jews from captivity and restoring the remnant.

In *verse 5* the Lord reaffirms to Cyrus that He is Jehovah, and that He girded, or equipped, him when he knew Him not. Such are the predetermined counsels of God, unthwartably carried into action at their appointed times.

The object for which the title was made known to the Gentile potentate was that people might know Him as Jehovah, the only true God, **"from the rising of the sun, and from the west"** *(v. 6)*, i.e., the whole habitable world. Cyrus' restoration of the Jews was designed to secure this. That restoration had a preparatory part in leading to the proclamation of a worldwide Gospel in these times.

When the Lord says, in *verse 7*, **"I form the light, and create darkness; I make peace, and create evil,"** His words are to be understood in the light of the context. He is speaking to Cyrus, whom He had appointed and empowered **"to subdue nations"** and to give deliverance to His earthly people.

The Persians believed in two coexistent principles virtually regarded as gods. The one, Ormuzd, good, symbolized by light, the other, Ahriman, evil, symbolized by darkness, both eternally in conflict, the world being the theater. Hence the present declaration by God addressed to Cyrus. Accordingly, the immediate reference is not to the evil of sin, which God did not create, but to the judgments of war with its consequent calamities, which, for instance, Cyrus was appointed to inflict upon Gentile powers, and to the peace which he, as

God's chosen instrument, would bestow upon Israel.

In *verse 8* the statement regarding peace is expanded in the assurance of blessing hereafter, when the skies will **"pour down righteousness,"** and salvation and righteousness **"will spring up together."**

At the *9th verse* the word of the Lord is addressed to those in Israel who were criticizing the ways of God (the message to Cyrus having been finished). The opening remonstrance should read as in the R.V. (the italicized words in the A.V. weaken the meaning). **"Woe unto him,"** says the Lord, **"that striveth with his Maker! A potsherd among the potsherds of the earth!"** He who complains of God is but a poor perishable vessel among others of the same sort. The word rendered "potsherd" signifies here the whole vessel, as in Proverbs 26:23 (R.V. "an earthen vessel overlaid with silver dross") and Jeremiah 19:1, where the same word is used.

Then follows the absurdity of a clay pot challenging its fashioner as to what he is making, and sneering at him as if he had no hands. The faultfinders had better leave the matters of His people in His competent hands. He had **"made the earth and created man upon it"** *(v. 12).* His hands had **"stretched out the heavens"** and **"commanded all their host."** Let the grumblers therefore drop their complaints and realize that everything depends absolutely upon God. He had raised up Cyrus in righteousness and would **"make straight all his ways,"** so that he could build God's city and let His exiles go free, and that without expecting price or reward. Such was the mighty work of the Spirit of God upon the heart of the eastern monarch *(v. 13).*

We have in this Scripture a passage, which, while establishing our hearts in the realization that everything is under the entire control of the Maker of Heaven and earth, and His purposes among the nations are unthwartable, may also be useful in our help to those who wonder if, after all, God is stronger than His foes, and will yet bring deliverance.

In *verse 14* the Lord's message passes from the immediate future relating to Cyrus to the then distant prospect of what will be accomplished in the coming day of Israel's restoration. This double view is a frequent feature of Old Testament prophecies, either in successive passages, as here, or in the same pronouncement.

Gentile nations will submit themselves to Israel, abandoning their idolatry, and Israel will be saved forever (verses 14–17). **"The labor** [i.e., the products] **of Egypt, and the merchandise** [i.e., the riches from trading] **of Ethiopia, and the Sabeans** [the men themselves, R.V.—a race in Upper Egypt], **with their prowess and strength, shall come over unto thee,"** i.e., will voluntarily surrender (cp. the same three in 43:3). How fully they will do so is shown in the five statements which follow. And what will lie behind it all will be their recognition of the presence of God among His people, **"Surely God is in thee; and there is none else, there is no God** [i.e., no other]."

The lesson for us in this is contained in the parallel in 1 Corinthians 14:25, where it is probable that the apostle had these words in Isaiah in mind. What will be true of Israel in the day to come is the will of the Lord for us now. The purpose of our testimony is edification, or building up. It is God's good pleasure for us to attract the souls of the ignorant and unconverted to Christ. The Spirit of God designs to operate in and through us collectively, that such may realize the presence of the Lord and become true worshipers.

In the *15th verse* Israel is the speaker, and not the Gentiles, as in the preceding verse. This verse is not a continuation of the future acknowledgment by the Gentile nations. To understand this verse we must observe that the statement **"Thou art a God that hidest Thyself"** is not a mournful utterance as if they thought that God had turned away His face from them in anger (as in 57:17). The meaning is that God is mysterious in His dealings and guides the affairs of nations in a way contrary to natural expectations and in a manner impossible to be discerned by mere human intelligence. Israel will be utterly astonished to find nations who have walked in heathen darkness and in alienation making supplication to them, acknowledging that God is among them and recognizing that He is the only God. It is as if they will say "Truly Thou hast acted in a marvelous way, passing our utmost comprehension." That is why they will address God as "Savior." He will be seen to be the Savior of the Gentiles as well as Israel universally in the establishment of the Millennial Kingdom.

This reminds us of the apostle's outburst of marvel at the depth of the riches of God's wisdom and knowledge, the unsearchable character of His judgments and the untraceable nature of His ways (Rom. 11:33). The theme of universal blessing is the same in both passages.

Have there not been times in our experience when, owing to circumstances of extreme disappointment and trial, God has seemed to hide His face? However dark our path may be from the earthly point of view, it can be ours so to live as to enjoy the light of His countenance and the smile of His approval, and all as a result of the work of grace accomplished for us on the Cross.

After this parenthetic verse 15 there follows a contrast between the doom of idol-makers and the unending blessedness of Israel. The former shall be ashamed, confounded and **"go into confusion,"** but Israel, **"saved with an everlasting salvation,"** shall **"not be ashamed nor confounded"** to everlasting ages *(v. 16)*. The restored nation will never apostatize again, and so will never know captivity and penal judgment.

The phrase **"world without end"** is not a happy rendering. Corresponding to that in the original (lit., "for ages") is the New Testament phrase rightly rendered "forever" (e.g., Rom. 11:36, lit., "unto the ages"). The literalizing of this and similar phrases is to be avoided.

The *17th verse* brings to a close this section (which began at 44:6) and brings to a consummation the prophecies therein contained giving promise of deliverance, glory and rejoicing to Israel. It gathers up much that has preceded. And firstly by way of the reaffirmation of God as the Creator of heaven and earth, and as being the only true God. The 18th verse first introduces God as the Speaker and then gives His own words: **"For thus saith the Lord that created the heavens; He is God** [the correct R.V. should be noted; it declares His absolute and exclusive Deity] **that formed** [the same word as in 37:26; 43:7, 21; 44:10, 21] **the earth and made it** [same word as in 37:16; 41:4; 43:7; the two words convey respectively the ideas of fashioning and finishing]; **He established it** [a word combining the ideas of establishing and maintaining]; **He created it not a waste** [a *tohu*, i.e., not as a desert or desolate place; the same word as in Gen. 1:2, R.V., "waste"], **He formed it to be inhabited."** The earth was not formed for its own sake. God had the creation of man in view.

What follows, to the end of the chapter, is again in the Lord's own words; He begins by confirming what had just been stated as to His exclusive Deity, making, however, the change from "He is God" to **"I am Jehovah,"** and adding "and there is none else" (cp. 44:8). **"I have not spoken in secret,"** He says, **"in a place of the land of darkness"**; that is to say, His utterances are not like those of soothsayers, nor do they issue from the lower regions, like the mutterings of spiritists and necromancers. **"I said not unto the seed of Jacob, Seek ye Me in vain."** The word rendered "in vain" is *tohu*, the same as in *verse 18* (R.V., "a waste"). Hence the meaning is that God did not say "Seek ye Me in a desert," i.e., without the prospect of deriving any benefit from the search. On the contrary He "speaks righteousness."

He gives promises to those who seek Him, which are fulfilled consistently with His righteous character; "He declares things that are right"; that is to say, His word is sure, and the blessing promised to His earthly people will verily be granted in His appointed time. See the New Testament parallel to this in 2 Corinthians 1:20; "For how many soever be the promises of God, in Him is the Yea: wherefore also through Him is the Amen, unto the glory of God through us."

Now again, just as in *verses 14–17*, the restoration of Israel will be followed by the enlightenment and deliverance of the Gentile nations. The Lord, having renewed His assurance to Israel, addresses a summons to those Gentiles who have escaped from the judgments upon the world and are brought into the blessing of the Millennial Kingdom. **"Assemble yourselves,"** He says, **"and come; draw near together, ye that are escaped of the nations."** None of these will have been worshipers of the Beast, for all such will be removed from the earth by Divine judgment through angelic ministry (Rev. 14:9–11; cp. Matt. 13:49).

In view of this the protest against their idolatry is renewed *(v. 20, as in v. 16)*, as also is the challenge issued to erstwhile idolaters to do what God alone can do, foretell the future (cp. 41:22, 26; 43:9; v. 21). Jehovah alone has done this, and now, declaring the salvation He is about to impart to the whole world, He says **"And there is no God else beside Me; a just God and a Savior; there is none beside Me."** This repeated statement stresses its tremendous import in view of the circumstances. Now follows the commanding invitation, **"Look unto Me, and be ye saved, all the ends of the earth,"** and a third time He declares **"for I am God, and there is none else"** (v. 22).

Deliverance from the period of Divine wrath upon the world (which will be coincidental with the great tribulation) and from pagan idolatry, will be followed by the worldwide acknowledgment of God. The prophecy of this is introduced by a Divine oath by which God, swearing by Himself, pledges the unthwartable accomplishment of His purpose: **"By Myself have I sworn, the word is gone forth from My mouth in** [or "of"; see R.V. margin] **righteousness** [cp. v. 19], **and shall not return, that unto Me every knee shall bow, every tongue shall swear"** (v. 23). This, which speaks of earthly Millennial conditions, is quoted (from the Septuagint Version) in Romans 14:11, which there, though of universal application, is used to refer to the fact that all believers will stand before the Judgment Seat of Christ. In the Romans passage the Divine oath is put in the form "as I live" (cp. Num. 14:21, 28; Deut. 32:40, R.V.), expressing God's power and authority. The bowing of the knee signifies the recognition of, and subjection to, the Lord's authority; the confession of the tongue indicates the acknowledgment of the inerrancy and rightfulness of His judgment.

After God's word has gone forth it never returns without fulfilling its purpose; that is the meaning of "shall not return" (see the extended assurance in 55:11).

The R.V. of *verse 24* is important. The bending of the knee and acknowledgment of the name of Jehovah in homage to God will be voluntary in the Millennial day: **"Only in the Lord, shall one say unto** [or "of"] **Me, is righteousness and strength"** [lit., "fullness of righteousness," i.e., righteousness completely fulfilled]. The foes of God will be compelled to bow (see Phil. 2:10, "things under the earth"), but that is not in view in this passage. "In the Lord" signifies voluntary acceptance and recognition of Jehovah in all His attributes, power and dealings. There is repeated emphasis on God's righteousness as the basis of His dealings—**"a just God and a Savior"**; in *verse 21,* righteousness and salvation; here righteousness and strength. Strength comes to us only as we walk in righteousness before Him.

Men will come to Him from every part of the world: antagonists will be put to shame. The seed of Israel will be justified (made righteous), not by works of the Law but "in the Lord," in a joyous acknowledgment of their Messiah by virtue of their relationship to Him. In Him they "shall glory," not in their superiority and prowess. And Israel will have a spiritual seed, all being justified on the ground of the atoning sacrifice of Calvary. That which is now being wrought out among Jew and Gentile in this day of gospel grace for the formation of the Church, will have its counterpart in the redeemed on earth in the Millennial Kingdom.

Chapter 46
Introductory Note

At this chapter there is a change in the subject. There are now three prophecies relating to Babylon. Yet there is a connection with what has preceded. For the prophet has been foretelling what was to be expected by Israel through the raising up and the administration of Cyrus. He is now going to show what Cyrus will carry out regarding Babylon. This potentate would be the instrument of the judgment of the Lord upon the gods of Babylon. At the same time the three prophecies contain matters relating to what is yet future in connection with Israel, and admonitions continue to God's people. The first prophecy occupies this chapter; the second is in chapter 47, the third in chapter 48. The first deals with the gods, the second with Babylon itself, the third with deliverance from Babylon.

Bel was the Jupiter of the Babylonians and was their tutelar deity. Nebo corresponded to the Roman Mercury and was the tutelar deity of the later Chaldean royal household.

Bel would "fall headlong"; Nebo would stoop till he shared the same fate. Instead of being carried in procession, their images would be a burden to the "beasts" (camels, dromedaries and elephants), and "cattle" (horses, oxen and asses). But even so the burdens would not arrive at their destination, they would not be delivered; in their flight from the conqueror they would be overtaken, and go into captivity (vv. 1, 2).

The rest of chapter 46 consists of three admonitions: the first is to all Israel (vv. 3–7); the second to apostates in the nation, associates with idolaters (vv. 8–11); the third to the rebellious (vv. 12, 13). The first and third are a call to "hearken," the second to "remember." God desires the ready ear to hear, the ready mind to recollect.

In the first admonition His people are reminded of their unique origin and support. Divinely formed as the seed of Abraham, they had been borne and cared for from their earliest existence onward. So much for the past. As to the future, He, the unchanging One ("I am He"), promises to bear them on His shoulder (a contrast to the Chaldean burdens in vv. 1 and 2), and to carry old age and hoar hairs, a figurative way of assuring the remnant that throughout their experiences His care would never fail them.

The statement in verse 4, "I have made" (or rather, "I have done it"), speaks not so much of His creative power, as of the fact that He has acted in the past so will He in the future. He is "the great, unchangeable I AM."

In accordance with this He immediately asks to whom they will liken and compare Him, putting another god side by side with Him so that they may be equal. Let them consider, and contrast the egregious and crass absurdity of fashioning, worshiping and appealing to images (vv. 6, 7).

The second admonition begins with a call, based upon the preceding, to those who are turning to idolatry, "to shew themselves men," i.e., to be firm instead of faltering. Let them call to mind "the former things," the great truths relating to His Person and His dealings of old in the history of the nation, His absolute Deity, evoking adoration, His sole power to declare "the end from the beginning, and from ancient times things that are not yet done" (v. 10; cp. 41:22, 26;

44:7; 45:21). He alone can say "My counsel shall stand, and I will do all My pleasure."

It is good for the believer to call to mind the former things, to remember the way the Lord has led and helped and delivered. It stirs the soul to renewed praise, and stimulates faith and hope as to the future.

In verse 11 this power to predict with absolute inerrancy is again illustrated in regard to Cyrus, as in 41:2–4. He is called the "the ravenous bird from the east" (Persia), "the man of My counsel from a far country" (Media, as in 13:5, 17). The potentates of earth, summoned on to the arena of history, are God's instruments to fulfill His counsel, whether for judgment or for deliverance; and Cyrus combined the two, judgment on Gentile nations, deliverance for the captives of Israel.

God's words are duly carried into action: "I have spoken, I will also bring it to pass"; so with His purposes: "I have purposed, I will also do it."

The third admonition addresses those who resist God's will in their ignorant obduracy. They are the "stouthearted," not courageous, but stiffnecked. They are "far from righteousness"; their unbelief has produced despair of the fulfillment of God's word, and banished desire for knowledge of it. Consequently they are without the salvation He grants on the basis of righteousness (v. 12).

There is, however, promise of salvation for those who accept His conditions. "I bring near," He says, "My righteousness it shall not be far off, and My salvation shall not tarry" (v. 13; cp. Deut. 30:13, with Rom. 10:6–10, which quotes from the Septuagint with certain modifications, and speaks of the same subjects of righteousness and salvation as in this Isaiah passage).

On the basis of His righteousness, established for Israel, as for us, on the ground of the death of Christ, God will "place [or give] salvation in Zion for Israel My glory," or "My glory to Israel" (R.V. margin). The glory of God which has departed from the nation (cp. Ezek. 9:3 and 11:23) will return to it, and that in full measure, so that Israel, shining in the divine splendor, will worthily reflect His glory.

Chapter 47

The 46th chapter pronounced judgment upon the gods of Babylon, the 47th declares the doom of Babylon itself. Her pride would be humbled in the dust. For the phrase **"sit on the ground,"** see 3:26. She had been noted for her luxury and debauchery, and called **"tender and delicate"** *(v. 1)*. Now she who was mistress must do the menial work of grinding at the mill. As a prisoner of war she would be compelled to abandon modesty and wade through her rivers.

All this Babylon would bring upon herself through her treatment of God's people. He is their "Redeemer," the Conqueror of their foes. He is **"Jehovah of hosts,"** possessed of absolute authority. He is "the Holy One of Israel," signifying their character as it should be in relation to Himself, and the unholy character of their oppressors *(v. 4)*.

Babylon had been looked upon as an Empress, "the lady of kingdoms" (the king of Babylon called himself "king of kings," Ezek. 26:7; cp. Dan. 2:37). Now she must go into darkness, hiding herself for shame. When the Lord used her as His instrument for the chastisement of His people *(v. 6)*, she exceeded her authority, mercilessly treating the aged and helpless.

This has been the case with all the potentates who have been permitted to occupy the land of Palestine and hold His people in captivity, and the same thing will obtain in regard to the Antichrist in the future.

Verses 8–10 depict further the character of the guilty city, her voluptuousness, her self-exaltation, as well as her self-deification in adopting the title **"I AM,"** which alone belongs to God, her false sense of security, her sorceries and enchantments (astrology had its origin in Babylonia), her seared conscience in declaring that no eye saw her wickedness, and so virtually denying the existence and omnipresence of God. Possessed of natural wisdom and knowledge, she had used these to pervert her ways.

Hence evil would come upon her, of which she would not **"know the dawning"** *(v. 11, R.V.)*, or rather, as in the margin, "know how

to charm away." Mischief would fall upon her which she could not expiate (see A.V. margin).

Enchantments and sorceries had been practiced there "from her youth" *(v. 12)*, i.e., from the time of the reestablishment of Babel by Nimrod (Gen. 10:10, which is historically subsequent to 11:9).* The practice of the black art would not deliver her from her doom. Her traffickers would wander each in his own way *(v. 15,* R.V. margin; cp. Rev. 18); they would flee to their own localities, leaving Babylon to its doom.

Chapter 48

This chapter is addressed especially to the Judaean captives who have **"Come forth (or** flowed) **out of the waters of Judah"**; that is, they had their source in Judah. They make great profession, but their ways do not conform thereto. They swear by the Name of Jehovah, and extol Him as the God of Israel, but **"not in truth, nor in righteousness." "They call themselves of the holy city,"** but its holiness placed them under an obligation to be holy themselves. They profess to rely upon God; but His name was **"the Lord of Sabaoth,"** a Name demanding reverence and submission, not external religion *(vv. 1, 2)*.

Now comes a renewal regarding God's sole power to predict with inerrancy. But there is a difference from similar previous statements. Those in 41:22; 42:9; 43:9 were contrasted with pagan idols and idolaters. That in 46:9, 10 was in contrast to Israelitic idolaters, but had special reference to Cyrus. Here *verses 3 to 5* speak of the Divine predictions of the apostasy and obstinacy of Israel. Further, the Lord would show them things which He was now creating, not those of long ago, though all were foreknown by Him, as were their treacherous dealings; they were transgressors from their earliest days *(vv. 6–8)*.

But the **"new things"** of *verse 6* include Israel's redemption. Had they their desert they would be cut off entirely. His mercy is ever consistent with His character; accordingly He says **"For My Name's sake** [His Name expresses His nature] **will I defer Mine anger, and for My praise will I re-**

---

*See Hislops's "Two Babylons."

frain for [i.e., hold back toward] **thee, that I cut thee not off"** *(v. 9).*

This dire captivity, like the coming time of their great tribulation, and like their present bitter experiences, constitute a refining process: **"Behold, I have refined thee** [this looks to the issue], **but not as silver** [the smelting was a higher character]; **I have chosen thee in the furnace of affliction"** *(v. 10).* The primary meaning of the verb rendered "I **have chosen**" is to prove with the object of approving, and hence the meaning of choice—not chosen for the purpose of affliction, but chosen in it with a view to approval as a result of it (some would render it "I have proved thee").

This is the gracious design of the Lord in our trials and afflictions. This will enable us to appreciate, and praise Him for, His grace and love therein, and will keep us from despondency. He only designs "our dross to consume, and our gold to refine" (see Zech. 13:9 and cp. 1 Pet. 1:7). This will have an end and a blessed issue, and will be accomplished for His own glory: **"For Mine own sake, for Mine own sake** [the repetition stresses the solemn importance of the fact], **will I do it** [i.e., bring about salvation]; **for how should My Name be profaned? and My glory will I not give to another"** *(v. 11).* The adversaries of the Lord and His people will never be afforded a ground for scoffing at God and His doings. His ways and acts constitute His glory, and this will never be relinquished.

A second time His people are called to hearken (see *v. 1* and, for the third and fourth, *vv. 14, 16*); and now for the following reasons: (1) *His absolute Deity*—**"I am He** (cp. 43:10); **I am the first, I also am the last"**—the eternal, the unchangeable (see 41:4; 44:6; Rev. 1:8, 17; 22:13); (2) *His power as Creator, (v. 13);* (3) *His power as the Director of events (vv. 14, 15):* it is He who has appointed the destroyer of Babylon and the Chaldeans. Of Cyrus, again, the Lord says He has loved, called and brought him, and **"he shall make his way prosperous"**; (4) *His power as the God of prophecy and its fulfillment (v. 16).*

The close of *verse 16* brings before us a striking instance of the work of the Trinity: **"and now the Lord God hath sent Me and His Spirit."** That Christ is the Speaker, and not the prophet, is to be gathered from a comparison with 61:1 (cp. 11:2; 42:1). His words are undoubtedly a prelude to what He is about to declare of Himself in chapter 49:5, 6. Jehovah, having prepared for the deliverance of His people by Cyrus, has sent His Servant acting by His Holy Spirit to accomplish a great deliverance for the nation and meanwhile to instruct and lead them. This is His message to His people: **"Thus saith the Lord, thy Redeemer, the Holy One of Israel; I am thy God, which teacheth thee to profit** [to do that which profiteth], **which leadeth thee by the way that thou shouldest go"** *(v. 17).*

This was the purpose of the trials and bitter experiences of captivity. This is the gracious design of the chastening given us by God: "He for our profit, that we may be partakers of His holiness" (Heb. 12:10). How often we fail to do "that which profiteth!" It is not mere guidance that is here spoken of, it is the disciplinary dealing that gives us instruction to cease from that which profiteth not, and brings our wandering feet into the path of conformity to His will.

Hence the ensuing appeal, **"Oh that thou wouldest hearken** [the R.V. margin gives this true rendering] **to My commandments! then should thy peace be as a river, and thy righteousness as the waves of the sea"** *(v. 18).* This is an appeal for the listening and obedient ear. Peace and true prosperity are conditional upon the contrition of heart and the responsive faith that accept and carry out the Word of God.

Peace is likened to the tranquil flowing of a river, *righteousness* to the power of the billows of the sea, *offspring* to the abundance of the grains (R.V.) of sand. What Israel might enjoy nationally, we may enjoy spiritually. Spiritual fruitfulness is dependent upon peace and righteousness.

To this end separation from evil is essential: **"Go ye forth of Babylon."** This is very significant. Suggestive also is the injunction to accompany the separation and deliverance with the voice of singing and with a joyful testimony. Israel was instructed to bear the news of their redemption **"even to the end of the earth."** This the godly remnant will do in a day to come. Meanwhile the worldwide testimony of the Gospel is committed to us. The blessings described at the end of *verse 20* and in *verse 21* suggest the very elements of the gospel messages.

This portion of the prophecy ends with the solemn statement, **"There is no peace, saith the Lord, unto the wicked."** This refers to the godless in Israel, and the word rendered "wicked" literally signifies "loose," indicating a careless moral condition which prevents the experience of peace and excludes such from blessings promised to the righteous.

This statement is repeated with one variation at the end of chapter fifty-seven. Here it marks the close of the testimony concerning Babylon, which began at 46:1. There is no further mention in the book either of Cyrus or Chaldea, or of the idolatry which had formed the subject of expostulation and remonstrance.

CHAPTER EIGHT

Part IIIb
Jehovah's Servant, His Sufferings and Glory
Chapters 49—57

Chapter 49

From this chapter to the end of chapter fifty-seven consists of nine prophecies. Chapter forty-nine contains the first and its subject is twofold:

The Self-witness of Jehovah's Servant (vv. 1–13), and a Comforting Promise in Zion's Despondency.

There is a renewed association of Israel as the servant of Jehovah with Christ in the same relation. While Israel is directly addressed in this way in *verse 3* in its restored condition, yet in *verses 5 and 6* the Servant of the Lord is marked as in distinction from the nation itself, and the statement there, **"that thou shouldest be My Servant to raise up the tribes of Jacob, and to restore the preserved of Israel,"** shows that Christ Himself is in view and not here the remnant of the nation. Moreover, *verse 6* is quoted in Acts 13:47 as directly applying to Christ, though there in connection with the Gospel. All this is entirely appropriate, inasmuch as Israel could not in its restored state act as the Lord's servant in the earth apart from identification with Christ Himself as their Messiah on the ground of His sacrificial and redemptive work at Calvary.

Since the evangelization of the Gentiles is in view, the message goes forth, **"Listen, O isles, unto Me; and hearken, ye peoples, from far"** *(v. 1)*, that is, the far distant nations (cp. 42:4, 10:12 and see 5:26). The twofold statement, **"the Lord hath called Me from the womb; from the bowels of My mother hath He made mention of My Name,"** is specifically true of the Lord Jesus (see Matt. 1:21). Moreover, it is noticeable

that everywhere else where Israel is thus spoken of, the phrase "from the womb" is used without the addition of the word "mother" (51:2 is not an exception).

The Speaker, as the Servant of Jehovah, now applies a simile and a metaphor to Himself as His Agent in this relationship. The Lord has made His mouth **"like a sharp sword,"** hid in the shadow of His hand, just as a sword is kept in the sheath, ready for use at the appointed time for the purpose of overcoming the enemy. He has made Him **"a polished shaft,"** keeping Him close in His quiver, so that in due time He may pierce the heart. That Christ Himself is in view and that the time is yet future is indicated in chapter 11:4 and 30:30–33 (cp. Hos. 6:5 and Heb. 4:12). The latter passage, together with these, and Revelation 1:16, show how closely identified are the personal word and the spoken word (see also Joel 2:10, 11; 3:16; 2 Thess. 2:8; Ps. 2:5).

In *verse 3* Christ identifies Himself with His people Israel, for it is in close association with Him that the restored nation is to become His servant, and it is in Israel that the Lord will yet be glorified on the earth.

In this relationship, and in view of the bitter experiences which will have preceded that time of glory, *verse 4* strikes a note almost of despondency, though it is only of a momentary character, and in a certain way it may be referred to Christ in the time of His suffering and rejection by Israel: **"But [R.V.] I said, I have labored in vain, I have spent My strength for nought and vanity [i.e., to no purpose]"**; but this is not an utterance of unbelief or despair, for immediately the heart expresses the assurance of the truth, **"yet**

surely My judgment is with the Lord, and My recompense with My God."

The service we seek to render often seems to produce little or no result. In addition to ineffectiveness there come circumstances of extreme difficulty and trial, which tend to weigh down the heart. And if Satan could accomplish his purpose, he would use all this to cast us down into despair and if possible cause us to cease from the work and turn back through perplexity and distress. Here then is a passage designed by the Spirit of God to give us to consider all such circumstances in the light of God's all-wise counsels, so that while in the midst of conflict we may be encouraged to share His vision and know that our judgment is with Him, and that with Him is the recompense for our seemingly fruitless work.

The language of *verse 5* and what follows is clearly that of the Messiah, who here bears testimony to the object for which He is the Servant of Jehovah, namely, **"to bring Jacob again to Him, and that Israel be gathered unto Him"** (R.V.). It is Christ alone who will do this, and a still wider purpose is in view in *verse 6*.

The parenthesis between (note the R.V. brackets) expresses the delight of the Lord Jesus in the Father's approval. His statement **"I am honorable in the eyes of the Lord, and My God is become My strength"** is introduced by the word "for," which expresses the fact that His work in the restoration of Israel is especially pleasing to the Father. It is clear, too, that His resurrection is in view. In the darkness of Calvary He said "My God, My God, why hast Thou forsaken Me?" He was "crucified through weakness." Now He declares that His God has become His strength. This is to be taken with chapter 52:13, which predicts that the Lord's Servant would be "exalted and extolled and be very high."

The **"Yea"** at the beginning of *verse 6* introduces an extension of the scope of Christ's work of salvation, as well as a confirmation of what has just been stated as to the salvation of Israel. The delighted heart of Jehovah looks on to the worldwide fullness of blessing: **"It is too light a thing** [or rather it is only a small thing] **that Thou shouldest be My Servant to raise up the tribes of Jacob, and to restore the preserved of Israel: I will also give Thee** [more expressive than "make Thee"] **for a light to the Gentiles, that Thou mayest be My salvation unto the end of the earth."**

This has a present application to the work of the Gospel in fulfillment of the command of the Lord Himself to go into all the world and preach the gospel, and to be His witnesses "unto the uttermost part of the earth." The complete fulfillment will take place in the Millennial age. Both are comprehended in Romans 11:12, where the present application is described as "the riches of the world" and "the riches of the Gentiles," and this is followed by the exclamatory prediction of what the restoration or "fullness" of Israel will mean for the world.

In *verse 7,* in the continuation of His utterance to His Servant (for it is still Christ who is primarily in view), we are reminded again of the time of His humiliation. That was a necessary basis for the carrying out of the work of saving grace. So He is called the One **"whom man despiseth"** [see 53:3 and cp. 50:6, 7], and **"whom the nation abhorreth,"** referring to His treatment by the Jews, and, thirdly, in a very suggestive phrase, **"a Servant of rulers."**

This provides an instance of the very real way in which the Lord Jesus identified Himself with the nation of Israel. That nation had become a servant of rulers. This was the result of its departure from God. At the same time there were men such as Daniel, Ezra, and Nehemiah who, while they were suffering with their people, served Gentile rulers in the fear of the Lord. So Christ, in the days of His flesh, made Himself subject to Roman rulers, handing Himself over to their will that He might fulfill the great purposes for which He had come. Included also are such beneficent deeds of mercy as that which He wrought for a centurion. In these many ways the verse points to His Self-humbling.

The outcome of it all will be seen in the coming day of glory, when **"Kings shall see and arise; princes, and they shall worship; because of the LORD that is faithful, *even* the Holy One of Israel, who hath chosen Thee"** (cp. 52:15, which foretells that kings shall shut their mouths because of Him, R.V. margin). How great the change of attitude from that of the present time! How startling will be the revelation of the Lord of glory in a world that has lain in darkness, superstition and alienation from God!

Verse 8 tells how Jehovah heard the prayer of His Servant when, in the lowly condition which He shared with His people, He "offered up prayers and supplications with strong crying and tears unto Him that was able to save Him from death" (Heb. 5:7). Here He says to Him: **"Thus saith the Lord, In an acceptable time** [in a time of favor] **have I answered Thee, and in a day of salvation have I helped Thee: and I will preserve Thee, and give Thee** [or set Thee] **for a covenant of the people, to raise up the land, to make them inherit the desolate heritages; saying to them that are bound, Go forth; to them that are in darkness Shew yourselves."** It was an acceptable time when God raised Him from the dead, and since Christ identifies Himself with Israel the words will become true of the nation in fellowship with Him in its restored condition.

That Christ Himself is made "a covenant of the people" indicates the Personal bond which will hereafter unite the nation to Him as the result of His having been heard and helped. The exiled prisoners will be freed and, being restored to their land, will manifest themselves as His people.

The verses which follow give one of the most glorious descriptions of the effects of Christ's Second Advent. The promises far exceed anything that took place in the return from captivity under Cyrus. The people are depicted as a flock returning home: **"They shall feed in the ways,"** that is to say, they will be able to have sufficient supplies of food on their journeys without going long distances to get food. **"On all bare heights shall be their pasture."**

They will know neither hunger nor thirst, nor will they suffer from the heat of the sun. And all this will be due to the fact that the Lord **"that hath mercy on them"** will lead them in Person; **"even by the springs of water shall He guide them"** *(v. 10)*.

In their return from all parts of the world their journeys will be characterized by entire freedom from obstacles and difficulties. **"And,"** He says, **"I will make all my mountains a way, and My high ways shall be exalted** *(v. 11)*. Comfortingly He speaks of "My mountains" and "My ways." They are His by creation and therefore He can order for their alteration so as to make everything favorable for the return of His people.

All this is applicable to our present experiences. The mountains of difficulty which face us in our pilgrim path can become highways of communion with God and of joyous fellowship with His people, if we trust in the Lord with all our heart and present to Him our whole being for the fulfillment of His will.

In the coming day Israel will be gathered to their appointed earthly center from all parts of the world: **"Lo, these shall come from far: and, lo, these from the north and from the west; and these from the land of Sinim"** *(v. 12)*. The west seems to be a comprehensive term, and would include districts in Africa as well as Western Europe and the Americas. Some regard Sinim as referring to the Near East. The Sinite is mentioned in Genesis 10:17. But there can be little doubt that the geographical scope is far wider, and that, as several Orientalists have maintained, the reference is to the land of China. In very ancient times Tsin was the name of a feudal kingdom in Shen-si, the first king of which began to reign in 897 B.C., and it is not at all improbable that the existence of the Chinese was well-known in Palestine and Western Asia generally. Accordingly the prophecy has in view the gathering of Jews from the uttermost parts of the world (cp. *v. 6*).

Such a prospect calls forth the jubilant summons to the heavens, the earth and the mountains to rejoice and to break forth into singing, **"for the Lord hath comforted** [a prophetic perfect tense] **His people, and will have compassion upon His afflicted"** *(v. 13)*. *Verse 14* records the grievous lament of the nation in its long period of suffering. The tribulation has been judicial indeed, but unbelief, instead of repentance toward God, complains of being forsaken by Jehovah and forgotten by the Lord.

The complaint elicits an expostulation and an assurance, to the effect that His love not only is as inalienable as a mother's love but exceeds it. So far from forgetting Zion (which again stands for its inhabitants), He says **"I have graven thee upon the palms of My hands: thy walls are continually before Me"** *(v. 16)*. Jews had a custom of marking on their hands, or elsewhere, a delineation of the city and the temple, as a sign of their devotion to, and perpetual remembrance of, them. The Lord graciously adopts the figure to confirm His assurance. However great the devastation wrought by Gentile powers might be, the walls are ever before Him in their restored and perfected condition in the future.

To be graven on the palms of His hands is suggestive of the closest identification with Himself, of His unchanging love, and of His constant mindfulness of us in all His emotions and activities. Often, in our unbelief, remissness and forgetfulness, we lose sight of our preciousness in His sight in Christ. What is here conveyed in figure finds its fullness of expression in the outflowing of the Lord's heart to the disciples in the upper room, "Even as the Father hath loved Me, I also have loved you: abide ye in My love" (John 15:9).

Verses 17 to 21 reaffirm the promise of the eventual gathering of the scattered outcasts of the nation back to their land. **"Thy children make haste"** (a variant reading is "thy builders"). The exiles enter: the destroyers and wasters go out. The children whom Zion thought she had lost come in crowds (*v. 18).* With a confirming oath Jehovah assures her that her people will be like the ornaments with which a woman decks herself and like the beautiful girdle which a bride fastens round her bridal attire (R.V.).

And the reason is (note the "For" of *v. 19*) that, notwithstanding the recovery and productiveness of the districts which had been desolated and rendered untenable and the removal of those that had swallowed her up, there will not be room for all her inhabitants. Her children will say in her hearing (i.e., will call to one another) that the place is too narrow, and room must be provided.

Her people had been exiles and wanderers and she had been left "solitary" (or "barren"). Now she finds herself surrounded by a multitude of her children. How, she wonders, had they been "borne" to her (R.V., margin—not "begotten")? Who had brought them up? **"Where were they?"** (R.V.). The answer is about to be given.

Sometimes the Lord refrains from manifesting His dealings and, in testing our faith, keeps us waiting till the appointed time for the disclosure of His actings and significance. Far

greater the joy when the unfolding comes than if there had been no mystery, no darksome circumstances, and far greater the glory of His grace.

"God moves in a mysterious way
His wonders to perform

Behind a frowning providence
He hides a smiling face

Blind unbelief is sure to err,
And scan His work in vain;
God is His own interpreter,
And He will make it plain."

The close of the forth-ninth chapter, from *verse 22,* gives the Lord's answer to the surprised questions arising from Zion in verse 21. He shows how the multitude of scattered Israelites will be delivered from their exile and those who oppressed them, and be gathered to their own land. He will employ the Gentile nations to take their part in accomplishing this gathering. **"Behold,"** He says, **"I will lift up Mine hand to the nations, and set up My ensign to the peoples."** The lifting up of His hand suggests that some marked sign or indication will be given to all the nations as to what is to be done. The setting up of a standard is a frequent figure in Isaiah: see 5:26; 11:10, 12; 18:3; 62:10 (one of the many indications that there was only one author of this book). The military metaphor may point to some connection with the Lord's interposition in the warfare of Armageddon (see end of the chapter).

Other metaphors follow. The nations will bring Zion's sons **"in their bosom,"** and her daughters **"shall be carried upon their shoulders."** Just as foster fathers give diligence to care for those committed to them, and nurses give their best in caring for the children they nourish, so will kings and princesses devote themselves to the welfare of God's ancient people. They will pay homage to them to the utmost, and subject themselves to them, doing them the most lowly and menial service. The statement that they shall **"lick the dust of Thy feet"** points to the submission of those who before had taken part in oppressing them (see Ps. 72:9; Mic. 7:17).

By all this Zion will recognize Jehovah and His ways: **"thou shalt know that I am the**

Lord." Then follows the comforting promise, **"and they that wait for Me shall not be ashamed."** In 40:31 the promise is that "they that wait upon the Lord shall renew their strength." In the present passage the promise is negative: they will not be put to shame. Here too the exercise of patience is in view, in the endurance of all that is difficult and adverse until the Lord's time for deliverance comes.

We wait *upon* Him in prayer. We wait *for* Him in the confident assurance that present conditions of trial and sorrow will have a future of joy and peace such as can come only by the direct and manifest intervention of the Lord Himself.

In the next verses the tyrants with all their power and malign intentions are in view. The rhetorical question in *verse 24* is divided into two distinct parts: **"Shall the prey be taken from the mighty"** (it certainly will, and not merely the Chaldeans are in view, but the Beasts of Rev. 13); "or the captive host of the righteous be delivered?" (margin). The captives are not lawful captives, as the text seems to indicate, though that would be true of those who had been taken into captivity by the Chaldeans under God's ordering; but the time in view is far beyond the return from captivity under Cyrus, and is yet future. Hence the marginal reading is to be preferred, which shows that the captives are the righteous ones whom the Lord will snatch from the hands of the Antichrist, whom Satan will instigate to endeavor to exterminate the Jews.

The assurance is given that the Lord Himself will contend with those that contend with His people. The passage again points to the time of Armageddon (Har-Magedon) and the Second Advent. With the statement **"I will feed them that oppress thee with their own flesh; and they shall be drunken with their own blood"** (cp. Rev. 14:20). All the world will discover and recognize that Jehovah is Israel's Savior and Redeemer, **"the mighty One of Jacob."**

All the efforts of the combined nations to establish "peace and safety" in the earth, however sincere the motive, however good the intention may be, are foredoomed to failure. The world's last great conflict, in which the Jewish question will be uppermost, will see the fulfillment of the Scriptures which make

known that righteousness can be established in the earth only by the Personal Advent of Christ in judgment upon the foes of God and in the deliverance of His people.

Chapter 50

Two facts stand out prominently in this chapter: (1) the responsibility attaching to Israel for her state of rejection, (2) the steadfastness and faithfulness of the Servant of Jehovah.

In *verse 1* the Lord asks two questions by way of protest, each repudiating the idea that the evils which had befallen the nation were the result of arbitrary dealings on His part. Nay, their state was due to their transgressions.

"Where," He says, **"is the bill of your mother's divorcement, wherewith I have put her away?"** (R.V.). This is a denial by the Lord that He had broken off the relation in which He stood to Zion (Israel's mother). He had betrothed Zion to Himself, and she had no bill of divorce to show, by means of which He had put her away, thus removing the possibility of receiving her back in case she should have married another (see Deut. 24:14, and especially v. 4). Her sad condition of being put away was not caused by any such proceedings.

Further, He asks **"or which of My creditors is it to whom I have sold you?"** That Israel was sold and exiled was true, but Jehovah had not been in the position of being indebted to creditors. In other words, His having given her into the hands of Gentile powers was not through His giving way to their constraint, as if He was discharging a debt by so doing. Nay, they were sold for their iniquities, and Zion, their mother, was put away for their transgression. The mother suffered through the perverseness of her children. Sinners often put down the evils that come upon them to any cause except their own transgressions.

But there are further questions, questions in a different manner of divine protestations, telling of Jehovah's power in the exercise of mercy, and all leading to a personal testimony by Messiah Himself.

"Wherefore, when I came, was there no man?" *(v. 2).* The past tense is prophetic. He "came," not merely by His prophets, nor would He come simply by deliverance from captivity. He would come in the Person of His Servant, the Messiah-Redeemer Himself. But how was it that there was no man, none willing to receive the message? (cp. 53:1). How was it that "when He called, there was none to answer"? His hand was not shortened (an emblem of weakness) that it could not redeem (cp. 59:1). He who could dry up the sea, make rivers a wilderness, clothe the heavens with blackness and make sackcloth their covering (telling especially of His retributive judgments upon Babylon), had power to deliver. And with this in view, He would send His Servant. Eventually He came, and declared at the outset of His ministry, that He had been sent "to proclaim release to the captives . . . to proclaim the acceptable year of the Lord" (Luke 4:18). Instead of receiving Him and His message, they cast Him forth to destroy Him.

So now there follows, in *verse 4,* in the words of Christ Himself, a description of His testimony as the Sent One, His obedience to Him who sent Him, His sufferings and His vindication.

God spake to prophets by special and periodic revelations, by visions and dreams. With the Servant of Jehovah it was different. Here He discloses the secret of His inner life in the days of His flesh, and the secret source of His ministry and ways: **"The Lord God hath given Me the tongue of them that are taught, that I should know how to sustain with words him that is weary: He wakeneth morning by morning, He wakeneth Mine ear to hear as they that are taught."** A joyous lowliness and condescension breathe through His illustration taken from discipleship. In the days of the fulfillment of this prophecy He says "My teaching is not Mine, but His that sent Me" (John 7:16); again, "as the Father hath taught Me, I speak these things" (8:28), and "I speak the things which I have seen with My Father" (8:38); and again, "the Father which sent Me, He hath given Me a commandment, what I should say, and what I should speak" (12:49; cp. 14:10, 24).

How He "sustained with words" the weary is told out in the Gospel narratives, both in His public ministry (e.g., Matt. 11:28) and in the comfort He gave to the widow, the diseased, the distressed and the tempest-tossed. The Lord daily listened to His Heavenly Father's voice. In this He sets us an example. It was His joy to say "I do always the things that are pleasing to Him" (John 8:29), and it is only as we are attentive to His voice day by day that we can fulfill His will, enabling us to say with the apostle, "we make it our aim . . . to be well-pleasing unto Him."

He says **"The Lord God hath opened Mine ear, and I was not rebellious, neither turned away backward"** *(v. 5).* This was the very perfection of obedience. Compare Psalm 40:6, where, however, the word rendered to open signifies to dig, which may either refer to the custom of boring a servant's ear, in token of perpetual service (Ex. 21:6), or be figurative simply of devotion to God's will. Here in Isaiah a different word is used, with the latter meaning. The Lord Jesus knew all the suffering that lay before Him, and with undeviating steadfastness He pursued His pathway to the Cross.

To that consummating act *verse 6* points: **"I gave My back to the smiters, and My cheeks to them that plucked off the hair: I hid not My face from shame and spitting."** With striking detail this prophecy predicts what the Lord actually endured as recorded in the Gospel. He set His face to His persecutors without faltering, knowing that the words that follow would be fulfilled, that the Lord God would help Him and that He would not be ashamed.

His example is an incentive to us, when called to suffer the pressure of fierce antagonism, so that with fixity of purpose we may fulfill that which the Lord has committed to us. We can never suffer as He did, but our life and testimony can be marked by the same characteristics as those which marked His. "We must through much tribulation enter the Kingdom," but to suffer for His sake makes it all a glory and joy.

He looked to the future with confidence, and so may we. He says, **"For the Lord God will help Me; therefore have I not been confounded** [He had not suffered Himself to be overcome by mockery and opposition]: **therefore have I set My face like a flint, and I know that I shall not be ashamed"** *(v. 7,* R.V.).

The design of our Father is to give us such confidence in Him and in the assurance of His help, that we may be free from every tendency to despair under the weight of trouble. If we are walking in the path of obedience we can ever be assured of His present help and of deliverance and victory in His own way and time.

The Lord knew that, in spite of every accusation both by man and by the spiritual foe, He would be triumphantly vindicated. He says **"He is near that justifieth Me; who will contend with Me? let us stand up together** [i.e., let the foe draw toward Me]: **who is Mine adversary? let him come near to Me"** (v. 8). He does not say "He will justify Me" but "He is near" that will do so, which declares His consciousness of the presence of His Father, as, for instance, when standing before Caiaphas and his associates and before Pilate and his men of war.

His justification took place in His resurrection. He was "declared to be the Son of God with power, according to the spirit of holiness (that is the sinlessness which marked Him as the Holy One of God), by the resurrection of the dead" (Rom. 1:4). This is further borne out by the clause in 1 Timothy 3:16, "justified in the spirit" (referring directly to His resurrection).

A second time He says **"Behold, the Lord God will help Me."** Such repeated expressions are characteristic of Isaiah's prophecies.

As for God's accusers and foes they shall all **"wax old,"** or rather, fall to pieces like a worn-out garment, a prey to the moth, an insect which, working slowly and imperceptibly, accomplishes thoroughly its deadly destruction (v. 9).

That finishes the testimony of Messiah Himself. Just as the chapter opened with the declaration of Jehovah, so it closes. Here it is addressed first to the believer who fears the Lord and obeys the voice of His servant, a title which looks back to what has been stated concerning Him in verses 4, 5 that is, to the one who follows in His steps (v. 10).

A believer may be walking in darkness circumstantially and have no light, and in such conditions may be tempted to despondency. Sometimes a situation seems hopeless. A variety of trials and adverse circumstances may crowd upon him. Here then is the message, uplifting and soul-stirring. **"Let him trust in the Name of the Lord, and stay upon His God."** True faith is tested faith, and proves its reality by standing the test. God is "a very present help in trouble." Faith not only accepts this as a fact, but learns to lean upon God Himself and to prove the power and love of His almighty arm. That turns our darkness into light. The heart is cheered and, more still, is empowered to rise victorious over all that opposes, rejoicing in the light of His countenance.

The next words (v. 11) are addressed to unbelievers and to their presumptuous self-confidence. They kindle a fire and gird themselves about with firebrands, and walk proudly in the flickering flame which they have kindled. Not only so, their fire is kindled against the Lord and against His Christ. For this the divine retribution is inevitable. They must suffer from the effects of the burnings which they have kindled. It comes from the hand of Jehovah Himself. Their activities, with all their malice and hard-heartedness are brought to a terrible end and they **"lie down in sorrow,"** a contrast to the joyous restfulness of the believer who stays himself upon His God!

Chapter 51

The subject of this chapter is the promise of salvation for Israel on a righteous basis and the removal of the cup of wrath. The Lord now addresses those among His people who are faithful and, following after righteousness, long for salvation and the fulfillment of the promise to Abraham. They share his spirit of faith in refraining from making mere earthly things and pursuits the objects of their ambition. Abraham was himself the rock from which the stones, of which the house of Jacob was built, had been hewn, and Sarah was the hollow of the pit from which they had been digged. For the reference here is to the fact that, in the advanced and barren condition of the married life of Abraham and Sarah, the Lord wrought by His own supernatural power in response to Abraham's faith (vv. 1, 2).

In this connection the R.V. of Romans 4:19–21 should be noted. Its correct rendering brings out more forcibly than the A.V. the character of Abraham's faith: "And without being weakened in faith he considered his own body now as good as dead (he being about a hundred years old), and the deadness of Sarah's womb:

yea, looking unto the promise of God, he wavered not through unbelief, but waxed strong through faith, giving glory to God and being fully assured that, what He had promised, He was able also to perform."

All this was the origin of the nation of Israel and the Lord calls them, in the figurative language of the rock and the pit, to remember this, and further reminds them that **"when he was but one I called him** [R.V.]**, and I blessed him and made him many."** Hence the strengthening assurance of comfort for Zion and her waste places and the blossoming out of her wilderness **"like Eden, and her desert like the garden of the Lord; joy and gladness shall be found therein, thanksgiving and the voice of melody"** *(v. 3)*. Just as joy came to Sarah after a long period of unfruitfulness, so Israel, after its long time of trouble and desolation, shall yet be made to rejoice.

The paragraph beginning at *verse 4* speaks of the times when the restoration of Israel will issue in blessing for all the world, and then later in the passing away of the whole of the old creation. The present message of the gospel is not here in view. The Lord makes the promise, **"a law shall go forth from Me, and I will make My judgment to rest for a light of the peoples** [i.e., the Gentiles]**"** *(v. 4)*. The law is not that of Sinai but stands for instruction which God will give through the instrumentality of Israel. That He will make His judgment to rest is, more literally, "I will make a place for My right." Hence the Lord declares that His righteousness is near, that His salvation is gone forth, and that His arms will judge the nations, that is, they will come under the judgment which His arms will inflict.

But the result of the judgment is that the remaining nations who survive it, even the far distant isles, will rely upon His arm. For that which ministered judgment will subsequently act in mercy and salvation. Thus the might of God's power, represented by His arm, will be exercised in two great contrasting ways *(v. 5)*.

Not only will sin exist during the Millennial age, the whole of the old creation has been defiled by it. The heavens are to vanish like smoke, the earth is to fall to pieces like a garment, and its inhabitants are to die out as if they were nothing (this seems to be the

meaning of the phrase rendered **"in like manner"**), *verse 6* (cp. 2 Pet. 3:13).

Those who are saved (these are comprehended in the phrase "My salvation") will never perish, and God's righteousness will stand forever. And now, in a striking parallel between this passage and the one in 2 Peter, there follows an appeal to those who know God's righteousness and share it, **"the people in whose heart is My law"** *(v. 7)*. In the Isaiah passage they are exhorted not to fear the reproach of mortals or to be alarmed at their revilings. The persecutors are to perish just as a garment is consumed by a moth and wool by a worm *(v. 8)*. A Jewish proverb says that "the worm is brother to the moth." God uses little things to accomplish great ends, whether by way of judgment or for purposes of grace.

The order here is salvation and righteousness; in the preceding verse it was righteousness and salvation. The whole is in the chiasmic order; the order is reversed again in *verse 8*.

These promises must have aroused in the hearts of the faithful a longing for the promised salvation *(v. 9)*. They knew that the arm of the Lord could bring it about. Was it not His arm that overthrew Pharaoh and his hosts? The mention of Rahab has reference to Egypt, and the dragon to Pharaoh himself, with an allusion doubtless to the power of Satan acting through him *(v. 10)*. The Egyptians are vividly described as having been cut into pieces. Pharaoh himself was not drowned in the waters but was "pierced." The memory of past deliverance and the assurance of future deliverance call forth the vivid appeal, uttered three times, for the arm of the Lord to awake.

It is good for the soul to recall the mercies of God in days gone by, but it is needful not to be occupied merely with a retrospect, but to let the power of the hope do its purifying work. The double view strengthens the power of prayer, prayer not merely for deliverance but for what will accomplish the glory of God. This meets with a response on His part far exceeding the mere expectation of deliverance.

What follows is scarcely exceeded anywhere in Scripture in the beauty of its language and in the sweetness of the assurance given to God's people as to their future. It begins not with the word "Therefore," but with "And," connecting the promise with the appeal, not by way of conclusion but with the closer combination, expressing the assurance more directly and decisively: **"And the ransomed of the Lord shall return and come with singing unto Zion; and everlasting joy shall be upon their heads: they shall obtain gladness and joy, and sorrow and sighing shall flee away"** (v. 11). All this speaks gloriously of the Millennial blessedness to be enjoyed by Israel. The prospect is enhanced and strengthened by the retrospect of past trials and sufferings.

So it is with the still brighter prospect that we enjoy who are members of the Church. Our present experiences of sore trial and affliction are brightened by the hope, a hope that "sweetens every bitter cup."

Verses 12 to 15 continue in a different way the comfort ministered by the Lord. Many of His people were in fear because of the oppressor, and doubtless in the coming day, in the time of "Jacob's trouble," the oppression of the man of sin will tend to have a similar effect. To this time the present passage seems to point. The Lord speaks of Himself as their Comforter. This being so, what had they to fear? **"Who art thou,"** He says, **"that thou art afraid of man that shall die, and of the son of man which shall be made as grass** (lit., "made a blade of grass")?" The tyranny of the Antichrist will be short-lived. The Lord has ever had His own way and time for delivering His earthly people.

Fear is the offspring of forgetfulness of God. The realization of the presence and power of the Lord is the all-sufficient antidote. Again and again the Lord reminds Israel that He was their Maker and that His power had stretched forth the heavens and laid the foundations of the earth. Why then should they continually stand in dread of the fury of the oppressor even when he was preparing to destroy?

The *14th verse* is rightly put in the R.V. as a promise: **"The captive exile** [lit., he that is bowed down, i.e., bound in fetters in prison] **shall speedily be loosed; and he shall not die and go down into the pit, neither shall his bread fail."** While the conquest of Babylon by Cyrus is probably immediately in view here, the prophecy will ultimately have its fulfillment in the coming time when Jews, suffering privation in exile among the nations under the Antichrist, will be set at liberty to come back to their land in recognition of their Redeemer Messiah.

The Lord pledges His all-sufficiency for this, in that He terrifies the sea when its waves roar, by putting His restraint upon it. That is probably the true meaning in *verse 15.* The Hebrew verb is the same as that rendered "rest" in verse 4. The reference here does not seem to be to the dividing of the sea when Israel was delivered from Egypt, but to the roaring of the waves which by His word are frightened into stillness. That is what the Lord did on Lake Galilee. The waters of the sea are interpreted in Scripture as symbolizing the restlessness and tossings of the nations (see Ps. 65:7; 98:7; Is. 17:12, 13; Ezek. 26:3; Luke 21:25, 26 and Rev. 17:15). The greatest turmoil among the nations will prevail during the latter part of the rule of the man of sin, and especially at the time of the warfare of Armageddon. But the Lord will still that tempest by His Personal intervention.

Verse 16 tells how the Jews will become His messengers. He will put His words in their mouth (the perfect tense is prophetic). He will cover them in the shadow of His hand, not only protecting them but equipping them for His purpose in view. This purpose is stated as follows: **"that I may plant the heavens and lay the foundations of the earth, and say unto Zion, Thou art My people."** The last clause refers to Millennial conditions and accordingly the planting of the heavens and the founding of the earth may point to changed conditions in the universe when the Kingdom of righteousness and peace is established. For the forces of nature both in the heavens and the earth will not be used any more for the exercise of divine judgments, as has often been the case and must again be so before the Lord comes in glory. There is doubtless also a reference to the new heavens and earth which are to be created hereafter.

The messenger of the gospel may apply to himself the comfort of the assurance "I have put My words in thy mouth." He is "the Lord's messenger in the Lord's message"; his testimony is effectual only as he adheres to the truth of Scripture. Again, as His messenger he is under His protecting care, covered by the shadow of His hand, indicating the pleasure the Lord has in one who rightly ministers His truth.

The last paragraph of this chapter, beginning at *verse 17*, describes in vivid language the effects of the judgments inflicted upon the nation as a result of its persistent rebellion against God. Jerusalem is depicted as a woman lying on the ground in a state of helpless stupefaction through having drained to the dregs the cup of staggering, the cup of the fury of the Lord. Not one among all her sons was able to guide her or, taking her by the hand, to lift her up. Devastation, ruin, famine and the sword had come upon her, and the prophet himself, like Jeremiah in his lamentations, could not find how to comfort her. Her sons, instead of assisting her, were lying helpless at the corners of all the streets, like an antelope taken in a hunter's net and exhausted by vain struggles to be free *(vv. 18–20)*.

Deliverance could come only from God, and in His pity and mercy He promises to bring it *(vv. 21–23)*. He remembers that they are His people, and describes Himself as the One who pleads, or, rather, conducts, their cause as their Advocate or Defender. And inasmuch as the nations whom He has used, and will yet use for the punishment of His people, overstep the limits of the power committed to them, and, acting as the agents of the evil one and priding themselves in their despotism, wreak their vengeance upon His people, God will take **"the cup of staggering, even the bowl of the cup of His fury,"** and will make their tormentors drink it. They thought they would trample upon the nation just as foes tread upon a street. God reverses the position and brings human pride down to utter degradation.

All this will yet be enacted in the coming time of "Jacob's trouble," when Satan's efforts to destroy Israel reach their height.

Chapter 52:1–12

Again the call of the Lord comes to Zion to awake and put on her strength and to Jerusalem to put on her beautiful garments. Here, as in the two preceding instances, the call is the result of what precedes. She has been in a state of utter prostration and covered with dust, powerless under the fury of her enemies

and robbed of her royal and priestly robes, wearing instead the chains of captivity around her neck. From all those who had defiled and degraded her she would be delivered.

But she was not only to arise but was to take her seat in a position of restful dignity and authority. Strangers will not be allowed to pass through her any more (cp. Joel 3:17; see also Nah. 1:15, where the R.V. rightly translates "the wicked one," i.e., the Antichrist). Babylon has sat as a queen but would be brought down to the dust; Jerusalem would be raised from her dust and sit upon her throne of glory *(vv. 1, 2)*.

The promises which follow in *verses 3 to 6* are set, with their comfort, in the background of past misery. The Lord's people are reminded that they **"were sold for nought"** (R.V.), they were handed over to Gentile powers; not that the Lord might gain any advantage from that; His sole purpose was to bring them to repentance under His chastening rod. No money would be paid for their redemption. That would be accomplished by His sovereign grace and almighty power. Their deliverance would emanate from Himself solely and absolutely.

So with redemption from the power of sin and Satan. Man can do nothing to effect it. It must be "according to the riches of His grace" (Eph. 1:7; Col. 1:14; 1 Pet. 1:18, 19).

As illustrations, the oppression of two Gentile powers is mentioned, Egypt and Assyria. For though the actual oppression is recorded only of the latter, it is evidently intimated in regard to the former, according to the principle of parallelism. Israel went down to Egypt "at the first" (R.V.) simply to sojourn there until the famine in Canaan was over. After their bondage, their deliverance was wrought by the outstretched arm of the Lord. They are reminded of this again and again throughout their history. On the other hand, the Assyrians invaded their territory and drove them into captivity as the instruments of God's disciplinary dealings. Let them remember each case, now that similar trouble had come upon them by Babylonian aggression.

The rhetorical question asked by the Lord Himself in *verse 5*, **"What do I here?"** has been interpreted in several ways. The right meaning seems to be "What advantage do I gain in the midst of My people?" as is indicated by the next clause, **"seeing that My people is taken away for nought."** And then as to the enemy themselves, **"they that rule over them do howl."** This is not the howling of misery (that idea seems to have led to the A.V. rendering "make them to howl"); here the verb is used of the blustering war cry of the oppressors and it was in that spirit that the Name of the Lord was blasphemed continually by them.

The shrieking and the blaspheming would be made to cease by the direct power of God. The Name so despised by the Gentiles will be made known to His people. His nature, character and power as represented by His Name will be revealed to them in the day of their redemption. His self-manifestation will cause them to know the voice of their Redeemer; see 63:1, where, in answer to the astonished question of His people as to who He is, He replies, "I that speak in righteousness, mighty to save." Here in *verse 6,* in view of that assured event, He says **"Behold, it is I,"** or, as in the margin, "Here I am." He will make known not only the character of His Person and attributes, but His very presence as their Deliverer.

This is how the Lord reveals Himself in our times of tribulation and difficulty. He uses such circumstances by way of increasing our knowledge of Himself, His character, His power and His grace. It is when we come to an end of ourselves that He makes Himself known to us. Wits' end corner provides the turning at which the Lord manifests to us not only our own helplessness but His almightiness. We may be like Peter, who, finding himself going down to a watery grave, cried out "Lord, save me." Christ planned the whole circumstance so that His ardent follower might know the strength of His arm and His power to do more than deliver. How often in the midst of the troubles of His disciples He said (that with which this passage in Isaiah ends) "It is I!"

Verses 7 to 10 consist of a triumphant exultation consequent upon the news of the great deliverance wrought for the Lord's people in the eyes of all nations. Wars will have been made to cease to the ends of the earth. Peace will prevail because God reigns and Jehovah is returning to Zion.

"How beautiful upon the mountains are the feet of him [or "them"—the pronoun is collective] **that bringeth good tidings, that publisheth peace!"** The feet of the messengers are lovely to behold (not the sound of the footsteps but the appearance of their feet), beautiful not only because of their buoyant rapidity, but because of the rapture of heart which lends character to their movement, and the very nature of their errand.

The mountains are those of the Land, and especially those north of Jerusalem. What are natural obstacles are made highways for God's heralds. He had declared "I will make all My mountains a way." The world will cry "peace and safety" (1 Thess. 5:3)—the old delusion, that man is his own savior! Destruction will come upon them, confounding their politics and chasing away their cherished dreams. God's Christ alone can bring deliverance, and at His Coming the messengers publish "peace and salvation." Not the "safety" of an imagined security, but the salvation wrought by the arm of the Savior Himself!

So it will be. But so it is now in respect of the messengers of the Gospel and its good news; and for this we have the confirmatory quotation in Romans 10:15, where "the mountains" is omitted, for the emblematic becomes the actual in the Gospel. The apostle exults in that in which he was himself such an assiduous messenger! And it is ours to share in the activity and the joy. The feet of one who goes forth with the evangel, at home or abroad, are lovely in the sight of Him who died to provide both the message and the messengers.

There are three blessings pronounced in the message, *peace, good,* and *salvation; peace* with God through the blood of Christ, instead of alienation; *good,* that which benefits and profits, instead of evil, the blighting effect of sin; *salvation,* which not only saves from death and judgment, but ministers continual preservation, with its eternal realization, instead of doom and eternal perdition.

The "watchmen" (or watchers) in *verse 8,* who **"lift up the voice together,"** rejoicing with singing, are the prophets (Isaiah himself being one), like those who look out into the distance as from a watch tower. They are distinct from the messengers just mentioned, who will bear the news of the Kingdom when Christ's Millennial reign is ushered in. Contrast the blind watchmen, the false prophets, in 56:10. These faithful watchers, who saw future events from afar, are described in 1 Peter 1:10–12 (cp. Is. 21:8, 11 and Hab. 2:1–3).

The day is coming when they will **"see, eye to eye, when** [or, rather, "how"] **Jehovah returns to Zion,"** lit., "makes Zion to return" (the same construction as in Ps. 85:4). They will see the Lord restoring Zion, as vividly as one person is to another when he looks straight into his eyes (see Num. 14:14, R.V. margin). No wonder they will join in a chorus of praise. Those who foretold these things apart from one another during the course of many centuries will, in one great company and in bodily presence, utter their joy before Him who has been the great Subject of these prophecies.

In *verse 9* the ruins of Jerusalem are called upon to do the same. The language is vivid, it visualizes and depicts the glory of restoration after the long periods of desolation: **"Break forth into jubilation, join in singing, ye ruins of Jerusalem."** And the reason is twofold, God's word and work: the word of consolation, **"The Lord hath comforted His people"**; the work of delivering power, **"He hath redeemed Jerusalem."** His word has been carried out in act. "Jesus . . . was mighty in deed and word" (Luke 24:19). Moses "was mighty in his words and works" (Acts 7:22). Compare 2 Thessalonians 2:17.

Comfort and deliverance, these are the constant ministration of the Holy Spirit in our sorrows and distresses, our trials and dangers: comfort *amidst* them, deliverance *from* them! We may rejoice in the consolation, and be confident of the deliverance.

Verse 10 first looks back from future fulfillment. **"Jehovah hath made bare His holy arm in the eyes of all the nations."** The metaphor is that of a warrior, removing all coverings and accoutrements from his arm so as to exert his power to the utmost. The foolish misconceptions the nations have had about God will be mightily dispelled. Their refusal to acknowledge the Person, facts and claims of His Son will meet the force of His direct interposition. **"All the ends of the earth shall see the salvation of our God."**

Verses 11 and 12 deal with another side of the circumstances, and give a view of the setting free of the exiles. They are bidden to go out from the scene of their captivity. The language of the command bears reference to Babylon, but Babylon here stands for more than the city itself, it speaks of world conditions, as the preceding context shows. They are commanded to touch no unclean thing. They are not to take with them the Babylonish gods, as they did when they took of the spoils of Egypt. The vessels they are to carry home are **"the vessels of the Lord."** This points to the return under the decree of Cyrus, when the vessels taken by Nebuchadnezzar were to be restored (Ezra 1:7–11). Again, unlike the exodus from Egypt, they would not go out in haste nor by flight. Their attitude, instead of that of fugitives, was to be one of complete preparedness for the resumption of the worship of the Lord in His Temple. For this the requisite is absolute purity.

Yet they would need His guidance and protection, and of this they are assured: **"for Jehovah will go before you; and the God of Israel will be your rearward."**

All this has its direct messages for those who, themselves vessels, set apart to the Lord for His use (2 Tim. 2:21), have a holy responsibility to keep themselves unspotted from the world, and to cleanse themselves "from all defilement of flesh and spirit, perfecting holiness in the fear of the Lord." And as to the promises, all that is here assured and much more, is gathered up in the pledge, "I will be to you a Father, and ye shall be to Me sons and daughters, saith the Lord Almighty." The relationship divinely established at the new birth finds its practical expression on His part in our experiences and circumstances in a manner impossible if the condition is not fulfilled.

Chapter 52:13–15 and Chapter 53

The division into chapters requires that what is marked as chapter 53 should begin here. These three verses and the twelve which are marked as chapter 53 comprise one great theme of the suffering, rejected, atoning and exalted Servant of Jehovah. The opening words **"Behold My Servant"** speak not of Israel but of Messiah, as in 50:10.

The connection with what has just preceded is significant. Deliverance from captivity has just been in view, deliverance from Bab-

...lon, and deliverance yet future and final. Bab-lon itself was not actually mentioned and is not spoken of again in Isaiah.

Deliverance can be wrought alone by Jeho-ah's Servant, whether for Jew or Gentile. So he Lord calls attention to Him, first to His prosperous dealing, then to His exalted posi-ion itself *(v. 13)*. There follows a brief mention of His humiliation as antecedent to the coming manifestation of His power and glory *(vv. 14, '5)*. And all this, in its condensed form, is the very theme which, having been thus intro-luced, is expanded in the twelve following verses.

"Behold, My Servant shall deal visely." Two meanings are contained in this vord, wisdom (one feature of which is pru-lence) and prosperity. These might be com-ined in a fuller rendering, "shall deal wisely, vith consequent prosperity." Strikingly this lescribes His life on earth, in all that He said nd did, with its prosperous effects, and in naintaining His testimony without surrender-ng His life till the appointed hour. No greater prosperity ever accrued from any act than from he giving up of that life in His voluntary and toning sacrifice.

"He shall be exalted and lifted up, nd shall be very high." Three stages are n view, His Resurrection (the word rendered exalted" signifies to rise up in exaltation), Iis Ascension (the thought is that of a glorious scent), and His position at the right hand of God (see Acts 2:33; Phil. 2:9; Heb. 1:3 and 3).

"Like as many were astonished at 'hee (with the change from a statement of ct concerning Him to an utterance addressed Him; cp. chap. 49, vv. 7, 8) **. . . so shall Ie startle** (R.V. margin) **many nations."** 'he similarity of the verbs in these corre-ponding statements is to be noted. In the egradation and disfigurement which man in-icted on Him many were astonished; in the oming manifestation of His glory He will as-nish (cause to leap and tremble in astonish-ent) many nations; "startle" is the meaning ere, not "sprinkle" (as the grammatical phra-eology makes clear).

The fact that **"His visage was so narred more than any man, and His rm more than the sons of men"** was the ause of the astonishment of those who beheld Him. The soldiers hit Him with a mock scep-ter one after another on His face and His thorn-crowned brow, till His features were un-recognizable. The form of scourging adminis-tered was that by means of which the flesh was cut away from breast as well as back. So Psalm 22:17 foretold: "I may tell all My bones; they look and stare upon Me."

In the coming Day the astonishment at His power and glory will be so great that kings will be overpowered into speechlessness, struck dumb at the sight of what they had never heard of. More still, they will be made to grasp the reality and significance of the stupendous man-ifestation: **"that which they had not heard shall they understand."**

There follows immediately the reason why they had not heard. The cause lay with Israel. They (not the prophet) are the mourning and repentant speakers in the next verse. They acknowledge with lamentation their unbelief. As a nation they had refused to believe the message proclaimed to them. That is the meaning of the rhetorical question rendered in our Versions, **"Who hath believed our report?"** *(v. 1)*. See the R.V. margin. The word rendered "report," means that which was heard, that which was declared, and the reference is to the Gospel preached at Pente-cost and afterwards, which was persistently rejected by the nation. Witness Paul's protests and lament (Acts 13:46; 18:6; 28:28; Rom. 9:1; 11:7, 8; 1 Thess. 2:14–18).

So with the manifestation of God's power in Christ: **"to whom hath the arm of the Lord been revealed?"** is a prophetic ques-tion expressing the confession to be made in the coming day of repentance, that Israel had in its unbelief failed to recognize what God had wrought in raising Christ from the dead. All that follows is a full acknowledgment to be made of the great facts concerning Him when the nation is restored.

They did not realize that **"He grew up before Him** [Jehovah] **as a tender plant, and as a root** [a sprouting root] **out of a dry ground"** *(v. 2)*.

The pleasantness of Christ in the eyes of Jehovah, in the days of His childhood and growth into manhood, as a tender twig and the verdant shoot, is set in contrast with the bar-ren and enslaved condition of the nation.

They saw nothing in His appearance to make

them feel naturally attracted to Him, nothing of comeliness or beauty to delight their natural senses. On the contrary, **"He was despised and rejected of men; a man of sorrows, and acquainted with grief"** (v. 3). The special meaning of the word rendered "grief" is sickness, or disease. The former clause marks His life as one characterized by the inward smart of experiencing the effects of the sins and sorrows of those around Him; the latter clause marks Him as One uniquely capable of complete acquaintance with various forms of illness.

The latter part of the verse expresses still more strongly the attitude of the people as a whole. It shows the character of their despisings: **"and as one from whom men hide their face He was despised, and we esteemed Him not."** Men hide the face from, or turn away from, that which is considered unbearable to behold. Their estimate of Him is put very strongly; they regarded Him as nothing. All this records the depths of remorse with which the nation hereafter will recall their attitude shown Him in the days of His flesh.

In *verses 4 to 6*, they enter into the subject more deeply, confessing that His sufferings were of quite a different nature from what they had supposed them to be. The sufferings of the Cross are now in view.

The change of their ideas is marked by the opening word **"Surely"** or **"Verily."** The statement **"He hath borne our griefs, and carried our sorrows,"** expresses more fully what was mentioned in the preceding verse as to His being a man of sorrows and acquainted with grief. It tells how the Lord bore in His own Person sufferings which were other than His own. Matthew quotes this in connection with His deeds of healing and deliverance (Matt. 8:16, 17). Yet that statement does not speak of His making a substitutionary atonement.

Verse 4 takes us directly to the Cross, for only to that could the statement apply, **"yet we did esteem Him stricken, smitten of God, and afflicted."** In their blindness they looked upon His sufferings as the punishment of His own sins, which they must have regarded as especially great.

But now, under the power of the revelation of the great facts, there comes an entire reversal of their opinions. This is marked in a special way by the series of emphatic personal pronouns in the plural in what follows. **"But He was wounded for our transgressions, He was bruised for our iniquities: the chastisement of our peace was upon Him"** (v. 5).

The words rendered "wounded" (or pierced) and "bruised" are the strongest terms to describe a violent and agonizing death. There is stress on the "our" in both statements. The chastisement which was administered to Him by God was that which makes for our peace (the word *shalom* is comprehensive and describes not simply a peaceful state, but well-being in general); **"and with His stripes we are healed"**—not the Roman scourging; the margin gives the literal rendering, "bruise" (so in the Septuagint, and see 1 Pet. 2:24, margin). The expression conveys in condensed form the stroke of Divine judgment inflicted upon Him. The healing, the spiritual soundness which we receive, is expressly set in direct contrast to the bruising or Divine stroke to which He submitted.

Now comes the climax of conscience stricken admission on the part of the penitent nation: **"All we like sheep have gone astray, we have turned every one to his own way,"** and then the grateful realization and recognition of the tremendous fact, **"and Jehovah hath laid on Him the iniquity of us all"** (v. 6).

What the nation will hereafter acknowledge is true of the whole human race. Man has substituted his own will for God's will. Being granted the power of self-determination, a feature which, among others, marks him as made in the image of God, he has used that power to go "his own way" and make himself egocentric instead of God-centric.

In this universal condition of guilt and misery the grace of God has interposed. Sending His own Son "in the likeness of sinful flesh and as an offering for sin" (Rom. 8:3, R.V.). He made to meet upon Him the whole weight of our iniquity and the righteous wrath due to it.

The third paragraph, *verses 7 to 9*, describes His sufferings, death and burial. **"He was oppressed** ["treated unsparingly"], **yet He humbled Himself** [i.e., He suffered voluntarily] **and opened not His mouth; as a lamb that is led to the slaughter, and as a sheep that before her shearers is dumb** yea, He opened not His mouth." This all expresses His voluntary endurance and is apparently set in striking antithesis to the straying away, in the first part of verse 6.

The scene passes next to the unrighteous judicial verdict passed upon Him, and from thence direct to Calvary. "By oppression and judgment [a hendiadys, i.e., one sentiment conveyed by two expressions, here signifying "by an oppressive judicial sentence"] He was taken away [Matt. 26:66; 27:22-31, and see Acts 8:33, which translates the Septuagint], and as for His generation, who among them considered that He was cut off out of the land of the living? for the transgression of my people was He stricken," or "was the stroke upon Him." This is preferable to the R.V. margin, "to whom the stroke was due." The stress of the passage is what Christ endured.

This section, which has described the character of His sufferings and the manner of His death, closes with a statement as to His burial: "And they [R.V.; i.e., "His generation"] made His grave with the wicked ["with sinners"], and with the rich ["a rich man"] in His death." The first part of this would seem to refer to the intention of the rulers, who would have had Him ignominiously buried with the two robbers. The Roman authorities, however, granted the body to Joseph of Arimathaea, the "rich man" (Matt. 27:57).

The Hebrew word rendered "death" is in the plural; this is expressive of the violent character, not to say the comprehensive nature, of His death.

In what follows, the A.V. rendering "because He had done no violence, neither was any deceit in His mouth" is probably correct, rather than the R.V., "although . . ." The clause is to be connected with what immediately precedes. The fact of His freedom from sin made it fitting that He should receive an honorable burial, instead of being cast into a criminal's grave, to which his enemies would have committed Him.

The last section of the chapter gives a threefold testimony concerning the experiences of His soul. We are taken into the inner sanctuary of His Being. Again, verses 10 and 12 speak of the dealings of Jehovah with Him, judicially in respect of His death and compensatingly in respect of His reward. Verse 11 speaks of the outcome of His Sacrifice and His own satisfaction therein and the justifying grace He ministers to others.

The statement "Yet it pleased the Lord to bruise Him" speaks of the determinate counsel of Jehovah in causing man's sin to be subservient to the actings of His grace, in the suffering inflicted upon His sinless Servant on the Cross. That He "put Him to grief" speaks of the extreme distress brought upon Him.

What follows is probably rightly rendered as in the margin: "When His soul shall make an offering for sin," i.e., a trespass offering, a sacrifice offered to God with the effect of clearing the sinner from his guilt. The sin offering was presented by the priest from the point of view of the offerer, but the trespass offering had especially in view the demands of God's justice. That is what is indicated here. This is the first of the three statements as to His soul.

This voluntary act of surrendering His life (a life with which God was ineffably pleased) to meet God's righteous demands concerning man's guilt, is shown to have the following results (in vv. 10-12) relating to Christ Himself:

1. "He shall see His seed." An Israelite was regarded as conspicuously blessed if he had a numerous posterity, and especially if he lived to see them (Gen. 48:11; Ps. 128:6). Here then we have an intimation of the exceeding joy of Christ in seeing the results of His sacrifice in the countless multitude of His spiritual posterity from among Jew and Gentile.

2. "He shall prolong His days," another blessing regarded as a high favor among Israelites (cp. Ps. 91:16; Prov. 3:2, 16). Here, however, the reference is to the unending resurrection life of the Lord, and to the joy that breathes through His words "I was dead, and behold I am alive forevermore" (Rev. 1:18).

3. "The pleasure of the Lord shall prosper in His hand." That is to say, the predeterminate counsels of God shall have their joyous realization. The phrase "in His hand" points to His Mediatorial and High Priestly work, as well as to the exercise of His authority and power in His Kingdom.

4. "He shall see of the travail of His soul, and shall be satisfied." This is the second mention of the soul of Christ in the passage. All the glory that follows and will fol-

low will be viewed by Him as the outcome of His atoning sufferings, which will never cease to be present to His mind as the all-necessary and all-sufficient means by which His heart is satisfied in the redemption of those that have become His own possession. This is true both in the progressive work of saving grace and in its entire fulfillment when the Church is complete and Israel is saved.

5. **"By His knowledge shall My righteous Servant justify many."** There is stress upon the word "righteous." There could be no justification for others, no reckoning of righteousness, were it not for His flawless righteousness, by which alone He was competent to render Himself voluntarily as a propitiatory Sacrifice.

The phrase translated "by His knowledge" may be rendered in two ways, either "by knowledge of Him" or "by His own knowledge." Regarding the former, to know Him is life eternal (John 17:3; 1 John 5:20; cp. 2 Pet. 1:3); this is the objective sense. The other is the subjective. In chapter 11:2, one of the seven spirits which were foretold as resting upon Christ is "the spirit of knowledge." Again, one of the qualifications of a priest is that his lips keep knowledge (Mal. 2:7), so that people may seek the law at his mouth. Further, in Matthew 11:27 the Lord says that knowledge of the Father belongs only to Himself and "to whomsoever the Son willeth to reveal Him." In the whole passage both the priestly and the mediatorial work of Christ is unfolded as well as the prospect of His regal glory (see 52:15 and 53:12). Because of what He is in His own Person as well as in this threefold office, and because of His absolute knowledge as the Son of God, He would effect the justification of many. That is to say, He would make righteous all that come unto God by Him. But only on the ground of His vicarious sacrifice, and this is why the statement **"And He shall bear their iniquities"** immediately follows. By reason of this He is an eternal Priest, qualified to dispense all that accrues from His offering.

There yet remains another glorious effect of His sacrificial death. Jehovah will **"divide Him a portion with the great, and He shall divide the spoil with the strong."** The Septuagint renders it, "I will give Him the mighty for a portion." The thought is not that of dividing into portions, but of assigning. "The great" and "the strong" are general terms, and do not specify particular individuals; they do not refer to specially prominent persons or those who are mightier than others, but to all who by reason of faithful adherence to His will are to be made sharers in His regal authority when His Kingdom is established.

The Father and the Son cooperate, and the Son will "divide the spoil with the strong." The latter are mentioned in Psalm 110:3 as volunteers in the day of His power, partaking with Him of the spoils of His triumph. The Septuagint renders this second statement, "He shall divide the spoils of the mighty" suggesting His triumph over His foes, and this meaning is accepted by many.

Again we are directed to the foundation work of His atoning sacrifice. The very establishment of His sovereign power in the earth will rest upon that finished work. It is here finally set forth in four statements. All the future glory, all that will accrue by way of reward to the faithful is because (1) **"He poured out His soul unto death"**; (2) **"He was numbered with the transgressors"**; (3) **"He bare the sin of many"**; (4) **"He made intercession for the transgressors."** The last two of these are set in striking contrast to the fact that He was numbered with the transgressors, and this is accurately set forth by the R.V. "yet" instead of "and." The former points to the unrighteous opinion of those who pronounced sentence upon Him and handed Him over to execution. Little did they realize that in what He endured on the Cross He was Himself the sin-bearer, and the closing statement refers especially to His intercessory prayer while He was being nailed to the tree. Then it was that He made intercession for the transgressors.

For the third time mention is made of His soul, and now in connection with His own act in pouring out His soul unto death. Concerning this He Himself said "I lay down My life for the sheep" and "I lay down My life that I may take it again. No one taketh it away from Me, but I lay it down of Myself. I have power to lay it down, and I have power to take it again" (John 10:15, 17, 18).

The details of this prophecy in chapter

fifty-three grow in vividness and reach a climax in these last three verses.

Chapter 54

Chapter fifty-four bursts out in exultation after the prophecies of the sufferings, sin-bearing and glory of the Servant of Jehovah in chapter fifty-three. Israel is called upon to rejoice with singing and shouting, as her state of barrenness would yield place to fruitfulness. The experiences of their ancestress Sarah had been a foreshadowing of this. The desolate condition of the people and their land was not to last indefinitely. Jehovah had not divorced her. The time will come when she will no more be termed "Forsaken" neither will the land be termed "Desolate," for **"as the bridegroom rejoiceth over the bride,"** so will God rejoice over her (62:4, 5) and her children will be more numerous than they were before she became desolate (v. 1).

She is therefore bidden to broaden out her tent and stretch out the curtains of her habitations, to lengthen her cords and strengthen her stakes, language metaphorically setting forth the extension of her territory so that there may be room for the increased population.

Accordingly the promise is given her, **"thou shalt spread abroad on the right hand and on the left; and thy seed shall possess the nations, and make the desolate cities to be inhabited"** (v. 3). The right hand and the left stands for both the south and the north, as in Genesis 15:18, Egypt and the Euphrates; also for the east and the west (see Gen. 28:14). There will be much more in the coming time than what was enjoyed in the reign of Solomon. They are to become the head of the nations, ruling over those who oppressed them (see Mic. 4:1–3). Cities desolated by war and pillage will become populous. Israel, repentant and converted, will then be the meek who shall inherit the earth.

Such are the Lord's ways. Enlargement follows curtailment when His chastening hand has done its work. When the disciplined soul learns to realize more fully what was accomplished at Calvary and bows in self-judgment before Him, spiritual enlargement is sure to result. Fruitfulness, which has suffered through impoverishment of soul, bursts forth in abundance, for the glory of the Lord and for the enrichment and blessing of others.

The passage that follows from *verse 4* onward is full of the tenderest promises and comfort, telling out the lovingkindness of the Lord, His covenant mercies, and the glorious future in store for the nation. Israel is no longer to fear, for she will not be put to shame. She is exhorted not to be confounded (or rather, as it may be rendered, "to bid defiance to reproach"). Her future will be so delightful that she will "forget the shame of her youth," the time when she was in bondage in Egypt. There she was like a virgin, but Jehovah who redeemed her betrothed her to Himself with a covenant of love (see Jer. 51:5), for her Husband was none other than her Maker (v. 5). He who had become her Husband was the One who brought her into existence, and He is **"the Lord of hosts,"** the One whose bidding the hosts above fulfill. In the Hebrew the words for Maker and Husband are plural, alike with *Elohim*, "God," the last divine title in the verse; they are thus expressive of the fullness of the relation and of His creatorial power.

Again, her Redeemer, the Holy One of Israel, is described as **"the God of the whole earth,"** indicating that the power to assist her belongs to Him and will be exercised because of the relation of love in which she stands to Him.

The relation had suffered a kind of disillusion, but Jehovah will yet call her back to Himself, **"as a wife forsaken and grieved in spirit, even a wife of youth, when she is cast off"** (v. 6). Wonderful is the restoring grace of God. He calls Israel back to Himself as a husband receives back the wife he loved in his youth. She has displeased Him, but she was not as one hated. On the contrary, the Lord regards the time in which He had forsaken her, the time of her captivity, as "a small moment" (v. 7).

The time of her captivity in the east had seemed long to the captives, and this is especially evinced in the intercessory prayer and supplications made by Daniel, who realized the terrible nature of God's disciplinary dealings in the time of the forsaking (see Dan. 9 and Jeremiah's Lamentations). Jeremiah says, "Wherefore dost Thou forget us forever, and forsake us so long time" (Lam. 5:20). Viewing the still longer period from the unalterable character of His mercy, God speaks of it as a moment. He says **"with great mercies will I gather thee"** *(vv. 7, 8).*

At the beginning of *verse 8* the R.V. rightly renders the phrase **"In overflowing wrath,"** that is, in the gushing forth of indignation. It is with this that His **"everlasting kindness"** is set in contrast. The Lord then gives a pledge that He will never again be wroth with Israel or rebuke her. Similarly, He says, He pledged Himself to Noah and His descendants that He would never cut off all the flesh again by the waters of a flood. Just as the already existent rainbow was then set as a token of a covenant between Himself and the earth and every living creature, so now He speaks of His "covenant of peace" as that which will never be removed, and conveys the assurance that likewise, even when the mountains have departed and the hills have been removed, His kindness shall never depart from Israel. For He is **"the Lord that hath mercy on thee"** *(v. 10).*

Just as Noah and his family came forth into a new world after the deluge, so after "the great tribulation" will God's redeemed earthly people come forth to Millennial blessedness. "Weeping may tarry [or come in to lodge] for the night, but joy cometh in the morning" (Ps. 30:5, where God's anger is said to last "but for a moment," just as here in Is. 54:7, 8; cp. 2 Cor. 4:17).

Thus does the Lord, while administering the necessary unjoyous chastening of His people, fix His heart and keep His eye upon the "peaceable fruit of righteousness." Never does He cease to have our highest and best interests in view.

From *verse 11* to the end of the chapter the future glory and happiness of God's earthly people is described in a beautiful variety of ways, which serve to set forth the coming deliverance and its issues in contrast to their present woes. This latter condition He describes in tender terms: **"O thou afflicted, tossed with tempest, and not comforted"** *(v. 11).* The tempest expresses the fury of Gentile powers in their Satanically inspired determination to crush Israel to the uttermost. Of Jerusalem, which at the height of the storm will become the center of the world's last great war, He says **"I will set thy stones in fair colors, and lay thy foundations with sapphires. And I will make thy pinnacles** [or minarets, not "windows," A.V.] **of rubies, and thy gates of carbuncles, and all thy border** [R.V.] **of pleasant stones."** All this represents the reflection of the glory of God Himself. The jewels which God has hidden in the earth, and which man has unearthed for purposes of his own avarice and self-glorification, have been designed for the purpose of setting forth the glory of Christ's attributes and character, and while they will be literally used to beautify the earthly Jerusalem, they will thereby be a continuous reminder and token to God's people of the glories and grace of Christ their Redeemer.

So the twelve precious stones, set in the breastplate of the high priest of old, set forth the glory and grace of Christ in His High Priestly ministry. And as from that breastplate the words of light and instruction were given for the impartation of the mind of the Lord to His people, so in the coming day the natural glory of Jerusalem, instead of ministering to human pride, will convey the mind and will of God as revealed in the Messiah.

This is what is immediately promised, for *verse 13* says: **"And all thy children shall be taught of the Lord; and great shall be the peace of thy children."** That is to say, they will all be disciples (see the R.V. margin). They will not need human instruction. This promise Christ Himself quoted when He said to the murmuring Jews: "Every one that hath heard from the Father, and hath learned, cometh unto Me," John 6:45. The two words in that verse in the original, "taught of God," are combined into one adjective in 1 Thessalonians 4:9, lit., "God-taught." Just as believers are taught of God to love one another, so in Israel, as those who will be "taught of the Lord," love will characterize them all. It naturally follows that peace will prevail. For where love is in exercise joy and peace inevitably exist (cp. Col. 3:14, 15).

All this is the outcome of the knowledge of the Lord. Israel will not need to teach every man his neighbor and every man his brother, saying, "know the Lord": for they will all know Him "from the least to the greatest" (Jer. 31:34). But all this happiness will be enjoyed on the basis of Divine righteousness: **"in** righteousness shalt thou be established," *verse 14* (see chap. 11:5).

No longer will foes oppress them. They will be far from oppression. They are not to fear a repetition of their troubles. They are to be far from terror; it will not come near them again. Their enemies may gather together, but all who dare to do so will fall because of them. Jerusalem will be invincible *(v. 15)*. God has created the smith who blows the coal fire and produces a weapon for his work (or "according to his trade"); He has also created the waster (or destroyer) to destroy *(v. 16)*. The very creative power of Jehovah is to be used to defend His people. Accordingly no weapon formed against them shall prosper. And then, just as every hostile weapon fails, so Jerusalem, quickened into the knowledge of the Lord, and therefore conscious of its Divine right, will convict every accuser as guilty and therefore subject to punishment. **"Every tongue that shall rise against thee in judgment thou shalt condemn"** *(v. 17)*.

The closing statement of the chapter sums up all the preceding promises, and describes them as **"the heritage of the servants of Jehovah."** What is the rightful reward of the great Servant of Jehovah in His exaltation, is differently described in respect of His servants, for their heritage is of grace. And whereas He is Himself "Jesus Christ the righteous," the righteousness granted to His people is likewise a matter of grace: **"their righteousness is of Me, saith Jehovah."** That is how Jerusalem is to be established. Israel will not be able to claim anything of this by their own merit, any more than we can who are "justified freely by His grace through the redemption that is in Christ Jesus."

Chapter 55

The prophet now issues an invitation to come and partake of the spiritual provision made by the Lord for those who are willing to turn from their own devices and activities and listen diligently to His voice. The invitation is to **"every one that thirsteth,"** and the provision made consists not of the material benefits of water, wine and milk. These are metaphorically used of higher things than the natural products. The spiritual significance of water has been mentioned in 44:3, where the reference is to the Holy Spirit, as in John 7:38. Similarly in regard to wine (see 25:6, 7). So we must understand the mention of milk (see 1 Pet. 2:2, where the reference is to the Word of God). In Scripture the Spirit of God and the Word of God are often associated.

Moreover, the purchase is to be made **"without money and without price"** *(v. 1)*. This is all of divine grace. The possession of the spiritual blessings is, from the point of view of the recipients, dependent solely upon a sense of need and a readiness to accept them.

With this invitation we may compare the words of the parable in Matthew 22:4, and the contrast, expressed in *verse 2* of this fifty-fifth chapter, reminds us of the contrast between grace and works in Romans 11:6. The paradox of buying without money is suggestive of spiritual bankruptcy. Israel was spending money and labor upon idols. Hence the solemn appeal of the opening word of the chapter; for the exclamation "Ho" is not simply a matter of invitation, it casts a reflection upon the state of those who are adopting their own devices instead of listening to the voice of the Lord.

The Lord follows His remonstrance with the gracious words **"hearken diligently unto Me, and eat ye that which is good, and let your soul delight itself in fatness"** *(v. 2)*. Often in Scripture where two commands are given the second suggests the good result of obeying the first (cp. Gen. 42:18).

The satisfaction of the soul can be obtained only in the path of the obedience of faith. By diligently listening to the voice of God and fulfilling His will we can enjoy real spiritual delight. Moreover, what the Lord here holds out is something more than meeting our need. He designs to give us an overflowing satisfaction. This is indicated by the word "fatness" (see, for instance, Pss. 36:8 and 63:5). This is "the riches of His grace."

He now bids His people to incline their ear and come unto Him, to hear, that their soul may live *(v. 3)* or revive (cp. John 14:6). Much the same thing was said later to the church in Laodicea. In such conditions the Lord calls upon the individual to hear His voice (Rev. 3:20), and the provision He makes for the responsive heart is to find in Him the very life and sustenance of the soul.

There is much in these first three verses of the chapter that affords matter for a Gospel message, but the appeal is directly to the backslider, whose soul needs the reviving that can be effected only by returning to the Lord.

"And I will make," He says, "an everlasting covenant with you, even the sure mercies of David." In human affairs a covenant is made and ratified by each of the parties to it. Here the Lord undertakes the obligations Himself, and the covenant is virtually a promise. So in Galatians 3:17, 18, where "covenant" and "promise" are used interchangeably. Moreover, the Greek word there used, *diatheke*, does not in itself contain the idea of joint obligation, it denotes that which is undertaken by one alone. The sole condition for the recipient is that he shall incline his ear and come. He will not thereby be putting his signature to a covenant; his acceptance of the invitation ensures the fulfillment of the "covenant of promise."

The phrase "the sure mercies of David" receives its interpretation in Acts 13:34, which quotes from the Septuagint: "I will give you the holy and sure *blessings* [lit., things] of David." Paul uses this as the second of three quotations from the O.T. to prove that they were fulfilled in the Person of Christ, the first foretelling His birth (v. 33, see the R.V.; there the raising up of Jesus speaks of His being raised up in the nation, in His life on earth, cp. v. 23), the second foretelling His resurrection, the third His incorruptibility. What God promised to David (e.g., in 2 Sam. 7:16), and will yet be fulfilled to him in the future earthly Kingdom, can be established in that day only in and through the Person of Christ Himself, by reason of His resurrection and exaltation, and in the glory of His Millennial reign.

David was, and yet will be, God's appointed "witness to the peoples" (the nations), and their "leader and commander" (see Ezek. 34:24; 37:24). Israel, possessed of worldwide dominion, will "call a nation that they knew not" (referring to Gentile peoples in general), and the nation that knew not Israel will run to them (indicative of swift means of travel), "because of Jehovah their God," and "for the Holy One of Israel." Now there is no such reciprocal recognition; the opposite is the case. But in the day of Messiah's reign, Israel will be glorified by Him *(vv. 4, 5)*. In

verse 6 there is a general appeal: "Seek ye the Lord while He may be found, call ye upon Him while He is near."

What follows is an appeal to the backslider; he is called upon to forsake his way and his thoughts, and to return unto the Lord. A return implies the retracing of one's steps to that which was formerly enjoyed. The unregenerate man can turn, but a return is for him who has gone back from that fellowship with God which he once experienced. He waits to have mercy upon him and to "pardon abundantly" (lit., "He will multiply to pardon"), *verse 7*.

The foregoing appeal to forsake their own way and thoughts, and, by returning to God, to yield themselves to Him, is urged by reason of the fact of the utter difference between the ways and thoughts of God and the self-willed and foolish ways and thoughts of men *(vv. 8, 9; cp. 40:27; 9:14)*.

The waywardness of the backslider plunges him into unbelief and misery. He finds that his purposes are frustrated by a mightier power than his, and the thorny path that he has chosen brings him into spiritual gloom and uncertainty.

To all this God sets His actings and decrees in striking contrast. Just as He has absolute control over the rain and the snow and the produce of the earth, and man can do nothing to alter that which God has established by His creative power, "so shall My word be," He says, "that goeth forth out of My mouth: it shall not return unto Me void [or, fruitless], but it shall accomplish [or, "till it has accomplished"] that which I please, and it shall prosper in [or, "has prosperously carried out"] the thing whereto I sent it." That is to say, it will not return without having achieved the purpose for which the Lord sent it *(vv. 10, 11)*.

His Word is His messenger (see 9:8; Pss. 107:20; 147:15–19). His Word is here personified. It runs like a swift messenger, accomplishing God's will with its vital power both in nature and amidst humanity. A word is the expression of thought. It is part of the person himself. So Christ is called the Word of God. He had declared Him (told Him out), John 1:18. "Everything that proceedeth out of the mouth of the Lord" provides spiritual food by which man lives (Deut. 8:3). Just as what comes from the soil of the earth is produced by the rain and the snow, so with the soil of the human heart and the Word of God.

How great a responsibility therefore devolves upon one who is God's messenger! If the messenger's heart is in full communion with the One who sends him, his message will accomplish God's pleasure and prosper in the object for which it is sent.

In *verse 12* the Lord graciously applies the principles relating to His Word to the promise of unspeakable blessing for Israel in the coming day. **"For ye shall go out with joy,"** that is to say, life's activities will be carried on without the haste of fear (cp. 52:12), **"and be led forth with peace"**: they will never again have to fight their way through foes or flee from them: **"the mountains and the hills shall break forth before you into singing, and all the trees of the field shall clap their hands."** Nature will be brought into unison with God's purposes of grace toward His people (cp. Ps. 98:8, where the clapping of the hands is applied to streams and billows of water). There will be a sympathy, so to speak, between nature and the joyous hearts of God's redeemed. No longer will the natural creation be subjected to vanity. The creation itself "shall be delivered from the bondage of corruption into the liberty of the glory of the children of God" (Rom. 8:21, R.V.).

"Instead of the thorn shall come up the fir tree [or cypress], **and instead of the briar shall come up the myrtle tree,"** a humble, sweet-smelling, beautiful evergreen; from the Hebrew word for it comes the name Hadassah, the original name of Esther (Esth. 2:7): **"and it shall be to the Lord for a name, for an everlasting sign** (or memorial) **that shall not be cut off"** *(v. 13).* What God will bring about in the blessedness of the Millennial Kingdom will have a twofold effect: it will tell forth His glory and will be a constant reminder to His people of His attributes and actings of grace and power.

Chapter 56

The opening words of this chapter, **"Keep ye judgment and do righteousness,"** recall the admonition in verses 6 and 7 of the preceding chapter. The thoughts and the ways of Israel were not those of the Lord *(v. 8).*

The glorious promises which followed in that chapter were incentives to the wicked to forsake his way and the unrighteous man his thoughts; they were also preparatory to the present injunctions. Let them fulfill practical righteousness and they would thus become conformed to the righteousness of God's character and dealings. And the reason why they should do so is twofold: **"for My salvation,"** He says, **"is near to come** [the salvation expressed in the preceding promises], **and My righteousness to be revealed."** Righteous dealing has as its basis the relationship into which God brings His people. It was a covenanted relation with Israel, involving the fulfillment of righteousness on each side. God fulfilled His part and He was ready to manifest it if they turned from their unrighteous ways and fell into line with His. If they only realized how near His salvation and His righteous dealings were in their manifestation, this itself should have impelled them to respond to His promise and command.

A special blessing is held out to him who keeps God's command, and to the son of man **"that holdeth fast by it, that keepeth the sabbath from polluting it, and keepeth his hand from doing any evil"** *(v. 2).*

As to the sabbath, ours is a perpetual sabbath keeping; "there remaineth [i.e., continueth perpetually] a sabbath rest for the people of God" (Heb. 4:9). We ourselves can only enjoy this rest in Christ if we keep our hand from doing evil.

The stranger who had joined himself to the Lord (and there were not a few who, professing the religion of Jehovah, had joined His people) might be tempted to fear that after Israel was restored to their land the Lord would separate him from them, depriving him of the privileges he had enjoyed. The fear was ill-founded, for if they "held fast by His covenant," God would bring them to His Holy mountain, and make them joyful in His house of prayer; their burnt offerings and sacrifices would be accepted upon His altar: for His house "would be called a house of prayer for all peoples." And He who will gather the outcasts of Israel, will gather others to him beside "his own" that were gathered *(vv. 6–8,* R.V.).

There were others who might be tempted to despair, considering their condition and all that was taking place. There were the eunuchs, concerning whom a prohibition was given in Deuteronomy 23:1. But even to these a promise is given of a **"memorial [A.V., place] and a name better than of sons, and of daughters,"** an everlasting name that would not be cut off *(vv. 4, 5)*, on condition that they refrained from profaning the sabbath and held fast by the Lord's covenant. The party wall would be pulled down, which separated the eunuchs from fellowship with the congregation of Israel. All humanly erected barriers to fellowship are destined to be removed in the coming day.

Verse 9, which the R.V. marks as the beginning of a paragraph, probably commences a new subject and forms the beginning of chapter 57. The watchman and the shepherds in Israel had given way to selfishness and debauchery. They had abandoned their responsibilities toward God's people and, instead of giving warning, they were blind to the impending danger. They were **"dumb dogs,"** unable to bark. Instead of watching they were **"dreaming, lying down, loving to slumber."** Accordingly the Lord gives an invitation to the beasts of the field and the forest, metaphorically representing Gentile powers, to come and devour *(vv. 9–12).*

All whom the Lord makes responsible to act as shepherds over His flock need to guard themselves against gradual decline from their duty and against either lording it over the charge allotted to them or becoming possessed of sordid aims to acquire filthy lucre (1 Pet. 5:2, 3).

Chapter 57

In contrast to the evil watchmen and shepherds and rulers, who were simply engaged in debauchery and self-indulgence, there were the righteous, who stand out conspicuously by reason of the fact that they are taken away from the coming evil, that is to say, from the impending Divine judgments. Their removal is unheeded. They are characterized as "merciful" (or rather, godly, R.V. margin). They **"enter into peace; they rest in their beds, each one that walketh in his uprightness"** (or "straight before him," *vv. 1, 2).* While the godly suffer by oppression, and by distress at what is going on around them, they do not lose their blessedness in the sight of

God or their reward hereafter. They die in faith and go to enjoy the eternal peace of the spirits of the just made perfect (Heb. 12:23).

Far better it is to suffer death for righteousness' sake than to endeavor to enjoy ease and freedom from trouble by making compromises with the world.

A striking change in the prophet's utterances follows. There is first a warning to the evildoers to draw near to listen to the voice of God *(v. 3).* Frequently in Scripture a man's moral character is indicated by a reference to his father (2 Kin. 6:32), or his mother (1 Sam. 20:30), or both parents (Job 30:8). Accordingly those who were in captivity and continued the idolatry which had brought upon their fathers the judgment of their overthrow by the Chaldeans, are called **"sons of the sorceress, the seed of the adulterer and the whore."**

All that follows, in *verses 4 to 11,* is addressed to those who had gone into captivity. The reference to the oaks and the green trees *(v. 5)* points to those forms of tree worship by which different trees were regarded as the special abodes of different deities. Abominable orgies were associated therewith. The slaughter of the children "in the valleys and under the clefts of the rocks" was not that carried out in sacrifice to Moloch in the valley of Hinnom, but that connected with the worship of Baal (Jer. 19:5; Ezek. 16:21). In *verse 6* the reference is to stone worship, end the libations poured out thereon. In *verses 7 to 9* the idolatrous worship is further described in the metaphorical phraseology of adultery, in its faithlessness toward God.

All this wickedness involved much toil and weariness *(v. 10);* yet the people were so far gone in their alienation from the Lord, that instead of realizing the hopelessness of their condition they found **"a quickening of their strength"** (R.V.), and continued to make alliances with the heathen. The longsuffering of God did not produce repentance, but His silence by way of helping His faithful ones would not be indefinitely postponed.

There are dangers in forming associations with those who do not adhere to the Word of God, under the pretext of being regarded as charitable, and, on the other hand, as a result of urgent advice that we must all make common cause against powerful adverse forces. Faithfulness to the Lord demands our maintaining the honor of His Name at whatever cost. And as the Lord came to the help of His faithful ones in captivity, so He will in these times of laxity and apostasy.

The alliances the people were making were the outcome of fear. They took refuge in lies and did not remember God; nor did they lay it to their heart *(v. 11)*. Forgetfulness of God and a seared conscience go together. The fact that God does not intervene by way of judgment leads the hardened heart to be void of the fear of the Lord: **"Have not I held My peace even of long time, and thou fearest Me not?"** He says.

In *verse 12* the statement **"I will declare thy righteousness"** does not indicate that those with whom God was remonstrating were themselves righteous. The very opposite was the case. It was what Israel in its blind condition regarded as their own righteousness. It was a lying righteousness and its true character would be declared, i.e., exposed and judged by the Lord. This is confirmed by what follows: **"and as for thy works, they shall not profit thee. When thou criest, let them which thou hast gathered deliver thee; but the wind shall take them, a breath shall carry them all away"** *(v. 13)*.

The Lord now addresses His faithful ones among His people in captivity, and gives the assurance, **"he that putteth his trust in Me shall possess the land, and shall inherit My holy mountain."** The way is to be made for the return of the captives, and the message to be given is, **"Cast ye up, Cast ye up, prepare the way, take up the stumbling block out of the way of My people."** This receives light from 62:10, which looks on to the final gathering of Israel from among the nations (cp. 40:3, 4). The stumbling block speaks of any and every obstruction standing in the way of the return *(v. 14)*.

In the last paragraph of the chapter the Lord gives a message of combined glory and grace, concerning His twofold dwelling place, the high and holy place in Heaven and the contrite and humble spirit on earth. The latter will be the condition of His earthly people after the restoration.

If we humble ourselves under the mighty hand of God (1 Pet. 5, 6). He will exalt us, or, as He says here in Isaiah, He will revive our spirit and our heart. Contrition and humility are as cause and effect. As one has said, "The selfish egotism which repentance breaks has its root in the heart; and the self-consciousness, from whose false elevation repentance brings down, has its seat in the spirit."

If the Lord were to contend continually and always be wroth, the spirit of the object of His righteous anger would fail before Him **"and the souls which He has made"** *(v. 16)*. Here significantly the Lord gives a reminder that the very existence of the soul is due to His creative power, and this is His touching appeal for contrition and humility before Him. In spite of His creative mercy, it became a necessity for Him to destroy the whole human race, save for eight souls, at the time of the Flood. The spread of the physical corruption consequent upon the unlicensed moral depravity of the race, and their persistent lack of repentance, would have terminated in a more terrible way than even by the Flood. The present statement seems to have a connection with the promise made after judgment had been inflicted, that God would not utterly destroy the race again.

Perhaps in fulfilling that promise, and certainly by reason of His covenant with Abraham and his seed, the Lord now makes a promise to Israel that, having smitten him for his covetousness (or rather, selfishness) and for the turning away of his own heart (margin), He would heal him, and lead him, and restore comforts unto him, and particularly to those who mourned by reason of their wanderings *(vv. 17, 18)*.

Verse 19 shows that the effects of God's dealings will divide the nation in twain. For those who became contrite and humble there would be "peace, peace," in all their scattered condition, those who were far offend those who were near. The doubling of the word conveys its perfection and perpetuity, i.e., "perfect peace," as in 26:3. This will produce worship and songs of praise; hence the Lord introduces the promise of peace by the statement, *"I create the fruit of the lips."*

On the other hand there will be the impenitent, the wicked, for whom there is no peace, who **"are like the troubled sea; for it cannot rest, and its waters cast up mire and dirt"** *(vv. 20, 21)*.

CHAPTER NINE

Part IIIc
The Godly and Ungodly in Israel
Chapters 58 to 66

Chapter 58

This chapter begins a new section of the prophecies, and in the first part the main features resemble those in what has preceded, namely, rebuke, warning, and promise. The prophet is commanded to cry around (lit., "with full throat"), to lift up his voice like a trumpet, in order to declare to Israel their transgression, and the sins of the house of Jacob. *Verse 2* exposes their self-righteousness. They were at all events outwardly conformed to the ways and ordinances of God; they even delighted in approaching Him in their external religion; but they made their professed conformity to His regulations a ground of complaint that God seemed to take no notice of them. As a matter of fact, there was no real exercise of heart before Him, no contrition and humility and true communion with the Lord. Even in the day of their fast, their external ritual (cp. Zech. 7:3; 8:19), they found their own pleasure instead of His. They oppressed their laborers, they engaged in strife and contention, smiting with the fist of wickedness. That was not the kind of fast which would make their voice to be heard on high; it was not the kind of fast which God had chosen, not the kind of fast by which a man would really afflict his soul, bow down his head as a rush, and spread sackcloth and ashes under him. The fast that God chose should lead to the loosing of the bonds of wickedness, the undoing of the bands of the yoke, letting the oppressed go free, breaking every yoke, dealing bread to the hungry, taking in the poor and homeless, clothing the naked, and not turning away from kith and kin.

If they were in fellowship with the Lord in these respects their light would break forth as the morning and their healing would spring forth speedily; their true righteousness would go before them as the precursor of blessing, and the glory of the Lord would be their reward. Their prayer would receive an answer and their cry to God would meet with His reply, "Here I am." Let them draw out their soul to the hungry (or bestow on the hungry what their soul desired); let them satisfy the afflicted. Then their light would rise in darkness, and their obscurity would be as the noonday *(vv. 6–10)*.

Mere external religion and outward conformity to ritual are easy. Moreover they tend to produce a spirit of self-satisfaction. What meets with God's approval is that obedience to His word which firstly keeps the soul in true exercise of heart before Him and then leads to the fulfillment of all righteousness in our ways and relationships with others. We may seek strictly to attend certain spiritual duties, while all the time the heart is not right with God, and there is sin in the life which His all-seeing eye does not fail to discern. This is the message and lesson of this passage.

Verse 11 resumes from verse 8 the promises of abundant blessings if the conditions are fulfilled. What is promised here is (1) uninterrupted guidance, (2) soul-satisfaction even in extreme drought or barrenness, (3) the impartation of strength, so that the very physical frame becomes an instrument of the fulfillment of His will, (4) the verdant beauty of a watered garden, setting forth the beauteous effects of the indwelling Spirit of God, (5) the outflowing of blessing by the Holy Spirit, represented as a spring or fountain of water, whose waters do not deceive (A.V. margin). While all this is promised to Israel the Lord graciously designs to make it good in the present life of the believer.

In *verse 12* there is promise of national revival. The phrase **"they that shall be of thee"** is another way of saying "thy people." These, returning from exile, will build up the old ruins and raise up what had been laid as foundations generations ago, so that the people shall receive the title **"The repairer of the breach, The restorer of paths to dwell in,"** or of streets, formerly places of habitation.

But again, there are conditions. The Israelite must hold back his foot from the sabbath and from doing his pleasure or business on God's holy day, calling the sabbath a delight, **"and the holy of the Lord honorable,"** honoring it by not doing his own will, or finding his own pleasure or business, or "speaking words" (that is, words of no value, a multitude of vain utterances such as boastings and mere gossip). The one who abstained from all this would delight himself in the Lord. So it was not merely a matter of keeping a commandment. The Lord Himself is inseparable from His Law. His commandment is but the expression of His own character.

As has been pointed out, our sabbath in this day of the indwelling Holy Spirit and His ministry, is not one day in the week; "there remaineth [i.e., abideth continually] a sabbath rest [a *sabbatismos*, a sabbath-keeping] for the people of God." Our rest is in the living and glorified Christ on the ground of His finished work at Calvary. This rest does not depend on special days, it is not intermittent. If kept uninterruptedly as God designs it for us, then our delight is in the Lord and we may enjoy constant fellowship with Him. We are ever to refrain from doing our pleasure, pursuing our own ways and engaging in any business as if it was our own. If we do so we cannot enjoy the privilege of rest in Christ. We are ever to abstain from useless talk of the lips, which "tendeth only to penury" (Prov. 14:23).

Delighting oneself in the Lord is the highest possible occupation. It is the privilege of the believer, whether in seasons of communion and worship or in the activity of service. But it is possible only as the admonitions which have preceded in this passage are fulfilled.

There are yet further promises: **"and I will make thee to ride upon the high places of the earth"** *(v. 14)*. This refers especially to Palestine for the restored people

and conveys the thought of their sovereign rights and dominant position, and that not only over the land but over the nations as well.

For us it speaks of our possessions with Christ in the Heavenly places *(Eph. 1:3)*. These spiritual blessings are our present possession and are realizable according as we renounce worldly advantages, taking up our cross daily and following Christ.

The next promise is **"I will feed thee with the heritage of Jacob thy father."** Israel has never yet been able to experience this. Their apostasy has prevented it. But it holds good for the godly remnant in the future, and its fulfillment is unthwartable, **"for the mouth of the Lord hath spoken it"** (cp. 1:20; 24:3; 40:5).

Chapter 59

This chapter continues and expands the subject of the perverseness and transgressions which have hindered the blessings promised, and which raise a barrier between God and His people. The Lord's hand was not shortened that it could not save; His power was ever ready to be put at their disposal. His ear was not heavy that it could not hear; He was only too willing to respond to their cry if they had hearkened to His word. But their iniquities had effected a separation from Him and had caused His face to be hid from them *(vv. 1, 2)*.

The Lord cannot hold communion with the willful heart. He cannot look down on sin with complacency. Perverseness of the will prevents the enjoyment of the light of His countenance.

The prophet now exposes their evil ways, their murders, lies and unrighteousness, and their trust in *tohu*, that is, in what is worthless *(vv. 3, 4)*. He then employs the twofold metaphor of the hatching of basilisks' eggs and weaving the spider's web (cp. Job 8:14). The former indicates the injurious character of all that they do. There is a twofold result; whoever eats of their eggs dies, and if an egg is trodden upon, it splits into an adder, which attacks the heel of the one who has disturbed it *(v. 5)*. The second metaphor signifies the valuelessness and injurious character of their activities. No garment is produced by their weaving and their works are characterized by iniquity and violence.

The next description of their evil doings *(vv. 7, 8)* is used by Paul in Romans 3:15–17, in a free rendering of the passage, to describe the universal guilt of mankind. Isaiah contrasts their ways of desolation and destruction with the way of peace, firstly in relation to God and then of their fellowmen, for whoever follows their paths does not know peace. He who loves peace makes it his aim to produce it both by example and effort.

From *verse 9 to verse 15* the prophet changes from the third person plural to the first, and includes himself with his people, both in acknowledging transgression and in stating the effects of judgments of God upon them. He says **"Therefore is judgment far from us, neither doth righteousness overtake us."** God was not dealing with Israel's enemies in the exercise of His righteous judgment upon the foe; hence His people were left undefended, though His salvation was ever near to come and His righteousness to be revealed (56:1). They looked for light, but behold darkness; for brightness, but they walked in obscurity (or rather, thick darkness). The words are the same as in 8:22 (see the R.V.), which, by the way, is one of the many testimonies to the unity of Isaiah. Those in exile hoped for release, but matters grew worse for them instead of better. They groped like blind men along a wall without finding an exit. They stumbled as if they were in the twilight, although God had given them the light of noonday.

Those who persist in error find no help from the light of God's truth, although it is there for them. Christ Himself and the very Scriptures have become a stumbling block to the Jews. So it is in Christendom: the Scriptures are read but not understood. The blinding power of ecclesiastical traditions obscures the light of God's word, and people who have the Bible remain in religious bondage, unable to enjoy the truth which would set them free if they faithfully listened to its voice instead of adhering to the systems of men.

The first part of *verse 11* depicts two conditions. Roaring like bears suggests impatience; mourning like doves suggests despondency; both are the very opposite to that peace of soul which arises from contrition of heart and submission to God's will. All this befell them because their transgressions were multiplied before the Lord and their sins bore witness against them. Moreover, it was not as if they sinned in ignorance. They knew that they were doing wrong *(v. 12)*, that they were denying the Lord, and turning away from following their God, and at the same time **"speaking oppression and revolt,"** or rather, untruth, the same word as in Deuteronomy 19:16, rendered "wrongdoing" (R.V.), margin, "rebellion," where the evil referred to is that of false accusation.

In *verse 14* the statements **"judgment is turned away backward and righteousness standeth afar off"** do not speak of God's retributive dealings, they continue the description of the evil condition of the people. Truth had fallen in the marketplace. Where righteous dealing should have been in evidence, not only was truth lacking, but anyone who departed from evil rendered himself the subject of plunder (the verb is usually rendered "to spoil"), *verse 15*.

The latter part of verse 15 should really begin verse 16, and from this to the end of verse 18 forms the third part of the chapter. We are now given to see the attitude of the Lord toward such a condition of things and the manner of His judicial intervention. **"The Lord saw it, and it displeased Him that there was no judgment** [or right]. **And He saw that there was no man,"** that is, that there was no man possessed of either the character or the ability to stem the tide of evil *(v. 16)*. For this use of the word "man" see Jeremiah 5:1. There is an old Jewish saying "Where there is no man, I strive to be a man."

God **"wondered** [or was astonished, expressing His displeasure rather than anything like human wonder] **that there was no intercessor,"** no one acting on the side of God on behalf of His people as against their abominations and the inevitable consequences *(v. 16)*.

In consequence of this God prepared Himself for judicial intervention. The description is vivid and striking. Different forms of expression are used: (1) direct statement, (2) similes and metaphors: (1) **"His own arm brought salvation unto Him; and His righteousness it upheld Him."** No one could be found to cooperate with Him in that form of salvation by which His cause would be vindicated; so His own arm brought it about. No one could be found to act in righteousness in fellowship with Him; so the self-sustaining power of His own righteousness wrought for the requisite end.

God uses sanctified human agents to engage in His work and fulfill His will toward others. Witness the testimony of the prophets, "messengers in the Lord's message" (Hag. 1:13; cp. Is. 44:26), and the employment by Christ of His disciples. Paul describes those who preach the gospel as "God's fellow workers" (2 Cor. 6:1).

Next are similes and metaphors: **"And He put on righteousness as a breastplate, and a helmet of salvation upon His head; and He put on garments of vengeance for clothing, and was clad with zeal as a cloak"** *(v. 17)*. There is nothing actually physical about this. The armor and the vesture depict the various manifestations of His character and power, the actings of His justice and His mercy (just as in Eph. 6 the believer's panoply describes the spiritual powers at our disposal to meet the foe).

In explanation of this there follows a prophecy unfolding in order the great events of the future in relation to Israel. Firstly, the Lord will deal with the rebellious in Israel, inflicting punishment upon those in the nation who will persistently associate themselves with the Antichrist. These are the adversaries referred to in the first part of *verse 18*. That seems clear from what has preceded in this chapter, especially *verses 14 and 15*. It is to these apostates that the statement refers, **"According to their deeds, accordingly He will repay, fury to his adversaries, recompense to His enemies."**

Secondly, judgments must fall upon the foes of God in the world of Gentiles. These are indicated by the term "the islands," or coastlands. This is an inclusive word, embracing the furthest nations of the Gentiles. They will be gathered together at the end of this age, "against the Lord and against His Christ." Similarly the isles and their inhabitants, in Isaiah 42:10, and the isles of Kittim, in Jeremiah 2:10, are joined with Kedar, to indicate all lands from west to east. This rebellion against the Lord on the part of the federated nations is described in the next verse: **"for he shall come as a rushing stream, which the breath of the Lord driveth"** (R.V.). How the Lord will intervene for the overthrow of His foes, how **"the Spirit of the Lord shall lift up a standard against him,"** is described further in chapter 63:1-6.

Thirdly, following these judgments, they that are left of the nations will **"fear the Name of the Lord from the west, and His glory from the rising of the sun"** *(v. 19)*. This will be compulsory subjection and recognition of the claims of God and of His Son. Fourthly, there will come the deliverance of God's earthly people, the remnant in the nation, who (unlike their godless fellow nationals, who will have perished with the Beast and the false prophet and their associates) will remain faithful to the Lord, multitudes of them having been converted to their coming Messiah through the testimony of the witnesses mentioned in Revelation 11:3-12 (see also 12:17). **"And a Redeemer shall come to Zion, and unto them that turn from transgression in Jacob, saith the Lord"** *(v. 20)*.

The chapter closes with the promise of the new covenant *(v. 21)*. It is based upon God's words to Abraham in Genesis 17:4. The message **"My Spirit that is upon thee . . ."** is addressed to the restored nation, who will testify for the Lord continually. They will never cease to declare His word and bear witness for Him. The terms of the covenant are fully given in Jeremiah 31:31-34, and Hebrews 8:10-12 and 10:16, 17.

Chapter 60

As a result of what has just preceded a rousing message comes at once to Zion. Long has it remained in darkness and desolation, but the Millennial glory is coming, and the command "Arise" *(v. 1)* is a word imparting power in the very command. She is to rise out of the dust and to shine, for her light, or Light-giver, is come, causing the glory of the Lord to rise upon her, a contrast to the condition in 59:10 (cp. ch. 2:5)!

Verse 2 reveals the condition of the Gentiles in their gross darkness which will exist especially under the Antichrist and which will linger until the Lord "arises upon Israel and His glory will be seen upon them." Then "nations shall come to their light, and kings to the brightness of their rising."

Until the Lord comes to receive His Church to Himself the light of Gospel testimony shines into individual hearts, while nations still lie in darkness. At the time of the removal of the Church, the deceptive power of the Devil and the rule of the Man of Sin will plunge them into gross darkness. Scripture does not justify the idea that the Gospel will spread through the world until whole nations receive the light. Only when Israel is restored will whole nations receive the light of Divine testimony and acknowledge the truth relating to the living God and His Christ. All earthly might will yield subjection by sheer compulsion, to the Lord and His glorified people.

Not only will the nations come up to Jerusalem as their center, but they will bring God's people from all the countries where they have been scattered. **"Thy sons shall come from far, and thy daughters shall be carried in the arms,"** probably as little ones cling to the side of those who are carrying them *(v. 4)*. Thus the passage recalls 49:22, 23. The statement is metaphorical of the care and security to be provided by Gentile powers.

Verse 5 describes the awestruck joy with which God's earthly people will find themselves delivered and so abundantly blessed. The prophecy **"Then thou shalt see and be lightened [R.V.], and thine heart shall tremble and be enlarged,"** is not suggestive of fear, but of a trembling for joy, as the following passage makes clear.

The tremendous change in the circumstances of the nation will produce not only a joyous thrill but an enlargment of heart to apprehend the infinite goodness of God. The Gentile nations will devote their energies to the enrichment of God's people, and above all the Lord will thereby glorify and beautify the House of His glory, and upon the altar raised in connection with it commemorative sacrifices will be offered continually *(v. 7)*.

The question in *verse 8,* **"Who are these that fly as a cloud, and as the doves to their windows?"** can well be realized in view of the enormous development of passenger aviation in our times. The transference of the scattered Jews to their own territory could

be accomplished in the course of a few days by this means.

"Surely the isles shall wait for Me" *(v. 9)*. This indicates that the far-off nations of the world will act under God's decree and direction and Gentile activity will be exercised in these matters, not by way merely of a political scheme, but with the definite object of honoring the Lord. They will minister of their wealth and substance, **"for the Name of the LORD thy God, and for the Holy One of Israel, because He hath glorified thee."**

In *verse 10* the promise **"strangers shall build up thy walls, and their kings shall minister unto thee"** does not refer to the post-captivity decrees of Cyrus, Darius and others, but to the beginning of the Millennium and the activity on the part of Gentile nations in rendering assistance to Israel. That such assistance will be voluntary rather than by way of subjection is indicated in verse 6.

The Lord then contrasts His mercy with His wrath, as in several other places in Scripture (see, e.g., 54:7, 8 and cp. 63:4). In a special sense mercy will glory against judgment (Jas. 2:13, R.V.).

That the gates of the city will be open continually *(v. 11)* implies a state of peace, of freedom from attack, so that the wealth of the nations (R.V.) may have free entrance, and that their kings may come in triumphal procession (cp. Rev. 21:25, 26).

Verse 12 shows that God's judgments will be exercised during the Millennium upon nations that manifest a spirit of rebellion and refuse to render help to Israel (see also Zech. 14:17–19).

The promise of this ministry of the Gentiles is resumed in *verse 14.* There is, however, an interlude in *verse 13,* in which the Lord delights to foretell the glory of His sanctuary, the beautiful Millennial Temple, and to indicate His presence there by speaking of it as **"the place of My feet."**

That the glory of Lebanon, with its splendid trees (cp. 41:19) will be brought to beautify the place of the sanctuary, would seem to indicate that these trees will be planted in the environment of the Temple, perhaps by way of avenues. What is referred to here is not timber for the structure itself, but "the place," that is, the vicinity.

Verse 14 briefly looks back to the time of the great tribulation, to those who afflicted

God's people. Now it will be their sons that come bending to them. Their fathers will have perished in the judgments of the day of the Lord. There will be a multitude of people who, while not having gathered themselves together against the Lord, will yet have despised God's people during the time of hostility. These will bow themselves down at the feet of Israel and will call Jerusalem "**The city of the Lord, the Zion of the Holy One of Israel.**" Instead of being forsaken and hated like a slighted wife (cp. Deut. 21:15), the Lord will make the city "**an eternal excellency, a joy of many generations**" *(v. 15)*. The nations and their kings will bestow their vital energy upon God's people, just as a mother gives her milk to a child. And above all, instead of being in a state of blind ignorance of God, they will recognize Jehovah as "**thy Savior and thy Redeemer, the Mighty One of Jacob.**"

We may gather from *verse 17* that (instead of wood and stone) gold, silver, bronze, and iron will be used for the building of the city, so that it will be indestructible by the elements of nature and by every sort of foe. Peace, here personified, will act as magistrates, and righteousness will act as bailiffs. Violence, desolation and destruction will be absent. The walls of the city will be called "Salvation," for the city will be impregnable; the gates will be called "Praise," for God will glorify His name there continually *(v. 18)*.

The sun and the moon will still exist, but will not be needed, owing to the effulgence radiating from the presence of the Lord and the Church, with His uncreated Shekinah glory *(v. 20;* cp. Rev. 22:5). This will be verily the triumph of light over darkness.

Under such conditions there could be no such thing as mourning; "**sorrow and sighing shall flee away,**" and will give place to everlasting joy (see 35:10). Joy is always intensified by the fact of the preceding sorrow and trial from which deliverance has come. The trusting believer can ever say of his trials "I was brought low, and He helped me."

In the Millennial state the fruitfulness and glory of nature will be accompanied by the moral excellence of the nation. The people will be "**all righteous**" *(v. 21)*. The word "Jew" will never again be a term of national and moral reproach. Israel will be in permanent possession of the land, and that by what is here meta-

phorically described as "**the Lord's planting.**" It will be by reason of this that they are righteous. They will be like a green shoot or sprout (Eng. text, "branch"). The same word is used of Christ in 11:1. God's grace will do the planting, and that for His glory.

The nation will become abundantly fruitful from the point of view of population; "**The little one** [perhaps the one with few children] **shall become a thousand, and the small one** [perhaps one in humble position] **a strong nation**" *(v. 22)*. That means not only numerical increase in population but the extension of joyous fellowship. Moreover all this blessedness will be accomplished with great rapidity: "**I the LORD will hasten it in its time.**"

Chapter 61

Up to the end of the last chapter the speaker was Jehovah. In the first verse of this chapter there comes a change; the speaker is not Isaiah but Christ the Messiah. In confirmation of this, what He says about Himself is identical with what has already been said about the Servant of Jehovah. He says, "**the Spirit of the Lord God is upon Me**" (see 42:1); "**the Lord hath anointed Me to preach good tidings unto the meek. He hath sent Me** [see 48:16] **to bind up the brokenhearted** [cp. 50:4], **to proclaim liberty to the captives, and the opening of the prison to them that are bound**" (see 42:7; 49:9). When the Lord Jesus was in the synagogue at Nazareth, having read this very passage, He closed the roll and said "Today hath this Scripture been fulfilled in your ears" (Luke 4:17–21).

This passage speaks of the Trinity. The Three in One are mentioned in the very first words uttered by the Lord. The title "the Lord God," Adonai Jehovah, is the same as is mentioned four times in 50:4–9. Some manuscripts omit "the Lord" here.

The anointing was probably what took place when, at His baptism, "the Holy Ghost descended in a bodily form, as a dove, upon Him" (Luke 3:22, together with 4:1, 18).

The word rendered "the meek" primarily signifies suffering ones. The binding up of the brokenhearted is that of applying a relieving bandage to heart wounds. The Gospel of Luke almost immediately records the Lord's tender acts in this respect (see 4:40; also the case of the widow of Nain, 7:13–15; the woman with the issue of blood, and the daughter of Jairus, 8:43–56; the women with the spirit of infirmity, 13:11–13; and the lepers in Samaria, 17:11–19).

So with the proclamation of liberty to the captive, those who were bound with the fetters of sin and of the Devil. The phrase rendered **"the opening of the prison"** should probably read as in the R.V. margin, "the opening of the eyes" (as in 35:5; 42:7). There were many who were spiritually imprisoned and blinded by the religions of the Pharisees, Scribes and Sadducees (the Lord remarks upon their blindness in Matt. 23:24).

Great the joy when the blinding film of human tradition and religion is removed by the power of the ascended Lord through the Spirit! great the gladness and gratitude in the possession of liberty and spiritual sight!

He was sent **"to proclaim the acceptable year of the LORD,"** (lit., "the year of the LORD'S good pleasure," *v. 2*). *The year* stands not for a particular date but for a season. That season lasted during the days of the Lord's testimony and subsequently in the proclamation of the Gospel to Israel; it applies in a wider sense to the whole period of Gospel grace. God in mercy will shorten the period of the exercise of His wrath. The Lord, in quoting this passage in the synagogue, finished His quotation at the preceding clause. He had not come to earth to usher in the day of vengeance. Later He foretold that the days of vengeance would come upon the nation, and that Jerusalem would be "trodden down of the Gentiles, until the times of the Gentiles be fulfilled" (Luke 21:22–24).

The objects next mentioned, **"to comfort all that mourn; to appoint unto them that mourn in Zion"** *(v. 3)* will be fulfilled after the time of "Jacob's trouble," when the godly remnant in Israel will have passed through their time of unprecedented sorrow. The Lord, coming as their Deliverer at His Second Advent, will delight to minister His comfort, giving them (what follows is the object of the verb "appoint," lit., to put upon, resumed in the verb to give) **"a garland for ashes,"** (lit., a diadem, to adorn the head). For the sprinkling of ashes on the head of those in sorrow see, e.g., 2 Samuel 13:19.

The oil of joy is emblematic of that which refreshes and cheers (see Ps. 45:7). This is to be imparted in the day when the Lord sets up His Kingdom over the world in the midst of His earthly people. He will clothe them with **"the garment of praise for** [i.e., instead of] **the spirit of heaviness"** (the word describes a condition burdensome enough to cause one's death). As a garment upon the body so will be the praise of the redeemed as the expression of inward jubilation.

The Lord who makes all things work together for good to them that love Him, turns our very sorrow into joy. There could be no such joy if there were no preceding sorrow. The dark cloud makes the following sunshine all the brighter.

The change wrought by the Lord in Israel will likewise be of a moral character. They will be called **"trees of righteousness."** Trees suggest firmness, fullness, verdure and fruit. So with the righteousness which will characterize the nation. This will not be their own doing, it will be **"the planting of the LORD, that He might be glorified"** (cp. 60:21).

Verses 4 to 9 foretell the restoration of Palestine and the exaltation of Israel to their appointed position of dignity and honor and authority over the Gentile nations. Places that were waste and desolate will be fertile and thickly populated. Those who belonged to nations that afflicted them in their time of trouble will now minister to them as shepherds of their flocks, farm laborers and cultivators.

They themselves will be what the Lord designed them to be from the beginning, "a kingdom of priests" (Ex. 19:6). Accordingly in this high service they will be, from the earthly point of view, associated with the Church in its priestly ministry. Not only so, the Gentile nations will recognize them as acting in this capacity and will acknowledge the God of Israel as the true God. All the Gentile powers who have in past periods used the world for their self-enrichment, will become the possession of His people, who will **"eat the wealth of the nations."** All that the Gentiles boasted in, glorying in their development and prowess and in the objects to which they devoted the products and deposits of the earth, vill be bestowed upon Israel under the benign nd firm administration of Christ.

This whole subject is described by the postle Paul in Romans 11:12 to 32. If their all and their present loss has meant the riches f the Gentiles through gospel grace and ministry, still greater will be the effect of their ullness, that is, the full national prosperity f Israel. "As touching the gospel, they are nemies for your sake: but as touching the election [the predestining counsel of God concerning them], they are beloved for the fahers' sake."

"For their shame they shall have double" *(v. 7).* They will have, so to speak, a louble posession in their land, which will be extended far beyond its former confines. Whereas formerly they were in confusion, the objects of reproach and contempt, they will be illed with exceeding and unending joy. There vill be altogether a double compensation for heir former sufferings.

In *verse 8* the Lord makes known that in all his blessing His own character will be vindiated. He declares that He loves judgment and ates robbery with iniquity (R.V.), referring to he cruel treatment which Israel had sustained rom their adversaries. In direct contrast to his He will give them their recompense in ruth and make an everlasting covenant with hem, with the result that they will be recogized among the nations as those whom the Lord has blessed—a complete reversal of resent conditions.

What follows in *verses 10 and 11* has been egarded by some as the utterance of the reeemed nation. It seems, however, almost ertain that the Speaker is the same Person s in the beginning of the chapter. It is surely Christ, speaking in identification with His peole and declaring His joy in Jehovah on their ehalf. He is regarding what will have been ccomplished in the coming day as if it were lready fulfilled. The garments of salvation vith which the godly ones in Israel will be lothed are His own garments. Just as a bridexroom **"decketh himself with a garland, nd as a bride adorneth herself with her ewels,"** so will the Lord manifest Himself in His glory and beauty in His relation to His edeemed people.

The word rendered "decketh" signifies to eck as a priest, and it is in that capacity that the Lord will act in the day when His righteousness is manifested in the earth. He will then be the revealed antitype of Melchizedek. He will act in the threefold capacity of a King, Priest and a Bridegroom. The picture of the bride adorning herself with her jewels especially portrays His earthly Kingdom as wedded to Himself. So with regard to the Church, He acts, and ever will act, as a royal Priest (Heb. 7:17; 9:11), and as her Heavenly Bridegroom (Eph. 5:25-32).

Just as the earth brings forth its sprouts and as the garden causes the things that are sown in it to sprout up, so the Lord GOD will cause righteousness and praise (or renown) to spring forth (or sprout up) before all the nations. It is God that causes the seed to germinate, and the Bearer of the seed is Jehovah's Servant. All these processes are at work through the gospel among all nations, but the immediate application here is the Millennial state of Israel.

Chapter 62

The Speaker here is not Isaiah but the LORD, as is clear from verse 6. He says He will not retain silence nor will He rest until Zion's righteousness shall go forth as the brightness of the morning and her salvation as a blazing torch. These are the actual comparisons in *verse 1*.

Verse 2 resumes what was said at the end of the preceding chapter concerning the righteousness and renown of the people as manifest to all the Gentiles. Again, the completely new position of the people will be marked by His bestowal of a new name, to correspond with their changed character. In Jeremiah 33:16 the name is mentioned as "Jehovah is our righteousness." Just as now in the case of the believer righteousness is reckoned by grace and manifested in character and conduct, so with redeemed Israel. This is what the whole passage from 61:10 to 62:2 sets forth.

The figurative language of *verse 3* is intensely beautiful. The metaphor which describes the condition of Zion is that of **"a crown** [or coronet] **of beauty in the hand of the Lord, and a royal diadem in the hand of thy God."** The word rendered "diadem" is used of the mitre, or rather, turban, of the High Priest (Ex. 28:4, 39; Zech. 3:5). Two different Hebrew words are used for the "hand" here, the first signifying the open hand, but indicating that which is held out for display. The two together set forth the intense delight in the heart of the Lord in manifesting the effects of His grace and redeeming power.

Again the two descriptions mark the combination of royal authority and priesthood, and in this twofold capacity Israel will share the authority of Christ. At various times in the world's history from that of Nimrod (Gen. 10:9) to that of the Antichrist (Rev. 13), men of renown have sought to exercise this double function, so as to have authority over both the religious and the civil life of those under them. The whole history is one of dismal failure and catastrophe.

In the day to come Jerusalem will no more be called "The Forsaken one" and the land will no longer be called "Desolate." The city will be known as **"Hephzi-bah"** (My delight in her) and the land **"Beulah"** (married); His love will be as strong and as full of joy as the love of the newly married. The thought in each part of the verse is that of winning an inalienable right by a bridegroom "to have and to hold" *(vv. 4, 5)*.

The same figure is used of what the believer should be in spiritual union with Christ (see Rom. 7:4). We are married (R.V., joined) "to Him who was raised from the dead, that we might bring forth fruit unto God." We are to live therefore as those in whom He can delight.

With a view to all this God has stationed watchmen upon the walls of Jerusalem who day and night intercede with Him until His purposes concerning His earthly people are accomplished. The watchmen symbolize those who pray for the peace of Jerusalem. That special intercession should be our constant occupation. The language is vivid: **"Ye that are the Lord's remembrancers, take ye no rest, and give Him no rest, till He establish, and till He make Jerusalem a praise in the earth"** *(vv. 6, 7)*. The word rendered "establish" signifies to make ready, to prepare for oneself (cp. 51:13, margin).

That such intercession is the will of God is confirmed by the statement of the Lord's oath in *verses 8 and 9*: **"The Lord hath sworn by His right hand and by the arm of His strength"** (i.e., His strong arm). With this compare Hebrews 6:13. He declares that Gentile powers shall never again pillage the land and rob its rightful owners of that which they have produced. On the contrary, His people who have garnered their grain **"shall eat it, and praise the Lord."**

Forcibly this reminds us that for all which the Lord bestows upon us by way of material benefits such as food and raiment, we should be in the habit of praising Him day by day. Our thanks at mealtimes should never become formal. It should be given out of the heart which ever recognizes the goodness of God. The food we eat is "sanctified by the Word of God and prayer" (1 Tim. 4:5).

Further, in the coming day these who have gathered in their wine **"shall drink it in the courts of My sanctuary."** They will delight to go up to the house of the Lord with hearts overwhelmed with gratitude.

This constant going up to the House of the Lord receives a vivid anticipation in the command in *verse 10* yet to be issued: **"Go through, go through the gates; prepare ye the way** [or clear the way] **of the people."** Obstacles in the way of ready entrance are to be removed: **"cast up, cast up the high way; gather out the stones."** The way of the people will be the way of the Lord (see 40:3). This has a spiritual application as well as a physical. Everything that is an obstacle to spiritual blessing will be removed from the hearts of Israel.

All that presents a stumbling block, all that hinders our enjoyment of free and constant access to the Throne of Grace, everything that stands in the way of our communion with God is to be removed. Often there is much rubbish to be cleared out, such as worldly associations and fleshly desires.

Verses 11 and 12 depict the fulfillment of these promises to Israel, a banner is to be lifted up to all the Gentile nations (the word at the end of verse 10 is plural, "peoples"). For the Lord will sound out tidings to the end of the earth. There is to be a general acknowledgment of the manifestation of God's power toward His people in that their salvation has come, that **"His reward is with Him, and His recompense before Him."** The nations will recognize Israel as **"The holy people,**

The redeemed of the Lord." The city which no one cared for will be called "Sought out, A city not forsaken." That is to say, men will resort to Jerusalem. They will go there to see its glory and beauty. The wonders of God's grace and power will be manifest to them. The city will be full of people, and the streets will be filled with boys and girls enjoying their play there (Zech. 8:4, 5).

Chapter 63

The first six verses of this chapter consist of a dialogue between the redeemed remnant of Israel, delivered from their great tribulation, and the Lord. The time is that of Christ's Personal intervention for the overthrow of the Gentile foes gathered under the Antichrist in Palestine. Accordingly the passage follows appropriately after the divine promises given in chapter 62.

The Jewish people, delivered from their enemies ask, with astonishment at the power and glory of their great Deliverer, "Who is this that cometh from Edom, with dyed garments from Bozrah? this that is glorious in His apparel, marching [R.V.] in the greatness of His strength? (v. 1). He comes not as a traveler (as in the A.V.), but as a Conqueror at the head of His armies (see Rev. 19:14).

But why does He come from Edom and Bozrah? The answer is to be found in a comparison of Psalm 29 with Daniel 11:45, in the latter of which the word rendered "palace" should be "encampment," the military base of the king of the North after his return from conquering Egypt, with a view to the overthrow of his national Gentile foes gathered under the ten-kingdomed confederacy of the Roman powers. All the Gentile nations are thus assembled at the warfare of Har-Magedon (Rev. 16:16). Psalm 29 describes poetically the complete overthrow of all the nations by the power of the voice of the Lord. The geography of that Psalm is interesting and significant. The overthrow begins in Lebanon (vv. 5 and 6) and sweeps down to the wilderness of Kadesh (v. 8), the center of which is Bozrah (cp. Num. 13:26). The destruction is swift and complete. The distance from Sirion in Lebanon to Bozrah in Edom is 200 miles,

or 1600 furlongs, which is the very distance foretold in Revelation 14:20 in a passage parallel to Isaiah 63, concerning the winepress of the wrath of God. The harmony of Scripture in its various parts is thus strikingly illustrated.

In reply to the question of the delivered nation, the Lord answers "I that speak in righteousness, mighty to save." The "I that speak" corresponds to "the voice of the Lord" in Psalm 29 (see also Ps. 2:5) and to the sword which comes forth out of His mouth, as mentioned in Revelation 19:21. His righteousness will then be manifested in the deliverance of His earthly people.

In verse 2 a second question is asked by them: "Wherefore art Thou red in Thine apparel, and Thy garments like him that treadeth in the winefat [or rather, winevat]?" The Lord's response to this in verses 3, 4 makes clear the time of the event, namely, the final destruction of Gentile powers before the Millennial reign. He says "I have trodden the winepress alone; and of the peoples [plural] there was no man with Me: yea, I trod them in Mine anger, and trampled them in My fury; and their lifeblood is sprinkled upon My garments, and I have stained all My raiment. For the day of vengeance was in Mine heart, and the year of My redeemed is come." With this vividly metaphorical description of the treading of the winepress compare Joel 3:9-16; Revelation 14:17-20 and 19:15. The day and the year are contrasted. The time of the Lord's wrath is short, for "the Lord will execute His word upon the earth, finishing it and cutting it short" (Rom. 9:28).

The tenderness of the heart of the Lord toward His people, His by covenant and promise, is manifested in the rest of His response to the second question, "And I looked, and there was none to help; and I wondered that there was none to uphold: therefore Mine own arm brought salvation unto Me; and My fury, it upheld Me. And I trod down the peoples in Mine anger, and made them drunk in My fury, and I poured out their life blood on the earth" (vv. 5, 6).

In the 7th verse Isaiah, speaking as representing his people at the time of their deliverance, as just mentioned in verses 1 to 6, and by way of response to the Lord's goodness, says "I will make mention of the loving-kindneses of the LORD, and the praises of the LORD, according to all that the LORD hath bestowed on us; and the great goodness toward the house of Israel which He hath bestowed on them according to His mercies, and according to the multitude of His lovingkindnesses."

Such language befits our lips who have been granted Heavenly and spiritual deliverances and blessings, in addition to earthly mercies.

Verse 8 expresses God's approval of His redeemed people, the righteous remnant who have waited for His salvation during the time of the great tribulation, in contrast to the many who will have remained in apostasy, owning allegiance to the Antichrist. This contrast is intimated in the Divine declaration, **"Surely, they are My people, children that will not deal falsely."** The prophet then records that for this reason **"He was their Savior,"** and proceeds to show how He acted as such: **"In all their affliction He was afflicted"** *(v. 9).*

Some manuscripts have the word "not" in the latter part of this statement, with the meaning that in all their adversity He was no adversary to them (see the R.V. margin). The weight of evidence, however, supports the rendering of our Versions. In a day long gone by, when Israel returned to the Lord in repentance for their sins as a result of His chastisements, "His soul was grieved for the misery of Israel" (Judg. 10:16; cp. 2:18). So in the coming time of Jacob's trouble His dealings will have in view both the overthrow of their enemies and the removal of His chastening hand at the appointed time. The statement reveals the tenderness of the Lord's compassions. His chastisements are ever ministered in love (Heb. 12:5–11). "The Lord doth not afflict willingly, nor grieve the children of men" (Lam. 3:33). It grieves Him to see their waywardnesses. It likewise grieves Him to be compelled to afflict them.

Next comes the actual mode of His delivering power; **"the Angel of His Presence saved them: in His love and in His pity He redeemed them"** *(v. 9).* Here the thought is carried not only to the future salvation, but back through the past history of His dealings. The presence of God was with His people of old in the pillar of cloud and fire and in the Tabernacle, and the Angel was none other than Christ Himself (see Ex. 23:20, 23; 32:34; 33:2). His presence was more than the mere existence of God in their midst, it indicated the manifestation of Himself in and through the accompanying Angel.

The metaphor of bearing and carrying them all the days of old, recalls verses 10 to 12 of the song of Moses in Deuteronomy 32, where he recounts God's goodness during their journey in the wilderness (cp. v. 10 with Deut. 32:19–25). **"They grieved His Holy Spirit"** *(v. 10),* a sin against which we are warned in Ephesians 4:30.

Verses 11 to 14 present the other side of God's dealings, His mercy to them in delivering them from Egypt and giving them rest so that His Name might become glorious. At the end of the 14th verse Isaiah addresses God, reminding Him of His goodness, and this forms an introduction to the prayer that follows.

The prayer for redemption and deliverance *(v. 15)* begins with the request that the Lord will "look down from Heaven, and behold from the habitation of His holiness and of His glory [or majesty]," indicating that He who had been with His people, manifesting His presence and power, had withdrawn Himself and was to be approached only in His Heavenly dwelling place. His holiness and His glory are specifically mentioned in contrast to the godlessness and shame of His people. This attitude of distance is borne out by the appeal, **"where is Thy zeal and Thy mighty acts? the yearning of Thy bowels and Thy compassions are restrained toward me."**

When God's people are in distress because of their waywardness, the necessity of His disciplinary acts and judgments does not remove His compassion; "whom the Lord loveth He chasteneth." He longs to relieve His people from their afflictions but sometimes necessarily puts a restraint upon His tender mercies.

It is noticeable that Isaiah speaks of himself as the subject of these dealings, thus identifying himself with the condition of his people. So it was with Moses (Ex. 32:31, 32), and again with Paul (Rom. 9:2, 3). So it is with every true intercessor in times when the Lord's people are in a spirit of declension from Him.

The prophet appeals in *verse 16* to the relationship of God with His people on the same ground. God has begotten His earthly people by His creative power and loving counsel. He was their Father, though Abraham knew them not, and Israel (i.e., Jacob) acknowledged them not. Abraham and Jacob were no longer present to have regard to their descendants. The words rendered "knoweth" (R.V.) and "acknowledge" convey the thought of intimate recognition and active regard (see, e.g., Deut. 33:9; Ruth 2:10, 19). The departed saints do not intercede for anyone. With the Lord, however, the case is different. The relationship is inalienable. So Isaiah repeats the statement **"Thou, O Lord, art our Father"**; His knowledge and recognition abide. He is their **"Redeemer,"** and His name **"is from everlasting,"** that is to say, in the counsels of the past eternity and in His gracious actings in history.

The prayer in *verse 17* now contains the startling appeal, **"O Lord, why dost Thou make us to err from Thy ways, and hardenest our heart from Thy fear** [or, so as not to fear Thee]?" Isaiah is not imputing to God the responsibility for the sin of His people. Persistent and obstinate rejection of God's will causes Him, consistently with His righteousness, to forego a continuation of His grace and mercy, giving those who have hardened their hearts against Him up to the effects of their own evil ways, rendering them incapable of faith and of walking in His fear. A striking example of this is the case of Pharaoh. The R.V. should be read in Exodus 7:13, as in both Versions in 8:19, 32. Again in 9:7 the statement is "the heart of Pharaoh was stubborn." Then comes the change in verse 12, where it says that God hardened his heart.

This was the case with the greater part of Israel. There were some, however, who remained faithful, and the prophet makes two appeals, first on behalf of these and then on the ground that the nation was God's inheritance: **"Return,"** he says, **"for Thy servants' sake, the tribes of Thine inheritance."** There was a remnant "according to the election of grace."

The Lord's people had possessed the land "but a little while" *(v. 18)*. Adversaries had trodden down His sanctuary, and the people had become **"as they over whom Thou never barest rule; as they that were not called by Thy Name"** *(v. 19)*. Their condition resembled that of Gentile nations.

Believers need to give heed against departing from the will of God and becoming conformed to the world. Persistent Laodicean lukewarmness makes us resemble the unregenerate, and the Lord has to withdraw Himself and stand outside the door (Rev. 3:15, 20).

Chapter 64

This chapter continues the prophet's prayer. He cries to God to manifest His power against His adversaries so that the Gentile powers might tremble at His presence. The language recalls the way in which the Lord manifested His presence and power at Sinai. There the mountain quaked (R.V. margin) at His presence. He descended upon the mount in fire; smoke ascended as out of a furnace (Ex. 19:16–19). Thus revealing His Name to His people, He made them tremble. Would He not now manifest His power and judgment against the foe? *(vv. 1–3)*.

The prayer is based upon the fact of the absoluteness and uniqueness of God and His attributes, and of His ways of grace toward those who walk in His fear, having Him in remembrance and seeking to please Him: **"For from of old men have not heard, nor perceived by the ear, neither hath the eye seen a God beside Thee, which worketh for him that waiteth for Him. Thou meetest** [that is, coming forth to shew favor; cp. Gen 32:1] **him that rejoiceth and worketh righteousness, those that remember Thee in Thy ways"** *(vv. 4, 5)*.

The threefold combination of joy and righteousness and the remembrance of God has a special significance. It is possible to walk in righteousness in strict adherence to religion, without delighting ourselves in the Lord. It is possible to do what is morally right and virtuous without actually having God Himself in remembrance. The enjoyment of the secret of His presence is the key to the manifestation of His power in effective service for Him. The Lord delights in those who know in practical experience what fellowship with Him is. His eye is upon them that fear Him. The apostle Paul precedes his desire for the realization of the power of His resurrection by the desire "that I may know Him." Enoch walked with God, and so had this testimony that he pleased

God. He "delighted himself in the Lord" and his life of witness in a godless world issued in his translation to the very presence of God.

In the latter part of the verse Isaiah acknowledges the guilt of his people both past and present, and, calling to mind the long continued state of their apostasy, he asks the question **"shall we be saved?"** (R.V.). This, his rhetorical question, makes acknowledgment that they have no claim to be delivered. They had **"all become as one that is unclean,"** and all their righteousnesses were **"as a polluted garment."** Consequently they all faded as a leaf and their iniquities like the wind had taken them away.

All this provides a warning as to the effects of persistent departure from the ways of God. Willful apostasy leads to forgetfulness of God. So it was in Israel. There was none that called upon His Name, that stirred up himself to take hold of God. Insensibility to sin produces insensibility to God's claims and to His mercies.

The consequence was that God withdrew His mercies from them, hid His face from them, and consumed them by means of their iniquities (*v. 7*, R.V.).

In the reality and power of this confession the prophet calls to remembrance the alienable relationship which the Lord had established between Himself and His people, and the way in which He had formed them according to His own counsel. **"But now,"** he says, **"O Lord Thou art our Father; we are the clay, and Thou our potter: and we all are the work of Thy hand"** (*v. 8*). This implies the possibility of the remaking of the marred national vessel. Certainly that will be the case when the Redeemer comes to Zion.

The national foe had been permitted under the retributive hand of God to make the cities of the land a wilderness and Jerusalem a desolation. The very dwelling place of God in Zion, which in days gone by had rung with the praises of the Lord, had been burned down. By God's appointment it had been indeed "a beautiful house" but it was so no longer (*vv. 10, 11*).

And now the prophet makes his closing appeal for deliverance and restoration: **"Wilt Thou refrain** [i.e., restrain] **Thyself for these things, O Lord? Wilt Thou hold Thy peace and afflict us very sore?"** (*v. 12*).

Chapter 65

The answer of the Lord was not immediately by way of the promise of restoration, though that was to be given (*vv. 8 to 10*). The condition of the people however was so grievous that further reproach and warnings of judgment were necessary, so obstinate and incessant had been their resistance to God's grace.

There are two ways of understanding the opening words of this chapter. Primarily the meaning of the Hebrew is by way of divine denunciation of Israel, and that is continued in the succeeding context, in *verses 2–7*. The original has the past tenses, as in the R.V. margin: **"I was inquired of** [or rather I was discernible] **by them that asked not for Me** [i.e., who refused to turn to God and seek Him]; **I was found** [to be found] **by them that sought Me not."** God was ever ready to reveal Himself, had there been a heart to approach Him in humble desire to walk in His ways. Further, **"I said, Behold Me, behold Me, unto a nation that hath not called upon My Name"** (R.V. margin). In keeping with this the Lord goes on to say **"I have spread out My hands all the day** [that is, throughout the long period of His dealings with Israel] **unto a rebellious people, which walketh in a way that is not good, after their own thoughts; a people that provoketh Me to My face continually"** (*v. 2*, R.V.).

With regard to the other interpretation, the Septuagint version is different, and we have to remember that the apostle Paul in Romans 10:20, 21, uses the Septuagint, as he frequently does elsewhere. Thus verse 1 is regarded as referring to the Gentiles; for it is of these that the statements are made, "I was found of them that sought Me not; I became manifest unto them that asked not of Me." It was by the direct guidance of the Holy Spirit that the great missionary to the Gentiles thus made use of this passage and in the next verse referred to the apostate conditions of Israel.

In the ensuing passage in *verses 3, 4* there is a terrible revelation of the idolatrous practices of God's people. Sitting among the graves probably had to do with a form of spiritism, in an effort to hold intercourse with the dead. Lodging in the secret places (R.V.) probably represents the practice, in crypts or caves, of a form of idolatry accompanied by abominable sacrificial meals.

Those who practiced these abominations were accustomed to boast in their own special sanctity and so to say to the uninitiated "**Stand by thyself** [or stop]: **come not near to me, for I am holier than thou**" *(v. 5)*. Such made themselves fuel for God's wrath and called forth the most grievous and righteous retribution.

In contrast to all this, the Lord now makes mention of those who were His faithful servants, for whose sake He would not bring about the universal destruction of the nation *(vv. 8–10)*. These, who foreshadow the godly remnant in the future time of Jacob's trouble, were like clusters of ripe grapes, in the midst of a degenerate vineyard producing sour grapes or fruitless tendrils. From amidst all God will bring forth **"a seed out of Jacob, and out of Judah an inheritor of My mountains** [representing the land of Israel; cp. Ezek. 6:2, 3]: **and My chosen shall inherit it, and My servants shall dwell there"** *(vv. 8, 9)*. Election always has an object in view. For example, the "elect of God the Father" according to His foreknowledge, are chosen "unto obedience and sprinkling of the blood of Jesus Christ" (1 Pet. 1:2).

In this connection mention is made in *verse 10* of two places, Sharon, the plain of rich pastures and famous for its flowers, stretching along the coastal region from Joppa to Carmel (see Josh. 17:9; 1 Chr. 5:16; Song 2:1; Is. 33:9; 35:2), and secondly the valley of Achor (a place lying in the plain of Jericho and associated with the sin of Achan, Josh. 7:1; called Achar in 1 Chr. 2:7). There the people humbled themselves before God, dissociating themselves from the evil. There, in the language of Hosea 2:15, the nation, in the days of her youth, made answer to God (R.V.). Consequently the valley is to become "A door of hope." The whole region is to become "a garden of the Lord," a scene of fertility and productiveness.

There is always hope for those who humble themselves in the sight of God and seek to walk in His fear (Ps. 33:18; 39:7).

In *verse 11* the prophecy returns to the guilty ones who were threatened in verses 1 to 7. They forsook the Lord, were unmindful of His worship, substituting for it idolatrous feasts. Two objects of their veneration are mentioned, Fortune and Destiny (R.V.). They prepared a table for the one and filled up mixed wine for the other. The reference is rather to the spreading of cushions upon which the images of the gods were placed during the feasts in their honor. Accordingly the Lord declares that He will **"destine"** them (the word rendered "number" in the A.V. is associated in idea with that rendered "Destiny") to the sword, and as they bowed down to their images so they would bow down to the slaughter.

The Lord was longsuffering with them: He called, but they did not answer. He spoke and they refused to hear but deliberately chose that in which He found no pleasure *(v. 12)*.

In *verses 13 to 16* the Lord presents a vivid contrast between them and His faithful ones who walked so as to please Him. They would eat and drink and rejoice and sing for joy, whereas those who turned away from God would suffer want and shame and anguish and vexation. Their name would become a curse, referring to the oath with which the priest had to administer the water of jealousy (see Num. 5:21–24), for Israel had acted as an adulteress. On the contrary, the Lord would call His servants by another name, so that He who blessed Himself in the land and He who uttered a solemn oath, would do so by **"the God of Amen"** (margin). That is, the God who fulfills His word and will carry out His covenant promises to His people. So now in Christ "how many soever be the promises of God, in Him is the Amen, unto the glory of God through us" (2 Cor. 1:20, R.V.; see also Rev. 3:14). In the coming day the redeemed nation will stand in firm and uninterrupted relationship with the Lord.

All this brings home the folly, futility and sinfulness of pursuing our own way, carrying out our own designs and turning after that in which God cannot take pleasure, instead of waiting upon Him, listening to His voice and delighting in the fulfillment of His will. Through our walking with God He fulfills, and will fulfill, all the promises of His Word. He responds to delighted confidence in Him, by adding an Amen to His assurance. The peace of an obedient heart and a trusting spirit is that which enjoys the sunshine of His countenance and the calmness of holy communion with Him.

With the assurance that the former troubles are to be forgotten and hidden from His eyes *(v. 16)*, the Lord now foretells the unspeakable blessedness and joy to be ministered to redeemed Israel in the coming Millennial day. But this, which begins at *verse 18*, is preceded by the declaration of what is to be brought about after the Millennial period is over. For it is only when God creates the new heavens and the new earth that unalloyed and perfect blessedness will be granted, and **"the former things shall not be remembered, nor come into mind."**

When the Lord sets up His Kingdom of righteousness and peace He will fulfill what is now about to be stated in a passage which, perhaps more than any other passage in Scripture, describes the prosperity and bliss of this coming time. He calls upon us to be glad and rejoice perpetually in what He is about to create, and says **"for, behold, I create Jerusalem a rejoicing, and her people a joy. And I will rejoice in Jerusalem, and joy in My people; and the voice of weeping shall be no more heard in her, nor the voice of crying"** *(v. 19)*.

True, there will be death and there will be sin, but these evils will be under severe restraint. And the explanation of this lies in the double fact that Christ and His Heavenly people as well as His earthly will be reigning, and, secondly, the evil one will have been cast into the abyss for the thousand years (Rev. 20:1–3). Under these conditions there will not be **"an infant of days** [that is a suckling only a few days old], **nor an old man that hath not filled his days: for the child shall die an hundred years old, and the sinner being an hundred years old shall be accursed"** *(v. 20)*. That is to say, that one who is a hundred years old will be a youth, and one who, being a sinner, will suffer death as punishment, will not come under this judgment before the hundredth year of his life. The longevity of the earliest times of human history will return.

The next promises, *(vv. 21–23)*, give the assurance that His people will enjoy what they have worked for and reap the fruits of their labor without plunder by foes; the duration of their life that of trees which lived for centuries. They will be a generation blessed of Jehovah and their children will share with them what

they enjoy, without being removed by premature death (cp. Job 21:8).

The Lord declares that before they call He will answer and while they are speaking He will hear *(v. 24)*. That is to say, the desire in the hearts of His redeemed will be in perfect harmony with His own will. Often now there is an interval between the prayer offered and the answer given, but not so in the day to come (cp. Dan. 9:20–23 and Is. 30:19). This provides a striking testimony to that which will be the outcome of the very presence of the Lord in their midst. Prayer that is the Lord's delight can only arise from the enjoyment of close fellowship with Him.

There is also to be a change in the nature of rapacious animals *(v. 25)*. Natural conditions have been full of discord, but then the wolf and the lamb will feed together. The fodder eaten by the ox will be that of the lion. This passage recalls in an abridged form what the prophet had said in 11:6–9. This and similar correspondences between the later portions of the book from chapter 40 onward, and the earlier, again give plain testimony to the unity of Isaiah in contrast to the higher critical suppositions.

What is new in the present passage is the prophecy that dust shall be the serpent's meat. Its form will be the same but it will have the food appointed for it in Genesis 3:14.

These conditions will not be the outcome of evolutionary processes but will result immediately from the decree and power of Israel's Messiah. To imagine that what is here said of the changed condition of creatures is mere allegory is utterly without foundation. Isaiah has not used allegory in any of his descriptions of the coming period.

Chapter 66

The opening part of this chapter is a continuation of the glorious vision of the future just given, but the great point of connection with the preceding chapter is the contrast between the true and faithful servant of God and the apostate and worldly character of most of the nation. It is to the latter and their ideas of establishing a temple in Jerusalem that the Lord protests that, as the Creator of heaven and earth, He does not stand in need of a house erected by man. What He looks for primarily is the spirit of contrition and godly fear: "**to this man will I look, even to Him that is poor and of a contrite spirit, and that trembleth at My word**" *(vv. 1, 2).* From those who are not so characterized He looks for no efforts at temple building and for no animal sacrifices. With scathing denunciation the Lord makes a comparison between the offering of hypocritical worshipers and gross iniquities; "**He that killeth an ox** [i.e., in sacrifice] **is as he that slayeth a man; he that sacrificeth a lamb, as he that breaketh a dog's neck; he that offereth an oblation** [or a meal offering], **as he that offereth swine's blood; he that burneth frankincense as he that blesseth an idol**" *(v. 3).*

They had chosen to follow the ways of the heathen in their abominations. To this the Lord replies that He has a choice to make, and will choose their mocking devices (A.V., and R.V., "delusions," but see the margins) and will bring their terrors upon them, because they made no answer when God called and refused to hear His Word *(v. 4).*

At *verse 5* the Lord turns to the minority, consisting of those who with reverence and awe tremble at His Word. He promises them that He will deal with their brethren who have hated them and persecuted them, thus enhancing the grievous character of their sin, and who with scornful unbelief dared to take the Lord's Name in vain, saying "**Let Jehovah be glorified** [or rather "Let Jehovah glorify Himself"], **that we may see your joy**" (the R.V. rightly so connects the clauses). These apostates regarded any hope in God as mere deception, but the Lord determined that they should "be ashamed." Whereas the city and the Temple were lying in ruins, the time will come when there will be a voice of tumult from the city, a voice from the Temple, and that a voice of the Lord rendering "**recompense to His enemies**" *(v. 6),* not only those of the Jewish people but the Gentile nations, who will hereafter be gathered together "against the Lord, and against His anointed" (Ps. 22, and for the voice see v. 5; cp. Joel 2:11; 3:16; Amos 1:2; Is. 63:1 and 2 Thess. 2:8).

In view of this mention is made in *verse 7* of the future time of Jacob's trouble and the fact of the Incarnation of Christ: "**Before she travailed** [before the great tribulation which the nation is yet to experience at the hands of the Antichrist] **she brought forth; before her pain came, she was delivered of a man child.**" This experience of the nation is contrary to conditions of natural birth. The order is reversed, and this draws forth the surprised questions, "**Who hath heard such a thing? who hath seen such things?**" There is evidently a connection with Revelation 12:1–6. The nation is spoken of as having brought forth a "man child." Some regard this as the godly remnant among the Jews in the coming day. Surely the reference is to the Lord Jesus. The Roman power, energized by Satan, fulfilled what is said in Revelation 12:4, and "stood before the woman which was about to be delivered, that when she was delivered he might devour her child." Herod would have accomplished this had he been able to, but the Man Child was to be "caught up to God and His Throne." This could scarcely be said of the remnant, who are to enjoy the Millennial reign. The birth, death, resurrection and ascension of Christ have already taken place. The great tribulation is yet future. This explains the inversion of the natural order of the circumstances of birth as mentioned in this Isaiah passage.

The next questions, in *verse 8,* point to the effect and issue of the travail of the nation. These two questions demand a positive answer, whereas the two preceding ones were asked so as to produce negative answers. Now it is asked "**shall a land be born in one day?**" Then follows the question, "**shall a nation be brought forth at once?**" The positive assurance is immediately given, "**for as soon as Zion travailed, she brought forth her children.**" First the birth pangs and then the birth, and thus different from the preceding circumstances!

Accordingly the immediate outcome of the great tribulation will be the issue of God's earthly people as a nation in peace and joy and righteousness under the mighty hand of its Messiah Deliverer. The nation thus delivered is not the same as the Man Child in verse 7.

In view of the certainty that His people will be delivered from their time of unprecedented trouble, and that speedily *(v. 9),* the Lord calls upon all who delight in Him and His purposes, all those who love His earthly people, to rejoice with Jerusalem, and be glad for her.

Those who mourn over her woeful condition are invited to rejoice for joy with her (v. 10). Those who on earth will thus feel for her in the coming time will themselves derive benefit when she is established in the earth.

In *verse 11* Jerusalem is looked upon as a mother, ministering of her personal nourishment to her children with an overflow for others. The Lord declares that He **"will extend peace to her like a river, and the glory of the nations like an overflowing stream."** Israel will receive the riches of the Gentiles, who will care for the nation with the utmost devotedness and attention (cp. 49:23 and 60:4). That is what is indicated in the promise, **"ye shall be borne upon the side, and shall be dandled upon the knees"** (v. 12).

In *verse 13* the Lord declares how He Himself will care for His people: **"As one whom his mother comforteth, so will I comfort you; and ye shall be comforted in Jerusalem."** Their heart will rejoice and their bones will flourish like the tender grass, a vivid description of the flourishing condition of Israel when the Lord reigns over the earth (v. 14).

How all this blessing will be brought about is described in *verses 15 and 16* by a renewal of the prophecies of the overthrow of their foes. In His indignation against His enemies **"the Lord will come with fire, and His chariots shall be like the whirlwind; to render His anger with fury, and His rebuke with flames of fire. For by fire will the Lord plead, and by His sword, with all flesh: and the slain of the Lord shall be many."**

In *verse 17* the Lord deals with those among His people who will have corrupted themselves and become like the heathen. They are to be brought to an end. They will share the doom of the adherents of the Antichrist.

Now by way of contrast the prophecy turns again to the future of Israel and to the favorable dealings of the Gentile nations with them in the Millennium. The statement that the Lord knows their works and their thoughts, forms a transition from the apostates in verse 17 to the redeemed nation and the way the Gentile peoples will assist them.

All nations and tongues are to be gathered to Palestine, and there they are to see the glory of the Lord (v. 18). To this end the Lord will set a sign among the Gentiles (v. 19), and this for the recovery of His people in far distant places. What the actual sign will be is not disclosed. From Exodus 10:2 and Psalms 78:43 and 105:27, where the R.V. renders by this very phrase, and where the reference is to the miracles wrought by God in delivering His people from Egypt, we may gather that there will be some form of supernatural intervention in the world's affairs. Moreover, God makes clear here that He will send out the Jews as His messengers to nations in all parts of the world, to Tarshish in the west, to Pul and Lud in the south, to Tubal and Javan in the north, and to far-off coastlands such as those in Asia and other continents, to peoples who have not heard His fame or seen His glory, that they may make known His glory in all the earth (v. 19).

The Gentile peoples will bring the Jews **"out of all the nations for an offering unto the Lord."** They will be brought to His holy mountain Jerusalem, just as the children of Israel were accustomed to bring their offerings in clean vessels into the Lord's house. A considerable variety of means of conveyance will be used, and it is quite possible that motor cars, etc., are referred to in the mention of chariots and litters. Further, what was said in chapter 60:8, in a passage similar to this, about those who will "fly as a cloud and as doves to their windows," is indicative of air travel. The mention of the clean vessel shows that all the Israelites who are brought into Millennial glory will have been purged from their old sins and brought to walk in the ways of the Lord, and accordingly He will take of them for **"priests and for Levites"** (v. 21).

Isaiah's prophecies end with a striking contrast. First there comes the pledge that **"as the new heavens and the new earth which God will create will remain before Him, so the seed of Israel and their name will remain"** (see 65:17). For Christ, who is of Israel as concerning the flesh, and who is "over all, God blessed forever" (Rom. 9:5), will be identified with His earthly people. Owing to His presence in their midst all flesh will come to worship before Him at every new moon and at every sabbath. There will in that day be every facility for speedy and frequent journeys from all parts of the world.

The nations will thus have a vivid reminder of the grievous nature and consequences of rebellion against God. For as they assemble in the land on the stated occasions, they will **"go forth, and look upon the carcasses of the men who have transgressed against Him,"** and the Lord declares that **"their worm shall not die, neither shall their fire be quenched; and they shall be an abhorring unto all flesh."** The region would seem to be the valley of Hinnom outside Jerusalem.

Yet in spite of this, such will be the spirit of dissatisfaction with the righteous and firm reign of the Lord, that the nations will break out in rebellion at the end of the thousand years, when, under the permissive will of God, Satan will be loosed from his prison to deceive them (Rev. 20:7, 8).

No merely natural conditions, however peaceful and blessed, can ever regenerate the human heart. This, with its consequent loyalty to Christ, must ever have as its foundation the efficacy of His atoning blood.

Some of the details that bind together the two parts of the book:

1. God's abhorrence of mere formal worship, 1:11, 13, and 66:3.
2. The Lord's Throne in the high and holy place, 6:1, and 57:15; 66:1.
3. His regard for the lowly soul, 6:5–7, and 57:15; 66:2.
4. His House and Mountain as a resort, 2:2, 3, and 56:7; 60:12–14.
5. His making every high thing low, 2:11, 17; 5:15, 16, and 40:4.
6. His overruling of human pride and violence, 10:5,7; 37:26, and 47:6; 54:16, 17.
7. The chastisement of rebellious Israel, 1:2, 5; 31:1, 2, and 63:8, 10.
8. The sickness and healing of the nation, 1:5, 6; 6:10, and 57:18, 19.
9. People and land forsaken, 6:12; 17:9; 27:10; 32:14, and 49:14; 54:6, 7; 62:4, 12.
10. Judicial deafness and blindness, 6:10; 29:18; 32:3; 35:5, and 42:7, 18.
11. A remnant saved, 1:27 (margin); 4:2, 3; 10:20, 22; 37:31, 32 and 59:20; 65:8, 9.
12. A sign or covenant concerning the sure mercies of David, 7:14; 9:6, 7, and 55:3, 4.
13. The Spirit of the Lord resting upon Messiah, 11:2, and 61:1.
14. Israel fruitful by the Spirit of God, 32:15, and 44:3, 4.
15. Waiting for God, who has hidden His face, 8:17, and 64:4, 7.
16. The setting up of a standard, 5:26; 11:10, 12; 18:3, and 49:22; 62:10.

The Leading Themes
of the Gospel of John

▪ PREFACE ▪

The following chapters consist of a series of papers written for *The Witness,* with a view to presenting for Bible students the chief subjects which run through the whole, or the greater part, of the Gospel of John. The writer has sought, as far as possible in the case of each subject, to refer to every place in the Gospel where the respective subjects are mentioned. In many of them a distinct progress in the teaching is traceable, and this is partly due to the fact that this fourth Gospel is clearly divided into two almost equal parts, the first consisting chiefly of the Lord's ministry in His public life and testimony, the second part comprising His private instruction to His disciples and containing also the narrative of His death, burial and resurrection.

The consummation of His public ministry is reached at the close of chapter eleven, in connection with the raising of Lazarus from the dead. That was a crisis in the witness given to the unbelieving Jews by means of His works. Their rejection of this manifestation of the authority of His claim to be the Son of God marks the close of His testimony to His opponents: "From that day forth they took counsel that they might put Him to death. Jesus therefore walked no more openly among the Jews, but departed thence into the country near to the wilderness, into a city called Ephraim, and there He tarried with His disciples." To the people in general He gave one more testimony subsequent to His public entry into Jerusalem (chap. twelve), but He had ceased to deal with the leaders of the people. The twelfth chapter marks a transition from all that has preceded to the circumstances of the night of His betrayal. His private teaching to His disciples in the upper room and after His resurrection contains a fuller, deeper range of instruction than what He had given in His earlier ministry. This is especially exemplified, for instance, in the subjects of "the Holy Spirit" and "Believing."

The manner in which the leading themes are handled and developed in this Gospel is itself an evidence of the operation of the Spirit of God in producing it. The aim of the apostle clearly is to bear witness to Christ as the Son of God, and to show how eternal life is obtained through and in Him. Yet neither of these themes is dealt with as an ordinary writer would set them forth whose object was to produce a treatise on either subject. The sacred themes are not treated academically or theologically, nor would they impress the heart of the reader by that means with the divine power which manifests itself in their presentation in the Gospel. The unbiased reader is convinced, as he peruses the apostle's record, of the Deity of the Person Whom it sets forth, and of the fact that the possession of eternal Life is possible only through faith in Him on the ground of His atoning sacrifice.

The object of the following pages is, not so much an exegesis of special passages, though the writer ventures to hope that some help will be afforded in this respect. His object rather has been to demonstrate the way in which the chief subjects are woven into the whole texture of the Gospel, giving it a unique character amongst the books of the sacred Volume. His desire above all is that the heart of the reader may be led into closer communion with the Lord Himself and be helped the more intelligently to adore Him Who loved us and gave Himself up for us.

Bath, 1924.

The Prologue of the Gospel

The great subject of this Gospel is clear from the very first statements. Christ is at once presented to us in the grandeur of His eternal Deity, His distinct personality in the Godhead, His essential oneness with the Father, and His power as Creator and as the Giver of life. The Gospel is verily a "revelation of Jesus Christ the Son of God." It depicts His glory and His grace. The marvels of His grace are enhanced by the unveiling of His glory. The sublime glories of His Deity and His power bring out the more strikingly the grace of His condescension and love toward man. No profounder truths concerning the Son of God are to be found in the contents of the Sacred Volume than those which are given in the first few verses of this Gospel.

All this, however, is soon seen to be preparatory to a series of revelations concerning Him which expand the theme of His glories and His grace. Each item in this series has its own special setting and its own immediate purpose. The details of the series are to a considerable extent briefly intimated, as we shall see, in the first chapter. Throughout the Gospel the doings and teachings of the Lord Jesus pass before us in a divinely arranged order.

The Purpose Stated

It is not, however, until we come almost to the close of the Gospel that the object for which it is written is definitely stated. This stands in remarkable contrast to the ordinary method of writing a book. The purpose of a book is customarily set forth in a preface or introduction, and in most of the writings of men this is necessary. Not so in this Gospel. That the mention of the reason why it was written should come near the end is entirely appropriate. "Many other signs therefore," says the apostle, "did Jesus in the presence of the disciples, which are not written in this book: but these are written, that ye may believe Jesus is the Christ, the Son of God; and that believing ye may have life in His name" (20:30, 31).

A reader to whom the Gospel story was new, carefully reading this short book straight through, would, by reason of the revelation thus given of Christ and His work, at least feel the tremendous force of this statement of the purpose of the book as applicable to his own case, if indeed, he had not, through the power of the Spirit of God, already accepted Christ as his Savior. The Gospel was written, then, for the purpose of bringing men into life by faith in the Son of God.

A Further Purpose

While the exercise of faith in Christ is the object for which the Gospel was written, the presentation of the Son of God in the way indicated above has another purpose. This, though not expressed by the author in so many words, becomes clear on careful perusal of the record. The various aspects of glory and power, of grace and love, in which the Lord is seen, have in almost every case a special bearing on the life and service of believers. Each revelation of Christ is connected with some particular purpose of God for His children. The teachings of the Lord given to His disciples, either directly in His private conversation with them, or indirectly in public testimony, constitute a development of truth as to the will of God for us, all being based upon the foundation truths relating to Christ.

It is our purpose to look somewhat closely into this development, as its order is not a little striking. Speaking broadly, the earlier presentations of Christ are preparatory to the later ones. The object in view is evidently efficiency in service, and the teachings concerning service (which occupy the latter portion of the Gospel) are preceded by a number of revelations and truths which bring home to the heart the glory and power of the Lord in a way that is calculated to establish and strengthen the faith of His servants.

The Past Eternity of the Son of God

We will consider first the way in which Christ is presented to us in the opening portion of the book as the initial declarations concerning Him bear very largely upon all that follows. Each truth stated at the beginning is unfolded in the course of the Gospel record. Each is like a bud opening out in fuller beauty under the sunlight of the Holy Spirit's revelations.

The initial words, "In the beginning," speak of the past eternity of the Son of God. This is expanded in His teachings as recorded subsequently. Thus, for instance, as expressive of the eternity of His Deity, He uses again and again the Jehovah title "I AM." When the Jews call into question His preexistence, He says, "Before Abraham was I am" (8:58). Again, He says to them, "Except ye believe that I am, ye shall die in your sins"; and further, "When ye have lifted up the Son of Man, then ye shall know that I am" (8:24, 28). Later on, when He is instructing His disciples in the upper room, after having washed their feet, He says, "From henceforth I tell you before it come to pass, that, when it is come to pass, ye may believe that I am" (13:19). The great truth of His eternity is finally told out in another and fuller way when He says in prayer to the Father, "And now, O Father, glorify Thou Me with Thine own self with the glory which I had with Thee before the world was"; and, "Thou lovedst Me before the foundation of the world." That is only a way of amplifying the words, "In the beginning." But the teaching is now expanded into the themes of His eternal glory and the eternal love with which the Father loved Him. How striking is the Holy Spirit's development of the first truth of the Gospel!

Christ as "the Word"

Let us now take the full statement, "In the beginning was the Word." A word is the ex-

pression of a thought. The mind of God is told out in and through Christ. This truth is developed almost immediately in this first chapter. "The only begotten Son which is in the bosom of the Father, He hath declared Him" (John 1:18). The Son of God, as the Word of God, has made known the Father. But it is as One in the very center of the affections of the Father that He has declared Him. Christ is "the heart of God revealed."

This title, "the Word of God," again receives a series of comments which run through the Gospel. John speaks of Him thus, "He whom God has sent speaketh the words of God" (3:34). Christ Himself opens up the theme as follows: He says to Nicodemus, "I tell you heavenly things" (3:12). Again, He says that hearing His Word and believing on Him that sent Him are conditions upon which life is granted (5:24). His Word, then, reveals the Father, and this leads to faith in the Father. By His word (who is the Word) He opens up to us the heart of the Father for our faith. His teaching was not His, but the Father's who sent Him. He spoke not from Himself (7:16–18). Again, He says, "The things which I heard from Him, these speak I unto the world. . . . As the Father taught Me, I speak these things. . . . I speak the things which I have seen with My Father" (8:26, 28, 38). And again, "The Father which sent Me, He hath given Me commandment, what I should say and what I should speak" (12:49). Further, to the disciples, "The words that I say unto you I speak not from Myself, but the Father abiding in Me doeth His works" (14:10).

There is clearly an advance in this truth as given to His disciples, beyond what He gave to the Jews. He declares now that the Father was in Him, expressing Himself by word and work. His works were at the same time teachings. Continuing the theme, He says, "The word which ye heard is not Mine, but the Father's who sent Me; . . . all things that I heard from My Father I have made known unto you" (14:24; 15:15). The subject of Christ as the Word of God is finally brought out in His prayer in the seventeenth chapter, when He says, "The words which Thou gavest Me I have given unto them. . . . I have given them Thy Word" (17:8, 14). Thus throughout the course of the Gospel the first introductory declaration is unfolded. The passages we have quoted are the amplification by the Spirit of God of the great truth, "In the beginning was the Word." They serve to emphasize the truth with increasing beauty and power, just as each touch of the painter's brush sets out in greater grandeur the central figure of a picture.

The words "In the beginning" convey no suggestion of a commencement of the existence of Christ. The apostle's meaning is, firstly, that Christ, as the Word of God, was coexistent with God, for He was God; and, secondly, that at whatsoever time any order of creatures came into being, Christ was preexistent to them, for "all things were made by Him." In the beginning of all else He was existent. The evangelist's statement is similar to what Wisdom utters in Proverbs 8:23, "The Lord possessed Me in the beginning of His way before His works of old." Wisdom is an unoriginated, attribute of God. So Christ is His unoriginated Son, one with Him in the Godhead.

Christft as the Word

Christ as the Word

What was pointed out in the last chapter in respect of the first declaration is borne out in the case of those that immediately follow. We must distinguish, however, between the way in which these doctrines are expanded, and the method we might expect to find in a theological treatise on foundations of the faith.

Though the apostle John begins by stating a series of facts concerning the Son of God, they are not given as so many articles of a creed upon which he is about to write. The Spirit of God is directing him, not to discourse on truth, but to bring before our gaze the Person and work of Him who is the Truth. We have no evidence that John's intention was to enlarge upon, or illustrate, the initial doctrines he states. On the other hand, the way in which they are unfolded in the Gospel reveals the supernatural design of the Divine Author. Here, then, is an important evidence of the divine inspiration of this Gospel.

"The Word"

We will now consider the second statement, **"The Word was with God."** This declares, firstly, the distinct personality of Christ in the Godhead, and, secondly, the eternal and unbroken fellowship existing between the Father and the Son. Thus the truth of His preexistence is here also implied. The Word was not, as early errorists taught, an eternal emanation proceeding from God. The Son had a proper personality, eternal, as was that of the Father. The preposition *"pros,"* rendered "with," is not the one which merely denotes the presence of one person with another. Its underlying idea is "toward." This may be illustrated by its use in 1 John 2:1, "We have an Advocate with *(pros)* the Father." It suggests attitude toward, and intimate intercourse with, the Father, as well as presence with Him.*

Let us now see how this truth is continued and expanded in John's Gospel. First it is repeated in verse 2, **"The same was in the beginning with God."** This is not a mere repetition of the words in verse 1. Firstly, it combines the truth of the first two statements of that verse, and then it forms, in its twofold doctrine, the basis of what is to follow as to the work of creation. **"All things were made by Him."** The creation could be effected only by One who was eternally existent, and actually was effected by the conjoint operation of the Father and the Son. **"Without Him** [apart from Him] **was not anything made that has been made."** Thus in creation "The Word was with God."

"The Only Begotten"

Further on in the prologue to the Gospel this truth is conveyed with the additional ideas of intimate communion and affection. These are contained in the title, "The Only Begotten." **"We beheld His glory,"** says the writer, **"glory as of the only begotten from the Father"** (v. 14).

The term "only begotten" implies, firstly, the eternal relation of the Son with the Father, and, secondly, the Father's delight in the Son. Both these ideas are likewise contained in the similar title "Firstborn," as used of Christ.†

---

*While we think of His distinct personality as the Son of God, we must remember the absolute oneness of the Father and the Son in the Godhead. This is made clear in the next statement.

†See Romans 8:29; Colossians 1:15, 18; Hebrews 1:6; Revelation 1:5; Psalm 89:27. The distinction between the two titles is that "Only Begotten" refers absolutely to His Divine relationship; "Firstborn" is used in reference to created beings, but distinguishes Him absolutely from all creatures, and relatively from those who are, or will be made, children of God by the grace.

This subject is still further developed in verse 18, and here the idea of affection receives special emphasis. Christ is now called "The only begotten Son, which is in the bosom of the Father." The Son, ever abiding in the seat of the Father's affection, was "daily His delight, rejoicing always before Him." Even while Christ was on earth in the days of His flesh, He did not cease to be in the bosom of the Father. Again, one of the keynotes of this Gospel is that the Father sent the Son into the world. The Lord constantly asserted it, and this implies that before He came He was "with God." The very term Father involves Sonship. If there was a Father who sent, there was a Son to send. If the Father was eternal, His Son must have been eternal too.

The continuance of the oneness and fellowship of the Father with the Son in the days of His flesh is really a further development of the subject. Christ says to the Jews, "My Father worketh even until now, and I work" (5:17). Three times He states that the Father is with Him, twice to the Jews and once to His disciples. To the former He says, "I am not alone, but I and the Father that sent Me" (8:16); and again, "He that sent Me is with Me; He hath not left Me alone" (8:29). And to the latter, "Behold, the hour cometh, yea, is come, that ye shall be scattered, every man to his own, and shall leave Me alone: and yet I am not alone, because the Father is with Me" (16:32).

To each of these three statements of the presence of the Father with the Son a special idea is attached. The first relates to the thoughts and words of Christ, the second to His deeds, and the third to His experiences.

The truth of the eternal presence of the Son with the Father before the Incarnation is further expanded in the Lord's prayer in the seventeenth chapter. He says, "And now, O Father, glorify Thou Me with Thine own self with the glory which I had with Thee before the world was" (17:5), and again, "Thou lovedst Me before the foundation of the world" (v. 24). Thus the themes of glory and love embodied in the teachings of the prologue concerning this second declaration stand out in their full light in these two utterances of the Lord in the closing portion of the Gospel.

"The Word—God"

The third statement is, "The Word was God." The Deity of Christ constitutes the great foundation doctrine of this Gospel. As in other parts of Scripture, the doctrine is sometimes directly expressed and sometimes implied. The latter cases are very numerous, and demand careful and reverent attention. In our present consideration of the subject we shall not sharply distinguish the two.

The Deity of Christ is at once implied in the third verse of the prologue, which declares that "all things were made by Him," and again in verse 10, "the world was made by Him." The Creator of all things must Himself be God. The same is true in reference to the statement in verse 12, "As many as received Him, to them gave He the right to become the children of God, even to them that believe on His Name." Only by God could such a right be bestowed. Again, His Deity is to be inferred from the title "The Only Begotten Son." Limitations of space prevent a full enumeration of the passages in the Gospel in which the Deity of the Lord is implied. Nathanael confessed it when he said, "Rabbi, Thou art the Son of God, the King of Israel" (1:49). Christ Himself directly declared it when He said, "My Father worketh even until now, and I work." In the opinion of the foes by whom He was confronted this was a claim to Deity. This it was that led them to seek the more to kill Him. To them His language was unambiguous—"He called God His own Father, making Himself equal with God." Their opposition to this truth, and their hardness of heart, drew from Him still stronger affirmations of His Deity.

"One with the Father"

The Lord proceeded to claim that equal honor was due to the Son and to the Father, and further stated that the Father had committed all judgment to Him (5:21-29). His essential Deity, implied in the truth of His oneness with the Father, forms the central teaching of His testimony to the Jews, and is continued in His subsequent discourse to the disciples, and again in His closing prayer. Thus He says to the Jews, "I and the Father are One." This claim to Deity they met by an attempt to stone Him, and when He further said, "The Father is in Me, and I in Him," they endeavored to seize Him (10:30, 31, 38). To the disciples He says, "If ye had known Me, ye would have known My Father also. From henceforth ye know Him, and have seen Him." And when Philip requests that He will show them the Father, He says, "Have I been so long time with you, and hast thou not known Me, Philip? He that hath seen Me hath seen the Father, . . . I am in the Father, and the Father in Me; . . . the Father abiding in Me doeth His works. Believe Me that I am in the Father, and the Father in Me: or else believe Me for the very works' sake" (14:7–11). Finally, in His prayer following that discourse He says, "Thou, Father, art in Me, and I in Thee; . . . we are One" (17:21, 22). Thus the truth of the opening declaration, "The Word was God," stands out in every part of the Gospel as its great leading theme.

· CHAPTER THREE ·

Christ as the Light

The first verses of the Gospel consist of statements concerning the Deity of Christ as the Word of God, His eternal oneness with the Father, and His power as Creator. We have shown how each of these themes is developed throughout the Gospel. In *verses 4 and 5* the subject of His relationship with mankind is introduced, and in this respect Christ is represented as Life and Light. "In Him was life, and the life was the light of men." This subject of eternal life in and through the Son of God is a special feature of this Gospel. We shall now endeavor to show how, as in the case of the preceding statements, this theme is expanded.

Light Shining into Darkness

In the first chapter of Genesis the mention of God's work of Creation is followed by a description of the darkness which existed therein, and the introduction of light into the scene. So here in the first chapter of John the fact of the creative power of the Son of God is followed by the mention of the world's darkness. Into this His life-giving light shone, and the darkness apprehended it not. There is more in this than a failure to "comprehend" the light, as the word is rendered in the Authorized Version. It most frequently means "to lay hold of," and implies an effort on the part of an opposing power to seize the light so as to hinder its benign effects (see margin of R.V., "overcome").

Unsuccessful Opposition

When Christ was born Satan, acting through Herod, sought to destroy Him. The darkness was endeavoring to overpower the light. Satan failed. He failed again in the wilderness. He failed again at the Cross. Never did the darkness apprehend the Light. Never will it do so. The light is now shining through the Church. The gates of Hades shall not prevail

against it. Satan's power is yet to reach its climax in this world, yet the darkness will not prevail. Nay, the light of the Lord's Second Advent will overpower it, Satan will be hurled into the abyss. Yet another effort at the close of the Millennium on the part of this great power of darkness, and he will be confined to the lake of fire. Never again will the darkness be able even to make an attempt to apprehend the light.

The Light as the Life

Continuing the subject as indicated in the prologue, we must notice the fundamental truth of this Gospel, that faith in Christ is the means of the possession of life. Through faith His life is imparted to us. So the aim of the ministry of John the Baptist was "that all men might believe" *(v. 7)*. That is at once the beginning of the development of the theme "the life was the light of men." The Light shone, but could not produce life unless men exercised faith. Without that the darkness continues. Yet the Light shone, and still shines. It shines forevery man.

Now that is just the point of the much misinterpreted *verse 9*. By the omission of a comma after "man" the Authorized Version has proved very misleading. The verse has been taken to mean that there is an inner light from God in every infant that is born into the world, and that thus there is the essence of eternal life in every man by natural birth. This of course is not the meaning of the verse at all. The Revisers rightly inserted a comma after the word "man"; the remaining part of the verse, "coming into the world," goes with the "light" and not with "man." Thus the verse rightly reads, "There was the true Light, even the Light which, coming into the world, lighteth every man." That is to say, the Light shines provisionally for every man; but only because it came into the world; otherwise man must have remained in spiritual darkness. That Christ came into the world forms one of the outstanding truths of the Gospel of John. Verse 9 gives the first definite mention of it, and here the Person is represented figuratively as the Light.

How Does Life Come?

The metaphor of the light served to introduce the subject of life, and the latter theme is now developed in association with that of faith. We are shown how the life is produced. "As many as received Him, to them gave He the right to become children* of God, even to them that believe on His Name; which were born, not of blood, nor of the will of the flesh, nor of the will of man, but of God" *(vv. 12, 13)*. Spiritual birth involves spiritual life. But the birth is effected by faith. Those who "believe on the Name" of Christ become "children of God." Life comes through faith.

The Necessity of the New Birth

That is how the theme of Christ as the life is introduced in the first chapter. It is resumed in the third. The first chapter reveals the *means* of life, the third reveals the *necessity* for it. This phase of the theme has its setting in the narrative of the dialogue between the Lord and the inquirer Nicodemus. "The same came to Jesus by night." Thus in the physical sense the light was to shine in the darkness. The darkness within the soul of the ruler of the Jews had its counterpart in the darkness without. The Light shone at once with its lifegiving power. The ruler's initial statement was met with the unexpected rejoinder, "Verily, verily, I say unto thee, except a man be born anew, he cannot see the Kingdom of God." This aroused inquiries, and the light flashed forth again, "Verily, verily, I say unto thee, Except a man be born of water and of the spirit, he cannot enter into the Kingdom of God." Literal water is not here in view. The new birth does not come by baptism. In whatever way the metaphor of the water is applied, whether to the Spirit ("and" being "even") or to the Word of God, the application is spiritual. This is clearly so elsewhere in the Gospel (see chaps.

4:10, 14; 7:38, 39; see further on p. 216). In the sixth verse the Lord confines the subject to the Spirit, "That which is born of the flesh is flesh; and that which is born of the Spirit is spirit." How this life was to come about He proceeds to show. If the Spirit's operation is essential the heart too must be receptive. Moreover, the life can come only by the death of Christ. "As Moses lifted up the serpent in the wilderness, even so must the Son of Man be lifted up: that whosoever believeth may in Him have eternal life."

The Consequence of Refusal

Yea, there must be faith in Himself and the only alternative to this is to perish. Moreover, it must be faith in Christ as the Son of God, "For God so loved the world, that He gave His only begotten Son, that whosoever believeth on Him should not perish, but have eternal life." But more, to perish is to perish under the judgment of God. "He that believeth not hath been judged already, because he hath not believed on the Name of the only begotten Son of God." God's provision in Christ is the very infinitude of mercy, the highest height of love. Here, where love is brought in, the theme of light is reintroduced. The light has revealed God's love. Only willful love of darkness could account for the rejection of such love. Love of darkness means hatred of light: and hatred of light can only be accounted for by the practice of evil (see v. 20, R.V., margin). Accordingly, "This is the judgment, that the light is come into the world, and men loved the darkness rather than the light, for their works were evil." God loved men; men loved darkness. How vast the depth to which man has fallen! Yet God's love, God's light, God's life, remain for all who will accept them. "He that believeth on the Son hath eternal life." "Verily, verily, I say unto you, he that heareth My word, and believeth on Him that sent Me, hath everlasting life, and shall not come into condemnation; but is passed from death unto life" (John 5:24). Refusal is disobedience to the Son. In that case sentence of judgment has been passed already, and wrath abides. "He that obeyeth not the Son shall not see life (let

---

*Not "sons" as in Authorized Version. In John's writings the word "children" not "sons," is always used to describe those who are born of God. The title "Son" is reserved by him for the Son of God.

the universalist take note!); but the wrath of God abideth on him" (3:36).

The Evidence of Life

There is a further expansion of the theme in this section of the Gospel. If light brings life, the life is evidenced in the doing of the truth. "He that doeth the truth cometh to the light"—not the initial coming for the acceptance of salvation, but "that his works may be made manifest, that they have been wrought in God" (3:21). Thus the first three chapters of this Gospel give us (1) the *provision* of life through the coming of the Light; (2) the *means* of life through the acceptance of the Light; (3) the *necessity* for the life in contrast to the rejection of the Light; and (4) the *evidence* of the life in coming to the Light.

Christic as the Life

In the preceding chapter we endeavored to show how the statement "In Him was life, and the life was the light of men" is developed in the first three chapters of the Gospel of John. We shall now see how the subject of Christ as the Life runs through the remainder of the Gospel and is expanded in its teachings. In the fourth chapter the coming of the Samaritan woman to fill her pitcher at the well becomes the occasion for the teaching of the Lord that He Himself is the Fountain of living water. The water that He gives becomes in the recipient a well of water springing up into eternal life. This is an advance on His teaching to Nicodemus. To him He made known that eternal life is a gift conditional upon faith; "Whosoever believeth in Him should not perish, but have eternal life" (3:16; cp. v. 36). To the woman of Samaria He reveals something more than the fact of the gift of life. He declares the character and the effect of the gift. The water of life will act as a springing fountain within the believer—a joyous refreshment, an energizing power.

Passing from that scene the Gospel now proceeds to show us how it is that Christ is the Life, and what further effects are derived from Him in this respect. In His discourse with the Jews, as mentioned in chapter five, He declares that the power to give life lies with Himself and that this power rests upon the fact that what belongs to the Father belongs likewise to Himself in essential union with the Father: "As the Father hath life in Himself, even so gave He to the Son also to have life in Himself" (5:26). Accordingly

The Blessing of Life

formerly offered to the Jews on condition of keeping the law, must, in view of their failure, come to them only from Himself. They searched the Scriptures thinking that in them they had eternal life. But these very Scriptures bore witness to Him. He must, therefore, be the Fountain of life, a life incommunicable save through Himself. They would not come to Him that they might have life, and therefore they remained without it (v. 40). Further, God the Father had confirmed the fact that the power for life rested in the Son. This is what underlies the statement, "Him the Father, even God, hath sealed" (6:27). For Christ states this as a proof that eternal life can be given them only by the Son of Man. Again, He shows that He is the Life by describing Himself as "The Living Bread" which, having come down from Heaven, is the necessary means of the sustenance of spiritual life for men. This sublime truth was elicited by the reference on the part of His critics to the manna provided for their fathers by God (6:30–35). Twice He declares "I am the Bread of Life" *(vv. 35 and 48)*, and in the latter case He points out that their fathers, even though they ate manna, died, whereas, on the contrary, to partake of Himself is to live forever (v. 51). That He is

The Embodiment of Life

equally with the Father is declared further in His words, "I live because of the Father" (v. 57).

Again, the words He speaks are spirit and life (v. 63). They are part of His being, and therefore they communicate life. When we feed upon His words we are feeding upon Himself. Our spiritual life is maintained thereby. Peter at once began to apprehend this when, immediately after the discussion now referred to, he said to Christ, "Lord, to whom shall we go? Thou hast words of eternal life" (v. 68, margin). On our part the sustenance of our spiritual life depends upon the exercise of faith.

The seventh chapter develops this truth in this way, that, in addition to the fact that Christ and His words are the sustaining element of our spiritual life, this life in us is

To Overflow in Lifegiving

enrichment to others. Jesus said, "He that believeth on Me, as the Scripture hath said, out of his belly shall flow rivers of living water. But this spake He of the Spirit, which they that believe on Him were to receive" (7:38, 39). The Holy Spirit is described by the apostle Paul as "the Spirit of life in Christ Jesus." Now Christ taught the disciples that the Spirit's work in and through the life of the believer could not be carried on until He Himself had been glorified. For, firstly, the Spirit would be sent forth by the Son of God as well as by the Father (16:7). Secondly, He would take of Christ's and declare it unto them, and this in order to glorify Him (16:14). Accordingly the flowing forth of the rivers of living water in the lives of believers is the glorifying of Christ by the Spirit in and through them.

The crowning point in the Lord's teaching concerning Himself as the means of life, was His statement to Martha, "I am

The Resurrection, and the Life

he that believeth on Me, though he die, yet shall He live; and whosoever liveth and believeth on Me shall never die" (11:25, 26). The resurrection of Lazarus from the dead was the crisis of the Lord's dealings with the Jews. They had ignored all His other works. Would they accept this greatest evidence of His power, and so acknowledge His claim to be the Son of God? They refused even this evidence. Nay, more, they took counsel together to put Him to death. From that time, therefore, the Lord ceased to deal with them, and left them to their darkness (11:53, 54). The resurrection of Lazarus, the greatest manifestation of His Deity up to that time, was, however, the occasion of the most comprehensive declaration of His power as the Lifegiver. He declared nothing less than that resurrection and life were embodied in His own Person, and that spiritual life, imparted

through faith in Him, excluded the possibility of death. In contrast to the rejection of His testimony by the Jews, even after the proof He gave of His power to raise the dead, stands the unquestioning acceptance by Martha of His tremendous claim, even before the event of her brother's resurrection. His declaration to her was an advance upon His preceding teaching concerning His power of resurrection. He had previously stated that He would quicken the dead, that they would hear His voice and live (5:21, 25); that He would raise up at the last day those who believe in Him (6:40, 44). But now He gathers up all this power into His own Person and says, "I am the Resurrection, and the Life."

This Transcendent Claim

is the climax of the teaching of the Gospel, regarding the initial and foundation truth of the introduction: "In Him was life" (1:4). After gathering His disciples around Him in the upper room prior to His crucifixion, He takes up the same theme with them, and declares that He is "the Way, the Truth, and the Life," and that in order to come to the Father it is necessary to come through Him (14:6). He tells them further that because He lives they shall live also (v. 19). Thus in two distinct statements He makes known to them what he had combined in His words to Martha, "I am the Resurrection and the Life."

In His prayer in chapter seventeen the theme of Christ as the source of life is further expounded. Not only has the Father given to the Son to have life in Himself, but He has given Him authority over all flesh, that He should give eternal life to all whom the Father has given Him. This specifies

The Recipients of Life

in a way not mentioned before. They are not simply those who believe, they were the gift of the Father to the Son from eternity. Moreover, the life which is derived from Christ is here defined as personal acquaintance with the Father and the Son. "This is the life eternal, that they should know Thee the only true God, and Him whom thou didst send, even Jesus Christ" (17:3). This is a new definition of life.

Spiritual vitality is not merely endless existence, it consists of the knowledge of God, a knowledge which molds character and determines action.

As the subject is brought to a close toward the end of the Gospel the apostle specifies the object for which it is written, and in doing so sums up the subject of Christ as the Life. He says, "These are written that ye may believe that Jesus is the Christ, the Son of God; and that believing ye may have life in His Name" (20:31). In the phrase "In His Name" are included all the preceding teachings of this Gospel which are developed from the statement "In Him was life." For His Name expresses what He is. It represents His character and attributes. It suggests that among other things

He is the embodiment and the fountain of life. The exercise of faith in Him brings His life into the soul. That life is therefore the light of men.

"In Him Was Life"

Yet He died. He yielded up His life. Only through His death could His life be communicated to man. A vicarious death it must be, too. For man was dead through sin. But since "in Him was life," death "could not hold or bind Him." He is "the resurrection, and the life." His life out of death brings life to us in our death. We have life out of His death. And because He lives we shall live also—a deathless life like His. May we know increasingly here, and now, the power of His resurrection!

CHAPTER FIVE

Christic the Sent One

A leading theme of this Gospel is that Christ came into the world as the One sent from the Father. This basic truth of the faith is stated in almost every chapter, and frequently in most of the chapters. The statement, as recorded by John, was constantly upon the Savior's lips. Its importance lies in this, that it implies His preexistence, and that it signalizes His coming into the world as distinct from that of every other being, and especially in this respect, that coming as the preexistent Son of God He was "of the full Deity possessed."

The Only-Begotten from the Father

Moreover, He came as "the only begotten from the Father" (1:14), a title indicating eternal relationship. God was eternally the Father, therefore the Son was eternal with the Father. Further, having come, He was still "in the bosom of the Father" (1:18); He was one with Him in the Godhead. He declared, "I and the Father are One" (10:30). His having been sent by the Father is a direct testimony to His distinct personality. Yet when He says to Philip, "He that hath seen Me hath seen the Father" (14:9), He declares His oneness with the Father in the Godhead.

His preexistence with the Father was constantly stated by Christ Himself. He described Himself as "the One who descended out of Heaven" (3:13), and again, as the One who is "from God" (6:46). He says further, "I am from above; . . . I am come forth, and am come from God" (8:23, 42). Again, in making acknowledgment to the disciples of their belief of this fact, and in assuring them that the Father loves them because of this belief, He repeats, "I came forth from the Father, . . . and am come into the world" (16:27, 28). His satisfaction with their belief comes out again in His closing prayer when He says, "They knew of a truth that I came forth from Thee, and they believed that Thou didst sent (a) Me" (17:8).* He states His preexistence in other ways. Putting it negatively He says, "I am not come of Myself but He . . . send (a) Me" (7:29 and 8:42).

Sanctified before Sent

The Father had sanctified Him before He sent (a) Him into the world (10:36). He was thus set apart for His mission before His incarnation. Again, He says that the Father who sent (p) Him gave Him commandment what He should say and speak (12:49). Further, His

---

*Two distinct words are used in John's Gospel for the verb "send," *pempo*, which is used 24 times, and *apostello* 17 times. They are sometimes used interchangeably. Any distinction lies in this, that *pempo* is a general term, without any special idea being necessarily attached to the relation between the sender and the one sent; *apostello*, from which the English word "apostle" is derived, expresses this relation, and suggests an official, authoritative sending. We shall indicate which word is used in the various passages by the letters (p) and (a). *Apostello*, not *pempo*, is always used when Christ is addressing the Father concerning His having sent Him. It is also noticeable that in direct statements, when "God," or the "Father," or the personal pronoun "He," is the immediate subject of the verb to send, *apostello* is used. When, on the contrary, the statement is not thus directly made, but is introduced by a relative pronoun, *pempo* is used. The use of the subordinate relative clause, that is, one introduced by a relative pronoun, comprises all the occurrences of the verb *pempo* in reference to Christ as the sent One, while, on the other hand, no relative clause, introduced by a relative pronoun, contains the word *apostello*. Now a relative clause (*e.g.*, "He that sent Me") necessarily gives much less stress in the expression of an idea than the direct statement of a principal clause (*e.g.*, "He sent Me"); in this latter the mission is the main thought, whereas in "He that sent Me is true," e.g., the main thought is not that of the mission. The above facts therefore serve to confirm the distinction already pointed out, and to show that *apostello* is the more expressive word of the two.

acts were done in the consciousness that He came forth from God and was going back to God (13:3). The fact of His return to the Father from whom He had come finds frequent mention in this Gospel, and is another link in the testimony both to His preexistence and to His Deity. For of no other could such statements be true. He says to the Jews, "Yet a little while am I with you, and I go unto Him that sent (p) Me" (7:33). This He repeats to the disciples, "Now I go unto Him that sent (p) Me; . . . I leave the world and go unto the Father" (16:5; cp. v. 28).

John's Gospel does not state the actual details of the manner of His coming. The record of that is found in the first and third Gospels. The omission of the facts relating to His birth is entirely appropriate to the character of this Gospel, the object of which is to present Christ as the eternal Son of God. In the paper under the heading of "Christ as the Light" we drew attention to the ninth verse of the first chapter, which states that Christ is a light for every man because He came into the world. This is the first direct mention of the truth of our present theme. The place to which He came is next mentioned. "He came unto His own things [Palestine, the land of God's choice] and they that were His own [the Jews, the people of God's choice] received Him not" (1:11). Then follows a statement of the mode of His coming, "The Word became flesh, and dwelt among us" (1:14). Thus in a threefold way the introduction to this Gospel presents the truth of the first Advent.

The first teaching given by the Lord Himself on the subject is in His conversation with Nicodemus, when He says, "God so loved the world that He gave His only begotten Son . . ."; this, with a statement of the purpose of the gift, He amplifies by saying that "God sent (a) not His Son into the world to judge the world; but that the world should be saved through Him." Here is given the first definite statement that the Father sent the Son. This great truth is stated over forty times in the Gospel. Its teaching upon the subject may be further set forth under the following heads: (I.) the purpose for which He came; (II.) the character He manifested; (III.) His identification with the Father; (IV.) the witness borne to Him.

I. The following are

The Purposes for Which He Came

(1) That the world might be saved through Him (3:17[a]). (2) To do not His own will, the will of Him that sent (p) Him (6:38). In this connection He declares that He seeks the glory of Him that sent (p) Him (7:18), and that He works the works of Him that sent (p) Him (9:4). (3) That He might give life unto the world (6:33). (4) That a man might eat of Him as the Living Bread, and not die (6:50); compare verses 51 and 58. (5) For judgment—not, that is to say, to judge the world, but—"that they which see not may see; and that they which see may become blind" (9:39). (6) That His sheep might have life, and have it abundantly (10:10). (7) That whosoever believeth in Him may not abide in the darkness (12:46) (8) That He might bear witness of the truth (18:37).

II. Associated with the fact of His being sent is

The Character He Manifested

This may be set forth in three ways, as to (1) His life, (2) His acts, (3) His words.

(1) The most notable feature in His character as the sent One is His perfect representation of the Father. This was the outcome of His entire obedience to His will. At the same time the Father manifested Himself in and through Him. He says "The living Father sent (a) Me, and I live because of the Father (6:57). Again He says "He that sent (p) Me is with Me" (8:29).

(2) Of His deeds He says, "My meat is to do the will of Him that sent (p) Me, and to accomplish His work" (4:34); "I seek not Mine own will, but the will of Him that sent (p) Me" (5:30); "I do always the things that are pleasing to Him" (8:29); "I must work the works of Him that sent (p) Me" (9:4). He was thus Himself the fulfillment of the promise of Jehovah to Israel that He would raise up from among them a prophet to whom they must hearken; for He would put His words in His mouth, and would speak all that He commanded (Deut. 18:15–18). That He did nothing of Himself is further shown in His statement that no one could come to Him ex-

cept the Father that sent Him drew him (6:44[p]).

(3) Of His words He says, "He whom God hath sent *(a)* speaketh the words of God" (3:34); "My teaching is not Mine, but His that sent *(p)* Me" (7:16); "He that sent *(p)* Me is true; and the things which I heard from Him, these speak I unto the world" (8:26). To the disciples He says, "The word which ye hear is not Mine, but the Father's who sent *(p)* Me" (14:24).

Thus His whole life bore testimony to the initial truth of the Gospel: "The only begotten Son, which is in the bosom of The Father, He hath declared Him." Men could never have learned the true character of God save through Him.

III. The following texts show

The Identification with the Father

as the One who sent Him: "He that honoreth not the Son honoreth not the Father which sent *(p)* Him" (5:23); (2) "He that believeth on Me, believeth not on Me, but on Him that sent *(p)* Me" (12:44); (3) "He that beholdeth Me beholdeth Him that sent *(p)* Me" (12:45); (4) "He that receiveth Me receiveth Him that sent Me" (13:20); (5) "This is life eternal, that they should know Thee the only true God, and Him whom Thou didst send *(a)*, even Jesus Christ," (17:3).

IV. Concerning

The Witness Borne to Him

He says: (1) "The very *works* that I do, bear witness of Me, that the Father hath sent *(a)* Me" (5:36); (2) "The *Father* that sent *(p)* Me beareth witness of Me" (8:18); (3) *Christ Himself* likewise bore this witness. It was not only the burden of His whole testimony, but He occasionally made certain statements in the hearing of men for the very purpose that they might believe that the Father had sent *(a)* Him (11:42). Though His testimony was generally rejected, and is still

rejected, yet the world is to be convinced that the Father sent *(a* in each verse) Him by the unity of all believers in Him (17:21 and 23). Amidst the cold refusal of the world to acknowledge His mission He expresses His delight in the fact that His followers believed in the truth of it (17:3, 25—*a* in each verse).

The Conclusion

The last statement in this Gospel in connection with this subject is the Lord's word to the disciples on the evening of the day of His Resurrection, when, having shown them His hands and His side, and thus rejoicing their hearts, He said, "Peace be unto you; as the Father hath sent *(a)* Me, even so send *(p)* I you (20:21).* A few evenings before He had said, "As Thou didst send *(a)* Me into the world, even so sent *(a)* I them into the world" (17:18). Now He confirms the words of His prayer. This statement He accompanied by breathing on them, and saying, "Receive ye the Holy Ghost (or, perhaps, holy breath): whose soever sins ye forgive, they are forgiven unto them; whose soever sins ye retain, they are retained" (20:21–23). That is to say, in their mission the Gospel they preached would be the means of forgiveness in the case of those who received it; it would be a savor of life unto life. On the other hand, the unbeliever, rejecting the Gospel, would remain in His sins, and it would thus be to him a savor of death unto death. Inasmuch as His sending us into the world bears a resemblance to His own mission from the Father, we have much to learn from the teaching of this Gospel on this subject as to what should be the character of our life and our work here. As it was His chief pleasure to do the will of Him who sent Him and worthily to represent Him, so may we unceasingly enter into the responsibility and privilege of doing the will of God and living to give a faithful witness for Him in this dark world of sin!

---

*In view of the precision with which the choice between *pempo* and *apostello* is made throughout the Gospel (see footnote on page 192), it cannot be gathered that the two words are used simply interchangeably in this verse. Even though in the corresponding statement in 17:18, the word *"apostello"* is used in both parts of the verse, yet the use of the two different verbs in 20:21, suggests the significance pointed out in the footnote referred to. Certainly, whatever distinction there is between the two words, the Lord does not observe the distinction when addressing the Father, but He does so when speaking to the disciples, suggesting perhaps, not a difference in the mode of sending but a difference in the relation between Himself and the Father on the one hand, and Himself and the disciples on the other.

· CHAPTER SIX ·

The Subject of Believing

Next to the person and work of the Son of God, the subject of "believing" is the chief and constant theme of this Gospel. It is definitely stated as the object for which the Gospel was written. This statement, instead of being given, as in ordinary books, in the introduction, or at the beginning of the book, is, as we have remarked, mentioned at the end. There the apostle, speaking of the words of Christ, says, "These are written, that ye may believe that Jesus is the Christ, the Son of God; and that believing ye may have life in His Name" (20:31). So the object of the writer is to lead to faith in the Son of God.

The reason why he mentioned this at the end instead of at the beginning is perhaps because his immediate purpose, under the guidance of the Spirit, is to present the Person of Christ in His glory and His grace, and hence any initial statement as to the reason why the Gospel is written is unnecessary. The way in which the Person and His work are depicted is in itself calculated to create faith in Him. So the mention of the purpose can be reserved till the story is told.*

The Introduction of the Gospel

To refer first to the introductory verses of this Gospel, we have remarked already that practically every leading theme therein has some express mention in the prologue, and this is the case with the present subject. The apostle introduces the theme of believing, first by stating that the purpose of John the Baptist's witness was that all might believe through Him (v. 7), and then by contrasting the treatment Christ received when He came unto His own with the effect of receiving Him

on the part of those who did so: "As many as received Him, to them gave He the right to become children of God, even to them that believe on His Name" (v. 12).

This expression "believing on" is the most important of all those that refer to belief. It involves more than mere "believing" or "believing in." Literally it is "believing into," and thus it suggests, not the mere acknowledgment of certain facts, but, at all events usually, an intimate union between the Person in whom faith is imposed and the one who exercises it; the phrase "believing on the Name" occurs elsewhere in this Gospel in 2:23 and 3:18. The Name is expressive of the character and authority of the Person referred to. In chapter 1:12 and chapter 3:18, to believe on the Name of Christ is to enter into the Divine relationship and to acknowledge His authority over the life, with the result that the character becomes manifested in the believer.

The passage in the first chapter makes it clear that to believe on the Name of Christ is (1) to receive Him, (2) to be born of God, and thus to become a child of God. The eighteenth verse of the third chapter shows, too, that to believe on His Name is (3) to be freed from condemnation. For "He that believeth on Him is not judged; he that believeth not hath been judged already, because he hath not believed on the Name of the only begotten Son of God."

In chapter 2:23 some are recorded as having "believed on His Name, beholding the signs which He did." These may perhaps not be regarded as having actually entered into the relationship referred to. Yet the phrase suggests that there was in their case at least such a recognition of His character and claims that it led to more than a mere acceptance of facts

*In this Gospel the apostle John nowhere uses the noun "faith"; he always speaks of the act of believing. The significance of this lies perhaps in the fact that in fulfilling his great object of presenting the Person in whom we are to believe, the act of believing is more appropriate than the mention of the abstract idea of faith. The subject of the Person Himself is antecedent to that of the exercise of faith.

concerning Him. There was doubtless such an outgoing of the heart to Him that possibly discipleship followed. True, it says that the Lord did not trust Himself to them, but that does not suggest that He had no confidence in them. The point is that He knew all men and needed not that man should bear witness concerning man (*see* R.V.). We know that only a few years after this His disciples numbered at least 500. Possibly those here referred to were among that number.

The first definite cases of believing with that faith which involves discipleship are those of Nathanael, who confessed Christ as the Son of God (1:49, 50), and of the disciples who witnessed His miracle in Cana of Galilee (2:11). These cases, and those mentioned in 2:23, are cited by John apparently as preliminary examples of the great theme of his Gospel.

Nicodemus

In the third chapter the case of Nicodemus is narrated because it opens up the teaching of the subject of believing. To him the Lord unfolds the great truths relating thereto in connection with the new birth. The important matter for Nicodemus and his fellow-Pharisees is expressed in the question, "How shall ye believe?" (v. 12). Whatever Nicodemus may have known about Jesus of Nazareth this was the essential thing. He must indeed be born anew, but this new birth depends on believing, and thereby on the death of the Son of Man. So the tremendous truth is stated that the present blessing and future destiny of Nicodemus are to be based upon the death of the One who is speaking to him. "The Son of man must be lifted up, that whosoever believeth may in Him have eternal life" (v. 14). Moreover, faith must be exercised in Christ Himself. "God so loved the world, that He gave His only begotten Son, that whosoever *believeth on Him* should not perish, but have eternal life" (v. 16). This effects deliverance from judgment (v. 18). These are the basic

truths of salvation by faith, and it seems clear that John took the case of Nicodemus in order thus to set them forth early in the Gospel.

The third chapter closes with a further narrative concerning John the Baptist and his testimony, the writer evidently of a purpose recalling our thoughts to the main subject of believing: "He that believeth on the Son hath eternal life; but he that obeyeth not the Son shall not see life, but the wrath of God abideth on him" (v. 36).

The Woman of Samaria

The fourth chapter records Christ's dealings with the woman of Samaria. To her the Lord mentions nothing about believing, yet the narrative shows how the Lord led her to exercise faith in Himself, and the result is recorded that many of the Samaritans believed on Him (vv. 39–42). Following this is the record of the faith of the nobleman whose sick son was healed (4:50–53). The account is now given, in chapter 5, of the healing of the impotent man, and this leads to

Christ's First Discussion with the Jews

(5:19–47). To those who were opposed to Him the Lord mentions nothing about *believing on Him*.* In other words, in dealing with His would-be murderers, Christ does not refer to that faith by which a person is brought into union with Him. He does state that the one who believes Him that sent Him (R.V. of v. 24) has eternal life and is freed from judgment, and this is indeed the faith that unites to Christ, but the Lord states here that the necessary preliminary to that is the acceptance of His Word. Hearing is in this case clearly the obedient hearing and not mere listening. Thus all the conditions for union which are involved in *believing on* Christ are here implied. This general statement, however, only stands out in contrast to what He says concerning the Jews themselves; in reference to His opponents He speaks of their believing, or their

---

*Except in verse 24, on which see above, the word "believe" is not used in this chapter with a preposition, but with the dative case only, suggesting an acceptance of the Lord's statements or of facts concerning Him (as clearly in v. 46), and not expressly the faith which unites the heart to Him, which seems to be the predominant idea with *eis*, upon, or into. *References are from the Revised Version.*

efusal to believe, as a matter of acceptance of facts. He says, "Whom He has sent, Him ye *believe* not; . . . if ye believed Moses, ye would *believe Me*. But if ye believe not His writings, how shall ye *believe My words?*" (vv. 38:45, 47). How could they believe who received glory one of another? (v. 44). They were not in the same state as Nicodemus, for instance; he was an inquirer, they were His foes. Nicodemus must be brought to the faith which gives life; they must be got first, if possible, simply to accept facts.

The Multitude Whom He Fed

In the sixth chapter His teaching was given to the people whom He had fed miraculously. Here He is not confronted with direct opponents as on the preceding occasion. At all events at the beginning of His remarks He speaks to them of that faith which involves union with Himself, and not of mere credence which accepts facts. Thus when they inquire what they must do to work the works of God He says, "This is the work of God, that ye *believe on Him* whom He hath sent" (6:29). In reply to this, however, they want to see a sign that they may *believe Him* (v. 30). They have no idea of the exercise of spiritual faith. Yet Christ still seeks to lead them into it, and tells them that the true bread is the bread of God, which comes down out of Heaven and gives light to the world. Drawn by this remark they say, "Lord, ever more give us this bread." He then says, "I am the Bread of life; he that cometh to Me shall not hunger, and he that believeth on Me shall never thirst" (v. 35). His word *"believeth on Me"* is the reply to their "that we may *believe* Thee." Again, He says, "This is the will of the Father that every one that beholdeth the Son, and *believeth on Him*, should have eternal life." This passage therefore makes clear the difference between believing Him and believing on Him.

This leads to

The Second Discussion with the Jews

They now murmur concerning Him. The more they resist His teaching the more difficult it becomes. He has little to say about believing. He simply says, "He that believeth

hath eternal life" (v. 47, R.V.). He tells them that they must eat His flesh and drink His blood, words purposely difficult for them, for no idea could be more repulsive to them as orthodox Jews. This teaching was therefore retributive. The remainder of this sixth chapter is occupied with the Lord's conversations with the disciples. There were some who were apparently not genuine disciples. He Himself says, "There are some of you that believe not" (v. 64). The difficulty of His language to the Jews had the double effect of hardening the Jews on the one hand, and on the other hand of separating the disciples, for there arose a murmuring among them (v. 64). Those who believed not "went back and walked no more with Him" (v. 66). On the contrary, in reply to the Lord's question to the twelve as to whether they should also go away, Peter says, "Lord, to whom shall we go? Thou hast the words of eternal life. And we have believed, and know that Thou art the Holy One of God" (vv. 67-69). What Peter here states as to believing is perhaps to be distinguished from the teaching of the Gospel as to believing on the Son of God and thus receiving life. The faith of the disciples was produced by a gradual process of recognition of Christ. Certainly Peter's statement marks a tremendous step in the process.

The Great Invitation

In chapter seven we are introduced to the Lord's unbelieving brethren (note that the A.V. of v. 5 "in Him" ought to be "on Him" as in R.V.). After they had gone up to the feast in Jerusalem, Christ went up secretly. In the middle of the feast, however, He went to the temple and taught, resulting in a further controversy among the people. The effect of this was that many of the people believed on Him (v. 31). On the last day of the feast the Lord publicly directed any who were in spiritual need to come to Him to have it met, and declared that the supply of the need must be by means of believing on Him. He says, "If any man thirst, let him come unto Me and drink. He that believeth on Me, as the Scripture has said, out of his belly shall flow rivers of living water" (vv. 37, 38).

This marks an important step in the development of the subject. The Lord now laid claim publicly to the faith of all who would receive spiritual life and power. There is an advance, too, upon the previous teaching of this Gospel. In the third chapter we learned that to believe on Him was to be born of the Spirit. Here Christ taught that those who believed on Him would receive the Spirit, and that thereby they would become a means of enrichment to others. Later in the Gospel this particular aspect of the subject is extended.

The Gospel of John may be divided into two parts. The first contains a series of discussions between the Lord and the hostile Jews. Their rejection of the witness of His greatest miracle, the raising of Lazarus, led Him to depart from them. This was the climax of their unbelief. From that time "Jesus walked no more openly among the Jews" (11:54). It is true that after His triumphant entry into Jerusalem He gave one more public testimony, but the Jews who opposed Him were left to fill up the cup of their iniquity. The latter part of the Gospel is occupied with His private dealings with His disciples, His betrayal, trial, death, and resurrection, and His subsequent testimony to His disciples.

This division of the Gospel has an important bearing on the subject of believing. We have seen how the theme developed up to His public invitation to the thirsty to come to Him and drink (7:37–39). Chapters five to seven contain three discussions with the skeptical Jews. We have observed that to them the Lord does not speak of *"believing on"* Him, but merely to believing or refusing to believe Him; that is, by way of mental acceptance of facts concerning Him. So in

The Fourth Discussion with the Jews

recorded in the eighth chapter, He says, "except ye believe that I am He ye shall die in your sins" (8:24). He then gave a special testimony of His relationship with the Father, as a result of which many of the people (not His opponents) *believed on* Him (v. 10). This verse marks the close of a section of the narrative. When it says in the next verse that Jesus addressed those Jews which had *believed* Him (R.V.), it is necessary to distinguish between these and the ones referred to in the preceding

verse as having *believed on* Him. The Revised Version accurately makes the distinction. The Jews who are spoken of in verses 31–59, and who eventually sought to stone Him, had not *believed on* Him as some of the people had done. They had, up to a certain point, agreed to some of His statements. Now that He began to talk about the power of the truth to set them free, their pride was wounded and they identified themselves with His would-be murderers. Accordingly to them the Lord merely speaks about *believing* Him, and not about the faith which leads to discipleship.

How different is the case with the blind man in the next chapter! Finding him after his excommunication, the Lord says, "Dost thou believe on the Son of God?" His "Lord, I believe" meant the saving of his soul. His case leads to

The Fifth Discussion with the Jews

recorded in the tenth chapter. Here again He makes no statement about believing on Him. He merely seeks to get them to accept His testimony. He says, "I told you and ye believe not; . . . ye *believe* not because ye are not of My sheep; . . . if I do not the works of My father, *believe* Me not. But if I do them, though ye *believe* not Me, *believe* the works" (vv. 25–38). In contrast to all this is the record at the close of the chapter, that as a result of His visit beyond Jordan "many *believed on* Him" (10:42). Having ceased to reason with the Jews, He will give them one more opportunity of believing Him, by a more striking miracle than any He had performed, that of the resurrection of Lazarus. That would be His last witness.

Incidental to the resurrection of Lazarus is the Lord's conversation with Martha. This strikingly illustrates the difference between His words to the opposing Jews concerning believing and those to His followers. He was purposely absent at the time of Lazarus' death in order that Martha and Mary might believe (11:15). The character of their faith is shown in what follows. To Martha, He says, "I am the Resurrection and the Life: he that *believeth on* Me, though he die, yet shall he live: and whosoever liveth and *believeth on* Me shall never die" (vv. 25, 26). He then draws from her the confession of faith, "I have be ieved that Thou art the Christ, the Son of God, even He that cometh into the world." She was still doubtful as to His power to raise her brother, even when He was standing before the tomb. Hence His remonstrance, "Said I not unto thee, that if thou believedst thou shouldst see the glory of God? (v. 40). His glory is ever revealed to believing souls.

This miracle was a touchstone for faith: (1) as to the multitudes, they must believe that the Father had sent Him (v. 42); that acknowledgment must come first; (2) as to the Jews who had come to Mary, many of them beholding what He had done *believed on* Him; (3) as for the rest, they reported the matter to the authorities and took counsel to put Him to death. This miracle, then, had a separating effect, turning some into opponents and others into disciples (v. 45).

Before finally gathering His disciples around Him He gives

One More Testimony

to the people generally. There is something very solemn about this final witness in the city of Jerusalem. The people cannot understand His teaching that the Son of man must be lifted up. Jesus replies by warning them that the light will be with them only a little while, and by exhorting them to *believe on* the light while they have it, so that they may become sons of light, and that the darkness may not overtake them. They refused to believe on Him, however, and thus the prophecy of Isaiah was fulfilled, "Lord, who hath believed our report?" and his further prediction of their blindness and hardness of heart. In contrast to this there were some of the rulers who *believed on Him,* but they remained His secret disciples, fearing excommunication. So the Lord finally says, "He that *believeth on* Me believeth . . . on Him that sent Me . . . I am come a light into the world, that whosoever *believeth on* Me may not abide in the darkness" (12:44–46). That was His closing testimony, He had now finished the work of dividing between those who refused to *believe* and those who *believed on* Him.

We now pass to the section of the Gospel which records

His Private Discourse with the Disciples

In His words to them on the subject of believing we note a distinct development in the theme. His first word, however, is simply that His prediction of what He is to pass through is in order that, as He says, after it is fulfilled, "Ye may believe that I am" (13:19; 14:29). At the beginning of chapter fourteen He utters the tremendous words, "Ye believe in God, believe also in Me." The Lord had never spoken even to His disciples just in this way before. He shows them that faith must be exercised in Him equally with the Father, a strong testimony to His own Deity. His next words on believing are closely connected with these, for they similarly declare His equality with the Father. The disciples are to believe that He is in the Father and the Father in Him, or they are to believe Him for the very works' sake (vv. 10, 11). Now follows

The Practical Effect of Believing

An intimation of this had been given, as we have seen, in His testimony at the feast that those who believed on Him would receive the Spirit and become channels of living water. Now He says, "He that believeth on Me, the works that I do, He shall do also; and greater works than these shall he do; because I go unto the Father" (14:12). His teaching in the upper room is calculated to confirm their faith in Himself and to make them effective and fruitful in their future ministry by the power of the Holy Spirit.

He further points out that the sin of the world lies in its not believing on Him (16:19). As for the disciples, they were the special objects of the Father's love because they had loved Him, the Son, and had believed that He came forth from God (v. 30). They listen to His prayer, and learn therein what joy He has in their faith. He tells the Father that they have received His Word, have known that He came forth from Him, and have believed that the Father is in Him (17:8). They hear Him pray also for those who will believe on Him through their word (v. 20). They learn that the union of all in the Father and in the Son has this object in view, that the world may believe that the Father sent Him (v. 21). After that prayer they have but to see the crucified One raised from the dead and present with them in resurrection life and power, and their faith will be perfected and unshakeable.

The Gospel next records His betrayal and trial,

His Crucifixion and Resurrection

John emphatically declares that he witnessed the details of the crucifixion, that his witness is true, and that he knows that he saith true in order that we may believe (19:35). After the resurrection the record again centers in the subject of believing. John follows Peter into the empty tomb. He sees there the clear evidences of the Lord's resurrection; Here are the bodycloths lying as they had been wrapped round His body, and the head napkin not lying with them, as if they had been put into a pile, but still folded as it had been round His head and lying where His head had been. The cloths were still in the shape of the body. John says that he himself followed, and, looking at the cloths as they were lying, he saw and believed.

Then follows the record of

The Absence of Thomas

in the evening of that day, from the company of the disciples, when the Lord came into their midst, and his refusal to believe unless he sees the Person Himself and actually feels the marks in His hands and side. He little knew that Christ was listening all the time he said it. So that day week the Lord comes among them when Thomas is there, and, repeating His words, invites him to handle Him, with the exhortation, "Be not unbelieving but believing." This is quite enough. Thomas confesses Him as "My Lord and My God." But the Lord, speaking of those who would afterwards believe on Him, says, "Because thou hath seen Me thou hast believed; blessed are they that have not seen, and yet have believed" (v. 29).

How blessed to be among that number and to be able to say of Christ, "Whom not having seen we love; on whom, though now we see Him not, yet believing, we rejoice greatly with joy unspeakable and full of glory!" Faith worketh by love. So may our faith lead us to respond to His love by the loving devotion of our whole being to Him, by taking up our cross and following Him with ardent, unstinted, and undying affection!

We have already referred to the closing mention of the subject in this Gospel where the apostle shows that it was written that we might believe that Jesus is the Christ, the Son of God, and believing might have life in His Name (v. 31).

Witnesses to Christ

The reader of the Gospel of John cannot fail to be struck with the constant reference therein to the subject of the witness born to Christ. Testimony to Christ is, of course, the very *raison d'etre* of all the Gospels, but with John the specific mention of the fact forms a characteristic feature of his Gospel. The same is true of his first Epistle. He there says, "If we receive the witness of men, the witness of God is greater" (1 John 5:9). Possibly he means by "the witness of men" the testimony of himself and his fellow apostles, though more probably he is stating as a general fact that men receive human witness on good evidence, and that therefore the witness of God is much more to be received. Even from the human standpoint the testimony to Christ is cumulatively of such a character that to reject it savors either of willful ignorance or blind antagonism.

Now John's testimony is very definite. It is twofold, and consists of proofs, firstly, that Christ is the Son of God, the sent One of the Father; and, secondly, that eternal life for men is in Him. This is stated pointedly in the Epistle: "The witness of God is this, that He hath borne witness concerning His Son; . . . that God gave unto us eternal life and this life is in His Son" (1 John 5:9–11).

It will perhaps be useful to go through the records of the Gospel on the subject, as we have done in the case of other leading themes.

The first witness is

John the Baptist

The earlier part of the Gospel is largely occupied with his testimony. In the introduction he is mentioned as the one who came "for a witness, that he might bear witness of the light that all might believe through him" (1:7). Obviously the record of the Baptist's testimony is designedly introductory to the whole theme of the witness to Christ. The apostle emphasizes the fact that the Baptist was not himself the Light, but "came that he might bear witness of the Light" (v. 8).

Next comes a preliminary record of his actual testimony. "John beareth witness of Him, and crieth, saying, This was He of whom I said, He that cometh after me has become before me: for He was before me" (v. 15). The next three sections of the first chapter (vv. 19–42) give a detailed report of the Baptist's witness and its effects. Verse 19 is a heading to the subject. "And this is the witness of John, when the Jews sent unto him from Jerusalem priests and Levites to ask him, Who art thou?" John the Baptist's testimony increases in definiteness; it is like a light which glows the more as it is turned on.

1. He denies that he is the Christ (v. 20).
2. He is preparing His way (v. 23).
3. One is in their midst who is incomparably superior to him (vv. 26, 27).
4. He is "the Lamb of God, which taketh away the sin of the world" (v. 29).
5. John has seen the Spirit descending upon Him, and He abides upon Him (v. 3).
6. He will baptize with the Holy Spirit (v. 33).
7. This Person is the Son of God (v. 34).

To show that this is the climax of his testimony he says, "And I have seen and have borne witness that this is the Son of God."

The increasing definiteness of all this is noticeable:

1. His first statement is purely negative.
2. The second shows John's relationship toward Christ.
3. The third signalizes Him, but indefinitely.

4. The fourth specifies him definitely, but symbolically.
5. The fifth declares the Divine testimony to His Godhead.
6. The sixth states His Divine power.
7. The seventh declares specifically that He is the Son of God.

There are two further references to John the Baptist's witness, one when, in reply to the remark of his disciples that all men were coming to Christ, he declared that since he himself was not the Christ, but was sent before Him, Christ must increase while he must decrease (3:26). The other is Christ's declaration of John, that he had borne witness unto the truth, as a burning and shining lamp, but that there was a still greater witness than that of John. The Lord's statement, "the witness which I receive is not from men" (v. 34), meant primarily that the witness of John the Baptist was not simply John's testimony, but that it came from God through him. The Authorized Version, "I receive not testimony from man," is a mistranslation, and does not convey the Lord's meaning.

A Series of Witnesses— The Father

He is here engaged in controversy with the opposing Jews, and now mentions one after another of those who have borne witness to Him. He declares that the testimony which he has given Himself is not His alone. He says, "If I bear witness of Myself, My witness is not true." Later on He says, "I am He that beareth witness of Myself and the Father that sent Me beareth witness of Me." Thus there are Two bearing witness, and, as he reminds the Pharisees from their law, the witness of two men is true. Here in the fifth chapter He lays stress upon the Father's witness: "It is another that beareth witness for Me; and I know that the witness which He witnesseth of Me is true . . . The Father which sent Me, He hath borne witness of Me" (5:31, 32, 37). The Lord was perhaps referring partly to the voice uttered by the Father on the occasion of His baptism, "Thou art My beloved Son: in Thee I am well pleased." But there seems to have been more in view than this. For He has

just said that His works bore witness of Him, and that these were given Him to do by the Father (v. 36), and subsequently He declared that the Father Himself dwelling in Him did the works (14:10). Accordingly the Father was bearing witness to Him by the works He wrought.

His Works

His works constitute the third of the witnesses of which the Lord speaks in this discourse. By His works He does not mean merely His miracles. Everything He did bore witness both to His Deity and His character, and to His mission as the One sent of the Father. "The very works that I do," He says, "bear witness of Me, that the Father hath sent Me" (v. 36). He tells the Jews that they had neither heard His voice at any time nor seen His form. There is perhaps here an intimation that they had never understood the messages God had given to the nation, and that now they completely misunderstood the Person who was now before them, in their refusal to recognize Him as His Son, and so neither did they understand the nature and significance of His works.

His works are called "signs." The word *sēmeion*, "sign," is more than a mere miracle. A miracle is that which excites wonder, but a sign is a significant appeal to the heart of man, used in this case by God to produce an acknowledgment of His existence, power, or character. So the miracles wrought by Christ were testimonies to the fact that He was the Son of God. Three in John's Gospel are recorded in a way which shows that they were specially wrought with a view to convince the Jews of the Lord's Divine Sonship and mission. The first of these three was that of the lame man by the pool of Bethesda. It was that miracle that led to the discussion now under consideration, in which the Lord spoke so much of the witness borne to Him. The second was the healing of the blind man, which led to the discussion as to whether Jesus had come from God or not, and which was followed by His declaration, in answer to their request that He would tell them plainly whether He was the Christ, "I told you, and ye believed not: the works that I do in My Father's Name, these bear witness of Me" (10:25). The third is the resurrection of Lazarus. That was, as we have already seen, His last testimony to them by this special means.

The Scriptures

The next witness mentioned by the Lord is the Scriptures. He says, "Ye search the Scriptures, for in them ye think ye have eternal life; and these are they which bear witness of Me" (5:39). The Jews looked to the law of Moses as a means of life, and prided themselves in the exclusive privileges God had given to them; but they read the sacred page with spiritually blinded eyes. Their table had become a snare, and the proof of their blindness was that they failed to see any correspondence between the One who was in their midst and the Scriptures which foretold of Him. Hence they would not come to Him that they might have life. It was a stupendous claim to make that the inspired records committed to the nation concentrated their testimony from beginning to end on a Person who had grown up in a humble, unobtrusive path of life in the nation, and had but recently come forth from a cottage home, the home of a laboring man. Yet all the circumstances of His life and ministry thus far only vindicated His claim. The various witnesses mentioned by Him in these discourses, the witness, that is to say, of the Father and of John the Baptist, of the Lord's own works and the Scriptures, blend together to form a light that shines with intense power, revealing to our worshiping hearts the glories of the Son of God.

Past, Present and Future

So far the witnesses to which the Gospel of John refers were either past or present. When we pass to the latter part of the Gospel the reference is to the future, that is, to testimony which was to be given after the Lord had ascended. This change in the subject is appropriate to the circumstances of the Lord's life on earth. For it was when He had ceased His public ministry and had gathered His disciples around Him, just before His crucifixion, that He told them of the witness that was yet to be borne to Him. It would be twofold.

The Holy Spirit

The Holy Spirit would bear witness, and, as a result of His operation, the Lord's followers would do so. He says, "When the Comforter is come, whom I will send unto you from the Father, He shall bear witness of Me; and ye also bear witness, because ye have been with Me from the beginning" (15:26, 27). It is the one object of the Holy Spirit in all His operations to glorify Christ. With that in view, those who are really yielded to God, so that the Holy Spirit can use them, will be led by Him to make it the great and constant object of their lives also to glorify Christ.

His Disciples

That was characteristic of His apostles. They had had proof positive in all their associations with Him in the days of His flesh, and subsequently after His resurrection, that He was the Son of God, the One sent of the Father, the Messiah of the nation, and the Lord of His people. They were Spirit-filled men, and the Holy Spirit was able to use them in bearing witness to Him. It was given to them to bear witness, not only by oral testimony, but by continuing and completing the Scriptures of truth, the Word of God. All the witness that believers have given since, both individually and collectively in the Churches, while it is due to the work of the Spirit of God in their hearts, is at the same time the outcome of the witness which was given by the first disciples of the Lord. When the Church is complete and removed at the Rapture, that particular testimony will cease, and the Holy Spirit will bear witness in another way.

The Seventh Witness

Thus far in this Gospel we have read of six witnesses to Christ: the Father, John the Baptist, the works of the Lord Himself, the Scriptures, the Holy Spirit, and the disciples. There is yet another. It is that of the writer of this Gospel. He records the supernatural circumstances in the death of Christ in that he saw blood and water coming out of the smitten side of the Crucified. He says, "And he that hath seen hath borne witness, and his witness is true; and he knoweth that He saith true, that ye also may believe" (19:35). This flowing of the water and the blood was not an evidence of mere physical suffering, it was a Divine and supernatural testimony to the fact of the impartation of life eternal. Concerning it John says: "This is He that came by water and blood, even Jesus Christ, not with the water only, but with the water and the blood. . . . There are three who bear witness: the Spirit, and the water, and the blood; and the three agree in one, . . . and the witness is this, that God gave unto us eternal life, and this life is in His Son" (1 John 5:6–11).

"Ye Are My Witnesses"

Finally, the apostle concludes his Gospel by a statement characteristic of his references therein to himself. It forms a kind of climax to his testimony. He says, "This is the disciple which beareth witness of those things, and wrote these things; and we know that His witness is true" (21:24). His Gospel is itself a wonderful fulfillment of the promise of the Lord on the day of His ascension, "Ye shall be My witnesses." May it be ours by sound doctrine and godliness of life to continue the witness!

CHAPTER EIGHT

Divine Love

That the apostle John should write about Divine love to a greater extent than any other writer of Scripture is what we might expect on reading his testimony of his personal experiences of the love of Christ to him. This disciple seems to have enjoyed the manifestation of His love in a special manner, he delights to call himself "the disciple whom Jesus loved" (13:23; 19:26; 20:2; 21:20). Not that there is any hint of favoritism in this. The Lord did not bestow His love upon John at the expense of His love to the other disciples. On the contrary, John himself says that Christ "loved His own which were in the world," and "He loved them unto the end" (13:1). Christ's affections went out indeed especially to him, but not so that the others were losers by it. If the beloved disciple was loved the more, they were not loved the less.

And yet, the love of the Lord Jesus was not a kind of indiscriminate benevolence, smiling on all alike, nor could it have been the outcome merely of a sovereign will. There was no doubt something in John that drew it forth in a special way. However that may have been the case, John himself apprehended the fact that Jesus loved him, and he appreciated it.

Nor, again, does his testimony concerning the love of Christ toward him savor of boastfulness in the slightest degree. Nay, verily, it breathes a tone of childlike humility. There is a complete lack of self-consciousness about his assertions—not a breath of protestation that he was unworthy of the love, nor any such disclaimer of merit. What he says is just the spontaneous expression of his enjoyment of the fact. This then is the disciple whom the Spirit of God used to write preeminently on the greatest of all themes.

Its Place in the Gospel

We have observed in the case of other subjects in this Gospel that there is a somewhat different treatment in the first half, which gives our Lord's public ministry; from that in the latter part, which gives His private instructions to His disciples, and so it is with the present subject. It naturally occupies a more prominent place in the latter part of the Gospel than the former. In the latter part the theme is almost continuous. Not so in the first half, the first ten chapters, though the love of God to men is recorded, contain no statement concerning the love of Christ. From the eleventh chapter onward the Gospel is full of it. And here in His private intimacy with His disciples He unlocks the treasures of the Father's heart toward them. Here love is not spoken of as the love of God; save where Christ's own love is mentioned, the love is always that of the Father.

The First Mention

Nothing could be more appropriate than that the theme should be introduced by the sublime testimony, "God so loved the world, that He gave His only begotten Son, that whosoever believeth on Him should not perish, but have eternal life" (3:16). That this should be the first mention is suggestive; we must learn of the love of God toward ourselves as sinners before we begin to learn of His love as our Father. It is fitting, too, that the next should consist of a statement of the love of the Father to the Son; it occurs in the same chapter, and, like the first statement, it is associated with believing "The Father loveth the Son, and hath given all things into His hand. He that believeth on the Son hath eternal life" (3:35, 36). "God so loved the world," and the evidence is that He gave His Son: "The Father loveth the Son," that suggests the value of His gift, and the evidence is that "He hath given all things into His hand."

Two Synonyms

The statement, "the Father loveth the Son," occurs again in chapter 5:20, in the Lord's controversy with the Jews. But here a different word, *phileō*, is used for "loveth"; it was *agapaō* in chapter 3:35. These two words are nowhere used simply interchangeably; each is used upon occasion to convey the thought of deep affection, but *phileō* suggests a still more emotional love than *agapaō*. The change of the word in chapter 5:20 is significant.*

In chapter 3:35 the Father's love to the Son is predicted in connection with His committal of all things into His hand. The similar statement in chapter 5:20 is the Lord's own testimony, not the writer's, and here He is speaking about the constant communion between Himself and His Father. The Son does what He sees the Father doing; the Father shows the Son what He Himself does. The word of deeper emotion is therefore entirely appropriate here.

The Eleventh Chapter

There is not much more about the love of God in this section of the Gospel, for the Lord is holding a controversy with His enemies. He says to them, "Ye have not the love of God in yourselves" (5:42); and again, "If God were your Father, ye would love Me" (8:42). Their attitude toward Him shows that God is not their Father. We pass now to the latter part of the Gospel. The eleventh chapter is transitional; it records Christ's final witness to the Jews in the resurrection of Lazarus, and also

the first of a series of private conversations with His followers. In regard to the latter, this chapter contains a touching testimony about the love of Christ in connection with the death of Lazarus. The message of the sisters is, "Lord, Behold he whom Thou lovest *(phileō)* is sick" (11:3). Then comes the testimony of John, the writer: "Now Jesus loved *(agapaō)* Martha, and her sister, and Lazarus." Bearing in mind that each word speaks of deep affection, it is again quite suitable that the more emotional word should be used by the sisters. So, too, when the Jews, seeing the intensity of the Lord's feelings, say, "Behold how He loved him!" they use the same word, *phileō* (v. 36). The writer is not changing the verb simply for the sake of variety or euphony.

The Upper Room

When we come to the Lord's conversation with the disciples in the upper room, the subject of Divine love becomes the prominent theme. This river, running through the Gospel record, here broadens out. The narrative begins with the statement of the love of Christ for His followers in all its sufficiency and permanency. "Jesus knowing that His hour was come that He should depart out of this world unto the Father, having loved His own which were in the world, He loved them unto the end" (13:1). This is the special love of which John delights to speak. The reader cannot fail to be struck with the way in which the Lord unfolds to His disciples the Father's love toward them and His own association with Him in it. He uses the Father's love toward Himself as a comparison of His own love to the disci-

---

*The two words are used in the same connection in three or four instances in this Gospel. The case which has received most notice is in the conversation between the Lord and Peter in chapter 21:15–17. The note in the Expositor's Greek Testament is to the effect that here at all events there can be no distinction between the words, as it could not be said, if there were, that Peter was grieved because Jesus *the third time* said, "Lovest *(phileō)* thou Me," when in the same question just before He used the other word *agapaō;* and that therefore the words are identical in meaning, and are "interchanged for the sake of euphony." This supposition is entirely unfounded. Firstly, it may not be concluded that the two words could not have a different meaning, because the same question was asked three times. The question would be practically the same even though the word "lovest" in the third expressed a more emotional feeling. Secondly, there is good reason to think that Christ did not address Peter in Greek. John's Greek was an inspired translation of the Lord's words, and the different words in the Gospel narrative express different shades of meaning conveyed in His original utterances. Thirdly, the idea about euphony must be ruled out; anyone who reads the Greek text through can see that there would be more euphony in verse 16 if *phileō* were used instead of *agapaō.* Fourthly, the commentator quotes a sentence from a nonbiblical writer to show the identity in meaning, which shows the very contrary. Moreover, Greek writers themselves point to the difference in meaning. Thus Dio Cassius says of the loyalty of the people to Caesar, "ye had affection *(phileō)* for him *as a father* and ye loved *(agapaō)* as a *benefactor*" (44:48). Aristotle plainly states that there is a distinction (Rhet. 1. 11, 17). The distinction must be observed in every case in John's Gospel.

ples. He says, "He that hath My commandments, and keepeth them, he it is that loveth Me: and he that loveth Me shall be loved of My Father, and I will love him, and will manifest Myself unto him." And again, "If a man love Me, he will keep My words: and My Father will love him, and we will come unto him, and make our abode with him" (14:21, 23). Following this assurance of the united love of the Father and the Son for those who fulfill His will, there comes the still more wonderful statement: "Even as the Father hath loved Me, I also have loved you: abide ye in My love. If ye keep My commandments, ye shall abide in My love; even as I have kept My Father's commandments, and abide in His love" (15:9, 10). This expresses the immeasurable degree of the love He is unfolding to them; it is the infinite love of the Father for the Son Himself. And this is the standard for our love to one another, for He gives it as His "commandment" that we love one another even as He has loved us (v. 12). Toward the close of His discourse to the disciples the Lord uses the more emotional word to express the Father's love, as being a response to the love they had shown to Him. He says, "The Father Himself loveth (phileō) you, because ye have loved Me, and have believed that I came forth from the Father" (16:27).

The Lord's Prayer

In His prayer which follows He renews the comparison of the Father's love to Him and His own love to them, only reversing the order. Previously He had said, "Even as the Father hath loved Me, I also have loved you"; now He says, "Thou lovedst them even as Thou lovedst Me" (17:23). But this love is to be realized in their experience. The close of this prayer is to the effect that the love wherewith the Father loved Him is to be in them and Christ Himself is to be in them. This then is to be the practical effect of that love. This, the closing utterance of His prayer, is also the close of this section of the Gospel. It begins and ends with the same theme of divine love, the unfailing love of Christ (13:1), and the abiding love of the Father and the Son (17:26). There can be no higher expression of divine love toward God's children than that He loves

them as He loves His own Son. Thus the theme of the Father's love to the Son gradually expands in the Gospel from the introductory statement in chapter 3:35 to the closing testimony in the seventeenth chapter.

The Last Chapter

As we consider this great subject the questions must arise, What response has this infinite love in our hearts and lives? Do we really love the Lord with that deep-rooted affection which will mold our very life and shape our conduct according to His own character? Is our path the path of the ardent follower? Are our acts impelled by a burning devotion that gives Christ the uppermost place in our lives, and makes it our one great purpose and ambition to be well-pleasing to Him in all things? These indeed are the questions suggested by the closing narrative of that Gospel. Peter had avowed to his Master that though all would forsake Him, yet would not he. Then came his time of temptation and his faithlessness, the time, too, of his restoration by the One whose look had already melted his heart, and after this the morning scene on the shore of the lake. "Simon, son of John," says the Lord, "lovest (agapaō) thou Me more than these?"—that is, more than the other disciples. Peter replies by using the other and still more tender word, phileō, to declare his love. The second time Christ asks the question with the same word He had already used. Again Peter insists. The third time the Lord touchingly uses Peter's word. This elicits a still stronger declaration in which the disciple naturally adheres to his same expression. The Master's work in His follower's heart is done, and done as He only could do it. The love that He gladly recognized in that heart is to manifest itself increasingly for others that belong to Him—the lambs and sheep of the flock.

The Lesson

This is the lesson for us all, enforced upon our own hearts as we come to the end of this Gospel. Christ must have the preeminent place if our lives are to be happy and useful, and only thus shall we be His instruments in blessing to others.

CHAPTER NINE

The Death of Christ

In the first three Gospels the reader goes through several chapters before direct reference is made to the death of Christ. Not so in the fourth Gospel. The very first chapter, which so definitely describes the glories of His Deity, His creative power, and the grace of His incarnation, foretells His death. This is given in the testimony of John the Baptist at the river Jordan. Here, where the Lord came to be baptized, and so, in obedience to the last command to Israel under the law, to identify Himself with the nation in this respect, His herald gave the first public announcement of His death, pointing Him out to the people as

"The Lamb of God"

This first mention is figurative. The phraseology would be familiar to the people, but how startling the personal application! Still more so the declaration that He was the One "who taketh away the sin of the world."

We cannot but be struck with the contrast in the titles ascribed to the Lord in this chapter. He who is declared to be the Word of God is also the Lamb of God. He is at once the Father's eternal Coequal and the voluntary Victim for the sin of the world.

The similar announcement made next day, "Behold the Lamb of God," had the effect of causing two of John's disciples to follow Jesus. They at least grasped something of the significance of the message. To point to Christ as the Lamb of God is the way to win men to be His followers.

"Destroy This Temple"

The next reference to His death is in connection with the cleansing of the Temple, recorded in the second chapter. Having drastically put a stop to the traffic of those who were defiling the house of God with their merchandise, He was asked by the Jews for a sign of the authority for His action. His reply contained a purposely veiled reference to His death. "Destroy this Temple," He said, "and in three days I will raise it up." They naturally took Him to mean the building in which His power had just been displayed. In reality His utterance was prophetic of the blind selfwill which would yet lead them to desecrate the still more sacred Temple of His Body.

"As Moses Lifted Up the Serpent"

In John's Gospel, then, the first mention of Christ's death is in the language of the Passover, the second is on the first occasion of the Passover feast itself after the inception of His public testimony. In each of the first two cases the language is symbolical. The third is a direct statement, associated with the Lord's conversation with Nicodemus. There was something in the well-known narrative of the brazen serpent which lay beyond the ken even of the ruler of the synagogue, at least if we take the paragraphing of the Revised Version, according to which the statement, "As Moses lifted up the serpent in the wilderness, even so must the Son of Man be lifted up," is part of what the Lord said to Nicodemus. Here the manner of His death is foretold, and though the actual mode is not named, yet probably Nicodemus would connect it with the Roman method of execution.*

"The Bread Which I Will Give"

The next reference to His death occurs in the Lord's second discussion with the Jews,

---

*Quite possibly the record of the Lord's conversation with Nicodemus ends at verse 12. We need not discuss the point here.

which resulted from the feeding of the five thousand. The conversation turns upon His statement that He is the Living Bread which came down from Heaven. The Jews had already begun to reject His testimony concerning His relationship with the Father (5:18), and the continuation of His witness met with still more determined opposition. The first part of this Gospel is largely a history of this controversy. One of its great lessons is that willful rejection of the truth leads to the impossibility of receiving it. The hardening of the heart is God's retributive answer to refusal to listen to His Word. This lies behind the increasing difficulty of the Lord's utterances to the Jews. Having declared that He is the Bread of Life which came down from Heaven (6:33; 35:41), He goes on to say that the bread which He will give is "His flesh for the life of the world" (v. 51). This is the first mention of His death in His conversations with them. The idea of His giving His flesh to eat was utterly impossible to them and created strife among them. "How," they said, "can this Man give us His flesh to eat"; "My flesh is meat indeed."

And now a still more difficult statement: "Verily, verily, I say unto you, Except ye eat the flesh of the Son of Man, and drink His blood, ye have not life in yourselves. He that eaten My flesh, and drinketh My blood, hath eternal life; and I will raise him up at the last day. For My flesh is meat indeed, and My blood is drink indeed. He that eateth My flesh, and drinketh My blood, abideth in Me, and I in him" (6:53-56). The Jews were expecting that their Messiah would simply liberate the nation from bondage to the Gentile yoke and establish the Kingdom of God in their midst. But Christ had come to tell them that salvation could be theirs only through His death, that the blessings which God had to give could be enjoyed only through spiritual life. Salvation for the Jews, and for all men, must be by regeneration, and this must be by means of His atoning death. They must eat the flesh and drink the blood of the Son of Man or they could have no life. His words, so difficult for their hardened hearts to grasp, meant that He Himself must die if they were to live. What could be more opposed to their religious scruples than to drink blood? Had not God's own Law strictly prohibited it? Yet "His flesh is meat indeed, and His blood is drink indeed."

Life Through His Death

His words, so difficult to His enemies, are clear in the light of the completed Scriptures. The words "flesh" and "blood" point to the fact of His death. Life is given by God to the sinner by means of it. To receive Christ as Savior is to acknowledge that the death sentence, due on account of one's sins, was carried out in the Person of Christ on the Cross. In this acknowledgment by faith we eat the flesh and drink the blood of Christ, and live unto God in Christ. Eating His flesh, coming to Him, believing on Him, all issue in eternal life. Not only is that life imparted by His death (v. 53), it is also sustained through it (v. 56). True it is that the constant nourishment we receive, and the spiritual life we live, are derived from the living Christ by the power of the Holy Spirit, but the maintenance of the spiritual life is nevertheless the result of constant feeding on the flesh and drinking of the blood of Christ. Spiritual life is maintained in communion with God by faith, and Christ is Himself our life, but this is because He died for us, and we must own His death as our death before we can enjoy His life as our life. "He that eateth My flesh, and drinketh My blood," He says, "abideth in Me, and I in him." The one who believes on Him is brought into permanent union with Him, and it is as we constantly realize the value and efficacy of His death that we really experience what abiding in Him is and He in us.

The tenses in verse 53 for "eat" and "drink" are different from those in the following verses. In verse 53 the words "eat" and "drink" are in the aorist or momentary tense, indicating the necessity of obtaining life once and for all on the ground of the death of Christ. In the following verses the tenses are continuous, showing that the one who has passed from death to life appropriates by constant experience as a believer the effects of His death, effects which are ministered by the Spirit of God. There is also a change in the verb. The word for "eat" in verse 53 is *phagein*, the ordinary word with that meaning; in the verses which follow it is *trōgein*, which denotes "to chew." The change of word suggests that in Aramaic the Lord expressed with similar emphasis to His opponents the necessity of their obtaining life through His death.

"The Blood Is the Life"

Our Lord's word as to "eating" His flesh and drinking His blood no doubt had direct reference to the Passover; the blood of the Lamb being the divinely appointed means of the deliverance of the nation from the doom of Egypt. The shedding of the blood involved the taking of the life of the animal, and, the blood having been sprinkled in the manner ordained of God, the Israelites fed on the flesh of the lamb roasted in the fire. So again, in subsequent sacrifices, they were to offer the flesh and blood of their burnt offerings upon the altar. The blood was to be poured out thereon, and they were to eat the flesh (Deut 12:27). They were not allowed to eat the blood, "for the blood is the life," and they were not to eat "the life with the flesh" (v. 23). How difficult, then, and purposely so, for the hardened Jews to receive the Lord's teaching! How blessed for us to enjoy the fullness of the reality which the Mosaic injunctions but dimly foreshadowed!

Christ's words to the Jews are to be distinguished from the teaching of the Lord's Supper. Both converge to the same point; both direct our hearts to the Cross; but we may not say when we are partaking of the bread and of the cup at the Lord's Table that we are thereby eating the flesh and drinking the blood of Christ. For by means of eating His flesh and drinking blood we have life, but we do not obtain life by partaking of the Lord's Supper. We proclaim His death, we declare that He died for us, we partake of that which is communion of His body and His blood; but that is not the same thing as what the Lord taught the Jews.

"His Hour Had Not Yet Come"

The next reference in the Gospel occurs in the fourth discussion with the Jews (chap. 8). The Lord's renewed testimony—now given in the Temple—to His unity with the Father, again aroused their animosity, and would have led to His immediate arrest, but no man took Him, because "His hour had not yet come"; that is to say, the appointed hour in which He would offer Himself in sacrifice. There may be a similar reference in the preceding chapter, where He says, "My time is not yet come"

(7:6, 8). But probably all that He meant there was that, while in the case of His brethren their arrangements were carried out according to their own inclinations, His were under the direction of His Father. Here again, in this fourth stage of the controversy, He intimates the mode of His death. "When ye have lifted up the Son of Man," He says, "then shall ye know that I am He, and that I do nothing of Myself but as the Father taught Me, I speak these things" (8:28). That Messiah should die was not in all their thoughts. Yet now He declared that His identity will be disclosed to them after they have put Him to death.

"The Good Shepherd"

In the fifth and last discussion with the Jews, resulting from the healing of the blind man, the Lord takes occasion to tell them of the parable of the Good Shepherd, basing His teaching on the fact that the man He had healed had become one of His own sheep. This is how He now speaks of His death: "I am the Good Shepherd: the Good Shepherd layeth down His life for the sheep." Again, He tells His critics, but now in a different way, that life must come by His death. Here His thoughts are occupied with His followers. He had come that they might have life, and might have it abundantly. But more, the laying down of His life for this purpose was to be the outcome of the most intimate communion with the Father. So when He says again, "I lay down My life for the sheep" (10:15), it is not a mere repetition of His word in verse 11. There He simply said that He had come to give them life through His death. Now He bases His statement on the fact that He knows His own and His own know Him, even as the Father knows Him and He knows the Father. And further, the Father's love is combined with the Father's omniscience, and He loves the Son because His death is a means to an end. "Therefore doth the Father love Me, because I lay down My life, that I may take it again. No one taketh it away from Me, but I lay it down of Myself. I have power to lay it down, and I have power to take it again. This commandment received I from My Father" (vv. 17, 18). He had given the Jews to understand that they would accomplish His death.

It was they who would lift up the Son of Man (8:28); but now He shows that they had no power to do this at all except by His permission. He gave them signal proof of their inability at the close of this discussion, in that though they sought again to take Him "He went forth out of their hand" (v. 39).

The Counsel of Caiaphas

Now comes the climax of the controversy. The raising of Lazarus was His last public testimony to His divine claims, His last offer to His critics to acknowledge Him. Instead the chief priests gather a council to decide what was to be done with Him, and this provides the occasion of the next statement concerning His death. It is the prophecy uttered by Caiaphas. His advice to the council, "It is expedient for you that one man should die for the people, and that the whole nation perish not," was, from his own point of view, simply an argument for getting rid of Christ. National ruin could be averted by His death. Political expediency was a pretext serving the purposes of the high priest's personal animosity against Him. Yet here was a higher Power controlling his utterance. "This he said not of himself." His personal motives were subservient to the counsels of God, who makes the wrath of man to praise Him. Upon occasion God compelled His foes to prophesy. The position of Caiaphas lent itself to this. He was in line of succession of the priests who had communicated divine messages from God by the Urim and Thummim. "Being high priest that year he prophesied that Jesus should die for the nation, and not for the nation only, but that He might also gather together into one the children of God that are scattered abroad." Probably, too, the fact that He was the high priest, the religious leader of the people, accounted to some extent for the divine influence over his utterances. Mark the immediate effects: "From that day forth they took counsel that they might put Him to death." No effort on their part could attain to success until His hour had come; but that hour was drawing near.

"The Day of My Burying"

The Gospel now gives us several intimations by the Lord that His death was at hand.

The first of these is at the supper at Bethany, where Mary anointed the feet of Jesus. The remonstrances of Judas at the waste of the ointment called forth the Lord's answer, "Suffer her to keep it against the day of My burying." The disciples knew well by this time that death was to be His lot. When He had decided to go to Jerusalem owing to the death of Lazarus, Thomas had said: "Let us also go that we may die with Him." The indications were becoming more numerous that the end was near.

"It Beareth Much Fruit"

His second utterance recorded in this chapter regarding His death is contained in His reply to those who told Him of the desire of the Greeks to see Him. Apparently their wish was not granted. The Lord was not there to gratify curiosity. The incident, however, drew forth some remarks which showed that He was thinking of that vast multitude of Gentiles which would be drawn to Him through His death. "The hour is come," He says, "that the Son of man should be glorified. Verily, verily, I say unto you, Except a grain of wheat fall into the earth and die, it abideth by itself alone; but if it die, it beareth much fruit" (12:24). The seed must die to produce the harvest. This is the law in both the physical and spiritual realms. In the latter it is a law of self-renunciation. Its fulfillment in the case of the Lord Jesus Christ stands alone, yet He lays it down as a law of life for His followers. "He that loveth his life loseth it; and he that hateth his life in this world shall keep it unto life eternal" (v. 25). The thought of "the hour," and all that it meant for Him was burdening His soul. Yet His "now is My soul troubled" was not a mere outburst of sorrow. His utterance had in view a testimony to His devotion to the Father. The burden was real and heavy, and He did not conceal it, but His one engrossing desire was the Father's glory. Hence His prayer, "Father, save Me from this hour," is followed by the confession, so full of redemptive truth, "but for this cause came I unto this hour," and by the prayer, so indicative of absolute submission to the Father's will, "Father, glorify Thy Name."

The Father's voice out of Heaven, the immediate answer to the prayer, was a witness to the people of His infinite approval of His Son, and of the unbroken union between them.

The Lord now shows to the people standing by that His death is to be the great crisis of the world's history.

The twelfth chapter of this Gospel gives us a series of momentous utterances by the Lord concerning His death. Firstly, there is the prediction of His burial (v. 7); secondly, the comparison of His death to the falling of a grain of corn into the earth to die, that it may bring forth fruit (v. 24); thirdly, the announcement that the hour was at hand for which He had come to glorify the Father (vv. 27, 28); fourthly, His declaration that His death would involve the world's judgment, that it would effect the casting out of Satan, and be the means of bringing all men within the scope of His own attractive power (vv. 31–33). The first three of these we considered in our last paper. Now as to the fourth, and with that we come to a parting of the ways as to the Lord's testimony.

"I, If I Be Lifted Up"

The Father's response from Heaven to the prayer of Christ, "Father, glorify Thy Name," came, He said, for the sake of the multitude that stood by. As the actual response was not revealed to them, the Lord explains the occurrence by saying, "Now is the judgment of this world; now shall the prince of this world be cast out. And I, if I be lifted up from the earth, will draw all men unto Myself." The word rendered "judgment" is *krisis*, which gives us our word "crisis." That may possibly be its meaning here, but only so because the death of Christ would, on the one hand, involve the condemnation of the world for its rejection of the Son of God, while on the other hand it would provide a means of deliverance from condemnation on the fulfillment of God's conditions. This would also involve deliverance from the world's spiritual tyrant: "Now shall the prince of this world be cast out." The death of Christ would judicially and potentially be the destruction of "him that had the power of death," and the annihilation of all his claims to authority over the world. Satan's claims were the outcome of man's rejection of the claims of God upon him. The death of Christ has abrogated the claims of Satan and opened the way for men to be drawn to the Savior: "I, if I be lifted up from the earth," He says, "will draw all men unto Myself." What a note of triumph sounds in the Redeemer's "I!" He sets Himself antithetically, and with strong emphasis, as the Conqueror of Satan and the Deliverer of men, and this by His own death.

Three times, as recorded in this Gospel, the Lord uses the term "lifted up," first at the beginning of His public career, when speaking to Nicodemus (3:14); then about halfway through it, when addressing the Jews who opposed Him (8:28); and now just as the end was drawing near, when addressing the multitude for the last time (12:32). Does not this itself reveal how continually the Cross occupied His mind?

The Lord points, then, to His death as the ground upon which He will exercise His attractive power. The multitude understood what was meant by His being "lifted up," but found it impossible to harmonize His Messianic claims with the fact that their Messiah would abide forever. How could the Son of man be lifted up? and who was this Son of man? Christ does not satisfy their inquiries. He simply warns them to make use of the light while it is with them.

The Upper Room

The crises had come. His public testimony must now cease. He will confine His attention from henceforth to His disciples.

John's preface to the discourse in the upper room views the Lord's approaching death and departure to the Father in the light of His infinite love: "Jesus, knowing that His hour was come that He should depart out of this world having loved His own which were in the world He loved them unto the end." These are the thoughts which pervade the discourse in what has been called "The Holy of holies" of the New Testament. Our consideration will here be limited to the references to His death.

Again and again in the course of His remarks He reminds them that He is about to leave them and go to the Father. True, He does not say in so many words that this is to be by way of the Cross, yet that is implied His journey to the Cross was His pathway back to the Father. This we may see more forcibl by putting together some of His utterances to His disciples at this time. He says, "Yet a little while I am with you" (13:33); "Wither I go thou canst not follow Me now; but thou shalt follow afterwards"—plainly a direct reference to his death (v. 36); "I go to prepare a place for you" (14:2)—we can scarcely take this as referring merely to a preparation in Heaven itself after He had ascended there. The great preparation for our reception into the Father's house hereafter lay in the work of the Cross. This is confirmed by the statement of the writer to the Hebrews when he says that it was necessary that the heavenly things should be cleansed with better sacrifices than those of the earthly tabernacle, the plural standing for the one Sacrifice in its various aspects. Our entrance there, now by faith, and eventually at the Lord's Coming, depends on the atoning work of the Cross. Moreover, the Lord reminded the disciples that they knew the way He was going, for He told them clearly about His death (v. 4). Again, He says, "Now I go unto him that sent Me" (16:5); "a little while, and ye behold Me no more . . . because I go to the Father" (vv. 16:17); "I leave the world and go unto the Father" (v. 28). Similarly in His prayer that follows He says, "I am no more in the world . . . I go to the Father" (17:11–13).

These utterances constitute most of His references in the upper room to His death. The four other utterances present

A Striking Contrast

when put together. After Judas had gone out, Jesus said, "Now is the Son of man glorified, and God is glorified in Him." What calm and majestic dignity there is in this remark concerning the deed which the traitor was just about to perpetrate, and its effect! The Lord was viewing His death in the light of its issues. His obedience to the Father and His redemption of sinners thereby would bring undying glory to His own Name, and thus also His Father would be glorified. With the same thoughts in His mind He says, at the beginning of His prayer, "Father, the hour is come; glorify Thy Son, that the Son may glorify Thee" (17:1); and, anticipating the accomplishment of what He was about to do, "I glorified Thee on the earth, having accomplished the work which Thou hast given Me to do" (v. 4).

Now contrast this with His remarks about His great spiritual foe. Still looking on the Cross, He says, "The prince of this world cometh: and He hath nothing in Me." There was nothing in Christ that responded to the Devil's temptations or claims. Never could the evil one achieve success by His efforts against the Lord. On the other hand, there was everything in Him that responded to the Father. His very meat, the sustenance of His life, was to do the will of the Father, and so His death would yield nothing to Satan. Nay, rather, by it the world would know that He loved the Father. It is particularly His death He has in view when He says, "And as the Father gave Me commandments, even so I do." That was His heart's desire, and the thought of its accomplishment leads Him to say, "Arise, let us go hence." His heart was fixed, His step was steadfast. It was as if He was ready to go immediately through the dread sufferings that were awaiting Him. How great is the contrast between those two utterances, "Now is the Son of man glorified, and God is glorified in Him," and, "The prince of the world hath nothing in Me!" The world, which was lying under his tyrannical sway, would learn to know that, by very reason of the Devil's effort against Him, He would deliver it from his grasp, and so display His love to the Father.

"Greater Love"

There is one more reference to His death in this upper room conversation, and this bears specially upon His followers, and their attitude one toward another. "This is My commandment," He says, "that ye love one another, even as I have loved you. Greater love hath no man than this, that a man lay down His life for His friends." His was the "greater love," and, in laying down His life for us as the great expression of His love, He puts before us His standard of our love one toward another. How far short have we come!

John's Narrative of the Death

Two things stand out prominently in regard to John's narrative of the death of Christ.

Firstly, he writes as one who was an eyewitness of all that happened. This, indeed, he himself states (19:35). There is more detail given by John than in any other Gospel. Secondly, those facts which John gives, and which are not supplied by the three Synoptists, contribute very largely to that testimony which is a characteristic feature of this Gospel, namely, that Jesus is the Son of God. For instance, it is John who mentions the reply of the Jews to Pilate, that death was the rightful penalty for Jesus, according to their law, because He made Himself the Son of God (19:4–7). In the details throughout the narrative there is a tone of dignity and exaltation consistent with His relationship to God as His Son. We notice this in His witness before Pontius Pilate, and again in such incidents of His actual crucifixion as His commendation of His mother to John (vv. 25–27); the statement that "knowing that all things were now finished, that the Scripture might be accomplished, He saith, I thirst"; His closing utterance, "It is finished"; the fact that He bowed (or reclined) His head before giving up His spirit—self-determined acts expressive of His submission to the Father's will; the fact that His legs were not broken; the flowing forth of the blood and water after the piercing of His side by the soldier, a further testimony to the supernatural character of His death, and significant of the fact that Christ by His death has become the Source not only of cleansing, but also of the impartation of life.

We may mention here, for reference, other details which are also supplied by John alone in connection with the death of Christ, namely, Pilate's "Behold the Man" (19:5); his "Behold your King" (19:14); Christ's bearing His own Cross (19:17); the part of the superscription "Jesus of Nazareth," and the fact that Pilate wrote it (19:19); the vessel of vinegar and hyssop (19:29); the quotation, "A bone of Him shall not be broken" and "They shall look on Him whom they have pierced" (19:37); the presence of Nicodemus at the burial and the part he took in it (19:39).

"The Water and the Blood"

The closing testimony regarding the death of Christ, *i.e,* as to the flowing of blood and water from His pierced side, is explained in the writer's first Epistle. "There are three who bear witness, the Spirit, and the water, and the blood: and the three agree in one . . . and the witness is this, that God gave unto us eternal life, and this life is in His Son" (1 John 5:8, 11, R.V.).

Putting now together the first and the last references in God's Gospel to the death of Christ, we see that each bears testimony to the means of eternal life. The first was the Lord's statement to Nicodemus that "the Son of man must be lifted up that whosoever believeth may in Him have eternal life." The last is the record by John that blood and water flowed from the Savior's side, symbolic of the cleansing and life provided for us through His death. John immediately says that the testimony of what he saw is given that we might believe (19:35). Life comes with faith, and comes by reason of His death. This is the sublime message of this great theme that runs through the fourth Gospel.

CHAPTER TEN

The Holy Spirit

A comparison of the Gospel of John with those of the Synoptists shows that the subject of the Holy Spirit forms a distinctive feature of this fourth Gospel. In the first three Gospels the statements concerning the Spirit are chiefly incidental to the Incarnation, Baptism, and Temptation of Christ. There is comparatively little teaching about the work of the Spirit and the character of His Person. The Gospels of Matthew, Mark, and Luke give the Lord's teaching concerning blasphemy against the Holy Ghost. All three record the promise to the disciples, that when they were brought before governors and kings the Spirit of the Father would speak in them. Matthew and Mark give the statement of Christ that David spoke by the Holy Spirit in the Psalms. Luke records Christ's declaration that the Spirit of the Lord was upon Him (4:18), and His promise that the Father would give the Holy Spirit to them that ask Him (11:13).

In John's Gospel the subject receives special treatment, in a way which indicates a development of doctrine.

The First Mention

The first mention brings us into touch with the records of the Synoptists in relation to the Baptism of Christ. That is the only incident mentioned in this Gospel of the actings of the Spirit in connection with the Personal circumstances of the Lord Jesus in the days of His flesh. The apostle does not state the details of Christ's baptism, but he adds the Baptist's testimony to the fact that he beheld the Spirit descending as a dove out of Heaven, that it abode upon Him, that he had received a message from God as to the means by which he would be able to identify the Lord as the One who "baptizeth with the Holy Spirit," and that "he saw and bare witness that He is the Son of God" (1:32, 34). It would seem that John the Baptist, even if he had seen and known the Lord in younger days, had no natural means of recognizing Him on this occasion, for he says "I knew Him not." But the visible descent of the Spirit upon Christ was not merely to enable John to recognize Him, it was in order that he might testify that Christ was He who would baptize with the Holy Spirit. Such a One could be none other than the Son of God. This prediction referred, no doubt, to the then future work of the Holy Spirit in the experience of those who, being born of God, are thereby identified with Christ, and become members of the Church (see 1 Cor. 12:13). This was potentially made good for the whole Church on the day of Pentecost.

The Two Parts of the Subject

Turning to the next passages relating to the subject, the Gospel sets forth the work of the Spirit of God in the hearts of men. Most of the teaching is contained in the ministry of Christ Himself. This we may divide into two parts in the same way as in other subjects. The first part consists of the Lord's instruction either to individuals or in public, and this is found in the third to the seventh chapters. The second part is contained in His discourse to the disciples in the upper room, from the fourteenth to the sixteenth chapters. In the earlier part we learn of the work of the Spirit in connection with the new birth. Then comes, in the seventh chapter, a statement anticipative of the upper room teaching. In the latter part the Lord speaks of the Spirit's operations first in the hearts and experiences of believers, and then in regard to the world. There is a distinct advance in the subject as communicated by the Lord privately to the disciples, in contrast to what has been given in the earlier part of the Gospel. This will be considered in its own place.

The New Birth

In the earlier part of the Gospel the first mention, subsequent to the first chapter, is in the Lord's interview with Nicodemus. He here speaks of the Spirit's work in connection with the new birth, an appropriate aspect of the subject at the outset of the Lord's testimony, as having to do with the initial work of the Spirit in a believer's experiences. The Lord is alone with a ruler of the Jews. The inquirer has come to learn more of this wonderful Teacher so recently arisen among the people. Christ's reply to his opening remark comes straight to the point of his spiritual need. Neither time nor word is wasted. "Except a man be born anew, he cannot see the Kingdom of God." To Nicodemus's surprised interrogation as to the possibility of such a thing the Lord replies, "Verily, verily, I say unto thee, Except a man be born of water and of the Spirit, he cannot enter into the Kingdom of God."

It may be that this statement was connected in the Lord's mind with Ezekiel 36, a passage which must have been well-known to Nicodemus, where, referring to the spiritual restoration of Israel, God promises that He will by means of water cleanse the nation from all its defilements and will put His Spirit within them, giving them a new heart and a new spirit. What there is applied to the nation is here applied to the individual. The water is symbolic of cleansing, and the Spirit is the means of impartation of life. These form the constituent elements in the new birth. There must be a removal of sin and the gift of life. John's baptism, too, was "a baptism of repentance unto the remission of sins," and this the Pharisees had rejected. Nicodemus must therefore dissociate himself from them and fulfill the command of God given to the nation through the Baptist.

The Lord goes on to describe the dignity of this new birth: "That which is born of the Spirit is spirit," a product entirely different from that which is dominated by the flesh. And the operation lies outside the range of human perception: "The wind bloweth where it listeth [this may also be rendered "the Spirit breatheth where He listeth," but the next words seem to show that Christ is referring to the wind by way of illustration], and thou hearest the sound thereof, but cannot tell whence it cometh, and whither it goeth: so is every one that is born of the Spirit" (3:8).

The Baptist's Second Testimony

The Lord says nothing in this discourse about the gift of the Spirit to the believer, He is occupied with the necessity of the new birth and the means whereby it is effected. The subject of the gift of the Spirit receives an incidental mention at the close of the chapter, in the testimony of John the Baptist to the Person and mission of the Lord Jesus. Stating a general principle he says, "He whom God hath sent speaketh the words of God, for God giveth not the Spirit by measure" (3:34). The words "unto Him" in the Authorized Version are not in the Original. It is true that primarily John the Baptist was speaking of Christ, to Whom the Holy Spirit had been given by the Father for His ministry on earth, in fulfillment of Isaiah 11:2 and 61:1, but the statement is of general application. The Spirit of God is not an influence pervading believers and ministered partly to one and partly to another. He is imparted Personally and entirely to everyone who believes, though it is sadly possible not to realize the fullness of His power, through failure to fulfill the exhortation "be filled with the Spirit" (Eph. 5:18). So far as the Gospel record is concerned, then, the order of the teaching regarding the Holy Spirit's work in the heart is significant. Firstly, His work in the new birth, and then the impartation of the Spirit Himself as a gift to the believer.

The Well of Living Water

This truth is now developed, first, by implication, in the Lord's discourse to the woman by the well (chap. 4), and then by specific mention in His public testimony at the feast in Jerusalem (chap. 7), two passages which are to be connected. In the former the Spirit is not actually mentioned, but when the Lord says that the water which He will give shall become in him who drinks "a well of water springing up into eternal life" (4:14), He is undoubtedly speaking of the Spirit. The water is more than the water of life. Life does come with the Holy Spirit, as the Lord states in the next mention in this Gospel, "It is the Spirit that quickeneth," i.e., "that maketh alive" (6:53). But there is more than this in His words to the Samaritan woman. The meaning of the springing well within is interpreted in the seventh chapter. The order there is the same as in His remarks to the woman; first there is the invitation to the thirsty to come and drink, just as He has intimated to her that, had she asked Him, He would have given her living water. Then comes the statement as to the inward spiritual activity, just as He had remarked to her about the springing well within, "He that believeth on Me, as the Scripture hath said, out of his belly shall flow rivers of living water. But this spake He of the Spirit, which they that believed on Him were to receive; for the Holy Spirit was not yet given; because Jesus was not yet glorified" (7:33, 39).

The Upper Room Discourse

This great pronouncement, and the interpretation given by the Evangelist, are expanded in the Lord's private discourse to His disciples in the upper room. That discourse contains four distinct passages relating to the Holy Spirit, and the Lord's instruction gradually broadens out as He proceeds.

The Promise of the Comforter

Firstly, after His initial promise that He would pray the Father and He would give them another Comforter, that He might be with them forever, "even the Spirit of truth," He tells them that, in contrast to the world which could not receive Him, they themselves knew Him, and He would abide with them and be in them (14:16, 17). Two things stand out here: (1) The Lord had been their Guide, Teacher, and Friend, but He had not been with them the whole time. What a relief to them to know that the other Comforter (One of the same character as the Lord) would be permanently with them, now that He Himself was about to leave them in a hostile world! (2) The Holy Spirit could be received only by those who were Divinely prepared to receive Him. The world could not do so. Being antagonistic to Him in its nature it was lacking in that which was requisite to the reception of the Spirit. Those who had responded to the Lord's claims

and to His work in their hearts were thereby ready to receive the priceless gift.

The Teacher Sent in the Lord's Name

Secondly, "The Comforter," He says, "even the Holy Spirit, whom the Father will send in My Name, He shall teach you all things, and bring to your remembrance all that I said unto you" (14:26). This is an advance on the preceding statement. The Spirit will not only be given to them, the Father will send Him in the Name of Jesus. This conveys a fundamental principle of the relation of the Holy Spirit to Christ. As Christ came in the Father's Name, so the Spirit has been sent in Christ's Name. Christ has revealed the Father; the Spirit reveals Christ. The Divine Name suggests both the Divine character and authority. Again, not only would the Spirit indwell them, He would teach them all things. He would unfold to them the meaning of the things which the Lord has spoken to them.

The Spirit of Truth

Thirdly, He Himself would send the Comforter from the Father, "even the Spirit of truth, which proceedeth from the Father," and the Spirit would bear witness of Jesus: they also would bear witness since they had been with Him from the beginning (15:26). Here again there is progress of teaching, both as to the nature of the Spirit and as to His work. Why does the Lord restate that He is the Spirit of truth? He has just spoken of the hatred of the world toward Himself and toward the Father, and of its persecution. The world would hate His followers also and persecute them. This would be the outcome of witness given by them, as it had been in His case. Yet their witness would be irresistible. For the Comforter, as the Spirit of truth, would be both their infallible Guide and the power by which their testimony would be effective. The truth would prevail. He would give them "a mouth and a witness their adversaries would be able neither to gainsay nor resist." He adds this point of comfort here, too, in view of the hostility with which they would meet that, He will Himself send the Holy Spirit from the Father. He Who had Himself suffered from the witness he gave, and had endured to the end, would send them the Spirit, by Whose aid they would be enabled to do likewise.

The "Procession from the Father"

Furthermore, He "proceedeth from the Father." This sacred mystery which has been termed the "Procession of the Holy Spirit," and which has been the subject of much controversy, cannot be explained by finite intelligences. We tread on holy ground. To quote the words of Bishop Moule, "It has to do with revelations of the mysterious inner blessedness of the 'Blissful God' (1 Tim. 1:11) . . . It has been adopted to denote the eternal origination of the Spirit from the fount of Godhead, the Father. That origination must be eternal, supernatural, necessary, or there would have been at some time a great change developed within God. It must on the other hand be origination; the Spirit, as a Person, is not His own cause, or He would be an independent God. As regards mode, the procession is wholly inscrutable. Only, it is not filiation. But every word touched in such an inquiry is a Divine secret. The procession is from the Father and the Son. What this says is, in effect, that while the Father is the eternal origin of the Spirit, the Son is concurrently His eternal origin; Deity is in the Spirit, eternally, because of the Son as well as because of the Father. The Scripture evidence for this is briefly as follows: The Spirit is repeatedly called "the Spirit of Christ," "the Spirit of the Son," just as He is called "the Spirit of God," "the Spirit of the Father." . . . And does not the work of the Spirit for us, in connection with the work of Christ, gain indefinitely in our view as we contemplate the dual procession? He who testifies of Christ, and glorifies Him, and imparts Him, does this, not only as His holy messenger and cooperator, but as the stream of love and life from Him the Fountain. Strong is the concord of such cooperation."

The Last Passage

Fourthly, in the last passage the Lord speaks on the subject at greater length. It consists of three parts: (a) in the first He shows what was necessary in order that the Spirit might be sent (16:7); (b) in the second He predicts the character of His work in the world (vv. 8-11); (c) in the third He shows how the

Spirit will glorify Him in ministering to His followers (vv. 12-15). These three we will now briefly consider.

The necessity for Christ's departure. (a) A terrible gloom had come over the hearts of the disciples at the prospect of their Master's departure and the subsequent events predicted by Him. True, He had promised that the Comforter would come, but why could not Christ stay with them and the Comforter come too? The Lord now points out that His departure and the sending of the Spirit were matters of cause and effect, He says, "Nevertheless I tell you the truth; it is expedient for you that I go away: for if I go not away, the Comforter will not come unto you; but if I go, I will send Him unto you" (16:7, R.V.). As Westcott says, "The departure was in itself a necessary condition for the coming of the Spirit. . . . The withdrawal of His limited bodily presence necessarily prepared the way for the recognition of a universal presence (*i.e.,* in the hearts of believers). It was necessary that the Son should disappear as an outward authority in order that He might appear as an inward principle of life."

Sin, righteousness, and judgment. (b) Secondly, as to the world, He would "convict the world in respect of sin, and of righteousness, and of judgment" (v. 8). Here the world stands for the whole system of humanity in relation to its responsibility to God. The judgment under which it lies is its rejection of the Son of God. The refusal to accept Him is the great sin of the world. The Holy Spirit would convict the world in respect of sin, "because," says the Lord, "they believe not on Me." The sending of the Spirit and His presence here are proof that the world stands convicted in the court of Heaven of the sin of refusing Christ. That is the world's position.

Next in respect of righteousness. That is God's side of the matter. His righteousness stands in contrast to the world's sin. "Of righteousness," the Lord says, "because I go to the Father, and ye behold Me no more." The exaltation of Christ to the right hand of the Father was the Father's vindication both of the righteous character of His Son as manifested here in the days of His flesh, and of the righteousness of God's judgment of sin at the

Cross in the Person of Christ. The sinless One, by His sacrifice for sin, there completed the work of atonement. On this account the Father raised Him from the dead and gave Him glory. The presence of the Holy Spirit here from Pentecost onward, therefore, shows that all this has been accomplished, and that while the world stands condemned for its rejection of Christ, God's righteousness is confirmed in His removal of His Son, in resurrection power, from the world which condemned and killed Him.

The third point of conviction is in respect of judgment, "because the Prince of this world has been judged." On the part of the world, sin; on the part of God, righteousness; but what of the sinister being which led the world to reject the Son of God? In his act of death Christ potentially destroyed "him who had the power of death," The utter defeat which Satan then sustained in His effort to thwart God's purposes of grace on the Cross was a ratification of the Divine sentence that had been passed upon Him. The proof of this is the presence of the Holy Spirit in this dark scene over which the evil one still has temporary control.

All this shows, then, how the departure of Christ to the Father's right hand was a necessary preliminary to the sending of the Holy Spirit, and how the Spirit's presence is a confirmation of the work of Calvary and of the exaltation of Christ in His resurrection and ascension.

The guide into all the truth. (c) Thirdly, "When He, the Spirit of Truth, is come, He shall guide you into all the truth" (v. 13). While His presence here in the Church is proof of the guilt of the world in rejecting Christ, and of the righteousness of God and of the judgment of Satan, on the other hand the Spirit is here to guide into all the truth those who have been delivered from the Devil's power and the world's darkness. "For He shall not speak from Himself," says the Lord. We should note the Revised Version here, in order that we may be clear that the rendering in the Authorized Version "of Himself" does not mean "about Himself." The Holy Spirit constantly speaks about Himself. The meaning is that He would not be Himself the source of His own teaching. "What things soever He shall hear this shall He speak: and He shall declare unto you the things that are to come." As Christ received His messages from the Father, so the Spirit would receive His from Christ. "He shall glorify Me," He says, "for He shall take of Mine, and shall declare it unto you." All the revelations that were to be given both prior to the completion of the Scriptures, and in order for their completion, would be given by the Spirit for the glorification of Christ, and so with all the subsequent unfoldings of the contents of the finished Book to the hearts of believers throughout the present era.

He finishes His subject with the confirmatory statement, "All things whatsoever the Father hath are Mine; therefore, said I, that He taketh of Mine and shall declare it unto you." In unfolding the glory of Christ the Holy Spirit would communicate that which belonged to Him as glorified with the Father. Practically everything Christ mentions about the Spirit in this discourse He states in connection with Himself. The Spirit would come in answer to His request (14:15); He would be sent in His Name (14:26); He would Himself send Him (15:26); He (the Spirit) would bear witness of Him (15:26); He would be sent only after Christ had ascended (16:7); His presence in the world would be testimony as to the meaning and power of His death, resurrection, and exaltation (16:8–11). He would be here to glorify Christ in receiving from Him and communicating to His followers (16:14, 15). How fully now the disciples could see that the Holy Spirit would take the place of Christ, as the Comforter, and that the blank which they foresaw would thus be more than filled!

John: His Record of Christ

Among the four Gospel writers two, Luke and John, mention the purpose for which they wrote. The former mentions his in the opening paragraph (1:4); the latter mentions his as he draws to a close. He states as his object "that ye may believe that Jesus is the Christ, the Son of God; and that believing ye may have life in His Name" (20:31).

The place of this is uniquely significant. No preface to the Gospel is required to express its object and scope. The very nature of the transcendent subject precludes such an opening. Here at the end, where the details are retrospective, there are recalled to the reader's mind the preceding unfoldings of the glories of the Person who constitutes the great subject the apostle has had before Him: (1) His Deity, He is "the Son of God"; (2) His humanity, He is "Jesus"; (3) His Messiahship, He is "Christ." Here, too, the apostle recalls that which the Gospel has repeatedly recorded in respect of human responsibility toward the Person: "that ye may believe"; and the effect, "that believing ye may have life."

The Great Subject

Each of these particulars is readily traceable throughout the Gospel. The paramount subject is Christ's relationship with the Father as the Son of God. In this respect the main parts of the Gospel present Him as follows:

(I) Preexistent and manifested in the flesh (1:1 to 14);

(II) Manifested as the Son revealing the Father in word and deed in public testimony (1:15 to 12:50);

(III) Manifested as such privately to His disciples (13:1 to 17:26);

(IV) Manifested as such in His Betrayal, Trial and Death (18:1 to 19:42);

(V) Vindicated as the Son of God in His Resurrection, and the subsequent revelation of Himself to His disciples (20:1 to 21:25).

The words and deeds of the Lord cannot be rightly appreciated, nor can their significance be understood, apart from the disclosures in the prologue, of the facts relating to the person. It has been well said that "What Christ did and said becomes explicable only by knowing what Christ is." The unfolding of the facts of His deity and His incarnation in the prologue throw light upon His ways as recorded in the rest of the Gospel. What, from the point of view of His humanity, might appear, in some of the incidents in the Gospel narrative, to be contradictory to the fact of His deity, becomes an evidence of a perfect and indissociable combination of both. We may take, for example, the statement, "And the Word became flesh and dwelt (or tabernacled) among us." "Became," be it noted, not "was made," as the A.V. renders it. He took upon Him the real and complete nature of man. This union of Godhood with manhood remained indissoluble forever.

This should prevent the unscriptural ideas that Christ did such and such a thing as God, and such and such a thing as man. We do well to remember that where His human qualities, characteristics and acts are prominent, these never involved the abandonment of any of His attributes of deity.

The Revised Version has been used throughout, but is especially noted in certain places.

JOHN

CHAPTER ONE

Verses 1 to 18

The Prologue

The Gospel begins by speaking of Him as "the Word" *(Logos)*, and the apostle proceeds not only to declare facts of His Godhood in this respect, but to identify Him thus as "the only begotten Son of the Father" (v. 18). Doubtless this introductory presentation was designed to counteract the erroneous teachings which had sprung up even in the apostle's times.

"**In the beginning was the Word**," He was uncreated and eternal: this opposes the Gnostic teaching that the *Logos* was created and temporal; "**and the Word was with God, and the Word was God**." He was personal and divine: this opposes the conception of the Platonic philosophy that the *Logos* was ideal and abstract. Verse 2 repeats the first and last clauses of verse 6 for the sake of emphasis.

"**All things were made by Him**"; He was creator and cause: this opposes the Judaistic philosophy, of which Philo was the great exponent, that "the Word" was the type and idea of God in creation; "**and without Him was not anything made that hath been made**." He was unique and was universally creative: one sect of the Gnostics taught that the Word was dualistic and only partially instrumental in creative acts.

Life

"**In Him was life**" (v. 4). This statement, the truth concerning which is developed throughout the Gospel, predicates, not simply that life existed in Him who is the Word, the Son of God, but that it was unoriginated and eternal in respect of, and by reason of, His self-existence as One in the Godhead. In this sense life is the very essence of Godhood. The implication of this is that He is the author, source and cause of life. The statement is retrospective, looking back to the fact of creation (v. 3), and prospective, in that "**the life was the light of men**." Physically life and light are distinct; light ministers to life. Spiritually the principle of life and the principle of light are indissociable. Life and Light, essential in the Son of God, are together communicated to those who believe upon Him.

The communication of life, spiritual and eternal, comes with the new birth, and that by faith, so that those who believe on His Name become there and then "children of God" (v. 12, R.V.). As the light He reveals to us the nature and the will of God. He discloses to us ourselves, our sins and errors; He reveals the remedy for our fallen condition and the salvation provided for us in Himself. He makes us glad with His countenance. Through what He has undertaken for us as the Son we are brought into relationship and union with Him as children of God.

Accordingly, in the first three chapters we are shown (1) the *provision* of life through the coming of the light, 1:9; (2) the *means* of life through the acceptance of the light, 1:12; (3) the *necessity* for life, in that without the light men abide in darkness, 3:15–19; (4) the *evidence* of life, in coming to the light, 3:20–21.

Light

The facts that are predicated of Him in verses 1 and 2 as "the Word" lead to the identification of Him as the Light that "**shineth in the darkness**" (v. 5).

"**and the darkness apprehended it not.**" The word might mean that the darkness did not understand it (A.V., "comprehended") Judging, however, from 12:35 (where the same word in the Greek is rendered "overtake") the meaning is "did not seize upon it" (see the R.V. margin). The darkness would thus signify the spiritual condition of the world as influenced by the spiritual powers of darkness.

The subject of witness-bearing is a characteristic of the writings of this apostle, and the paramount purpose in this respect is to testify that Jesus Christ is the Son of God (cp. John 3:31). There is first the witness of John the

Baptist. He was "**a man sent from God**" and "**came for witness, that he might bear witness of the Light, that all might believe through him**" (vv. 6. to 8). This is introductory. It is followed by the record of his actual testimony (vv. 15, 19, 29).

"**He was not the light, but** *came* **that he might bear witness of the light. There was the true light, even the light which lighteth every man, coming into the world.**" Because of Christ's "coming into the world," He is a light for everyone. The R.V. of this verse is important, and the comma placed after "every man" should be noted; it serves to attach the phrase "coming into the world" to the mention of the light; the A.V. connects it with "every man," which lends support to the erroneous view that everyone is possessed, from birth, of an inner light, which simply requires development; moreover the clause "that cometh into the world," if predicated of "every man," becomes meaningless, as suggesting a distinction between those who come into the world and another class of men that do not.

Children of God

"**He was in the world, and the world was made by Him, and the world knew Him not**" (v. 10). The word *kosmos,* world, had various meanings in the N.T. Besides signifying an ornament (1 Pet. 3:3) and the ordered universe (Rom. 1:20), and the inhabitants of the earth (v. 29; 4:42), it means the earth, as in the second statement in this verse, and the world of men alienated from God, as in the last statement. They ought to have known Him. The verb rendered "knew" is *ginōskō,* to get to know, to recognize. The world did not acquire knowledge of Him. "**He came unto His own** [neuter plural, His own property] **and His** own [masculine plural, His own people] **received Him not.**" Men in general did not recognize Him, but the Jews, to whom He was especially sent, did not receive Him (*paralambanō,* a strong word, "did not give Him a welcome"). "**But as many as received Him** [*lambanō,* a simple but spontaneous acceptance from individuals, whether Jews or Gentiles, and so a simpler verb than that used before of the Jewish nation], **to them gave He the right to be-**

come children of God,"—not *dunamis,* power, but *exousia,* a right (*dunamis* expresses the faculty, the capacity, but the right is bestowed to those who receive Him), "**even to them that believe on His Name**" (v. 12). Believers become children of God by faith. Christ did not become the Son of God, He was that in eternal preexistence. The preposition *eis* expresses more than "on," it indicates motion toward, and rest upon, the object of belief. It therefore expresses the strongest belief, involving a union with Him. His Name expresses His attributes, character and actings.

"**which were born,**" or rather, "**begotten,**" "**not of blood,**" the element which is the means of physical life (Lev. 17:11): the plural "bloods" in the original is idiomatic and emphatic, it does not indicate the two sexes: "**nor of the will of the flesh,**" *i.e.,* not from a natural impulse: "**nor of the will of man,**" the word stands for the male sex, and stresses the human determination; "**but of God.**" Three times John declares that human generation has nothing to do with divine and spiritual generation.

From this the prologue passes to the fact of the "Word" as becoming Incarnate (v. 14). "**The Word became flesh, and dwelt** [Greek, "tabernacled"] **among us.**" He was possessed of real and permanent manhood: this was counteractive of the theory held by the Docetic sect of the Gnostics, that "the Word" was intangible and visionary.

Grace, Truth, Glory

In contrast to all these heretical views the prologue of this Gospel proceeds step by step to demonstrate the identification of "the Word" with "the Son of God." According to the A.V. and R.V. rendering what follows is put in brackets and the clause "**full of grace and truth,**" at the end of the verse, is taken as in connection with "dwelt among us." That fact is true indeed. There is, however, no need to separate it from the immediately preceding words (in spite of a certain grammatical irregularity); it would thus describe His character and acts, *i.e.,* His glory, as in the relationship mentioned. Grace is seen in connection with Him as the life, and truth as the light.

"and we beheld His glory,"—glory, when used of God, the Father or the Son, is the shining forth. of nature and power, of character and operation. So it was in all the ways of the Son of God. Here John describes it as **"glory as of the only begotten from the Father"** (v. 13). The R.V. margin is to be noted. Literally the description is "an only begotten from a Father." There are no definite articles in the original, and their absence serves to lay stress upon what is specified in the nouns.

"John beareth witness of Him, and crieth saying, This was he of whom I said, He that cometh after me is come before me, for He was before me" (v. 15), i.e., "He who comes after me as to date (in His birth and ministry) has become before me (in dignity and preeminence), for He was before me (in eternal preexistence)." Here the Baptist declares Christ's superiority both in position and time. His preexistence issued in His becoming before him (R.V.). The first word "before" is *emprosthen,* which here means superior in dignity; the second word "before" is *prōtos,* which refers to time; the phrase is literally "first of me," which is an idiom. Not priority of birth is indicated but confirmed by the explanation immediately given; **"For of His fullness we all received, and grace for grace."** The fullness signifies the totality of the attributes and powers of God. Out of that fullness every believer is supplied (see Eph. 1:23 and Col. 1:19). Here John the writer is speaking and not the Baptist. The phrase "grace for grace" may be understood either as one grace leading on to another or perhaps, rather, grace answering to the grace which is His attribute.

"For the law was given by Moses; grace and truth came by Jesus Christ." The apostle adds truth to grace as in verse 14, for Christ was the revealer of all truth as well as the minister of grace.

The Only Begotten Son

This statement, to the effect that the truth became known by Jesus Christ, leads at once to the confirmatory double declaration, first negative, that **"No man hath seen God at any time,"** second positive, that **"the only begotten Son, which is in the bosom of the Father, He hath declared** (or rather, interpreted) **Him"** (v. 18). This closing statement of the introduction to the Gospel, as the visible manifestation of the invisible God, the way by which grace and truth came, brings to a consummation the subject of the Incarnation of the Word. (There is strong MS. evidence for the rendering "the only begotten God.")

The phrase rendered "which is in the bosom of the Father" (lit., the One being in . . .) describes a timeless state, an eternal condition and relation of the fullest intimacy, affection and fellowship, and implies the unbroken continuation of it in the days of His flesh. He it is who has become the manifestation and representation of all that the Father is. The clause sets forth the eternally preexistent Sonship of Christ.

Verses 19 to 51

The Baptist's Testimony

Following the introduction, or prologue, comes the first main division of this Gospel, from 1:19 to the end of chapter 12. This especially narrates the public testimony of Christ, by word and work. The narrative begins by resuming the witness of John the Baptist, now to priests and Levites sent by the Pharisees to Bethany beyond Jordan where John was baptizing.

John had by this time drawn the attention of the Sanhedrin. He had proclaimed the approach of a new era (Matt. 3:2). Hence the sending of the priests and Levites to inquire whether he himself was the Messiah. These came from the Pharisees; The Sadducees were not so interested, they were more submissive to the Roman power. For the Baptist it was a time of crisis. Hence his emphatic declaration, that he was neither the Messiah nor Elijah nor **"that prophet"** (Deut. 18:15) but **"the voice of one crying in the wilderness** [an intimation of the spiritual state of the nation], **Make straight the way of the Lord, as said Isaiah the prophet"** (v. 23).

Then came the question as to the reason for his baptizing. It had the appearance of treating Jews as if they were mere proselytes, and of implying that they were defiled and needed cleansing. The answer he gives reveals that to him the Lord Jesus is more than all His credentials. He has no time to argue about himself; his answer is to point them to Christ. **"I baptize with water; in the midst of you standeth One whom ye** (emphatic) **know not, even He that cometh after me, the latchet of whose shoe** [i.e., the thong of whose sandal] **I am not worthy to unloose"** (vv. 26, 27), one of the most menial acts of slaves.

The Lamb of God

Verse 29 begins the Baptist's testimony to the people, by reason of Christ's coming on the scene in person on the following day. And now He who has been described as the Word, the Creator, the Son of God, is pointed out as **"the Lamb of God,"** the one **"who taketh away the sin of the world."** The **"Behold"** is an interjection, not a command. His hearers would understand what the mention of a lamb signified, and might recall the language of Isaiah 53. But they must know that He is the Lamb of God, and that as such, that is by the atoning efficacy of His sacrifice, He takes away, not merely the sin of Israel ("my people," Is. 53:8), but the sin of the world. Christ will restore the world's broken relation with God. In this matter it has been necessary for God to take the fact of sin into consideration, but Christ's sacrifice will be the eternal foundation of the renewed relation.

It was given to John the Baptist for the first time to designate Him as "the Lamb of God." The phrase is not found in the Old Testament, though typical intimations and foreshadowings abound therein. The nearest expression is in Genesis 22:8. The verb rendered "taketh away" denotes either to lift and bear or to take away, here both senses may be combined, for the word points to Christ's expiatory sacrifice and its effects. This is here said of "the sin of the world"; not the sins, but that which has existed from the time of the Fall, and in regard to which God has had judicial dealings with the world; hereafter the sin of the world will be replaced by everlasting righteousness.

John recalls his testimony of the previous day (v. 15) and the reason why he baptized with water (v. 31); it was that Christ was to be manifested to Israel. But there was more than this. That which would identify to the Baptist the person in a twofold way was the descent of the Holy Spirit upon Him.

The Son of God

This was the crowning point of his witness, namely, that the Lamb of God is the Son of God: **"And John bare witness, saying, I have beheld the Spirit descending as a dove out of heaven; and it** [He] **abode upon Him. And I knew Him not: but He** [God the Father] **that sent me to baptize with water, He said unto me, Upon whomsoever thou shalt see the Spirit descending, and abiding upon Him, the same is He that baptizeth with the Holy Spirit. And I have seen, and have borne witness that this is the Son of God"** (1:31 to 34). The two facts regarding Him were that he was the One who would baptize, not in water, but with the Holy Ghost, and that was none other than the Son of God. He says, "I have seen," in contrast to "I knew Him not."

The three persons in the Godhead combine in making John the Baptist the instrument of this witness. The Father sent him as His messenger (1:6); the Holy Spirit directed him by His supernatural demonstration; Christ Himself was the center and object of the testimony, as to (1) His deity as the Son of God (v. 34); (2) His humanity, "a Man which is become before me" (v. 30); (3) His atoning death as the Lamb of God (v. 29); (4) His exaltation as "the Baptizer with the Holy Spirit" (v. 33).

The Third Day

Now comes the third day (v. 35). On the first Christ was proclaimed; on the second He was pointed out; on the third He was followed by disciples. John still proclaimed Him as the Lamb. **"He looked** [fastened his gaze] **upon Jesus as He walked** [not now coming to him] **and saith, Behold, the Lamb of God"** (v. 36). Nothing is added now. That was a sufficient intimation to the two who had been his disciples that a greater than he must now become their Master. Christ's first disciples were won by the testimony to His atoning sacrifice. He is mentioned as the Lamb elsewhere only in 1 Peter 1:19 and in the Apocalypse. There, however, the word is always *arnion* (not *amnos* as here), a diminutive term, but the diminutive idea is not to be pressed; it lost its diminutive significance. The difference between *amnos* and *arnion* lies in this, the *amnos* points to the fact, the nature and character of His sacrifice; *arnion* presents Him, on the ground indeed of His sacrifice, but in His acquired majesty, dignity, honor, authority and power.

The Choosing of Disciples

The two disciples who **"followed Jesus"** were Andrew and, no doubt, John (the writer). From the conversation that ensued (vv. 38, 39) two things arise. Firstly, just as the disciples' knowledge of Christ only gradually increased (they knew Him just as the Messiah, v. 41), so he who receives Christ by faith receives Him in the fullness of His person, but the perception of His excellences, His power and glory is gradual. Secondly, Christ's knowledge of them and His direction of their lives give intimation of His authority and headship. **"And Jesus turned, and beheld them following and saith unto them, What seek ye?"** He did not ask, "Whom seek ye?" That they were seeking Him was evident. He asked them what they sought in Him. His invitation and their acceptance, resulting in their abiding with Him for that day, must have meant a wonderful unfolding by Him of the truth relating to Him.

That third day produces three, if not four, disciples, Andrew, John, Peter, and perhaps James. Peter was not the first to become one. Cephas (v. 43) is the Aramaic name. *Petros,* Peter, denotes, not a mass of rock, but a detached stone or boulder (easily thrown or moved); in Matthew 16:18 the word *Petra,* a mass of rock, is used of Christ, figuratively of a sure foundation, not of Peter, who is spoken of as *Petros*.

On the fourth day a new circumstance arises; for the Lord Himself goes to seek a disciple. Hitherto they had come or had been brought to Him. Now **"He was minded** [or as the word *thelō* commonly means, He willed] **to go forth into Galilee."** He finds Philip, who was of the same city as Andrew and Peter and bids him follow Him. Philip finds Nathanael (a name meaning gift of God) and gives a special testimony to Christ, firstly, as the subject of the Law and the Prophets, secondly as to His coming from Nazareth, thirdly as to the belief about His being the son of Joseph.

Nathanael's Confession

To say the least, Galileans were the objects of contempt owing to their lack of culture, their rude dialect and their association with Gentiles. Hence Nathanael's surprised question, **"Can any good come out of Nazareth?"** Philip does not stop to argue but bids him come and see. At the interview the Lord immediately reveals His divine powers of knowledge, which at once elicits the confession, **"Rabbi, Thou art the Son of God; Thou art King of Israel."** The absence of the definite article before "King," while grammatically serving to stress His kingship, perhaps indicates Nathanael's hope of an earthly king.

The fig tree under which he was is doubtless figurative of the nation of Israel, fruitless under the old covenant, though Nathanael himself is representative of the godly remnant in the nation. In this connection the promise that he and other believers would see the **"Heaven opened, and the angels of God ascending and descending upon the Son of man,"** points to the coming day when Christ will come in His glory and manifest Himself as the King of Israel in a far higher sphere than was in the mind of Nathanael. The Lord was thinking of Millennial scenes.

Chapters 2 to 9

The following four events which took place as recorded in chapters 2, 3, and 4 are significant in their order. There is first the marriage in Cana; next the cleansing of the temple; then the testimony to Nicodemus; finally the conversation with the woman of Samaria. The four events form a counterpart to the victories of Christ over Satan's temptation in the wilderness. The first of these was the suggestion to *turn stones into bread to satisfy Himself* (Matt. 4:3); now He *turns water into wine to satisfy others*. The second temptation was to cast Himself down from *the pinnacle of the temple* to declare to the people below His supernatural power; now, instead of performing a miracle *outside* the temple for His own glory, He cleanses the *inside* for the glory of His Father. The third temptation was an offer to have all the *kingdoms* of the world on the single condition that He should fall down and do an act of *worship* to His tempter; now to Nicodemus He is giving teaching concerning the heavenly, spiritual and eternal *kingdom,* a kingdom of far wider scope and importance than the kingdom of this world. Finally in the fourth chapter He is occupying the attention and interest of a Samaritan woman with the subject of *worship* to the Father.

There is something very suggestive about all this as recorded in the fourth Gospel. In this Gospel Christ is revealed especially as the Son of God; that is just the relationship concerning which the evil one challenged Him in the wilderness, saying, "If Thou be the Son of God." Again, this fourth Gospel marks the Lord especially as delightedly fulfilling the will of His Father instead of fulfilling Satan's suggestions that He should act according to His own will.

JOHN

▪ CHAPTER TWO ▪

Verses 1 to 11

The Galilee Week

The "third day" (2:1) was the third day of His stay in Galilee, making a week altogether (1:29, 35, 43). There is much in the details of the marriage feast in Cana that is indicative of things beyond the actual circumstances. The third day is suggestive of the coming period of resurrection life and millennial glory. In a special sense in the future celebration on earth of the spiritual and heavenly marriage between Christ and His saints, the water of purification for Israel (i.e., the godly remnant of the nation) will be turned into the wine of joy. Then indeed the nation will say **"Thou hast kept the good wine until now."**

Again, the word to His mother, **"Woman what have I to do with thee? Mine hour is not yet come,"** can only be rightly understood in the way it points to His relation to Israel. His mother was the natural connection with the nation under the law. His relation with Israel will in a coming day be a matter of grace. But that could be brought about only through His sacrificial and atoning death. To that He referred when He said "Mine hour is not yet come." That "hour" would and will be the means of bringing about the new relationship of grace. Figuratively and anticipatively therefore He indicates that which will be greater and more blessed than the natural tie of kinship.

His Signs

That all this, and more, is indicated, is set forth in the statement, **"This beginning of His signs did Jesus . . . and manifested His glory"** (v. 11). The word *sēmeion* is rightly rendered "sign"; it is more than a miracle; it is a miracle with a significance. Christ's signs were (1) evidences of His combined Godhood and manhood, (2) evidences of the character of His mission, (3) symbolical of spiritual truths. Eight are recorded by John.

This at Cana was the first, and being a sign, its details conveyed the spiritual teachings above mentioned. In this, too, He manifested His "glory." The glory of the Lord is the shining forth of His character and His power, the presentation of His nature and His actings. The manifestation of His glory was at the same time the manifestation of the glory of His Father.

He graces our gatherings with His presence spiritually, not only at the marriage of two of God's children, but wherever any are gathered in His Name. He never fails to fulfil His promise to be "in the midst." His sanctifying presence imparts the utmost blessedness at every such gathering.

He gives His best to the lowly. They were a humble folk at the Cana feast. There was no outstanding display. Cana itself was an obscure village. It was in the rustic home that the Lord displayed the glory of His power. He "came to minister." He loves "to revive the spirit of the humble" (Is. 57:15).

A Full Supply

He is ready to meet our needs. The need was great. To run short of wine, to be unable to provide adequate entertainment, was a grievous predicament. Our lives are largely made up of needs. He knows them all. They are designed to cast us upon Him. Nothing is too hard for the Lord.

He gives a full supply. **"Fill the water pots with water." "They filled them up to the brim."** That was what He intended. There would be enough for all. If our hearts and lives are empty of self, His fullness will fill us.

He transmutes natural things, making them ministers of joy and gladness. He makes water become wine. Our daily routine of work, so often dull and even dreary in our poor estimate, our round of labor, our "common task," can all become radiant with joy and gladness if we live in the light of His countenance and enjoy true fellowship with Him.

He uses home circumstances as a means of blessing to others. The closing statement of the narrative is, **"His disciples believed on Him"** (v. 11). They were guests at the wedding. What the Lord had wrought had marked effect on them. It established their faith in Him. Thus the union of the married pair was made by Him a means of blessing to others than those of the family circle.

Verses 12 to 22

The Cleansing of the Temple

This was the public display of Christ's authority and power. His glory had been exhibited privately at the marriage at Cana. Now He came forth in official manifestation to the place where God had set His Name in the nation, the place where He would dwell among them, where shone the glory of His own uncreated light. At Cana He had manifested His grace; now He was about to manifest His truth.

The Occasion

The occasion was **"the Passover of the Jews"** (v. 13). Three times the apostle (and he alone of the Gospel writers) designates the Passover feast thus (see 6:4 and 11:55, and cp. 5:1 and 7:2), a plain reflection upon the deplorable condition of the people and their religious rulers. What was by His own declaration "the Lord's Passover" (Ex. 12:11), had become by national departure and the desecration of the temple, "the Passover of the Jews."

Pilgrims had assembled in Jerusalem in immense numbers for their great national feast. On the eve of the occasion the head of every family had assiduously collected all the leaven in the house and given the dwelling place a general cleansing. How vastly different was the condition of God's house at this time! Again, the divinely appointed half-shekel atonement money would be paid into the temple treasury. The payment sealed to each his status as a member of the divinely chosen nation, and religious fervor reached its height. But now the offering was desecrated by the jingling of the coins of the money changer swindlers. The glory of the temple had been robbed of its spiritual significance and power. How could a man bring his lamb to God amidst the hindrances of such unholy confusion? Commerce, supported by the priests, robbed the poor of their privileges.

This kind of corruption has been reproduced in Christendom. Priestcraft, perhaps commercially the most paying concern in the world, has perverted the cause of the humble believer, by striding across the path of his free access to God through the one mediator on the ground of His expiatory sacrifice.

The Startling Interposition

Now the Lord suddenly comes to His temple. He finds in the temple those that sold oxen and sheep and doves and the changers of money sitting. The place of prayer for all nations resounds with the noisy traffic of a cattle market, with all its filth and stench. The covetous hearts of the dealers in small change gloat over their ill-gotten gains. What a sickening sight for the devoted pilgrim as he entered the court of the temple! How he must have longed for the time when the promise would be fulfilled, "there shall be no more a Canaanite (a trafficker) in the House of the Lord of Host" (Zech. 14:21)! How much greater was the holy indignation of Him who thus beheld the unutterable desecration of His Father's house!

In the midst of all the desecration He appears whose "eyes are as a flame of fire," and whose heart burned with zeal for the glory of His Father's house. He makes a scourge the instrument of the exercise of His authority. Was it emblematic of a greater scourge destined to chastise rulers and people, when the Romans would destroy both temple and city? Certainly the paramount significance of this cleansing process, this divine attack upon the vested interests of the evildoers, was the vindication of the Name of God and the honors of His house, His hatred and condemnation of sin. And on this account the Lord's act was the presage and pledge of God's mercy to men in the eventual freedom of access into His presence on His conditions of grace in and through Christ. While the actual cleansing was not that of the inner sanctuary (the *naos*) but of the precincts, the outer court, yet it stood for the reconsecration of the entire building for the holy purposes designed of God.

Evidence of His Divine Power

But there was a deeper significance in this supernatural act; for such it was. The expulsion by a single person of the hosts of avaricious traffickers and their belongings, the overthrow of the tables and scattering of their money piles, notwithstanding the fact that their sordid business had the sanction and support of those who had legal possession of the whole place, was proof of His divine power; this indeed was tacitly acknowledged by the surprised religious authorities in their question recorded in verse 18. And the deeper significance is this, that whatsoever is consecrated to God for His service is to be freed from mere worldly profit. The veneer of religion is often but a covering to hide the selfish interests of those who promote it. Personal advantage can only act as a defiling influence in any church or assembly. The sheep, the oxen and the doves were sold for sacrificial purposes, but the motive and methods of the business were an abomination in the eyes of the Lord. Mere conformity to religious rites and ceremonies may make their appeal to the natural, the religious, the sentimental mind, but human motives and ambitions are doomed to meet the exposure and judgment of Him who searches the hearts.

A church is a temple of God, the dwelling place of His Spirit (1 Cor. 3:16), and he who mars it will be marred of its owner (v. 17). "For the temple of God is holy, which temple ye are."

The Effect of the Sign

The temple authorities dared not question the moral rectitude of the Lord's action in cleansing it. Taken by surprise at the display of His power and authority, they decided to ask Him for a sign in confirmation thereof. For them the value of a sign would consist in its being simply indicative of the triumph and greatness of the chosen nation.

Their blindness, consequent upon their hardness of heart, is evinced in their failure to recognize that He was, by the very character of His dealings, the greatest possible sign Himself. According to their request (He absolutely refused it later when their persistent refusal to recognize His claims had reached its height, Matt. 16:1 to 4), He gives them a sign,

but not in accordance with their expectations: **"Destroy this temple, and in three days I will raise it up"** (*naos* is the word here, the inner sanctuary, not *hieron*, the entire building), and this was appropriate to His reference to **"the temple of His body."** And such His body was. In it shone the abiding Shekinah, the glory of the Lord. "In Him dwelleth all the fullness of the Godhead bodily."

Voluntarily He would hand over this holy temple for them to "destroy" (*luo*, to loosen, was sometimes used with reference to a structure; cp. Eph. 2:14, where it is used of the breaking down of a wall). How constantly His impending death and what it involved formed the subject of His utterances! Here also He mentions "the glory that would follow," foretelling withal His own part in His Resurrection. This, too, was a clear indication, for those to whom the fact would be revealed, of His oneness with the Father in Godhood. For in the act of His resurrection the Father and the Son were, as ever, inseparable. The Jews eagerly laid hold of what they considered a discrepancy in His utterance. Conviction, however, eventually was borne in upon them. That is recorded by Matthew (27:63).

The Effect upon the Disciples

The significance of His act of cleansing the temple was realized by the disciples immediately. They remembered that it was written, **"The zeal of Thine House shall eat Me up"** (R.V.). The significance of His reply to the Jews was realized after His resurrection. The disciples then remembered His utterance **"and they believed the Scripture, and the word which Jesus had said."** As for the people, many believed on Him, but with a shallow if sincere credence.

Here, then, we observe the contrasting effects which so constantly marked the Lord's public ministry of work and word, and still mark those of His faithful witnesses, namely, rejection and reception. If by grace we have received Him, let us on our part follow the path He trod.

There were more signs wrought by Him at that time in Jerusalem, purposively unrecorded in this Gospel, and these caused many to believe on His Name, by way of sincere conviction, a natural recognition of facts; but this did not alter their spiritual condition, and **"Jesus did not trust Himself to them." "He knew all men"** and **"He Himself knew what was in man."** The same emphasis "He Himself" should be expressed in both statements. The Lord knew the state and character of every man. He knew man's moral nature.

JOHN

• CHAPTER THREE •

Verses 1 to 21

Nicodemus

"**B**ut there was a man" who was an exception. Chapter three continues the last paragraph of chapter two by this contrast. The connecting word should be "But," not "Now," as in the R.V. (it should not be omitted as the A.V. does). "Now" suggests a completely new subject.

The contrast was twofold. Nicodemus was not a case of mere acknowledgment of the facts about Christ because of the signs He wrought. His conscience was reached; he felt his soul's need. And Christ on His part, in response to this need, opened His heart to meet it, trusting Himself in this way to His inquirer.

Nicodemus begins by expressing an assurance concerning Jesus, based upon the signs He did (v. 2). This utterance was an evidence of exercise of heart which he dared not disclose to his fellows. It is "night" with us when we fail to witness for fear of the world. The Lord goes at once to the root of the matter. He did not stop to give mere mental instruction to him. How can anyone be spiritually blessed by patching up the "old man"? The old is carnal and cannot discern spiritual things. Nicodemus doubtless thought the Lord's signs were indication of the approaching earthly kingdom. Hence the reply, **"Except a man be born anew, he cannot see the kingdom of God."** The word *anothen* may mean "from above" (R.V. margin), as in 19:11; James 1:17; 3:15, 17 (a very probable meaning here), or "again," anew, as in Galatians 4:9.

The Natural and the Spiritual

The thoughts of Nicodemus are occupied with the natural (v. 4). The Lord points to the spiritual: **"Except a man be born of water and the Spirit, he cannot enter the kingdom of God."** He first said **"cannot see,"** for Nicodemus was occupied with the visible. Now He goes deeper. Water is a means of cleansing. Cleansing is by the Word of God. "Ye are clean," says the Lord, "through the word which I have spoken unto you." Christ sanctifies the Church by cleansing it "through the washing of water by the Word." The Spirit of God applies the Word of God to the heart. There is another possible interpretation. The *kai*, "and," may mean "even," as it does sometimes. The effect of regeneration by the Holy Spirit is to produce a corresponding spiritual life. What God creates may be material; but what He begets partakes of His spiritual nature and likeness. **"That which is born of the Spirit is spirit."** The origin determines the nature. Accordingly baptism cannot produce the new birth and beget a child of God. Baptism is first a sign of death. The Lord gives the illustration of the wind (the R.V. and A.V. renderings are doubtless right).

How could **"the teacher** [the representative of such] **of Israel"** grasp **heavenly things,** if notwithstanding his reading of the prophets, he did not understand **earthly things?** Christ and those associated with Him spoke what they knew (the "we" is not the plural of majesty); they bore witness of that which they had seen—a witness rejected. The origin was heavenly. No one had ascended into heaven to receive these heavenly things and bear witness of them. The only One possible was He who **"descended out of Heaven,"** and who while still on the earth, was **"the Son of Man, which is in Heaven."** He was the very embodiment of the heavenly and in His combined Godhood and manhood was the manifestation of the heavenly to men. Therefore to understand these things Nicodemus must be related to Christ by the new birth, and that would involve a share in the witness.

The Means of Life

But the Lord has a further and still more explicit word to say about the new life (imparted in the new birth), and gives "the teacher of Israel" a fact from the Old Testament (which he had often read without getting any further than the earthly circumstance), in order that he may perceive the great foundation application and realize its eternal importance: **"And as Moses lifted up the serpent in the wilderness, even so must the Son of Man be lifted up: that whosoever believeth may in Him have eternal life"** (vv. 14, 15). There is something necessary then before the new birth can take place. Truly the new birth brings life eternal, and this comes by faith. But this can be brought about only by the remission of sin. There could be no life without that. For that purpose this very person, the Son of man, whom Nicodemus had sought, **"must be lifted up."** He must be made sin to take sin away. He must become a curse, the very antitype of the serpent in the wilderness. For this purpose He had come down from heaven. Whosoever rejected Him, for such there could be no remission of sins, no removal of the curse, no new birth, no eternal life, no entrance into the kingdom. The Son of God, the Son of man, alone knew the character and requirements of God against whom man had sinned and from whom he was alienated.

The great fact of the means for this is immediately stated in another way.* To accomplish this, and meet the need of the new birth for Nicodemus and for all who are brought to realize their need, **"God so loved the world, that He gave His only begotten Son, that whosoever believeth on Him should not perish, but have eternal life."** Man's sinful condition and God's holy character and requirement, and His infinite love, all meet at the Cross.

All this goes beyond the limits of His dealing with the Jewish people: God sent His Son into the world **"not to judge the world; but that the world should be saved through Him"** (v. 17).

The purpose of Christ's coming was not to pass sentence but to bring salvation. As for the believer no sentence can be passed on him; as for the unbeliever, he stands self-condemned, for he has refused to accept the self-revelation, the Name, **"of the only begotten Son of God."** His Name is the expression of His very person (v. 18).

The Cause of Refusal

But it is more than a case of refusal to accept the Divine testimony; **"men loved the darkness rather than the light"**; that is to say, they hated the light; and that because their works were evil (*ponēra*, a word which combines the ideas of base and baneful; *ponēros* describes the character of Satan as "the evil one," 17:15; 1 John 2:13, 14; 3:12; 5:18, 19). **"For every one that doeth** [*prasso* means to practice, to do a thing by way of constant activity] **ill** [here the word is *phaula*, which signifies worthless things, good-for-nothing] **hateth the light, and cometh not to the light** [a hatred exhibited in a deliberate refusal to come], **lest his deeds** [his works] **should be reproved** [or rather, convicted, i.e., of being what they actually are, by being exposed in their true character and so meeting with condemnation]."

The contrary is the case with the true believer. As to the nature of his activity, he **"doeth the truth"** (the truth in its moral aspect). As to the character of his walk, he **"cometh to the light"** (he loves the presence and fellowship of Him who is the Light). As to the purpose of his coming, **"that his deeds may be made manifest** [he is attracted to that which marks the character of his doings], **that they have been wrought in God,"** that is, in fellowship with, in the presence of, and by the power of, God.

Verses 22 to 36

The Baptist's Further Testimony

The next part of the chapter gives a beautiful picture of John the Baptist, by reason of his faithfulness and devotion to Christ, his delight in Christ's superiority in antecedence, in position, and in purpose, and his joy in the privilege appointed to him of being as near to Him as he was. To him Jesus was everything; His exaltation and His interests were his consuming object. When a question arose between John's disciples and a Jew about purifying, and they reported that Christ was attracting everybody, he presented with true humility and with

---

*The present writer regards the passage from verse 16 to verse 21 as a continuation of the Lord's discourse to Nicodemus, rather than remarks made by John the writer of this Gospel.

manifest satisfaction (1) the truth as to the source of any revelation, verse 27; (2) the facts of his past witness, verse 28, and its present fulfillment, verse 29; (3) the contrast in position: he was simply a forerunner, sent before the Messiah Himself; (4) the contrast in relationship: Christ was the Bridegroom, John was but the friend of the Bridegroom, His devoted attendant and listener, (5) his joy of heart in every word spoken by the Bridegroom, verse 29; (6) the increase of the One for whose sake he testified, (7) his own decrease in the very path of his devotedness, verse 30.

In this lowliness and satisfaction John the Baptist is an example to us. The intimacy of our relationship to the Bridegroom is no doubt greater positionally than his. It should be so with us as it was with him, the only thing that should matter should be that Christ is glorified by us and in all our ways and circumstances. That Christ may be magnified in our bodies—if that dominates our desires, aims and ambitions, all will be well with us, no matter how greatly we may be despised, no matter how great may be our suffering and trial.

Three Further Contrasts

The closing part of the chapter continues the contrasts, first in regard to Christ and John, then between the effects of the witness, and finally between the eternal destinies of men. Firstly, Christ came from above and bore witness of what He had seen and heard. John's witness was that of one whose origin and condition were of the earth. Secondly, Christ's witness was generally rejected; whosoever received His witness **"hath set his seal to this, that God is true"** (v. 33); he solemnly confirms his acceptance of, and adherence to, the great fact. And the evidence of the fact is seen in the testimony of the Lord Jesus as the One whom God sent. **"For He whom God hath sent speaketh the words of God,"** not the testimony in general but each detail of each statement of it; moreover this is the operation of the Holy Spirit. Firstly, not only was He sent by God, there is deeper fuller truth than this; He is the Son, to whom the Father **"hath given all things."** This is introductory to the statement of the third contrast, between destinies. For since all things are in the hands of the Son, the destiny of every human being is under His control. But this, again, depends upon the attitude of each toward Him. **"He that believeth on the Son hath eternal life; but he that obeyeth not the Son shall not see life, but the wrath of God abideth on him"** (v. 36).

All this from verse 22 to the end is introductory to the more public testimony of the Lord. There was a special beginning of this after John was cast into prison (3:24). The introductory character of that portion lies in this, that it has stated the way in which He came, His position, His glory, the nature of His witness, the great purpose of His coming, His being "lifted up," man's condition regarding this, the Father's love for Him and His committal of all things into His hands. The following chapters illustrate and amplify the closing statement as to those who believe and have life and those who refuse and endure divine wrath.

JOHN

CHAPTER FOUR

Verses 1 to 42

The Woman of Samaria

The "therefore" in the first verse of chapter four connects this chapter, not merely with 3:22 and the details of the baptizings by John and by Christ's disciples, but with all the last part of chapter three. There is another change of scene, but now Christ begins a ministry outside the limits of the Jewish people. The jealousy of the Pharisees leads to this, but whatever the Lord did always had a significance beyond the actual doing. This visit to and ministry in Samaria recalls the "whosoever" of 3:15, 16, and the wide sphere of the world, 3:17, and gives a foreshadowing of the worldwide message after His ascension and the coming of the Spirit. Again, the fact that **"He left Judaea,"** though only for a time, was suggestive of an attitude caused by the hardened condition of the Jews. The word rendered "left" signifies more than mere departure, it really means "He let it go," *i.e.*, He left it to itself.

Everything was by divine counsel and appointing, each fact the Son's fulfillment of the Father's will: the weariness, the thirst, the locality (the plot of land bought by Abraham, given by Jacob to Joseph, and Joseph's burying place, Gen. 33:19; 48:22; Josh. 24:32). Christ's ministry of grace there was a particular fulfillment of Genesis 49:22, "a fruitful bough by a well" and a branch running "over the wall," i.e., of Judaism. The side of the well, the time of day, everything was ready for the one who now becomes the object of God's grace and mercy.

The Opening of the Dialogue

The beginning of the flowing forth of the fountain of grace was by way of a request, **"Give Me to drink."** The blessed Savior had a spiritual thirst as well as the physical. His request had more than a natural significance. How satisfying to the spirit is the salvation of a soul!

There is no discrepancy between the statement that **"Jews have no dealings with Samaritans"** (there are no definite articles in the original) and the fact that the disciples had gone into Samaria to buy food. Even the Pharisees allowed fruit, vegetables, etc., to come from Samaria. Moreover, Galileans were less strict.

The surprise of the Samaritan woman meets with the response, **"If thou knewest the gift of God, and who it is** (not who I am) **that saith to thee, Give me to drink; thou wouldest have asked of Him, and He would have given thee living water."** This combines the glory of His Godhood with the evidences of the reality of His manhood, and the lowliness of His stoop in that respect. The combination enhances the grace by which the Lord seeks to meet her spiritual need. For the "living water" see Genesis 26:19 (R.V., margin); Leviticus 14:5 (margin); Jeremiah 2:13; 17:13; Zechariah 14:8.

Different Waters

Her thoughts are occupied solely with her natural circumstances and surroundings. "The natural man understandeth not the things of the Spirit." That Jacob gave the well, as she said, was a Samaritan tradition. In her opinion the well was good enough for him and his; could this tired person provide a better one? **"Art Thou greater . . . ?"** The "Thou" is very emphatic. He does not answer her question concerning comparative greatness, He develops His subject, pressing home the contrast between the natural and the spiritual, between that which provides no permanent satisfaction and that which involves the placing of the spiritual well within a person himself. **"Every one that drinketh of this water shall thirst again: but whosoever drinketh of the water that I shall give him shall never thirst, but the water that I shall give him shall become in him a well of water springing up unto eternal life."** There is a noticeable change of tense: **"every one that drinketh"** (v. 13) is in the present tense, drinketh habitually; but the verb in the original **"whosoever drinketh"** (v. 14) is in the perfect tense, "whosoever hath drunk," an act with an abiding result. The negative in **"—shall never thirst"** is very strong, and the rendering might well be *"shall certainly not thirst forever."*

This would surely take her mind off the natural. But no! Whatever it is He can provide let it provide an antidote to thirst and put an end to her daily toil and weariness, so that she does not **"come all the way hither to draw"** (R.V.).

A Turn in the Conversation

Now begins the second stage of His dealings. He will now deal with her conscience. One word, and it leads to the tremendous disclosure that her whole life lies open to His eye. Her limited recognition, that He was a prophet, makes clear that she realized that she had come face to face with a messenger from God. Yet she shrinks from anything further along this line and turns to the subject of the right place for worship.

The Samaritans claimed that on Mount Gerizim Abraham offered up Isaac and here he met Melchizedek. The Lord speaks no more of her sinful life, but leads her thoughts again, and in another way, to the spiritual realm, taking up the question to which she had turned. This was grace indeed, and wisdom, too, for He would lead her to the realities of His own person, and it is this great revelation which brings the blessings of salvation. Sufficient had been said to bring home the sinfulness of her life. The Lord would not probe that further.

He shows that it is not a question whether Jerusalem or Gerizim is the appointed spot for worship. The Samaritans were ignorant even of the person to be worshiped. It was not so with the Jews; for **"salvation is from the Jews."** They were God's people, and salvation comes from them by reason of promises to Abraham and Isaac. True worship must accord with the nature of Him who is to be worshiped. **"God is Spirit"** and must be approached by means of that part of our being which is spirit. There are no limitations of space and locality with Him. He must be worshiped in truth, not in ignorance, superstition, and sectarianism. There must be submission of thought, feeling

and desire to His will; **"spirit and truth"** present two aspects of the one fact. **"For such** [an emphatic word] **doth the Father seek to be His worshipers,"** that is to say, true worship must answer to the nature of His being. And how this is to be brought about has been made known by grace in the person and work of His Son.

It was not in any spirit of contradiction to the Lord's words **"ye know not"** (v. 22) that the woman now said **"I know."** She was thoroughly arrested in her ideas by the great truth which Christ had just uttered. She was sure that all this and more would be declared by the Messiah when He came. This instruction concerning worship would be confirmed by Him and everything else would be made clear.

The Great Revelation

Now comes the climax: For this the Lord had been preparing. It is when Christ is revealed to the needy soul that the work of grace accomplishes its end. So it had been in other ways with John the Baptist, with Nathanael and other disciples, and with Nicodemus. So it was now with the woman. **"Jesus saith unto her, I that speak unto thee am He."** There are immediate evidences that His saving work was done. The water of life had been poured into her soul. She forgot her water pot and the temporal requirements. The customary toil gave place to a quick step back to the city. She becomes a messenger to others. An invitation had not long since been given to a very different person, "Come and see." **"Come, see,"** she says, **"a man, which told me all things that ever I did. Can this be the Christ?"** (the R.V. is correct). Her heart was occupied with Him and He became her satisfying portion. She confessed Him with her mouth and thus confirmed her faith. She attracted the men of the city to Him.

Spiritual Harvest

While they **"were coming to Him"** (v. 30), the disciples, who had come upon the scene marveling, were begging Him to allay His hunger. He found His nourishment from another source. His food consisted in doing the will of Him who sent Him and accomplishing His work. They were occupied with mundane matters. Firstly, they wondered whether, while they had come with food which they had gone to Samaria to buy, someone else had supplied Him. Secondly, they were discussing the time of the year and the prospect of harvest. They must wait four months before bread became cheaper (perhaps they had paid a good price for what they had brought from the city).

But there was reaping to be done that day, for the spiritual fields were **"white unto harvest."** There were wages for laborers and **"fruit unto life eternal."** Those who had prepared by sowing and those who enjoyed the counterpart by reaping could **"rejoice together."** The Baptist had sown, Christ had sown, and now the woman had sown. The disciples could join in the reaping. That was better than buying food. It is one thing to trade with folks, and quite proper withal, but another thing to win their souls to Christ.

The woman's testimony produced abundant fruit. Many believed on Christ (there must have been a large crowd from the city). They asked Him to go back with them and stay, and He stayed two days. More reaping was done. Many more believed, rejoicing in having the witness of the woman confirmed by hearing Him themselves, and acknowledging Him as, more than the Messiah, **"the Savior of the world"** (v. 42).

Verses 43 to 54

The Second Sign

After the two days He goes to Galilee, where the people received Him because they had seen the things He did in Jerusalem. It did not mean that they honored Him. He knew they would not (v. 44), but He did not go there to get that, He went to bear witness. And He bore witness by another sign.

The "second sign" which Christ did in Galilee, the healing of the "nobleman's" son, has at least this significance, that it marks a striking difference between the ground upon which faith was now exercised and that which created faith in the heart of the Samaritan woman and her fellow townsfolk. This nobleman (or rather, king's officer, R.V., margin, an official

under Herod Antipas, a tetrarch who held his father's title of king) urged Him to come and heal his dying son. His faith rested upon the signs and wonders wrought by Christ, news of which had reached him from Judaea (v. 47). That this was so is clear from the Lord's remonstrance, **"Except ye see signs and wonders ye will not believe."** A faith based on miracles was not of such value as that manifested by the woman, which was the result, not of news of His wonder workings in Judaea, but of His own testimony and teaching. She and the other Samaritans believed because of the truth He spoke; the officer rested his hopes upon Christ's miraculous acts. The Lord would not reject his faith, but He found less pleasure in that which rested on His power to deliver from calamity than in that which rested in His own person, and was established by His character and teaching.

Christ did not go to the sickbed to accomplish the healing and receive acknowledgment as acting in the capacity of a healer. He simply said, **"Go thy way, thy son liveth,"** and the man departed believing.

The different words used to describe the sick lad are characteristic: the father speaks of him as his *paidion* (v. 49), a term of endearment; the servants use the word *pais,* a boy, a term of ordinary familiarity (v. 51); the Lord and the writer John call him *huios,* "son," a term of dignity.

The Chief Factor

The important point in the discovery that the healing was coincidental with the Lord's utterance, is the power of His word. That which caused the man and his household to believe was not so much the fact of the supernatural deed, but the personal word of the Lord. The person Himself is ever greater than the deeds wrought by Him.

The two signs wrought in Galilee represent the twofold way in which the Lord manifested His delivering power and grace when on earth, and will yet manifest them in the restoration of His earthly people. The one was by intervention in circumstances of difficulty, the other by healing. The Jews will yet find in Him the One who can remove their natural difficulties and can give them spiritual recovery.

JOHN

CHAPTER FIVE

Verses 1 to 9

The Healing of the Impotent Man

The occasion the Lord chose for this sign was **"a feast of the Jews."** Various suggestions have been made as to which feast it was. It could scarcely have been that of Purim, as there was no Sabbath connected with that feast. That of Pentecost, "the feast of weeks" (Deut. 16:10–16), seems not unlikely, especially if the Lord used in turn the three greatest feasts in the year for the fulfillment of the witness which Moses bore to Him. The first was the Passover (2:13); the third was the Feast of Tabernacles (7:2).

The apostle John, however, does not specify the time, simply mentioning it as "a feast of the Jews," their religious functions being observed with punctilious exactitude, as if all was right with God. Yet their ways were not His ways, nor their thoughts His thoughts.

"The Glory That Excelleth"

Perhaps they considered that the miraculous powers of the pool of Bethesda in their city were a token of their enjoyment of the divine favor. Thither accordingly the Lord goes to give a sign that a different kind of healing was necessary for "the daughter of Zion" from that which the Bethesda waters indicated. The pool is to be disregarded. The healer Himself was in their midst. Their sabbath-keeping would avail nothing for their salvation. As has been well said, "The poverty of the pool is exposed. It is seen to be nothing but a beggarly element. It has no glory by reason of the glory that excelleth . . . Jesus is there standing . . . in contrast with all that system of ordinances and observances which had gone before, and He exposes them in all their impotency and poverty."

There among the multitude of the diseased and infirm in the five porches or colonnades, He singles out the man who shall be both the object of His compassion and the means of His witness. He is touched with the feeling of his infirmity. He knew all about his past and his constant disappointments. There is no entreaty on the man's part. Christ takes the initiative. He asks him **"Wouldst thou be made whole?"** He knew what the answer would be, knew that the invalid's thoughts would still be concentrated on the pool. It is futile expectancy that looks for other resources than the Lord.

Faith Expressed in Action

Most frequently Christ made some remark concerning the requisite of faith. In this case He immediately bids him **"Arise, take up thy bed, and walk."** Faith was indeed necessary, and faith was there. The word was with power, power to heal, power likewise to elicit the obedience of faith. **"And straightway the man was made whole, and took up his bed and walked."** Here was faith without wavering, faith that turned from the pool to the person.

The carrying of his mat was a testimony to his miraculous restoration. More than this, it declared the boldness of a faith that ignored the startling spectacle of a Jew carrying a "burden" on a Sabbath! It bore eloquent testimony to his sense of indebtedness to his healer.

Verses 10 to 15

The Lord of the Sabbath

The Sabbath day! The Jews at once seized upon the breach of the Law. It was enough for him that His healer had bidden him carry his mat. The healer was in his eyes greater than the law of the sabbath, and the healer Himself testified on another occasion that He, the Son of man, was "Lord of the Sabbath," a repudiation of the punctilious observances of their traditional exactitudes, regarding the letter of the law to the neglect of the spirit of it (Matt. 12:8). They do not ask the man as to who cured him, but as to who told him to break the Sabbath.

The Lord **"conveyed Himself away,"** not to escape from danger, but to avoid the applause of the crowd, and with the object of dealing further with the man in private. Augustine remarks that "it is difficult in a crowd to see Christ, a certain solitude is necessary for our mind."

Why Did the Man Tell the Jews?

The healer of his body finds him in the temple to deal with his soul. **"Behold,"** He says, **"thou art made whole: sin no more** [continue no longer in sin], **lest a worse thing befall thee."** He who "searcheth the hearts" knew the past history of the man's life. The disclosure involved in this command was more than a conclusion drawn simply from the nature of the man's disease. "He knew what was in man." Upon this **"the man went away and told the Jews that it was Jesus which had made him whole."**

The connection between this and the warning just given him by the Lord does not afford sufficient ground for an assumption of any spirit of retaliation on the man's part. He had probably come into the temple to fulfill the duty of thanksgiving. He may have felt himself under an obligation to show obedience to the religious authorities.

There was, however, the danger of falling back into sin. Past habits of evil have a way of reasserting themselves after deliverance. Only the power of Christ and His Word can give sufficient strength for overcoming. Was not His warning given to the man with this very design? And to us the Spirit of God has been imparted that we may heed the injunction "Walk by the Spirit, and ye shall not fulfill the lust of the flesh. For the flesh lusteth against the Spirit, and the Spirit against the flesh; for these are contrary the one to the other, that ye may not do the things that ye would" (Gal. 5:16, 17).

Verses 16 to 47

That this miracle was wrought on a Sabbath day roused the fierce hostility of the Jews. They were "up in arms to defend their favorite piece of legalism." **"For this cause did the Jews persecute** [imperfect tense, continued to persecute] **Jesus, because He did these things on the sabbath."** Their religious zeal utterly outweighed any consideration of the marvelous deliverance granted to the cripple and his joy and comfort in his healing. Religion is the greatest persecuting force in the world. From the days of Cain onward it is in religion that the innate enmity of the natural mind toward God is particularly manifested, and as each sign disclosed something of what God is in the person of His Son there was a rising tide of opposition to the One thus revealed and the great incomprehensible depths of mercy and grace of God.

Christ's Reply to His Persecutors

With sublime dignity and calm the Lord, in response to their antagonism, begins to disclose His great prerogatives as the Son of God, His perfect oneness with the Father, the love of the Father for Him, the uninterrupted communion existing between them, and His entire and delighted submission to the Father's will.

He here makes no comment on the sabbath law, as on other occasions. He had something more important to deal with, and His testimony constitutes an essential feature of the fabric of this Gospel. **"My Father,"** He says, **"worketh even until now, and I work"** (v. 17). This reveals the character of the sign just accomplished. It was one instance of the co-work of the Father and the Son. That God should break the sabbath law was impossible. In censuring the Son they were censuring the Father. The work of the Son was as indispensable as that of the Father, and was the Father's work. The declaration exposed at once the untenable character of their position.

Law and Grace

But more than the one incident was involved. The co-work was "even until now." God could not find rest where sin existed, save by the atoning sacrifice of His Son. Had it not been so the race must have perished entirely. Ever since sin entered, God had anticipatively wrought in grace. Of this the miracle of healing just wrought was an instance. So the work of the Son was the work of the Father with Him. The obligation regarding the Sabbath under the law did not nullify the actings of grace. Nay, the law, by its inability to justify men and give them true rest, served to enhance the power of grace. The Jews' method of keeping the Sabbath must be exposed and set aside, to reveal the mercy of God in Christ and the true nature of the mercy in the joint operation of the Father and the Son.

The claim made in His statement is at once clear to them. It intensifies their antagonism. They cannot deny the miracle. Ignoring its significance, they resort to the additional charge of blasphemy and endeavor to act accordingly. **"For this cause the Jews sought the more to kill Him, because He not only brake the sabbath, but also called God His own Father, making Himself equal with God."**

THE FIRST PUBLIC DISCOURSE
Introduction

The way is now open for the most comprehensive public witness given by the Lord concerning the Father and Himself and Their dealings with man, both now and hereafter.

The Lord's discourse consists of two parts: (A) verses 19 to 29, (B) verses 30 to 47. In (A) He speaks of (1) His relation to the Father in Their unity of counsel and action (vv. 19, 20); (2) His resulting dealings with individuals as lifegiver and judge (vv. 21–27); (3) His position and power in the future resurrection of the dead to life or judgment (vv. 28, 29). (B) consists of (1) a restatement of His entire dependence on the Father, involving, firstly, the righteousness of His judgment, secondly, the fact that He does not bear witness from Himself (vv. 30, 31); (2) a declaration of the witness borne to Him (vv. 32–39); (3) a remonstrance against the unbelief of His hearers (vv. 40–47).

Verses 19 to 29

The Oneness of the Father and the Son

The first part, (A), is characterized by a threefold **"Verily, verily"** (vv. 19, 24, 25). This is a translation of the Hebrew word "Amen," which signifies "truth." The repeated word (used by the Lord twenty-five times as recorded in this Gospel and not found

thus elsewhere in the New Testament) always introduces a solemn pronouncement demanding the utmost attention.

The first of the three in this discourse is followed by declarations which govern all that follows. They are foundation truths predicating (1) the impossibility of His acting independently of the Father: **"the Son can do nothing of Himself,"** (2) the intimacy and unbroken continuity of their communion— **"but what He seeth the Father doing,"** (3) the coincidence and coextension of Their work **"for what things soever He doeth, these the Son doeth in like manner,"** (4) the love of the Father for the Son as the causative element characterizing this unity, communion, and cooperation: **"For the Father loveth the Son** [note the connecting word, "For," gathering up the preceding truths into the underlying cause]**, and sheweth Him all things that Himself doeth"**: as the Son does nothing without the Father, so the Father keeps nothing secret from the Son; this, coupled with the earlier statement as to the preexistent cooperation, **"My Father worketh even until now, and I work,"** clearly establishes the eternal preexistence of the relationship; (5) the increasing nature of the work as further revealing the intimacy now made known, and challenging the acknowledgment of the beholders: **"and greater works than these will He show Him, that ye may marvel."** These "greater works" are mentioned in what follows.

Resurrection, Spiritual and Physical

Having made known that what He did represented the joint work of the Father with Himself (as exemplified in the healing of the impotent man on the Sabbath), and that the great feature of this divine cooperation was the love of the Father for Him, a love which involved the unbroken and most intimate communication to Him of all that the Father did (5:19, 20), the Lord now confirms all this, for the attention of His critics, by instancing the most transcendent operations of God, those, namely, of resurrection, spiritual, and physical; these He describes as "greater works" (i.e., than those of healing the sick). This is dealt with in the first part of the discourse

(vv. 21 to 29), first as to spiritual resurrection (vv. 21 to 27), then as to the physical (vv. 28, 29).

"For as the Father raiseth the dead and quickeneth them, even so the Son also quickeneth whom He will." This at once constitutes a positive and explicit claim to deity. Not only are the Father and the Son conjointly engaged in the salvation of the souls of men and the impartation to them of spiritual life from their dead condition, but this impartation is the effect of the will of the Son, not apart from the Father, but determined in equality of mind and counsel with Him. This is the significance also in His "whom He will," that there is no limit to His life-bestowing power to those who accept the condition of faith in Him, a condition which He is just about to state.

How to Obtain Eternal Life

As the quickening involves the raising, there is a definite connection between His power as the imparter of life and His capacity as judge, as is obvious from the "For" introducing verse 22: **"For neither doth the Father judge any man, but He hath given all judgment unto the Son."** And the connection surely lies in this, that, as the bestowment of spiritual life depends upon the will and act of the Son, His knowledge as to who is to receive life from Him and who is to remain without it, constitutes Him an infallible judge in determining the destiny of all. Hence He says (though without a prior and very important declaration, v. 23), **"Verily, verily I say unto you, He that heareth My Word, and believeth Him that sent Me, hath eternal life, and cometh not into judgment, but hath passed out of death into life"** (v. 24, R.V.). Note that it is not "believed on Him," as in the A.V., but "believeth Him," that is to say, "believeth God's Word respecting His Son."

Now this makes clear that the "whom He will" in verse 21 is not a matter of arbitrary selection. Each one is responsible to decide whether he will believe and thus receive life, or not. This is open to all who hear. God's interposition in and through His Son has alone made it possible. The case of the impotent man was illustrative of this. His condition was

the outcome of sin and was hopeless, but for Christ's intervention. His "Wilt thou be made whole?" is typical of the human responsibility to accept. Nevertheless salvation must be the effect of His Word. The obligation rested with His hearers to see the significance, and to place themselves among the recipients of life from Him.

The Son's Equality of Honor

The Lord precedes this glorious truth of the Gospel by a statement as to the great reason why the Father has committed all judgment to Him. It is not simply that He may act as the judge of men, nor that He may give eternal life to all who believe, but **"that all may honor the Son, even as they honor the Father,"** and this He substantiates by the declaration, **"He that honoreth not the Son honoreth not the Father which sent Him"** (v. 23). This is of paramount importance in view of the variety of tenets, arguments, and propaganda which detract from the honor of the Son. He it is against whom the arch-spiritual foe exerts his fiercest and unremitting antagonism.

"The obligation of honoring the Son is defined to be just as stringent as the obligation of honoring the Father. Whatever form that honor may take, be it thought, or language, or outward act, or devotion of the affections or submission of the will, or that union of thought and heart and will into one complex act of self-prostration before finite greatness, which we of the present day usually mean by the term adoration, such honor is due to the Son no less than to the Father. How fearful is such a claim if the Son be only human! how natural, how moderate, how just, if He is in very deed Divine!" (Liddon).

Since the Father does nothing apart from the Son, and the Son nothing apart from the Father (vv. 19, 20), this unity of operation demands equality of honor. To this honor of the Son all will be inevitably constrained, either in full and gladsome recognition by those who have eternal life, or compulsorily in the case of all rejectors, human and spiritual. It is the unthwartable determination of God that every tongue shall "confess that Jesus Christ is Lord to the glory of God the Father" (Phil. 2:11).

The Lifegiver and Judge

The hour of verse 25 is already 1,900 years long. The authority of **"the voice of the Son of God"** in the bestowment of life on dead souls rests upon two great facts, (1) that **"as the Father hath life in Himself, even so gave He to the Son also to have life in Himself,"** (2) that **"He gave Him authority to execute judgment, because He is the Son of Man"** (vv. 26, 27). The first does not imply that the Father had imparted life to the Son, it declares that as the Father is the source of life, so the Son in incarnation is the source, by reason of the appointment of the Father. Life stands here for the vivifying power. The life, the Divine counsels and operations, everything centers in Christ, and by reason of this and of His incarnation and what results from it, spiritual life becomes communicable only through Him.

The second statement, that His authority to act as the judge of all men is based upon the fact that He is **"the Son of Man"** (not here indicating His messiahship but His humanity) receives especial stress from the absence of the article in the original before both "Son" and "Man." He will judge as being in full understanding experimentally of human conditions, sin apart, and thus as sharing the nature of those He judges. Being Son of God He knows what only God knows, the possibilities of man (Matt. 11:21). He who is judge must be God and man.

The Two Resurrections

The astonishment of the Jews at such claims met with a still more startling proclamation. **"Marvel not at this,"** He says, **"for the hour cometh, in which all that are in the tombs shall hear His voice, and shall come forth; they that have done** [*poieō*] **good, unto the ["a"] resurrection of life; and they that have done** [*prassō*, have practiced] **ill, unto ["a"] resurrection of judgment."** The two resurrections, distinct in character (stressed by the absence of the article in each case), are shown in other Scriptures to be separated in time, *e.g.,* Revelation 20:4 to 6. What the Lord had already taught governs the statements as to doing good and ill. Doing good (plural) is that which marks the lives of those who have believed

and so have passed from death unto life (v. 24); doing evil (plural) is that which characterizes unbelievers, the unregenerate (Rom. 3:9; Gal. 3:10). The distinction between "have done" (*poieō*) and "have practiced" (*prassō*) lies in this, that *poieō* denotes an act complete in itself, while *prassō* denotes a habit (cp. 3:20, 21, where the same distinction is made).

Verses 30 to 38

Having declared His authority to execute judgment upon all men, the Lord repudiates any idea that this is a matter simply of His own will and doing, reiterating what He had said in verse 19. There, however, He said, "What I see the Father doing I do"; now He says, **"As I hear, I judge."** This is an additional attestation of the essential unity of the Father and Himself. Nevertheless He was here in entire and delighted subjection to the Father's will, which in itself was the guarantee of the infallible equity of His judgment: **"and My judgment,"** He says, **"is righteous; because I seek not Mine own will, but the will of Him that sent Me"** (v. 30). The judgment passed by the Jews was perverted because they sought their own will. The accuracy of our judgment in anything depends upon our entire subservience to the will of God.

In the latter part of this discourse (vv. 31–47) the Lord pointedly rebukes the unbelief of the Jews. The great force of His rebuke lies, however, in the continuation of His claims to His oneness with the Father, still answering the charge that He had made Himself equal with God.

The chief point in this vindication is

The Witness Given
Him by the Father

"If I bear witness of Myself, My witness is not true. It is Another that beareth witness of Me: and I know that the witness which He witnesseth of Me is true" (vv. 31, 32). As to the question who this "other" is, the answer is provided in verse 37. He designedly postpones the actual mention of the person, so that it may come the more forcefully by reason of the contrast to human witness, particularly that of John the Baptist, concerning whom they had sent making special inquiries (1:19). Moreover, the immediate necessity was to rebut any imputation that He was the sole source of His testimony. In that case, while the testimony would be true, it would be invalid. So for the moment He speaks of "Another," and proceeds with "and I know (*oida,* I have perfect knowledge) that the witness which He witnesseth of Me is true." The essence of His knowledge consisted in His unity with Him to whose voice He listened and whose will was His unremitting delight.

The Source of the Baptist's Light

He valued, as He alone could, and far more than they did, the witness of the Baptist; **"he hath borne witness** [perfect tense, expressing the enduring effect] **unto the truth." "He was the lamp** [*luchnos,* not a torch, but a portable lamp] **that burneth and shineth"** (v. 35). Christ Himself is the Light. From Him John, the human lamp, derived his light. Their rejoicing in John's witness was ephemeral and unproductive. If only they would realize and recognize that the source of his light was now testifying to them! **"I say these things that ye may be saved."** How wonderfully this exhibits the tender compassion of His heart, even toward the hardhearted and antagonistic! Verily these are words of One who was "full of grace and truth."

And now the Lord leads up to the definite statement as to the witness borne to Him by the Father, by speaking of the witness of His works. They are not simply His own doing **"the works which the Father hath given Me to accomplish, the very works that I do bear witness of Me that the Father hath sent Me."** This recalls verse 20, and, in the light of that, the works clearly are comprehensive not only of those of healing and similar signs but of the impartation of life, affecting the character and conduct of His followers, works accomplished by His teaching (as in the case of the conversion of the Samaritan woman, see 4:34). In His prayer in chapter 17 He sums up all, including the sacrifice of the Cross, in the phrase "the work" ("the work which Thou hast given Me to do," 17:4).

The comprehensive character of His reference to His works here is intimated in His statement that they are those "which the Fa-

ther hath given Me to accomplish," lit., "in order that I may accomplish." This being so, the way is now open for Him to make clear to whom He had referred when He said, "It is another that beareth witness of Me" (v. 32). **"And the Father which sent Me, He hath borne witness of Me."** There is the strongest emphasis both upon "the Father" and upon "He." This is

The Keystone of His Declarations

as to the various kinds of witness borne to Him. It manifests His keen pleasure in glorifying the Father. The witness of the Father was given not simply by the works which He wrought through Christ, it was especially borne, for instance, on the occasion of His baptism, when **"a voice came out of heaven, Thou art My beloved Son; in Thee I am well pleased"** (Luke 3:22).

Now, in His capacity as their judge, He proceeds to pronounce His judgment upon them. His remonstrances follow in solemn sequence. **"Ye have neither heard His voice at any time, nor seen His form. And ye have not His word abiding in you: for whom He sent Him ye believe not"** (vv. 37, 38). This is all closely connected. That they had neither heard the Father's voice nor seen His form, is reminiscent of God's words concerning Moses in Numbers 12:8, Moses combining in himself the promulgation of the Law and the function of the prophet. The Jews, who had neither understood nor heeded the voice of God to their nation, and especially that of Moses, on whom they had set their hope (v. 45), failed now to apprehend that the Father was speaking to them in and through the Son (cp. Heb: 1:2), and that the Son, whom they were refusing, was Himself the manifestation of the Father (*eidos,* the visible form or representation).

The connection between the voice and the form is repeated in what follows. As to the voice, *"Ye have not His word abiding in you,"* as to the person, **"whom the Father sent ye believe not."**

Verses 39 to 47

The Lord had spoken to His critical and unbelieving audience of three kinds of witness which had been borne to Him, that of John the Baptist, that of the Father, and that of His works. John's witness they simply made the subject of an inquiry. To the witness of the Father their unbelief blinded them. The witness of the works of Christ met with their criticism of His person and His claims, a criticism fostered by the misconceptions and prejudices of human tradition.

An Erroneous Use of Scripture

There was a further witness to Him, one with which they had been longer and more intimately acquainted than those already mentioned. To this He now draws attention. **"Ye search the Scriptures,"** He says, **"because** ye [emphatic] **think that in them** [emphatic] **ye have eternal life; and these** [emphatic—the objects of your search] **are they which bear witness of Me; and ye will not** [ye are not willing to] **come to Me, that ye may have life"** (vv. 39, 40). Whether the opening verb be regarded as indicative, "Ye search," or imperative, "Search" (and either is possible), the great point is that, while the Scriptures were theirs for their guidance, they were so out of touch with the mind of God therein revealed, that they failed to grasp their purport, that, namely of witnessing to Christ. They imagined that they had life simply by their possession of the Word of God, by their devotion to the letter of the Law, and by a formal perusal of the Scriptures, the real and divine purpose of which is to lead the reader to the lifegiver. In this lies the connection between His statements **"these are they which bear witness of Me,"** and **"ye will not come to Me that ye may have life."** The revelation and ministry of Christ to the soul are ever the paramount objects and power of the sacred page.

The True Source of Glory

The Lord follows this with the statement, **"I receive not glory from men."** As to the bearing of this upon the course of His remarks, the preposition *para*, "from," in this construction, indicates the source or origin. This at once suggests that the source of glory He received was not human; it was divine, it came from God (v. 44). Even the Scriptures, the import of which the Jews grievously

missed in not finding them a means of coming to Him to obtain eternal life, were not of human origin.

Now the true recognition of this and the consequent apprehension and application of the Scriptures as pointing to Christ, would produce the love of God in the heart, as they ever do when so applied. In all this His hearers utterly failed. **"But I know you,"** He says, **"that ye have not the love of God in yourselves"** (v. 42). It was all very well to boast in the Scriptures, but what did their use of them avail when they had not the love of God and refused to receive His Son, to whom the Scriptures bore witness? He had come in His Father's Name (as the personal presentation of, and with the authority of, the Father), and they received Him not.

But there was more than this in His declaration that He received not glory from men. That was just where the Jews erred. And their error lay at the root of their unbelief. **"How can ye believe,"** He says, **"which receive glory one of another, and the glory that cometh from the only God ye seek not?"** It was not want of proof that hindered faith on their part, it was pride, vanity and earthly desires, alienating their heart from God. Their rejection of Christ nationally would ultimately put them under the delusive power of the Antichrist: **"If another shall come in His own name, him ye will receive."** While that points on to the future national reception of the man of sin, the evil principle was working in their own hearts, and they were forerunners of the nation's final apostasy. To come in one's own name is to attract honor to oneself and seek human applause, and that is the very negation of the love of God. Christ had come to manifest the Father and to do nothing but His will. Hence the Father's glory ever shone transcendently in Him. With them there was neither the love of God nor the faith which worketh by love (v. 44). There is no neutral ground. Men must either receive Christ or suffer the blinding delusions of the powers of darkness and stand on the side of His foes.

The Great Subject of the Pentateuch

At the close of His discourse the Lord knocks away the very foundation of their false confidence. He increases the force of His blow by preceding it with the negative statement that He will not Himself act as their accuser to the Father (v. 45). Nay, His immediate object was their salvation (v. 34). Their accuser was Moses, on whom they had "set their hope." They imagined that in accusing Christ of breaking the sabbath they were defending the Law of Moses, which, however, condemned them (cp. Deut. 31:21, 26; 32:28). Their rejection of Christ was, in point of fact, a rejection of Moses. **"For if,"** He says, **"ye believed Moses, ye would believe Me; for he wrote of Me."**

In this He states the outstanding subject of the whole Pentateuch, testifying at the same time to its authorship, authority and divine inspiration. The emphasis may be brought out by the rendering "It was of Me that he wrote." His statement (which recalls His words as to all the Scriptures, v. 39) affords us the great guide to a right understanding of the much-criticized and misunderstood Pentateuch. Happy is he who, assured of a response, breathes the prayer.

> *Teach me to love the sacred page*
> *And view my Savior there.*

With what solemn abruptness the Lord closes His discourse! "For if ye believe not his writings how shall ye believe My words?" It is virtually an exclamatory protest, and in it He puts the writings of Moses in the same divine category as His own words. He demands the acceptance of each as a matter of faith. Refusal means the loss of valid hope of salvation.

A Review

Reviewing this discourse we may observe that it contains twelve great subjects: (1) The essential relation between the Father and the Son (vv. 19-21); (2) The commission, authority and dignity of the Son (vv. 22, 23); (3) The everlasting blessings of those who believe (v. 24); (4) Spiritual resurrection (v. 25); (5) Christ the lawgiver (v. 26); (6) Christ the judge (v. 27); (7) Universal physical resurrection (vv. 28, 29); (8) The infallible judgment of Christ (v. 30); (9) Witness to Christ, by the Father, John the Baptist, Christ's works, the Scriptures (vv. 31, 39); (10) Man's perverse will and consequent ruin (vv. 38, 40-43); (11) The love of man's praise as the cause of unbelief (v. 44); (12) The importance, claims and object of the writings of Moses (vv. 45, 46).

JOHN

▪ CHAPTER SIX ▪

Introduction

In chapter five the Lord is seen as the source of life, and that in respect of His relation to the Father. In chapter six He is seen as the supporter of life, and that by reason of His relation to the believer. In this chapter there is again, as in chapter five, first a sign, or miracle, and then a discourse arising from it, but now the results of the discourse are narrated. In addition to the sign given in public, that of the feeding of the five thousand, there is a sign privately to the disciples, that of His walking on the water.

Verses 1 to 25

Again the Lord turns His back on Judaism and goes to Galilee. The Lord had been doing signs continually (the verb rendered **"He did,"** v. 2, is in the imperfect tense, "He was doing"), especially in the healing of the sick. As a result of this **"a great multitude"** was following Him. As the Passover, here called **"the feast of the Jews,"** was drawing near, there would be large numbers of people going up to Jerusalem, and it is just possible that the crowd would be augmented thereby.

Now it seems evident from verse 1 that the Lord had gone away to get rest and quiet, and to pray (see Matthew and Mark). When, however, He saw the multitude toiling up the hill, whither He had gone with His disciples, His heart, instead of being disturbed by the interruption, was moved with compassion. He had known everything beforehand and His many signs were wrought so as to lead up to this great act with all its spiritual significance.

Dependence on Christ

But the Lord had His eye on the disciples, and especially now upon Philip. So He asks him, **"Whence are we to buy loaves that these may eat?"** the object being to test his

faith and turn his mind from mere material resources to Himself as the great personal means of meeting every need, and so lead him to be occupied more with Himself, His power and grace, than with circumstances. That is just what we all need. The heart must realize its dependence upon Christ Himself and be occupied with Him more than with difficulties and exigencies. He desired to make Philip and his fellow disciples grasp the fact that, though they had neither loaves nor money adequate for the occasion, they had the Lord Himself.

Philip remarked that even about a year's wages* would not buy enough loaves for all that multitude. Andrew, like Philip, is occupied with material things and their insufficiency. How meager are such thoughts! And what a majestic contrast is presented by the Lord as He says, **"Make the people sit down"** (v. 10)! The word *anthrōpous* is rightly rendered "people," for it includes both sexes, whereas in the latter part of the verse the word is *andres*, men. That was His one preparation for the manifestation of His powers of godhood, and of His grace and mercy.

Divine Economy

As the people, now in orderly groups, witnessed how He gave thanks and how their need was more than supplied, they were preparing to make Him their messianic king, regarding Him as the promised prophet, foretold in Deuteronomy 18:15. There was one thing that must have impressed the disciples especially, if not the people themselves, in that, while He could minister bountifully, it was not a case of mere lavishness, this was economy: nor a case of mere wonder-work, every detail had divine significance. The fragments must be gathered up "that nothing be lost." What need was there for this, considering that the Lord could multiply food at His will? There was the lesson to be learnt, that there must be no waste. No idea must be entertained that,

---

*Publisher's note: The original says, "£8."

considering what was possible as to further acts of bounty, there must be no disregard for what might naturally be considered as superfluous. For everything had a significance; no act was without its meaning. The provision of such supplies of bread was introductory to spiritual teaching of the utmost importance concerning the Bread of Life.

In this connection John purposely omits reference to the fragments of fish (whereas Mark mentions them, Mark 6:43), for the spiritual application to follow is a matter of that life of the nourishment of which the bread was symbolical.

The High Priest of His Disciples

And now the great provider has to withdraw from all this popular excitement regarding Him. Instead of becoming the people's king, and that in a way contrary to the Father's will and to Scripture testimony, He takes a position which sets Him forth as the high priest of His people. He goes up into the mountain, from whence He can consider the needs of His followers, pray for them, and come to their assistance in a time of danger (v. 15).

Evening had come on; it had become dark; the disciples had entered a boat and were well on their way across the sea to go to Capernaum.

The Purpose of the Storm

So now, having become the object of their faith in the matter of providing food, He makes Himself the object of their faith amidst peril. The creator of bread was likewise the creator of the waters, and whether they were too tempestuous or calm His power was to be in evidence in each respect. The trust of His followers must be amplified.

He stills their fears with His **"It is I; be not afraid,"** and stills the storm. His will to pass them by (Mark 6:8), to deepen their confidence in Him, issues in their will to receive Him into their boat. **"They were willing"** to do so (R.V.). But there is an additional act in the sign given to them. The boat immediately arrives at its destination. Distance is nullified by His powers. His presence is both protection and deliverance. So He bringeth them at once "to their desired haven."

There follows the incident of the efforts of the multitude to seek for Jesus. They had remained in the locality where the Lord had provided the bread, and next day, finding that He and the disciples had gone, the people took boats and came to Capernaum, astonished to find that He was there already. All this, and their question as to when He came across, is both the sequel to what had taken place on the mountain slope, and introductory to His discourse concerning Himself as the means of life.

THE SECOND PUBLIC DISCOURSE
Verses 26 to 59

Introduction

This discourse is divided into two parts: (1) verses 26 to 40, (2) verses 43 to 59. The first answers the application of the multitude to Him because of the miracle that He had wrought; the second is a reply to the murmuring of the Jews.

Each part contains the same two leading truths, (1) that Christ is the Bread of Life, (2) that as such He came from Heaven to earth to give life to men. These subjects are conveyed in four distinct statements in each section. They are as follows.

In the first part: (1) **"My Father giveth you the true bread out of Heaven"** (v. 32); (2) **"The bread of God is that which cometh out of Heaven and giveth life unto the world"** (v. 33); (3) **"I am the bread of life"** (v. 35); (4) **"I am come down from Heaven"** (v. 38).

In the second part: (1) **"I am the bread of life"** (v. 48); (2) **"This is the bread which cometh down out of Heaven, that a man may eat thereof and not die"** (v. 50); (3) **"I am the living bread which came down out of Heaven: if any man eat of this bread he shall live forever"** (v. 51); (4) **"This is the bread which came down out of Heaven . . . he that eateth this bread shall live forever"** (v. 58).

Other Similar Details in Each Part

In addition to these statements concerning Christ as the Bread of Life, (1) each division of the discourse contains "Verily, verily" twice: those in the first part both introduce denials of the suppositions entertained by the Lord's hearers (vv. 26, 32); those in the second part introduce the conditions for the possession of eternal life (vv. 47, 53). (2) In each He speaks of the provision of life for the world (vv. 33, 51). (3) Each contains a twofold statement concerning coming to Christ; they are as follows: **"Him that cometh to Me I will in no wise cast out"** (vv. 37); in the second part: **"No man can come to me, except the Father which sent Me draw him"** (v. 44); **"everyone that hath heard from the Father and hath learned, cometh unto Me"** (v. 45). (4) Again, in the first part there are two statements concerning seeing the Father; the two in the first part form a contrast: **"ye have seen Me, and yet believe not"** (v. 36); **"everyone that beholdeth** [a different word from that in v. 36, which we notice later; the difference is missed in the A.V.] **the Son and believeth on Him . . . "** (v. 40). The distinction is between unbelievers and believers. In the second part the Lord speaks of Himself as the only One who has seen the Father. **"Not that any man hath seen the Father, save He which is from God, He hath seen the Father"** (v. 46). (5) Each of the divisions contains a reference to the provision of the manna in the wilderness (vv. 32, 58). (6) Each contains the assurance that the Lord Himself will raise from the dead those who believe upon Him (vv. 40, 54).

Outstanding Facts and Contrasts

The whole discourse may be viewed under the following headings:

I. The contrast between natural bread and Christ the spiritual bread (vv. 26–35).

II. Christ the spiritual bread in relation to the Father (vv. 32, 40).

III. The contrast between the manna and Christ the spiritual bread, with an extended definition of the latter (vv. 43–51).

IV. The flesh and blood of Christ (with reference to His death), the means of spiritual nourishment: a final contrast between the manna and Christ the spiritual bread (vv. 53–58).

The Second Public Discourse in Detail
Verses 26, 27

Discarding the question of the multitude, the Lord replies by exposing to themselves their actual motive for seeking Him, and proceeds to urge upon them the deeper needs of their souls. He begins with a "Verily, verily," lit., "Amen, Amen," a mode of arresting attention which was frequently upon His lips. It introduces a subject of pressing urgency by reason of its essential importance, and usually because it runs counter to, or exceeds, the ideas in the minds of His hearers.

"Verily, verily, I say unto you. Ye seek Me," He says, **"not because ye saw signs, but because ye ate of the loaves, and were filled. Work not for the meat which perisheth, but for the meat which abideth unto eternal life, which the Son of Man shall give unto you: for Him the Father, even God, hath sealed"** (vv. 36, 27). His "work not" has a comparative force: the spiritual nourishment is a matter of far greater concern than the material. And what toil they had given themselves in endeavoring to find Him! With a view doubtless to obtaining more bread! His injunction was certainly not against earning their living; the R.V. rightly has "work" instead of "labor," as the same word is used by His hearers in the next verse. Let their pursuits be directed to obtaining the spiritual food. It abides. A hint perhaps against their idea of getting continual supplies of material bread from Him! The spiritual bread abides unto eternal life: it sustains forever. And there it was for the having. Let them do the real seeking and they shall find. The Son of man gives it. He is the provider of the vastly more important spiritual sustenance.

The Sealing of the Bread of Life

The sealing here signifies the authentication, the commissioning with authority, by God, of the Son of man as the sole giver of eternal life. The allusion may be to the impress of a mark by bakers upon their loaves, or, with a typical reference, to the testing and sealing of lambs for sacrifice, foreshadowing Christ as the Passover Lamb (other suggestions seem less satisfactory).

Verses 28 to 35

The Lord's admonition to the Jews to **"work . . . for the meat which abideth unto eternal life,"** elicited from them the apparently acquiescent inquiry (earnest enough, we may suppose), **"What must we do that we may work the works of God?"** They perceived that His remarks had a moral implication in contrast to their materialistic conceptions. How then should they act so as to do works pleasing to God and then obtain the imperishable spiritual bread?

"And That Not of Yourselves"

His reply strikes immediately at the idea, so innate in the hearts of men, that the favor and mercy of God are conditional upon human merit and self-effort. Man's fallen condition should of itself suffice to demolish such expectations. But that is just what men fail to recognize. Man must be ruled out; God alone can meet the need. And God has met it, and that in the person and work of His Son, His sent One. But this requires a divine revelation. God has given it. He has "spoken unto us in His Son." But this again requires faith. And God who bestowed upon man the faculty of faith, has given "assurance unto all men (this word *pistis* in Acts 17:31, which ordinarily denotes faith, here signifies a ground for faith), in that He hath raised Him from the dead."

Accordingly, the Lord states directly and specifically that **"This is the work of God, that ye believe on Him whom He hath sent"** (v. 29). The reply is anticipative of the great doctrine for which the apostle Paul contends in Romans and Galatians, justification by faith, in contrast to the futility of works. It is not "do" but "trust."

The Jews, like many others, could not look upon things that way. They must have tangible evidence, something for the natural vision. Seeing is believing. Such is blind unbelief. **"What then,"** they say, **"doest Thou for a sign, that we may see, and believe Thee? What workest Thou?"** Moreover, had not their fathers been granted through Moses something for the natural sight, and bread for the natural man? If then the One who addressed them was the Messiah and therein greater than Moses, would He not demonstrate this by a confirmatory sign?

"The True Bread"

Again, the Lord repudiates their ideas with a **"Verily, verily, I say unto you,"** and with a denial and a contrast: **"It was not Moses that gave you the bread out of Heaven: but My Father giveth you the true bread out of Heaven."** The word *alēthinos* denotes true, not in the sense of actual, or true to fact *(alēthēs),* but of that which is ideal, as well as genuine; it is also used of Christ in 1:9; 15:1; 1 John 2:8; 5:20 (thrice); Revelation 3:7, 14; 19:11. Just as to the Samaritan woman He had contrasted the "living water" with that of the well sacred to the name of Jacob, so now He contrasts Himself as the true bread, with that which they attributed to the provision made by Moses.

Reserving for the moment the specific identification of Himself as this "true Bread," He confirms its character as follows: **"For the bread of God is that which cometh down out of heaven, and giveth life unto the world"** (v. 33). Two contrasts stand out in this: (1) whereas the manna is spoken of as "bread from Heaven" (Ps. 78:24), and "the bread of Heaven" (Ps. 105:40), the Lord stresses His "coming down out of Heaven" attesting the fact of His descent to earth by His incarnation as the Son of man and as the One sent by the Father (vv. 27, 29); (2) whereas the manna could not prevent their "fathers" from dying ("their carcasses fell in the wilderness"), the true bread imparts an imperishable life; and whereas the manna was the exclusive privilege of Israel, the true bread ministers life to the world, that is to all who partake of it, racial distinctions being ruled out.

An Earnest Request and the Great Disclosure

This elicits from them the request **"Lord,** (why was it not rendered "Sir," as in the utterance of the Samaritan woman in 4:15? They were not addressing Him as humble followers in willing submission to His authority), **evermore give us this bread."** The request was sincere enough; they believed in His power, though they disbelieved His mission.

The Lord answers this by a climax of stupendous disclosures concerning Himself which constitute the remainder of the first part of this discourse. As, again, to the Samaritan woman, He had turned upon Himself the full light of His revelations, when He said, "I that speak unto thee am He," so now He says to the people, **"I am the bread of life: he that cometh to Me shall not hunger, and he that believeth on Me shall never thirst."** This claim, so unambiguous, so authoritative, so imperative, could have but one of two effects upon His hearers. Life abundant, unendingly sustained, would be theirs upon believing on Him by coming to Him. Refusal, with its evidence of lack of appetite for the bread He gives, involved the spiritual death of separation from Him. Their choice is made clear in the rest of the chapter. The alternatives still remain for all to whom the offer comes.

Coming and Believing

The Lord's two statements are in the couplet form of Hebrew parallelisms. In the original each contains the same strong double negative (*ou mē*, "by no means"), and the combined declarations close with the strongly stressed "never" (*pōpote*), which, standing in its emphatic position at the end, governs both, as if to say, "He that cometh to Me shall by no means hunger, and he that believeth on Me shall by no means thirst, no never." As hungering and thirsting express what can be met conjointly by natural supplies, so coming to Christ and believing on Him are the indissociable means of the supply of spiritual need.

The figure He uses is of paramount significance. Bread means nourishment, sustenance, strength, the building up of the very tissues of life. And this, spiritually, is what Christ becomes to the believer. Communicating His life to us He becomes part of our very selves, the strength of our soul. He is the adequate supply of every spiritual need, the full satisfaction of every spiritual desire. We cannot live the natural life without bread. We cannot live the spiritual life without Christ. He who is thus sustained by Him can say with the apostle, "Christ liveth in me." And what possibilities this holds for one who knows the joy and power of this holy union of life and love! Such can truly say, "I can do all things in Him that strengtheneth me."

Verses 36 to 40

The promises, conditional upon coming to Christ, of never hungering or thirsting, were hindered of fulfillment in the case of the Jews by their persistent unbelief. This He forcibly brought home to them by His contrasting statement, **"But I said unto you, that ye have seen Me, and yet believe not"** (6:36), the reference probably being to their having seen Him as the miraculous provider of bread, without their having entered into any relation with Him by faith (vv. 26–29). Their hearts, naked and open to Him, entirely lacked any appreciation of the real character of His person, His acts, and His ways. How many hear of Him and get no farther than they did!

Divine Election and Human Free Will

His next words make clear, however, that their unbelief did not argue any frustration of His mission: **"All that which the Father giveth Me shall come to Me: and him that cometh to Me I will in no wise cast out"** (v. 37). This sublime utterance conveys two fundamental facts regarding God and man, (1) the eternal foreknowledge and electing purpose of God in salvation, (2) the exercise of human free will to accept God's conditions or to reject them. Human experience confirms both verities. There is no inconsistency therein. The twofold operation is expressed in the well-known words, "the grace of God by Christ preventing us, that we may have a good will, and working with us, when we have that good will."

Note the change from "all that which" to "him that." The former, expressed in the neuter, views the whole body of believers as an entity and unity foreseen and predetermined by the Father, stressing this apart from the offer made to, and accepted or refused by, individuals (see also v. 39, and cp. the same use of the neuter in 17:2, "whatsoever," and 17:24, "that which Thou hast given Me"). Then follows the masculine, speaking of each individual who, exercising his will to accept the offer, decides to come to Christ (cp. again the same change to the personal in 17:2 and 24).

There is a change also in the verbs rendered "shall come" and "cometh." The former *(hekō)* stresses the arrival and the being present, and here from the Father's point of view; the latter *(erchomai)* presents the act of coming and marks the voluntary decision of the comer.

The strong negative "in no wise" suggests that, so far from casting out a believer, the Lord will embrace and protect him; it conveys something more than the promise to receive, it carries with it the assurance of eternal security, and intimates the delight of the Lord in his grace toward what is given Him by the Father (for the confirmation of the irreversible and unending security of the believer, see also 1:25, 26).

The Will of the Father

All this, with His assurances of resurrection, He now bases upon (1) the fact of His having come from heaven to do the Father's will, (2) the design of His will. He says, **"For I am come down from Heaven, not to do Mine own will, but the will of Him that sent Me. And this is the will of Him that sent Me, that I should lose nothing, but should raise it up at the last day. For this is the will of My Father, that every one that beholdeth the Son and believeth on Him, should have eternal life; and I will raise him up at the last day"** (vv. 38–40).

The significance of the connecting "For" lies in this, that His having come from heaven to carry out the will of the Father in the eternal salvation of those who come to Him, rules out the possibility of His casting out one such. Four times the Lord speaks of His coming down from heaven, here and verses 50, 51, 58. He thus precludes the idea that He is expressing simply His own opinion or speaking for Himself.

Again the neuter is used, signifying the complete company of believers viewed as an entity. That He will not lose any implies His guarding care (cp. 17:12; 18:9). This negative is followed by the positive declaration of His consummating act in their resurrection, an act which confirms the assurance of their eternal security.

The statement as to resurrection is repeated, with the same change as has been noted above. When He says, firstly, that it is the Father's will that He should raise up at the last day all that which He has given Him (the entire company), He is declaring the salvation of believers from the Father's point of view. When He repeats His assurance, and says "I will raise him [the individual believer] up at the last day," He is regarding the matter from the point of view of the believer himself as one that "beholdeth the Son and believeth on Him." In the first pronouncement He gives the assurance that He will lose nothing, all is the gift of the Father; in the second each one has eternal life, as the result of his faith.

No Outer Darkness for Any Believer

This pledge that everyone will be raised, as the result of having been given Him irrevocably, utterly refutes the erroneous doctrine that certain believers will be cast into the outer darkness during the millennium on account of their state of unwatchfulness at the time of His Second Coming.

The verb rendered "beholdeth" is *theōreō* (not the simple verb *horaō*, to see, as in the A.V.); it indicates a close contemplation or careful perusal, and the meaning is, "everyone who contemplates the Son with the effect of believing on Him." It was not so with the Jews. They had seen Him *(horaō)* and did not believe. A person cannot believe in the Lord Jesus Christ and be saved without that measure of consideration of His person and work of redeeming grace which results in faith in Him. No mere passing consideration is sufficient.

As to the phrase "at the last day," the word is used to mark the time in which all who have part in the first resurrection will be raised, both those at the Rapture (1 Thess. 4:16) and those who, having suffered death during "the time of Jacob's trouble" or "the great tribulation," will be raised subsequently (Rev. 20:4–6). The Lord did not disclose such details to the Jews. Nor would they have received it. And though He revealed the subject more fully to His disciples later in the Upper Room, the full revelation was reserved for apostolic ministry after churches had been formed. This gradual process of the unfolding of prophetic truth at different times in the course of divine revelation demands consideration in order for a right perspective of the purposes of God.

Verses 41 to 46

The interruption in the Lord's remarks, by the murmuring of the Jews, is suggestive of their dissatisfaction with His exposure of the condition of their hearts. The immediate reason was His claim involving their deprivation of eternal life through their refusal to accept Him. They evidently felt this. As a matter of fact, His guarantee of resurrection to life is the crowning point of the truth that He is the Bread of Life.

Unbelief's Excuses

Unbelief is ever ready to make excuses. Accordingly, ignoring the implication of His assurances of life eternal and resurrection for those whom He contrasted with their own guilty attitude, they support their self-complacency by the mutterings of their presumed acquaintance with the circumstances of His birth: **"Is not this Jesus, the Son of Joseph, whose father and mother we know? How doth He now say, I am come down out of Heaven?"** Their plausible questioning, virtually impugning His veracity, was simply an evasion of the chief point of His testimony.

A Lesson for the Preacher

While briefly rebuking their grumbling, He does not answer their objections, nor does He convey the facts of His birth, or repudiate the calumnies of the Jews concerning it. To do so would have but plunged them deeper into their darkness. The matters of immediate and paramount importance are their own spiritual need and danger, not the mode of His coming into the world, but the means of their coming to Him. What a lesson for the preacher of the gospel when confronted with skeptical arguments on side issues of theology!

"Murmur not among yourselves," He says. **"No man can come to Me, except the Father draw him."** This necessity of the drawing power of the Father presses home again the sovereignty of God, while what follows enforces the responsibility of man to come to, that is, to believe on, His Son

(vv. 45–51), just as the same two facts were combined in verse 37. The power of the Father to draw is available for those who are willing to come.

Then, for the third time, stressing the tremendous importance of the fact for His hearers, He declares that He will raise up at the last day him who comes. The divine attracting begins the work of salvation; resurrection will complete it.

How the Lord Appealed to Scripture

He now directs them to the Scriptures, with a deeply significant connection with, and continuance of, the subject of coming to Him; **"It is written in the prophets, And they shall all be taught of God. Everyone that hath heard from the Father, and hath learned, cometh unto Me"** (v. 45). Here the Lord uses the prophecy of Isaiah 54:13 (a passage foretelling millennial blessing) to show that God draws men by teaching, not by legal statutes, nor by outward vision, nor by mere action on the emotions, but by gracious instruction, and that His teaching has Christ Himself as its object. His quotation does not imply that the Scripture provides Him with His doctrine; nay, He confirms His doctrine by appealing to the Scripture.

The Necessity of Coming to the Son

Later on to the disciples He says, **"No one cometh unto the Father but by Me"** (14:6). Now He says, No one cometh unto Me but by the Father (v. 44). Yet it remains the responsibility of men to hear and learn, and so, by the Father's instruction, to come to the Son, in whom all the counsels of grace and glory center.

But why does He now say, **"Not that any man hath seen the Father, save He which is from God; He hath seen the Father"**? Firstly, to prevent any idea that the Son is to be dissociated from the Father. Their unity He stresses in a subsequent discourse (10:30). Secondly, to show that the revelation of the Father is by the Son: "The only begotten Son, which is in the bosom of the Father, He hath declared Him" (1:18): "He that hath seen Me hath seen the Father" (14:9). Thirdly, to show that any access to the Father s to be distinguished absolutely from that open, immediate and uninterrupted vision enjoyed alone by the Son. He thus puts Himself above Moses, whom the Lord knew only "face to face" (Deut. 34:10). Fourthly, to enforce upon His hearers not only the fact of His deity as the Son, but the necessity of coming to the Son as the One who, in virtue of this, can alone be the means of spiritual life and subsistence.

The preposition *para*, "from," in the phrase "He which is from God," signifies "from beside," "from (being) with"; it indicates source of origin (cp. 15:26, of the Holy Spirit). While pondering over such phraseology, we need to bear in mind the unity of the Three in One Godhead. As has been well said, They are "neither three Gods, nor three parts of God. Rather they are God threefoldly, God tripersonally. The personal distinction in the Godhead is a distinction within, and of, unity, not a distinction which qualifies unity, or usurps the place of it, or destroys it." All this remained true and in continuity throughout the life of Christ on earth.

Verses 47 to 51

In verse 47 we come to the Lord's third "Verily, verily," each being, as we have noticed, designed to arrest the attention of His hearers in a particular way. In what follows He declares still more explicitly certain facts which He had before stated. Albeit His teaching leads up to a point (concerning His "flesh") which, owing to their unbelief and hardness of heart, becomes judicially more difficult and unacceptable to their prejudiced minds. And this, as we shall see, increases as He proceeds further toward the close of His discourse. Persistent unbelief makes truth all the harder to grasp.

The Living Bread: The Provision and Purpose

"Verily, verily, I say unto you, He that believeth hath eternal life. I am the bread of life." The first statement recalls more definitely what He said in verse 40. It is now not "should have" but "hath." His second statement reiterates what He said in verse 35. The repetition is due to the fact that this was the special point of their murmuring (v. 41). He then refers again to the subject of the manna. When they had remarked that their fathers "ate the manna in the wilderness," His reply presented the subject from the point of view of gifts from God, both the manna and Himself, the true bread as the gift of the Father. Now He states the contrast in regard to the receivers. Their fathers ate the manna and "died." Even the manna, the typical bread, did not suffice to maintain physical life in perpetuity. He, the Antitype, is "the bread which cometh down out of Heaven, that a man [anyone] may eat thereof and not die [the divine purpose, and the unbounded provision]." "I am," He says, "the living Bread which came down out of Heaven" (vv. 50, 51). It is important to notice the difference between the present tense, "cometh down," and the aorist, the past definite, "came down." The former does not signify a continual coming down, it indicates the inherent characteristic of the bread, defining (as the article with the present participle does) that which is essential to its nature and to the circumstances indicated. The past tense denotes the historic fact of the descent, the act by which He became incarnate (cp. v. 33). In verse 38 the perfect tense is used, "I have come down," expressing the fact with stress upon the abiding effects.

Again, in each part of this discourse the Lord couples with the fact that the Father sent Him His own voluntary act in coming, in delighted fulfillment of the Father's will. He "sent Me" (v. 44); "I . . . came down" (v. 51). We must note, too, the change from "I am the bread" (v. 48) to "This is the bread" (v. 50), and the change from that again to "I am" in verse 51. The "This is" suggests a demonstrative reference to their ignorant reasoning, "Is not this Jesus, the son of Joseph?" (v. 42).

The Sending and the Coming

Further, He had hitherto said "I am the bread of life" (vv. 35, 48). Now He says "I am the living Bread," with special stress on "living." There is a difference. The former statement stresses the impartation of life by reason of the characteristic nature and productive power of His person: the latter stresses the essential principle and quality of life which is inherent in Himself.

What a contrast to the lifeless manna, which, under certain conditions, went to corruption! It sustained life just for the day. For those who by faith receive Christ, the living bread, He becomes in them a veritable principle of imperishable life, causing them to live forever.

This confirms positively the preceding negative, **"that a man may live and not die."** So that more than spiritual life is therein assured. To live forever involves the resurrection life hereafter, the eternal life of the whole person, body, soul and spirit. With this in view He had given the assurance, **"I will raise him up at the last day"** (v. 40).

A Climax and a Parallel

His teaching now reaches a climax, in statements more difficult of apprehension for His incredulous hearers than anything He had said hitherto. And the difficulty increases as He proceeds after their interruption. He says, **"Yea, and the bread which I will give is My flesh, for the life of the world."** His "flesh"! In this addition lay a staggering difficulty for them, and they are not alone in experiencing it.

The statement, coupled with what follows, is exhaustive and forms the subject of the next chapter. We may now notice the parallelism between verses 48 to 50 and 51.

(a) **"I am the bread of life"** (v. 48):
(b) **"I am the living bread"** (v. 51).

(a) **"Your fathers did eat manna and died"** (v. 49):
(b) **"If any man eat of this Bread, he shall live forever"** (v. 51).

(a) **"which cometh down out of Heaven"** (v. 50):
(b) **"which came down out of Heaven"** (v. 51).

(a) **"that a man may eat thereof and not die"** (v. 50):
(b) **"the bread which I will give is My flesh, for the life of the world"** (v. 51).

Feasting on the Living Bread

How fully He is able to supply our spiritual needs! What an infinite wealth of provision resides in Him for our growth and development, our strength and refreshment, enabling us to "grow up into Him," becoming conformed to His image (Rom. 8:29)! And all the outcome of His going down into death that we, having been identified with Him therein, and "becoming conformed unto His death," might here and now, in the power of His resurrection, walk in newness of life. May we ever feast upon the living bread. Only so can we in any measure here and now "attain unto the resurrection from the dead" (Phil. 3:11).

A Summing Up

The Lord now sums up His discourse by reaffirming, with three reminders, the main facts of His discourse: (1) He is **"the bread which came down from Heaven,"** (2) their fathers ate manna and yet died, (3) **"He that eateth this bread** [Himself "the true Bread," v. 32, "the living bread," v. 51] **shall live forever."** He thus makes a closing appeal for faith in Him.

All this was said in the Capernaum synagogue. The congregation included a considerable number of disciples (many more than the twelve), not a few of whom regarded His speech (logos would seem to include the discourse as a whole), as "hard," i.e., difficult to accept, an obstacle to their faith; who could listen to it? They were talking to one another in a low tone.

"But Jesus, knowing in Himself [intuitively perceiving] **that His disciples murmured at this, said unto them, Doth this cause you to stumble? What then if ye should behold the Son of Man ascending where He was before?"** He refers to His ascension. He does not say that they would see it. His rhetorical question did, however, apply to those in the company who actually witnessed it.

His question carries with it the implication of His resurrection and the certainty of His ascension. That event would be the complete vindication and ratification of all His testimony.

Having conveyed the fact of the spiritual and vital import of what He had stated regarding Himself as the Bread of Life and His flesh and blood as the means of life, He reveals the separative effect of His message, separative because of the faith of some and the unbelief of others: **"But there are some of you that believe not."** He **"knew from the beginning who they were that believed not, and,"** among them, in contradistinction to the eleven of His inner circle of disciples, **"who it was that should betray Him."** He knew in precise detail the way in which His death would be accomplished. The shadow of Calvary ever lay across His soul!

Apostasy or Fidelity?

The separative power of His ministry is seen in regard not only to believers but to professed followers. For, following upon His repeated declaration that no one could come to Him **"except it be given of the Father** [all who believe are known to God as such before and to those it is given to come], **many of His disciples went back and walked no more with Him."** Defection or devotion? The choice lies with us in our day.

So it has ever been. The gospel is either the word of life to those who accept it, or a ministry of death to those who refuse: it is "the power of God" to those "who are being saved," but "foolishness" to "them that are perishing."

Verses 52 to 71

When the Lord said to His unbelieving hearers **"the bread which I will give is My flesh,"** He knew that this would meet with a stronger objection on their part than anything He had said previously. Their unbelief retributively made the unfolding of the mystery of His person and purpose for which He had come into the world the more difficult for them to understand. And the difficulty was enhanced when, after their altercation with one another and the skeptical nature of their question, **"How can this man give His flesh to eat?"** He went further and said, **"Verily, verily, I say unto you, except ye eat the flesh of the Son of Man and drink His blood, ye have not life in yourselves. He that eateth My flesh and drinketh My blood hath eternal life; and I will raise him up at the last day. For My flesh is meat indeed, and My blood is drink indeed,"** an astonishing statement to Jews in view of Leviticus 17:10 to 16!

What was a stumbling block to them, and has been the subject of much misinterpretation in Christendom, receives its true interpretation, not from the bias of ecclesiastical tradition, but from the Scriptures themselves, and indeed from the Lord's subsequent remarks to His disciples. The Jews persistently took His statements to refer to literal blood and flesh and to the physical acts of eating and drinking. This erroneous view He repudiated in the explanation, **"It is the spirit that quickeneth; the flesh profiteth nothing: the words that I have spoken unto you are spirit, and are life. But there are some of you that believe not."**

His Flesh and His Blood

His "flesh" stands here, not simply for His bodily frame, but for the entire manhood, spirit, soul and body of the Son of man, Who, by giving Himself up to the death of the cross, provided Himself thereby as the means of eternal life and sustenance. His "blood" represents, not simply the physical element, but the giving up of His life by atoning sacrifice, in the shedding of His blood. The blood is essential to life. "For the life of the flesh is in the blood . . . for it is the blood that maketh atonement by reason of life" (Lev. 17:11, R.V.). Thus the saving efficacy of the death of Christ depends upon the fact that by the shedding of His blood He gave His life (Matt. 20:28), that "He gave Himself up" (Gal. 2:20).

Not the Lord's Supper: A Distinction

What He says in this sixth chapter has no reference to the Lord's Supper. And for the following reasons: (a) Had the Supper been in view, to eat of the bread of the Supper would constitute the participant a partaker of eternal life apart from the condition of faith in Christ; (b) the paramount subject in this part of the discourse is eternal life: that subject is never mentioned in connection with the Lord's Supper; (c) to take His teaching to refer to that, is to give a literal application, whereas He plainly indicates that His words concerning His flesh and blood were not so intended; (d) He says that the giving of His flesh is "for the life of the world"; the Lord's Supper was instituted not for the world but for His disciples; (e) in His instruction concerning the Supper He speaks of His body, whereas here He speaks of His flesh.

Five Resulting Benefits

The solemn warning in verse 53 of the consequences of not partaking of His flesh and blood is followed by a series of gracious assurances as to the blessedness of doing so:

1. To eat His flesh and drink His blood, that is, to appropriate to oneself the saving efficacy of His death, is to be in *possession of eternal life*. In verse 54 the word for eating is changed from the general term *phagō*, which was used previously, to *trōgō*, which is used in the rest of the discourse. This verb, primarily signifying to chew, lays stress upon the process of eating; it is thus more intensive than *phagō*, and the change marks an increase in the difficulty of His language for His skeptical audience.

2. He will *raise him up at the last day*. For the third time, and with evident joy in the repetition and in the assured prospect of His mighty act, the Lord looks on to His final victory over death.

3. **"For My flesh is meat indeed, and My blood is drink indeed"**—or, closely to the original, *"true food"* and *"true drink"* (see R.V. margin; cp. v. 32).

4. **"He that eateth My flesh, and drinketh My blood, abideth in Me, and I in him,"** *a mutual indwelling* of which the Lord speaks more fully to the disciples later in the Upper Room, a permanent oneness of life and the deepest intimacy of communion. The believer finds his life in Christ, and Christ imparts His to the believer.

5. **"As the living Father sent Me, and I live because of the Father; so he that eateth Me, he also shall live because of Me."** The phrase "the living Father" implies His self-existence and describes Him as the One in whom life, unoriginated, resides essentially. He is therefore also the center and source of life. So with the Son, Who is one with the Father (10:30). Here He testifies that, as the Son, the sent one, who had become man, He lives **"because of** [or by reason of, not "by," as in the A.V.] **the Father"** (see 5:26). And since the Son communicates life to the one who by faith appropriates Him to himself the believer lives and ever will live by reason of Him.

Christ and the Twelve

In verses 67 to 71 there is a distinction between the Twelve and those disciples who ceased to walk with Christ. This is the first mention of the Twelve as such. Here Peter's fidelity becomes conspicuous. When the Lord says "Would ye also go away?" (not "will ye?" as if a future possibility), He means "Surely ye also do not desire to go." He knew their loyalty. The whole passage marks His omniscience.

Peter's answer has three reasons why they cannot leave Him, and these in designed order: (1) His uniqueness as the master, (2) His fullness as the teacher, (3) His divine personality: (1) **"to whom shall we go?"** (no teacher remained since the Baptist had gone); (2) **"Thou hast (the) words of eternal life"**; He is sufficient to meet all need; (3) **"And we have believed and know** [have come to know, *ginōskō*] **that Thou art the Holy One of God"**; He fulfilled His messiahship completely. Christ's answer is to them all (v. 70): **"Did not I choose you, the twelve?"** Both pronouns are emphatic. The question mark should come here. He then reveals His divine knowledge of the character and course of Judas, by which he identified himself with the arch-spiritual foe. The apostle adds a striking confirmatory testimony, marking him as **"one of the twelve."**

JOHN

CHAPTER SEVEN

THE THIRD PUBLIC DISCOURSE
Verses 1 to 24

In chapter seven the scene of Christ's controversy with the Jews shifts from Galilee to Jerusalem. The crisis grows in intensity. The circumstances are now connected with the Feast of Tabernacles, with its immense concourse of the people, and, as we have already remarked, the Jewish feasts in the Gospel of John in connection with the Lord's testimony seem to occur in their chronological order. While in Galilee, His brethren, who, in their worldly wisdom, did not believe on Him, had bidden Him go into Judea, that He might give an exhibition of His works to His followers, manifest Himself to the world, and so restore the national glory of Israel. To this He pointedly replied that their ideas and ways were contrary to His. They were yet on the side of the world (though that attitude was not to continue indefinitely). He bade them go to the feast; He Himself would be absent from its beginning. After they had gone He went up Himself **"not publicly, but as it were in secret,"** fully cognizant of the trend which the renewed controversy would take, and purposely ordering His movements with the eventual issues in view leading to His death. He knew that the Jews would be seeking Him at the feast, and so they did (v. 11).

The Source of Truth and Light

To the crowds, and particularly those who had come up from Galilee, He was the subject of much discussion and of very divergent ideas. There was **"much murmuring among them."** Some regarded Him as **"a good man,"** but they had to keep their discussions quiet through fear of the religious leaders and their "Gestapo" agents. Others declaimed Him as a deceiver and dangerous. The close of this part of the controversy issues in an actual attempt, instigated by the hierarchy through the said agents, to seize Him,

an attempt in which some of the multitude themselves were ready to take part (vv. 30, 32, 44, 45). At the appointed time, the midst of the feast, the Lord goes right up into the temple and begins to preach. In what follows in this and the next few chapters the Lord reveals Himself as the source of truth and light, just as in the preceding discourse He had revealed Himself as the source and support of life.

There are really four public discourses in chapter seven, the first in reply to the Jews (vv. 14–24), the second in reply to some of the people in Jerusalem (vv. 25–31), the third after the officials from the Sanhedrin had come to take Him (vv. 32–36), the fourth, on the last day of the feast (vv. 37–39).

"I Delight to Do Thy Will"

The teaching He gave in the temple aroused the astonishment of the Jews: **"How knoweth this man letters,"** they said, **"having never learned?"** "This man" was contemptuous, as in 6:42. Their astonishment lay in the fact that He had manifested such learning without having attended the rabbinical schools, to receive the usual instruction from the recognized representatives of traditional religion. The Lord, ever delighting to glorify the Father (see 17:4), at once replies, **"My teaching is not Mine, but His that sent Me"** (cp. 5:19, as to His deeds; 5:30, as to His judgment; 6:38, as to His will; 6:57, as to His life; 8:26, 28, 38, as to His words).

How insignificant was the rabbinical instruction compared with this! Here was a source unique; for it lay in the absolute and unbroken oneness of the Son with Him who had sent Him. Both the evidence of His teaching and His own testimony concerning it should have silenced all cavils.

The Will to Do God's Will

He proceeds at once to bring home to them the responsibility to receive His teaching and the condition upon which that responsibility can be discharged: **"If any man** (anyone) **willeth** (not simply the future "will," but the exercise of the human will, the definite intention) **to do His will, he shall know of the teaching, whether it be of God, or whether I speak from Myself"** (v. 17). To know that He spoke from God was to realize that His teaching was the voice of God to men. His teaching and our doing are to be conjoint. And the condition for this lies in our willingness. The doing of God's will is not merely a matter of faith, but of a heart in harmony with Himself: It is neither mechanical nor compulsory, but intelligent and voluntary. This was not to be obtained simply in the rabbinical schools; nor is it acquired merely by courses of theological study.

The Lord now states the motival evidence of the source of His teaching. The test of its validity lay in its motive. **"He that speaketh from** (not "of," in the sense of "concerning") **himself seeketh his own glory: but He that seeketh the glory of Him that sent Him, the same is true, and no unrighteousness is in Him."** This was true only of Christ. Human teachers who are possessors of the highest motives are not thereby free from error. Any ambassador who seeks the glory of his master is "true," and carries out his commission righteously. But the Lord alone perfectly fulfilled the criterion. His, and His only, was undeviatingly selfless obedience to the Father.

In the next verse He does not pass to a different subject, He illustrates what He has just said by the utter contrast in their case. They gloried in the Law as being distinctively their national possession, and had they sought the glory of God they would have been possessed of a will to fulfill His commandments. With them it was otherwise. **"Did not Moses give you the Law, and yet none of you doeth the Law? Why seek ye to kill Me?"** (cp. Acts 7:53).

Once in seven years, at the Feast of Tabernacles, the whole Law was publicly read daily (Deut. 31:10-13). Whether that took place on this occasion or not (though it is quite possible), there was doubtless a reference to it in the charge He made. The first part of the Law as customarily read, namely, Deuteronomy 1:1 to 6:3, contained the command, "Thou shalt not kill," an injunction they were breaking in their intention concerning Him.

"The Meekness and Gentleness of Christ"

At this, the multitude, whether ignorant of the fact, or under the influence of their religious leaders, broke in with the insulting rejoinder of His being demon-possessed. With what dignified meekness He meets it! Meekness under insult is the most potent weapon to bring home the guilt of the offense. He simply recalls their attitude on the occasion of His healing of the impotent man at the pool of Bethesda, and their accusation against Him of sabbath-breaking. **"I did one work,"** He says, **"and ye all marvel. For this cause** (the text is to be preferred to the R.V. margin) **hath Moses given you circumcision (not that it is of Moses, but of the fathers;)** perhaps a reference to the rabbinical technicalities of interpretation; the rabbis had a saying that "Circumcision gives away the sabbath"; **and on the sabbath ye circumcise a man. If a man receiveth circumcision on the sabbath, that the Law of Moses may not be broken, are ye wroth with Me, because I made a man every whit whole on the sabbath? Judge not according to appearance, but judge righteous judgment"** (vv. 21-24).

If the Sabbath yielded place to a ceremonial ordinance, how much more a deed of mercy! (The word *cholao,* here only in the New Testament, signifies to be bitterly resentful; cp. English "choler.") His gracious act was a breach of the Sabbath only in outward appearance. Their view of the deed was the negation of righteous judgment.

Verses 25 to 38

The Lord's vindication of Himself and His work of healing (7:21-24) was again interrupted by a questioning on the part of some of the Jerusalem residents (perhaps proud of their local connection, in contrast to the numerous visitors) as to why the rulers (the hierarchy) had not taken measures against Him. Surely they could not "have come to know" *(ginōskō)* that He was the Messiah (v. 26). **"Howbeit,"** they say, **"we know (***oida,* **we** are perfectly aware of) **this man whence He is, but when the Christ cometh, no one knoweth whence He is.**" In their opinion that was a sufficient answer to their question. They may have referred to His parentage. The belief had been disseminated among the Jews that since the Messiah would appear in the manner foretold, e.g., in Daniel 7:13 and Malachi 3:1, His origin would be unknown.

A Serious Lack of Knowledge

Taking up the words of their objection the Lord concedes to them their knowledge as to the external facts concerning Himself, but they lack the all-important knowledge, the higher truths of His being. **"Ye both know Me, and know whence I am; and** [here a word of contrast, as often in John's writings] **I am not come to Myself, but He that sent Me is true** [i.e., He has fulfilled His Word in sending Me], **whom ye know not. I know Him** [*oida*, I have absolute knowledge of Him], **because I am from Him and He sent Me**" (cp. vv. 16, 17).

A Climax in His Testimony

He declares His complete consciousness of His eternal Sonship, His unoriginated preexistence with the Father, and His combined deity and humanity as the Father's sent one.

This aroused an intense enmity against Him on the part of the fanatical Jews, who would have seized Him there and then, and were only just not bold enough to do so, through force of circumstances. Their action was impossible because **"His hour was not yet come."** The attitude of the multitude was different. Many had been favorably impressed and **"believed on Him,"** admitting, that is to say, His claim to be the Messiah (v. 31). This was too much for the hierarchy. Christ's influence was clearly in the ascendant. Accordingly they issued a warrant for His arrest and sent temple officers to seize Him (the chief priests are here mentioned for the first time by John). This He calmly and boldly met with a declaration anticipative of His death, at the same time continuing His testimony as to the Father and intimating the terrible doom of His opponents: **'Yet a little while am I with you, and I go unto Him that sent Me. Ye shall seek Me, and shall not find Me; and where I**

am ye cannot come.'' An impassable barrier would be placed between Him and them, both as to any purpose or desire regarding Him, whether hostile or otherwise, and as to any possibility of their ever being in His presence in His Father's glory (cp. 8:21; 13:33; and Luke 17:26).

A Scoff with an Unintentional Reality

This met with scorn. Where would **"this man"** (a scoffing epithet) go? Would He go to their Hellenistic fellow-nationals scattered among gentile peoples? Would He, forsooth, even teach the Gentiles? How ignorantly their sarcasm anticipated the very thing He would do by the mission of the Spirit through His gospel messengers after His ascension!

The controversy died down till the last day, **"the great day of the Feast,"** the Hosanna Rabba. The eighth day was, like the first, observed as a Sabbath (Lev. 23:39); special sacrifices were offered (Num. 29:36–38). During the seven days preceding, pilgrims, leaving their booths, marched in procession seven times round the city, shouting "Hosanna." Crowds followed the priests and Levites daily bearing the golden vessels to the brook of Siloam to carry the water thereof up to the temple, where it would be poured into a silver vessel on the eastern side of the altar of burnt offering, and all to the chanting of Isaiah's words, **"Ho, every one that thirsteth, come ye to the waters,"** and **"With joy shall ye draw water out of the wells of salvation."**

This ritual was apparently not observed on the eighth day, for whereas the preceding ritual symbolized the water from the rock in the wilderness, the eighth day commemorated their entrance into the **"land of springs of water."**

"Rivers of Living Water"

This day therefore provided the occasion for the giver of the water of life to interpose His invitation to the spiritually needy. Standing before the crowds with a solemn and authoritative dignity, and with a kindly summons that rang out over the whole scene, He cried, **"If any man thirst, let Him come unto Me, and drink. He that believeth on Me, as** the Scripture hath said, out of his belly shall flow the rivers of living water" (v. 38).

The Lord thus promises a twofold source of refreshment and satisfaction: He Himself satisfies the thirsty soul, and by the indwelling Holy Spirit the believer is to be the means of satisfying others. To the Samaritan woman He had spoken of the water bestowed by Him as becoming in the recipient "a well of water springing up unto eternal life"; now He enlarges the promise: the believer is to be a channel of the fullness of life-giving ministry and enrichment to needy souls. He does not say "a river of living water," but "rivers." What a contrast to the ewer of water poured out each day of the feast!

How great the possibilities of a Spirit-filled life! How important that we should permit nothing to clog the channel! This being "filled with the Spirit" is not an attainment securing a condition of permanent freedom from any defect on our part, it necessitates recourse to the efficacy of the cleansing blood of Christ (1 John 1:7), and the renewing of our mind (Rom. 12:2). The purpose of the Spirit is to glorify Christ (John 16:14) and this ministry He fulfills in and through the believer who, seeking to refrain from grieving the Spirit, presents his body to God as a living sacrifice.

So let us thirst, come, be filled, and be a channel of supply. The "living waters" were figurative of the Holy Spirit (v. 38) and the Lord was promising what would, and did, take place at Pentecost, and from that time onward. The Spirit would not be given thus till the Lord Jesus was glorified. There is no mention here of the Church; only the individual believer is in view. Further, what is here mentioned is not the Spirit's work of regeneration. He was to be a gift to those who were already believers when Christ was on earth. What takes place since Pentecost is that when we believe and are born of the Spirit, He indwells us and becomes a river flowing through us in blessing to others.

Division Owing to His Teaching

The reasonings and discussions which follow concerning Christ on the part of the multitude (vv. 40–44) are only samples of what has occurred ever since. The world by its wisdom, religious or otherwise, knows Him not.

The "multitude" are to be distinguished from "the Jews." The latter desired to take His life. Some of the people would have arrested Him. In respect the effects of His testimony upon the people afforded a sample of what has ever taken place since: **"there arose a division because of Him."** Such divisions have been numerous. Just as failure to understand His teaching produced such divisive results, so failure to understand and accept the Scriptures concerning Him have produced the numerous sects and parties of Christendom.

The officers sent by the chief priests and Pharisees to arrest Him failed in their purpose, apparently through timidity. His testimony was such as to prevent His being taken before the divinely appointed time. **"Never man so spake."** True it was, and ever has been. His words have ever had differing but decisive effects, either winning the heart or hardening it.

The religious leaders, the Sanhedrin, condemned all who dared to differ from them or who rejected their authority, a great characteristic of the potentates of traditional ecclesiastical systems. The multitude, regarded as ignorant of the law, were accounted "accursed." Even Nicodemus, who could speak from a position of equality and pointed out that while they were pleading for "the law" they were themselves breaking it (v. 51), became the object of their scorn. Was he, forsooth, of Galilee? No prophet, they said, arose from Galilee. But Jonah came from Galilee, and probably Hosea and Nahum, to say nothing of others.

JOHN

CHAPTER EIGHT

Verses 1 to 11

The Woman Taken in Adultery

As to the narrative concerning the woman brought by the scribes and Pharisees to the Lord because of adultery, whatever may be said about the MSS. and versions, the narrative bears its own witness to the likelihood of the facts. The criticisms against its validity are plainly futile. The enemies of the Lord were not bringing her before Him as a judge to try a case involving the presence of witnesses; their appeal was to one regarded as a prophet, who should know the mind of God and speak accordingly. They were filled with madness against Him. They had just failed to have Him seized openly (7:32-40). They therefore contrived an ingenious plan by which He either would, by condemning the woman, give evidence of lack of grace and failure to act as a Savior the "Friend of publicans and sinners," and thus bring condemnation upon Himself in this respect, or, by letting her go, fail to uphold the Law. The people must choose Moses or Him, and they would cling to Moses. If His foes entangled Him they could have a pretext for bringing Him before the Sanhedrin.

They little knew that they were dealing with One who Himself searches the heart, and who knew the secret history of their own lives. The Lord makes no oral answer at first, thereby the more forcibly to bring them to commit themselves. They could not have considered Him embarrassed; at first they gave the appearance of misunderstanding Him, and kept plying their question. Can they have discerned what He wrote on the ground? If so they must have hardened their hearts against His testimony.

Teacher, Not a Judge

He lifts Himself up (not standing erect) therefore and addresses them. He does not nullify the edict of the Law of Moses; let it be obeyed, but those who execute it must have unstained hands and pure hearts. "He that is without sin among you, let him first cast a stone at her." This is the voice of a teacher, not a judge. Moreover a judge has to deal with the accused, not with the executioner. This teacher deals with the accusers. He finds them out, and uses the Law to do it. And as for the manifestation of grace, about which they sought to expose Him, they were the very ones who needed it.

Again He stoops down and writes on the dust of the floor, the very dust being a veritable suggestion of their physical doom. Conviction is designed to lead to repentance. But their hearts know nothing of this. They flee from the light, it is too much for them. "The wicked shall be silenced in darkness." The elder ones go out first, they would be the older in sin; the younger follow. The Lord is left alone and the woman by Him where they had brought her. He says to her, **"Woman where are they? did no man condemn thee? And she said, No man, Lord." And Jesus said, "Neither do I condemn thee: go thy way; from henceforth sin no more."**

Here then was a notable example of His fullness of *"grace and truth"; truth* in that instead of counteracting the Law He maintained it: *grace* in that in the rights of His own prerogative He did not condemn the woman but bade her sin no more.

The Light of the World

Clearly, then, this passage is seen to be an integral part of this Gospel. It is essentially connected both with what precedes and with what follows. As to the former, it was the Pharisees who had failed in their open attack upon Him (7:44-49), and it was the Pharisees who, changing their tactics, adopted the subtle method of attack. They failed again, and that because His holy light had shone into their seared consciences, and into the woman's soul. In contrast therefore to the darkness of His foes, who were under the Law, and breakers of it, He immediately says to the people, **"I am the light of the world: he that followeth Me shall not walk in the dark-**

ness, but shall have the light of life" (8:12). This constituted a direct claim to be the Messiah.

THE FOURTH PUBLIC DISCOURSE
Verses 12 to 18

Not improbably this statement in verse 12 had reference to another ceremony of the Feast of Tabernacles, just as His proclamation concerning the "living water" had reference to the carrying of water from the pool of Siloam. On the evenings of the Feast, except the last, the Court of the Women was brilliantly illuminated, in commemoration of the pillar of fire which guided Israel in the trackless desert, and the night was given up to dancing and festivity. Christ had appropriated to Himself the type of the rock; now He does the same with the pillar of fire. The city shone in the glow of the ceremonial light; He declares Himself to be "the Light of the world." The fiery pillar was Israel's guide for night journeying, to be a follower of Jesus is to have "the light of life."

Light and Life

Day by day, step by step, he who "follows His steps" (1 Pet. 2:21) will "see light in His light." Yea more, since Christ is Himself the light of life, the light that dispenses life, he who lives in Him and partakes of His life, himself becomes light, "light in the Lord," walking as a "child of light" (Eph. 5:8). And this is to love even as He loves. "He that loveth his brother abideth in the light, and there is none occasion of stumbling in him." Christ taught, then, that He was the Bread of Life, for nourishment; the Water of Life, for the thirsty, the Light of Life, for His followers.

"The Faithful and True Witness"

And now there follows a whole series of interruptions in His discourse. The controversy becomes keener. The claim to be the Light of the World, and to minister the Light of Life, aroused a fierce objection on the part of the Pharisees: **"Thou bearest witness of Thyself; Thy witness is not true."** They were doubtless recalling His words, **"If**

I bear witness of Myself, My witness is not true" (5:31). With that His present reply, **"Even if I** [the pronoun is emphatic] **bear witness of Myself, My witness is true,"** is perfectly consistent. In 5:31 He had referred to their law of evidence, and had declared His fulfillment of its requirements.

The evidence of one may be perfectly true but is not valid without corroboration which is afforded in the fuller way. The Lord's testimony was never single: **"I am One that beareth witness of Myself,"** He says **"and the Father that sent Me beareth witness."** He shows that His evidence is true, because of the unique character of His being and destiny. In 5:31 He appealed to the dual witness of His Father and His own. Now when He precedes the reaffirmation of this by saying that even if he does bear witness of Himself His witness is true, He shows that in the very essentials of His being the knowledge of His critics is deficient. For His own testimony is the outcome of His divine preexistence, His divine consciousness and futurity. Of all this they were entirely ignorant. About it only He Himself could bear witness. **"My witness is true,"** He says, **"for I know whence I came, and whither I go; but ye know not whence I come, or whither I go."** The change of tense from "I came" to "I come" is to be noted. As to His own knowledge He refers to His preexistence and His incarnation. In regard to their ignorance He speaks of His coming as in the present. Accordingly, though they could not know the former, they could recognize the present evidences and acknowledge the authority of the One who had sent Him.

They judged **"after the flesh,"** treating Him as a mere man and so rejecting His witness as invalid. **"I judge no man,"** He says. He had come not to judge but to save. **"Yea and if I judge, My judgment is true; for I am not alone, but I and the Father that sent Me."** The requirement as to the twofold witness was therefore fulfilled. But why does He say "your law," and not "the Law," in the matter of the validity of the witness of "two men"? (Deut. 19:15). He was in no way repudiating the Law; the point of the "your" law in this, that they were professed expounders of it and charged Him with failure to fulfill it.

Verses 19 to 25

Equal Honor to the Father and the Son

Christ's constant testimony to the fact that the Father had sent Him elicits, in 8:19, the scornful question, **"Where is Thy Father?"** as if to suggest "Granted, then, that you are one witness; let us see the other, Him of whom you speak as your Father. Thus you will evidentially fulfill the requirements of the Law!" This is an instance of the use of the Word of God to support erroneous ideas and prejudices! How very differently, on a later occasion, one of His disciples made the request "Show us the Father" (14:8)!

The Lord replies, **"Ye know neither Me, nor My Father; if ye knew Me, ye would know My Father also."** Their ideas of the dual witness to which He had referred were utterly awry. His statement conveys a vital truth. To ignore Him in the reality of His person and work is to be ignorant of God the Father. It is through the Son that the Father reveals Himself. The Son is the one and only means of knowing the Father. To claim God as Father while neglecting the Son is fatal blindness. Men are largely ready to talk about God, and to appeal to God, while failing to recognize and acknowledge His Son, Jesus Christ, and His demand that all men should "honor the Son, even as they honor the Father" (5:23).

Dying in Sin

The dialogue was in public. The crowd could hear it. Christ was speaking "in the Treasury," called so because of the bronze chests placed for the reception of gifts in the Court of the Women, one of the most frequented parts of the temple. Close by, the Sanhedrin was in session planning His arrest. Their object failed **"because His hour was not yet come"** (v. 20).

Accordingly He continues His teaching, and now with solemn denunciation of His detractors. **"I go away,"** He says, **"and ye shall seek Me, and shall die in your sin: whither I go, ye cannot come."** "Away" is the right rendering; there is no pronoun representing "My" in the original. There is special stress on the "I," however. The feast was drawing to its close. Considerable numbers of the people would be leaving for various

destinations. So, in the hearing of the crowd, He says to His critics, "I [I too] am going away," not that He was leaving there and then. His words had another significance, as is clear from His solemn declaration that whither He was going they could not come.

They would die in their sin: the singular, the right rendering of the original, points to the state of sin, not here to the acts, as in verse 24. The singular is used again in verse 34 and presents sin as a unity in essence though the effects are manifold.

They ignore His warning as to their sin, and ask, with malicious scorn, indicative of increasing hardness of heart, **"Will He kill Himself, that He saith, Whither I go, ye cannot come?"** The implication in this was that by suicide He would utterly perish, and therefore of course they, as Abraham's descendants bound for paradise, could certainly not go where He was going.

The "I Am"

The Lord showed at once that He knew their hearts, and says **"Ye are from beneath; I am from above: ye are of this world; I am not of this world."** These statements are not parallel, as if "from beneath" is the same as "of this world." The first contrast presents extreme opposites, and is to be understood in the light of His words, **"Ye are of your father the devil"** (v. 44). Here in verse 23 the Lord passes, for the moment, from the more solemn declaration of their evil spiritual connection, to their identification with the world as alienated from God. And having thus patiently met their scornful remark, He impugns their refusal to believe, as the reason why they would suffer eternal doom: **"I said therefore unto you, that ye shall die in your sins** [plural now, expressing, not a condition, as in verse 21, but details of the life which mark conduct]; **for except ye believe that I am He, ye shall die in your sins."**

There is no word in the Greek representing "He." We must therefore take the "I am" as it stands; and while there is perhaps a connection with His word "I am from above," there is more in it than this. He is disclosing the essential nature of His being, as in the Name Jehovah, the "I am" of Exodus 3:14. It conveys the thought, "I am what I am," and carries with it the truth of His unoriginated preexistence and immutability. See verse 58 and the sequel. This acceptance of the fact of His deity is essential to salvation.

The Embodiment of His Teaching

The declaration is so stupendous that they ask, with malicious violence, and with great emphasis on the "Thou," **"Who art Thou?"** or, more expressively, "Thou, who art Thou?" Their ignorance was their death. To know Him is "Life eternal" (17:3).

His reply is rendered in the A.V., "Even the same that I said unto you from the beginning," and in the R.V., **"Even that which I have spoken unto you from the beginning."** Certainly He did not mean that He was what He had told them at first. In the clause, "Even that which I have spoken unto you," the tense is not the perfect but the present, and the meaning, thus far, is that He is the embodiment, the personal expression, of what He speaks. His doctrine is Himself, it is inseparable from His being, His attributes and character. He says "I am that which I speak." Now as to the phrase rendered "from the beginning," in the clause in the original there is nothing representing "from." The Lord is not referring to what He had said from a special beginning, but to the essential character of what He speaks to them. The phrase has the meaning "absolutely" or "altogether."

Accordingly the meaning is "I am essentially and undeviatingly what I speak to you." It stood in direct contrast to the character of their religious leaders and to all with whom principles are one thing and practice another, to anyone who has the effrontery to intimate to his hearers that they must do as he says but not as he does. But of Christ alone could it be true that altogether what He spoke was the expression of what He was. This is in keeping with the main trend of all His testimony in these discourses (see especially the immediately following vv. 26, 28, 29), and with His later declaration, "I am the truth."

Verses 26 to 35

The Coming Judge

Had it not been for their hardness of heart, Christ might have enlarged upon the matter of discipleship and explained more fully the nature of His being. Instead of this He has matters about which to speak concerning themselves. Hence the apparent break in the connection. They wanted to find out something by which they could judge Him. He shows that there are things in their own life which He has to reveal, and upon which He has to pronounce judgment: **"I have many things to speak and to judge concerning you"** (v. 26). Let the critic of Christ and the denier of His deity beware. Such will yet find Him to be their judge.

The time for His judicial dealings with the Pharisees had not come. His immediate object was to continue bearing witness concerning the Father and His unity with Him. Accordingly He proceeds with declarations to this end: **"howbeit He that sent Me is true and the things which I heard from Him, these speak I unto the world."** What they needed was a right understanding of His ministry and of its source. Had they apprehended this it would have adjusted their views in conformity with the teaching of the Old Testament Scriptures. But just here they failed, as many have done since: **"They perceived not that He spake to them of the Father"** (v. 27). Their hearts were so hardened that His words produced no awakening of their conscience.

Accordingly He at once points to the consummating act of their iniquity, and its effects, declaring at the same time His power to reveal the future: **"Jesus therefore said, When ye have lifted up the Son of Man, then shall ye know that I am, and that I do nothing of Myself, but as the Father taught Me, I speak these things."** His Crucifixion (cp. 3:14; 12:32, 34) would issue in the manifest vindication of the truth relating to His person ("I am") and therefore to His messiahship as the One sent of the Father. It would issue, too, in their recognition of what He had taught concerning His relationship with the Father in regard both to His works ("I do") and His words ("I speak"). All this was fulfilled at Pentecost and subsequently, and will have its final accomplishment hereafter in the restored nation.

A Further Claim

To confirm it all He declares that He who had sent Him was with Him, a fact utterly incomprehensible to minds occupied with merely mundane expectations. Yet it expressed His own consolation and His joy in the love of the Father amidst the sorrow of His pathway to Calvary: **"The Father hath not left Me alone** (the aorist is perfective in meaning, and should not be rendered "did not leave"); **for I do always the things that are pleasing to Him."** Here are two coextensive and simultaneous conditions, undeviating fulfillment of the Father's will, and consequently uninterrupted enjoyment of His presence. And the principle holds good for those who are Christ's followers, though we come far short of His perfect standard. Our realization and enjoyment of the presence of the Lord is conditioned by our devoted obedience to Him. Let us then make it our aim ever "to be well-pleasing unto Him" (2 Cor. 5:9).

The Effects

The ministry of Christ had widely different effects, as has ever since been the case with testimony concerning Him. A difference is noted by the apostle as he makes a break in the record of the discourse in chapter eight. This is brought out in the R.V. of verses 30, 31. What Christ had said caused many to believe "on Him." It is otherwise with those Jews mentioned in verse 31; they had merely "believed Him." The former had full faith in Him; the latter were simply disposed to believe what He said.

To these the Lord applies a test designed to raise their credence to a higher level. One crucial point, one essential condition, and their credence collapsed: **"If ye abide in My word,"** He says, **"then are ye truly My disciples."** Faith that saves produces discipleship. Discipleship depends upon the permanent application of His teaching to oneself. Passing impulses do not make disciples. The first "ye" and the first "My" have special emphasis: "If you on your part abide in the word that is Mine. . . ."

The Liberty of Subject Will

Now comes that part of the test that disclosed the actual state of their hearts: **"and ye shall know the truth, and the truth shall make you free."** How true it is! Acceptance of, and adherence to, the Word of God shake off the shackles not only of sin, but of human tradition, ecclesiastical bondage, and mere religion. Every truth received prepares for the unfolding of more truth, and each brings its own liberating power. Behind the acceptance is the will to accept. Let the will be unfettered, and we shall enjoy the liberty of devoted subjection to His will.

The idea of being made free was too much for their pride. They answered Him, **"We be Abraham's seed, and have never yet been in bondage to any man: how sayest Thou** [emphatic], **Ye shall be made free?"** Pride blinds the mind to facts. What about their times of oppression, their captivity, and their then-present subjugation to the Roman yoke? The Lord, however, goes deeper than all this. The needs of the soul outweigh material considerations: **"Jesus answered them, Verily, verily, I say unto you, Everyone that committeth sin is the bondservant of sin. And the bondservant abideth not in the house forever: the Son abideth forever"** (vv. 34, 35).

The tense of the verb rendered "committeth" signifies not the committal of an act, but a course of sin; the better rendering would be, "everyone who continueth to do sin." That is what constitutes slavery to sin (so in 1 John 3:4, 6, 7, 9, which should be read in the R.V.). True it is that the willful committal of a sinful act indicates a condition of heart which involves slavery to sin, but that differs from being overtaken by temptation and the committal of an unpremeditated act. Such bondage was the condition of His hearers, despite their high national ancestry.

Verses 36 to 44

Just as a slave is not a member of a family and has no claim to be in the house, so they, Jews though they were, were outside God's spiritual family. To be sons of God we must be spiritually related and united to the Son of God by faith. Thus it is that the Son makes us free from bondage to sin. Whosoever is begotten of God does not continue the practice of sin (1 John 3:9). If a person practices sin, whatever his profession may be, he has not been born again.

Identification with the ever-abiding Son gives us ever-abiding freedom. Hence He says, **"If therefore the Son shall make you free, ye shall be free indeed,"** in reality (v. 36). It is "the law (or invigorating principle) of the Spirit of life in Christ Jesus" that makes us "free from the law of sin and death" (Rom. 8:2).

Accordingly, the Lord exposes to them the entire inconsistence of their illusory appeal to Abraham with their determination to kill Him. And the secret of it all was that His word had **"no free course"** in them (v. 37, R.V.).

A Tremendous Contrast

He then applies a further test to them: **"I speak the things which I** (emphatic: I on My part) **have seen with My Father,"** and reveals their actual and appalling spiritual parentage: **"and ye** (emphatic: you on your part) **also do the things which ye heard from your father."** Though the definite article is used for the possessive pronoun in each part in the original, the English Versions are right in supplying the possessive pronouns, as they are really involved in the emphatic words "I" and "ye." The "also" is likewise to be noted. It stresses the parallel in the principle involved in the relationships. Yet how great are the contrasts! He, in the infinitely blessed, ineffable, and eternal union as Son with the Father, representing Him here and delighting in fulfilling with unclouded vision His will: they, in a relationship consequent upon their sinful state and their willful persistence in evil, characterizing themselves, in their murderous intent, with the characteristics of the evil one!

The change of the tense is to be noted: "I have seen" (perfect tense), indicating divine counsels in the timeless past, carried into permanent effect in His teachings: "ye heard" (aorist or point tense), a communication proceeding from the devil, made when they became the bondslaves of sin, and issuing in the foul act they were ready to carry out and eventually accomplished!

They repeat their claim in respect of Abraham (v. 39), and then make the higher claim of having **"one Father, even God"** (v. 41). This indicates that their statement **"We were**

not born of fornication"** had a spiritual reference to idolatry, with perhaps a hint as to the Samaritans (cp. v. 48). He repudiates both claims. They did not the works of Abraham. The principle of like father like son had no application in that respect. And as to the greater claim, He says: **"If God were your Father, ye would love Me for I came forth and am come from God: for neither have I come of Myself, but He sent Me"** (v. 42).

Of Whom Is God the Father?

What a proof this gives of the falsity of the doctrine of the universal fatherhood of God! What a rebuke to the rationalist who professes belief in the fatherhood of God and yet sets Christ aside! Such belief is pure assumption, void of any foundation of fact. The relationship is dependent upon faith in Christ (Gal. 3:26), and is evidentially established by devotion to Him, not in mere sentiment but in true discipleship. To miss the object for which the Father sent Him, and to fail in the response of love to Him, is to be void of any claim to have God as one's Father. True children of God necessarily love Him who is the Son of God.

The Lord's statement, **"I came forth and am come from God,"** is anticipative of His similar and still more comprehensive words later to His disciples, **"I came forth from the Father. I came out from the Father, and am come into the world"** (16:27, 28). The two passages show that He was in eternally preexistent relationship as the Son with the Father, and that this relationship did not take inception at His Birth.

His necessarily stern denunciation of these opposing Jews reveals more even than previously their terrible spiritual condition. They could not hear His word (*logos,* the matter or substance of His speech), and hence could not understand His speech (*lalia,* the manner of language of His speech), verse 43. Refusal to listen to the voice of the Lord dulls the intelligence. "They were of their father the Devil, and the lusts of their father it was their will to do" (R.V.; cp. 1 John 3:8, 10, which perhaps recalls Christ's words). Their resemblance to the evil one as his spiritual offspring was twofold: **"He was a murderer from the beginning** [i.e., from the time of his jealous attack upon the human soul at the Fall, and permanently since], **and stood not in the truth"**; the true reading is probably "standeth not," as in the R.V. margin, which is confirmed by the next statement, **"because there is no truth in him."** That is to say, he continues to be what he was at the beginning referred to. **"When he speaketh a lie** [not that he ever speaks the truth, for, as the Lord has just stated, it is not in him], **he speaketh of his own** [the fallen nature and qualities which are characteristically his]; **for he is a liar** [e.g., Gen. 3:4] **and the father thereof"** (or, rather, as it may be rendered, "of him," i.e., of the liar—that with which the Lord was charging them).

A Double Guilt Exposed

Of these two sins, then, they were guilty: they were murderers because of their determination to do away with Him; they were liars because they said God was their Father (see vv. 54, 55, where He marks this as their lie). **"But,"** He says, **"because I say** [*legō*, referring to all His teaching] **the truth, ye believe Me not"** (v. 45). The "I" is very strongly emphatic, as the order in the original brings out—"But I [or, as for Me], because I say the truth." Just as the devil does not stand in the truth through his natural dissociation from it, so they, by reason of their relationship to him, refused to accept the truth from Christ's lips.

The absolute truth of His teaching was the effect of His sinlessness. His sinless life gave proof of the truth of His doctrine. Accordingly, untruthfulness being sin, He issues the challenge, **"Which of you convicteth Me of sin?"** (not simply the sin of falsehood) and waits (so we may gather) for an answer. Only Christ, the sinless one, could utter such a challenge. And with what sublime majesty and dignified patience He does so! What grace and humility to submit such a question to such men!

No answer on their part is recorded. Accordingly He proceeds with the cogent question, **"If I say truth, why do ye** [emphatic] **not believe Me."** Since He was free from sin, He was free from falsehood. What then was the reason for their unbelief? His question was not so much an appeal for their faith as a preparation for the consummating proof that

they were not God's children: **"He that is of God heareth the words of God: for this cause ye hear them not, because ye are not of God"** (v. 47).

Instead of yielding to the gracious, though firm, humility by which the Lord resisted their pride, they proceed further in evil and vilify and blaspheme, charging Him with being **"a Samaritan"** (ignorant, that is to say, of the God of Israel and apostate from the faith), and with being demon-possessed.

The Meekness of Christ

His reply was the essence of meekness and forbearance. He first simply denies their foul second vilification and then passes to the vindication of the Father's honor, and to words of warning and virtual appeal. He does not reply to the accusation of being a Samaritan; He refrains from any denial which would endorse their contempt of the Samaritans. Had He not Himself carried on a lifegiving ministry among them (chap. 4)? We will quote His words, and then Peter's comment upon His meekness. And let us seek to carry home to our hearts the lesson of His example. He says **"I have not a demon; but I honor My Father, and ye dishonor Me** [i.e., "you dishonor My Father in dishonoring Me"]. **But I seek not Mine own glory** [i.e., "My saying that you dishonor Me does not imply that I am seeking My own glory"]: **there is One that seeketh and judgeth** [that is to say, "He it is who seeks glory for Me and pronounces judgment on you"]. **Verily, verily, I say unto you, If a man keep my word, he shall never see death."** This last, which was still addressed to them, graciously held out an offer of mercy.

Such a reply is one outstanding illustration of the testimony afterwards borne by Peter to Him, in that "when He was reviled, reviled not again; when He suffered He threatened not" (1 Pet. 2:23). In this the apostle exhorts us to "follow His steps," that the example He left us may have its character-shaping effects upon us.

The Deathlessness of the Believer

To keep His word is not merely to bear it in mind, but to pay such regard to it as diligently to obey and fulfill it. The combined phrases in the original, rendered "never," are very strong and the statement more fully rendered would be "shall certainly not see death forever," *i.e.*, shall not know the experience of death. The negation is a way of expressing the positive assurance of eternal life. For in 11:26 the Lord makes clear that it is solely conditional upon believing upon Him (cp. 5:24 and 6:40). He who thus receives Christ enters upon a life which is essentially characterized by keeping His word. This was what He now held out to His hearers. He referred, not to physical death, but to a life in which physical death, so far from causing a cessation, issues immediately in a fuller realization of life.

The Jews construed His words as if they signified physical death, and exaggerated His language accordingly, changing His "see" into "taste of." Then, repeating their blasphemous calumny, they charged Him with vainglory. This He repudiates, declaring its worthlessness, and the fact that it is the Father who glorifies Him, whom they claimed as their God (v. 54). The Father glorified His Son by His double testimony, at His baptism and His transfiguration, "This is My beloved Son, in whom I am well pleased" (Matt. 3:17 and 17:5), and by the signs and wonders which He wrought (Acts 2:22), and by His resurrection and exaltation (1 Pet. 1:21).

A Difference in Knowledge

In His next statement there is a noticeable difference in the verbs rendered to know, a difference which makes an immeasurable distance between Him and them. He says **"and ye have not known Him** [*ginōskō*, to get to know: they had not even begun to know Him]: **but I know Him** [*oida*, here, of Christ, to have full knowledge; cp. 6:6, 64; i.e., "I know Him absolutely"; a knowledge not progressive but essential]." To deny this (and it made Him greater than Abraham and the prophets) would, He says, have made Him, like them, a liar. So He says again **"but I know Him,"** and adds **"and keep His word,"** the very condition (perfectly fulfilled in Him) which He had laid down as essential for the relation of His followers to Himself.

And as to Abraham, he exulted (that is the force of the word rendered **"rejoiced"**) in the anticipation of the coming of the Christ (**"My Day,"** the day when Christ in person would fulfill in both His advents the promises made by God). That was the goal toward which Abraham's life was set (cp. Heb. 11:10).

JOHN

CHAPTER NINE

Introduction

The opening words of chapter nine show that the healing of the man who had been blind from his birth took place immediately after the Lord's controversy with the Jews in the temple, as recorded in the preceding chapter, and therefore at the close of the Feast of the Tabernacles. His opponents had been just about to stone Him. But He **"hid Himself, and went out of the Temple."** This was a judicial blindness inflicted upon them, and indicative of their spiritual blindness, which refused to recognize His claims and the evidences He gave of their validity.

Verses 1 to 41

He had claimed to be the Light of the World (8:12). They had refused this testimony, and accordingly the Lord, seeing a blind man as He passed by, decided to use his case both as illustrative of the condition of the Jews and as a means of vindicating His claim. This would confirm the faith of the many who had believed and might be the means of carrying home the truth to the heart of skeptics.

A Curious Question and Its Answer

Previous to the act of healing, the disciples asked Him who had sinned, as the cause of his blindness. Repudiating the thought that the man's condition was the outcome of some special sin, the Lord reveals the divine purpose of it all, namely, **"that the works of God should be made manifest in him."**

There is a lesson for us in this. There may be a lurking tendency to seek to find some reprehensible cause for another person's suffering, to say nothing of the possibility of a natural feeling of self-satisfaction with the case. The Lord's reply is a rebuke to all that kind of thing, and points the way to finding a means of dealing effectually with sorrow and misery.

The Time Appointed for Service

There is something suggestive in this connection in the Lord's remark, as rendered in the R.V., **"We must work the works of Him that sent Me."** The most authentic texts have the plural of the pronoun (not infrequently the more difficult reading has the better MS. evidence). While He here refrains from identifying His disciples with His mission from the Father, He does associate them (and ourselves too) with Himself in fulfilling the works of God. He was sent by the Father, but He himself sent His disciples (20:21). There lay the distinction.

The work must be done **"while it is day,"** not merely the natural period as distinct from the night, but the period of opportunity afforded during the lifetime. The Lord applies this to Himself in regard to His life here in the days of His flesh, and connects it with the immediate act He was about to perform, in relation to the great subject of His testimony to Himself as the Light: **"When** [different from "while" or "so long as," as in v. 4] **I am in the world, I am the light of the world."** The absence of the emphatic personal pronoun in the original stresses the fact and effects of His presence in the world rather than His person.

Significance of the Lord's Acts

The facts that the Lord, instead of restoring the man's sight by a word, spat on the ground, and made clay of the spittle, and anointed the man's eyes with the clay, telling him to go and wash in the Pool of Siloam, have a special significance. Doubtless all would help the man's faith. At the same time the process adopted by the Lord suggests the character of the spiritual condition of the Jews, to whom light must come by a process, granted that they were willing even yet to receive His testimony. The man must needs grope his way to get to the pool, a circumstance illustrative of the darkness that blinded the eyes of the Jews. Moreover, that the meaning of the name Siloam (sent) is given in the Gospel narrative, is undoubtedly purposive. The meaning is evidently to be connected with Christ's valid claim to be the sent one.

Again, as to the man himself, the method the Lord chose to use must have brought home to his heart his need of cleansing, as he went on his way to the water. Here then were the great requisites for salvation, a Savior to save, the realization of need, and the obedience of faith. The sequel introduces us to the next great controversy between Christ and the Pharisees. The Lord had given a practical demonstration of His power to heal, and with it a vivid parable of His power to give the light of life to men, as well as a testimony to His authority as Lord of the Sabbath.

The Controversy

The curiosity, not to say perplexity, of the neighbors is aroused. Their question is twofold. How was the healing done? and where was the healer? The man can answer the first but not the second. So now he is brought to the Pharisees. The consequent discussion is full of interest. They first affirm that a sabbath-breaker cannot be from God. Some of them argue, however, that the accomplishment of such signs was impossible on the part of a sinner. Hence a division among them. And this is by no means unique. The person and work of Christ have constantly been matters of controversy and of divided opinions. Happy are those who have the confidence of faith and the experience of Christ's power to deliver, and are able to bear such a courageous testimony as was given by this subject of the Lord's healing mercy.

The man's parents did not share that courage, fearing excommunication by their religious leaders. Their son shall answer for himself. So the man is called again, and receives a command and a confident statement about his healer: **"Give glory to God. We know that this man is a sinner."** The man knew better than to give glory to God by agreeing to this. Regardless of scorn, and altogether independent of the opinions of his examiners, he meets their bullyings with trenchant argument and even sarcasm. The facts of his healing were incontrovertible. How futile and foolish to deny them! Yet the only answer of these "blind leaders of the blind" was to denounce him as **"altogether born in sins"** (as if forsooth their own state was quite otherwise), and scornfully to repudiate the very idea of his teaching them. Accordingly they excommunicate him from all attendance in the temple and synagogues, and from participation in all religious privileges.

The Spiritual Healing and Its Lessons

The Lord makes a special point of finding him after this, so as to reveal to him more fully who He Himself was. He would more than make up to him for what he had lost. To know Him is life eternal, and to enjoy the secret of His friendship outweighs everything else that the natural mind deems valuable.

This spiritual opening of his eyes made him at once a worshiper, and upon this the Lord issues a declaration in the very hearing of the Pharisees who were present, which introduces the discourse recorded in chapter ten. **"For judgment,"** He says, **"came I into this world, that they which see not may see; and that they which see may become blind"** (v. 39). These are the two companies formed by contact with Christ, the seeing and the blind. Christ is the great divider as well as the great uniter. This is the twofold effect of testimony concerning Him. The self-satisfied, whether religious or otherwise, confident in their complacent imaginings that they have true sight, remain in their blindness; the humble souls who realize their actual spiritual condition and, exercising their simple faith, become His followers, have their eyes opened.

Four Lessons

Obedience to Christ's call to come for cleansing, life and light, leads to personal acquaintance and relationship with Him. Refusal to accept the call means death and darkness. That is the first great lesson of the miracle. Mere religion and the traditions of men blind their adherents to true spiritual conception. Mere ritualistic ordinances are as futile as the clay on the blind man's eyes would have been if he had never washed. That is the next great lesson. Thirdly, we cannot but marvel at the gracious desire and loving care shown by the

Lord to beget faith in the heart. His patience, forbearance and longsuffering render the state of the impenitent all the more terrible. Fourthly, the design of the grace that enlightens the soul is to make the recipient a simple but effective witness to Christ. Such a one finds no place or time for discussions with rationalistic quibblers. He has no place for the wisdom of words as a means of dealing with skeptics. Christ is made to him "wisdom from God, and righteousness and sanctification and redemption."

JOHN

Verses 1 to 10

The tenth chapter is a direct continuation of the Lord's controversy with the Jews arising from His healing of the man born blind, but in this chapter the Lord goes more deeply than before into the joy of the relationship between Himself and those who have been brought from nature's darkness to become His followers. He expresses His delight in having them as His own and in what He becomes to them, and what will issue similarly in the case of others as the result of the laying down of His life for them. All this He sets forth in what is really an allegory (or an enlarged metaphor, called in our Versions a "parable," margin "proverb"), under the figure of the shepherd and the sheep.*

The Good Shepherd and the Bad Shepherds

In His collision with His critics, whom He has just charged with abiding in a state of sin (the very thing that they had imputed to the man to whom the Lord had given sight, 9:34), the Lord introduces His allegory by a clear intimation that spiritually they belong to the class of the thief and the robber. He begins with His characteristic **"Verily, verily, I say unto you."** The Pharisees were bad shepherds; the blind man had found the Good Shepherd. They had not entered by the door into the fold of the sheep, but, like the thief and the robber, had climbed up some other way.

The Lord applies two details in the allegory to Himself in unfolding its meaning. He first says, **"I am the door"** (vv. 7, 9), and then **"I am the good Shepherd"** (vv. 11–14). If it is necessary to obtain an interpretation as to the porter (v. 3), it seems best to regard

the figure as signifying the Holy Spirit, for it is His work to introduce sheep into the fold. In the East the intimacy between a shepherd and his sheep is very close, and the practice of the naming of the sheep is quite ancient. With the Lord's word, **"He calleth His own sheep by name,"** we may compare Isaiah 43:1; 45:3; 49:1; and Revelation 3:5.

Two words are used to express the act of the Shepherd in regard to the going forth of the sheep. **"He leadeth them out"** (v. 3) by going before them, but he first **"putteth them forth"** (v. 4). There is a striking significance in the latter expression. The verb in the original is the same as that rendered "they cast him out" (9:34, 35). False shepherds put them out to lighten the burden of caring for them; true shepherds put them forth to see that they are well fed. The intimacy just referred to is beautifully set forth further, first, by the fact that the shepherd goes before the sheep and they follow him (just as Paul, the faithful undershepherd, could say "Be ye imitators of me even as I am of Christ," 1 Cor. 11:1; cp. Phil. 3:17; 1 Thess. 1:6; 2 Thess. 3:7–9); secondly, in that they know the voice of their shepherd in contrast to that of strangers, from whom they flee. A Scottish traveler once changed clothes with a Jerusalem shepherd and endeavored to lead the sheep; they refused however to follow the shepherd's clothes on the stranger, in spite of all that he did to draw them; but they readily followed the voice of their own shepherd, in spite of the change of his garment.

Thieves and Robbers

The Pharisees failed to understand what the Lord had been talking about (v. 6). Their treatment of the man whose sight was restored made clear that their characteristics

---

*A parable literally denotes "a placing alongside," and consists of putting one thing beside another by way of comparison. It is generally, as in the present instance, a narrative drawn from nature or human circumstances, in order to convey a spiritual lesson. We must carefully enter into the analogy if we are to gather the instruction. Two dangers are to be avoided in regard to the interpretation, firstly, that of ignoring the important features, and secondly, that of seeking to make every detail mean something.

were entirely foreign to those of true shepherds. Accordingly the Lord now repeats the allegory, unfolding the special details and applying them to Himself. **"Jesus therefore said unto them again, Verily, verily; I say unto you, I am the door of the sheep."** The "I" bears special emphasis, just as in 4:26; 6:35, 41, 48, 51, etc. In each case what the Lord implies is, "I and no other." Here He declares that He is the one and only door through which both sheep and shepherds enter. His next statement, **"All that came before Me are thieves and robbers,"** refers not, of course, to those who had previously been sent of God, but to those who had misled the people, serving their own ends instead of God and His truth, false prophets who had come in sheep's clothing, but inwardly were ravening wolves (Matt. 7:15), men who had shut the kingdom of heaven, neither entering themselves, nor suffering others to enter (23:13), who took away the key of knowledge and hindered people from possessing it (Luke 11:52). The present tense, "are," indicates that they were the men of the time when He was upon earth; compare however Ezekiel 34, **"But the sheep did not hear them."** There were many who listened to them, but His own followers, the remnant in Israel, found nothing to benefit in what these ecclesiastical authorities taught.

The Happiness of Entering

Now He states the blessedness of those who do enter in, and precedes it with an emphatic repetition of the fact that He is the one and only door. **"By Me,"** He says, **"if any man enter in, he shall be saved, and shall go in and go out, and find pasture."** He does not say "If any man enter in by Me," but puts the "by Me" first, placing the greatest stress upon the uniqueness and absoluteness of His own Person. How comprehensive is His word, "If any man [or, rather, anyone]!" His mind goes beyond Jews to Gentiles. There are not limitations either of sex or nationality.

He who enters in "shall be saved." This is more than being delivered from perdition; it points to the state of salvation consequent upon the step of entering. To go in and to go out is suggestive both of security and liberty. The double expression is used frequently in the Old Testament for describing the free activity of daily life (see, *e.g.,* Deut. 28:6, 19; 31:2; 1 Sam. 18:16; Ps. 121:8; Jer. 37:4). The same Hebraistic phrase is used in Acts 1:21; 9:28. The finding of pasture is descriptive of the feeding upon Christ, both by means of the Scriptures and in the daily appropriation of Christ in the life of communion with Him. The benefits are threefold: deliverance, freedom, and nourishment.

Radical Differences

All this is followed by one of the most striking contrasts in Scripture. It lies between the motives and acts of the thief and those of the Good Shepherd. The former are described by way of a climax of selfish cruelty—stealing, killing, destroying—selfishness, bloodlust, brutality. The killing is not for sacrificial purposes, as some suggest, but for murderous intent. The destroying is more than the killing, it means the utter ruin of the flock.

The twofold motive of the Good Shepherd is in inverse antithesis to all that. He came (1) that they might have life; that stands in contrast to the killing and destroying; He does not take life, He gives it; (2) that they might have it **"abundantly"** (not "more abundantly," as in the A.V.: the word "more" has no MS. authority: it is not a matter of greater instead of less, but of a full supply of all that sustains life); instead of stealing He imparts abundance.

But there are two more contrasts. There is that of the emphatic "I," purposely set in contrast to "the thief." Then there are the different tenses. The thief **"cometh"**; he pays his visits, whensoever he finds possibility of attempting his fell design; **"I came,"** says the Good Shepherd; He had come by one great voluntary act of grace and compassionate love.

Verses 11 to 21

"I am the good Shepherd." The word *kalos,* "good," conveys all the attributes and characteristics of what is ideal, or of what is well adapted to its purposes because it is intrinsically good. Christ is the "good" Shepherd in each respect. His character is manifested, and His purpose fulfilled, in laying down His life for the sheep. His description of

Himself as more fully rendered, is strikingly expressive: "I am the Shepherd, the good one"; this stands out in contrast to the hireling.

At the same time it breathes His delight in, and tender thought and care for, His flock. They are "His own," as intimated in His negative descriptions of the hireling who is **"not a shepherd"** and **"whose own the sheep are not."**

The Hireling

The hireling acts simply in his own interests. He saves his life by leaving the sheep to their destroyer. The Good Shepherd lays down His life that His sheep may not perish. The one saves himself by sacrificing his charge; the other sacrifices Himself to save His charge. Just there lay the difference between the religious authorities and Christ, in their respective treatment of the blind man.

A Twofold Mutual Intimacy

In verse 14 He repeats His statement, **"I am the good Shepherd,"** but now to introduce the subject of the intimacy between Himself and His sheep. There should be no break between verses 14 and 15, the one runs on into the other: **"I know Mine own, and Mine own know Me, even as the Father knoweth Me, and I know the Father."** The mutual "knowing" is thus twofold, and the former has its source in the latter. The mutual intimacy between Christ and His followers is but the overflow and extension of the unoriginated and infinite mutual intimacy between the Father and the Son.

The verb in each of the four statements is *ginōskō*, expressing knowledge existent through constant experience (and here involving mutual appreciation), as distinct from *oida*, which conveys the idea of complete or absolute knowledge. As the Father delights in the full recognition and appreciation of all that the Son is to Him, and the Son in all that the Father is to Him, so the Son, as the Good Shepherd, delights in the full recognition and appreciation of all that His sheep are to Him, and the sheep in their recognition and appreciation of what He is to them. This latter mutuality finds its basis in the great sacrificial act of the Shep-

herd, and for this reason He says again, **"I lay down My life for the sheep."**

The "Other Sheep" and the "One Flock"

In view of His death His thoughts and tender affections go out to those **"other sheep,"** other than Jewish believers. They were already His own though they had not come into being. They had been given to Him by the Father (17:7). Hence He says **"Other sheep I have"** (cp. Acts 18:10; 28:28). The Jews had derisively asked, "Will He go . . . and teach the Greeks?" (7:35). He affirms that there are His own among the despised Gentiles. As Bengel remarks, "He does not say, who are out of or in another fold." And in His statement **"which are not of this fold,"** the emphasis is upon "fold," not upon "this" (which readers frequently stress). There is not a Gentile fold.

"Them also," He says, **"I must bring** [or rather, "lead"], **and they shall hear My voice** [see v. 3], **and they shall become one flock, one Shepherd."** Not "one fold," but "one flock." The oneness is not to be brought about by an external union of the sects and systems of Christendom (described in mistaken religious parlance as The Church). Scripture never speaks of "the Church on earth," consisting of all the believers in the world. The phrase "the Church on earth" is utterly unscriptural and is responsible for many a mistaken idea. The Church has never been on earth; heaven is its destiny and dwelling place. For its true unity and destination, see 17:22 to 24. This is the will of the "One Shepherd," that **"where I am, they also may be with Me; that they may behold My glory."** That is the destiny.

His Raising of the Temple of His Body

Therefore, in repeating the fact of the laying down of His life, He adds that of His resurrection, and that by His own power: **"That I may take it again,"** assigning this as a special reason for the Father's love: **"Therefore doth the Father love me, because I lay down My life, that I may take it again."** Speaking of the temple of His body He had said, **"Destroy this temple, and in three** days I will raise it up" (2:19, 21). This power in His resurrection He shares with the Father: "No one taketh it away from Me, but I [with special emphasis] lay it down of Myself. I have power [or authority] to lay it down, and I have power to take it again. This commandment received I from My Father." His resurrection was therefore an essential act in fulfillment of the Father's will, which He had come to accomplish (6:38).

For this reason He is "the Good Shepherd," "the Great Shepherd," "the Chief Shepherd," and will be the "One Shepherd," with His one complete "flock."

Never Perish

So in the next statement, "My sheep ["the sheep which are Mine"] hear My voice [cp. 10:4] and I know them, and they follow Me and I give unto them eternal life." Not "I will give," as if the bestowment of life was a promise conditional upon following Him. That interpretation has been put forward by some, but it is contradictory to 5:24, where the Lord declared that eternal life was imparted upon hearing His word and believing. The present tense indicates the possession of life already enjoyed. The enjoyment of life hereafter is a continuation of present spiritual life: "And they shall never perish, and no one shall snatch them out of My hand." The negative is very emphatic: "they shall never by any means perish" (so in 8:51 and 11:26).

There are, in two respects,

Three Successive Facts

As to the sheep: (a) they hear His voice, (b) they follow Him, (c) they shall never perish; and as to the Shepherd: (a) He knows them, (b) He gives them eternal life, (c) He holds them securely in His hand.

Then, as usual, the Lord leads up to teaching concerning the Father, whom He ever glorified: "My Father, which hath given them unto Me, is greater than all"; not here with reference to the Son (as in 14:28), for see the next verse, but as having complete control over all adverse powers. That His sheep are the gift of the Father ensures their eternal safety. Note the perfect tense, "hath

given," denoting an accomplished act with permanent results.

"And no one is able to snatch them out of the Father's hand. I and the Father are one" (vv. 29–30). Those who are in the hands of the Son, having been given to Him by the Father, remain likewise in the hands of the Father, and this is a potent demonstration of the unity of the two. The Father and the Son, being one in godhood, are therein one in the infinitude of power, a power exerted against all adversaries. As Liddon says, "a unity like this must be a dynamic unity, as distinct from any mere moral and intellectual union, such as might exist in a real sense between a creature and its God. Deny this dynamic unity, and you destroy the internal connection of the passage. Admit this dynamic unity, and you admit, by necessary implication, a unity of essence. The power of the Son, which shields the redeemed from the foes of their salvation is the very power of the Father: and this identity of power is itself the outflow and the manifestation of a oneness of nature."

THE FIFTH PUBLIC DISCOURSE
Verses 22 to 39

The preceding discourse produced a division among the Jews. Some blasphemously accused the Lord of being demon-possessed and mad; others repudiated the idea, on two grounds, His teaching, and His cure of the blind man. This was the third division resulting from His testimony. The first was among the multitude at the Feast of Tabernacles (7:43); the second was among the Pharisees, consequent upon His act of imparting sight on the Sabbath day (9:16); the third was among the Jews, for the reasons just mentioned (10:19–21).

It was now "the feast of the dedication," a feast observed to commemorate the purification and restoration of the temple after its defilement by Antiochus Epiphanes. It lasted eight days, from December 20th. The mention of its being winter (v. 22) seems to be connected with the fact that "Jesus was walking in Solomon's porch," a cloister on the east side of the temple.

The Increase of Antagonism to Christ

The occasions of the feasts mark a progress of hostility to Him till the climax is reached. At the first feast they prosecuted Him and sought to kill Him (5:1, 16, 18). At the next the chief priests and Pharisees took the step of sending officers to take Him (7:2, 14, 32). On the present occasion the Jews prepared to stone Him, and attempted to lay hands on Him (10:31, 39). At the last they accomplished His death. The occasions, therefore, which had been designed for the glory of God and the blessing of His people, were turned by their hardness of heart into occasions for the utter rejection of His Son.

So now they come round about Him and say, **"How long dost Thou hold us in suspense? If Thou** [with special stress on the word] **art the Christ, tell us plainly."** To this He replies, **"I told you, and ye believe not"**—a completed testimony, a continued unbelief—**"the works that I** [with stress on the pronoun] **do in My Father's Name, these bear witness of Me"** (v. 25; cp. 5:36). The clause "in My Father's Name" has this significance, that, contrary to their ideas and expectations concerning the Christ, He had come as His Father's representative, and His works, wrought in this capacity, revealed His true character as the Christ, that is to say, what kind of a Christ the Father had actually sent.

What Characterizes the True Sheep

He now resumes the subject about which He had spoken to them before concerning His sheep. This and the preceding discourse are therefore closely connected. **"But ye** [with stress on the word] **believe not, because ye are not of My sheep,"** an emphatic phrase, more literally, "the sheep which are Mine."

There are no persons so obdurate as religious fanatics. The Jews prepare to stone Him. To this He replies, with calm dignity: **"Many good works have I showed you from the Father: for which of these works do ye**

stone Me?"** They base their act on what they regard as His one claim to deity. The Lord knew all their arguments. They failed to discern that His works were part and parcel of His divine nature itself and were not the acts of a kindly man. They were essentially a witness to His deity. To prove the validity of their charge they ought to have prepared to stone Him on the ground of His works as much as on the ground of His statement.

A Final Word

He has one word more for them before leaving them. The manner in which He absolutely rebuts the charge of blasphemy evinces His divine wisdom. He refers them to Psalm 82:6, speaking of the quotation as part of **"your law."** They prided themselves in their knowledge of Scripture. How little they really apprehended its truth! From their own principles and from the Scriptures they were wrong: **"If He** [God] **called them gods, unto whom the Word of God came (and the Scripture cannot be broken), say ye of Him whom the Father sanctified and sent into the world, Thou blasphemest; because I said, I am the Son of God?"** It is abundantly clear that the Jews did not expect the Messiah to be possessed of deity. The whole controversy between Christ and them shows that.

Accordingly, the Lord, in closing, makes His claim as clear as it could be made: **"If I do not the works of My Father, believe Me not. But if I do them, though ye believe not Me, believe the works: that ye may know and understand, that the Father is in Me, and I in the Father."** That statement brought the matter to a climax. It was both retrospective and anticipative: retrospective regarding all His "signs," and especially that of giving the blind man sight: anticipative regarding the next and last sign, the raising of a man from the tomb (see 11:42).

They made one more effort to take Him, but it was true for some days that His "time had not yet come." Escaping therefore from their grasp, He went beyond Jordan, where John had baptized, and abode there. Many came to Him and believed on Him.

JOHN

CHAPTER ELEVEN

Verses 1 to 26

The Raising of Lazarus

This was the consummating act of the Lord's signs recorded in this Gospel, as a testimony to His deity as the Son of God (v. 4). The narrative exhibits both His tender compassion and His almighty power, evidences at once of His veritable godhood and His true manhood.

Faith's Testing

This crown of His miracles was both a witness to His critics and a means of establishing the faith of His followers. True faith is tested faith. Hearing that Lazarus was sick, Jesus **"abode at that time two days in the place where he was"** (R.V.). The Lord's testings are always proofs of His love. **"Jesus loved Martha, and her sister, and Lazarus . . . Therefore He abode . . . where He was."** But beyond His love for them He honored them by putting them in the furnace of affliction for the completion of His final witness to the people.

The case with His disciples was different. Upon His decision to go, they would have stayed Him so as to deliver Him from danger. The Lord uses their devoted representations to give them a lesson concerning the highest motive of service. To be faithful to God is to walk in the light. To be governed by mere expediency is to walk in the darkness and to stumble.

The Highest Motive

But everything must be the outcome of faith and, as with the sisters, that was the immediate need of the disciples. So, after an explanation of the actual meaning of His statement, **"Our friend Lazarus is fallen asleep,"** He says, **"I am glad for your sakes that I was not there, to the intent ye may believe."** Thomas was anxious to believe. His, **"Let us also go, that we may die with Him,"** evoked by Christ's decision

to go, was not a case of melancholy foreboding, but of downright and cheerful loyalty. Jesus was more to him than life itself. What a lesson for us! Activity in His cause is valueless if it is not subordinated to love for Christ Himself. Let the preciousness of His person ever be the dominating motive of our service for Him.

"Jesus Wept"

This intense attachment to Him is touchingly evinced in both Martha and Mary. The one goes to meet Him, the other stays to receive Him. Martha's attitude is that of reverent confidence and entire submission. She combines the recognition of His power with that of His love: **"And even now I know that whatsoever Thou wilt ask of God, God will give it Thee."** His question, **"Where have ye laid him?"** betokened, not a lack of knowledge, but a kindly design to kindle their expectations. **"They say unto Him, Lord, come and see"**—a combination of expectancy and earnest desire, but withal a natural ignorance of the actual power possessed by Him. **"Jesus wept."** There was more than the sight of human sorrow in this, more even than sympathy with the sorrowing. Sympathy there was indeed. He knew the feelings and emotions of every heart in the company, but He knew more than this. He knew all the circumstances of fallen humanity that brought about death and all its woe. The sin and ignorance of all were laid open to His infinite mind. The touching detail, so briefly told, discloses His combined deity and humanity.

The Jews regarded His tears merely as the evidence of His love for Lazarus. Others were skeptical. One who had given sight to a man born blind could surely have prevented Lazarus from death. Since He let him die, how could He really love him so much? **"Jesus therefore again groaning in Himself** [a preferable rendering to the R.V. margin] **cometh to the tomb."**

"The Glory of God"

His command to take away the stone would have two different effects. It would encourage faith, for it was clear that something was about to be done. At the same time, to touch a grave would be running the risk of defilement, so faith might be tested. Yet the act of obedience indicated that He had drawn them into harmony with His will.

Martha's shrinking from the effects draws forth His gentle rebuke to her unbelief: **"Said I not unto thee that, if thou believedst, thou shouldst see the glory of God?"** This gathers up what He had said in the course of His conversation, concerning the glory of God (v. 4) and of the assurance of resurrection (vv. 25, 26). To know that they were going to see the act which would exhibit the glory of God, must have banished all misgivings.

The stone having been removed, the Lord lifts up His eyes and says, **"Father, I thank Thee that Thou hast heard Me, and I** [with special stress on the pronoun] **knew that Thou hearest Me always; but because of the multitude which standeth around I said it, that they may believe that Thou** [with stress also] **didst send Me."** By this the Lord intended that all around should know that what He was about to do was combined work of the Father and Himself, and that the impending event was of such importance, that it would finally substantiate His claims for the acceptance of faith. He had never preceded a miracle by any such utterance.

The Greatest of His Signs

And now the mighty deed is done. He cries with a loud voice, **"Lazarus, come forth."** The spirit returns to the body. The resurrected brother comes forth, the gravecloths still around him. This and the command to loose him were designed to give directions and force to the testimony. That he was still bound with the cloths was convincing proof to any skeptical and hostile Jews that he had actually been dead. He is to be "let go," suggesting his retirement from immediate and idle curiosity.

The miracle foreshadowed the death and resurrection of Christ, which would effect both the present spiritual resurrection of believers with their loosening from the binding power of sin, and their coming physical resurrection, when with His mighty shout He brings all together to meet Him in the air.

But the immediate effect was decisive. It was the crisis which finally gave rise to the greatest crime in the nation's history. Many of the Jews believed on Him. But some went their way to report it all to the Pharisees. Thus did Christ become, as He has ever been, the dividing line among men.

JOHN

CHAPTER TWELVE

Verses 1 to 25

The twelfth chapter forms an interlude between the last great sign accomplished by the Lord in the resurrection of Lazarus and His private discourses to His disciples in the Upper Room.

All the details in this chapter have a bearing in one way or another upon the subject of His death. These details with their accompanying circumstances we will now consider.

Service, Rest, Affection

The first is the scene in the house in Bethany six days before the Passover, the last of these great feasts before Christ Himself became our Passover. At the supper which was made for Him, Martha served, Lazarus sat (*i.e.*, reclined) at the table (R.V., "at meat"). Mary took the opportunity of using her pound of ointment of very precious spikenard to anoint the feet of Jesus and wipe them with her hair—three positions, serving, reclining and affectionate devotion, the last of the three being the greatest.

They all have lessons for us. Each has its place in our Christian life, whether of service or of rest or of intimate devotion to His person. It was this last by which **"the house was filled with the odor of the ointment."** So in the spiritual house, an assembly of God's people, occupation with Christ Himself in heart devotion is that which lends its fragrance to the whole gathering. Where each believer is in the enjoyment of being occupied with Christ in loving devotion during the week the effect cannot but be felt when we gather together to meet Him and worship in spirit and truth, while "at His table sits the Lord."

The Grumbling Traitor

Now comes the Lord's own reference to His death, and this is the outcome of the murmuring of covetous, treacherous Judas. Of the four Gospel writers John alone points out Judas as the grumbler. His complaint that the ointment had not been sold for three hundred pence [300 silver coins*] and given to the poor, was sheer hypocrisy; he had no care for the poor, but was a thief and robbed the common purse of Christ and His disciples of some of the contents from time to time. The Lord did not expose him but simply remonstrated saying **"suffer her to keep it against the day of my burying"** (R.V., margin, "let her alone: it was that she might keep it against the day"). **"For the poor ye have always with you; but Me ye have not always."**

This does not imply, of course, that Mary did not use the whole of the ointment at that time. She poured it all out upon Him. Her spending was keeping. Her devotion was deeper than to hold the ointment for His embalming. Her discerning mind knew what the issue of the hatred of the Jews would be. She would manifest her affection while her Lord was living and able to appreciate it. He was everything to her. Should He not be so to us?

Different Public Attitudes

The rest of the narrative reveals a variety of attitudes toward Him. There was the curiosity of "the common people"; there was the murderous envy of the chief priests; and now the excited enthusiasm of the multitude. There were often, it is said, some three million persons at Jerusalem at Passover time. His great miracle of the raising of Lazarus must be celebrated by a procession into the city. That would be quite to their liking. Moreover, who could this great person be but the king of Israel?

The Lord, fully knowing the issue, was willing to offer Himself as their king Messiah, and thus fulfill the prophecy of Zechariah 9:9. The people would have the opportunity of receiving Him, though His thoughts were not their thoughts. His arrangements were not made by

*Publishers note: The original has "about £10.12s.6p."

the suggestion of the disciples. They, for the time being, did not understand why He chose this manner of declaring His messiahship.

Greek Aspirations

The issues would involve the bringing in of Gentiles. There were certain Greeks who had come to worship in Jerusalem. They were proselytes, Gentiles by birth, and had adopted the Jewish religion. They wanted to see Jesus, not simply to get a view of Him, that was easy enough, but to have an interview with Him, probably as to whether He could satisfy their aspirations. Now Philip had a Greek name, and being "of Bethsaida, of Galilee" ("Galilee of the nations"), he knew their language well, so they approached him; he saw the meaning of their request sufficiently to associate Andrew with himself in applying to Christ. Moreover, would the Lord be willing, considering that on a recent occasion He had bidden His disciples not to go among Gentiles?

Gentile wise men from the east came to Christ's cradle; gentile men from the west came to His cross. His reply to Philip and Andrew was not a refusal. The cross was occupying His heart. It was the only means of securing for Gentiles far greater benefits than these Greeks were seeking, the blessings of their salvation; and to secure this would be His very glory. Accordingly He immediately says, **"The hour is come, that the Son of Man should be glorified. Verily, verily, I say unto you, except a grain of wheat fall into the earth and die, it abideth alone; but if it die, it beareth much fruit."** The inquiring Greeks would get to know Him, and to realize His power, and thus would have the fulfillment of more than their aspirations, and that not by His miracles but by His death.

The Lord gives two lessons in His reply. His death provides the productive power of the life that is in Him, risen and exalted. That is His first lesson. But while His falling into the ground, with the consequent fruitfulness of His act, was unique and absolute, it provided an illustrative principle, to be realized in the lives of His faithful followers. That is His second lesson. In this respect He says **"He that loveth his life, loseth it; and he that hateth his life in this world shall keep it unto life eternal."** If the seed grain is eaten instead of being sown, it produces no fruit. If we consume our lives for our self-gratification, neither are we fruitful here, nor shall we reap the reward in the life beyond. He who sows his life for Christ on behalf of others loses much worldly advantage but keeps it in the fruit it produces unto eternal life, the effect and power of which he himself will enjoy forever.

Verses 26 to 36

The occasion of the desire of some Greeks to make Christ's acquaintance leads to His last two testimonies in public. This, the last but one (vv. 26–36), contains constant references to His impending death.

A High Calling

Following His promise that he who hates his life shall keep it unto life eternal, a promise which He had illustrated by fruitfulness, He shows, firstly, what this means in practical experience, what kind of life we are called upon to live, and, secondly, what is the special feature of the life beyond. **"If any man serve Me, let Him follow Me."** There is emphasis on the "Me" in both clauses. It is He who is the object of the heart's true devotion and it is He who has trod the path before. His example has been set. True service means hating one's life instead of loving it. Self-love is self-destruction. He has given up His life for us; let us give up our lives to Him, cost what it may. This estimate of our life does not mean carelessness in the matter of our body and health, but it does mean absolute self-denial. It means taking up our cross and following Him, and that daily (see Luke 9:23 and 14:27). If we follow not the path He has trod we walk in darkness.

As to the future, He says, **"where I am, there shall also My servant be."** That is not merely future. It is the height of present privilege, honor and bliss. "'Tis heaven where Jesus is." That is so now. It will be so in eternity. It is Christ Himself Who will make heaven our delightful paradise.

He then says, **"If any man serve Me, Him will the Father honor."** Here the emphasis is on the verbs "serve" and "honor." It is the Father's will ever to glorify His Son;

therefore service for the Son will receive honor from the Father. We should ever seek to realize what the apostle Paul calls "the prize of the high calling of God in Christ Jesus."

The Prelude to the Sacrifice

The Lord's mention of His approaching death leads to an utterance which has been described as the prelude of the conflict in Gethsemane. It marvelously combines the deepest trouble with the highest desire. He says **"Now is My soul troubled** [lit., has been and is troubled]; **and what shall I say? Father, save Me from this hour. But for this cause came I unto this hour. Father, glorify Thy Name"** (vv. 27, 28).

Some would put a question mark after "hour," as if the Lord meant "Shall I say, Father save Me from this hour?" While this is possible, the rendering as it stands in our versions seems right. The hour was the time of the impending sufferings of His atoning sacrifice, and of the divine judgment for sin upon His sinless soul. He knew all that was coming upon Him. That was sufficient to elicit the prayer "Father, save Me from this hour." It was an expression of the utmost stirring of His soul. It seems inappropriate to regard it as a question, as if the Lord was deliberating as to what He should say. He similarly prayed in Gethsemane, "If it be possible, let this cup pass away from Me" (Matt. 26:39). There too He said immediately "Nevertheless, not as I will, but as Thou wilt." That prayer conveyed no deviation from submission to the Father's will. So in the present instance He at once asserts the reason for His coming to that hour: "But for this cause came I unto this hour." Is not the cause the laying down of His life that the Father's Name might be glorified (combining what He had taught in v. 25 with what immediately now follows in v. 28)? Not simply in submission to the will of the Father, but in His heart's perfect devotion to Him He says, "Father, glorify Thy name."

His Greatest Desire

That was ever His undeviating motive, and His prayer meets with an immediate double response: **"I have both glorified it, and will glorify it again."** The Father had glorified it in the past life of the obedience of His Son, reaching its climax in His death, which seems to be included in that statement as an accomplished fact. It covers both His life and His death. He would also glorify it in raising Him from the dead and seating Him at His right hand.

The crowd around imagined there had been a clap of thunder. Some thought an angel had spoken to Him. He declared that the voice had come especially for their sakes, with the object that they might believe (see v. 36). His thoughts center again in His death. **"Now is the judgment of this world."** The "now" vividly points to that which is impending. The judgment of this world means the sentence to be passed upon it, not the opinion expressed by it. While in God's love and mercy He gave His only-begotten Son to die for the world, there could be nothing else than condemnation for all rejecters, both those who actually determined upon His death, and all since who by unbelief have taken sides with them.

Verses 37 to 50

The closing portion of chapter twelve consists of two parts: (1) verses 37 to 43, describing, as a climax, the persistent unbelief of the Jews, (2) verses 44 to 50, giving as a consummation the Lord's public testimony to them. These form the two great subjects of all the preceding part of this Gospel from 5:10 to 12:36, and they are mentioned here by way of bringing the record of these circumstances to a head. The crisis had been reached. (1) The Christ-rejecting Jews must go on in their darkness. (2) Yet He holds out hope for any who would even now believe and turn to Him. His testimony is the very height of long-suffering and merciful warning.

As to the multitude, **"though He had done so many signs before them, yet they believed not on Him."** The apostle declares that this unbelief was in order that two prophecies of Isaiah might be fulfilled, 53:1, and 6:10 (so, by the way, Isaiah wrote both parts of that book!).

Human Responsibility

Now this seems, at a cursory glance, as if the Jews were helpless in the matter; Isaiah had foretold their state, so it must be! Such an idea loses sight of the great foundation fact of the absolute foreknowledge of God. God foreknew that the Jews would harden themselves, spurning His long-suffering and mercy, despising their privileges and foregoing their responsibility. God, foreseeing their perverseness and the consequent necessity of His retributive dealings in blinding their eyes and hardening their hearts, caused Isaiah to put it all on record centuries before. That was the infallible Word of God. It could not "be broken." Being His Word it must be fulfilled. The foreknown and foretold issue was inevitable, not because God had determined their condition, but because of their sinful self-will and their own determination to reject His overtures and offers. Their unbelief was their own act.

There is a limit to God's long-suffering, a limit consistent with His perfect character and attributes. When a man oversteps that limit he comes under judicial hardening by God. The most striking instance of this is the case of Pharaoh. See the R.V. in Exodus 7:13 (the correctness of which is confirmed by v. 14); 7:22; 8:15, 19; 9:7. At that juncture he overstepped the limit and 9:12 declares that God hardened his heart (see also 10:1, 20, 27; 11:10; 14:4).

That Isaiah spoke of the blindness and hardening of Israel in his own time, after the death of Uzziah, is clear in the passage in chapter six. That John applies it to the Jews in the time of Christ and declares that Isaiah saw the glory of Christ and spake of Him, shows that, as with many other prophecies of the Old Testament, there is a double application, one immediate, the other remote, to be fulfilled in a later period.

The Fear of Man

Amidst the general apostasy many even of the rulers believed in Christ, but feared to confess Him lest the religious leaders should excommunicate them: **"they loved the glory of men (**R.V.**) more than the glory of God."** This snare is easy to fall into. Let us guard against allowing our attitude to God to be governed by human considerations. To set a greater value upon the esteem of men than upon the glory of God blights the spiritual life. Let Christ's love dominate our affections

and we shall not fear man, but shall esteem reproach for His sake our highest honor.

An Epitome

Verses 44 to 50 give the Lord's testimony in the form of an epitome of all that He had taught, every word as He spoke it, but not necessarily after the occasion in verse 36 when He hid Himself from the multitude. The great points in the epitome are as follows:

Firstly, the true believer He directs to the Father (vv. 44, 45). He ever sought to glorify Him. The glory of the Father is the great theme of the whole passage.

Secondly, as to the believer's own condition, His having come as a Light safeguards him against abiding in darkness (v. 46). **"I am come a light into the world."** There is great emphasis on the "I."

Thirdly, as to the unbeliever, the rejecter of His sayings, let none be surprised at His refraining from passing sentence of condemnation upon such; He had come, not as judge but as Savior (v. 47). Judgment will come in the last day, and then everything will depend upon the way His Word has been treated (v. 48). His "word" is the sum and substance of all His teaching. To reject that must bring sentence of condemnation. So it is with the gospel, which ever since has, in its fullness, proclaimed all that He taught.

Fourthly, the gravity of the rejection lies in this, that all that He uttered was by commandment of the Father, both the doctrine **("what I should say")** and the phraseology in which it was expressed **("what I should speak"),** verse 49. The R.V. **"from myself"** is preferable to the A.V., "of Myself," which might mean "about Myself": Christ was not Himself the source of His teaching.

Fifthly, the Father's commandment, here signifying, not a specific command, but all that Christ had been given to speak, has as its object the bestowment of life eternal (v. 50). That is the gracious purpose of the Father's commission to the Son and of the Son's faithful ministry.

This brings to a close the first part of this Gospel. The public witness has been given, the works have been accomplished, the judgment has been pronounced. All must now be concentrated privately upon the disciples.

JOHN

CHAPTER THIRTEEN

Verses 1 to 17

The first verse of chapter thirteen contains, by way of introduction, the prominent ideas found in the five chapters thirteen to seventeen. There are five particulars: (1) the time: **"Now before the feast of the Passover,"** (2) the person: **"Jesus,"** (3) His foreknowledge, **"knowing that His hour was come that He should depart out of this world unto the Father,"** (4) the objects of His love, **"having loved His own which were in the world,"** (5) the continuity and degree of His love: **"He loved them unto the end."**

His thoughts center, not in His impending sufferings, but in the Father and "His own." This latter phrase refers to different objects from "His own" in 1:11; there it spoke of His natural property and kin, here it speaks of those who were the Father's spiritual gift to Him. The great key word here is "love."

As to the immediate circumstances, the A.V., "supper being ended" does not represent the original. There are only two possible renderings, either "when supper was come" or "when supper was taking place." The R.V. **"during supper,"** is probably right. The indication is that it was the early part of the meal. The opening words of the chapter point to the supper as being that of the paschal feast. The scene is full of preparations. The Lord, who knew all that was coming upon Him, and who had, only a day or two before, told the disciples that in this Passover period He would be delivered up to be crucified (Matt. 26:1), had prepared all the arrangements for this Upper Room occasion. Satan had been preparing. He had already put it into the heart of Judas Iscariot to betray Him. Other human agents of the evil one were busy making preparations, and holding a council of death.

"Jesus, Knowing"

What is said about the devil and Judas is followed by a statement for the second time as to the Lord's knowledge, and the two very different subjects are combined as an introduction to the washing of the disciples' feet; **"Jesus, knowing that the Father had given all things into His hands, and that He came forth from God, and goeth unto God, riseth from supper, and layeth aside His garments; and He took a towel, and girded Himself."** This was another preparation, a preparation, first by act and then by teaching, for the life the Eleven were to live after He had gone, and the testimony they were to give in their service after the coming of the Holy Spirit at Pentecost. Hence the three statements as to the Lord's knowledge.

The vivid present tense is used, almost entirely, to depict the circumstances. Every act had its special significance. His laying aside His garments spoke of the fact that He who ever was "in the form of God" took "the form of a servant" (Phil. 2:6, 7). It does not seem to have entered the minds of the disciples that they might wash one another's feet. Indeed they do not appear to have been in a mood for it (see Luke 22:24). If, as Edersheim thinks, Judas, as the manager for the company, took the first place, the Lord may have washed his feet first. In any case here was malice met with kindness. Here was long-suffering manifested with grace and dignity. It has been well remarked, "Jesus at the feet of the traitor—what a picture! What lessons for us!"

Cleansed to Render Service

The feet-washing was designed to teach two distinct things in the Christian life, first the need of cleansing from sin, second the need of serving one another with humility. The first is brought out by Peter's exclamatory question, **"Lord, dost Thou wash my feet?"** by his impetuous remonstrance, **"Thou shalt never wash my feet"**; and (on hearing that without this he can have no part with Him) by his impulsive desire, **"Lord, not my feet only, but also my hands and my head."**

In answer to the question, the Lord says, **"What I do thou knowest not now; but thou shalt understand hereafter."** The

"I" and the "thou" are emphatic. The R.V. brings out the distinction between the verbs, *oida,* to perceive intuitively, and *ginōskō,* to understand by learning. In the reply to the remonstrance the Lord reveals the deep significance of the washing. To have no part with Him means the lack of more than the external washing of the feet. The answer to the impulsive desire makes clear the difference between the initial removal of the defilement of sin at the time of the new birth, and the need of renewed cleansing consequent upon the committal of an act.

The Lord immediately distinguishes between the condition of the Eleven, who had all been bathed and were thus **"clean every whit,"** and the one who, because his heart was defiled, had not been bathed. So, knowing who would betray Him, He said **"Ye are not all clean"** (v. 11). After resuming His place at the table He gives the second explanation of His act. **"Ye call Me,"** He says, **"Master** [teacher, a term of respect and recognition of instruction] **and Lord** [a term of honor and recognition of authority]." If He, with all that these titles meant, did what He had now done, there rests upon them, as upon us all, a sacred obligation, consequent both upon His example and upon the claims of nature common to all (**"one another"**).

True Blessedness

The apostle Peter recalls this scene, when he says, "Yea, all of you, gird yourselves with humility to serve one another" (1 Pet. 5:5). It speaks of freedom from high-mindedness, of self-forgetting love, of submitting to one another in the fear of God, of putting on "a heart of compassion, kindness, humbleness of mind, meekness, long-suffering." For a servant is not greater than his lord, nor one that is sent greater than he that sent him. **"If ye know these things,"** He says (and they did, and we do), **"blessed are ye** [a better rendering than "happy," as it conveys not mere joy but the sense of divine favor that carries its reward] **if ye do them."**

Verses 18 to 30

There was now to be another kind of purification. The spiritual atmosphere must be cleansed before the Lord's Supper could be instituted, and the Eleven prepared for that ministry for which they were to be sent into the world. How could one be so prepared who had definitely identified himself with the world? The statement **"I speak not of you all"** seems to be connected with what He had just said about sending. Judas was not to be "one that is sent." Moreover, Christ was going to say something further about sending (v. 20).

Judas could not deceive Him: **"I [emphatic] know whom [plural] I have chosen"** [or, as it should be, I chose], He says. He knew them all, each one, and as for Judas see 6:70, 71. He chose them to be His immediate companions and followers. He chose Judas by a divine deliberation in the fulfillment of His Father's will, and, consistently with it, in fulfillment of Psalm 41:9. His object in telling them beforehand was for their best interests, and their best interests lay in their faith in Him. **"I tell you . . . that, when it is come to pass, ye may believe that I am."** There is no pronoun "He" after "I am." They would find both that He was all that he had declared concerning His essential attributes, and that He was to them all that He had promised to be, as the One who would send them. They would know Him in their experiences in this respect. And this was so important that He attaches a "Verily, verily" to it: **"Verily, verily, I say unto you, He that receiveth whomsoever I send receiveth Him that sent Me"** (v. 20). They could not enjoy a more intimate union with Him and with the Father.

The Disclosures of the Betrayal

It cost the Lord much to make the disclosure as to who would be the instrument of His betrayal: **"He was troubled in spirit** [in 11:33, in seeing the sorrows of others, "He troubled Himself"], **and testified, and said, Verily, verily, I say unto you, that one of you shall betray Me."** The statement evinces His sorrow more than the guilt of the act. More than this, it shows the voluntary nature of His suffering. He could have suggested a way of escape, or some mode of prevention or resistance; but there is nothing of all this. It was part of the predetermined path toward the accomplishment of that for which He came into the world.

The disciples are stirred to sorrowful and bewildered anxiety (an emotion absent from Judas) as to which of them would be the cause. Peter makes a sign to John (who was leaning on the bosom of the Lord) to find out, and says **"Tell us who it is of whom He speaketh."** So John, **"leaning back** [a different word from that in v. 23, "reclining"], **as he was on Jesus' breast** [the R.V. "as he was" represents the single word, *houtōs,* "thus," which the A.V. omits, but this adverb would rather indicate that John, having paid attention to Peter's request, did what he wished (the "thus" referring to his so doing as Peter had desired), and, leaning back again (the change in the tense, to the aorist, points to this)] **saith unto Him, Lord, who is it?"**

"Jesus therefore answereth [and the narratives in Matthew and Mark show that the answer was not given privately to John alone], **He it is, for whom I shall dip the sop, and give it to him."** The definite article "the" is to be noticed. It specifies the regular act at the Feast of the Passover (the A.V. "a sop" misses this, and gives the idea of a passing act). According to custom, the sop, prepared by the head of the household, was delivered at the proper moment to the person chosen by him. Apparently Judas had dipped his hand in the dish (Matt 26:23, R.V.). The Lord dips the sop and hands it to him. Quite possibly Judas had chosen the chief couch for himself and acted accordingly.

"That Thou Doest"

Thereupon Satan enters into him. He had prepared himself for this climax. The Lord was fully cognizant of this act on the part of the spiritual foe: **"Jesus therefore** [i.e., because of Satan's entry] **said unto him, That thou doest, do quickly."** All that was required for the removal of the traitor was said; nothing more, nothing less. All is known between Christ and Judas. Judas sees both that the master is not deceived and that he himself is discovered. Yes, discovered, but not exposed; he has admonition, but freedom to act; separation, but not expulsion. Much was prevented which would have deprived the disciples of that ministry which they were about to receive. Self-humbled, they are not roused to animosity against the culprit. He allows their ideas to be mistaken (vv. 28, 29).

What an example (an additional example) the Lord set us! What self-restraint, what forbearance, what freedom from severity of judgment and strong judicial action! Much would never have happened in the past, much would not be taking place now, if the spirit the Lord manifested had characterized believers.

The language of the original in Christ's command "That thou doest, do quickly" is striking. Firstly, there is a change of tenses in the verb: the first is the present continuous, i.e., "What thou art doing" (what thou art engaged in doing); the second is the aorist tense, the tense of definite act, i.e., "go and do it." The first views the doing, the process of betrayal, as a whole; the second views it as a single deed. Again, the word "quickly" is in the comparative degree (lit., "more quickly"), suggesting the possibility of interruptions or hindrances, which might arise from Christ's intervention. But He will not so interfere. He is the controller of the whole situation.

"It Was Night"

Judas, **"having received the sop went out straightway: and it was night"**—nature's night around him, moral and spiritual, night in his soul, the precursor of a darker night to follow, and all to do with the darkest and greatest crime in human history.

And now the atmosphere is cleansed. The immediate burden is lightened. The reserve, hitherto necessary, can yield place to the outflow of affection, to the unfolding of the deepest truths, and, almost at the beginning of it all, the institution of that love-feast, "the Lord's Supper."

The opening statements disclose the highest truths, truths that are basic to all that follows to the end of the seventeenth chapter: **"Now is the Son of man glorified, and God is glorified in Him."** In the original the verbs are in the aorist tense, which gives the literal rendering "Now was the Son of man glorified, and God was glorified in Him" (see the R.V. margin). But they are not simply statements of past events. What is indicated is that the events that are to follow, both the immediate events in connection with the Cross, and the succeeding events in both the near and the distant future are regarded and spoken of as assured and accomplished facts. The Lord was looking through all that was then actually in course of preparation for His death, and the circumstances and effects of His death. And having used this comprehensive form of expression, He proceeds to a direct statement of the future: **"and God shall glorify Him in Himself, and straightway shall he glorify Him."** In all that the Father is essentially, in His own being, the Son will ever be glorified in perfect oneness with Him. He straightway glorified Him in that "He raised Him from the dead and gave Him glory."

The Lord's Supper

Taking into consideration the Synoptic narratives of the institution of the Lord's Supper, and the circumstances recorded by John in chapter thirteen, it seems probable that this institution took place just after Judas had gone out, and Christ had made the immediately consequent remarks mentioned in verse 32, and previously to His addressing the disciples as mentioned in verse 33. This is more probable than after what He says in verse 35, as verse 36 is linked with verse 33.

The omission is purposive. The teachings of the Lord in that room do not refer to sacrifice for sin, the body and the blood of Christ, and the new covenant. The leading subjects are our immediate relations with Him. There are manifest correspondences and connections between the institution and the Lord's discourses, as, for instance, in the instruction concerning His coming again.

A New Commandment

How suitably, after they had partaken from His hands the emblems of His body and His blood, the symbols of His death, and had heard His promise to return, come the words, **"Little children, yet a little while I am with you . . . A new commandment I give unto you, that ye love one another; even as I have loved you . . . I go to prepare a place for you, And . . . I come again, and will receive you unto Myself!"**

He had announced to His enemies His going, but had forewarned them of eternal separation from Him (8:21); His announcement here to His disciples of His going is accompanied by the assurance of eternal reunion. He addresses them as "little children" for the first time. John uses it seven times in his first epistle. It conveys four ideas, (1) affection, (2) parental care, (3) compassion, (4) family intimacy.

He gives a "new commandment" to love one another according to the standard of His own love (v. 34). Seven times in the whole discourse He speaks of His commandments, and in each place associates them with the subject of love (here; 14:15, 21, 23; 15:10, 12, 14 with 13). His love provides both *the motive* and *the measure* of our love. As exhibited in us it both displays *the character* of real discipleship and gives the testimony of it to the world: **"By this shall all men know that ye are My disciples, if ye have love one to another."** In this we are to be His representatives here.

The word *kainos,* "new," signifies not newness in time, recent *(neos),* but newness of nature and quality, superior to the old. The love of which the Lord speaks is therefore not obedience to the letter of the Law but the very spring and power of the new life, "the law of the Spirit of life in Christ Jesus."

Peter is occupied especially with the staggering fact that the Lord was going away. His answer elicits that disciple's impetuous but faithful assurance of the utmost loyalty. This, in turn, produces another revelation of the Lord's complete foreknowledge, and now of all that would affect the circumstances of them all.

The Lord checks mere impulse and self-confidence. His prediction of Peter's threefold denial does this. But both this prediction and other details of His disclosures produce foreboding in the hearts of all. It was all purposively preparatory on His part to the words of consolation and blessed assurance He would minister to them and to all His own ever since, and the revelation of Himself, His character, His ways and doings, which form the great essence of the following discourse.

JOHN

CHAPTER FOURTEEN

Verses 1 to 11

Unity of the Godhead

Consolation and revelation: this is His double ministry throughout. They are the features of His twofold message which opens that part of His discourse at the beginning of chapter fourteen: **"Let not your heart be troubled"**; that is the consolation; **"ye believe in God, believe also in Me"**: that is revelation. Consolation to the hearts of His followers, revelation of His own heart! Since, however, the verb rendered "Ye believe" has also the form of the imperative, and since His ministry is that of consolation to troubled hearts, it is better to regard each part as a command: **"believe in God, believe also in Me."** It is a faith that goes much further than an acceptance of a truth, it cleaves to the speaker. And what the Lord reveals is the unity between the Father and the Son. Faith in both is a necessity. Without this there is no salvation in any sense of the term.

The unity of the persons and yet their distinctive personalities are further declared: **"In My Father's House"** means that what is the Father's is likewise the Son's, and it is the prerogative of the Son both to prepare the abode and to come and convey thither those for whom it is prepared: **"I go to prepare a place for you . . . I come again** [vivid present tense in both parts, giving assurance of the future facts], **and will receive you unto Myself; that where I am, there ye may be also."** This is more than a reception to meet Him in the air (1 Thess. 4:17). That will be so, but He takes us, surely, from the place of meeting in the air, into the Father's house, to be with Him. He says, "where I am"; this is "within the veil, whither as forerunner Jesus entered for us" (Heb. 6:20). That place is "the Father's House" (see also 17:24).

His Coming Again

The Lord is not referring to the falling asleep of the individual believer. He is speaking of the time of the Rapture of all believers at the completion of the Church. He thus, at the beginning of His discourse, carries the thoughts of the disciples right on to the time of consummation, so that this promise may cast its rays upon all that intervenes, as dealt with in the remainder of His teachings.

In His wisdom the Lord states the assumption that they know the way He is going: the R.V. is right, **"And whither I go, ye know the way."** He knew that this would cause Thomas to demur (v. 5). Christ had ready His self-revelation, so personal, so comprehensive: not, "I make the way, I reveal the truth, I give the life," but **"I am the way, and the truth, and the life."** And the fact that He is the truth and the life because He is the way, is confirmed by His additional statement, **"No one cometh unto the Father, but by Me"**; that has to do with the way alone, it is the way to the Father, and means the consequent experience of Christ as the truth and the life.

He thus goes further than the way to the Father's house. He occupies our thoughts with the Father Himself and the present experience of coming voluntarily and by faith to Him, through Christ. "By Me" conveys the twofold thought both of His immediate personal mediation and of what He has wrought so as to bring this about, that is, His incarnation, life, atoning death, resurrection and ascension (see Rom. 5:2; Eph. 2:13, 15, 18; Heb. 7:25; 10:19–21). Accordingly this statement goes far beyond what it had meant for Old Testament saints to come to God.

Knowing the Two in One

The Lord now presses home the profound truth He had uttered in public (8:19), but with a difference. Here He says, **"If ye had known** [ginōskō] **Me, ye would have known** [oida] **My Father also."** The first verb expresses a knowledge progressive and gained, the second a knowledge immediate and perceptive. In 8:19 the verb is *oida* in both parts. With the opposing Pharisees the very idea of getting to know Him is altogether set aside. No knowledge whatever was possible to them. To the disciples He can and does say, **"from henceforth ye know him"** (*ginōskete*, ye are getting to know); they had entered upon the process and would increase in the acquisition. Moreover they had "seen Him." Christ, as the Son, was the personal manifestation of the Father, and in reply to Philip's earnest request that Christ would show Him He says, **"he that hath seen Me hath seen the Father"** (v. 9).

Here again a different verb, *horaō,* is used from that in 12:45 *(theōreō). Theōreō* denotes to be a spectator of: it stresses the action of the beholder; *horaō* lays more emphasis on the object beheld, upon the direction in which the vision goes. This is especially exemplified in the Lord's word here to the disciples, that the Father manifests Himself in the Son (cp. 1:17, 18). It must be so by reason of the mutual indwelling, **"I am in the Father, and the Father in Me,"** repeated here and again in 17:23, in the prayer. The essential unity of their nature in the Godhead, involving unity of mind, will and action, is conveyed in this great foundation statement by the Lord.

Our Highest Occupation

True, this unity, this mutual indwelling, exceeds the limits of natural comprehension, and for this very reason He adds **"believe Me for the very works' sake."** This He had said in public (10:37, 38), but here there is more to follow. First the person, then the works—these are the combined motives for faith. To the Jews they had been presented as alternatives; to the disciples the works provide a supplementary motive to the faith: "believe Me on account of [i.e., by reason of, not for the sake of, as in the Versions] the very works." Nicodemus draws a conclusion from the works (3:2), and that by way of observation and reasoning. The disciples acknowledge Him apart from His works (1:41-48). Our highest occupation is with Christ Himself and our personal and increasing knowledge of Him. This is strengthened by the experience of His dealings with us.

Verses 12 to 31

Greater Works

From the mention of His works He opens their minds again to the future, but now concerning their service. He passes from Himself as the object of faith to their life of faith in dependence upon His presence with the Father. And again the greatness and newness of the theme is marked by His **"Verily, verily, I say unto you."** His self-revelation continues: **"he that believeth on Me, the works that I do shall He do also; and greater *works* than these shall he do; because I go unto the Father"** (v. 12). There is continuity and increase, but He is the author and means of both.

The fact that the works will be greater is due to His exaltation. They also become greater because of their extent in the world and because by them the Church, the Body of Christ, is in process of formation, the greatest of all the creative works of God.

Asking in His Name

In this connection the Lord associates prayer with works, indicating the necessity of the former for the effectiveness of the latter. There are three factors essential in this respect: (1) requests are to be made in His name; (2) He will Himself fulfill them; (3) the Father is thus to be glorified in the Son. In this repetition of the first two He says, **"If ye shall ask Me anything in My Name"** (v. 14, R.V.), expressing in another way His unity with the Father in the Godhead.

To make a request in His Name does not mean simply appending the phrase to a petition or prayer, it involves the experience of that relationship to, and fellowship with, Him, that resemblance to His character and delight in His will which His Name implies; it means the appropriation of His merits, His rights, His claims. This imparted a new character and power and sweetness to prayer which they had not experienced hitherto.

With this His next statement is not disconnected, **"If ye love Me, ye will keep My commandments."** Asking in His Name is a mere shibboleth if we do not keep His commandments. For in departing from them we fail to represent Him and therefore fail to do anything in His Name.

The Trinity

But for this we cannot rely upon our own wills, however determined we may be to be obedient. Accordingly, it is just here that the Lord introduces the subject of the promised presence and power of the Holy Spirit: **"Ye will keep My commandments, and I will pray the Father** ["make request of"—a different word from "ask" in vv. 13 and 14: *aiteō*, there, suggests the petition of an inferior to a superior, *erōtaō*, here, suggests a right to expect the fulfillment], **and He shall give you another Comforter** [not *heteros*, another of a different kind, but *allos*, another of similar nature], **that He may be with you forever, even the Spirit of truth."**

Obedience, then, is the obedience of love, love that expresses itself in an act that fulfills His will. The authority of His will and the affections of the heart are as cause and effect in those who are "in law (*ennomos*, the literal word in 1 Cor. 9:21) to Christ." For this He promises the Holy Spirit. In this matter again He reveals His oneness and equality with the Father. For in verse 26 He says, as here, "Whom the Father will send in My Name." In 15:26 and 16:7 He says, "Whom I will send." What is this but the Trinity, the three acting in one? For what He is going to reveal concerning the Holy Spirit is nothing short of a predication of His deity. The Father acts in and through the Son, the Son acts as in the Father, and the Spirit acts in perfect unison of being and action with the Father and the Son.

The Paraclete

The Name given to the Spirit is "the Paraclete," lit., one called to the side (of another); but the work expresses the purpose for which He comes, the kindly act He does. There are two meanings, the one signifying, as it does in the four occurrences in this part of the Gospel, one who by His presence and companionship imparts encouragement, strength and support. "Comforter" is the right rendering, only it means more than merely giving comfort. The other meaning is advocate, one who undertakes our cause and pleads for us; that is its meaning in 1 John 2:1.

When He says "another Comforter" (using the word which means another of like nature), He is recalling the fact that He has been to them all that the word signifies in the first of the two meanings just mentioned. The same ministry will be continued by the Spirit, and that "forever," both here and hereafter. He is "the Spirit of truth"; that is to say, He will be the power in their testimony to the truth, thus fulfilling both the divine counsels and human needs. For in a world of darkness, devilry and deception, man's great need is the truth. For this Christ came into the world (8:32) and He is Himself, as He has just said, "the Truth." "The Spirit beareth witness," witness to Christ and all that this means, "because the Spirit is truth" (1 John 5:7).

The World—A Contrast

Just here it is that the Lord contrasts them and the world. The world **"cannot receive"** the Spirit, **"for it beholdeth Him not, neither knoweth Him."** The very condition of the world rendered impossible any recognition of Him. The disciples did behold in Christ and His ways and works the manifestation of the Holy Spirit's person and power. Instead of knowing Him, the world charged Christ with being demon-possessed (8:52). The disciples knew the Spirit, for they had already experienced His power, as well as seeing His works in their master. **"He abideth with you,"** that was already true, **"and shall be in you,"** that would be true from Pentecost onward. They would realize Him as the comforter, empowering their witness and operating in the written testimony of such as would take part in the completion of the Scriptures of truth. "With" and "in"! What a power for every experience in life!

But that did not mean that He would take the place of Christ Himself. He assures them of this immediately, and says, **"I will not leave you desolate** (lit., orphans): **I come unto you."** The Spirit Himself is the very minister of Christ. If the Spirit of Christ indwells us, Christ Himself does. This means a vision of Christ; not physical, but very real. The spiritual would replace the physical for the disciples. **"Yet a little while, and the world beholdeth Me no more; but ye behold Me."** The world had seen Him only to mistake Him, because of their sinful state. The disciples, and we like them, have a different faculty of sight, the sight of faith.

Life Indeed

But His presence with us and in us, according to His promise, is just the very essence and vitality of life, spiritual life: **"because I live, ye shall live also."** That means, in the later words of the apostle Paul, "To me to live is Christ." It carries with it more than mere spiritual life. It is the constant personal experience of the risen and living Christ, producing His living power within our daily life. In the present enjoyment of this it is given to us to enjoy the blessed promise, **"Ye shall know that I am in My Father, and ye in Me, and I in you"** (v. 20). For the further experience of this mutual indwelling see 15:4 to 7.

All this is a matter of carrying out His commandments; not mere sentiment, but the enjoyment of love as the spring of obedience, and obedience as the proof of love. So the Lord says, **"He that loveth Me shall be loved of My Father, and I will love him, and will manifest Myself unto Him"** (v. 21). This practical love on the part of a believer brings a special manifestation of the love of the Father and the Son, and not only of their love but of their very nature and character as revealed in the Son. "In the keeping of His commandments there is great reward," and there can be no greater reward than the communion enjoyed in the fulfillment of this promise. There comes a wonderful disclosure to the true heart. The verb rendered "I will manifest" is not the ordinary word *phaneroo,* it is *emphanizo,* which suggests more than an appearance, it carries the thought of a disclosure of what the person is in His own nature, character, counsel and work.

The Religious World

This drew forth an inquiry from Judas (not Iscariot) as to what had happened to bring about this distinction between themselves and the world (v. 22). Publicity, self-advertisement to gain applause, is characteristic of mere religion; it is the negation of the character and way of Christ. Accordingly, His reply shows how utterly impossible what He had in mind for them is for the world. The world has no

room for Christ all through this period, any more than it had for Him when He was on earth. It has its religious ideas of Him, but their conception of Him is radically distinct from what He is Himself. Jesus answered him, **"If a man love Me, He will keep My word** [not My words, but the whole Word as an entity]; **and My Father will love him, and We will come unto him, and make Our abode with him"** (v. 23). There is now a dwelling place on earth both for Father and Son. It is in the heart and life of anyone who carries the whole truth of the Word of God, not some particular doctrine or practice, nor a special set of doctrines, attaching importance to some while making little or nothing of others. The "Word" is the whole teaching.

This brings from the Father and the Son, not an external display of power and attractive activity, but the inward disclosure of their love, producing likeness to the character of Him who is "meek and lowly in heart," and the real power of the Spirit of God. The idea of an "abode" is not something ephemeral, but habitual and permanent. So John wrote later, "He that abideth in the teaching, the same hath both the Father and the Son" (2 John 9, R.V.). And the Lord finished His reply by combining, in a negative statement, the love and the obedience: **"He that loveth Me not keepeth not My words** [plural now, the various parts which make up the whole]: **and the word which ye hear is not Mine, but the Father's who sent Me."** It was indeed Christ's word but only as it was that of the Father, in their perfect unity.

The Holy Spirit—A Person

What He had told them was only a beginning. They themselves must have felt the need of more, and He assures them that the need would be met. His teaching would not end with His being here with them: **"But the Comforter, even the Holy Spirit, whom the Father will send in My Name, He shall teach you all things, and bring to your remembrance all that I have said unto you"** (vv. 25, 26). This makes clear that the Spirit is not a mere influence, He is a person, who Himself acts as the minister of comfort and instruction. The two are inseparable. Instruction imparts all that is conveyed by the comprehensive term "Comforter." He would teach all things, that is, the truth of Scripture in its entirety, and would recall all that Christ taught. This latter contains the basis of all the truth that was to follow, from the Acts to the Apocalypse (cp. Heb. 2:3). All the rest of the New Testament serves to confirm the authenticity of the Gospels.

This promise pointed to the responsibility of the disciples to recollect what Christ had taught, but this as being under the superintending control of the Holy Spirit (cp. 12:16). This places the writings of the apostles beyond the scope of mere recollection and contemplation.

The Peace of Christ

Following this assurance the Lord ministers a word of strong comfort to them. When He says "Peace I leave with you" (v. 27), He is not giving them simply a farewell message. The word rendered "I leave" is the same in the original as when He said "I will not leave you desolate." The peace is a bequest, and that not merely of freedom from anxiety as to circumstances, but of all that makes for mental and spiritual welfare.

But there is a special character about the peace. When He further says, **"My peace I give unto you,"** He uses a phrase the force of which is not expressed in our versions. Literally it is "the peace, the Mine," a very emphatic way of speaking of His peace as that which characterizes Him in a special manner and to a special degree, an inward peace which is His own possession, a peace not to be upset by foes or by the world. More than this, it is that which He imparts as being in accordance with His own nature. It has been described as consisting of "the composure of a holy affection, the sunshine of a settled purpose, and the sunshine of unclouded communion with God." He describes His love and His joy in the same phraseology (15:10, 12).

"Not as the world giveth," He says, **"give I unto you."** There is more than one contrast. As to the mode of giving, the world gives it conventionally, and often merely superficially. As to the means, it does not possess real, lasting peace, and it cannot give what it has not got. As to the source, the peace the Lord gives has been procured for us at the cost of His atoning sacrifice; this provides the right for believers to receive it from Him. As to the nature, it is not only a peace of conscience, it is a peace of rest in the will of God, not merely resignation to it, but delight in it, rest in all His dealings.

Fearfulness or Love

He then adds an exhortation against that which is the very negation of peace, namely, a troubled or a fearful heart. He here repeats what He said at the beginning (there in a different connection) and adds the words, **"neither let it be afraid."** The verb is *deiliaō* (here only in the N.T.), not a passing fear, but a condition of fearfulness (cp. 2 Tim. 1:7).

All fearfulness should yield place to love, for two reasons, (1) because Christ has gone to the Father, (2) because He is coming again (cp. 14:3). **"Ye heard how I said unto you, I go away, and I come unto you. If ye loved Me, ye would have rejoiced, because I go unto the Father for the Father is greater than I"** (v. 28). This last statement gives the consummating reason for love to, and joy in, Christ, as powers that banish anxiety and fear. That the Father is "greater" is not said with regard to the relations in the persons of the Trinity. The Lord has been speaking of Himself as the one sent by the Father, and who fulfills His commandments, the way that leads to the Father, and the one who reveals the Father. Of all this the Father is the authority and the object. In all these respects the Father is greater than the Son, but not greater in essence and Godhood.

That these assurances actually created the love and rejoicing to which the Lord exhorted them is told out in Luke 24:53 and in the opening chapters of the Acts. We should so live, too, that these blessings may operate in our hearts continually and give effect to our testimony.

But all is a matter of faith, faith that realizes and appropriates the unseen: **"And now I have told you before it come to pass, that when it is come to pass ye may believe"** (v. 29).

The Power of Darkness

For the disciples the scene was about to change; this companionship and intimate converse were about to terminate for the time.

The powers of darkness were mustering for the attack. **"The prince of the world"** was coming; he had come to Him with a claim to this title in the wilderness at the beginning of His public testimony. The claim was not then denied by the victorious Lord. And now with his permitted authority over rebellious man, over the world in its persistent hardness of heart against all divine revelation and command, Satan was hastening to the crucial attack, and using the leading human powers among the Jews as his instruments.

Yet if this prince of the world had claims upon men, he had none upon the Son of God: **"and he hath nothing in Me,"** He says; he could not find, as he did in the world, something that would answer morally to his own nature; the very fact that men are sinners makes them partakers with the evil one, who "sinneth from the beginning." So it was with the first human sin, and men have ever since thrown open the avenues of their being to him. But he found no means of ingress in Him in whom "is no sin." Therefore while Satan could make an attempt, subject to the permissive will of God, he had no right to do so.

The Great Issue

That he should do so at this time was, by such permission, voluntarily granted. Therefore there must be a divine purpose in it. This is seen in the Lord's next words, **"but that the world may know that I love the Father, and as the Father gave Me commandment, so I do"** (v. 31). Therefore the doing was not merely by voluntary consent, but by loving obedience. Here was a display of grace indeed. This is something more than the fact that God so loved the world that He gave His only begotten Son for the salvation of any-one who would believe. The world was to know that, in giving up His life that men might be saved, He was giving evidence of His love to the Father. Here then was a proof of the grace of Father and Son toward a guilty world.

That the Lord now said **"Arise, let us go hence,"** does not necessitate the idea that the company immediately left the room. The greater likelihood is that they lingered there or at least in the premises while He continued His discourse and prayed His prayer. Perhaps at this point they sang the Hallel. If after they rose they stayed in the recesses of the house, there would very likely be a vine growing on the sides, and this may have led to His remarks at the beginning of chapter fifteen. What is noticeable is that immediately upon His mentioning that "the prince of the world was coming," He says, "Arise, let us go hence," suggesting His readiness to meet the attack and fulfill all that was now to be accomplished.

The purpose in the narrative, however, is clearly the continuity of the discourse; there is so much in what follows that recalls and expands what He had previously spoken of, and this He now applies by way of practical exhortation, and that not only for the Eleven but for all believers.

The great subject of the next two chapters is the relation of believers to the Lord Himself as the one by whose power their lives are to be lived. The relationship is fivefold; they are sharers in His life and fruitfulness as His members (vv. 1–8), in His love and joy as His friends (vv. 9, 19), in His work and ways as His associates (15:20–16:3), in His ministry and spirit as His disciples (16:4–15), in His conflict and victory as His adherents (16:16–33).

CHAPTER FIFTEEN

Verses 1 to 8

Life and Fruitfulness

In speaking of Himself as **"the true vine"** (lit., the vine, the true one) He signifies that He is the one who is the very essence of spiritual life and fruitfulness, and from whom alone these can be possessed and produced. The nation had become barren and dead. He was the twig out of the stump (Is. 11:1, 2). But He changes the metaphors, because now He includes all those who, as His members, partake of His life and its products, showing that there is a vital union between Himself and them.

But this union and fruitfulness must be maintained in practical apprehension by their abiding in Him. Yet fruitfulness does not lie merely within their own power. They are entirely dependent on the vine. Hence, He says, **"My Father is the Husbandman."** There are two sorts of branches, the non-fruitbearing and the fruitbearing. The former He takes away, the latter He cleanses. There is no thought here of the loss of eternal life. The Lord is picturing the use of the pruning-knife, in the one case, and the removal of such things as parasites and mildew, in the case of the other.

"He shows the disciples that, walking on earth, they should be pruned by the Father, and be cut off if they bore no fruit; for the subject here is not that relationship with Christ in Heaven by the Holy Ghost, which cannot be broken, but of that link which even then was formed here below, which might be vital and eternal, or which might not. Fruit should be the proof" (J.N.D.).

Abiding in Him

The eleven disciples were already clean; their faith in Christ had made them branches in the vine. They had become clean because of the word He had spoken to them. They would yet need cleansing to bear **"more fruit."** The secret of all this lay in His command **"Abide in Me."** This implies the exercise of the will, a voluntary and conscious perseverance, and makes clear the possibility of spiritual dangers, lest anything should be allowed to interrupt or hinder the continual experience of this union. Moreover the relation is mutual. There is a promise conditional upon fulfillment of the command. He says, **"Abide in Me, and I in you."** This is a condition, not of sentiment but of activity. In 14:20, "ye in Me, and I in you" signified a state. Here the relation is that which expresses itself in practical result, the activity being the outcome of the realization of the state.

Thus soul-energy finds its effect in loving obedience to all His commands, and this is the life of Christ bearing fruit: **"As the branch cannot bear fruit of itself, except it abide in the vine; so neither can ye, except ye abide in Me. I am the vine, ye are the branches: he that abideth in Me, and I in him, the same beareth much fruit: for apart from** [i.e., severed from] **Me ye can do nothing"** (vv. 4, 5).

Our Insufficiency

A distinction is necessary between the subject of the life of the believer as being inseparable from Christ from the day on which he receives Him by faith, and the relation of the believer to Him in the matter of spiritual fruitbearing. As to the former the Lord made the imperishable life of the believer clear in chapter ten, in declaring that His sheep could never perish. What He is now showing is that no believer can bring forth fruit from his own resources or by his own initiative. As the apostle Paul says, "I labored . . . yet not I, but the grace of God which was with me." "We are not sufficient of ourselves to think anything as of ourselves." "I live, yet not I, but Christ liveth in me."

The Lord compares one who abides not in Him to a withered branch. That kind of branch men gather and burn. The aorist tenses of the verbs rendered **"he is cast forth"** and **"is** withered," suggest a twofold significance, (1) the decisive character of the acts (no other course being practicable), (2) the all-knowing mind of the speaker (as one who knew what must take place before it became a fact).

The fruitlessness may be caused by lethargy of soul, or by unbelief, or by willful apostasy. The latter had been the case with the betrayer; avarice, then discontent, then definite antagonism!

Conditions for Power in Prayer

Now the Lord deals with the fruitfulness of enjoyed union and communion, and shows that the indwelling of His words means power in prayer, and that the truly prayerful life is the fruitful life: **"If ye abide in Me, and My words abide in you, ask* whatsoever ye will, and it shall be done unto you"** (v. 7). His words are vital principles; they are designed to inspire our motives and to direct our thoughts and prompt our acts. To have His words abiding in us gives us such communion with God that we can count upon His answers to our prayers. And this inevitably means productiveness. It is the very opposite to fruitlessness.

This asking and obtaining never affords self-gratulation. What it does effect is true discipleship of Christ, whose one and only motive was the glory of the Father. "Herein is My Father glorified, that ye bear much fruit; and so shall ye be My disciples" (v. 8). Their discipleship had begun, but there was to be development and progress.

Verses 9 to 13

The Key to Love, Joy and Friendship

Passing for the moment from His subject of the vine and the branches, with its significance of vital and constant union of His members with Himself for fruitfulness, He now speaks of His love for them as His friends, and its practical effect in them. "Abiding" is the continued keynote. As they must abide in Him as their life, so they must abide in His love.

Firstly, as to the source, **"Even as the Father hath loved Me"**; secondly, as to the mediating bestowment, **"I also have loved you"**; thirdly, as to the enjoyed element, **"Abide ye in My love,"** fourthly, as to the means, **"If ye keep My commandments ye shall abide in My love:"** fifthly, as to the example, **"even as I have kept My Father's commandments, and abide in His love"** (vv. 9, 10).

All this makes clear that our obedience does not create the Lord's love, any more than walking in sunshine creates the sun's light. The light is there, His love is there all the time. Obedience gives the realization of it. Disobedience, turning from the path of His commandments, hinders our enjoyment of His love. It rests upon him who walks as He walked.

His Joy

It is just this which leads on to the subject of His joy, for it was His joy to do the Father's will, and in our case a life of obedience is a life of joy: **"These things have I spoken unto you, that My joy may be in you, and that your joy may be fulfilled"** (v. 11). That the former purpose means that the joy which is His own may be imparted to them (rather than that His joy in them may continue) is confirmed in two respects: firstly, by the striking character of the full phrase in the original, which describes the uniqueness of His joy, lit., "the joy, the Mine"; secondly, by His prayer in 17:13, "that they may have My joy fulfilled in themselves." It is not "that your joy may be full"; that rendering misses the important point. That His followers would live and work in full fellowship with Him in seeing the extension of His kingdom, would mean that His joy in the outworking of the will of the Father would be fulfilled in each of their lives.

This is abundantly illustrated in the Epistles. To take one example, when Paul says of the Thessalonian believers "Ye are our glory and joy" (1 Thess. 2:20), this is but the Lord's own joy being fulfilled in the hearts of the apostle and his fellow laborers.

His Friends

But it is to be fulfilled by the mutual love of fellow believers, and this it is which leads to

---

*The better reading in the original is *aitesasthe,* the aorist imperative, "ask ye."

His reminder that those who act like this are His friends: **"This is My commandment, that ye love one another, even as I have loved you. Greater love hath no man than this, that a man lay down his life for his friends"** (vv. 12, 13). He uses again the same kind of striking phrase concerning His commandment as He has done of love, joy and peace: "This is the commandment, the Mine" ("that which is especially Mine").

The question has been raised as to whether, in this thirteenth verse, the Lord was actually making reference to His own atoning sacrifice, or whether, in enjoining upon the disciples the exercise of mutual love, He was simply giving the highest example of merely human self-sacrifice. This calls for careful consideration. True it is that there is no other direct reference, in this discourse in the Upper Room, to His death. It has been asked, too, whether, since Christ died for all men, "died for the ungodly," died for the whole world, He would have spoken of His death as a giving up of His life for His "friends."

The Reference to His Own Death

It is necessary first to consider the main purpose of the Lord's message to His disciples. One cannot read through this discourse without noticing that His great object was to comfort, strengthen and instruct them in view of their coming experiences, trials, and vicissitudes, after He had gone to the Father, and so to prepare them for their service and testimony. This would not mean the entire withholding of an intimation of His death (that would be improbable), but it would mean keeping the subject in a certain amount of reserve. The circumstances and meaning of His death they had already known to some extent ("the way ye know"), but the facts and their implications would be clear in a few hours, and in due time their full explanation would be made known to them. For that immediate occasion there was manifested therefore in His messages a divinely wise economy of treatment. To have handled the subject of His death as an offering for the world, a giving up of His life "for the ungodly," would have been to exceed the scope and method of His immediate teachings.

Consistently with this, and so far from keeping secret the subject of His death, He addresses His disciples as His "friends" in this connection. He had used that term for them long before (Luke 12:4). While therefore He is instructing them as to how they should manifest their love one to another, it is in keeping with the nature of His instructions that He should include a reference to His own death as the giving up of His life for His "friends." Such indeed it was with regard to the Eleven who were listening to Him, and there is nothing theologically erroneous, or doctrinally inconsistent with the subject of His expiatory sacrifice as set forth elsewhere in Scripture, in regarding His general statement, "Greater love hath no man than this, that a man lay down his life for his friends," as including a reference to His own act with its special significance. The fact that its general character, as bearing upon their love one to another, involved the mention of the giving up of life as the act of "a man," in no way detracts from the expiatory efficacy of His death, as if suggesting that His act was that of a mere man. On the contrary the natural illustration involved the use of such phraseology. As a matter of fact the word "man" is not in the Greek in any part of the verse. The words are "no one" and "anyone."

The crowning exemplification made the inclusion of His own deed, with its special instruction, most appropriate. And how wisely and suitably He intimated it! That His statement did not preclude an intimation of His own act, with its expiatory uniqueness, is confirmed by what His "beloved disciple" says in his first Epistle, in words which surely contain an echo of the very words of Him on whose breast he leaned, "Hereby know we love, because He laid down His life for us: and we ought to lay down our lives for the brethren" (1 John 3:16). We may observe that the apostle narrows the subject to believers, instead of referring to the world as that for which the Lord died, just as Christ Himself did on the evening when He spoke to His disciples.

Verses 14 to 16

The Intimacy of Friendship

In the deeper intimacy established by the Lord in this discourse He now unfolded more fully to His disciples what their being His "friends" involved. He had already made clear that it meant their doing all that pleased Him. But there was to be more than this. Accordingly He says, **"No longer do I call you servants; for the servant knoweth not what his lord doeth: but I have called you friends."**

This did not mean that they were no longer His servants. Such they continued to be, and they ever delighted so to describe themselves (*douloi,* bondservants; see 1 Pet. 1:1; Jude 5:1; Rom. 1:1). With the believer the capacity of being a servant carries with it the intimacy and communion of friendship. The servant (*doulos*) as such does not know what his master is doing; his knowledge is limited to his duty. If, however, his master takes him into his confidence, the scene is changed. There is cooperation and sympathy and fellowship. A friendship is established. And this is just what the Lord now says: **"I have called you friends for all things that I heard from My Father I have made known unto you"** (v. 15).

By this communication of the Father's counsels and ways, a communication constantly being made to us by the Spirit through the Word, Christ brings us into partnership with Himself, in His purposes, interests and operations, we are His friends. This is more than the friendship produced by loving obedience. To be partners is a greater privilege than to be servants.

His next word provides a beautiful connection. In making them His friends to share in His thoughts and purpose He it was who took the initiative: "Ye did not choose Me, but I chose you, and appointed you, that ye should go and bear fruit, and that your fruit should abide: that whatsoever ye shall ask of the Father in My Name He may give it you" (v. 16). This is not election to eternal life, it is choice for service and fruitfulness. The statement looks back to two facts, one to the immediately preceding subject of the combined service and friendship, consequent upon the communication of the Father's counsels and operations made to the disciples through the Son, the other to the first part of the chapter, where the Lord was speaking of the union with Himself as the requisite for fruitbearing.

Private Communion and Visible Power

This metaphor is resumed. The word rendered "appointed" is, literally, "set in" (*i.e.,* "I set you in Me"). But now there is more than the union of branches with the stem. There is all the consequent activity of the mission which lay before them.

With all true believers there is the double condition necessary, first the privacy of vital and intimate communion, with the realization of partnership with Him, and then, and then only, the spiritual and visible activity of producing results for His glory; not for spectacular display, but by the quiet yet earnest response to the guidance and power of the Holy Spirit. Such fruitfulness goes on from time into eternity. And the secret of it all is the power of prayer, prevailing prayer.

Verses 17 to 27

The World's Enmity

The renewal of the command in verse 17 to love one another is a connecting link between what has preceded and what now follows (cp. 14:25; 15:11; 16:1, 25, 33). As to the preceding, the one thing compatible with those who know what union and friendship with the Lord are, is that they should love one another. But this the more so owing to the antagonism of the world (cp. 1 John 3:11 to 14). Outer hatred! Inner love! In all this their identification with Christ is exemplified. **"If the world hateth you, ye know that it hath hated Me before it hated you"** (v. 18). This introduces certain principles, spiritual truths governing the condition; these principles are the subject of 15:18 to 27. In 16:1 to 15 the Lord gives details of actions.

We have seen how He speaks to His own, first as His *members* participating in His *life,* then as His *friends* participating in His *love.* Now He shows that they are to be His *followers,* participating in His *work.* But this last means opposition and hatred from the world and consequent experiences of suffering and trial. But that means triumph and glory through the ministry of the Comforter.

"If the world hateth you"; the "if" expresses, not a possibility, but a fact. And the explanation is clear: **"If ye were of the world, the world would love its own but because ye are not of the world, but I chose you out of the world, therefore the world hateth you"** (v. 19). There is in the world a pervading characteristic, a sort of affection for those who naturally belong to it, and this is indicated by the phrase "its own." The verb *phileō*, here used of its love, indicates what is merely natural, in contrast to *agapaō*, to love by way of moral choice. The fellowship created by Christ in choosing His disciples out of the world and uniting them to Himself, conforming them to His own likeness, is radically and essentially contrary to the spirit of the world. Therefore it hates both Him and them. The fivefold mention of the "world" emphasizes what He says of it. Similarly five times John speaks of it in his first Epistle.

The Lord now reminds them of what He had already said, **"A servant is not greater than his lord."** Before, this statement inculcated likeness to His in lowliness of service; now it speaks of identification with Him in treatment by the world: **"If they persecuted Me, they will also persecute you; if they kept My word** (which they had certainly not done), **they will keep yours."** The change to "they" is noticeable; the term "the world" suggested its oneness in nature and attitude, the plural suggests its varied antagonistic efforts: **"But all these things will they do unto you for My Name's sake** (because of My Name)." His Name is expressive of His character and ways, all being contrary to those of the world.

His Witness Against the World

In both respects He revealed the Father who sent Him. In both respects His followers represent Him. Having no real knowledge of the sender, the world failed to recognize the sent. The sent one came in person and spoke to them; hence the extreme degree of their sin. **"If I had not come and spoken unto them, they had not had sin: but now they have no excuse for their sin."** The Lord thus showed that He was ready to make allowance were it possible. Their sin was unbelief.

They could not plead ignorance. Their unbelief developed into hatred.

The evidence He had given was twofold and overwhelming. He had Himself borne witness that He and the Father were one. In hating Him they hated His Father also (v. 23). Then there was the witness of His works: **"If I had not done among them the works which none other had done, they had not had sin: but now they have both seen and hated both Me and My Father."** Their unbelieving malice had therefore a double condemnation.

Behind all this witness was that of the Scripture, which He speaks of as **"their law."** They boasted in it, blind to the fact that it testified against themselves: **"They hated Me without a cause."**

Additional Witness

This instruction concerning the world and its treatment of them had been imparted with regard to the witness that was yet to be given in it by them. For this object adequate provision would be made. The contrasting "But" connects the past with the future: **"But when the Comforter is come, whom I will send unto you from the Father, even the Spirit of truth, which proceedeth from the Father, He shall bear witness of Me, and ye also bear witness, because ye have been with Me from the beginning"** (vv. 26, 27).

There is strong emphasis on the pronouns "I" and "He," the first stressing the Lord's own action, the second the importance of the Holy Spirit's action. The Lord speaks of Him now as "The Spirit of truth"; this is additional to what He mentioned in 14:16 and 26, and is appropriate to the subject of the witness to be given, for the truth describes the matter of the witness. Also He "proceedeth from the Father," this describes a going forth that is constant, but of which His coming at the promised time was to be a special act. The witness of the apostles would be by reason of their having been with Christ from the beginning, that is, from the beginning of His public manifestation and ministry (Acts 1:2, 21, 22; 5:32; 1 John 1:1–3).

JOHN

CHAPTER SIXTEEN

Verses 1 to 11

The Establishing Word

The very fact that they would be witnessing to Him amidst fierce hostility produces the reminder that He was about to leave them, and that this was necessary if they were to experience the provision He was about to make for them, so that they might be both delivered and empowered. If they were to have the help they must be alive to the danger.

"These things have I spoken unto you [i.e., especially vv. 18–27 of chap. 15] that ye should not be made to stumble" (16:1); the word here is a warning, not against being tripped up in the path, but against a sorrowful reaction of thought in being disappointed at not seeing the kingdom set up in the world through the conversion of Israel. Let not their faith be staggered by the hostile fanaticism of Jewish leaders in excommunicating them, and even killing them as an act of service to God (vv. 1, 2). Let them bear in mind the reason for it all, namely, ignorance of the Father and Himself. Let them remember, when the antagonism burst upon them, that it was but fulfilling what He had foretold, and thus let the very adversities be but reminders of His ministry of love that very evening (vv. 3, 4).

"These things," He says, "I said not unto you from the beginning, because I was with you." The phrase "from the beginning" is to be noted; it is not "at the beginning" (as in the A.V.). He *had* told them "at the beginning" (see Matt. 10:16 to 25), but He had not continued all along to do so and thus disconcert their minds. For He was with them, and what they needed was His person and His teachings concerning Himself. One forewarning was enough.

A Warning

This has its lesson for us. We must never allow difficulties and distresses in the future so to preoccupy our minds that we shall lose our enjoyment of His own person and love and power. Let not dark circumstances obscure the light of His countenance and glory.

Now He was going to Him who sent Him, and, instead of faith and hope, nothing but sorrow filled their hearts. True, they had asked whither He was going (13:36 and 14:5), but the inquiries were by way of despair and perplexity, not of hope. "Nevertheless," He says, "I tell you the truth; it is expedient for you that I go away [the pronouns "I" are emphatic]: for if I go not away, the Comforter will not come unto you; but if I go, I will send Him unto you." It was expedient in more ways than one. The very loss would be gain. Sight would give place to faith, the all-important factor in present service. They would pass from a stage of training to qualified activity. Their earthly companying with the Lord would be exchanged for the power of the indwelling Spirit of God, ministering Christ to and through them.

Two different words are rendered "go" in verse 7; twice the verb *apeltho* indicates departure from the place left, i.e., from the world; the last verb *poreutho* indicates the journey to the place and the object in view, heaven and God. The former suggests the inevitable, the latter the purposive.

A Threefold Conviction

Verses 8 to 15 present two contrasting operations of the Holy Spirit after His coming. The former has to do with the world, the latter with the disciples. As to the world He would convict it "in respect of sin, and of righteousness and of judgment: of sin, because they believe not on Me; of righteousness, because I go to the Father, and ye behold Me no more; of judgment, because the prince of this world hath been judged." The significance of the word rendered "convict," is to bring home the evils of false notions and gross errors.

The three subjects pertain to the realm of conscience. They have to do with the state and attitude of man in regard to God and His claims. They are factors in the ancient and continued controversy between God and man from the beginning of human sin onward. But the Lord shows that, since His own coming into the scene, a new and special test is applied. The test relates to, and centers in, Himself: It is applied by the Holy Spirit. As to the first, conviction in respect of sin is not of a transgression of God's law; it goes deeper, it goes to the root of sin, namely, unbelief. For all sin is essentially unbelief. That was so with Adam and Eve and had been so all along. But now, with the new test, the evil consists in refusal to believe on Christ: "because they believe not on Me."

As to the second, conviction in respect of righteousness is not because man has departed from the right ways of God. That is so. But now in Christ righteousness had been realized in man for the first time and was duly to be vindicated by His enthronement at the right hand of God: "of righteousness, because I go to the Father" (a different word again for "go": *hupagō*, which might fully be rendered "I go My way"; cp. John 8:21; 16:5). The world had refused to recognize His righteousness; they counted Him a demon-possessed blasphemer and numbered Him among the transgressors. As to His right to be raised from the tomb, with the issues at the right hand of the Father, they concocted a lying fable about that. The Lord adds very significantly "and ye behold Me no longer" ("behold," *theōreō*, is the word). That meant faith; and the life of faith is a life of practical righteousness; it is a witness to the world of what true righteousness is. Therefore, it is a veritable part of the convicting work of the Spirit in regard to the world. Appropriately therefore, the Lord associates the life of believers here with His presence with the Father, as an essential factor in this second process of conviction.

As to the third, conviction in respect of judgment is the crowning operation. The world dares to pronounce its judgment on its affairs as if its directing policy would issue in the vindication of the rights of humanity. The present is "man's day," that is, the time in which man seeks to walk by the light of his own counsels. But man's estimate is marred by his alienation from God. "The whole world lieth in the evil one" (1 John 5:19, R.V.). The world will yet find that out. But the evil one, its prince, met his doom at the Cross. Then was fulfilled the word of the Lord, "the prince of this world cometh, and hath nothing in Me." The triumph of Christ at Calvary meant the casting out of Satan (cp. Col. 2:15). Since the being who is the "the deceiver of the nations" (Rev. 20:3) has been judged, the world is to be convicted by the Spirit in respect of judgment, the falseness of its own judgment and the righteous judgment of God.

Verses 12 to 15

As to the Spirit's work in the case of believers, the Lord had much to say, but that was not the time: **"Ye cannot bear them now"** (*arti*, just at the present time). There is a divine economy in the process of revelation. The Lord had now disclosed matters which He had hitherto withheld. Trust is tempered to suit the mind's stage of development. The fullness of truth was to be given when further experiences relative to Christ had fitted the disciples for it. **"Howbeit when He, the Spirit of truth, is come, He shall guide you into all the truth: for He shall not speak from Himself; but what things soever He shall hear, these shall He speak and He shall declare unto you the things that are to come"** (v. 13).

Finality of Revelation

The first "He" is emphatic (*ekeinos*, the person, not an influence). He is "the Spirit of truth." Truth is His nature, and that is the guarantee of the character of what He teaches. He would not only be sent, He would "come," by His own power. He would guide into the truth, leading into its facts and their meanings by divinely arranged progress. Moreover it would be completely given to them in their lifetime. Nothing would remain to be added by the Church. It would be sufficient for all generations (Jude 3, R.V.). Just as Christ spoke that which He heard from the Father (8:38; 15:15), so would the Spirit. He is not a separate deity, originating truth. The three are one. He would declare the coming things, i.e., all things relative to this period and the coming ages.

As to the world the Lord said, **"He shall bear witness of me,"** and as to the mode of His ministry, **"for He shall take of Mine** (more fully, out of that which is Mine), **and shall declare it unto you''** (v. 14). The whole of the New Testament is the great proof of the fulfillment of this, and by means of the entire Scriptures the Spirit of truth has been fulfilling it to and through believers ever since. Yet not all has been unfolded thus far. The *ek*, out of, is to be taken literally. There remains yet more in the ages to come.

He gives a reason for this promise in repeating it, and the reason is this: **"All things whatsoever the Father hath are Mine"** (v. 15). He thus shows not only the unity between the Father and Himself in Godhood, but points out the vastness of the storehouse of divine possessions from which the revelations and unfoldings are to be made. "The Spirit searches all things, yea the deep things of God."

Verses 16 to 33

Sorrow to Be Turned into Joy

The ministry of the Spirit would be given amidst seasons of sorrow and trial for all believers. The Lord now prepares the disciples for this. He first reminds them that He is about to leave them, but there is joy to come from His own person: **"A little while, and ye behold Me no more; and again a little while, and ye shall see Me"** (v. 16). The first "little while" was a few hours, and then after some days He would cease to be seen of them (in the sense of the verb *theōreō*, a visible beholding). He would be seen by the eye of faith indeed. But there is surely more than this in the *opsesthe*, "ye shall see (Me)." The apostle John uses this very verb and the same tense in 1 John 3:2, and the Lord doubtless had in mind His future return, as He had said in 14:3. For the time being the disciples were perplexed. The Lord noted that they were inquiring among themselves, and satisfied their questionings by His further disclosures (vv. 17 to 22).

They would indeed weep and lament, while the world rejoiced, but Christ Himself, first by His resurrection and appearances, would turn their sorrow into joy, and since everything centered in His death and resurrection, the very cause of their sorrow would be the cause of their joy. For Him and for them the experiences found their analogy in the birth pangs of a woman in her travail with the resulting joy in the birth of her son. His own bitter hours on the cross and the triumphant joy of the vacant tomb were to have their counterpart in their experiences, for He had identified them with Himself. He "saw of the travail of His soul and was satisfied." God loosed the birth pangs of death, because it was not possible that He should be holden of it (Acts 2:24).

He did see them again, their heart did rejoice, and no one could take their joy from them (see *e.g.*, Acts 5:41). But what was experienced in that way, and has been ever since, is not the complete fulfillment of the Lord's reassuring words of promise. The best, the complete, fulfillment will be brought about when He comes to receive us to Himself and takes us into His Father's house above.

Communion, Suffering, Victory

The Lord now completes His confirmatory comfort and assurance. The intercourse they had enjoyed with Him in bodily presence was about to be changed, not to end, but to continue in a different condition. There was an intercourse during the forty days after His resurrection (Acts 1:1 to 8), but the new experience was to be marked by a different mode of access and by a new mode of communion. **"And in that day ye shall ask Me nothing** [margin, ask Me no question]. **Verily, verily, I say unto you, if ye shall ask anything of the Father, He will give it to you in My Name. Hitherto have ye asked nothing in My Name: ask, and ye shall receive, that your joy may be fulfilled"** (vv. 23, 24). This all combines immediate access and mediation (see Eph. 2:18; 3:12).

Concerning Prayer

There is a change in the verbs to ask. The first, *erōtaō*, primarily means to ask by way of inquiry, and then by request. The second, *aiteō*, means to ask by way of petition. A nearer relation is involved in *erōtaō* than in *aiteō*. *Erōtaō* had been used of the disciples with regard to Christ (v. 19) and is used in verse 26 of Christ's address to the Father; so in 17:9, 15, 20 (cp. the change in 1 John 5:16). The Lord did not mean that no prayer must be offered to Him afterwards. They did address Him in prayer (Acts 1:24; 7:59; 9:13,

JOHN 16:16-33 • 303

etc.). What He does stress particularly is His own ministry of mediation and the effect of prayer addressed to the Father. What He gives He does so in the Name of the Lord Jesus, that is, by reason of all that the Name implies in relation to the Father (see on 14:14, 26; 15:16). The conditions for prayer being thus fulfilled, the answers are designed to fill the heart with joy, a joy of which no foe, no adverse circumstance, can deprive us.

But there was to be a change in the nature of the unfoldings of truth. The Lord would not again adopt the use of "proverbs," a word including different modes of figurative language. He would speak "plainly" of the Father. The word is to be taken in its wider sense of freedom of speech. The time for fullness of utterance was coming. No longer would the mind be needing a gradual process of training. The communications would impart a full assurance of understanding. All this became characteristic of the ministry of the Spirit to and through the apostles. The subject is "the Father," and the Lord at once communicates plain and direct truth concerning Him.

He says, **"In that day ye shall ask in My Name, and I say not unto you that I will pray** [make request of] **the Father for you: for the Father Himself loveth you, because ye have loved Me and have believed that I came forth from the Father"** (vv. 26, 27). Firstly, He does not say He will *not* pray the Father, He actually proceeded to do so (ch. 17), and He "maketh intercession for us" (Rom. 8:34); His negative way of putting it "I say not . . ." is simply a way of preparing for the strong positive assurance which immediately follows. Secondly, the preposition *peri* here means "concerning" ("I will pray the Father concerning you"). The same preposition He has just used in regard to telling them concerning the Father. Thirdly, He gives a reason for His interest concerning them, in that the Father Himself loves them because of their love for Christ and their faith regarding Him.

Unoriginated Sonship of Christ

Now follow His plain statements concerning the Father and Himself, fundamental facts of the utmost importance, a climax in His communication: **"I came out from the Father,**

and am come into the world: again, I leave the world, and go unto the Father" (v. 28). These four facts summarize the history of Christ. The first takes us to His past eternity. There is a significant change of preposition. In verse 27 He said, "Ye have believed that I came forth from (*para*, from with) the Father" (so the R.V., instead of "from God"). But now He says "I came out from (*ek*) the Father." This is a deeper truth, it is more than a recognition of the faith of the disciples. The *ek* indicates a complete oneness of essence, of the Father and the Son, in the past eternity. Those who deny the preeternal Sonship of Christ fail, for one thing among others, to discern the significance of this *ek;* it definitely implies the essential relationship of Christ as the Son of the Father before He became incarnate, He did not become the Son at His birth.

The second covers the facts of His birth, incarnation, death, burial and resurrection. The third marks His ascension, the fourth His return to the Father, to the One standing in the same relation to Him as in the eternal past. His coming out and His return are each inseparable from His Sonship. The coming out does not suggest that the Father ceased to be with Him. It could not be so. He said "I and the Father are One." "The Father hath not left Me alone."

The doubts were cleared away from the minds of the disciples. They use a third form of preposition in asserting their faith that He came from God, the preposition *apo,* the least definite of the three; it gives the general view, as stated by the disciples; *para* is more close in the relation; *ek,* the Lord's other word, is the most intimate.

A Closing Message

His answer, **"Do ye now believe?"** (not a statement, "Ye do now believe") is not a doubt or denial. It is equivalent to an exclamation, in view of what He is going to state as to the impending danger and their being scattered: **"Behold, the hour cometh, yea, is come, that ye shall be scattered, every man to his own, and shall leave Me alone; and yet,"** He says, in giving a closing message of comfort, **"I am not alone, because the Father is with Me."** This He designed to be a reassuring word for them and for all those who, like Him, pass through conditions of trial and solitude. For He says, with reference both to this word and all that He had given them, **"These things have I spoken unto you, that in Me ye may have peace. In the world ye shall have tribulation: but be of good cheer; I have overcome the world"** (v. 33).

This sums up much of what He had said. He had given them a legacy of His own peace (see 14:27). He had reminded them of world antagonism (15:18–25; 16:1–4). He had assured them of the issue in His own case (14:3, 18, 20, 21; 16:22) and of His victory over the prince of the world (14:30). His very word "Be of good cheer" suggests that naturally there would be cause for depression of heart. But against this He is Himself the antidote. He had been through it all, and had defeated the influences of the world. He had vindicated truth and righteousness in the fact of its deceit and iniquity. The morrow was to see the crowning triumph, over the devil, the world and death, and His word "I have overcome" looks to the accomplished victory.

But they were to share the victory, and we are to share it, and the means for this is to fulfill our identification with Him and thus to obey His command of promise and assurance, "Be of good cheer." We are to be "more than conquerors through Him that loved us." And our victory that overcomes is faith (1 John 5:4, 5). It is just our joy in Christ Himself, our good cheer, that gives us to be more than mere conquerors. Christ points to this very super-victory in this His closing word. Victory can bring content. Joy in Christ gives more than the satisfaction of victory (see Rev. 3:21).

JOHN

CHAPTER SEVENTEEN

Verses 1 to 3

Introductory

"These things spake Jesus: and lifting up His eyes to Heaven, He said, Father the hour is come." The mention of His lifting up His eyes immediately upon His closing word to the disciples, shows that there was no break in the circumstances. The prayer follows the discourse as a consummation of the teaching given, linking it all with the throne. All that has preceded receives now its interpretation and ratification. The disciples hear how the Father and the Son contemplate their condition, how their prospects are regarded by them, how their highest interests are the subjects of effective intercession, and how others with them are to be brought into the same sphere of eternal blessing and into the bliss of ineffable oneness in both Father and Son.

In this prayer there is nothing giving the slightest intimation of infirmity, demerit or defect. Even the tone of entreaty is absent. There is nothing but the consciousness of a life of the constant, uninterrupted fulfillment of the Father's will, summed up in the statement, "I have glorified Thee on the earth." This is but one of the many such statements of the perfect accomplishment of the divine will and counsel: "I have finished the work." "I have manifested Thy Name." "I have given them the words." "I have kept (them)." These are declarations and assertions of will impossible to a mere human being. When He says "Father, I will," He expresses a claim with the complete consciousness of the right of its accomplishment, as being equally the will of Him whom He is addressing.

It is the prayer of our "Apostle and High Priest," the apostle as sent from God to men, the high priest interceding for men to God.

There are three interwoven subjects, (1) concerning Himself (especially vv. 1–5): (2) concerning His followers and messengers (vv. 6–20); (3) concerning other believers (v. 20 to end). Matters concerning Himself involve those relating to the apostles and others. These three correspond to those mentioned after Judas had gone out; (1) 13:31, 32; (2) 13:33; (3) 13:34, 35. This marks the order and connection throughout.

The Glory of the Persons and the Work

The opening words at once indicate that everything is based upon, and determined by, the eternal relation "Father . . . Thy Son." There is also the consummating word of time, "The hour." It is the predetermined hour, fulfilling the past, conditioning the future. It is the hour of the overthrow of Satan, the hour of atonement and redemption, bearing their eternal issues. "The hour is come; glorify Thy Son, that the Son may glorify Thee." The answer is seen in His resurrection, ascension, and mediatorial work, and in giving Him all authority in heaven and on earth. In the exercise of this authority and work, with all that it accomplishes; the Son glorified and will glorify the Father.

Life Eternal

But this receives its especial expression in what follows: "even as Thou gavest Him authority over all flesh [i.e., all mankind in its weak state], that whatsoever Thou hast given Him, to them He should give eternal life" (v. 2). The "whatsoever" is, lit., "all that which," viewing the gift in its collective aspect and not in its individual parts (cp. 6:28 and see again 17:23, 24). But in the giving of eternal life the individual recipients are in view (cp. 10:10, 28). The life is not mere existence, it is an enjoyed possession of capacities and activities, of affection and devoted energy. This is brought out in His next words (and His own words they are, despite arguments assigning them to the writer). This is His own pronouncement of what really constitutes eternal life: "And this is life eternal, that they should know Thee the only true God, and Him whom Thou didst send, *even* **Jesus Christ**" (v. 3). The word *ginōskō*, "know," indicates a knowledge acquired by experience. The tense of the verb here signifies a continuous course of progressive knowledge. Moreover, it is a knowledge of persons, not simply of facts, and this involves personal contact and intercourse. It is *our* mind answering to *His* mind, *our* heart to *His* heart, our appropriating to ourselves all that God makes known to us, the Father and the Son revealing themselves to us by the Holy Spirit.

Not the Father Without the Son

The oneness of Christ with the Father in godhood is implied in what the Lord says in regard to the experience of knowing Him, and is confirmed by the apostle's testimony, "We know that the Son of God is come, and hath given us an understanding, that we know Him that is true, and we are in Him that is true, even in His Son Jesus Christ. This is the true God and eternal life" (1 John 5:20). There is no such thing as knowing the Father without knowing the Son. No one can know the true God apart from the Son whom He sent, and who is in Himself the personal embodiment and manifestation of the true God. His two Names Jesus Christ, here mentioned by the Lord concerning Himself in His prayer, contain the title of deity, the work for which He came, and the confirmation of it by God the Father. Hence the appropriateness of the Names to His immediate utterances. It is His coming as the Son from the Father and all that His Names convey that make the knowledge of the one inseparable from the knowledge of the other.

He is "the true God." All other objects of veneration are false gods, and any conception of God which does not accept the oneness of the Son with the Father in the Godhead, and the oneness of the Spirit in the same Godhead, as taught by the Lord and in the Scriptures of truth, is a misconception. There is no eternal life possible without the knowledge of the Father and the Son in this oneness by the operation of the Spirit.

Verses 4 and 5

Glorifying and Glory

The statement "whom Thou didst send" leads to the mention of the fulfillment of that for which He was sent **"I glorified Thee on the earth, having accomplished the work which Thou hast given Me to do."** Up till now he had used the third person with reference to Himself, giving an introductory review of the great facts concerning His relation as the Son, and the plan of the ministry of eternal life through Him. Now He changes to the first person "I." The contrast of circumstances is striking. "I glorified Thee:"—a life of unsullied brightness of glory in fulfilling the Father's will: "on the earth,"—a scene of grossest darkness in the human rejection of Himself and His testimony.

He finished the work, not simply bringing it to an end, but perfectly fulfilling it and achieving its object. It was His meat to do the will of Him who sent Him and to accomplish His work (4:34). This is His example for every true follower who realizes that what he engages in doing is given him to be fulfilled for His glory.

The Glory of Preexistent Sonship

And now comes the sequel, expressed in a desire certain of its fulfillment, a desire that, looking to the immediate future, goes back to the eternal past: **"And now, O Father, glorify Thou Me with Thine own self with the glory which I had with Thee before the world was"** (v. 5). There are three parts of this which call for reverent attention: (1) the bestowment of honors merited by, and consequent upon, the perfected work—"glorify Thou Me"; (2) "with Thine own self" not "by," but "with" *para,* expressing presence with (the same word as in the next clause, "with Thee"); (3) "with the glory which I had with Thee," not merely before He came as the sent One, but before the world had its being from the Creator's hands. This is the glory of essential and unoriginated deity, of a being uncreated, a personal being and not an ideal existence, and an eternal relationship as the Son; for it is a glory "with Thee," the Father—a clause in itself exposing the errors of Arianism, Socinianism, present-day cults, and the denial of the eternal Sonship of Christ. It was a glory which "I had," not which "I received."

Verses 6 to 8

Facts Concerning the Disciples

The Lord now mentions seven facts concerning His followers: (1) He had manifested the Father's Name to them; (2) they were the Father's gifts to Him out of the world; (3) they had kept His word; (4) they had known that what belonged to the Son came from the Father; (5) the words given them by the Son were given Him by the Father; (6) they had received them; (7) they knew that He came forth from the Father as sent by Him.

It is clear that the purpose in all this was to prepare these men for their service as instruments in bearing testimony for Him, with all its consequences. In manifesting the Name he had declared all that God is, His nature, counsels, and ways and works (cp. 1:18). His disciples were given Him **"out of the world,"** humanity in its alienation from God and in its darkness. They belonged to the Father, not merely as being foreknown by Him, but by being actually and personally related to Him. They were given to Him not merely by divine purpose, but as delivered by the Father to Him for His possession, care and instruction. With joy He could say, that they had responded to it; **"they have kept Thy word."** And not merely the teaching as a whole but the very words of which it consisted.

These teachings were not simply His; He taught every detail as that which He received from the Father. In receiving His words they had accepted the truth concerning His person as the one who came forth from the Father and was sent by Him. That was the great preparation for their mission. They were raised above the perplexities, the cavils and criticisms of false teachers.

Verses 9 to 19

A Radical Distinction

They were to be left, but not without the divine help they would need. So the Lord begins with His own high priestly intercession: **"I pray** [*erōtaō,* I make request] **for them** [the "I" is especially emphatic]: **I pray not for the world, but for those whom Thou has given Me; for they are Thine."** The distinction is solemn and radical—the disci-

ples—the world. Not that He had not the interests of the world before Him. He was about to send them into it that all men might believe and be saved. But the uppermost and immediate interests are those of His own. They are equally the Father's and His: **"and all things that are Mine are Thine, and Thine are Mine."** To say, "whatever is mine is Thine," is possible for any believer, but no one but the Son of God could ever say, "all things that are Thine are Mine."

The next words **"and I am glorified in them"** would seem to refer to the disciples; for Christ was, and continued to be, glorified in them. It is possible, however, to read thus: "All things that are Thine are Mine, and I am glorified in them," for God orders all things so that they may be for the glory of His Son.

Kept in the Name

Now comes the special point of His intercession for the disciples as those who are to be still in the world, with all that this entails: **"And I am no more in the world, and these are in the world, and I come to Thee; Holy Father, keep them in Thy Name which Thou hast given Me, that they may be one, even as We are"** (v. 11). He had Himself experienced all the hostility and adverse conditions of the world, and He feels for those who are to be in it still. It is full of everything unholy and unwholesome, baneful to the spiritual life and antagonistic to endurance and power. All the time He was with them, He kept them, **"in Thy Name,"** He says, **"which Thou hast given Me and I guarded them, and not one of them perished, but the son of perdition; that the Scripture might be fulfilled"** (v. 12). How He kept them, teaching and training them amidst all the circumstances of an adverse character in the nation's condition is brought out in the narratives of the Gospels. So to the end (see 18:8, 9).

But He kept them in the Name the Father had given Him. That is the better reading. Since the Name conveys all that God is as revealed in Christ, all the truth concerning Him, in nature, character and ways, had been the very sphere and element in which the Lord had guarded, taught and trained these men. For the subject of the Name see further at verse 26 and at Exodus 33:19 and 34:5, 6. The fullness of the Name is again and again mentioned in the Epistles as "Christ Jesus (or Jesus Christ) our Lord" (see, e.g., Rom. 5:11, 21; 6:11, 23). In all that this meant He made request that they might still be kept. And on their behalf He addresses the Father as "Holy Father," for they were, and we are to be, holy, for He is holy. They were, and we are, by nature unholy and in an unholy world.

Holiness

Holiness is a quality which is essential to true spiritual unity; anything short of it makes for division and discord. The unity is designed for believers, and will be manifested hereafter. It is not simply likemindedness, nor mere acknowledgment of the truth; it is the very character of God manifested in all circumstances and activities.

The "son of perdition" stands out in contrast. That kind of phrase describes the character and effect of a man's moral state, as the manner of his life (e.g., 1 Sam. 25:17; Matt. 23:31; Luke 6:35; Eph. 2:2), and not a destiny. The Scripture, being God-breathed, has the character of accurate prediction; it has never been, and could not be, falsified. Christ had shown, in regard to this very person that He, the living Word, was possessed of divine powers of knowledge (13:18).

Joy

But they were not only to be kept, it was His desire that they might be filled with joy, His own joy experienced in them: **"But now I come to Thee; and these things I speak in the world, that they may have My joy fulfilled in themselves"** (v. 13). This plainly intimates that the Lord purposely spoke these things in their hearing. But why does He say "in the world" instead of "in their hearing"? He had expressed the same desire to them directly (15:11). The world, however, was the scene of so much that would tend to cast down and depress (and He was leaving them in it), that He repeats this great desire, addressing it to Him to whom He was coming, that the joy that characterized Him might continue and be fulfilled in them.

But not only was His own sustaining joy to be theirs, it would be maintained by the Word

He had given them, the Father's Word. The Word of God, accepted and kept, ministers joy to the heart. To keep His Word is, however, contrary to the spirit of the world and produces its hatred: **"I have given them Thy Word; and the world hated them, because they are not of the world, even as I am not of the world. I pray not that Thou shouldest take them from the world, but that Thou shouldest keep them from the evil one"** (vv. 14, 15). To remove them from the world would leave the effects of their presence and of their very mission unaccomplished. But the negative way first of making the request served only to stress the urgency of the positive desire. For the being who had sought to hinder and defeat Him was still active, and would be, in spite of his initial overthrow at the Cross. There lay, and there lies, the great danger.

The Evil One

The Lord had spoken of the evil one (Matt. 13:19), not as a sinister influence, but as a person, and the Epistles bear this out in frequent passages. The apostle Paul assures the church at Thessalonica that God would guard them "from the evil one" (2 Thess. 3:3). The apostle John speaks of him five times thus and says in the closing passage of his first epistle, in words which reecho the Lord's, "We know that whosoever is begotten of God sinneth not (present continuous tense, "doth not go on doing sin"); but He that was begotten of God (i.e., the Son of God, 4:9) keepeth him (R.V.), and the evil one toucheth him not. We know that we are of God, and the whole world lieth in the evil one" (1 John 5:18, 19).

The preposition "from" in "from the evil one" is *ek*, out of, and is used of deliverance from persons, e.g., Acts 26:17.

Sanctification

In verse 16 the Lord says again, **"They are not of the world, even as I am not of the world,"** and this precedes a request for their deliverance: **"Sanctify them in the truth: Thy word is truth."** Sanctification is a state of separation to God; all believers enter into this state when they are born of God; but sanctification is also used of the practical experience of this separation to God, and is the effect of the Word of God as learned by the Holy Spirit, and is to be pursued by the believer earnestly (1 Tim. 2:15; Heb. 12:14). In this sense of the word the Lord prays here; and here it has in view the setting apart of believers for the purpose for which they are sent into the world: **"As Thou didst send Me into the world, even so send I them into the world. And for their sakes I sanctify Myself, that they themselves also may be sanctified in truth"** (v. 18, 19). That He set apart Himself for the purpose for which He was sent, is both the basis and the condition of our being set apart for that for which *we* are sent (cp. 10:36). His sanctification is the pattern of, and the power for, ours. The sending and the sanctifying are inseparable. The words "in truth" mean "in reality," i.e., in practical experience (as in Matt. 22:16; Col. 1:6; 2 John 1).

Verses 20 to 24

Prayer for All Believers

"Neither for these only do I pray, but for them also that believe on Me through their word." The Lord uses the present tense "them that believe," as He views the vast company forming the Church, the outcome of their initial ministry by tongue and by pen, the latter inclusive of the Gospels as well as the Epistles. In this connection the foundations of the future city of glory have on them the names of "The Twelve Apostles of the Lamb." The purpose of the request is the same as that made for those who were listening to Him that evening, **"that they all may be one; even as Thou, Father, art in Me, and I in Thee, that they also may be in Us"** (v. 21), lit., "one thing" in us (neuter), not indicating the elimination of individual life, but the oneness as of a body in its various members, each developing its activity as part of the whole.

The great object looks on to the time when the Church will be completed and manifested with Him in glory at His Second Advent. The world will then be brought to accept all the facts involved in His being sent, and that for the very purpose He has expressed. There are three purposes, (1) oneness in themselves as with the Father and Son; (2) oneness in

them ("in Us"), the essential sphere and relation of the oneness; (3) recognition by the world.

Imparted Glory Expressed in Unity

This is confirmed and expanded in His next words, **"And the glory which Thou hast given Me I have given unto them; that they may be one, even as We are one; I in them, and Thou in Me, that they may be perfected into one; that the world may know that Thou didst send Me, and lovedst them, even as Thou lovedst Me"** (vv. 22, 23). What this imparted glory is receives an explanation from 1 Peter 1:21, "God . . . raised Him from the dead and gave Him glory." It is the glory therefore of resurrection and reception into His presence. How the Lord Jesus will impart this glory to all believers is stated in 1 Thessalonians 4:16, 17. He will "fashion anew the body of our humiliation, that it may be conformed to the body of His glory" (Phil. 3:21). At that moment and from that time believers will be one, even as the Father and the Son are one. The fulfillment and completeness is to be realized in the indwelling of Christ and the Father in each and all "I in them, and Thou in Me." The perfecting into one will be accomplished by, and consist in, our being "like Him; for we shall see Him even as He is" (1 John 3:2). There will be a participation by all in this perfect likeness. Then will be fulfilled the word, "whom He justified, them He also glorified" (Rom. 8:30).

Then will the world be made to recognize not only the great truths concerning Christ as the One sent by the Father (see v. 21), but that all that is accomplished is the effect of the love of God the Father toward believers, as definite as His love for His Son (see v. 26). For the fulfillment in regard to the world see, *e.g.,* 2 Thessalonians 1:10; Revelation 1:7. For the love of Christ as that which is to be recognized by the world, see Revelation 3:9.

The Lord's Will

Thus far the Lord has said three times "I pray" (I make request); now He says "I will": **"Father, that which Thou hast given Me, I will that, where I am, they also may be with Me."** This and what follows are a consummation of all that has preceded regarding those who are His. It brings everything to the complete fruition of all the divine counsels and operations on their behalf. Accordingly His desires now find their expression in a word which conveys the equality of the Son and the Father in counsel and purpose. Again He speaks of His people first as a totality, a complete entity, **"that which Thou hast given Me,"** and then as a company of individuals, **"that they may be with Me."**

His will concerning them is twofold: (1) their being with Him, (2) that they may behold His glory, each is involved in his relation to Him. Of the first He had given them a promise (14:3), and now His will completes all that He has added: **"that they may behold My glory, which Thou hast given Me: for Thou lovedst Me before the foundation of the world"** (v. 24). This is the glory already mentioned in verse 22, a glory given, and now as a proof that the Father loved Him "before [not "from," as in Matt. 25:34, as to the earthly Kingdom] the foundation of the world." To behold His glory will be to be like Him (cp. Ps. 17:15).

Verses 25, 26

The Concluding Facts and Purpose

Just as the title "Holy Father" was used as appropriate to the holiness of His followers (v. 11), so now regarding the world and its unrighteous state of ignorance of God, the Lord says, **"O righteous Father."** God had endowed man with a capacity for knowing Him,

with resulting fulfillment of His will and obedience to His command. He would thus have been "right with God." The world refused to have Him in knowledge (Rom. 1:28). To the Jews He said "ye have not known Him, but I know Him" (8:55). So now He says **"the world indeed [*kai*] knew Thee not, but I knew Thee** [looking back on the contrast experienced in the days of His flesh]; **and these knew that Thou didst send me"** (v. 25).

Then comes the close; it is retrospective, prospective and purposive. That which He had been doing for His own, He will continue to do, and that with one great object: **"and I made known unto them Thy Name** [cp. 15:15], **and will make it known** [see 14:26 and 16:13]; **that the love wherewith Thou lovedst Me may be in them, and I in them."** He continued to make the Name known during the forty days after His resurrection; He continued to do so by the Holy Spirit through the apostles after Pentecost; He has done so ever since by the ministry of the Spirit in and through the Scriptures of truth; and this will not cease in the ages to come.

Finally, as to the purpose, the love of the Father to Him is designed to dwell in us by reason of the perpetual indwelling of Christ Himself. Were our hearts in such a condition that this love might be the controlling power over our lives, we should learn to love as He loves, to love one another fervently with a pure heart, and so to manifest the very life and character of Christ. That kind of life it is which will meet with the highest reward hereafter.

JOHN

CHAPTER EIGHTEEN

Verses 1 to 11

It was in a garden where God had walked with man in perfect communion that man treacherously handed over the springs of his being to the spiritual foe and was at enmity with God. It was again in a garden, where Christ had held communion with His disciples, that one of them, having treacherously handed over his being to the human foe, manifested his enmity against the Son of God and betrayed Him.

The Traitor's Precautions

Judas had had experience of the power of Christ in various ways. Determined therefore to make sure of the carrying out of his object, he obtained **"a band of soldiers,"** a Roman cohort together with officers, or the temple guard, from the chief priests (Luke includes some of the latter themselves) and Pharisees, and guided this large company, carrying lanterns and torches, to the familiar spot. These elaborate preparations were perhaps made because of the possibility that Jesus might do as He had done before, and hide Himself and escape. There was no need for all this precaution: **"Jesus . . . knowing all the things that were coming upon Him, went forth, and saith unto them. Whom seek ye? They answered Him, Jesus of Nazareth. Jesus saith unto them, I am He."**

Three facts stand out conspicuously in these circumstances. The form of the verb rendered "betrayed" in verses 2 and 5 indicates the whole process of the treachery of Judas. It is, literally, "the one betraying Him," and while it is almost equivalent to a title, it indicates the whole course of his procedure.

The Effect of the Jehovah Name

Secondly, that Jesus went forth to meet the company indicates the voluntary character of His sacrifice. The hour had come for the great fulfillment of His becoming obedient even unto death. Hence the significance of His word to Peter, **"Put up the sword into the sheath; the cup which the Father hath given Me, shall I not drink it?"** (v. 11).

Thirdly, there is the striking effect of the Lord's reply to His foes, who stated that they were seeking Jesus of Nazareth. The words *egō eimi,* "I am," were to Jewish ears the equivalent of the name Jehovah. That the company went backward and fell to the ground, was the effect, not of guilt confronted with innocence, but of the majesty and power of His utterance. The fact that He permitted them to rise again and seize Him serves to confirm the voluntary character of His giving Himself up to death.

And now He shows His loving care for, and His power to defend, His followers, as a shepherd cares for his sheep: He says, **"if therefore ye seek Me, let these go their way,"** thus fulfilling His own word in 17:12, with a change from "not one of them perished" to "I lost not one," which brings out forcibly the Lord's own act in intervening on their behalf.

Verses 12 to 27

The Ecclesiastical Tribunals

The Lord is seized by the cohort ("the band") under their commander, the military tribune, "the chief captain," as well as the Jewish officials, and taken before Annas. He was the most influential member of the hierarchy. He secured the high priesthood for Caiaphas, his son-in-law, and for five of his own sons, the last of whom, also named Annas, put James to death. There were several deposed high priests in the Sanhedrin, Annas was the acting president. The attitude Caiaphas would adopt was clear from his statement in 11:50, an unconscious prophecy, doubtless too an advice that if Jesus were put to death the Romans would postpone their enslavement of the nation and devastation of the land.

The court into which Christ was taken, and into which the disciple mentioned in verse 15 (almost certainly John) entered was quadrangular, and around it the high priest's house was built. There was a passage running from the street through the front part of the house. This was closed at the street end by a gate with a wicket, which on this occasion was kept by a maid. The rooms round the court were open in front; in one of these Jesus was being examined, and the Lord could see and hear Peter. John had seen Peter following at a distance and went to the maid with a request to let him in. She, knowing that the one was a disciple, naturally greets Peter with the question, **"Art thou also one of this man's disciples?"** In confusion at being confronted by such a hostile crowd, and remembering the blow he had struck in the garden, Peter denies any such connection. One denial prepared for more.

The Effect of Impulse

The impetuous act of using the sword in the garden was no inconsiderable factor in bringing about the terrible circumstances of these denials. We need to be on our guard against acting by sudden impulse on any occasion. One act of mistaken zeal in the energy of the flesh may have a bearing upon ensuing circumstances which are fraught with dire consequences.

Had Peter been void of self-confidence, and had he heeded the Lord's warning, he might have acted otherwise than remaining in the company of the servants and officers warming himself with them by the fire. That was a position full of danger. The repetition of the fact in the record is very suggestive: **"Peter also was with them, standing and warming himself"** (v. 18), and again, after an interval, **"Now Simon Peter was standing and warming himself"** (v. 25).

In the conversation his Galilean accent was readily detected. **"They said therefore unto him, Art thou also one of His disciples?"** That produced a second denial. In the groups was a servant of the high priest, a relative of the man whose ear Peter had cut off. **"Did not I see thee,"** he says, **"in the garden with Him?"** Peter therefore denied again: and straightway the cock [rather, "a cock"] **crew."** This, Luke tells us, was about an hour after the second denial. Then it was that the Lord turned and looked on Peter, either from the room looking out into the court, or as He was being led across the court. That brought Peter to himself and he went out and wept bitterly. The tenderness of

the look brought home the terrible nature of the guilt, and saved him from blank despair.

This is all written for our admonition, a warning against self-confidence, against planning our own steps, against associating with the world even with a good motive, and a strong reminder that, should we fail to take heed to ourselves and fall, He who went to the Cross for our sakes, yearns for our restoration and has provided the means for it.

Jewish Illegalities

The record of the trial before Annas and Caiaphas is brief. Nothing could be done until Pilate's ratification. Every detail of the trial was illegal to hold it at night at all. The high priest asked Jesus both about His disciples and about His teaching. He answers nothing concerning them, shielding them from the unscrupulous ways of these foes. Concerning Himself His statements as to the openness of His teaching stand in contrast to their secret method. **"Why askest thou Me?"** He says. **"Ask them that heard Me"** (not the disciples, but witnesses present). Witnesses for the defense should be heard first.

The act of the attendant officer who struck Jesus with the palm of his hand (not with a rod, as R.V., margin) was particularly noted by John. The meek yet firm reply of the Lord was sufficient to finish that part of the proceedings. **"Annas therefore sent Him bound unto Caiaphas."**

A Summary of 18:28 to 19:16

Pilate and the Jews

John describes this scene at some length. He records what is elsewhere omitted, the conference between Pilate and the Jews (18:28 to 32) and the two private examinations by Pilate (18:33–38 and 19:8–11).

Caiaphas had passed sentence of death on Christ, and now they led Him into the Praetorium, the official residence of the procurator. The circumstances which follow are partly outside this place, partly inside: in verses 28 to 32 Pilate deals with the Jews, the accusers outside; in 33 to 37 he deals with Christ inside; in 38 to 40, with the accusers outside; in 19:1 to 3, with Christ inside (now the scourging and cruelty take place); in 4 to 7 outside with the accusers; in 8 to 11 with Christ inside (when the Lord's testimony produces a climax); in 12 to 16 with the Jews outside.

Verses 28 to 40

The significance of the statement in verse 28, **"and it was early,"** is as follows. A Roman court could be held after sunrise. The occasion being critical, Pilate would be ready to open the court, say, between 4:00 and 5:00 A.M. The Sanhedrin officials were in a difficulty, as a whole day must intervene between their sentence and execution. Hence they go at once to Pilate. If he agrees to execute he can fix the time. So they transferred the breach of their law from themselves to him.

Their supercilious adherence to the Law prevented their entering a polluted house, uncleansed from leaven (Ex. 12:15). **"Pilate therefore went out unto them,"** lit., "went out . . . outside unto them," with emphasis on the verb "went out," marking his concession to their religiousness and his anxiety to avoid disturbance.

Pilate's Interview

His question as to the accusation (v. 29) has an air of judicial formality. At the same time the prisoner looked very unlike a criminal. On their refusing to name their charge, and with a combination of contempt and irritation, he tells them to judge Him by their law. Upon this they raised an accusation with regard to the Roman power, that He forbade to give tribute to Caesar and claimed to be a king. Could they not have stoned Him otherwise? However that may be viewed, the point is that Christ had foretold by what manner of death He would die. They said it was not lawful for them to do the execution. He had said He must be "lifted up."

The private interview inside the Praetorium therefore takes place, and Pilate puts the question **"Art Thou the King of the Jews?"** There is stress on "Thou," and the question indicates surprise. Christ demands that the responsibility of making the charge should be put upon the right persons (v. 34). Pilate says, **"Am I a Jew?"** (with stress on the "I"), brusquely repudiating the idea that he has any

interest in Jewish affairs. So he emphatically says, **"Thine own nation** [the nation that is thine] **and the chief priests delivered Thee unto me. What hast Thou done?"**

Three times over in His reply the Lord says, with similar emphasis, **"The Kingdom that is Mine,"** and likewise, **"The servants** [or officers] **that are Mine,"** setting Himself and His affairs in direct contrast to the world. The "now" in verse 26 indicates that there is to be a kingdom hereafter. He shows therefore that His kingdom could not engage in conflict with the kingdom represented by Pilate. The latter scornfully asks **"Art Thou a king, then?"** with stress on the "Thou." If he had any lurking fear of some secret society, it is removed by Christ's reply, that a king He is, that He had been born for this, and has come into the world also to bear witness to the truth. There is special emphasis upon the "I" in the statement **"I have been born to this end."** Moreover, He has authority, His voice has power, everyone who is of the truth (the characteristic of His kingdom) is subject to Him, listens to His voice.

Pilate's Injustice

All this is essentially different from what Pilate had expected. There is nothing but innocence in such statements. And as for truth, that sort of thing has no place in the Roman procurator's mind. With a sort of combination of impatience and pity, and not in jest or serious inquiry, he says **"What is truth?"** Upon this he goes out again to the Jews, declaring the innocence of the prisoner and suggesting His release, according to custom at the Passover. To pronounce the accused guiltless and then to try and propitiate the savage accusers was the extreme of weakness. Injustice removed the one means of resisting their bloodthirstiness.

Barabbas

Barabbas was popular, he was a bandit *(lēstēs),* a man of violence (not a thief). He rose against the Romans, that which Christ refused to do. The accusation by the Jews was that Jesus was dangerous to the Roman government; in reality one great reason for their antagonism was that He was not against the government.

JOHN

• CHAPTER NINETEEN •

Verses 1 to 16

According to Luke 23, Pilate had sent Christ to Herod before this, and Herod, with his troops, maltreated Him and sent Him back to Pilate. Pilate "took Jesus, and scourged Him." This was not the immediate preliminary to execution. He doubtless hoped that this might somehow satisfy the fury of the Jews. This form of Roman scourging (not that of the lictors' rods; Pilate had no lictors) was barbarously cruel. The heavy things were loaded with metal, and bone was woven into them, a piece of metal being fastened at the tip. Every cut tore the flesh from the bones, chest and back (see Ps. 22:17). Eusebius tells how he saw martyrs sinking down in death under the lashes of this kind of scourging.

Brutal Mockery by Troops

Upon this followed the cruelty of the soldiers, who **"plaited a crown of thorns, and put it on His head, and arrayed Him in a purple garment"** (a military cloak), and saluting Him in mockery as a king, put, as Matthew says, a reed (a stout rod, as a scepter) in His right hand, spat upon Him, and taking the reed, one after another, from His hand, smote Him on the head (imperfect tense in the Greek, *i.e.*, they kept on doing it). See Isaiah 50:6. All was intentionally a cruel caricature of Jewish hopes of a king.

Ecce Homo

Pilate now brought Him out, still arrayed (previously he had left Him inside), and declared again His guiltlessness. With pity rather than contempt he says **"Behold the man."** The chief priests and the Sanhedrin officers, perhaps fearing some signs of compassion among the people, begin at once to shout **"Crucify, crucify."** Pilate, goaded into taunting them, tells them to do it themselves, a thing he knew they dared not do. They were clever enough to advance a new accusation, held in reserve, which might appeal to his fears. When therefore, they brought the accusation that He made Himself the Son of God, and so broke their law, fear laid hold of Pilate, by very reason of this word (*logos*, not a mere saying, *rhēma*). There was the combination of his wife's message, the awesomeness of Christ's demeanor throughout, the possibility that, even according to Roman religion, he had been dealing with the offspring of a god. Apprehensive about it all he took Jesus into the Praetorium again and said **"Whence art Thou?"**

To this Christ gave no answer. For one thing, the information would have been useless in Pilate's case. For another, the injustice of his actions could now have only one issue: no explanation would have altered what was a foregone conclusion. In the next question, **"Speakest Thou not unto me?"** the special emphasis is on "me." The Roman governor could naturally claim power to release or to crucify. And now, in Christ's last word to him, He shows His judge that He is Himself the judge. Any exercise of power by Pilate depended on the permissive will of a power **"from above."** And his prisoner could pronounce and measure guilt. The sin of Caiaphas was declared to be greater than Pilate's.

The Final Argument

Going again outside he made efforts (more than one, as the imperfect tense shows) to release Him. At this the accusers played their last card. To release the prisoner would endanger the governor's position. A report would go to a suspicious emperor (his fear of the emperor was real). The political argument succeeded. Pilate brought Christ out and prepared to pass sentence; it must be passed in public. He sat down on the judgment seat (probably a temporary one; there is no definite article, as everywhere else in the N.T. with *bēma*), on a tessellated pavement, called in Aramaic Gabbatha (or raised). His **"Behold, your king!"** was uttered in bitter irony. They shouted in one loud cry (aorist or definite tense), **"Away with *Him*, away with *Him*, crucify, crucify."**

In declaring that their only king is the heathen emperor, the chief priests, the official exponents of Israel's religion, with blasphemous callousness renounce the faith of their nation. If Pilate was guilty of judicial murder, they were guilty of suicide. In his delivering Christ **"unto them to be crucified"** (v. 16), the actual execution would be done by soldiers.

Verses 17 to 37

The Death of Christ

"They took Jesus (*paralambanō*, to receive, is used in 1:11 of not receiving the Father's gift of His Son; here, of receiving Him from Pilate; in 14:3, of His coming to receive His own to Himself); **and He went out, bearing the cross** [*stauros*, a single beam, a stake, a tree trunk, not a two-pieced cross, a thing of later arrangement from pagan sources], **for Himself,"** R.V. (the A.V. misses this point), that is to say, like the vilest felon. Yet there is in this an underlying intimation of His voluntariness.

Jesus in the Midst

The name Golgotha, **"The place of a skull,"** refers to the configuration and markings of the place. At the same time it suggests the emptiness of all mere human ideas, methods, aims and schemes. John describes more fully than the Synoptists the fact that the cross of Christ was the central one: **"They crucified Him, and with Him two others, on either side one, and Jesus in the midst"** (v. 18). The position assigned may have been a Roman mockery. Yet it serves to make prominent both the contrasting sinlessness of Christ, and His actual bearing of our sins, His being "made sin" for us. But further, it indicates the eternal separation between repentant, saved sinners, as represented by the converted robber on the one side, and unrepentant, unsaved sinners, represented by the other on the other side.

Pilate carried on further mockery, writing a title in Hebrew, Latin and Greek, for the cosmopolitan crowd to read, and putting it on the cross: **"Jesus of Nazareth, the King of the Jews."** The Septuagint in Psalm 96:10 has that "the Lord reigned from the tree." Pilate's contemptuous reply to the objection raised by **"the chief priests of the Jews"** (a phrase here only in the N.T.) shows that, now that his personal interests were not at stake, he could be obstinate instead of vacillating.

The Seamless Robe

Four soldiers (a small force was sufficient, as there was no more danger of an outbreak of the mob) divided Christ's garments. These were the legal perquisites of soldiers who carried out executions. In casting lots for the seamless tunic they fulfilled Psalm 22:18. As the high priest's robe was seamless (Ex. 28:6–8), the detailed mention of this by the apostle John would suggest that this garment of Christ was symbolic of His high priesthood (Heb. 8:3).

In the Greek in the closing statement of verse 24 and the first statement of verse 25, there are two particles setting in marked contrast the callous doings of the four soldiers and the devoted attitude of the four women standing by the cross. This is partly expressed by the "But." That John here again calls himself the disciple whom Jesus loved is definitely connected with the Lord's loving committal of His mother to him. It was a mark of Christ's love for His disciple, that He should thus give him a mother and her a son. John takes her at once to his own home, sparing her from seeing the end.

"I Thirst"

One prophecy remained to be fulfilled. True, He experienced in terrible measure the physical anguish of thirst. Spiritually, too, he felt the drought of the condition of being forsaken of God. What, however, John mentions is that He said **"I thirst, knowing that all things are now finished** (or rather have been completed), **that the Scripture might be accomplished."**

The stupefying draft mentioned in Matthew 27:34 He refused. He did not refuse the vinegar or hyssop. Hyssop was appointed in connection with the Passover lamb (Ex. 12:22). Thereupon He said **"It is finished"**; all the will of the Father, all the types and prophecies, all the redemptive work, He declared to have been fulfilled; **"and He bowed His head,"** He reclined *(klinō)* His head, putting it into a position of rest, with face turned heavenward, indicative of the rest He found in the fulfillment of the will of His Father, **"and gave up His spirit,"** a voluntary act, committing His spirit to the Father. No other crucified person ever died thus. In every other case the head dropped forward helplessly on the chest. He had said of His life, "No one taketh it from Me, but I lay it down of Myself" (10:18).

The request of the Jews, in their scrupulosity as to the sabbath, had been forestalled in the case of Christ by Psalm 34:20; Exodus 12:46; Numbers 9:12. But a soldier pierced His side with a spear, **"and straightway there came out blood and water."** God, overruling the act of human enmity, testified to the efficacy of the death of Christ. The blood speaks of redemption, and cleansing, the water speaks of the new birth and separation. Both tell of life, life bestowed through the giving up of His life in propitiatory sacrifice;

"it is the blood that maketh atonement by reason of the life" (Lev. 17:11, R.V.), and life is bestowed by the water or regeneration (Titus 3:5). Accordingly the apostle lays special stress on his own evidence: **"his witness is true** [*alethine*, not simply truthful, but real, genuine, fulfilling the conditions of valid evidence], **and he knoweth that he saith true** [*alethe*, true things], **that ye also may believe"** (v. 35).

Verses 38 to 42

The Burial

Joseph of Arimathaea and Nicodemus, of whom we hear nothing afterwards, are representatives of a future remnant of repentant Israel. Nicodemus would now certainly understand the significance of the brazen serpent (3:14). The tomb was "new" (*kainos*, fresh, not newly hewn out), no body ever having been laid in it. Matthew speaks of its newness, Luke of its freshness.

JOHN

CHAPTER TWENTY

Verses 1 to 10

The First Evidence
of the Resurrection

The first day of the week, the third from the burial, was the day on which Abraham typically received his son as from the dead; it was also the day of Jonah's deliverance, and is the day of Israel's future revival (Hos. 6:2). Mary Magdalene knew Christ as yet only "after the flesh." Hence her message to Peter. What he saw on entering the tomb was the evidence, in the very condition of the clothes, of resurrection. There had not been a tidying of the wrappings. They had not been disturbed, any more than the tomb and the stone, when the Lord arose. His body, possessed of supranatural resurrection power, left the wrappings, not in a heap, but in the shape in which they had been. Every detail gave proof of resurrection. That revealed the fact to both Peter and John (vv. 6 to 8). What they failed to learn and understand from the Scripture they realized from what they saw. There was no need to stay and make inquiry: so they went home.

Verses 11 to 18

The Second Evidence
of the Resurrection

The outstanding fact about Mary Magdalene is the utter absorption of her mind and heart in the person of Christ, whom she regards as dead and whose lifeless body she wants. She **"continued standing,"** after the others had gone. Even the appearance of the two angels in the tomb did not startle her, nor did their question to her distract her from her preoccupation. Even though she was thinking only of the body, the lifeless form was still to her **"my Lord."** Turning herself and thinking that the person who asked her the same question as did the angels, was the gardener (Christ's risen body was so changed that He was not recognized by those who had known

Him), she wanted to know, should he have taken the body out, where he had put it (she says "Him") and she would take Him away, the wrappings and the hundred pounds weight of spices and all. **"Jesus saith unto her, Mary."** That awakened the ecstasy of her heart. "He calleth His own sheep by name." She turned again (she had evidently turned away while thinking she was talking to the gardener), addressed Him as **"Rabboni,"** in the language used by the Lord and His followers, and reached out to hold Him. His command, rendered **"Touch Me not,"** is used in the present continuous tense and is to be understood with the meaning "Do not hold Me" (or "Do not be clinging to Me"). **"For I am not yet ascended,"** He says, **"unto the Father."** The former intermittent intercourse is to be replaced by the new and continuous intercourse, but this cannot be till He is with the Father.

He was going to place them in the same position as His own, of relationship with His Father and His God. Hence He sends this devoted soul as His first messenger to His **"brethren,"** to say **"I ascend unto My Father and your Father, and My God and your God."** Heavenly, eternal and infinitely intimate relationship, with all the joy of the love of the Father and the power of God realized and enjoyed in Christ.

Verses 19 to 23

The Third Evidence
of the Resurrection

The **"therefore"** in verse 19 indicates that it was owing to her testimony that the disciples assembled. If the news reached the authorities it would excite their hostility. They gathered **"for fear of the Jews."** It was **"evening,"** late in the day; it was **"that day,"** the memorable day, but it was still **"the first day of the week"** (not the second, though the second had begun in the evening by Jewish reckoning). A new week-period had begun; it was the Resurrection day, not the sabbath, there was beginning a perpetual sabbath-keeping of rest in Christ (Heb. 4:9). **"The doors were shut"**; that marks two things, a protection against the Jews and the supernatural entrance of the Lord. **"Jesus came and stood in the midst, and saith unto them, Peace be unto you."** Peace was His last message to them before He went with them to Gethsemane; it was His first word to them after His resurrection.

He then showed them **"His hands and His side,"** and Luke says His feet (24:39). Whatever other scars there had been were obliterated at His resurrection, but not these marks of His crucifixion and the significant wound in the side. Their sorrow is turned into joy. He repeats to them what they had heard Him say to the Father (vv. 17, 18, 21). Thereupon **"He breathed on them."** The same word (here only in the N.T.) is used in the Septuagint in Genesis 2:7; that was more than natural life, it was spiritual life as well.

His word **"Receive ye the Holy Spirit"** (R.V. margin) referred not merely to His own breath, it was symbolic of the Holy Spirit as about to be sent at Pentecost. It was connected with their being sent into the world, and with the effect of their ministry of the gospel in the forgiveness of sins by the Spirit's power, or the retention of sins by the rejection of the message (vv. 23, 24). It was a prophetic act as well as symbolic.

Verses 24 to 31

The Fourth Evidence of the Resurrection

When Thomas, who had been absent, rejoined his brethren, they repeatedly told him (imperfect tense, *elegon*, they kept telling him) that they had seen the Lord. He had only one reply to make (aorist tense; *eipen*), it was decisive. Doubtless they told him that Christ had bidden them handle Him and see. Hence his persistent asseveration, **"Except I shall see in His hands the print of the nails, and put my finger into the print of the nails, and put my hand into His side, I will not** (a strong negative, I will in no wise) **believe."**

A week later, the next first day of the week, Thomas being present, the Lord appears again in the midst, and shows him, by quoting his words, that He had heard the condition he laid down. This draws forth immediately the acknowledgment of the authority of Christ as his Lord and of His deity as God. Christ accepts both titles (just as He accepted the charge of the Jews in 5:18, that He made Himself equal with God), and proclaims the blessedness of the multitudes of those who, not having seen, have yet believed.

Here the apostle looks back over the whole book he has been writing, recording the fact that the Lord did many other signs (a miracle was a sign) in the presence of His disciples. What he wrote was not a history of Christ, or the life of Christ, but just those facts which would enable readers throughout this period to believe **"that Jesus is the Christ, the Son of God** [the outstanding fact and feature of this Gospel]; **and that believing ye may have life in His Name."** Were He not the Son of God, He would not be the Christ, the Messiah. Jehovah's anointed must be very God as well as very man. "In His Name" indicates that the gift of life comes by reason of His character, His attributes and His dealings.

JOHN

CHAPTER TWENTY-ONE

Verses 1 to 14

The Fifth Evidence of the Resurrection

The narrative (miscalled an epilogue) continues the proofs of the reality of Christ's resurrection. The manner in which the Lord manifested Himself at the Sea of Tiberias after His resurrection, forms the closing act, as recorded in this Gospel, of the preparation of His disciples for their service. On this occasion there were seven of them. What memories the lakeside had for them. There they had listened to His teaching. There they had seen wonders of His glory. Thither their boat had been safely and suddenly brought from out of the storm that threatened to overwhelm them.

Deciding to pursue their former occupation they had gone **"a fishing,"** had toiled all night, and taken nothing (cp. Luke 5:5). Natural skill and persistent effort avail nothing apart from the will and power of the Lord. God brings us to an end of ourselves that He may give us to see His all-sufficiency to meet our need. "Man's extremity is God's opportunity."

The Withholding and the Revealing

"But when day was now breaking, Jesus stood on the beach: howbeit the disciples knew not that it was Jesus" (v. 4, R.V.). As He had dealt with Mary Magdalene at the tomb and with the two on the road to Emmaus, so now with these seven. In each case the initial withholding of His identity had the design of imparting the greater assurance, in the immediately succeeding manifestation, of the fact of His resurrection. The brightness of a light is rendered more vivid by an antecedent darkness. As the natural dawn that morning shone out upon the darkness of the weary night, so He first veiled the reality of His person that the power of the disclosure might be the more effective.

Accordingly, permitting them to regard Him as an ordinary bystander, He addresses them in the customary and familiar manner of such. Our English versions render His question **"Children have ye aught to eat?"** (A.V., any meat). The word *paidion*, translated "children," was used variously, e.g., of a newborn infant, a more advanced child, a son. In affectionate, colloquial address, as in the present instance, our term "lads" would almost represent it.

In response to their somewhat cheerless **"No."** He says, **"Cast the net on the right side of the boat, and ye shall find."** There was still nothing in that to make His identity known, nothing more than the natural interest any stranger might take in a fishing enterprise.

A Ready Recognition

But now the surprising and magnificent haul, rendering it impossible to draw the net into the boat, immediately effects in **"that disciple . . . whom Jesus loved"** the recognition characteristic of strong and intimate attachment. John's frequent mention of himself in this way was not, as some have suggested, indicative of the soft character of a weakling. How could it be so? Was he not described by his Master as "a son of thunder"? Nor was it a vaunt of superiority over his fellow disciples. He does seem to have had a readier, if not fuller, grasp of spiritual verities. **"It is the Lord,"** he says to Peter. Ardent, impetuous Peter, first at the sepulcher, and now first to make for the Lord, girds his coat about him and casts himself into the water. He had cast himself before into the waters of the same lake to reach Him in very different circumstances. Acts reveal character. The impulse which made him leave all behind to go to his Master was the eagerness of love. This was a renewal, with the added attractiveness of the risen Christ, of that former renunciation of all things for Him, concerning which he had afterwards said, "Lo, we have left our own, and followed Thee" (Luke 18:28, R.V.).

Provision and Cooperation

Leaving the larger boat in which they had spent the night, the other disciples come **"in the little boat . . . dragging the net full of fishes."** Getting out upon the land, with the net and its catch left for the moment in the water, they see **"a fire of coals . . . and fish** [less in size than the "great" fish of their catch] **laid thereon, and bread."** Their guide becomes their host.

Nothing is said as to how the Lord provided the repast, and surmisings are fruitless. There is no indication of the miraculous in this respect. That He bade them bring of the fish which they had taken would remove feelings of mere awe and prevent any misgivings. This token of fellowship on His part added to the homely intimacy of the feast. Besides this, the kindly gesture serves to remind us how the Lord delights to use our cooperation in His ministrations, the more fully to reveal Himself to us in His grace and love.

Lessons of Dependence on the Lord

Then there were the lessons of their entire dependence upon Himself in all that lay before them, and of His sufficiency to meet their needs in all the details of their life and service. That is what the Lord would likewise have us learn. How futile are our own schemes for bettering ourselves! How constant and ready are the provisions of our great El Shaddai!

The details were so vividly impressed on the mind of the apostle John that some sixty years later he could remember the precise number of fish caught. Speculations as to the significance of the number tend to obscure the true force and meaning of the facts. The very simplicity of the narrative, the brevity in the recounting of the details, the freedom from undue enlargement upon the miraculous, give eloquent evidence of the reality of His risen person. That was the Lord's design in all that He did, besides the confirmation of their faith in Him and in His power to meet their need.

Reassurance of His Resurrection

After the counting, the customary thing with the fishers upon occasion, the Lord bids them **"Come and break your fast."** The homeliness of the welcome, given in the same gracious tone with which they were familiar in days gone by, at once leads to the statement, **"And none of the disciples durst inquire of Him, Who art Thou? knowing that it was the Lord."** There might have been some ground for the question. The Lord's body was not the former natural body, though still real, corporeal, and tangible. But the character of His utterances and His acts, His ministration of the bread and the fish, together with the marks of His identity, dispelled all possible misgivings, and the way was now opened for further and different ministry.

"We walk by faith, not by sight." "Blessed are they that have not seen and yet have believed." It is ours not only to believe in the fact of the resurrection of Christ, but to experience the joy and power of His presence, as the apostles did of old when, after His ascension, His promise was fulfilled for them, as it is for us, "Lo, I am with you all the days even unto the end of the age." Let us lay hold of the significance for us of this post-resurrection sign. Let us learn day by day our entire dependence upon Him both for our temporal needs and for all that is involved in our occupations as His followers and servants. May we realize that the same loving heart that planned for the disciples, cared for them with tender affection, taught and disciplined them and attached them to His own glorious person, does the same for us if we, as they did, follow Him with Spirit-filled devotion.

Verses 15 to 25

Christ and Peter

Peter's relation to his Master had been established. He is now to be reinstated in view of his responsibility as an apostle and as one who could strengthen his brethren, his self-confidence having been banished. Three times he had denied his Lord. Three times the Lord says **"Lovest Thou Me."** The first time he says **"Lovest thou Me more than these?"** Grammatically the "these" might refer either to persons, fellow disciples, or to things. But (1) Peter had boasted that he was a more ardent disciple than the others: they might deny their Master, but he would not, (2) to speak of loving the matters connected with fishing does not give a sufficient application to the meaning; (3) would the Lord be likely to ask the question with this in mind, considering that the moment Peter saw it was the Lord he left the boat and the nets and swam ashore to be with his Master?

Agapaō and Phileō

As to the change of verb in Peter's reply to the Lord's question, "Lovest thou Me?" Christ uses *agapaō* in His first two questions; Peter uses *phileō* in all three answers. *Phileō* expresses a natural affection, and in this Peter is perfectly sure of himself and is keenly desirous of stating his affection, particularly after his denials. This the Lord fully appreciates; but He is thinking of the practical manifestations and effects as well, as is evident from His commands And the verb *agapaō* combines the two meanings: it expresses a real affection, but likewise raises it to the thought of an active and devoted exercise of it on behalf of others. Accordingly He first says **"Feed My lambs"** (showing that the love is the expression of mind in action). So again, when Peter adheres to *phileō*, Christ replies, **"Tend My sheep."** Shepherd work (all that is involved in tending sheep) must exhibit the love. The commands show how fully reinstated Peter was.

The third time the Lord adopts Peter's word, and this grieved him. It was not that Christ had asked three times, but that now the third time, in using Peter's word, He should even seem to question the deeply felt, genuine affection he felt for Him. This is confirmed by the statement Peter makes, **"Thou knowest all things** ["Thou knowest intuitively," *oida*]; **Thou knowest** [*ginōskō*, "Thou dost recognize"] **that I love Thee** [*phileō*].

The Call to Follow

In what the Lord now says He takes up both the aspects of love, the practical and the deep-seated, affectionate and emotional love. First He adheres to the practical: **"Feed My sheep."** Then He foretells how Peter will manifest his affection in laying down his life after all for his Master's sake. Thus it would be given him to do what he had in self-confidence boasted he would do. And it was devotion to his Master that made him say it. The being

girded and carried **"whither thou wouldest not"** did not imply unwillingness to die, but a natural shrinking from a cruel death, especially crucifixion as a criminal.

That the Lord said to him **"Follow Me"** (v. 19) may have had a literal meaning, as the same word in the next verse has, but it certainly had a figurative sense; it was a call to follow in the path of testimony and suffering (see 13:36). The apostle now clearly discloses his identity. In telling how, as the Lord moved away and Peter after Him, John himself followed, intimating his own devotion, he recalls how he leaned on Christ's breast at the supper, and asked as to who would betray Him.

Fellow Apostles

In John's record concerning Peter and the Lord's reply to his question regarding himself we cannot but note the continued and special intimacy between these two disciples, an intimacy which would be seen in the earliest apostolic testimony. Noticeable also are the Lord's combined foreknowledge of, and authority over, the future lives of His servants. He not only foretells Peter's martyrdom, but says that the length of John's life depends upon what He wills (vv. 22, 23). In verse 22, the "he" and the "thou" are emphatic and set in contrast: "whatever concerning *him* My will may be, *thou* must follow Me." In the last utterance of Christ recorded in this Gospel He speaks of His coming, and the Lord holds out to us the possibility that it may take place during our lifetime.

As to the statement in verse 24, the mode of expressing his identity is characteristic of John. The **"these things"** probably refers to all the contents of this Gospel. The change of tense from **"beareth witness"** to **"wrote,"** shows that though the writing was finished, the witness was continuing. The use of the plural "we" in **"we know"** is quite in keeping with John's style (cp. 1 John 5:18–20); as there so here, he includes all the believers of his time.

The last verse expresses a note of appreciation and admiration regarding all that Christ wrought during the whole course of His life here including the period after His resurrection, and an overwhelming sense of the infinitude of His person and His activities.

Romans

The Theme and Analysis of the Epistle

In the Epistle to the Romans the apostle Paul vindicates the *righteousness of God* in His dealings with men, especially His righteousness as shown in the gospel, in which is revealed, as the apostle says in his introduction, "a righteousness of God by faith unto faith" (1:17). With this in view he sets forth the character and effects of the gospel, showing the means God has adopted by which righteousness can be reckoned to men in spite of their sinful state, and further, by which His grace and mercy, now brought alike to Jew and Gentile individually, will yet be ministered to them nationally. The prominent teaching of the Epistle is that this plan of salvation is consistent with God's own character and attributes.

With this then before him, the apostle, after his prefatory remarks, firstly sets forth the condition of the human race in its alienation from God, showing the effects of the Fall and of the refusal of man to recognize and acknowledge his Creator in the revelation He has given of Himself in nature. In this part of his Epistle he vindicates the righteousness of God in visiting men with wrath because of their sin. Jew and Gentile are thus alike brought under the judgment of God.

All this, however, is only preparatory to an exhibition of the way in which the dislocated relationship between man and God can be adjusted. This has a twofold side to it—on God's part the means provided in the vicarious death of His Son, on man's part the one thing necessary, faith. Having laid the foundation of the adjustment of the relationship between man and Himself in the death of Christ, God calls upon the sinner to respond to His mercy simply by exercising faith. Faith introduces him into a life in Christ Jesus, which is freely given to him on the ground of His death. This is the subject of the section of the Epistle from chapter 3:21 to the end of chapter five.

The character and power of this new life are shown in the sixth and eighth chapters. In this connection the apostle takes up in the seventh chapter the subject of the Law, by way of contrast. While showing its inherent perfection he at the same time shows its inability to reestablish the lost relation between God and man, to impart eternal life and to produce righteousness in the life. It is an external force, the effect of which is to reveal the power and exceeding sinfulness of sin. In contrast to this is the internal force of the new life in Christ, which operates by the indwelling of Christ Himself through the Holy Spirit. In the next part of the Epistle, chapters nine to eleven, still "justifying the ways of God with men," he shows how the divine dealings with the nation of Israel and the gentile nations are consistent with God's own sovereignty and righteousness, and how salvation is to be brought to all solely on the ground of faith. In these eleven chapters the apostle displays the sovereign grace of God in spite of the Fall and its consequences, first in the case of those who accept the divine conditions and then eventually in national deliverance and blessing in the coming age.

From the twelfth chapter onward the Epistle is occupied with the effects of the gospel as seen in the conduct of Christians in their various relations and duties Godward and manward. These constitute the outward expressions and manifestations of the inward life received in Christ through the Gospel.

The whole Epistle thus may be viewed under the three headings of *light, love* and *life,* in that order. The first part reveals God as light, in all His holiness and righteousness, and in contrast to the darkness of man's state. Then comes the revelation of God's love in Christ as exhibited at the Cross. Thirdly, as the outcome of the divine love, we see the divine life, into which the believer is brought through union with Christ and the effects of which are seen in his conduct.

ROMANS

・ CHAPTER ONE ・

Introduction, 1:1–16

1:1 Paul, a servant of Jesus Christ,—
Doulos is, strictly, a bondservant; it is rendered "bond" in contrast to "free" in 1 Corinthians 12:13, and "bondman" in Revelation 6:15. "Jesus" (Heb. "Joshua") denotes "Jehovah is salvation."

The order of the titles Jesus Christ and Christ Jesus is always significant: "Christ Jesus" describes the one who was with the Father in eternal glory, and who came to earth, becoming incarnate; "Jesus Christ" describes Him as the One who humbled Himself, who was despised and rejected, and endured the cross, but who was afterwards exalted and glorified. "Christ Jesus" testifies to His preexistence; "Jesus Christ" to His resurrection and exaltation.

called to be an apostle, separated unto the gospel of God,—He was separated, firstly, in the purpose of God, prior to his conversion (Gal. 1:15); secondly, in actual experience, at his conversion; thirdly, at Antioch, by the Holy Spirit, for his life's service in the Gospel (Acts 13:1).

1:2–6

This passage contains an outline of the subject of the gospel. There are four headings, and these correspond respectively to the four parts of the Scriptures: (1) the promise of the gospel (v. 2); (2) the person of the gospel, (vv. 3, 4); (3) the preaching of the gospel, (vv. 4, 5); (4) the product of the gospel, (v. 6).

The promise is conveyed in the Old Testament, the Person is the special theme of the four Gospels; the preaching is recorded in the Acts; the product consists of those to whom the remainder of the New Testament is addressed.

1:2 which He promised afore by His prophet—The work of the prophet is to tell forth spiritual truth, whether predictive or otherwise. Thus of Aaron God said to Moses,

"he shall be thy prophet," i.e., "thy mouthpiece" (Ex. 7:1; cp. 4:16).

in the holy Scriptures,—Though the article is absent in the Greek it should be retained in translating. The Scriptures are referred to seven times in this Epistle, three times in the plural (1:2; 15:4; 16:26), and four times in the singular, pointing to a definite text (4:3; 9:17; 10:11; 11:2).

This term is here used, as elsewhere, technically, to denote the collection of writings of the Old Testament.

1:3 concerning His Son,—To be connected with what immediately precedes. This title distinguishes the person from all others, since it indicates in His case, a unique relationship. His Sonship is coexistent with the Fatherhood of God. The timeless existence of the latter involves the timeless existence of the former, for God could not be an everlasting Father had He not an everlasting Son.

who was born—Not "was made," as in the A.V. (cp. "born of a woman, born under the law," Gal. 4:4). So always in the matter of His birth. On the other hand, "He was made sin" (2 Cor. 5:21).

The word *ginomai* literally denotes "to become." This is used not only of persons but also of events. Hence what is conveyed here is not merely that Christ was born: the word carries with it all that He underwent both in circumstances as well as in person, all, that is to say, that was involved in His leaving the glory and coming to earth to be born of a woman.

of the seed of David according to the flesh,—The Gospel of Matthew begins with the description of Christ as "the Son of David," and the book of Revelation closes with His own declaration that He is "the Root and Offspring of David" (Rev. 22:16).

The word "flesh" is here used to denote humanity. It is that by which the Lord Jesus identified Himself with the human race. This statement as to His humanity is preparatory to the testimony which follows as to His Deity.

1:4 who was declared—*Horizō:* this verb has two meanings in the N.T., (1) to ordain, or appoint (as in Acts 10:42; 17:31). This meaning would not suit the present passage, as Christ was never appointed as the Son of God.

(2) to mark out, determine or define, in distinction from others, as the "horizon" marks the distinction between earth and sky. So Christ was marked out as, or shown to be, the Son of God "by the resurrection of the dead."

to be the Son of God with power,—"With power" is literally, "in power," power which was His both in the days of His flesh and in His resurrection.

according to the spirit of holiness,—Christ was distinguished from all other beings as the Son of God in two respects. Firstly, by His life, a life of perfect holiness; secondly, by His death and resurrection. The spirit of Christ, distinct, and yet inseparable, from the Holy Spirit, was essentially and absolutely holy. His sinlessness marked Him off from all merely human beings. This uniqueness involves the supernatural character of His birth. All who have been born naturally have been tainted with sin. He was sinless (Heb. 4:15; 1 Pet. 2:22; 1 John 3:5). Therefore His birth was supernatural. Preexistent as Son of God, and therefore Himself essentially one in godhood with the Father, He became incarnate as a human descendant of David. His sinlessness, admitted by friend and foe alike, both during the days of His flesh and ever since, testifies to His deity, as the Son of God.

by the resurrection of the dead;—This is the second fact which distinguishes Him from all others as the Son of God. His resurrection was an inevitable result of His sinlessness. Death is the consequence of sin. He had none. His death was self-imposed. He laid down His own life, bearing sins, not His own, but ours. His death was unique (1) in that it marked the close of a sinless life on earth, (2) in that He voluntarily yielded to it, enduring it by way of vicarious sacrifice. Consequently resurrection was His divine prerogative, and not a matter of divine favor, as in the case of others. Since

He was His holy one, God did not suffer Him to see corruption (Ps. 16:10). Death could not keep its hold in His case. Thus, both by His sinless life and in His resurrection, He was determined as the Son of God.

But not only so, His power, in the resurrection of others, coupled with the fact of the resurrection of saints at His death (recorded in Matt. 27:52), as well as His own part in His resurrection (John 2:19), were evidences of His deity, as the Son of God; possibly, too, the phrase has in view the fact that His resurrection was both an example and guarantee of that of others.

even Jesus Christ our Lord,—This has the position of emphasis coming as it does at the end of the statements concerning His incarnation, life, death and resurrection.

1:5 through whom we receive grace and apostleship,—i.e., from the Father as the source, through the instrumentality of the Son (cp. 1 Tim. 1:1 and see Gal. 1:1).

Grace supplied the capability of the work; apostleship was the resulting function in which the work was to be carried out.

unto obedience of faith—Two translations are possible here, the one given in the text, or the one given in the margin, "unto obedience to the faith." As faith is one of the main subjects of the Epistle, and considering that this is part of the introduction, the rendering given in the text is probably to be preferred. Faith is the first act of obedience in the new life.

among all the nations, for His name's sake:—This is the paramount consideration in all gospel work. While the gospel is intended to accomplish the salvation of souls, yet, above and beyond this, its object is the glory of the Redeemer. The proclamation of the Gospel is a witness for His Name. His Name expresses what He is, and it is His character that shines out not only in the nature of the Gospel itself but also in the results which it achieves. Those who yield to the gospel the obedience of faith, therein reflect the character of Him whom it preaches and whom they receive. Thence onward their lives, as they show forth His glory, bring honor to His Name (see Acts 15:14).

1:6 among whom are ye also, called to be Jesus Christ's:—i.e., "you are of those who among the nations have obeyed the gospel" (v. 5). The comma after "also" is important. This word goes with its own clause, not with "called to be Jesus Christ's." We are not here said to be called by Him, though that is true, but called to be His possession. In the language of the Acts and Epistles the word "called" always denotes an effectual calling, and therefore suggests both the call given by God and obedience to it on the part of believers. Paul has drawn attention in the first verse to the dignity of his own position in relationship to Christ; he now speaks of the dignity of their position in this relationship. If he had received a call, they had also, and that through the voice of God in the Gospel.

1:7 to all that are in Rome, beloved of God,—God has a special love for those who are the called (John 14:21, 23; 16:27). The measure of God's love to such is the measure of His love to His Son (John 17:23).

called to be saints:—The saints are such by divine calling. They are not called to live a holy life in order to be saints, but because they are so, as a result of the sanctifying power of the Spirit of God. Holiness is a condition of separatedness to God by divine call. To be saints is to partake of the character of God, and so to represent Him worthily. The character of those who belong to Him is the outcome of their relation to Him. The word "saint," in reference to an individual believer, is not found in the New Testament. In Philippians 4:41, where the singular is used, the saints collectively are in view.

Grace to you and peace—Grace is God's free unmerited favor toward man. Peace is the result to those who respond to His grace. Our hearts are kept in peace as we realize that the favor of God is upon us.

from God our Father and the Lord Jesus Christ.—What comes from the one comes equally from the other, a striking testimony to the deity of Christ. This opening section of the Epistle contains several foundation truths of the faith: (1) that the writers of Holy Scripture spoke from God, (2) that Christ was and is the Son of God, (3) that He became incarnate, (4) that He was sinless, (5) that He was

raised from the dead, (6) that the Gospel is God's call to man for the obedience of faith, (7) that the Gospel claims men for Christ, (8) that Christ is God.

1:8 First, I thank my God . . . for you all, through Jesus Christ—The mediator, through whose person and work thanksgiving to God is alone possible. The order of the titles brings His incarnation and death, His resurrection and ascension, into prominence as the basis of thanksgiving.

that your faith is proclaimed throughout the whole world.—*Kosmos* here denotes mankind in general. That the word here signifies the Roman Empire is not likely. Paul probably means that wherever he goes he hears of their faith.

1:9 For God is my witness, whom I serve—*Latreuō,* and its corresponding noun *latreia,* originally signified the work of a hired servant, as distinguished from the compulsory service of the slave, but in the course of time it largely lost that significance, and in its usage in Scripture the thought of adoration was added to that of free obedience. Used of the service of God, the word gained the idea of a service characterized by worship (see, e.g., Phil. 3:3; Heb. 8:5; 9:9, 14; 10:2; 12:28; 13:10; Rev. 7:15; 22:3).

in my spirit—That is, in contrast to the service of ritual in the tabernacle and the temple. Paul's service was not mechanical; it was a matter of worship to, and communion with, God, and therefore was rendered essentially in His spirit.

in the gospel of His Son,—This marks the special feature of his service. That the gospel of God is equally the gospel of His Son is a testimony to the deity of Christ.

how unceasingly I make mention of you,—Constantly recurring prayer is the meaning. *Mneia,* rendered "mention" (here and in Eph. 1:16; 1 Thess. 1:2; Philem. 4), also means "remembrance" (Phil. 1:3; 1 Thess. 3:6; 2 Tim. 1:3), in which last it is used of prayer, as here.

always in my prayers—This is probably to be connected with the following words in verse 10.

1:10 making request, if by any means now at length I may be prospered—*Euadoumai*, literally, "to have a good journey" is used, (a) of the removal of difficulties in the way, as here; (b) of material prosperity in the daily avocation, 1 Corinthians 16:2; (c) of physical health, 3 John 2; (d) of spiritual health. (id.)

by the will of God to come unto you.—*Thelēma*, when used of God, signifies a gracious design (cp. 2:18; 12:2; 15:32); the similar word *boulēma* denotes a determined resolve (see 9:19). Submission to the will of God is not inconsistent with constant prayer. Prayer is often answered in a manner unanticipated by us.

1:11 For I long to see you, that I may impart unto you—The word suggests the idea of sharing rather than giving (cp. 12:8; Luke 3:11; Eph. 4:28; 1 Thess. 2:8). Paul would give of that which God had already given to him.

some spiritual gift,—*Charisma* denotes a gift of grace (cp. 5:15, 16; 6:23; 11:29). What Paul desired to impart came as a gracious gift from God to him by the operation of the Spirit of God upon his spirit. In this way the gift was spiritual (cp. John 7:38, 39).

to the end ye may be established;—*Stērizō*, from *stērix*, a prop. A strengthened form is *episterizo* (for which see Acts 14:22; 15:32, 41; 18:23). To establish is to cause to lean by supporting. Ministry of God's Word which leads us into fuller dependence on God, is ministry which establishes us. The Hebrew word for "believe" literally means "to lean upon" (cp. 2 Chr. 20:20); "Believe in the Lord your God, so shall ye be established," where "believe" and "established" represent the same word. The means of this constant confirmation, then, is the impartation of spiritual benefit, and the response of faith (see next verse).

1:12 that is, that I with you may be comforted in you,—Establishing produces comfort, both for those who are ministering and for those who are ministered to.

each of us by the other's faith, both yours and mine.—The evidence of faith in another believer is a means of comfort to the one who witnesses it.

1:13 And I would not have you ignorant, brethren,—This refers to believers without distinction of sex. The word "sisters" is used of believers in 1 Timothy 5:2 only, and there the subject in hand requires it. Here it includes both brethren and sisters in the Lord (cp. Acts 1:15, 16; 1 Thess. 1:4).

that oftentimes I purposed to come unto you *(and was hindered hitherto),*—He had entertained the hope for several years (15:23). What the hindrance was we are not told (cp. 1 Thess. 2:18, where Satan is mentioned as the hinderer). In Acts 16:6 a hindrance is recorded as imposed by the Holy Spirit.

that I might have some fruit in you also, even as in the rest of the Gentiles.—The apostle seems to have had in view the fruit not only of gospel work in the conversion of souls, but, as the preceding context suggests, that of the edification of the saints.

1:14 I am debtor—He was under an obligation to preach the gospel, as one to whom a stewardship had been committed (1 Cor. 9:16, 17; Eph. 3:2, 7-9).

both to Greeks and to Barbarians,—These were his spiritual creditors; not, of course, merely the people of Greece, as that would mean that the Romans were barbarians, an idea far from the apostle's thoughts; nor Gentiles as a whole, for he distinguishes them from the barbarians. Inasmuch as Greek was a universal language amongst the civilized nations of the Roman Empire, he means all such nations, including the Romans themselves, in contradistinction to the barbarians, the uncivilized nations.

both to the wise and to the foolish.—The difference here is that between the cultured and uncultured, from the educational and philosophic point of view.

1:15 So, as much as in me is, I am ready—*Prothumos* denotes a willing alacrity, not only readiness, but an inclination.

to preach the gospel to you also that are in Rome.—"To preach the gospel" represents the one word in the original *euaggelizomai*. A synonym is *kērussō*, which denotes "to give a proclamation as by a herald." This word is not used invariably for the preaching of the Gospel (e.g., at 2:21).

1:16 For I am not ashamed of the gospel:—A negative expression is often used as a forceful method of stating a positive fact: he glories in the Gospel (cp. Gal. 6:14).

for it is the power of God,—The power of God is now mentioned for the second time. The first was in connection with the resurrection of Christ (v. 4); here it characterizes and conditions the Gospel. The second is the outcome of the first. In the twentieth verse, it has reference to the essential attribute of the Godhead as demonstrated in creation.

unto salvation—Salvation is not only deliverance from the punishment of sin. It describes the effects of the eternal deliverance bestowed by God through His grace in Christ Jesus upon those who believe. It therefore includes deliverance from the bondage of sin (2 Cor. 2:15; Heb. 7:25; James 1:21) and all that is involved in this in the present life of the believer, and further, the culminating act of divine grace in the redemption of the body, and all that issues therefrom (5:9, 10; 13:11; 1 Cor. 3:15; 5:5; Phil. 3:20; Heb. 9:28; 1 Pet. 1:5).

to every one that believeth; to the Jew first, and also to the Greek—It was necessary that the word of God should first be preached to the Jews (Acts 13:46). This had been the command of the Lord to His disciples just before He ascended. He had told them that repentance and remission of sins were to be preached in His Name unto all the nations, "beginning from Jerusalem" (Luke 24:47). They were to be His witnesses first in all Judaea and Samaria, and then unto the uttermost parts of the earth (Acts 1:8). Inasmuch as the Jews were the heirs of the promises of God to Abraham, and these promises included the blessings of the gospel, the good tidings must first be proclaimed to them. On the other hand, the Jew must, at the same time, find his place in the scheme of God's grace through the gospel on the same ground as the Gentiles. The privilege of the Jew in this respect was merely that of priority of time and not of superiority of condition. That the gospel was to be preached "to the Jew first" shows both the faithfulness of God in fulfilling His promise to the chosen seed and His grace toward those

who had despised the privileges granted them, and had rejected their Messiah.

The Righteousness of God, 1:17 to 11:36

God's Righteousness Seen in the Gospel, 1:17

1:17 For therein is revealed—The tense is continuous "is being revealed," i.e., to each fresh discoverer.

a righteousness of God—The absence of the article suggests a different kind of manifestation of God's righteousness from that given at Mount Sinai. The character of God is invariable, but is manifested in different ways, and especially in the two contrasting modes of manifestation in the Law and in grace. The gospel is provided on a righteous basis equally with that of the Law, and the righteous character of God is vindicated alike in each, but His righteousness is displayed differently.

by faith unto faith:—Literally, "from faith unto faith," see margin. God's righteousness, revealed in the gospel, is manifested apart from law, and solely on the principle of faith. Such a mode of justification can be proposed only to faith, for faith is the only alternative to works. The words "unto faith" may be understood in one of two ways: (a) the effects of the gospel begin by faith; but the first exercise of faith is only the first step in the path of faith. The first step is implied in the words, "from faith"; the phrase "to faith" concerns the subsequent life and is involved in the quotation which follows, "the righteous shall live by faith." "From faith" points to the initial act; "to faith" to that life of faith which issues from it. Thus the phrase "by faith to faith" would embrace the entire Christian course; (b) the righteousness of God is revealed "by faith," i.e., on the principle of faith, "unto faith," i.e., so as to be received by faith. Faith alone can participate in the blessing, if there is to be a revelation of divine righteousness, and consequently it is to faith, wherever faith may be. The man that has faith gets the blessing. The latter meaning seems preferable, as Paul is here simply speaking of the way in which man is made righteous and lives.

as it is written, But the righteous shall live by faith.—This statement from Habakkuk 2:4 is quoted three times in the New Testament. Here the point of the quotation is that a man who is righteous has life, not because of his adherence to law, but by faith. In Galatians 3:11 the apostle is teaching the same thing, but there he is combating Judaism, and the force of his argument is that no man, however virtuous, can be justified by lawkeeping. In Hebrews 10:38, faith is again emphasized as an essential thing. The prophet Habakkuk showed that deliverance from impending national danger would be granted to the man who had faith in God. In the New Testament, the teaching is transferred from the material blessing of deliverance from national danger to the spiritual blessing of eternal life.

God's Righteousness in Judging Sin, 1:18 to 3:20

Introductory Note

In the next part of the Epistle (from 1:18 to 3:20), the apostle draws a picture of man's unrighteousness, firstly in order to vindicate the righteousness of God in His retributive dealings, and secondly as a preliminary to the exposition of the gospel as the instrument of God's unmerited favor to man on a ground consistent with divine righteousness.

The Sinful State of the Gentiles, 1:18–32

1:18 For the wrath of God—While the gospel declares the message of salvation (vv. 16, 17), it is a salvation granted by one who is a judge and who, consistently with His own character, has proclaimed, and must carry out, the doom of the ungodly. This is not an arbitrary manifestation of wrath, but the necessary exercise of the infallible judgment of the judge of men.

The subject of the wrath of God recurs throughout the first part of the Epistle (see 2:5, 8; 3:5; 4:15; 5:9; 9:22). In this Epistle, which treats especially of the gospel, the differing attributes of God are set forth in a manner which reveals His character as a whole. While the gospel reveals Him as infinitely merciful, His mercy is not characterized by leniency toward sin. The Scriptures never reveal one attribute of God at the expense of another. The revelation of His wrath is essential to a right understanding of His ways in grace.

is revealed from heaven—Present tense, denoting a constantly recurring manifestation (cp. the similar statement concerning God's righteousness in v. 17). The revelation of His wrath is constant, though two great expressions of it await the human race, one at the end of this age the other after the succeeding millennial age.

against all ungodliness and unrighteousness of men,—Two aspects of sin are here particularized, (1) as against God, (2) as against man, though unrighteousness is likewise sin against God. *Asebeia,* ungodliness, impiety (lit., irreverence) suggests a disregard of the existence of God, a refusal to retain Him in knowledge; that habit of mind leads to open rebellion. *Adikia,* unrighteousness (lit., unrightness) is a condition of not being right, or straight, with God, judged by the standard of His holiness, or with man, judged by the standard of what man knows to be right, through his conscience.

who hold down the truth in unrighteousness;—*Katechō* is "to hold fast," whether by avoiding the relinquishing of something (as in 1 Thess. 5:21), or by suppressing it so that it may not reach others. Here the latter is in view, and the idea is that of purposive suppression of the truth (see 7:6; 2 Thess. 2:6).

1:19 because that which may be known of God—Literally, "that which is knowable of God," referring to the physical universe, in the creation of which God has made Himself known in a particular manner—knowable, that is to say, by the exercise of man's natural faculties, and without such supernatural revelations as those given to Israel. The reference here is to the witness of the truth to the conscience, through creation (cp. Ps. 19).

is manifest in them;—That is, as beings possessed of faculties capable of receiving what may be known of God; not "among them." God gives an external manifestation of Himself, and has provided men with the faculty to receive it. Hence the Scripture regards ignorance of God as a willful sin.

for God manifested it unto them.—The tense is the aorist (or past definite), viewing the revelation of God in creation as a complete act. The effect of the aorist tense here, however, is much the same as that of the perfect, which signifies the abiding results of an act, only the aorist stresses the decisive and definite character of the manifestation.

1:20 For the invisible things of Him—That is, the invisible nature of God in its different characteristics and qualities (see Job 23:8, 9; John 1:18; 5:37; Col. 1:15; 1 Tim. 1:17).

since the creation of the world—This has been understood in two ways, (a) as referring to time, i.e., "since the world was created," but this has comparatively little force and is somewhat tautological; (b) as indicating the natural source from whence the knowledge can be derived. This seems to be the apostle's meaning. From the visible the mind was intended to conceive of the invisible. The physical creation provides the basis upon which certain attributes of God are made known to the mind, and thereby the conscience is affected.

are clearly seen, being perceived through the things that are made, even His everlasting power—*Aidios,* everlasting, is used elsewhere in the New Testament only in Jude 6. Both the unchangeableness and omnipotence of God are here in view, as exhibited in creation.

and divinity;—*Theiotēs,* used here only in the New Testament, is associated in meaning with *theotēs,* Godhead, which is used only in Colossians 2:9. There is, however, a certain distinction in meaning and accordingly the former is here translated "divinity" and the latter "godhead." The difference in the words is appropriate to the respective passages. Here Paul is speaking of the revelation which God has given in nature of His divine attributes. Man can thereby know certain facts about Him, such as His divinity, but cannot know God personally. Such knowledge can come only through the Son of God (cp. John 17:25 with John 1:18). In Colossians 2:9 Paul is speaking of the absolute Godhead of Christ, the fullness of which dwells in Him, and not of an external revelation of His divine attributes.

Hence the suitability of *theotēs,* deity, in that verse.

that they may be without excuse:—It is difficult to choose between this rendering and that of the margin, which is the A.V. test. Grammatically the R.V. text translates according to the regular construction (as in 1:11; 4:16; 6:1, etc.) and the meaning is that it was the purpose of God to remove from man all possible excuse for ignorance of Himself (cp. 3:19). This seems to be correct.

1:21 because that, knowing God,—*Ginōskō* here suggests, not an intimate and personal acquaintance, which would be conveyed by the word *oida,* but a knowledge of the existence of God and of those attributes already referred to. Man began with knowledge, not ignorance, of God's being and character. He has become alienated (Eph. 4:18). The Fall implies a descent from the light into mental and moral folly. Man was not created thus; his present condition is not a primary state but one self-induced.

they glorified Him not as God,—The natural creation was intended to lead man to glorify God and to express gratitude to Him. Cessation from praise and thanksgiving to God leads to disastrous consequences, which the apostle now enumerates. When we leave off praising and thanking God, we open the way for every form of evil.

neither gave thanks;—Thanklessness toward God is a proof of the alienation of man from Him. Thanksgiving is the expression of gratitude toward, and joy in, God, and the acknowledgment of the blessedness of His will (see 1 Thess. 5:18).

but became vain—*Mataioō* signifies to become useless; the corresponding adjective is *mataios,* which is used in the LXX for the Hebrew word *habal,* rendered "vanity" or "vanities," and frequently applied to idols. Both verb and adjective occur in 2 Kings 17:15, "they walked after vanities and became vain," and again in Jeremiah 2:5. The word is used to express King Saul's admission of guilt, "I have played the fool" (1 Sam. 26:21). Refusal to recognize God leads to a condition of uselessness, of futility for the purposes for which He created man.

in their reasonings,—*Dialogismos,* chiefly in the N.T. in an evil sense, of reasonings that are the outcome of self-will, reasonings of the natural mind in independence of God. So in the LXX (e.g., Lam. 3:60), "imaginations." Here it denotes the false notions about God, entertained in opposition to the facts revealed concerning Him in nature.

and their senseless heart—*Asunetos* is, literally, "unintelligent" or "without understanding" and is so translated in verse 31 and elsewhere in the New Testament (see 10:19; Matt. 15:16; Mark 7:18). The heart is frequently spoken of figuratively to indicate the hidden springs of the personal life. Here it is used simply of the understanding (as also in Matt. 13:15).

was darkened.—*Skotizomai* is used of spiritual darkness again in 11:10 and elsewhere in the New Testament only in Ephesians 4:18. The light that God had given men in nature became darkness in them. The faculty of reason becomes impaired by its abuse (see Matt. 6:23).

1:22 Professing themselves to be wise, they became fools.—Mere profession of wisdom is spiritual hallucination. The condition of heathenism is the consequence of departure from the primitive acknowledgment of God and the recognition of His attributes as revealed in creation; it is not a state from which men have advanced by stages to attain the knowledge of God.

1:23 and changed—*Allatō* signifies to exchange one thing for another. They could not actually change the glory of God into anything. His glory is immutable. They made an exchange (cp. Ps. 106:20, R.V.).

the glory—Referring to His everlasting power and divinity (as in v. 20), and thus denoting the attributes of God as revealed through creation.

of the incorruptible God—*Aphthartos* is used of God (here and 1 Tim. 1:17; wrongly translated "immortal" in the A.V.).

for the likeness—*Homoiōma,* a resemblance. The association of the two similar words "likeness of an image," while practically the same thing as "for an image" serves to enhance the contrast with "the glory of the incorruptible God," and is expressive of contempt.

of an image—Man is essentially constituted to be a worshiper. If he abandons the worship of God, some other object will be found to take the place of the Creator. In the Old Testament the voices of the prophets are raised sarcastically against the folly of idolatry, for God is remonstrating with His own people for turning from Him and falling thus to the level of the nations around them. Sarcasm is, however, conspicuous by its absence when the subject is mentioned in the New Testament. The manner in which Paul appeals to the Greeks on Mars Hill is not sarcastic, he is simply stating as a fact the folly of idolatry. The Gentiles, though originally turning from the worship of the Creator, were not guilty of folly to the same extent as Israel. Gentiles are brought up in idolatry. Hence sarcasm is not used in appeal to, or remonstrance with, them.

of corruptible man,—The words "incorruptible" and "corruptible" are inserted in order to expose more vividly in the contrast the folly of the exchange.

and of birds, and fourfooted beasts, and creeping things.—The order of the objects of worship is suggestive of the progressive degradation of the worshipers.

In whatever way idolaters regard their idols, whether as mere symbols of the beings they actually worship or as indwelt and energized by these beings, Scripture knows no such distinction. All such worship is transgression against God.

1:24 Wherefore God gave them up—Civilization provides no remedy for, or safeguard against, the evil. The more civilized men became, the more vicious became their idolatry. The knowledge of God is the only means of leading man to purity of heart. The sanctity of the body is implied in the teaching of this verse.

Paradidōmi signifies to hand over to the power of another. The statement is repeated in verses 26 and 28. The same word is used in reference to the death of Christ at 4:25 and at 8:32 (see also 6:17). In this passage the reference is to the divine retribution following upon the sin of exchanging God for an idol. To abandon God is to open a way for complete moral degradation. This retributive dealing is not the outcome of mere despotism on the part of God; for the acknowledgment and worship of the Creator are the means of human happiness. Atheism and polytheism tend inevitably to moral disease. Our moral nature is governed by laws which God has Himself put therein as part of our very constitution. God works in and by these laws in human experience. In acting against them man sins against God as his Creator and sins against himself as the creature. He therefore lays himself open to the divine retribution expressed in this verse. The process described is not that of mere natural law, it is designed by God and the issue is reached under His control.

It must be remembered that in the solemn description given in this passage, of the consequences of idolatry, the apostle is not presenting what is necessarily an irretrievable condition, for the gospel proves to be the power of God unto salvation even from such degradation. Indeed the whole description is a dark background to the revelation of the grace of God in and through the gospel.

in the lusts of their hearts—That is, in their condition characterized by the lusts of their hearts.

unto uncleanness,—See 9:19 (cp. the phrases in vv. 26 and 28 in this chapter).

that their bodies should be dishonored among themselves:—This dishonor is the retributive effect of their dishonor done to God.

1:25 for that they exchanged—*Metallassō*, in the N.T. only here and in the next verse, denotes the giving up of one thing (here the truth of God) in order to receive another (a lie). See note on "changed" (v. 23). The verb here is but a stronger form of the verb *allassō* there.

the truth of God—This corresponds to the "glory of God" (in v. 23). The phrase signifies, not "the truth concerning God," but "God whose existence is a verity," that is to say, the true God, as revealed to man by creation.

for a lie,—A terse expression used by metonymy (the substitution of a word describing the nature or significance of an object instead of the object itself) for an idol. Isaiah speaks of the idolater as failing to perceive that there is "a lie in his right hand" (Is. 44:20); Jeremiah calls the molten image falsehood (Jer. 10:14; 13:25; cp. 16:19, 20); so "their lies" (Amos 2:4).

and worshiped—*Sebacomai* is used here only in the New Testament. It primarily denotes "to hold in reverence," and so "to give honor to."

and served—For *latreuō* see note on verse 9. The order "worship," and "serve" is constant in Scripture (e.g., 6:13, 14). Acknowledgment of the person Himself must have precedence over activity in His service. Service to God derives its effectivity from engagement of the heart with God.

the creature . . . the Creator,—The difference between the two is immeasurable. The Creator is self-existent, unconditioned and unlimited in power and knowledge. To the Creator the creature not only owes its existence, but by Him it is conditioned; from Him it received its power and its knowledge, and those limitations by reason of which it enjoys the blessing of dependence on its Creator. To substitute the worship of the creature for that of the Creator is therefore the very height of perverseness and folly, meriting the retribution mentioned in the passage.

rather than—That is, "instead of," not a matter of comparison, but of the abandonment of one thing for another. Compare "lovers of pleasure rather than (instead of) lovers of God" (2 Tim. 3:4).

who is blessed—*Eulogētos*, used of God, indicates praise and adoration on the part of the creature, in recognition of the power and prerogatives of the Creator, and the privileges enjoyed at His hands. The word is thus to be distinguished from *makarios*, also translated "blessed," which, when referring to God, signifies His absolute blessedness in all the perfections of His attributes.

forever,—Literally, "unto the ages." The literal translation, however, is to be avoided, as, firstly, it tends to indicate a defined period, an impossible significance in the present instance, and, secondly, because it does not adequately express the phrase as understood in the mind of the Greek-speaking peoples. With them the expression denoted undefined duration. Plato, for instance, uses this terminology to contrast something with that which comes to an end. So the word *aiōnios* is contrasted with *proskairos* (temporary) in 2 Corinthians 4:18. Infinite duration is always the significance, unless precluded by the context.

Amen.—This is a transliteration of a Hebrew word, signifying, when used by men, "So let it be." When said by God it means "It is and shall be so." In Isaiah 65:16 it is used to describe the character of God as a Being who is faithful to His Word (see R.V. margin). In Revelation 3:14, it is a title of Christ, as through Him the divine purposes are established.

1:26, 27 For this cause God gave them up unto vile passions . . . receiving in themselves that recompense of their error which was due.—Self-will brings its own suffering. Natural laws have a self-executing power in a corresponding requital, like the Law of Sinai (Heb. 2:2).

1:28 And even as they refused to have God in their knowledge,—The subject of the effects of rejecting the divine revelation is further developed. The refusal (*adokimazō*, literally, signifies "not to approve of a thing") was not through indifference, but was a self-willed choice after a definite consideration of the circumstances. Men preferred sin to the knowledge of God held out to them by means of both the physical universe and their own natural constitution.

God gave them up—This is stated the third time, each marking a further phase in the retributive justice of God.

unto a reprobate mind,—*Adokimos* is an adjectival form of the verb rendered "refused." If man rejects God, God makes him reprobate, rejects him, as having failed to stand the test. A mind which is reprobate, worthless, useless, is unable to fulfill its natural functions as designed by God; it confuses right and wrong, failing to distinguish what is pleasing to Him from what is displeasing.

to do those things which are not fitting;—Determination to refuse the knowledge

of God leads, according to the righteous principles and decrees of the divine counsels, to the pursuit and practice of sin. The very influences which would restrain the ungodly are retributively withdrawn from them. The word *kathēkō* "to be fit," is here used of what befits the nature of man as God's creature and his responsibility toward his Creator.

1:29 being filled—The tense is the perfect, "having been filled," indicating, in the four evils about to be mentioned, a state which produced the sins and evil characters to be enumerated.

with all unrighteousness, wickedness, covetousness, maliciousness;—The additional word "fornication," in the A.V., is rightly omitted; it is absent from the best MSS.; it also introduces a specific act into a list of evils of a general character.

For the word *adikia,* unrighteousness, see at verses 17, 18; *ponēria,* wickedness, is used seven times in the New Testament (twice in the plural, Mark 7:22; Acts 3:26) to signify all kinds of evil. Covetousness (*pleonexia,* lit., "a desire for more") is associated with *ponēria* in Mark 7:22: it is described as idolatry in Colossians 3:5. *Kakia,* "maliciousness," the noun corresponding to the adjective *kokos,* evil, is a comprehensive term for all evil, especially moral evil (see, e.g., 1 Pet. 2:1, R.V. "wickedness").

full of—*Mestos* signifies full up, full to the utmost (cp. and contrast 15:14); elsewhere of moral qualities (only in Matt. 23:28; James 3:8, 17; 2 Pet. 2:14).

envy, murder, strife, deceit, malignity;—These five evils are of a more specific character. Envy is discontent with, or mortification at, the knowledge or sight of another person's superiority or advantage. For "strife," *eris,* see also 13:13.

whisperers,—This begins a list consisting chiefly, though not entirely, of personal characters. The verb is used here only in the New Testament, and the corresponding noun "whisperers" in 2 Corinthians 12:20 only. The evil is that of secretly conveying information, whether true or false, detrimental to the character or welfare of others.

1:30 backbiter,—Literally, "evil speakers." The word, here only in the New Testament, does not necessarily involve the absence of the person attacked.

hateful to God,—This represents the one word *theostugēs,* here only in the New Testament. The marginal and A.V. rendering "haters of God" is quite possible, and is appropriate to what is expressed by the next two words.

insolent, haughty, boastful,—The first word, elsewhere in the New Testament only at 1 Timothy 1:13 (injurious), is used of injury done whether by word or deed. The word *huperēphanos,* haughty, proud, is associated with boastfulness also in 2 Timothy 3:2.

inventors of evil things,—Literally "inventors of evils." What is indicated is not merely invention by human ingenuity, but also the discovery of things suggested by the powers of darkness.

disobedient to parents,—See, e.g., Exodus 20:12; Leviticus 19:3; Matthew 15:4; 19:19; Ephesians 6:2; and compare Jeremiah 35:18, 19; 2 Timothy 3:2; *apeithēs,* disobedient, is, literally, "not to be persuaded by."

1:31 without understanding, covenant-breaker, without natural affection, unmerciful:—These phrases represent four words in the original. We may render the second "non-covenant-keeping." Some MSS., not the most authentic, have the addition *"aspondous,"* implacable, as in the A.V.

1:32 who, knowing the ordinance of God,—That is, what God has declared to be right *(dikaiōma),* here referring to His decree of retribution. The relative pronoun "who," as in verse 25, suggests that what is now to be stated concerning the sinners mentioned is the cause of the evils just enumerated. The evils are the effect of the refusal to accept and follow what they know to be right. Man's conscience and experience tell him of the evil character and effects of impurity and cruelty, and their Divine condemnation.

Dikaiōma is used elsewhere in this Epistle in its other meaning of "righteousness" (see 2:26; 5:16, 18; 8:4); its meaning "ordinance" is found in Luke 1:6; Hebrews 9:1, 10.

that they which practice such things—The verb *prassō,* to practice, is to be distinguished from *poieō,* to do, as expressing a course of conduct, whereas the present tense of *poieō* expresses a series of repeated acts. In John's Epistles the present continuous tense of *poieō* takes the place of *prassō,* and should not be rendered "commit," as in the A.V. (e.g., in 1 John 3:8, 9).

are worthy of death,—Not simply the natural termination of life, but the execution of the divine penalty upon sin. This statement is explanatory of "the ordinance of God."

not only do the same,—Present tense of *poieō.*

but also consent with them that practice them—*Suneudokeo,* to consent, expresses a hearty approval of a thing (cp. Luke 11:48). In such cases not only is the voice of conscience stifled, but the mind has become absolutely callous regarding the moral degradation and ruin of others, and takes pleasure in their sinfulness.

ROMANS

CHAPTER TWO

The Sinful State of the Jews, 2:1–29

Introductory Note

In this chapter the apostle deals especially with the subject of the Jews, showing that they, alike with the Gentiles, are guilty before God. The argument is thus carried to the point that the whole world is brought under the judgment of God. The Jew's was an increased guilt because of the privileges granted him. Moreover, while condemning the sins of the Gentiles, the Jews were guilty of doing the same things, in spite of the light they had received from God.

(a) The Divine Judgment, 2:1–5

2:1 Wherefore—That is to say, because of the universal facts of the voice of conscience and the knowledge of the divine condemnation and punishment of sin and of the consequences of practicing evil and consenting with it, in spite of that knowledge.

thou art without excuse.—This recalls 1:20. If the Gentiles are without excuse, so are those Jews who, while judging the Gentiles for their rejection of God, are guilty of the same sins as stand to the condemnation of Gentiles.

O man,—That is, anyone who takes the place of a judge. The Jew is in view, but is not yet specifically mentioned. To have mentioned Jews just here would have marred the trend of the argument.

whosoever thou art that judgest:—*Krinō*, "to judge," primarily signifies to distinguish; then, to distinguish between right and wrong, without necessarily passing an adverse sentence, though this is usually involved.

for wherein thou judgest another, thou condemnest thyself;—*Katakrinō*, a strengthened form of *krinō*; always denotes "to pass an adverse sentence" (e.g., 8:3, 34; 14:23).

for thou that judgest dost practice the same things.—The reference is not, of course, to the same kind of idolatry as the Gentiles, for that particular evil had been purged from the Jewish nation during their captivity, but to such sins of moral obliquity as are enumerated in 1:29–31.

2:2 And we know that the judgment of God—*Krina* here, and almost invariably in the New Testament, signifies an adverse sentence (see above, on "judgest"). Sometimes it includes the carrying out of the sentence (see next verse).

is according to truth against them that practice such things.—That is, it is according both to facts and the unerring estimate of them by God.

2:3 And reckonest thou this,—*Logizomai* signifies the result of a deliberate process of reasoning (as distinct from the simpler verb *dokeō*, "to think").

O man, who judgest them that practice such things, and doest the same, that thou shalt escape the judgment of God?—There is strong stress on the pronoun "thou." The judgment here points to the execution of the sentence. The idea that membership of the Jewish race ensured the favor of God and spiritual privilege, was deep-rooted in the national sentiment.

2:4 Or despisest thou—The word "despisest" bears stress; it stands in implied contrast to the responsibility of glorifying God for His goodness.

the riches of His goodness—*Chrēstotēs* denotes the kindliness which disposes one to do good (cp. 11:22). It is used of God also in Ephesians 2:7 and Titus 3:4, and of believers in 2 Corinthians 6:6; Galatians 5:22; Colossians 3:12.

and forbearance—*Anochē*, is, literally, "holding up," and so a withholding of punishment.

and longsuffering,—*Makrothumia,* literally, "long-temper." If forbearance denotes delay in executing judgment, long-suffering denotes the particular disposition which delays it.

not knowing,—*Agnoeō* signifies "to be ignorant," suggesting not only a failure to recognize, but a willful ignoring of the fact.

that the goodness of God—*Chrēstos* is a shorter form of the word *chrēstotēs* just used. The Lord used it to describe the easy character of His yoke, a yoke not only easy, therefore, but kindly (Matt. 11:30). The same word is used elsewhere of God, in Luke 6:35, and 1 Peter 2:3, "gracious," and of believers in 4:32.

leadeth thee to repentance?—*Metanoia* is, literally, "a change of mind," but is usually associated with the idea of sorrow for sin. God wills that all men should come to repentance (2 Pet. 3:9). Here the special privileges granted to the Jews are in view, as a means of leading them to repentance.

2:5 but after thy hardness and impenitent heart—"After" means "according to." The word *sklērotēs,* hardness, i.e., insensibility to God's goodness, is used here only in the New Testament.

treasurest up for thyself wrath—An allusion to the riches of God's goodness (v. 4); the idea is that of amassing an accumulation of divine wrath. The responsibility for his doom lies with the sinner himself, "for thyself" bears stress.

in the day of wrath—That is, the time when the Lord will judge the world in righteousness. The word "day" here and in several other passages covers a more or less extended period, and is frequently associated with judgment. It is daylight that presents nature in its true aspect, in contrast to its appearance in the obscurity of night. Thus the present period is called "man's day" (1 Cor. 4:3, margin). Therein man forms his opinions and passes judgment upon things, a judgment, however, that is guided by natural and therefore finite reasoning, and perverted by sin. "Man's day" is to be superseded by the "Day of the Lord," the Day when the Lord will be manifested to execute His divine and unerring judgment upon men. Prior to this "the Day of Christ"

(Phil. 1:10; 2:16) will begin. This period has solely to do with the Church, and thus is to be distinguished from "the Day of the Lord."

and revelation of the righteous judgment of God;—In these words the apostle shows that the wrath of God is not vindictive or arbitrary, but that the day mentioned will bring a revelation of a judgment passed by one who is infallible in His estimation. Thus in describing the universal sinfulness of the human heart the apostle at the same time vindicates the holiness of God, and His righteousness in dealing with sin.

(b) The Means of Life, 2:6–11

Introductory Note

These verses appear at first to present a difficulty in this respect, that they give no indication of the foundation truth of the gospel, that the gift of eternal life is bestowed on condition of faith in Christ (John 3:15, 16, 36, etc.). Here eternal life is said to be bestowed as the result of seeking for glory and honor and incorruption and of patience in well doing.

Now (1) the subject of the whole passage is not the means of obtaining eternal life, but the righteous judgment of God against man's sin, and in this respect what is mentioned in verses 8 and 9, as to the punishment of those who do not obey the truth, is perfectly consistent with the teaching of the rest of Scripture on the subject. "He that obeyeth not the Son shall not see life, but the wrath of God abideth on Him" (John 3:36).

(2) It is a fundamental principle, in finding the meaning of a passage of Scripture, that no explanation is legitimate which contradicts the plain teaching of the rest of the Word of God; on the contrary, the passage in question must be understood in the light of plain statements elsewhere given.

(3) That eternal life is conditional upon believing on the Son of God, is plainly taught in numerous passages in the New Testament. Nor is the declaration in the present passage, that eternal life is to be the portion of those who seek for glory, honor and incorruption by patience in well doing, inconsistent with the teaching of the gospel, that the gift of eternal life is bestowed upon the condition of faith; for

faith is the initial act by which a believer enters upon a life that is necessarily characterized by patience in well doing and seeking for glory, indeed, if this is absent from the life of one who professes faith in Christ the essential evidence of the genuineness of his faith and of his possession of eternal life is lacking. But the apostle is not here dealing with the subject of justification and the gift of life through faith in Christ; that subject he takes up later in the Epistle. Here he is showing that the Jew and the Gentile are on the same ground in the sight of God in the matter of sin, and he is merely stating, in an anticipatory way, that they must both have deliverance in the same manner.

(4) Again, when he says that God will render glory, honor and peace to every man that worketh good, whether Jew or Gentile, we cannot take this as an absolute statement apart from the truth of the gospel. It is consistent with the gospel in that, in the estimation of God, that alone is good which is wrought in and through His Son. The very first requirement by God of good works on the part of man is that he believes in the Son of God (John 6:29). Therefore, according to the divine estimate, a man must be in Christ in order to receive glory, honor and peace, and on no other condition can he obtain these benefits. It is, however, not to the apostle's point to give these details in this passage. To do so would be an unnecessary digression.

(5) Clearly, a reading of the two verses 7 and 10 together shows that the apostle is not speaking of the bestowment of eternal life as conditional upon faith.

It is therefore, misleading to suggest that Paul is speaking of the manner in which the destiny of men would be determined if there were no gospel. The various revelations given in Scripture of the purposes and dealings of God are never inconsistent with one another.

2:6 who will render to every man according to his works:—This is predicated as the act of Christ in Matthew 16:27, and is word for word the same, except for the singular, "doing" (see R.V. margin), instead of the plural "works." Thus the two passages provide a testimony to the equality of the Son of God with the Father, and so to His deity (see also Rev. 22:12).

2:7 to them that by patience in well doing seek for glory and honor and incorruption,—"Glory" describes the character of the future of the kingdom of God and the rewards assigned to the faithful in connection therewith in relation to Christ. "Honor" is inseparably connected with glory, and signifies the token of God's estimate. The word rendered "incorruption" is found elsewhere in 1 Corinthians 15:42, 50, 53, 54; Ephesians 6:24; 2 Timothy 1:10; Titus 2:7. The word denotes the absence of decay or destruction, but when used of the state of a believer, it carries with it also the idea of a condition of happiness.

eternal life:—Not mere endless existence, but a life in the enjoyment of communion with God and the experience of His power. The word *aiōnios,* "eternal," denotes indefinite, and so unending, duration. "Age-long" does not express the meaning as understood by the Greeks.

2:8 but unto them that are factious,—Literally, "to those who are of strife" (cp. "everyone that is of the truth," John 18:37). *Eritheia* here signifies the spirit that resists the will and way of God, and for this reason disobedience to the truth is coupled with it.

and obey not the truth, but obey unrighteousness,—The construction used in the words "obey" in each case signifies an habitual course of conduct. Such yield themselves to unrighteousness and cooperate with it, fulfilling their sinful impulses. Dislike for the truth leads to its rejection.

shall be wrath and indignation,—The former suggests the feeling, the latter the manifestation of it God seeks, by a revelation of Himself and of the truth, to lead men to bow to His will. Man in his sinful condition resists God and yields to His enemy, the climax of which is the righteous exercise of divine wrath.

2:9 tribulation—*Thlipsis* is the suffering which results from what presses hard on the soul. The word occurs elsewhere in this Epistle at 5:3; 8:35; 12:12.

and anguish,—*Stenochōria,* literally, signifies the condition of one who is shut up without the possibility of escape, and hence it comes to denote a condition of distress. The four words suggest a series of cause and effect.

The first indicates God's attitude toward sin, the second the expression of that attitude, the third the result therefrom, the fourth the realization of entire helplessness. The whole is set in contrast to eternal life. In each respect there is a conscious experience either of woe or of blessedness.

upon every soul of man that worketh evil,—That is, upon every man, the soul standing for the person, as in Acts 2:41, 43 (cp. Lev. 24:18; lit., "soul for soul"). The word *katergazomai,* "worketh," is a strengthened form of the simple verb *ergazomai* (see next verse) and here indicates perseverance in sin.

of the Jew first, and also of the Greek;—Compare 1:6. The Jew was the subject of greater privileges, and consequently his was greater responsibility. The word "first" apparently means "especially."

2:10 but glory and honor and peace—This is set in contrast to tribulation and anguish. Note the parallel (with a change in the third word) to "glory and honor and incorruption" in verse 7; the reward exceeds the aim and effort. "Peace" is to be understood in the widest sense, both of acceptance with God and all the happiness resulting therefrom.

to every man that worketh good,—*Ergazomai* is the simple form (see above). The change from the stronger to the simpler serves to bring out the grace and mercy of God. To the one who works good (were it possible), with a simple effort to accomplish it, the reward is proffered, whereas it is one who persists in working evil who is punished.

to the Jew first, and also to the Greek:—The repetition of these words serves to give prominence to the distinction between Jew and Gentile and thereby lends force to Paul's argument by which he breaks down the distinction between the two in the matter of sin, proving that they are alike guilty before God.

2:11 for there is no respect of persons with God.—Literally, "acceptance of the face," the opposite to impartiality. God will pronounce sentence without regard to circumstances of birth (see also Deut. 10:17; 2 Chr. 19:7; Job 34:19; Eph. 6:9; Col. 3:23; James

2:1, 2). The remainder of this chapter is a development of this truth.

(c) The Impartiality of God's Judgment, 2:12–29

Introductory Note

The Gentiles, who have sinned without external law, must perish without the Law; the Jews who had an external Law, will be judged by it. The Gentiles have the law of conscience, and that law is equivalent to the Law given to the Jews (vv. 12–15). All men must therefore be judged in the day when God shall judge the secrets of men by Christ (vv. 12, 16).

Guilt is then laid to the charge of the Jew from the point of view that, while he glories in his privileges and has a form of knowledge of the truth and preaches to others, he himself is a transgressor and causes God's name to be blasphemed (vv. 17–24). So Jews are equally liable to judgment and righteous Gentiles will condemn them (vv. 25–29).

2:12 For as many as have sinned—Literally, "sinned," aorist tense, pointing back from the future time of judgment to the sins viewed culminatively during the life on earth.

without law—That is, in the absence of some specifically revealed law, like the Law of Sinai. That there is no definite article suggests that law is viewed here as a general principle. The Law is a declaration of God's will concerning man's conduct. The Gentiles were without that. Yet that fact will not save them from doom. God's wrath against them will be just, but their judgment will be administered altogether apart from the Law of Sinai. They are to be judged by another standard. Man will never be subject to condemnation through ignorance of that which has not been made known to him.

shall also perish—*Apollumi,* signifies ruin in regard to condition, loss of well-being, not loss of being. Neither this nor any other word in Scripture denotes annihilation. The gospel promises everlasting life for him who believes. The failure to possess this life will involve the utter ruin of those that perish.

without law:—See note above. The reference is to an external law, not the law of conscience, for that is the standard by which Gentiles are actually to be judged. The apostle shows that the fact that God has given the Law to one section of the race, constitutes no departure from the truth that there is no respect of persons with Him. He appeals now to a principle which includes all law, and which therefore applies equally to the Jews and the Gentiles. In other words, he is speaking here not specifically of the Law of Moses but of law as a principle which affects God's relations with man. The matter is viewed here as regards responsibility and not privilege. For the immediate subject is sin and its effects.

and as many as have sinned under law—Literally, "in law," i.e., within the scope of the precepts of a law, the reference being to the Law of Sinai.

shall be judged by law;—The judgment includes here the passing of the sentence, the standard of right and wrong being the moral law Divinely revealed.

2:13 for—This follows probably in immediate connection with verse 12.

not the hearers of a law are just before God, but the doers of a law shall be justified:—This is the first occurrence of the word "justify" in this Epistle. The context in each case explains its meaning. The application here is legal and the meaning is "free from all ground of condemnation," "pronounced righteous." The apostle has not yet begun to develop his subject of justification by faith. He is now affirming a general principle, and is making a conditional statement which is in strict accordance with the words of Leviticus 18:5. For an Old Testament use of "justify" in this sense, see Deuteronomy 25:1.

2:14 for when Gentiles—The principle of verses 12 and 13 is now applied to Gentiles in order to show its universality. By the absence of the article attention is drawn more particularly to the condition of Gentiles as distinct from that of Jews. With Gentiles conscience takes the place of an external revelation.

which have no law—They have no documentary revelation such as was given at Sinai.

do by nature—That is, according to natural impulse, in contrast to obedience to the decrees of God given by an external law. The subject is not nature in contrast to the dealings of grace.

the things of the law,—The Law of Sinai. The conduct of Gentiles is the result of internal forces, incident upon their natural constitution.

these, having no law, are a law unto themselves;—Their conscience guides them instead of an external revelation. Conscience in their case is what the law is to the Jews. As far as their conduct is right, it is a proof of the existence of this inner law. Conscience becomes a guide not only to each man individually but leads to a mutual understanding with others as to what is right and what is wrong.

2:15 in that they shew the work of the law written in their hearts—There are two possible meanings to this, (1) what is done in obedience to the Law, (2) what the Law itself does, its practical effect. The latter seems to be the meaning. They show the work, though they are not possessed of the actual letter.

their conscience—Conscience is the mental faculty by which man judges his actions and passes sentence thereon. "Conscience" (lit., "co-knowledge") is a knowledge of the right or wrong of an act.

bearing witness therewith,—That is, bearing witness in agreement with a moral standard generally recognized among them, unwritten, but corresponding to the Law of Sinai.

and their thoughts—*Logismos,* elsewhere in the New Testament only at 2 Corinthians 10:5, denotes "reasonings."

one with another—That is, one person with another, not one thought with another.

accusing or else excusing them;—"accusing" is put first because a condemnatory verdict in man's judgment upon his fellows is far more frequent than the opposite. All this goes to show that man is inwardly possessed of a law which corresponds to the Law of Sinai, and which therefore provides a standard by which he must be judged hereafter.

2:16 in the day—See note on verse 5. In this verse, if connected with what immediately precedes, the apostle is viewing the standard of conscience as that by which the Gentiles are to be judged.

when God shall judge the secrets of men,—The hidden things upon which men have passed sentence according to their own conscience, and so the inner motives of their actions. Compare "the hidden things of darkness" (1 Cor. 4:5), where the same word is used (see Eccl. 12:14).

according to my Gospel,—The gospel not only preaches salvation, it also proclaims principles upon which God will exercise judgment hereafter. Paul's preaching and teaching constantly maintained this truth (see, e.g., Acts 17:31; 1 Cor. 4:5; 2 Cor. 5:10).

by Jesus Christ.—The order of titles suggests that the one who is going to act as the Judge is the one who became incarnate (thus entering personally into the experience of human nature) and then ascended to God's right hand.

2:17 But if—This introduces a supposition regarding the Jew the answer to which is given at verse 21. This paragraph is really a continuation of the proof that God's judgment will be exercised without distinction of persons. It would be futile for a Jew to argue that God Himself made the distinction, for the Jew has abused his privileges.

thou bearest the name of a Jew,—"Jew" stands here as equivalent to Israelite. It was, however, a name of which the Jews were proud (Gal. 2:15, and see Rev. 2:9; 3:9, and v. 28 below). The name "Jew" first occurs in 2 Kings 16:6.

and restest upon the law,—Although the Law put the Jews into a special relationship to God, it became a ground of self-confidence, even though they transgressed it. For an illustration see the parable of the Pharisee and the Publican. Such Jews regarded the Law as an evidence of God's favor rather than as a guide for conscience and conduct (cp. Mic. 3:11, where the Septuagint has the same word for "lean upon" as here).

and gloriest in God,—The believer rightly glories in God when he acknowledges His greatness and power, His mercy and love. Hence, however, the thought is that the Jew boasts in Jehovah as the God of his race, and yet, living in sin, comes under the condemnation of the very being in whom he exults.

2:18 and knowest His will,—Literally, "the will" perhaps a term in general use among the Jews for the will of God, the perfect will.

and approvest—Approving is the result of proving. The process of proving is to distinguish between one thing and another. The approval here mentioned results in a mere acquaintance and a vain compliance with the Law.

the things that are excellent,—This is preferable to the more literal rendering, "the things that differ"; for the Jew would naturally boast, not in a mere capability of distinguishing things, but in the moral sentiment by which he approved of the excellent.

being instructed out of the law,—*Katēcheō*, to instruct, whence our words "catechize," etc., primarily denotes oral instruction. The Law, the Old Testament Scriptures, was read and explained every Sabbath.

2:19 and art confident—Literally, "art persuaded," suggesting that what follows is the result of an idea not only of superiority but of self-complacency.

that thou thyself art a guide of the blind,—*Hodēgos*, literally, "a wayleader" (cp. Matt. 15:14; 23:16). He was ready to undertake the training of those who lacked the light he himself had received.

a light of them that are in darkness,—The reference is especially to the state of the Gentiles (cp. Is. 42:6; 49:6; 60:3). See, however, concerning the darkness of the Jews (Is. 9:2; 59:9).

2:20 a corrector—*Paideutēs* is, literally, "a trainer," one who does all that ought to be done for the young. It includes instruction as well as correction.

of the foolish,—*Aphrōn* is here used of those who are immature in things moral and religious (cp. the Lord's use of the word in Luke 11:40).

a teacher of babes,—There is doubtless a special reference to proselytes.

having in the law the form of knowledge and of the truth;—*Morphōsis,* form, is that by which the inward character of a thing is made known to our senses. The word, however, had a tendency to attach special significance to the outward presentation. Here the contrast between the outward and inward is not emphasized; the mere appearance is not in view, but rather the expression of the truth contained in the Law and therefore of the knowledge imparted by it.

Perhaps knowledge is put first as a suggestion that the Jew was inclined to attach much importance to it.

2:21 thou therefore that teachest another,—Stress is not on the "thou" (the pronoun is not in the original) but on "teachest," literally, "the teacher of another."

teachest thou not thyself?—The claims of the Jew were valid though they increased his responsibility not to leave himself untaught, while presuming to occupy the position of professed holiness. Compare the Lord's remonstrance against the Pharisees (Luke 11:40).

thou that preachest a man should not steal, dost thou steal?—*Kērussō* ("preachest") is "to herald a message." A herald acts as the medium of the authority of the one whose proclamation he makes. The Jew professed to act thus for God, and yet committed the very things which he himself condemned.

2:22 thou that sayest a man should not commit adultery, dost thou commit adultery?—Including a reference to the sin mentioned in Matthew 19:8, 9. The great vindication of the faith is a holy life.

thou that abhorrest idols,—The Jews had been taught, by the severe discipline of the Captivity, to obey God's decree against idolatry. The nation had been purged from its grossness in this respect, and so the Jew learned to share the divine detestation of idols.

dost thou rob temples?—*Hierosuleō* signifies "to commit sacrilege" (see the corresponding noun in Acts 19:37). The treasures of the idol temples perhaps attracted the avarice of the Jews, who would excuse themselves on the score of the wickedness of idolatry.

2:23 thou who gloriest in the law,—Literally, "in law," suggesting that, while the Law of Sinai is in view, yet the Jew made much of it merely as a matter of law, adding his tradition to it. The phrase thus stands in contrast with those that follow in which the article is used.

through thy transgression of the law dishonorest thou God?—This is explained in the next verse. Each word, "dishonorest" and "God," bears stress in the original (cp. the Lord's words to the Jews, in John 8:49).

2:24 For the name of God is blasphemed among the Gentiles because of you, even as it is written.—The quotation is from the Septuagint of Isaiah 52:5 (see also Ezek. 36:23). Isaiah, Ezekiel, Paul, all declare that with the people of God His character and honor are at stake, opinion of Him on the part of others being formed from the condition and conduct of those who own His Name. The captivity of Israel and Judah, consequent upon their sins, caused the Gentiles to scoff at God. The word by Isaiah had, then, a prophetic application to the normal conditions of the Jews in the apostle's time.

2:25 For circumcision—This was the seal of God's covenant with Abraham and his descendants, and therefore another token, besides the Law, of the special privileges which were granted to the Jew and in which they gloried.

indeed profiteth,—See 3:1. The position of a circumcised Jew was superior to that of an uncircumcised Gentile, granted that the Jew kept the Law.

If thou be a doer of the law:—Not the absolute fulfillment of every commandment is in view, but a sincere endeavor to live in conformity to the Law.

but if thou be a transgressor of the law, thy circumcision is become uncircumcision.—Here, again, the reference is to a habit of life and not a condition resulting from a breach of one point of the Law.

2:26 If therefore the uncircumcision— This carries the argument a step further and views the subject from the standpoint of a Gentile, who seeks to spend his life in conformity with what he knows to be right in the sight of God.

keep the ordinances of the law,— This does not imply sinless obedience but an effort to act rightly according to the dictates of conscience, and so practically according to the Law of God (see Acts 10:35). The word *phullasso*, "to keep," suggests the assiduous care of one who is guarding something.

shall not his uncircumcision be reckoned—The self-constituted judge was practicing what he condemned in others. Did he reckon to escape God's judgment? God is true, His reckoning is unerring and just. The apostle compels an answer from the Jew in recognition of the fact.

for circumcision?—That is, as equivalent of circumcision. The value of an ordinance is measured by the moral end at which it aims.

2:27 and shall not the uncircumcision which is by nature,— That is, as the outcome of circumstances incident to nature, in contrast to external influences such as the Law given to the Jews.

if it fulfill the law, judge thee, who with the letter and circumcision art a transgressor of the law?—Compare the case of Cornelius. *Krinō* here denotes "to pronounce sentence upon." Compare the teaching of the Lord about the men of Nineveh and the queen of the South (Matt. 12:41, 42), where, however, *katakrino*, "to condemn," is used.

Stress is thrown upon each word, "judge" and "thee."

2:28 For he is not a Jew, which is one outwardly; neither is that circumcision, which is outward in the flesh;— The distinctive feature implied in spiritual circumcision cannot be determined by natural circumstances. God looks on the heart. Nothing external constitutes spiritual relationship to Him.

2:29 but he is a Jew, which is one inwardly;— Literally, "in secret"; i.e., the Jew in secret is a Jew in reality. The same phrase occurs in Matthew 6:4, 8.

and circumcision is that of the heart,— This is parallel to, and confirmatory of, the preceding statement. Circumcision of the heart is spoken of in Deuteronomy 10:16, and 30:6, utterances which, albeit they were made under the Law, yet contained anticipatory intimations of the Gospel.

in the spirit, not in the letter,— The spirit is that part of the believer's being upon which the Holy Spirit acts. The phrase "in the spirit" is practically explanatory of "the heart," and at the same time prepares for the contrast of "the letter" (see 7:6 and cp. 2 Cor. 3:6–8. Here "the letter" signifies the command relating to the rite of circumcision. The apostle shows that the God-fearing Gentile is viewed in the sight of God as on the same ground as a God-fearing Jew.

whose praise is not of men, but of God.— The word Jew is derived from "Judah," for the meaning of which see Genesis 29:35, and 49:8. The play on the word "Jew" leads to a statement of the divine verdict. The self-complacency of the Jew is thus finally rebuked.

ROMANS

CHAPTER THREE

None Righteous by Works of Law, 3:1–20

The argument is advanced by the method of question and answer. There are four questions in the first nine verses. The first asks what advantage the Jew has, and the reply is that God gave to the Jew His oracles. He will always prevail in judgment. The second question is whether, considering that human unrighteousness commends God's righteousness, it is right that He should punish man for what makes for His glory. The answer is that God is judge and therefore must punish sin. If this were not the case He could not be God. The third is that if a lie actually enhances God's truthfulness, why should man not do evil that good might come. The answer exposes the wrong of such a principle. God's position as judge is impregnable. The fourth is whether, after all, the Jews are actually in a worse condition than the Gentiles (see R.V.). The reply is in the negative, for both Jew and Gentile are unsaved. The apostle guards his teaching hitherto against perversion, and in doing so vindicates the character of the Law of God.

(a) A Question and Its Answer, 3:1–4

3:1 What advantage then hath the Jew? or what is the profit of circumcision?—The argument is as follows: if circumcision is really inward and not outward, and yet God enjoined circumcision on the Jew as an outward ordinance, wherein lies the privilege and benefit of it; The former question has regard to superiority over others, the latter to personal benefit derived.

3:2 Much every way: first of all,—Not necessarily the first in a list, but rather "principally." One thing is mentioned, but the intimation is that others are in view.

that they were intrusted—That is, not only on their own account but on behalf of others as well.

with the oracles of God.—*Logia* is, literally, "utterances," a word used by the Greeks for the prophetic utterances supposed to be given by their gods, by way of oracular response to inquiries. Here it refers not merely to the Law of Sinai but to all the written utterances of God through the instrumentality of the Jews. That God revealed His purposes in this way was due to their being brought into covenant relationship with Him through circumcision. That the Scriptures are thus spoken of is a testimony to their uniqueness, dignity and divine origin.

For a similar use of the word see Acts 7:36; Hebrews 5:12; 1 Peter 4:11.

3:3 For what if some were without faith?—The argument seems to be as follows: Certainly the Jew has advantages in being entrusted with the oracles of God. Is then the fact that numbers of the Jews proved unfaithful going to invalidate the faithfulness of God, in causing Him to refrain from fulfilling His promises? It surely is impossible that man's unbelief will militate against one of the attributes of God. The reply goes to show both that God's character remains consistent and that He is free to fulfill His promises according as He pleases.

shall their want of faith make of none effect—*Katargeō*. The literal meaning of this word is "to reduce to inactivity." It is rendered in a number of ways—cumber (Luke 13:7), make of none effect (here and at v. 31 and 4:14), be done away (6:6), discharged (7:2, 6), bring to nought (1 Cor. 1:28; 2:6; 6:13; 2 Thess. 2:8; Heb. 2:14), done away (1 Cor. 3:14; 10:1; 13:8; Gal. 5:11), put away (1 Cor. 13:11), abolish (1 Cor. 15:24, 26; Eph. 2:15; 2 Tim. 1:10), passing away (2 Cor. 3:7, 11, 13), disannul (Gal. 3:17), severed from (Gal. 5:4). The word never means "to annihilate." The general idea in the word is that of depriving a thing of the use for which it is intended. Thus it implies, not loss of being, but loss of well-being.

the faithfulness of God?—*Pistis* may signify either "faith" or "faithfulness." The latter is the meaning here, for the reference is to the consistency of God's character, which is a guarantee of the fulfillment of His promises.

3:4 God forbid: yea, let God be found true, but every man a liar;—Literally, "may it not be . . ." A person is true when his words are in perfect accordance with facts. It is impossible for God to lie (Heb. 6:18; Titus 1:2; Num. 23:19). He cannot deny Himself (2 Tim. 2:13). If God's methods seem to be contradictory to man's ideas or expectations, he has reason only to impute failure and inconsistency to himself and to acknowledge the faithfulness of God. Here, this is involved, that a believing Jew can claim the fulfillment of God's covenant and pledge, in spite of the fact that large numbers of his nation have turned away from God. Albeit his nation is at present in unbelief, that does not nullify the advantages of belonging to a people to whom God has committed His oracles and given His promises.

as it is written,—Scripture invariably vindicates the character of God, a fact which testifies to its divine origin.

That Thou mightest be justified in Thy words, and mightest prevail when Thou comest into judgment.—The quotation is from the LXX of Psalm 51:4. David's confession there is made, not to establish God's truth, but that God might be seen to be righteous. David's sin had the effect of vindicating the unerring character of God's dealings. David was willing to condemn himself to the utmost, that the justice of God's punishment might become evident. The words of the quotation suggest a lawcourt scene in which the righteousness of the verdict of the judge compels an acknowledgment on the part of the accused. This must inevitably be the case where God is judge. The effect of the quotation is to show that the apostle's argument is consistent with the teaching of the Old Testament. That God had given His promises to Israel did not provide a guarantee that any unrepentant Jew would escape doom.

This first section of the chapter incidentally provides a strong comfort to the believer that,

in spite of all adverse circumstances, God's words will assuredly be fulfilled.

(b) An Objection and Its Answer, 3:5–18

3:5 But if our unrighteousness—The apostle has just been speaking of unbelief; he now expands this into the broader subject of unrighteousness, which includes unbelief.

commendeth the righteousness of God,—God is a judge, and as such is righteous. His righteousness is brought into greater prominence by man's unrighteousness. The present aspect of the righteousness of God is not the same as in 1:17; there the gospel was viewed as a revelation of the righteousness of God in showing mercy, and that is the general teaching of the Epistle on the subject. In the present passage the gospel is not the subject; here God's righteousness is simply contrasted with man's unrighteousness. Since God's dealings with mankind in the matter of sin are in conformity with the principles of His law, man is compelled to justify God.

what shall we say? Is God unrighteous who visiteth with wrath?—The argument is that since man's unrighteousness only brings into greater prominence God's righteousness, how can God consistently punish men for that which makes for His glory?

We might have expected the objector to say "Is God not unrighteous?" In which case the objector would look for the answer "Yes." Instead of this, with a view to vindicate the character of God, the question is put in a way which demands a negative reply.

(I speak after the manner of men).—This does not suggest that the apostle's words were not inspired. He merely means that he is presenting a human point of view. For to argue in any way whatever, as to whether God is right or wrong, is to speak merely as a man and to give evidence of the unfruitfulness of the human mind.

3:6 God forbid: for then how shall God judge the world?—The stress in this sentence is on the word "judge." In view of the objection that, since man's sin only gives evidence of the holiness of God, how is He just in punishing sin? The answer is that, were it otherwise, God would not be a judge at all. Now it is an attribute of God, that He is judge of man's ways. That God will judge the world is an axiomatic truth with the writers of Scripture. Moreover, God is righteous. Therefore His estimation as judge is undeniably accurate. His acts of punishment are in every case just. Therefore the inference derived from the fact that man's sin only brings out God's righteousness, is wrong, and the argument falls to the ground. With this passage chapter 9:14-24 should be compared. In both passages Paul is vindicating the sovereignty of God.

3:7 But if—This verse gives a further proof that, were God unrighteous in visiting His wrath, He could not exercise the function of judge. The question now to be asked is an extension of the preceding one, and covers the first section of the argument of this chapter.

the truth of God—This stands for the truthfulness of God (cp. v. 4).

through my lie—That is, through the lie with which his detractors charged the apostle.

abounded unto His glory,—That is, so that He is glorified. The sentence is parallel to the first question in verse 5.

why am I also still judged as a sinner?—That is, when it is recognized that the effect of his sin is to enhance God's glory. The pronoun bears stress.

3:8 and why not (as we be slanderously reported, and as some affirm that we say), Let us do evil, that good may come? whose condemnation is just.—His adversaries charged the apostle, on the ground of the gospel he preached, with encouraging sin as a means of enhancing the glory of God's grace. The argument of his question and answer does two things: (1) it shows that so far from being delivered from judgment, on the ground that the (supposed) lie makes for God's glory, he must thereby himself come under divine judgment, and (2) it dooms his detractors to judgment, for they stand condemned in their very condemnation of him. Since, for example, David's sin only vindicated God's justice (v. 5) all sin will do the same.

3:9 What then? are we in worse case than they?—That is to say, if this is so, is the argument to lead to the conclusion that the Jews, so far from being better off than the Gentiles, are in such a position that their very privileges bring them into greater condemnation than that which the Gentiles will suffer? The A.V. is misleading here.

No, in no wise: for we before laid to the charge both of Jews and Greeks, that they are all under sin;—*Hamartia* is, literally, "a missing of the mark." The word, however, is used in a comprehensive way for sin in general. Sin, virtually personified, is viewed here as a power controlling man, from which escape on his part is impossible.

3:10 as it is written, There is none righteous, no, not one;—The apostle shows that the sinful state, of both the Jew and the Gentile, is confirmed by the testimony of Scripture. This first quotation is introductory, and is a free rendering of Psalm 14:1-3, which states the universality of sin. In the following quotations there is perhaps a more special reference to Israel, but the tenor of the whole passage is an enforcement of the fact that both Jew and Gentile are under sin. The quotations consist of (a) generalizations, verses 10-12; (b) specific sins, verses 13-15; (c) three statements of a general condition, verses 16-18.

3:11 There is none that understandeth, There is none that seeketh after God;—The quotation is from Isaiah 52:15 (contrast Rom. 15:21). Here lack of understanding is shown to be characteristic of the unregenerate condition; in 15:21 the possession of understanding is shown to be the effect of the Gospel.

3:12 They have all turned aside, They are together become unprofitable; there is none that doeth good, no, not so much as one:—The word *achreioomai* is a translation of a Hebrew word meaning "to turn aside," and so "to become useless." The corresponding adjective, *achreios*, "useless," "good for nothing," is found in Matthew 25:30 and Luke 17:10 only; an associated word, *achrēstos*, only in Philemon 11. That latter means lacking in what is good, while *achreios* means lacking in utility.

3:13 Their throat is an open sepulcher;—Jeremiah 5:16 describes the quiver of the Chaldeans as an "open sepulcher," but there the phrase is symbolic of power of destruction. Here (as in Ps. 5:9) the reference is to the noxious character of that which proceeds from their mouths, as of exhalations from a grave.

With their tongues they have used deceit:—This is from the LXX of Psalm 5:9; the Hebrew has "they make smooth their tongue." The tense of the verb in the Greek is the imperfect, signifying continuous action.

The poison of asps is under their lips:—This is from the LXX of Psalm 140:3. The suggestion is that of the malicious infliction of pain.

3:14 Whose mouth is full of cursing and bitterness:—A shortened quotation from the LXX of Psalm 10:7, which adds the word "deceit." The Hebrew has "deceit and oppression." *Gemō*, "to be full of," conveys the idea of being heavily laden with. It is to be contrasted with the passive form of *plēroō*, which simply means "to be filled" (cp. Matt. 23:25, 27).

3:15 Their feet are swift to shed blood;—a free rendering of Isaiah 59:7, where the LXX and the Hebrew agree. The suggestion is that of murder committed on the slightest provocation.

3:16 Destruction and misery are in their ways;—This points to the desolation and distress which mark their tracks. *Suntrimma*, destruction, primarily a bruising, is found here only in the New Testament.

3:17 And the way of peace have they not known:—That is, the way that is characterized by peace (cp. Luke 1:79).

3:18 There is no fear of God before their eyes.—This is from the LXX of Psalm 36:1. This last quotation sums up the whole condition just described. God, whose very presence should inspire men with the fear of doing wrong, is entirely disregarded by them. They are destitute of any sense of His presence, let alone any regard for Him.

(c) The Impossibility of Justification by the Law, 3:19, 20

3:19 Now we know that what things soever the law saith,—*Oida*, "we know intuitively," it is a matter of common knowledge. The preceding quotations, taken from the Psalms and Isaiah, indicate that by the Law is to be understood the Old Testament as a whole.

it speaketh to them that are under the law;—The word rendered "speaketh" is *laleō*, in contrast to *legō*, "saith." See preceding note. The difference, broadly speaking, is that *laleō* signifies the utterance of speech, as opposed to silence, while *legō* declares what the speaker actually says. The two verbs occur together with this distinction in Mark 6:50; Luke 24:6, e.g. In the present passage "saith" suggests the contents of the message, "speaketh" the fact of the utterance.

that every mouth—Jews "as well as Gentiles," with special reference to the Jew, who regarded the Gentiles as sinners. See Galatians 2:15, where the apostle speaks ironically, taking the Judaizers on their own ground.

may be stopped,—*Phrassō* is said physically of the mouths of lions, in Hebrews 11:33. The only other place where it is found in the New Testament is 2 Corinthians 11:10, where the literal rendering is "This boasting shall not be stopped to me." Here the meaning is that all excuse is taken away, both from Jew and Gentile.

and all the world may be brought under the judgment of God:—"The world" stands for humanity in general. A literal rendering is "may become under judgment to God." The phrase "subject to the judgment" represents the one word *hupodikos*, which is found here only in the New Testament. Man, being without excuse for sin, remains exposed to punishment from God, under the searchlight of divine revelation, such revelation being given whether by creation (1:20) and being made known to conscience (2:14, 15), or by the written Law itself.

3:20 because by the works of the law—The absence of the definite article before "works" and "law" indicates that, while the Mosaic Law is prominently in view, yet all efforts to fulfill law divinely imparted, whether externally or internally, are referred to. This comprehensive view is confirmed by what follows.

shall no flesh—"Flesh" here stands for mankind, in the totality of all that is essential to manhood, spirit, soul and body. For this sense see also Matthew 24:22; John 1:13. Thus the word stands for humanity conditioned by that through which actions are performed. There is perhaps also a suggestion of the weakness of the creature.

be justified in His sight:—*Dikaioō* is "to show, or declare, to be right." In the N.T. it mostly signifies "to declare a person to be righteous before God." Ideally the fulfillment of the Law of God would provide a basis of justification in the sight of God (see 2:13). The apostle has already shown that actually no such case has occurred in mere human experience. If a man should keep the whole Law and yet stumble in one point he is guilty of all (James 2:10). All men, whether Jew or Gentile, have failed to secure the approval of the sole lawgiver and judge. The quotation is from Psalm 143:2, and the apostle thereby shows that the Old Testament gives its *imprimatur* to what is being set forth.

for through the law cometh the knowledge of sin.—The human conscience convicts man of the fact of sin, but the external revelation of the will of God by the Law only intensifies the consciousness of sin. This subject is extended in chapter 7. The word for "knowledge," is *epignōsis,* "full knowledge."

A Righteousness of God by Faith, 3:21—5:21

Introductory Note

The following passage shows, by a striking contrast, how the righteousness of God has been manifested in a different way from that of the giving of the Law. It is necessary to distinguish between the righteousness of God (subjective) as a divine attribute and the righteousness (objective) which He reckons to a believing sinner by the means which He has

adopted consistently with His own attributes. The former is specially in view in verse 25. The primary object of the Epistle is to vindicate God's righteous character and then to show how, consistently with this, the sinner is reckoned righteous. We are thus introduced to the subject of God's grace, through the redemption that is in Christ Jesus, and this stands out in contrast to the universality of human sin.

(1) Justification through Faith, 3:21–26

3:21 But now apart from the law—Literally "apart from law," *i.e.,* apart from the works of law.

a righteousness of God hath been manifested,—Compare 1:17. The reference is to the character of God. His righteousness was revealed in the Law, the decrees of which were an expression of His own character. Now through the gospel His righteousness is revealed in another way, and is expressed in the means by which He has provided a ground upon which righteousness can be reckoned to a sinner. "Is manifested" is, literally, "has been manifested"; that is, at the Cross.

being witnessed by the law and the prophets;—"The Law" here signifies the Pentateuch, and "the Prophets" includes the Psalms; the expression therefore includes the whole of the Old Testament. An example of each case of this witness is given in chapter four, first in regard to Abraham and then from one of the Psalms of David. The statement shows that the gospel, so far from being incompatible with the Old Testament and the position of Israel under the Law, receives confirmation from it.

3:22 even the righteousness of God through faith in Jesus Christ—More closely to the original we might read "and (or but) a righteousness of God." Whatever connecting word is used, it is explanatory of verse 21, marking at the same time a contrast to the manifestation of God's righteousness under the Law. Here the phrase "the righteousness of God" still points to His character as the Just One, calling for faith, instead of for obedience to a law, which could not be rendered. "Faith in Jesus Christ" is the correct rendering and not as in the A.V.

unto all them that believe;—Manuscript evidence supports the single preposition "unto," as in the R.V., rather than "unto and upon," as in the A.V. The ministry of divine grace is fully comprehended in the single preposition. Faith is the means by which God's righteousness is brought to bear on men in their favor whether Jew or Gentile.

for there is no distinction;—That is, between Jew and Gentile, whether in the matter of sin, or in the display of God's holy character in the gospel and the terms upon which righteousness is reckoned by God to the sinner.

The following contrasts in this passage should be noted—(a) "the Law," verse 19, and "grace," verse 24; (b) "through the Law," verse 20, and "through redemption," verse 24; (c) "under judgment," verse 19, and "justified freely," verse 24; (d) "the works of the Law," verse 20, and "faith in Jesus Christ," verse 22; (e) "all the world," verse 19, and "them that believe," verse 22.

3:23 for all have sinned,—This provides a proof that there is no distinction. The original has the aorist, or point, tense, which simply adds precision and definiteness to the fact. The English perfect, "have sinned," gives an adequate rendering.

and fall short—Present continuous tense; "fall" is a preferable rendering to "come," as the latter presents an ambiguity in the matter of past or present time.

of the glory of God;—*Doxa* stands for the moral glory, the perfections of His character, which present a standard, with its requirements, for man, who has been made in the image of God (cp. and contrast 1:23, and see 6:4).

3:24 being justified—This brings before us the subjective side of justification. God has been shown to be just, and now the apostle shows how we can be just with God. Justification is here the legal and formal acquittal from guilt by God as judge, and the pronouncement of the believing sinner as righteous in His sight. The verb is in the present continuous tense and thus indicates a constant process of justification in the succession of those who believe and are justified.

freely—*Dōrean* is, literally, "as gift," "gratis." It indicates the absence of any cause in the person who is the object of the action.

by His Grace—Grace is God's free, unmerited favor toward man. This is the character of His justification of the believing sinner.

through the redemption that is in Christ Jesus;—*Apolutrōsis* is a strengthened form of *lutrōsis*, which signifies "deliverance," here deliverance from the guilt of sin. The corresponding verb is *lutroō*, "to deliver," "to redeem" (lit., "to buy up"). A person may be purchased without actually being set free. *Exagorazō*, to redeem, lays stress upon the price paid. *Apolutrōsis* lays stress upon the actual deliverance. The two sides of redemption should be kept distinct. The purchase price was the blood of Christ. The full redemption is the deliverance accomplished. Here both price and redemption are in view.

3:25 whom God set forth—*Protithēmi* may mean either "to determine," to "purpose" or "to set forth," so as to be manifest. Either sense would convey a scriptural view here, but the context bears out the latter meaning. The verb is in the middle voice, which lays stress upon the personal interest which God had in doing what is said, as predetermined in His eternal purpose. The aorist tense indicates the definiteness of the act in the past.

to be a propitiation,—*Hilastērion* here signifies an expiatory sacrifice. The word is used elsewhere in the New Testament only in Hebrews 9:5, where it denotes the mercy seat. The lid of the ark in the Holy of Holies was sprinkled with the blood of the expiatory victim on the Day of Atonement, the significance being that the life of the victim, not chargeable with the sin of the offerer, was presented to God, and that on the ground of this offering God provided a means of the acceptance of the people in His sight and on that account passed over their sins.

The corresponding Hebrew word primarily signifies "a covering" (cp. Ps. 32:1). Here the word is not simply antitypical, but stands directly for Christ as Himself the propitiatory sacrifice, Christ being, in His sacrifice on the cross, the means divinely appointed for the gratuitous justification of the sinner consistently with God's justice.

through faith, by His blood,—These words are to be taken with "propitiation." The commas which precede and follow "through faith" are important. The rendering "faith in His blood" is incorrect. Faith is never said to be in the blood. Faith is imposed in a living person. Faith is the means of making the pardon ours; the blood is the means of its effect. The preposition *en* of the original is instrumental. The phrase "by His blood" expresses the means of propitiation. The blood of Christ stands not simply for the physical element, nor merely for a life surrendered, but for His sacrificial death under the judgment of God by means of the shedding of His blood. Since blood is essential to life (Lev. 17:11), the shedding of blood involves the taking, or in His case the giving up, of life in sacrifice. It is not merely that death takes place, but it is the giving up of a life as a victim or sacrifice in expiation of sin. This was the significance of the sacrifice of victims under the old covenant.

"The fundamental principle on which God deals with sinners is expressed in the words 'apart from shedding of blood,' i.e., unless a death takes place, 'there is no remission' of sins (Heb. 9:22). But whereas the essential of the type lay in the fact that blood was shed, the essential of the antitype lies in this, that the blood shed was the blood of Christ. Hence, in connection with the Jewish sacrifices, 'the blood' is mentioned without reference to the victim from which it flowed, but in connection with the great antitypical sacrifice of the New Testament the words 'the blood' never stand alone; the One who shed the blood is invariably specified, for it is the person that gives value to the work; the saving efficacy of the death depends entirely upon the fact that He who died was the Son of God" (Notes on Thessalonians, by Hogg and Vine, Vol. 3).

to shew His righteousness,—This is explained in verse 26. Now He makes known to all that He was righteous in doing what He did in view of the work of Christ. This was not clearly manifested before.

because of the passing over of the sins done aforetime,—The word *paresis,* "passing over," is used here only in the New Testament. It signifies, not the remission of sins, but the withholding of punishment. It is somewhat distinct from *aphesis,* "remission." Those who sinned in the period from the Fall to the Cross could receive mercy from God only prospectively, in view of the sacrifice of Christ. Through the Cross it is seen that God was righteous in His forbearance, but until the Cross this was not demonstrated.

in the forbearance of God;—*i.e.,* a temporary suspension of God's retributive dealings (see 2:4).

3:26 for the shewing, *I say,* **of His righteousness at this present season;**—The original has a change of preposition from *eis* in verse 25 to *pros* here. In the former case we might render "for an exhibition," and here "with a view to an exhibition." We should probably take this phrase at the beginning of verse 26 in immediate connection with the end of verse 25. Thus the phrase "for the shewing of His righteousness" is not a mere repetition of what is said in the first part of verse 25, for the phrase "at this present season" stands in contrast to "aforetime" in the preceding verse.

that He might Himself be just, and the justifier—This explains what has just been said about the exhibition of God's righteousness as the design for which He set forth Christ Jesus to be a propitiation, and as the reason of His forbearance. The two words "just" and "Justifier" express, first, the character of God as judge, and then the pronouncement of His sentence consistently with His character as judge. Stress is laid upon His character by the word "Himself." The word "and" should not be taken to mean "and yet," as if the two thoughts of the righteousness of God and His act in justifying were set in contrast. Instead, what is set forth is that His act is consistent with His character. No act more fully displays His righteousness than His justification of the believing sinner. Again, we cannot take the word to mean "and therefore." There is no reason to insert any other word. God's righteousness in providing a propitiation, and His justification of the believing sinner, are shown to be perfectly harmonious. Without the death of Christ justification would have been unjust and impossible; for to justify sinners is forbidden in the Law (Deut. 25:1). On the basis of His death, that is both possible and consistent with the attributes of God.

of him that hath faith in Jesus.—Literally, "of the one [who is] of faith in Jesus," that is to say, every one who is characterized by faith, whose character is formed by faith in Him.

(2) All Boasting Excluded, 3:27–31

Introductory Note

In the following passage faith is regarded as a law, or principle, which excludes all human glorying. It shuts out all possibility of works as a means of justification (vv. 27, 28). Hence in the matter of faith Gentiles are on the same ground as Jews, and the confirmation of this lies in the fact that "God is One"; that is to say, there is not one God for the Jew and one for the Gentile. The argument is based not only on His character but upon His work, which is consistent therewith.

3:27 Where then is the glorying?—*Kauchēsis* is the act of glorying, whereas *kauchēma* is the ground or matter of glorying, as in 4:2.

It is excluded.—Literally, "It was shut out." The aorist, or point, tense indicates the completeness of the act. The divine means of justification excludes absolutely all self-approbation.

By what manner of law?—That is to say, "by what sort of principle has the glorying been excluded?" Law here stands for a principle of procedure.

of works? Nay: but by a law of faith,—That is, "is glorying excluded by a sort of principle of works obtained by merit? Nay, but by a principle which demands faith only on man's part." The phrase "law of faith" stands for the gospel. There should be no definite article, as in the A.V. The absence of the article, instead of stressing a particular law, lays stress upon the two contrasting laws or principles themselves.

3:28 We reckon therefore—The Sinaitic MS. and other MSS. confirm the reading "for" instead of "therefore." That is to say, verse 28 introduces, not a conclusion, but a confirmation of what has just been stated. "We reckon" conveys the idea of confident assurance.

that a man is justified—*Anthropos,* "man," stands, not for man in distinction from other beings, but for anybody of the human race, whether Jew or Gentile, without reference to sex or nationality.

by faith apart from works of the law.—Faith and works of law, as a ground of justification, are mutually exclusive (see Gal. 2:16). The definite article here shows that the Law refers to the Mosaic Law, and that in its entirety, both ceremonial and moral.

3:29 Or is God *the God* **of Jews only? Is He not** *the God* **of Gentiles also? Yea, of Gentiles also:**—The first question suggests the alternative. Faith is not a national quality, so neither is God merely a national God. Justification is not granted on a condition which only those under the Law can fulfill.

3:30 if so be that God is one.—That is to say, there is not one God for the Jew and one for the Gentile. The "if so be" does not imply any uncertainty, but signifies that it is left for the readers to recognize the fact. It was a foundation truth of the Jews' religion that there is only one God (see Deut. 6:4; Is. 42:8; 44:6).

and He shall justify the circumcision by faith, and the uncircumcision through faith.—The future tense "shall justify" does not indicate mere futurity, it suggests an unalterable principle, upon which God acts, a principle with which His acts are ever consistent. The first part of this verse states the great attribute of God, His unity, the second His action, His mode of justification. The two are entirely harmonious. His acts are the expression of His attributes. Then as to man's condition, since Jew and Gentile have sinned, and there is only one God over all, the means of justification are the same for all. The change of preposition from "by faith" to "through faith" is to be noted. It is not, as has been suggested, simply an alternative without distinction. In the case of the circumcision the phrase is, literally, "out of faith," and this seems to suggest that justification is not "out of" the law, as a suggested source from which Jews could seek righteousness. They had been tried on the principle of works of the Law, which the Gentiles have not been. There was no such external source possible to be suggested for the Gentile, so the uncircumcision is said to be justified simply "by means of" faith.

3:31 Do we then make the law of none effect through faith? God forbid: nay, we establish the law.—Since the apostle is obviously anticipating an objection on the part of a Jew (for he has been specially appealing to Jews in this passage), the word "law" here, in spite of the fact that there is no definite article in the original, would seem to refer to all that is embodied in the Old Testament as the divine standard of right and wrong. The question asked is whether the effect of the preaching of salvation by faith is to deprive of their authority the moral enactments of the Law.

ROMANS

• CHAPTER FOUR •

Evidences the Righteousness Is Reckoned on the Condition of Faith

Introductory Note

Two instances are now given from the Old Testament to confirm the truth that a sinner is pronounced righteous by God on the ground of faith apart from works. There is first the case of Abraham, and then the testimony of David in Psalm 32—a witness from the Law and the Prophets. In connection with these examples of the way in which the Old Testament confirms the Gospel, two facts are next set forth to advance the argument. Firstly, the blessedness of the forgiveness of sin cannot be confined to the Jewish nation, for righteousness was reckoned to Abraham while yet in uncircumcision. Circumcision, which was a seal of his righteousness, could not be a condition upon which it was granted. The divine purpose in reckoning him righteous apart from circumcision was that he might be the Father of all who believe, whether Jew or Gentile. The Jew, who claims natural descent from Abraham, must receive spiritual blessing on the same ground as the believing Gentile (v. 12). Secondly, the promise given to Abraham concerning his seed was made before the giving of the Law. It was therefore conditional solely upon faith, and was a matter of grace. Hence, again, the promise is secured to Abraham's spiritual children.

The latter part of chapter four deals, firstly, with the character of Abraham's faith. The importance of the written record is first stressed, and then its purposes (vv. 23–25). It was written, not for Abraham's sake only, but for our sakes, so that we might believe on Him who raised up Jesus from the dead (v. 24). This leads to a statement of the two great foundations of the Christian faith, namely, the death and resurrection of Christ, and their connection with human need. This forms an introduction to chapter five.

(a) Twofold Witness from the Law and the Prophets, 4:1–8

4:1 What then shall we say that Abraham, our forefather according to the flesh, hath found?—Abraham was the progenitor of the Messiah and regarded as head of the Jewish race.

The phrase "according to the flesh" can be taken grammatically either with "our forefather" or with "hath found." Opinions regarding the choice differ. If the latter connection is taken, the question asks what righteousness Abraham obtained by works, that is, by natural effort and attainment. This is in keeping with what follows in verse 2. If the phrase is connected with "our forefather," it signifies natural relationship in contrast to the spiritual relationship established by faith, a contrast stressed in verse 11.

4:2 For if Abraham was justified by works, he hath whereof to glory;—That Abraham was justified is agreed both by the apostle and the Jew who objects. If Abraham's justification were by works his works would provide him with a ground of glorying. The present tense "he hath" draws attention to the record as it stands prominently in Scripture.

but not toward God.—For Abraham would have done no more than it was his duty to do. His glorying would be in his own righteousness, and God would be simply a paymaster, but all such glorying is excluded (3:27).

4:3 For what saith the scripture?—The Scripture is here virtually personified (see 9:17; John 19:37; James 4:5). For the apostle and his readers the Scripture was the final and infallible court of appeal.

And Abraham believed God, and it was reckoned unto him for righteousness.—Abraham took God at His word (a fact represented by the word "it"), and so his faith was the instrument in his justification.

The word *logizō*, "to reckon," is best so rendered, rather than by the varying words "count" and "impute." Whatever is reckoned to a person cannot have been his originally and naturally (cp. Rom. 2:26). Abraham, in common with all the descendants of Adam, was a sinner (Rom. 5:12); that is to say, viewed from the divine standpoint, he was destitute of a personal righteousness. Hence, if his relationship with God was to be rectified, and this is what is meant by justification in such a case, it must be accomplished otherwise than by his own meritorious deeds.

The preposition "for" does not mean "as" or "instead of." That would make faith an act of merit as equivalent to righteousness. It has already been shown (in chaps. 2:15–17 and 3) that men are incapable of doing anything as a ground of justification in God's sight.

Righteousness thus far in the Epistle has been mentioned only as an attribute of God (1:17; 3:5, 21, 22, 25, 26). Now for the first time it is spoken of as that which is reckoned to one who believes.

The man who trusts in Christ becomes "the righteousness of God in Him" (2 Cor. 5:21), becomes in Christ all that God requires a man to be, all that he could never be in himself: Because Abraham accepted the word of God, God accepted him as one who fulfilled the whole of His requirements.

4:4 Now to him that worketh,—This and the next verse confirm the statement that Abraham was justified apart from works. At the same time what is now stated is by way of a general principle. "Worketh" means the fulfillment of the requirements of the Law.

the reward is not reckoned as of grace, but as of debt.—Inasmuch as that cannot be given as a favor to a man which is owed him as a debt, Abraham's faith and the faith of his spiritual children set them outside the category of those who seek to be justified by self-effort.

4:5 But to him that worketh not,—This specifies in contrast the company to which Abraham actually belongs.

but believeth on Him that justifieth the ungodly,—*Asebēs*, ungodly, is, literally, "impious" (cp. the noun in 1:18). Not that Abraham is marked out as an ungodly man: the word is used generally, as characterizing mankind lying universally in sin, and the strong term is chosen in order to set in the greatest contrast man in his own worthlessness and God in His mercy in justifying by faith. Moreover, where faith is not exercised, man remains ungodly and therefore exposed to the wrath of God.

his faith is reckoned for righteousness.—Faith, then, involves the recognition of one's sinnership and the reliance upon God's mercy to justify a person on His own conditions.

4:6 Even as David also—Introducing the second witness. The "even as" connects the statement immediately with that at the close of verse 5, and shows that it is sinners whom God justifies, when, like believing Abraham, they put faith in God.

pronounceth blessing upon the man,—The word *legō*, "to say," "to speak," signifies here a formal declaration, and this exactly describes the opening of Psalm 32. The word "blessing" signifies, not simply the state of being happy, but the declaration of blessedness as bestowed by God. It is rendered "gratulation" in 4:15.

unto whom God reckoneth righteousness apart from works,—See notes on verses 3–5. That God reckons righteousness to a person is another way of saying that God reckons him righteous. The effect is the same, namely justification, a pronouncement by the judge of freedom from guilt.

4:7 *Saying.* Blessed are they whose iniquities are forgiven,—The quotation is from the LXX. The word rendered "are forgiven" is in the aorist tense, expressing the definiteness of the act.

And whose sins are covered.—The aorist tense again. The word *epikaluptō* is a strengthened form of *kaluptō*, "to hide." It is used here only in the New Testament and is the equivalent to the Hebrew word for "to atone." It signifies, not merely a covering, but the removal of guilt under the covering; this involves the removal of divine wrath from the sinner. The English word "atonement" is not to be split into its parts as if it stood for "at-one-ment." "At-one-ment" is the effect of atonement. The atonement stands for the sacrifice itself of Christ (see note on "propitiation," 3:25).

4:8 Blessed is the man to whom the Lord will not reckon sin.—This is a negative way of expressing the reckoning of righteousness. It does not indeed convey all that is involved in justification, but it implies it. So in Ephesians 1:7, redemption is described as the forgiveness of sins, though the latter does not express all that redemption signifies.

(b) Twofold Proof from History, 4:9–16

4:9 Is this blessing then pronounced upon the circumcision, or upon the uncircumcision also? for we say, To Abraham his faith was reckoned for righteousness.—The subject of circumcision here relates to Abraham, and the question arises as to whether the blessing of justification granted to Abraham, and confirmed by his descendant David, is limited to Abraham's natural descendants.

4:10 How then was it reckoned? when he was in circumcision, or in uncircumcision? Not in circumcision, but in uncircumcision:—Genesis 15, which records Abraham's justification, has no mention of circumcision. That took place about fourteen years later, and is recorded in Genesis 17; so that the relationship between God and Abraham, confirmed by a covenant (Gen. 15:18), was established simply on the ground of faith.

4:11 and he received the sign of circumcision,—A sign that betokened the accomplished fact of his justification and the covenant relationship into which he had entered (see Gen. 15:18 and 17:11).

a seal of the righteousness of the faith which he had while he was in uncircumcision.—Literally, "a seal of the righteousness of the faith, that, namely, which was his in uncircumcision." The rabbis spoke of circumcision as the seal of Abraham. A seal was primarily used to authenticate and ratify a covenant. Metaphorically it is used here of an external attestation of what had been decreed or covenanted.

that he might be the father of all them that believe, though they be in uncircumcision, that righteousness might be reckoned unto them;—That is to say, Abraham is thus viewed as the spiritual father of all who believe, and that altogether independently of circumcision. Believing Gentiles are thus spiritual heirs of the promise given to him.

4:12 and the father of circumcision to them who not only are of the circumcision,—That is, who not merely have the outward sign in the flesh. The words "to them," instead of "of them," indicate the advantages of the relationship as well as the relationship itself.

but who also walk in the steps—The word "walk" is figuratively used to describe the activities and conduct of the life. The word in the original here is *stoicheō*, which signifies the general conduct of a person in relation to others. The more frequent word *peripateō* signifies activities and conduct of the individual life, that is to say, apart from relation to others.

of that faith of our father Abraham which he had in uncircumcision.—That is, whoever as a Jew is to enjoy spiritual descent from Abraham, with all the blessings it brings, must do so, not on the ground of natural relationship, but on the same ground as believing Gentiles.

4:13 For not through the law was the promise to Abraham or to his seed, that he should be heir of the world,—The R.V. rightly stresses the phrase "not through the law," and, while the immediate reference is to the Law of Sinai, yet the article is not used, and therefore "law" is here represented as a principle. The argument is continued and extended now with reference to the Law of Sinai. As the blessings divinely promised to Abraham have been shown to be independent of circumcision, so now they are shown to be independent of the Law. In Galatians 3:16 the apostle speaks of Abraham's seed as signifying Christ. Here the word "seed" is used in the collective sense of descendants (as in Gal. 3:29). The promise is particularly that mentioned in Genesis 15:5, 6. The promise which is spoken of in this chapter was ratified at the time recorded in Genesis 17:5.

but through the righteousness of faith.—
See note on verse 11. Here it is set in contrast
to obedience to law.

**4:14 For if they which are of the law be
heirs, faith is made void,**—Perfect tense,
"hath been made void," *kenoō* signifies either
to empty (as in Phil. 2:7) or to make empty
or void, to deprive of force (1 Cor. 1:17; 9:15;
2 Cor. 9:3 only).

**and the promise is made of none ef-
fect:**—For *katargeō* see notes at 3:3, 31. The
verb is again in the perfect tense. Faith and
the promise go together, and in line with these
is justification. All are nullified by law (cp. Gal.
3:18).

4:15 for the law worketh wrath;—That
is, the Law brings men under condemnation
and therefore renders them subject to the
wrath of God. The Law serves but to stimulate
sin (see 7:9).

**but where there is no law, neither is
there transgression.**—*Parabasis,* transgression (lit., "a stepping over"), always implies a breach of law, and especially of the Law
of Moses (as in 2:23; Heb. 2:2; 9:15). It is
used of the prohibition in Eden (Rom. 5:14;
1 Tim. 2:14).

4:16 For this cause *it is* **of faith,**—Because the law worketh wrath, and the promise
given to faith would thereby be made of none
effect; the promise, with all that it brings, is
conditional upon faith only.

that *it may be* **according to grace;**—That is
to say, that the fulfillment of the promise may
not be according to man's merit, but to God's
unmerited favor. The mention of grace indicates that there is no intrinsic merit in faith.
The promise, faith and grace, are set in direct
contrast to law, works and merit.

**to the end that the promise may be
sure**—Faith was made a condition of the
promise, that its fulfillment, apart from human
merit, might be secured for the recipients.
Had its fulfillment depended upon human
works or merit, it could not have been assured, because it could not have been attain-
able thus.

**to all the seed; not to that only which is
of the law, but to that also which is of**
the faith of Abraham, who is the father
of us all**—The seed (see note on v. 13) here
stands for all the children of Abraham who
accept God's condition of faith, whether Jews
or Gentiles. The promise given to Abraham
will be secured to the nation of the Jews, but
not on the ground of lawkeeping, and meanwhile all believing Jews are, alike with believing Gentiles, the spiritual children of Abraham.

(c) The Character and Effect of Abraham's Faith, 4:17–22

**4:17 (as it is written, A father of many
nations have I made thee)**—The quotation
is from the LXX of Genesis 17:15.

before Him whom he believed,—This
goes with the clause at the end of verse 16,
"who is the father of us all." More literally it
is "in the presence of Him," that is to say, in
the sight of, in the judgment of. In God's view
the future is alike with the present. He foreknew every member of the whole multitude of
Abraham's seed. The words "he believed"
may be taken as referring both to Genesis 15
and 22. The faith Abraham exercised as recorded in the fifteenth chapter determined his
attitude in the circumstances of the seventeenth.

even God, who quickeneth the dead,—
That is, makes the dead to live (see vv. 19,
20). The prerogative and power for this belong
to God alone, for it is an act which requires
almighty power (Deut. 32:39; 1 Sam. 2:6;
2 Kin. 5:7; Ps. 68:20). Faith in God as the
One who exercises this prerogative, enabled
Abraham to look forward with assurance to an
innumerable seed.

**and calleth the things that are not, as
though they were.**—The simplest explanation of this is that God speaks of, and so treats,
nonexistent things, upon which He has determined, as being already existent. A possible
meaning is that God commands the things, etc.

**4:18 Who in hope believed against
hope,**—The order in the original is "who
against hope in hope believed." "Against
hope," that is, contrary to human expectation;
"in hope" (lit., "upon hope"), that is, on the
basis of a hope inspired by God's promise,

God being regarded by him as the one who could do what is impossible to nature.

to the end that he might become a father of many nations, according to that which had been spoken, So shall thy seed be.— The "So" refers to what God had said about the stars (see Gen. 15:5).

4:19 And without being weakened in faith—This verse sets forth the object of the phrase "against hope" in verse 18. Verses 20 and 21 set forth the meaning of "in hope."

he considered his own body now as good as dead—This follows the reading of the oldest MSS. and the Syriac Version. The word "not" seems to have been put in by some copyist in order to make sense. The point, however, is that Abraham was not blind to facts, nor did he ignore difficulties; "he did consider carefully" (*katanoeō*, a strengthened form of *noeō*, "to consider") the whole situation, but the circumstances, so impossible to nature, in no way weakened his faith. The phrase "without being weakened in faith" itself supports the omission of the "not."

(he being about a hundred years old), and the deadness of Sarah's womb:—The word "being" is, in the original, not *eimi*, the verb "to be," but *huparchō*, which always suggests more than the mere fact of being; the suggestion here is that he was confessedly that age; that is to say, the fact was recognized by himself; and has received general recognition. This is a fundamental fact in the circumstances. The reference is to Genesis 17, an event thirteen years later than the birth of Ishmael.

4:20 yea, looking unto the promise of God, he wavered not through unbelief,— There is no word corresponding to "looking" in the original, but the phrase there suggests it, rather than, as some would render, "with regard to" the promise of God. The clause is in a position of emphasis, and requires something more definite than that rendering. Faith turns from natural impossibilities to rely upon the word of God. Faith therefore becomes the instrument of man's part in putting him into definite relationship with God Himself.

but waxed strong through faith,—Literally, "was made strong." It was the promise of God which was the primary means of his strength. Hence in the original the phrase "through faith" is not put in an emphatically instrumental form.

giving glory to God,—Abraham, by relying upon the word of God, acknowledged the attributes of God, and thus adopted a right attitude toward Him. This is the immediate effect of faith (see notes on 3:21–26).

4:21 and being fully assured that, what He had promised, He was able also to perform.—The word *plērophoreō;* the particular form of which is here rendered "being fully assured," literally signifies "to carry fully." This suggests that spontaneity and liberty of soul which, unhindered by obstacles, grasps the promises of God and His ability to fulfill them.

4:22 Wherefore also it was reckoned unto him for righteousness.—The "Wherefore" refers especially to what is contained in verses 18–21. What is now said is not actually recorded in Genesis 17 but is expanded from Genesis 15 and embraces Genesis 17, the condition of faith being fulfilled by Abraham in each case. It is just that acceptance of God's word in regard to the Lord Jesus Christ and the supranatural facts relating to Him, as, for instance, His atoning death and Resurrection, that puts right with God him who believes, bringing to him at once the justifying efficacy of Christ's death and the impartation of eternal life. This is therefore the same spirit of faith in regard to Christ that was exercised by Abraham in regard to the promise of God.

(d) The Purposes of the Record, 4:23–25

4:23 Now it was not written for his sake alone, that it was reckoned unto him;— At the beginning of this chapter the apostle asked "What saith the Scripture?" (v. 3). After answering the question from the Genesis record, he now shows that the Old Testament Scriptures are not merely a record of facts, but that they are permanently designed for the benefit of all believers (cp. 15:4).

4:24 but for our sake also, unto whom it shall be reckoned,—The phrase is not simply the future tense. It might be rendered more fully thus: "For whom it is appointed to be reckoned." The reference is not to a day still future, but to the design of God concerning all believers, past, present and future.

who believe on Him—More literally, "the believers upon." The preposition *epi*, "upon," signifies, not merely the acceptance of a statement, but the restfulness of faith that leans upon the person Himself.

that raised Jesus our Lord from the dead,—Abraham's faith rested upon God as the One who quickeneth the dead, *i.e.,* who could bring life out of natural deadness. We also believe in Him who quickens the dead, but in this case His almighty power has been already put forth in the Resurrection of Christ (cp. 1 Pet. 1:21 and Eph. 1:19, 20). The Resurrection of Christ is the cornerstone of gospel truth (1 Cor. 15:4, etc.). It unites all the other facts of the gospel. The verb is *egeirō,* to awake.

4:25 who was delivered up—The word *paradidōmi*, "to deliver up," is the same as that in 1:24, 26, 28. It is used in the New Testament of the act of the Lord Jesus Christ in submitting to death (Gal. 2:20; Eph. 5:2, 25) and of the act of God in sending Him with

that in view (as here and 8:32). Sometimes it is used of the act of men in delivering Christ up (Matt. 10:4; 27:2, 26; Acts 3:13).

for our trespasses,—Or "because of our trespasses"; that is to say, because of the fact that we had committed trespasses. The statement of the fact in this way is in keeping with what was set forth in 3:9–23.

and was raised for our justification.—Literally, "because of our justification"; the same construction as in the preceding clause "because of our trespasses." The clauses are parallel. Christ was raised because all that was necessary on God's part for our justification had been effected in the death of Christ. We had sinned, and therefore Christ was delivered up. The ground of our justification was completely provided in the death of Christ, and therefore He was raised. It is true that the believer is justified only when he exercises faith, but that is not the point of this verse. The stress is on that which has secured justification for the believer, namely, the death of Christ. The propitiation was complete (John 19:30), and His resurrection was the ratifying counterpart, the confirmation of the absolute completeness of the atonement (cp. 1:4, and see notes there).

ROMANS

The Effects of the Remedy, 5:1–11

Introductory Note

The great subject of this chapter is the effect of faith: firstly, with regard to the individual, 5:1-11, secondly with regard to the race, 5:12-21. Again, the fifth chapter shows what we have through Christ, while the sixth shows us what we are in Christ (see R.V.). "Through Christ" is the keynote of chapter five. This chapter unfolds the subjects of the effects of the death and resurrection of Christ, all being based on the doctrine of 3:21-26. The opening sentence of the chapter is at once deduced from the closing statements of chapter four. The leading thought, "through our Lord Jesus Christ," is expressed at both the beginning and end of the first part of the chapter (v. 1-11), and at the end of the second part (v. 21), the order of the titles being changed there, so as to emphasize the title "Lord," the special stress on this title being introductory to chapter six.

5:1 Being therefore justified by faith.—The verb rendered "being justified" is in the aorist tense, and indicates the definite time at which each believer, upon the exercise of faith, was justified in the sight of God.

let us have peace with God—The preponderance of MS. evidence, being in favor of this rendering, the Revisers adopted it. Exegetically much has been said to support the rendering which gives a statement rather than an exhortation, "we have peace." It has been argued, for instance, that an exhortation seems out of place in this part of the Epistle, which is of a didactic character. Yet as the apostle, having in a considerable argument laid the basis of the divine mode of justification, now begins to deal with its subjective effects in the heart of the believer, especially effects which are experienced in varying degrees in the case of different believers, there is nothing inappropriate in an exhortation here, nor is it incompatible with an immediate return to further statements concerning the death of Christ and God's grace therein. The point of the exhortation is not our submission to God, but the conscious and constant enjoyment of the justification which has been procured for us.

through our Lord Jesus Christ;—This is the keynote of this chapter; see the introductory note above.

5:2 through whom also—A continuation of the leading thought of the chapter (see the preceding note and link with 3:24).

we have had our access by faith—*Prōsagogē*, access, is, literally, a bringing in, an introduction. Here in Romans 5:2, the thought is rather that of our acceptance with God and the enjoyment of His grace, as those who have been justified.

into this grace wherein we stand;—This is expressive of the permanency of our position as justified ones, in contrast to our former state of condemnation.

and let us rejoice—Here the word in the original may be translated either "we rejoice," or "let us rejoice." It is not a case of difference of form or spelling in the Greek word; for the word is the same, whichever rendering is given to it. This was not so in the case of the phrase in verse 1, "let us have peace." The decision does not therefore rest on MS. evidence. Yet, again, the exhortation "let us rejoice," as already noticed in verse 1, is not inappropriate, for the justification and access granted to us are incentives to rejoicing.

in hope of the glory of God.—The preposition *epi*, rendered "in," is really "on," that is to say, "on the basis of"; the hope provides the ground of our exultation. The glory of God, when referring especially to the glory which He possesses, is the outward and visible expression of His essential attributes and character. When used objectively, of that which He bestows, it refers to that state of blessedness by which the believer will enjoy hereafter the realization of these attributes.

5:3 And not only so, but let us also rejoice in our tribulations:—The change from the thought of future glory to present sufferings serves only to enhance the reality of the believer's triumphant exultation. The joyful endurance of tribulations is a fitting accompaniment of the assurance of coming glory.

knowing—*Oida*, "to know" (from *eidō*, "to see"), signifies a clear perception of a fact, and so means "to be fully aware" (in contrast to *ginōskō*, which denotes a discriminating apprehension of circumstances, etc.).

that tribulation worketh patience;—To rejoice in tribulation is not to rejoice in the midst of them, but as being actuated by them. The meaning is that endurance, the effect of tribulation, is not something transient or partial, but thorough and abiding.

5:4 and patience, probation; and probation, hope:—*Dokimē*, when used in an active sense, denotes "a proving," "a trial" (as in 2 Cor. 8:2); but here it has its other meaning, of approval, as a result of proving (see also 2 Cor. 2:9; 9:13; Phil. 2:22), the condition of one who is conscious of having endured tribulations effectually, the spiritual state resulting being in accordance with God's designs.

5:5 and hope putteth not to shame;—The article is used with the word "hope," as if signifying the hope just mentioned and produced by the process in verses 3 and 4. That hope does not put the believer to shame suggests that, on the contrary, being freed from illusion and despair, he is able to go boldly on his course through this life, knowing that he will not be disappointed.

because the love of God hath been shed abroad in our hearts—This is the first mention of love in this Epistle, and the reference here is to God's love to us (see v. 8; 8:35, 39). This love is "shed," *ekchunō*, literally, "poured out." The word is used of the gift of the Holy Spirit (in Acts 10:45). Since the heart is the chief organ of physical life, the word is used figuratively for the inner springs of the personal life, the seat of the affections.

through the Holy Ghost which was given unto us.—This is really the first mention of the Holy Spirit in the Epistle (see note at 1:4). Each believer received the Holy Spirit when he believed (John 7:39; cp. Acts 5:32 and chap. 8:9 of this Epistle). Since the believer was then "born of the Spirit" (John 3:6), and lives by the Spirit (Gal. 5:25), He is his inalienable possession.

5:6 For while we were yet weak,—This introduces a proof that God loves us (vv. 6–8), and that the hope based on His love cannot fail (vv. 9, 10). The phrase "while we were yet weak" is a reminder of our powerlessness to obtain justification by works as set forth in the passage 3:19 to 14:25. The word rendered "weak" is, literally, "strengthless." The immediate cause lies in this, that we had not received the Spirit of God, and so were unable to please God.

in due season—Literally, "according to season," that is to say, a time divinely appointed as opportune for the manifestation of God's love in Christ.

Christ died—There is stress on each of these words, as indicated by their order in the Greek sentence. The order is, significantly, as follows: "Christ, we being weak, in due season, for ungodly ones, died." The death of Christ is expressed in various ways in the New Testament. It is stated as here in 2 Corinthians 5:15.

for the ungodly.—*Huper*, on behalf of, in the interests of; the same preposition is used of the death of Christ (in v. 8, below, and 8:32 and 14:15). This preposition is not equivalent to *anti*, which means "instead of" (see Matt. 20:28; 1 Tim. 2:6).

There is no article before the word "ungodly" in the Greek, and its absence indicates that those who are mentioned are not a distinct class from the godly, but that the term describes mankind in general; the meaning is that Christ died for all as being ungodly. The description, by the very vividness of its reality, serves to bring out more forcibly the character of God's love.

5:7 For scarcely for a righteous man will one die;—This continues to present, by way of contrast, the greatness of God's love.

The word *dikaiōs*, righteous, rightwise, here denotes one who is right in his general conduct. See 1:17, where, as in Galatians 3:17, the word describes one who does right according to human standards. The meaning is different in 5:19 (where see note).

for peradventure for the good man some-one would even dare to die.—The word *agathos*, denotes one who acts beneficially toward others, devoting himself to their welfare. For the distinction between *agathos* and *kalos*, the admirable, that which is intrinsically good, beautiful (see at 7:18), where both words are used.

Justice is the empowering motive of the righteous man; love is that which inspires the good man. The former meets with respect, the latter meets with affection. Bearing this in mind, and with regard to the "for" before "peradventure" at the beginning of this second statement, the meaning may be set forth somewhat as follows: "To die for a righteous man is difficult—perhaps the idea may be considered improbable in any case—and yet I would not say this, for peradventure for the good man some one would even dare to die." This meaning has regard to the difference between the righteous and the good, as well as to the fact that both sentences begin with "for." In the Greek there is no definite article before "righteous," but there is before "good," and this serves to bring out the distinction as in the explanation.

5:8 But God commendeth His own love toward us,—This continues and expands the subject of the love of God, presenting it now by way of contrast between what we can conceive might be done for the good man and what Christ has already done for sinners. For *sunistēmi*, "to commend," "to give a proof of," see 3:5, and contrast what is said there about that which gives proof of God's righteousness, with what is here mentioned as a proof of His love. There is stress on the pronoun "His," which necessitates the rendering "His own love," and brings out both its divine origin and its uniqueness. There is stress also on the word "God," standing as it does, in the original, at the end of the clause.

in that, while we were yet sinners,—*Hamartōlos* is, literally, "one who has missed the mark," the most general term used to describe the fallen condition of the human race.

Christ died for us.—For *huper*, "on behalf of," see note on verse 6. The unique and conspicuous character of the love of God lies, firstly, in the relationship of Christ to Him as His Son (this is brought out in 8:32); secondly, in that Christ has died for ungodly sinners.

5:9 Much more then,—The phrase rendered "much more," when used in a comparison regarding quantity, denotes a greater abundance (see 11:12). Otherwise, as here, it denotes a greater certainty (cp. vv. 10, 15, 17).

being now justified by His blood,—For the phrase "by His blood" see note on 3:25. The preposition *en* (lit., "in") is instrumental here as there.

shall we be saved from the wrath *of God* **through Him.**—This is the first mention of the verb *sōzō*, to save, in the Epistle. Here salvation is the object of hope, as it will be fulfilled, when the Lord comes (see 13:11; 1 Cor. 3:15; 5:5; Phil. 3:20; Heb. 9:28; 1 Pet. 1:5).

The wrath of God from which we shall be saved includes the wrath that is coming upon the world at the close of the present age. The Church is to be delivered from that (see 1 Thess. 1:10, R.V., and 5:9, 10). This deliverance will be their portion at the *Parousia* of the Lord Jesus (1 Cor. 15:51–56).

5:10 For if, while we were enemies,—The "if" is virtually "since." The word "enemies," while true of our hostile attitude toward God, signified also that we were under condemnation, exposed to His wrath (John 3:36). Note the three expressions "ungodly" (v. 6), "sinners" (v. 8), "enemies" (v. 10). The last word anticipates the mention of reconciliation.

we were reconciled to God through the death of His Son,—The significance of the word "reconciled" is clear from the context. The subject is that of justification and of the grace of God in pronouncing us clear of guilt. In verse 11, reconciliation is seen to be something that we have received. It is therefore a mercy which God bestows.

Again, in 2 Corinthians 5:19 reconciliation is said to be what God accomplishes. What is especially in view, therefore, is the exercise of His grace on the ground of the death of Christ (see also Eph. 2:16; Col. 1:21). The laying aside of our hostility is not here stressed, but the exhibition of the love of God in the death of Christ.

much more, being reconciled, shall we be saved by His life;—Our justification cost the death of His Son. Our present preservation and our future deliverance are dependent upon Himself as the living one. The love that was displayed in His death is the guarantee not only of our present maintenance but of our future redemption, the redemption of the body (8:23; see also Heb. 7:25).

5:11 and not only so, but we also rejoice in God through our Lord Jesus Christ,—The leading phrase of the chapter. This, and the preceding phrase "in God" afford the ground and point of all true rejoicing or glorying.

through whom we have now received the reconciliation.—with the noun *katallage*, "reconciliation," compare the corresponding verb *katallasso*, "to reconcile" (v. 10). The reconciliation is the effect of the death of Christ. That we have received the reconciliation stresses the attitude of God's favor toward us. The rendering "atonement" is incorrect. Atonement is the offering itself of Christ in sacrifice on the Cross.

Death through Adam's Sin, and Life through Christ's Death, 5:12–21

Introductory Note

In this second part of chapter five the apostle continues the subject of the effects of the death of Christ, with references to the human race. The chief themes before us now are, on the one hand, sin, death and the Law, on the other hand, righteousness, life and grace, all serving to illustrate the great subject of the justification of sinners on a basis of divine righteousness.

The main point in the whole section is the comparison between Adam and Christ, in this respect, that as Adam was the means of bring-

ing in sin and death, Christ has brought in justification and life.

First then as to Adam, the argument is as follows: (1) a penalty implies a broken law; (2) death is a penalty; (3) now sin is not imputed where there is no law; (4) Adam's sin was the transgression of a law, so were the sins of the people of Israel under the Mosaic Law; (5) between Adam and the time of Moses sin did not partake of the character of transgression, for there was no law (the law of conscience is not in view here); (6) yet death reigned from Adam to Moses; (7) as then death is a penalty of a broken law, all men were subject to death because of Adam's transgression, his posterity sharing thus in the effects of the act done by the head of the race (vv. 13, 14). That point being established, the parallel between Adam and Christ can now be stated. Adam was a figure of Christ (v. 14). As we are condemned in Adam, so we are justified in Christ. The apostle is not here speaking of the effects of the Law; this he does later. He is showing how sin and death have become universal because of Adam's sin. As these came through the act of another, so justification and life can, in like manner, become ours only through the act of another, even Christ.

5:12 Therefore, as through one man sin entered into the world,—This, which arises from the first part of this chapter, takes up the whole subject of human sin and how God has dealt with it, as set forth in the preceding part of the Epistle, and introduces a comparison and contrast in regard to Adam and Christ and their connection with the race.

The word *anthrōpos*, "man," is to be distinguished from *anēr*, "a man," "a male," i.e., as indicating his sex, and signifies a member of the human race, without reference either to sex or nationality. That sin "entered into the world" conveys not only the idea that sin began its course in the world, but that mankind became universally sinful.

and death through sin;—The reference is primarily to the death of the body, as is indicated in verse 14. The term may, however, have a more general sense, as including death spiritual and eternal; for these are the penal consequences of sin, and the whole argument points to death as a penalty thereof. Moreover, the life which is brought to the believer through Christ is set in contrast to death (v. 17) and this eternal life is more than simply antithetic to physical death.

and so death passed unto all men, for that all sinned:—This has been understood to mean, either that all sinned in Adam's sin, or else, that all have been guilty of acts of sin. The apostle has laid it down that sin is the cause of universal death, and that by reason of the solidarity of the human race, sin and its consequence have been transmitted from one to all. The sin of the head of the race is thus attributed to all the members, and this is what seems to be implied in the aorist tense. The fact of universal death presupposes both the principle of sin in general, and actual sin in all.

5:13 for until the law sin was in the world: but sin is not imputed when there is no law.—The verb *ellogeō* is found elsewhere in the New Testament, only in Philemon 18, where it is rendered "put to account." It here signifies to lay to one's charge. The principle here enunciated applies to the Law. Between Adam's transgression and the time of the Law of Sinai sin did not partake of the character of transgression; for there was no Law. It is true that the law of conscience existed, but that is not in view here.

5:14 Nevertheless death reigned from Adam until Moses,—Death is here personified. The word "reigned" bears stress in the original and the figure employed suggests the unmitigated tyranny of death.

even over them that had not sinned after the likeness of Adam's transgression,—Adam's transgression was the breach of a revealed commandment of God. That was not the case with those who lived in the time between Adam and the Law. Death in their case was the effect of Adam's sin; in Adam, sin and death had been inseparably joined.

who is a figure of Him that was to come.—*Tupos,* English "type," signifies a "mold," "pattern." It primarily signified a mark or impression made by a stroke or blow. Here it is used to signify that the characteristics of a person, or the circumstances connected with him, bear a correspondence to those connected with another.

5:15 But not as the trespass, so also is the free gift.—The comparison between Adam and Christ is now changed to a contrast. The point of similarity is that each stands at the head of a race, and that the effects of their influence has been upon all those who are under their respective headships. The dissimilarity lies in the character of their acts and the effects thereof.

For if by the trespass of the one the many died,—"The many" here stands for all mankind; they are spoken of as "many," not only because of the largeness of the number, but as standing in contrast to the one man, Adam. The "if" is equivalent to "since." The past definite tense, "died," expresses cumulatively the effect of Adam's transgression.

much more—This introduces, by way of contrast, a statement expressive, not of a greater degree of efficacy, but of legal certainty.

did the grace of God, and the gift by the grace of the one man, Jesus Christ, abound unto the many.—The word rendered "gift" is *dōrea,* which is derived from *didomi,* "to give," and stands simply for a gift in the general sense of the word. Contrast *charisma* in the preceding part of the verse. The phrase "the gift by the grace" is, literally, "the gift in grace." The grace of God expresses the source. The gift by (lit., in) "the grace of the one Man" expresses both the instrument and the channel by means of which the grace comes.

The article before "one man," which has been omitted in the A.V., is important. It stresses, firstly, the fact of His grace in becoming man, in order that through His death the gift of justification might be granted, and, secondly, the fact of His headship over the new race (the "many brethren" of 8:29; cp. 1 Cor. 15:45), in contrast to Adam's headship over the fallen race. "The many" again expresses the large number of those who actually partake of the effects of the death of Christ, and come thereby under His one headship.

5:16 And not as through one that sinned, so is the gift:—This introduces the second contrast and extends the first statement in verse 15. The contrast to the gift in this first part of verse 16 is the judgment by which condemnation was passed upon Adam and his descendants, as the latter part of the verse shows.

for the judgment came of one unto condemnation,—The word *krima*, "judgment," signifies judgment carried out (see 2:2; 3:3, 8). The "one" may be either masculine or neuter. The contrast presented in the remainder of the verse points to the neuter, that is to say, "one trespass." If "the one" is regarded as masculine, it must be taken with the preceding part of the verse, where "the one" speaks of Adam.

but the free gift *came* **of many trespasses unto justification.**—This second contrast is one of quality. Condemnation was passed as a result of one trespass; justification is declared in regard to many trespasses.

5:17 For if, by the trespass of the one, death reigned through the one;—This, which confirms verse 16, introduces a third contrast, not as previously between one and many, but between the legal effects of the one trespass and the effect of the abundance of grace in the future destiny of the justified.

much more shall they that receive the abundance of grace and of the gift of righteousness—This makes clear that only that part of the race which consists of believers, actually receives justification and life. The word "receive" bears stress. The limitation has a bearing on what follows. On the one hand sin and death are universal, on the other hand life is bestowed only upon those who receive grace.

reign in life through the one, *even* **Jesus Christ.**—The precise contrast to "death reigned" would have been "life shall reign," but the contrast is far greater than this. It is not that life reigns instead of death, but that those who receive grace will themselves reign in life. That we are to reign in life involves much more than participation in eternal life; it indicates the activity of life in fellowship with Christ in His kingdom.

5:18 So then as through one trespass *the judgment came* **unto all men to condemnation;**—The way has been opened in verses 13 to 17 for the resumption and completion of the comparison introduced in

verse 12. What has intervened leads to certain alterations in the first part of the comparison: "as through one trespass" is put instead of "as through one man," in view of what is said in verses 15–17; "condemnation" is put instead of "death," in view of what is said in verse 16, namely, "the judgment came of one unto condemnation."

even so through one act of righteousness—The R.V. rendering is important. The word *dikaiōma* is rightly rendered "act of righteousness." It refers to that which Christ accomplished at His death, and stands in contrast to *dikaiosunē*, righteousness simply as a quality. That the reference is to the death of Christ is clear from verses 8–10. Moreover, we are never said to be justified by the righteousness of Christ, but by the righteous act on the Cross. Some would take *dikaiōma* to mean a decree of righteousness, as in verse 16, but the meaning of "act of righteousness" stands in immediate contrast to the trespass of Adam.

the free gift came **unto all men to justification of life.**—The italicized words, "the free gift came," are necessary in the English Versions, and are rightly taken from verse 16. That the gift came unto all men must not be taken to mean that, as all men came under condemnation so all men become possessed of the free gift. The gift was free for all, but only those who accept it are justified. It was provisionally, but not actually, for all, but not all accept it. The universality of the expressions is not coextensive. Moreover, the apostle is not here bringing out the subjective side of justification, that is to say, the actual appropriation of the divine gift on the part of believers, with the effect of their justification, but the objective side, the provision made by God. The limitation in regard to those who believe and are thereby justified, is intimated in the change to "the many" in verse 19, where see note. The limitation is moreover enforced by the whole line of reasoning in the Epistle, which in this respect reaches its culmination in 8:30. The phrase "justification of life" signifies "justification which results in life."

5:19 For as through the one man's disobedience the many were made sinners,—The immediate purpose of verse 19 is to show the means by which the effects of God's grace were brought about, and to set forth the precise contrast to the effects of the one trespass. *Kathistēmi*, here rendered "were made," signifies "to set down," "to constitute," and so "to render," or "cause to be." This would seem to be the meaning here rather than that they were regarded or treated as sinners.

even so through the obedience of the one—Here again the reference is not to the life of Christ but to the culminating act of His obedience in His death on the cross, the same act as is described in verse 18 as "one act of righteousness." That is the means of justification (see 5:9). The description "act of righteousness" presents the legal aspect of the death of Christ. That it was an act of obedience presents its moral aspect.

Shall the many be made righteous.—As with reference to "all men," in the two parts of verse 18, so with regard to "the many," in the two parts of this verse, the company comprehended in the latter is not coextensive with that in the former. Because "the many" in the first part of the sentence embraces all mankind, we may not conclude that "the many" in the last part does so. The subject is here regarded from the point of view of the result, for evil or for good, of the acts of the heads of the representative companies, and the apostle is here speaking of the effect of these representative acts respectively of disobedience and obedience, upon those ranged under the two heads. The latter part of verse 18 presented the matter of the free gift as provisional. Here the actual effect is stated. Hence the change from "all men" to "the many"; it is said, "As all were made sinners, so all shall be made righteous."

Again, the word *kathistēmi*, "be made," denotes "constituted," as in some other places in the Epistle, does not merely signify futurity, as of something that is to take place hereafter, but rather the inevitable consequences,

viewed as resulting from a special act, here the death of Christ.

5:20 And the law came in beside,—The subject of the Law is now reintroduced that it may have its bearing upon the abundance of God's grace. The mention of the Law is thus to be connected with verse 13. It entered in addition to sin.

that the trespass might abound;—The Law does not make men sinners, for sin was already in the world, but it does make them transgressors. It not only multiplies the trespass numerically, it brings out the character of sin, causing it to be revealed in a form in which it could not be mistaken. The statement here is expanded in chapter seven. The Law was given that the trespass, as such, might be shown up in its true character.

but where sin abounded,—The change from *paraptōma*, "trespass," to *hamartia*, "sin," takes us back to the subject of sin as viewed in its general aspect. The change to the word "sin" is made with a view to what is to be said about sin in verse 21, as to its reign in death.

grace did abound more exceedingly:—The phrase "to abound more exceedingly" is a translation of the one verb *huperperisseuō*, a strengthened form of the simple verb *perisseuō*, which corresponds to *perisseia*, "abundance" (v. 17). Great stress is thereby laid upon the operation of grace. It has far surpassed the increase of sin (v. 21).

5:21 that, as sin reigned in death, even so might grace reign through righteousness unto eternal life through Jesus Christ our Lord.—Grace exercises its royal power in securing eternal life, life for the believer, and this is brought out "by means of" *(dia)* righteousness, that is to say, the exercise of God's righteousness in reckoning the believing sinner righteous on the ground of the death of Christ.

ROMANS

Life in Christ and Its Effect in Righteousness of Conduct, 6:1 to 8:39

Introductory Note

The apostle's aim in this chapter is to show the inconsistency of continuing in sin after being justified by grace. He makes clear that newness of life and continuance in sin are a contradiction of the new life in Christ. Chapter five constitutes the basis of the teaching of chapter six. Chapter five speaks of the means by which God has bestowed spiritual life, chapter six of how we are to live the life.

The leading theme of this chapter is identification with Christ; that is the very essence of the new life. While the keynote of chapter five is "through Christ," that of chapter six is "in Christ." The R.V. rendering "in," instead of "through," in verses 11 and 23 is to be noted. There we should read, not "through Jesus Christ" as in chapter five, but "in Christ Jesus." In the fifth chapter the order of the titles is suggestive of the fact that the one who here accomplished our redemption through His death, is now in exaltation and glory. Here in chapter six the order is reversed throughout. "In Christ" (vv. 3, 11, 23) suggests that we are in union of life with Him in the glory, on the ground of what He accomplished on the cross.

Chapter six has another keynote, namely, "unto God." That expresses how the new life is to be lived (see vv. 10, 11, 13, 22). Hence a suitable heading to chapter six is "In Christ unto God." The immediate basis of the subject of chapter six regarding life in Christ is to be found in the closing verses of chapter five.

6:1 What shall we say then? Shall we continue in sin,—*Epimenō*, "to continue," is a strengthened form of *meno*, "to abide" (it is incorrect to stress the literal meaning of *epi*, as if it meant "upon"; it simply intensifies the verb), and indicates persistence in what is referred to.

that grace may abound?—The question is whether we are to endeavor to further God's designs of grace by continuance in sin, on the ground that such continuance will only enhance His superabounding grace in our justification.

6:2 God forbid. We who died to sin, how shall we any longer live therein?—There is special stress on the pronoun "We," and indeed on the whole clause, which gives a description characteristic of believers, and intimates at once the preposterousness of continuing in sin. The reference is to a definite occasion in our past, namely, when through faith in Christ we passed from death unto life. Death to sin liberates for a new life, involves separation from, and discontinuance of relation to, sin. As material objects do not affect the dead physical body, so spiritually a believer is to consider himself as having entered into a corresponding spiritual state with regard to sin.

6:3 Or are ye ignorant that all we who were baptized—Not singling out some believers from others, but implying what was recognized as true of all. The word *baptizo* was necessarily transliterated into English, as there was no equivalent in our language. "To immerse" would be simply "to plunge into." To baptize is to put into water and take out again. It involves immersion, submersion, and emergence—death, burial and resurrection. The word was used among the heathen Greeks of articles which underwent submersion and emergence, as in the case of the dyeing of a garment.

into Christ Jesus—Spiritually the first moment of faith in Christ is the moment of resurrection. There and then the believer passes out of death into Christ. This is followed in experience by the ordinance of baptism. In Galatians 3:27 the phrase is "baptized into Christ." Here the double title is used, suggesting that the believer is baptized unto Him as the exalted and glorified one (Christ) who came forth for our salvation (Jesus). It stresses therefore the fact that baptism is into Christ, the living one, on the ground of His death.

were baptized into His death?—He not only died vicariously as the Bearer of sin's penalty, He also died to set us free from the old power that had enslaved us. In this respect the believer is identified with Him, and is legally to be regarded as having died to sin.

6:4 We were buried therefore with Him through baptism into death:—This statement alone makes clear the Scriptural mode of baptism. Burial is the natural consequence of death and the attestation of its fact. The words "into death" go with the word "baptism" rather than with "we were buried." This connection is confirmed by the close of verse 3, which states that we were baptized into His death. The article in the original before the word "death" is not to be translated, as death is used in its abstract sense here, though the reference is to the death of Christ.

A person must have life in Christ in order to realize his death with Christ, and his identification with Christ in His resurrection; that is what the teaching of chapter six specially stresses. Ideally, spiritual life in Christ, which is imparted on the ground of faith, and death to the former state, are simultaneous, but in baptism it is one who has life in Christ who expresses his identification with Him figuratively in the threefold way of death, burial and resurrection.

that like as Christ was raised from the dead through the glory of the Father,—The resurrection of Christ is most frequently mentioned as the act of God the Father (as, e.g., Acts 2:24, 32; 3:26; 10:40; 13:30; 2 Cor. 4:14; Eph. 1:20; Col. 2:12; 1 Pet. 1:21; see also Rom. 8:11; 10:9; for the word *egeirō*, used here, see notes on 4:24). The same word is used by Christ Himself (with reference to His resurrection as His act) when speaking to the Jews of His body as a temple, which, while they would destroy it, He would raise up in three days (John 2:19; cp. also 10:17, 18). This fact makes clear the absolute oneness of the Son with the Father. The word *doxa*, "glory," stands here for the excellence of God's almighty power as manifested in the res-

urrection of Christ. "The glory of the Father" involves a reference to Christ as His Son.

so we also might walk in newness of life.—This states both our identification with Christ in His resurrection and the effects thereof in our life in Christ. The word *kainotes,* "newness," is from *kainos,* new in quality, which is to be distinguished from *neos,* new in time.

6:5 For if we have become united with *Him* **by the likeness of His death,**—This phrase gives a confirmation of what has just been stated in verse 4. The word *sumphutos,* "united together" is found here only in the New Testament. It literally means "planted together," (from *sun,* "with," and *phuō,* "to bring forth," "beget," "grow"). Hence its second meaning "to be united together with." The R.V. is right in supplying "Him" here; for the point of the whole passage is our identification with Christ.

we shall be also—This does not merely refer to the future, though the future is included, but expresses rather the inevitable consequence, both now and hereafter, of our identification with Christ in His death. This is confirmed in verses 6, 7.

by the likeness **of His resurrection;**—As His resurrection was the assured sequence of His death, so our union with Him in resurrection is the inevitable sequence of our having died with Him. The phrase rendered "by the likeness of" goes, in the original, both with "His death" and "His resurrection." The "newness of life" in verse 4 is expressed now in the phrase "the likeness of His resurrection."

6:6 knowing this, that our old man—That is, our former self, what we were before we were in Christ.

was crucified with *Him,*—Christ in His crucifixion was judicially dealt with as to the question of sin. He who believes on Christ acknowledges God's judgment against sin to be righteous, and accepts the death of Christ as the execution of that judgment upon his "old man."

that the body of sin—The word *sōma* denotes the body as the organic instrument of natural life; it is here used figuratively with that as its essential significance (see also 7:24; 1 Cor. 12:12; Eph. 1:23, etc.). In the phrase "the body of sin," then, sin is regarded as an organized power, acting through the members of the body, though the seat of sin is in the will.

might be done away,—For the word *katargeō*, "to render inactive," see notes at 3:3, 31. That the body is to be rendered inactive as the instrument of sin, is the effect of the believer's death with Christ.

that so we should no longer be in bondage to sin;—*Douloō* signifies to fulfill the duties of a slave, for whom there was no choice either as to the kind or length of his service. Crucifixion would bring an end to all that, rendering the body useless for the purpose of sin, and this is how the believer is to regard his body in the matter of sin.

6:7 for he that hath died is justified from sin.—That is, in the legal sense. There is no legitimate method of terminating sin's claims except by death. Death both snaps all bonds and annuls all obligations. The statement of this verse covers the whole of the preceding argument and does not apply merely to the figure of bondage as just mentioned. The special reference is to the subject of crucifixion, the death penalty which Christ endured. Our identification with Christ, as the One who endured the penalty for us, removes the legal sentence from us and thereby delivers us from a condition of bondage to sin. There is both the removal of the penalty and the deliverance from the power. A corpse can neither be punished nor can it become subservient to the will of another.

6:8 But if we died with Christ, we believe that we shall also live with Him;—This again, as in verse 5, is not a matter of mere futurity, but the inevitable result of our having died with Christ. There can be no other consequence of this, than that we live with Him now, and shall do so forever. This is confirmed in the next verses. Life with Christ, upon which the believer enters when he is born of God, never ceases. Its continuance rests not upon our efforts any more than salvation by grace does.

6:9 knowing that Christ being raised from the dead dieth no more;—His voluntary submission to the power of death is a thing of the past forever. His resurrection, being the abiding seal of the work He accomplished in His death, is the guarantee of the resurrection life of those who are His.

death no more hath dominion over Him.—*Kurieuō* signifies to have the power of a lord *(kurios)* over another. The word is used again in this Epistle in 6:14; 7:1; 14:9. To this power of death Christ voluntarily submitted Himself. This second statement of the verse is made for the sake of emphasis, and in it the word "Him" is emphatic.

6:10 For the death that He died, He died unto sin—In His death he had to do with sin. As the sinless One who had refused all the claims of sin, He could stand forth as our representative and render up His life—not forfeited like ours, but free—to set us free. The prominent thought in the statement here is separation.

once:—*Ephapax*, "once for all," once and completely, to be distinguished from *pote*, "once upon a time." It is a strengthened form of *hapax*, which has the same significance, "once for all," and is used with reference to the death of Christ in Hebrews 9:26, 28; 1 Peter 3:18. The word in this respect marks the absolute sufficiency and finality of the death of Christ for all the purposes for which He died.

but the life that He liveth,—This phrase suggests all that is involved in His life, its fullness and power.

He liveth unto God.—The contrast between this and the death that He died is in the matter of relation to sin. He has nothing more to do with that. His life as being "unto God" makes good the effects of His sacrifice in the case of those who believe on him.

6:11 Even so reckon ye also yourselves—Since what we are to reckon is a matter of Divine revelation to us, it is necessarily likewise a matter of faith on our part, governing our conscience and will. There is stress on the word "ye."

to be dead unto sin,—This should be expressed more fully, as in the original, "to be dead indeed" (i.e., on the one hand) unto sin. The work *nekros*, "dead," describes a permanent state and here signifies the spiritual condition of believers in relation to sin. The condition is not merely that of freedom from the penalty, it constitutes the believer's whole attitude toward sin. Whenever the old master claims our service, we are to reckon ourselves corpses.

but alive unto God in Christ Jesus.—The phrase "in Christ Jesus" should be noted (in contrast to the incorrect rendering "through" in the A.V.; *en* is not "through" but "in"). It expresses here the believer's spiritual and eternal position in his identification with Christ. This verse sums up the whole of the first section of this chapter, bringing to bear upon us all that has been set forth by way of baptism with its threefold significance, and all as an argument against the preposterous idea of continuing in sin.

6:12 Let not sin therefore reign in your mortal body,—It is now mentioned as mortal, not simply because it is liable to death, but because it is the organ in and through which sin carries on its death-producing activities.

that ye should obey the lusts thereof:—*Epithumia*, usually rendered "lust," signifies desire of whatever character. It is used of a good desire only in Luke 22:15 and Philippians 1:3. Everywhere else it has a bad sense, and here refers to those evil desires which are ready to express themselves in bodily activity. They are equally "the desires of the flesh" (Gal. 5:16, 24; and Eph. 2:3), a phrase which describes the inner emotions of the soul, the natural tendency toward things evil. Such lusts are not necessarily base and immoral; they may be refined in character, but are evil if inconsistent with the will of God.

6:13 neither present your members unto sin—"Present" is in the continuous sense, indicating the normal condition of the unregenerate state. *Paristēmi* signifies "to put a thing at the disposal of another," and so voluntarily to present (see further at 12:2). The word "members" is virtually equivalent to "the body" but expresses the differing powers of the bodily organs.

as **instruments of unrighteousness;**—*Hoplon* is, primarily, an "implement," and more generally was used to denote a military weapon. Here the military metaphor is not necessarily to be pressed. Unrighteousness is personified as a power which can make use of our bodily members for the purpose of sin.

but present yourselves unto God,—The tense is now changed from the present to the aorist, indicating an act carried out with definite decision and abiding results. The whole being is thus to be presented.

as alive from the dead,—Literally, "as living (ones) from dead (ones)." Both words bear stress. The meaning is, "as those who no longer are destitute of spiritual life, dead through trespasses and sins, but as those who have been spiritually raised into life in Christ."

and your members as **instruments of righteousness unto God.**—*Dikaiosunē*, "righteousness," here stands for right action, as in the remaining four occurrences of the word in this chapter. God is to have the complete use of all that we are and have.

6:14 For sin shall not have dominion over you:—This is set in contrast to the words "unto God." The statement is not a command or an exhortation, but a promise.

for ye are not under law, but under grace.—The absence of the article before "law" shows that it here stands for law as a principle.

6:15 What then? shall we sin, because we are not under law, but under grace? God forbid.—This recalls the question in verse 1, and introduces an answer based upon the teaching in verses 2-14. There is a natural tendency to feel that sin can be committed with impunity because of the dominion of grace. We need to guard against the idea that we can sin without fear or restraint. Such laxity can result only in turning the grace of God into lasciviousness (Jude 4).

6:16 Know ye not, that to whom ye present yourselves as **servants unto obedience,**—For the word "present" see verse 13. The word rendered "servant" is *doulos* (as in 1:1). Obedience is the certain effect of the presentation. The word is not a verb, as in the A.V.

his servants ye are whom ye obey;—"No man can serve two masters," with stress upon the word "masters" (Matt. 6:24). Here stress is upon the word "servants." The slave is the property exclusively of his master.

whether of sin unto death,—Sin is personified. The effect of such mastery is death (cp. 5:12, 17, 21). Death here signifies the death of both body and soul.

or of obedience unto righteousness?—Obedience is personified as the alternative master, in the former part of the verse obedience was the effect and was not personified. The effect of service to obedience is righteousness. *Dikaiosunē* is not here "justification," for that is the outcome of faith on the ground of the sacrifice of Christ, righteousness is here right conduct.

6:17 but thanks be to God, that, whereas ye were servants of sin,—The special stress in the original, on "ye were" necessitates the addition of the word "whereas" in English, so as to introduce and emphasize the necessary contrast between the former state of the readers and that of their new life as believers. The apostle's gratitude to God lies in that their former condition is a thing of the past. The contrast expresses the absolute incompatibility of living in sin on the part of the believer.

ye became obedient—Literally, "ye obeyed," aorist or past definite tense, pointing to the time when they believed the gospel and indicating it as an act of decision leading to permanent results.

from the heart—Expressive of the voluntary and earnest character of their acceptance of the truth.

to that form of teaching whereunto ye were delivered;—*Tupos,* "a form" (Eng. "type"), is here used metaphorically of a cast, or frame, into which molten material is poured, so as to take its shape. The believers themselves are likened to the molten material and the truths of the gospel are the mold. To become obedient to it is to be conformed to Christ through its teachings. The Word of God

not only brings deliverance from all our former state, but shapes our character. We were delivered from bondservice to sin and handed over to the truth, that it might accomplish the Divine purposes in us.

6:18 and being made free from sin,—Literally, "being freed," continuing the metaphor of bondservice.

ye became servants of righteousness.—"Ye became servants" translates a single form of the verb in the passive voice and might be rendered "ye were made servants." The change of masters was not their own act; it was consequent upon faith on their part. The power of God wrought the change.

6:19 I speak after the manner of men—Literally, "I speak humanly"; that is, he adopts common phraseology, referring to his figurative use of terms of slavery.

because of the infirmity of your flesh:—The word "flesh" stands here for the weaker element in human nature. The meaning of "infirmity" is to be gathered from what is next stated in the verse; considering their manner of life in their unregenerate state, there would be a tendency to yield to its influence and not to apprehend what was involved in the change to the new service into which they had been brought.

for as ye presented your members *as* **servants to uncleanness and to iniquity**—Sin, which was spoken of as unrighteousness, is now regarded in the two aspects of impurity and iniquity (lit., "lawlessness"). The former defiles the being, the latter violates the law of God. *Anomia,* "lawlessness," signifies, not merely the abstract idea, but disregard for, or actual breach of, the law of God. In 1 John 3:4 lawlessness is stated as a definition of sin (see end of verse, R.V.).

unto iniquity,—This may express either a purpose, "with a view to a course of lawlessness," or the effect, "with the result of a course of lawlessness." The phrase in verse 22, "your fruit unto holiness," would point to effect as the meaning here. Sin has a power of development; it goes beyond the primary intentions of those who give themselves to it.

even so now present your members *as* servants to righteousness unto sanctification.—*Hagiasmos* signifies (1) separation to God, as in 1 Corinthians 1:30; 2 Thessalonians 2:13; 1 Peter 1:2; (2) the course of life which benefits those who have been separated to God. This is its meaning here and in verse 22. Sanctification is a state which God has predetermined for believers, and is the state into which in grace He calls them and in which they begin their course as believers. On this account they are called saints, *hagioi,* "sanctified ones." Whereas formerly their behavior bore witness to their standing in the world in separation from God, now their behavior should bear witness to their standing before God in separation from the world.

As there are no degrees of justification, so there are no degrees of sanctification; a thing is set apart for God, or it is not, there is no middle course; a person is either in Christ Jesus, justified and sanctified, or he is out of Christ, in his sins and alienated from God. But while there are no degrees of sanctification, it is evident there can and should be progress therein; hence the believer is urged to "follow after . . . sanctification" and is warned that without it "no man shall see the Lord," Hebrews 12:14.

6:20 For when ye were servants of sin, ye were free in regard of righteousness.—Literally, "free to righteousness"; that is to say, righteousness laid no sort of bond upon them, they had no relation to it in any way.

6:21 What fruit then had ye at that time in the things whereof ye are now ashamed?—Some would punctuate as follows: "What fruit then had ye at that time? Of which things ye are now ashamed." This is possible as a rendering, but that given under the text is preferable and is confirmed by the strong contrast between "at that time" and "now."

for the end of those things is death.—*Telos,* "end," marks the limit, either at which

a thing ceases to be what it was up to that point, or at which it ceases its activities hitherto, or expresses the final issue or result of a condition or process. Here the word is used not merely of physical death but in its most comprehensive sense.

6:22 But now being made free from sin, and become servants to God,—The phrase "become servants" represents the verb *douloō,* as in verse 18.

ye have your fruit unto sanctification,—For *hagiasmos* see note on verse 19.

and the end eternal life.—The "end" is here, again, the issue of present experience (see note above). The future is in view, when the believer will be with the Lord. The word *aiōnios,* "eternal," which is derived from the noun *aiōn,* "age," a period of undefined duration, is used here, as in most of its occurrences in the New Testament, to signify that which is undefined because endless. It is used of the resurrection body of the believer (see 2 Cor. 5:1), which is also said to be "immortal" (1 Cor. 15:53).

6:23 For the wages of sin is death;—This verse expresses in general terms the subject which has been dealt with in the preceding passage. The former metaphor of unpaid slavery, expressed in the word "bondservants," is changed to that of service that is paid for, thus intimating that sin deserves death which is sin's just wages. Both figures of speech depict the disastrous nature of sin.

but the free gift of God is eternal life—Not a mere prolongation of existence, any more than that death is a cessation of existence. Death, as the wages of sin, is a change of state involving separation from God; eternal life is the enjoyment of activity in communion with God.

in Christ Jesus our Lord.—Not "through" as in the A.V (see note on verse 11). That was the key word in chapter five (see 5:11, 21).

ROMANS

The New Life in Christ in Relation to the Law, 7:1–13

Introductory Note

To understand the seventh chapter it must be read as a development of the teaching of the fifth and sixth, and further as introductory to the eighth. The fifth chapter showed what grace has wrought in bringing us into justification and life. The sixth defended this new position against the presumptuous argument as to the possibility of continuing in sin, and showed that, as we are under grace and not under law, our newness of life both demands service to God and empowers us to render it. The seventh chapter proves the truth of this position, first making clear, by an illustration from nature, how it is that we have been set free from the Law (vv. 1–6). The latter part of this chapter guards against the idea that our freedom from the Law argued a defect in it. The passage, on the contrary, vindicates its authority.

7:1 Or are ye ignorant, brethren—The connecting conjunction shows how closely this chapter is joined to the last. The opening words are to be taken especially in connection with 6:14. The alternative introduced is this, either let them acknowledge the truth that they are no longer under the Law, with all that that freedom involves, or they must be ignorant of the very nature of law.

(for I speak to men that know the law),—There is no article in the original before the word "law," and this points to law as a principle. The passage does refer to the Law of Moses. At the same time the apostle is speaking of those who, whether Jews or Gentiles by birth, were acquainted with the principles of law, and so were familiar with what is conveyed in the following statement.

how that the law hath dominion over a man for so long time as he liveth? The phrase "for so long time as he liveth" lays stress upon the permanent claim of the law up to the time of death.

7:2 For the woman that hath a husband is bound by law to the husband while he liveth;—The word *hupandros*, rendered "that hath a husband," literally signifies "under (i.e., subject to) a man." It occurs here only in the New Testament. The phrase "to the husband while he liveth" is, literally, "to the living husband." That the authority of law is binding as long as life lasts, is strikingly illustrated by the law of marriage.

but if the husband die, she is discharged from the law of the husband.—The word rendered "is discharged" is *katargeō*, to make ineffective (See at 3:3, 31; 4:14 and 6:6). The tense is the perfect, literally, "she has been discharged."

The phrase "the law of the husband" means the law concerning the husband (cp. "the law of the leper," Lev. 14:2; "the law of the Nazarite," Num. 6:13). The basis of this law is the primary institution given in Eden (Gen. 2:24); its legal enactment is the seventh commandment (Ex. 20:14). For the connected regulations see Leviticus 18:20; Deuteronomy 24:1, 4; Matthew 5:27–32. The death of a woman's first husband makes void her status as a wife in the eyes of the Law.

7:3 So then if, while the husband liveth, she be joined to another man, she shall be called an adulteress: but if the husband die, she is free from the law, so that she is no adulteress, though she be joined to another man.—The phrase rendered "so that she is" can be alternatively rendered "so that she may be," as expressive of the purpose of the freedom consequent upon the husband's death. This would be especially consistent with the analogy in what follows. Perhaps, however, so far as verse 3 itself is concerned, the preference is to be given to the text.

7:4 Wherefore, my brethren, ye also were made dead to the law through the

body of Christ;—The body of Christ is that which was nailed to the tree, in sacrifice for our sins. It stands here as the physical instrument of His death. For the purpose of His death and for our sakes He partook of flesh and blood, thus assuming a body and identifying Himself with man in the constituent elements of manhood (Heb. 2:14). The word "body" is used instead of "death," with this especially in view and as appropriate to the analogy here drawn. By the death of Christ believers were made dead, literally, "were put to death," to the Law, as that under which they were held as bondservants.

that we should be joined to another,—The literal rendering is "that we should become for another," a phrase used in reference to marriage in the LXX of Leviticus 22:12, 13; Ruth 1:12; Ezekiel 23:4. Hence the union of the believer with Christ may be regarded figuratively in this way in continuation of what was set forth in verse 3. The spiritual application to the believer in verse 4 runs parallel to the illustration in verse 3, with one exception. In spiritual experience the three conditions are: (1) the union between the Law and the person as he was in the flesh; (2) the death of the latter "through the body of Christ," dissolving that union; (3) the new union of the person with Christ.

To put it more fully, and to note the exception in the analogy: (1) parallel to the union between the first husband and the wife is the union between the Law and our old self; (2) parallel in idea, but in point of fact in contrast, to the death of the first husband, is the death of our former self. The contrast lies in this, that in the illustration the husband lies, in the application the latter remains, but our former self died; (3) parallel to the marriage between the wife and the second husband is the union between the believer and Christ. Some take the first husband to be our old nature, "the old man," to which as long as it was alive we were bound under the Law, just as the wife is bound to her husband by law. But this explanation, while it may seem simpler, is hardly consistent with the sixth verse, which says that we have died "to that in which we were holden," that is to say, the Law. The R.V. "having died" gives the correct rendering, as the Law does not die.

even **to Him who was raised from the dead, that we might bring forth fruit unto God.**—This recalls 6:4, 5, 9. The resurrection of Christ is stressed here, firstly, to set it in contrast to the reference to His death in the first part of the verse, "the body of Christ"; secondly, to confirm the fact that the believer is united by faith to the living and life-imparting Son of God.

7:5 For when we were in the flesh,—"The flesh," *sarx,* stands here for the unregenerate state of man (see again at 8:8, 9). The clause is just another way of saying "when we were united to the Law."

the sinful passions,—Literally, "passions of sins"; *pathēma* has two distinct meanings, (1) a suffering, or affliction, (2) a passion, affection, emotion; the latter is the meaning here, and in Galatians 5:24.

which were through the law,—When we were in the flesh, the Law served, by its prohibitions and commandments, to kindle inward desires to do the very things that were forbidden (see vv. 7, 8.)

wrought in our members to bring forth fruit unto death.—The members are those of our body, as in 6:13, 19. "To bring forth fruit" expresses the result of the excitement of passions of sin by the Law, the effect being to swell the garners of death.

7:6 But now we have been discharged from the law,—*Katargeō,* the same word as that in verse 2.

having died to that wherein we were holden;—This is the accurate rendering, not, "that being dead," as in the A.V., speaking of the Law, it is not the Law that has died but the believer, who has been made dead to the claims of the Law through the body of Christ, in contrast to, and yet parallel with, the woman in verse 3.

so that we serve—The metaphor changes from that of marriage to that of service again, as in 6:22.

in newness of the spirit,—While "newness of spirit" may stand for the new state or the new life of the believer, as in 8:4, yet it is impossible to dissociate this from the Holy

Spirit, by whose power the believer renders his service.

and not in oldness of the letter.—"The letter," *gramma,* here stands for the Law with its external rules of conduct, mere outward conformity to which has yielded place, in the believer's service, to a response to the operation of the Holy Spirit (cp. 2 Cor. 3:3, 6).

7:7 What shall we say then? Is the Law sin?—That is to say, can it be that, as the sinful passions were through the Law (v. 5), the Law is itself a principle of sin? In other words, is the Law evil? For this use of the word "sin" compare Micah 1:5.

God forbid. Howbeit,—This is the correct rendering, instead of the A.V. "Nay"; for it introduces, as a contrast, after the denial that the Law is sin, the fact that the Law was the means of making sin known.

I had not known sin, except through the law:—While the apostle uses the first person singular, he refers to his own experience, not simply in a rhetorical manner, nor as representing an ideal conflict, but as typical of what is common to all believers.

for I had not known coveting,—*Oida,* in contrast to *ginōskō* above, suggests a knowledge gained by intuition.

except the law had said, Thou shalt not covet:—The tenth commandment is quoted here, not as a sample of what the Law says, but as containing a principle involved in all the rest. The very prohibition stirred up the desire to do the wrong thing. The commandment not only made known the evil as such, but also revealed its evil source within.

7:8 but sin, finding occasion,—Sin is here viewed as the corrupt source of action, an inward element producing acts. The word *aphormē* was frequently used to denote a "base of operations" in war. The commandment, then, provided sin with a base of operations, an attack upon the soul.

wrought in me through the commandment all manner of coveting:—The aorist tense does not here express one act of crisis, but serves to give definiteness to all the past action of the principle of sin. The phrase

"through the commandment" goes with the verb "wrought," as in the R.V.

for apart from the law sin *is* dead.—Not that a person is sinless without the Law, what is conveyed is that sin as a principle is not roused to activity. Such a state of powerlessness is here suggested by the term "dead." Without a commandment the sinfulness of sin is not realized.

7:9 And I was alive apart from the law once:—There is stress on the pronoun "I," and this stands in contrast to "sin" as mentioned in verse 8 (see also v. 20). "I was alive" translates the imperfect tense of the verb "to live," and refers to a continuous experience in the past. The condition referred to is that of freedom from a disturbing conscience, a condition of supposed happiness through the absence of a realization of alienation from God.

but when the commandment came,—That is to say, when it presented itself to conscience and so broke in upon the fancied state of freedom, imposing its restriction upon the natural tendencies.

sin revived,—Literally, lived, came to life again; it sprang into activity, manifesting all the evil inherent in it.

and I died;—That is to say, "became conscious of the sinfulness of sin and realized that I was in a state of separation from God." Separation is the essential feature of death; physical death is the separation of the soul from the body; spiritual death is the separation of the spirit from God. This condition of alienation from God involved the absence of any ability to work righteousness and the realization of condemnation and doom.

7:10 and the commandment which *was* unto life,—It promised life as a reward for obedience. For the commandment was given by the author of life, who said "this do and thou shalt live." Life, as here mentioned, is not merely a principle of activity, it is first and essentially life as God has it, and as the Son of God manifested it. From that man became alienated through the Fall (Eph. 4:18). Inseparable from that life are its moral associations of holiness and righteousness.

this I found *to be* unto death:—This explains what has been said in verses 8, 9. This was the actual effect of the commandment in the experience mentioned. The former imagined state of happiness had given place to a realization of the actual condition in the sight of God.

7:11 for sin, finding occasion, through the commandment beguiled me, and through it slew me.—This runs parallel to verse 8, but contains greater detail. In the original the order is altered. There the first and emphatic word was "occasion"; here it is "sin." On the other hand, just as in verse 8 the phrase "through the commandment" goes with the word "wrought," so here the same phrase goes with the word "beguiled." The verb *exapatao* is an intensive form of *apataō*, "to deceive." There is evidently a reference here to Genesis 3:13, and this is borne out by the use of the two verbs in 1 Timothy 2:14, where they may be distinguished by paraphrasing thus: "Adam was not beguiled, but the woman being thoroughly beguiled," etc. So what is said in Genesis 3, of Satan, is here said of sin.

7:12 So that the law is holy,—It partakes of the nature and character of God Himself, for it exposes the true character of sin.

and the commandment—viewing the Law in its detail.

holy, and righteous, and good,—This expresses, in a threefold way and with vivid descriptiveness, the character of the Law in its specific commandments. Besides being holy, it reveals the righteous character of the Lawgiver. Thirdly, it is good, *agathos*, not simply that which is intrinsically good *(kalos)*, but that which is also beneficial in its effect. All three words express the character of Him whose commandment it is.

7:13 Did then that which is good become death unto me?—God forbid. But sin, that it might be shewn to be sin,—That is to say, "but sin became death unto me, etc." The purpose was that sin might be exposed in all its heinous character.

by working death to me through that which is good; that through the commandment sin might become exceeding

sinful.—This is the third occurrence of the phrase, "through the commandment" in this passage, the fifth if we include the phrase "through the Law" or "through law," in verses 5-7; now the phrase is thrown into a position of great emphasis. What was wrought by sin was the working of a divine purpose by the Law in the manifestation, to the human conscience, of the true nature of sin and its effects, the indication being given, at the same time, of the perfect character of the Law, the very holiness of which was instrumental in bringing about the purpose intended.

The Inability of the Law to Deliver from Sin, 7:14-25

Introductory Note

The apostle speaks of his own experiences. This he does, not as in distinction from those of other believers, but as representing what is common to all believers. Again, his main subject is not that of the conflict between the old nature and the new; he is showing the impossibility of fulfilling the Law by self-effort and so escaping its condemnation. He gives these experiences as a warning that, if a person puts himself under the Law, he will only find how fearful is the power of sin within him.

It is not a case of Paul's speaking of himself as he was in his unregenerate condition, nor of his speaking of some particular phase in his Christian life. He is giving a vivid description of the character and energy of sin in relationship to the Law, so that he may lead up to a statement as to the power of Christ to deliver (v. 25), and the power of the Holy Spirit to enable the believer to mind the things of the spirit and to mortify the deeds of the body (8:1-13).

This section consists of three parts: (a) verses 14-17, here he shows his inability to keep himself from doing what he disapproves of; (b) verses 18-20, here he shows his inability to carry out that which he approves of; (c) verses 21-25, finally, bringing his discussion to its appointed conclusion, he shows how deliverance from this condition is to be effected.

7:14 For we know that the law is spiritual:—There are two ideas essentially connected with this word, *pneumatikos*, those of invisibility and power. It is said of that which owes its origin to God and is therefore in harmony with His character. Here the word "spiritual" sums up the three qualities, holy, righteous, and good, in verse 12.

but I am carnal,—*Sarkikos* is "fleshly," in the ethical sense, in contrast to *sarkinos*, which is "fleshly" in the material sense, *i.e.*, consisting of flesh. It is said of human nature rather than character. It suggests that one who is under the Law is dominated by the weaker element in nature, in contrast to the spiritual, which finds its origin and source in God, and is in affinity with God.

sold under sin.—That is to say, as fully under the domination of sin as a slave is under his master. What is expressed is not the condemnation of the unregenerate state, but the evil of bondage to a corrupt nature, and the futility of making use of the Law as a means of deliverance.

7:15 For that which I do I know not:—The verb rendered "know" is *ginōskō*, to recognize as a result of experience. This is the result of being like a slave, who is the instrument of another man's will. He does not discern the true character and effects of what has been wrought.

for not what I would, that do I practice;—This is the true order and emphasizes the clauses in a way which the A.V. rendering fails to bring out. "Practice" (not "do" as in the A.V.) expresses the constant activity which operates in the working out just mentioned.

but what I hate, that I do.—The word now rendered "do" is *poieō*, which, while it still describes a habit, differs from the preceding word *prassō* in this, that *prassō* implies that the practice has a conscious aim in view, while *poieō* simply describes a series of acts which may be void of such conscious aim and be merely mechanical. Such language as is contained in this verse, and in the passage as a whole, represents an experience possible in the case of any believer in a time of spiritual conflict, in a struggle against adverse moral and spiritual influences.

7:16 But if what I would not, that I do, I consent unto the law that it is good.—

Kalos signifies the moral excellence of the Law. This verse again points to the experience of a believer. He finds himself in agreement with the Law by his disapproval of that which is forbidden by it. That he acts contrary to it is no evidence that he has a bad opinion of it. The conflict is not between the Law and the believer, it is between the believer and what the Law condemns.

7:17 So now—The "now" means "this being the case." It is not here an expression of time.

it is no more I that do it, but sin which dwelleth in me.—The "I" is again emphatic. It expresses the true self. "Do" is here *katergazomai*, as in verse 15. As with the "now," the "no more" is not an expression of time, but of argument, as if to say "it can no longer be maintained that . . ." There is great stress on the word "sin." This verse provides no ground of excuse on the part of anyone for sinning, as if it was not the person who did it but the responsibility lay upon an inward principle. That is not the apostle's meaning at all. Moreover, it runs contrary to his whole line of argument, which represents the believer as in a struggle under the realization of the sinfulness of sin as evoked by the Law and as one who disapproves of the act.

7:18 For I know that in me, that is, in my flesh,—The flesh is here the weaker element in human nature, as in 6:19, and stands for such nature considered as the man himself apart from Divine influence.

dwelleth no good thing:—There is stress on the word "good." Whatever may be considered good from the purely natural point of view, is in reality void of that quality in the absence of right relationship with God. The statement affords a further proof of the fact of indwelling sin. "Good" here is *agathos*, see 5:17.

for to will is present with me, but to do that which is good *is* **not.**—*Katergazomai* as in verse 16. "Good" here is *kalos*.

7:19 For the good which I would I do not:—*Poieō*, as in verses 15, 16. This verse is similar to verse 15, with this difference, that in verse 15 the contrast is between good desire and bad act, here it is between good desire and failure to act.

but the evil which I would not, that I practice.—As with the word "good" in the preceding sentence, so here the word "evil" is marked by emphasis.

7:20 But if what I would not, that I do, it is no more I that do it, but sin which dwelleth in me.—Compare and contrast verses 16 and 17. Here again the pronoun. "I" bears stress. The first "do" is *poieō*; the second "do" is *katergazomai,* corresponding to the order of the verbs in verses 15 and 16.

7:21 I find then the law, that, to me who would do good, evil is present.—The law which he now mentions is probably to be understood as a controlling principle defined by the statement which follows. Possibly, however, "the law" refers to the Mosaic Law, and this may be supported by the fact that the conjunction "that" comes, in the original, after "to me who would do good," and before the clause "evil is present." On the whole the preference is to be given to the former meaning.

7:22 For I delight in the law of God after the inward man:—This expression approximates to "the mind," as mentioned in the next verse. The law of the mind guides the inward man, i.e., the inner self of the believer, as approving of the law of God.

7:23 but I see a different law in my members,—This is a principle by which evil is present despite the desire to do good. It is the same as the law of sin, in the latter part of the verse.

warring against the law of my mind,—This corresponds to that delight in the law of God mentioned in verse 22. The *nous,* "mind," stands for the new nature which belongs to the believer, in virtue of new birth. It stands in contrast to the flesh.

and bringing me into captivity under the law of sin which is in my members.—This is the "different law" of verse 23. It is set in opposition to the law of God: two opposing

masters, each with a law. For the word *melos,* "member," see verse 5. There are three different laws mentioned in verses 21–23, corresponding respectively to the three subjects mentioned in verses 14–20; these were (1) the law of God, the man struggling under the law, (2) the law of the mind, i.e., of the man who intellectually consents to the law of God, (3) the law of sin, a principle of evil, keeping the will captive.

7:24 O wretched man that I am!—Literally, "miserable I!" This expression introduces a consummation of the leading thought in the whole chapter, namely the still imperfect condition of the believer in his conflict with sin.

who shall deliver me out of the body of this death?—For *ek,* out of, see preceding note. The body is the physical body, the instrument of sin, which produces death, a slave shackle, by which sin brings one into death See note on 6:6.

7:25 I thank God through Jesus Christ our Lord.—That is to say, "I thank God that deliverance will come through Jesus Christ our Lord." This will take place when the Lord returns. Then the body will be redeemed. The apostle is anticipating, not death, but the Lord's return. This expression of thanks foreshadows the references to His Second Coming in chapter eight.

So then I myself—Here the apostle, speaking as before, as a representative believer, sums up in the concluding statement his line of argument, going back to present experiences from future anticipation as just expressed in his thanks to God.

with the mind serve the law of God; but with the flesh the law of sin.—For notes on the mind, and the law of God, and the law of sin, see on verses 22, 23. In this verse the phrases "the Law of God" and "the law of sin" are, in the original, without the definite article, and this has the effect of stressing the nature of each law, the first law as that which was given by God, the second law, as a principle of evil acting with the authority of sin.

ROMANS

CHAPTER EIGHT

Life in Christ in Relation to the Spirit, 8:1–39

The Spirit as the Means of Life and the Power for Righteousness, 8:1–11

Introductory Note

In this chapter the apostle continues the central theme of his Epistle, regarding life in Christ. In chapter five he showed the basis of this life; in chapter six its practical effect Godward; in chapter seven the inability of the Law to effect the deliverance necessary for its fullness. In chapter eight he shows (a) the character of this new life under the operation of the Spirit of God, and (b) the future issues, all exhibiting the effects of deliverance from the power of the Law through Jesus Christ our Lord. In thus setting forth the power of the indwelling Spirit of God in contrast to the inability of the Law, he teaches at the same time the eternal security of the believer.

There is a fivefold division of the chapter, somewhat clearly marked by the references to the glory which awaits us, in each case a climax.

The first section ends with verse 11. The aspect of glory there presented is the quickening of our mortal bodies. The second section ends with verse 17. The aspect of glory there is our joint-heirship with Christ as the issue from present suffering with Him. The third section ends with verse 23, pointing to the redemption of our bodies and its issue in the deliverance of the groaning creation. The fourth section ends with verse 30, telling of our being glorified with Christ as the crowning act of God's grace toward us. The fifth section closes with the assurance of our indissoluble enjoyment of the love of God in Christ.

8:1 There is therefore now—The inference is immediately derived from what has just been stated in chapter seven, though at the same time it introduces a conclusion based upon the whole of the preceding argument from chapter 3:19 onward.

no condemnation to them that are in Christ Jesus.—The word "no" stands in the position of very marked stress, and is an emphatic negative. For *katakrima*, condemnation, see 5:16, 18. The meaning "handicap," which has been suggested, is to be rejected. In the A.V. the latter part of the first verse is wrongly inserted. According to the most authoritative MSS. the right position of that clause is at the end of verse 4.

8:2 For the law of the Spirit of life—There is a new law for the new life. It is here the animating principle by which the Holy Spirit acts as the imparter of life. The phrase "the Spirit of life," is not subjective, "the Spirit who has life," but objective, "the Spirit who gives life." "It is the Spirit who quickeneth" (John 6:63). Cp. the phrases "justification of life" (Rom. 5:18), and "the Bread of life." i.e., "the Bread which nourishes life" (John 6:35).

in Christ Jesus—This is probably to be taken with the following words "hath made me free." There is peculiar stress on the phrase in the original, as if to say, "Certain it is that in Christ the believer is set free." Compare the same emphasis in 1 Corinthians 4:15 and Galatians 5:6; The phrase "in Christ Jesus" here sets forth the spiritual union of believers with the Lord through His death and resurrection. What is involved in this was set forth in chapter 6:3–11.

hath made me free—The tense is aorist, marking a definite time in past experience. Into this freedom from bondage the believer enters when he receives Christ by faith. He is to enter into the realization and power of it, and looks forward to its consummation in the redemption of his body.

from the law of sin and death—As set forth in the preceding chapter; see especially verses 13, 21, 23, 25.

8:3 For what the law could not do,—Literally, "the inability of the Law." The meaning may be either "the weakness of the law," or "that which was impossible for the Law." The latter is perhaps preferable. The significance is the same in effect; the Law could not give freedom from condemnation, could neither justify nor impart life. Literalism is impossible in rendering, but the sense is clear.

in that it was weak through the flesh,—Literally, "in which ["wherein," R.V. margin], it was weak." i.e., in its inability it was weak by means of the flesh, weak, that is to say, to accomplish, by means of the flesh, that which God alone could do and has done. Not the reason of the inability is stated, but the point of its powerlessness. The inability and its cause have been set forth in 7:14–25. The Law itself is perfect. It could not, however, through the instrumentality of the flesh, effect the end in view. "The flesh," the weaker element in human nature, as in 6:19.

God, sending—The "sending" is that from the glory which He had with the Father into the world, by way of the Incarnation, and not a sending out into the world subsequent to the Incarnation. So in John 3:17, 5:36, etc. It was as the Son in relationship to the Father that He was sent and came into the world. He did not become the Son of God at His incarnation.

His own Son—This phrase bears stress. It expresses not simply the closeness and dearness of the relationship, but the greatness and power of the person who was sent, and this is what is set in contrast to the weakness of the Law.

in the likeness of sinful flesh—There is stress on the word *homōioma*, "likeness," which conveys the thought not merely of resemblance but that of form. The phrase, literally, is "in likeness of flesh of sin." The flesh stands for the human body, which in man has become the seat of indwelling sin. Sin, however, is not inherent in man's nature, as created by God. What is here set forth is, that Christ took true human flesh, "of the substance of the Virgin Mary His Mother," apart from sinfulness, which has been acquired in fallen man. The flesh, in the likeness of which Christ came, was the same as that of which man consists. The likeness, then, expresses,

not the semblance, but the reality. The reality was His, sin apart. There is both identification and contrast: identification in regard to the flesh, contrast in regard to sin, and both points are stressed here.

and *as an offering* **for sin,**—The italicized words have been rightly added in the R.V., as the phrase is frequently used in the Septuagint as regards a sin-offering (see, e.g., Lev. 4:32; 5:6, 7, 8, 9; 2 Chr. 29:24; Ps. 40:6; see also Heb. 10:6, 8).

With this verse 3:25 should be compared. There Christ is spoken of as a propitiation . . . by His blood (see notes). The sacrifice was expiatory, and Christ, the person Himself is in this respect the basis upon which God shows mercy to the sinner. In the Old Testament the offerings are frequently spoken of as "making an atonement," literally, "a covering." In the fuller unfolding of the subject in the New Testament the word "atonement" is not found. In 5:11, the only place where "atonement" is found in the A.V., the word should be "reconciliation," as in the R.V.

condemned sin in the flesh:—This has been understood in various ways. The preceding context would lead us to understand the phrase "in the flesh" as referring to the fact that Christ, having taken human nature (sin apart), and having lived a sinless life, died under the judgment due to our sin. God thus condemned sin both by the sinless life of Christ (not that Christ bore our sins in His life, but that His life was a veritable condemnation of sin) and then in the crucifixion and death of His own Son. Both these points are in accordance with the two preceding clauses, "in likeness of flesh of sin" and "as an offering for sin."

8:4 that the ordinance of the law—*Dikaiōma* here stands collectively for the precepts of the Law, all that it demands as right. Distinguish the meaning here from that in 1:32 and 5:16 and 18.

might be fulfilled in us,—The fulfillment is "in" us, not simply "by" us, for it is primarily the work of God in us, accomplished by the indwelling of the Holy Spirit (vv. 2 and 9), and this operation is designed to meet with a willing response on our part. Not simply justification seems to be in view here, as if the opening words of the chapter were being amplified; for the apostle is leading up to the character of the life and work of the believer, a life in which he is to please God (v. 8). Further, the "in us" is not simply "in our case." It is that, with the additional thought of the response on our part just referred to. That believers do not in point of fact attain to sinless perfection in this life, is not an objection to this view, for what is here set forth is God's design in the sending of His Son, and the ideal standard set before us, as an outcome of His death and the gift of the Holy Spirit.

who walk not after the flesh, but after the spirit.—*Peripateō*, "to walk," describes the whole activity of the believer's life. The flesh here stands for corrupt human nature, the dominating element in unregenerate man. The spirit would here seem to stand for the renewed inward man, as mentioned in 7:22 (see vv. 10 and 16 below), which in the believer is to be the dominating factor instead of the flesh. To walk "after the spirit" is indeed to walk under the operating power of the Spirit of God (Gal. 5:18); for the spirit of the believer is the sphere of the operations of the Holy Spirit (v. 16 below).

The whole phrase "who walk not after the flesh, but after the spirit," describes those in whom alone the ordinance of the Law can be fulfilled, on the ground of the death of Christ and by the law of the Spirit of life in Christ Jesus, and as those who in Him are freed from condemnation (vv. 1–3).

Four Contrasts, 8:5–8

Introductory Note

These contrasts distinguish the regenerate from the unregenerate. They are as follows: (1) a contrast in persons (v. 5a), (2) a contrast in aims (v. 5b), (3) a contrast in effects (v. 6), (4) a contrast in conditions (vv. 7, 8).

8:5 For they that are after the flesh— That is, those who live in accordance with the dominating principle of the corrupt nature in man.

do mind the things of the flesh; but they that are after the spirit the things of the spirit.—*Phroneō*, to think, to feel, here means to regulate one's mind by something, to seek the instruction or guidance of. See notes on verse 4.

8:6 For the mind of the flesh is death;— *Phronēma*, "mind," is the noun corresponding to *phroneō* in the preceding verse. It is found in the New Testament only in this chapter, in this verse and verses 7, 27. It signifies that which one has in mind, the thoughts and purposes, and is to be distinguished from *phronēsis*, and understanding, prudence. For the subject of death see 6:21; Here not only eventual doom is in view, but the present experience of alienation from God (see v. 7 and cp. 1 Tim. 5:6).

but the mind of the spirit is life and peace:—Peace is not here the act of reconciliation, accomplished through the death of Christ, as in 5:1, but the enjoyment of the condition of reconciliation itself.

8:7 because the mind of the flesh is enmity against God;—The reader is now directed, not simply to a present condition as such, but to the attitude toward God. This is the all-important matter. To that point Scripture in all its teaching leads. The Bible is not a book of moral philosophy. Everything hinges upon God's view of things and upon the condition of persons in His sight. The mind of the flesh is therefore set in antagonism against God, refusing to acknowledge His claims.

for it is not subject to the law of God,— The tense is present continuous, expressing a constant or normal condition. The verb is in the middle voice, signifying the voluntary subjection of oneself to the will of another. The meaning, then, is that the mind of the flesh does not submit itself to the Law of God; it refuses to be controlled thereby. What is involved is not mere indifference but actual hostility.

neither indeed can it be:—As a matter of essential characteristic the mind of the flesh is not subject to God's law, and as a matter of inherent nature it cannot be so; it is impossible to improve it into being subject to Him. The natural man neither receiveth the things of the Spirit nor can he know them (1 Cor. 2:14).

8:8 and they that are in the flesh cannot please God.—The word "and" instead of the A.V. "so then," should be noted. It links this statement with the first in verse 7, which it confirms; "not to please God" is to be at enmity against Him. "They that are in the flesh" is another way of describing those who are "after the flesh" (v. 5). The one expresses the state, the other expresses the characteristic effects.

8:9 But ye are not in the flesh, but in the spirit,—As the phrase "in the flesh" expresses the state of those who are "after the flesh," so "in the spirit" expresses the state of those who are "after the spirit" (v. 5). The contrast is between the dominating elements which govern the different kinds of persons (see notes on vv. 4-7).

if so be that the Spirit of God dwelleth in you.—This does not express a condition according to which the believer may be in the spirit, it states a fact true of every believer, for this passage distinguishes between the regenerate and the unregenerate, as the next statement shows.

But if any man hath not the Spirit of Christ, he is none of His.—This teaches the doctrine of the tri-unity of the Godhead; for the Holy Spirit is both the Spirit of God and the Spirit of Christ. To have the Spirit of God indwelling us is to have the Spirit of Christ. The Holy Spirit is given to all believers from the moment of their regeneration, to indwell them; "having believed" (i.e., upon believing) they are "sealed with the Holy Spirit of promise" (Eph. 1:13). Since He is the Spirit of Christ, to be without Him is not to belong to Christ. See 2 Corinthians 13:5; The contrasting conditions are, "not in the flesh" and "none of His."

8:10 And if Christ is in you,—That the indwelling of the Holy Spirit is the indwelling of Christ Himself, see Ephesians 3:16, 17.

the body is dead because of sin;—The body, the human frame, contains the seeds of decay and is mortal, i.e., doomed to death, in the ordinary course of events, on account of sin. Cp. 5:12, 14. The body of the believer is said to be dead (albeit he is living in the body), so as to set forth the inevitableness of the fact.

but the spirit is life—The spirit, having been quickened at regeneration, is possessed of the inalienable principle of life, but only as being secured to it eternally in virtue of the power of the Spirit of God.

because of righteousness.—That is to say, on account of the fact that righteousness is reckoned by God to him who believes.

8:11 But if the Spirit of Him that raised up Jesus from the dead dwelleth in you,—This is the longest title of the Holy Spirit in the New Testament. For the subject of the resurrection of Christ, see 4:24, 25; 6:4, 9; 7:4. As in the other places, so here, "from the dead" is literally, "from among" *(ek)*.

This is the second and only other place in this Epistle where the single title "Jesus" is used. The first was in 3:26 and was there used to describe Him as the object of faith. Here, in connection with His resurrection, it is used of Him as the One who is pledge of all that is secured in Him for the believer.

He that raised up Christ Jesus from the dead shall quicken also your mortal bodies—For the double title of Christ, as in the R.V., see notes on 1:1. For the word *zōopoieō* see note at 4:17. It does not denote reinvigoration. The reference is not to the impartation of some special energy of life and power to our bodies in their present state, but to the effect upon them of the shout of the Lord at the time of the Rapture (1 Thess. 4:17; Phil. 3:20, 21; 1 Cor. 15:52, 53). What is mortal will then be "swallowed up of life." The statement in this eleventh verse is to be put in connection with that at the close of the seventh chapter, where the assurance is given that Christ will deliver us "out of the body of this death" (7:24).

through His Spirit that dwelleth in you.—The well-supported marginal reading, "because of His Spirit," is to be regarded as correct. Scripture does not speak of the Holy Spirit as the One who will raise the dead and change the living saints. He is not the means but the cause. Their coming glory is assured to them first by the resurrection of Christ and then by the fact of the indwelling Spirit. There are two references to this in the second Epistle to the Corinthians, one in 1:22, "God . . .

sealed us and gave us the earnest of the Spirit in our hearts"; the other in 5:5, "He that wrought us for this very thing is God, who gave us the earnest of the Spirit." The power that wrought in Christ is the power that will accomplish the quickening of our death-doomed bodies (Eph. 1:18–20).

The Spirit, the Means of Sonship and the Pledge of Future Glory, 8:12–27

Introductory Note

This section is divided in two parts. Verses 1–11 have spoken of the indwelling of the Spirit of God; now follows an unfolding of the operation of the Spirit within us in a two-fold way, firstly as to His leading and the ef-fects of our response thereto (vv. 12–14); secondly, as to the inward witness given by the Holy Spirit, that we are the children of God, and the effects of this, issuing in our being glorified with Christ (vv. 15–27).

8:12 So then, brethren, we are debtors, not to the flesh, to live after the flesh:—Believers owe nothing to the flesh. What they derive from that is death. They are therefore under no obligation to it.

8:13 for if ye live after the flesh, ye must die;—The contrast, in the word "live," at the end of the verse, indicates that the death here is not merely that of the body. Cp. 1 Timothy 5:6.

but if by the Spirit ye mortify the deeds of the body, ye shall live.—The contrasting parallel to verse 12 would have been "we are debtors to live after the spirit"; the conclusion is, however, put in a very striking way, and with a change from "we" to "ye," recalling the similar change in verse 9. The "Spirit" now mentioned is the Holy Spirit, not the hu-man spirit. The verb *thanatoō*, "to put to death," is the same as in 7:4, where it is used in the passive voice. That was the act of God through the death of Christ. This verse states the responsibility of the believer himself. The power for this is not his own, but that of the Holy Spirit.

In Colossians 3:9 the believer is said to have "put off the old man with his doings."

That is recorded as the initial act of the new life, to be followed by the constant fulfillment of the putting to death of the deeds of the body as mentioned in this verse. The body is here regarded as the instrument of the flesh, the principle which tends to animate it.

8:14 For as many as are led by the Spirit of God,—The word *agō*, "to lead," is almost always used in the New Testament of persons, and implies cooperation on their part with the one who is leading, or is associated in the object in view. Here, therefore, the wholehearted response to the leading of the Holy Spirit, is suggested. To be led by the Spirit of God is to walk after the spirit (v. 4).

these are sons of God.—The emphatic "these" signifies "these and none but these." The word *huios*, "son," signifies primarily the relationship of offspring to parent (see John 9:18–20; Gal. 4:30); but it is frequently used in a sense suggestive of distinct moral charac-teristics. The moral characteristic in evidence here is that of being led by the Spirit of God. For the contrasting word *teknon*, see verse 16, below. *Huios* expresses the dignity of the posi-tion into which the child is brought, and the character which is consistent therewith. In his standing a believer is a child of God; in his state he should be a son of God, and only as he gives evidence that he is a son of God can he really claim to be a child of God. The Lord Jesus brought out the special significance of *huios* in His remarks in what is called the Ser-mon on the Mount, e.g., in Matthew 5:9, 44, 45. See also 2 Corinthians 6:17, 18, and verse 19 below.

8:15 For ye received not the spirit of bondage,—There is no definite article before "spirit"; we may therefore render the clause "not a spirit of bondage." That is a spirit pos-sessed by, and characteristic of, slaves.

again unto fear,—That is, tending to fear, the fear of death, for instance (Heb. 2:14, 15), such a fear as characterized them in their un-regenerate state (cp. 1:4, 18), the fear of an unwilling slave.

but ye received the spirit of adoption,—*Huiothesia* is, literally, "son-placing" (from *huios*, "a son," and *tithēmi*, "to place"), i.e., a place and state of a son, given to one to whom it does not belong by natural descent (see 9:4). That very fact indicates that the Holy Spirit is in view here, by whom alone the relationship is established in the case of the believer. Just as natural relationship is established upon the event of natural birth, so spiritual relationship is established immediately upon spiritual birth.

whereby we cry Abba, Father.—In the parallel passage in Galatians 4:6 it is the Holy Spirit that is said to cry this. So intimate is the relationship between the divine Spirit and the human spirit in the regenerate, that what is said in one place of the former is said in another place of the latter. It is the action of the Spirit of the Son on the spirits of the sons that enables them to cry "Abba! Father!" Cp. 8:26, 27.

"Abba" is the cry of the infant, the simple, helpless utterance of unreasoning trust, the effect of feeling, rather than knowledge. It is an Aramaic word (cp. English "papa"). It was a form of address forbidden among the Jews to be used by a slave to the head of the family. "Father" (Greek and Latin, *"pater"*) is not a translation of "Abba." It is another mode of address. It is relationship intelligently realized by the one who utters it, a word of filial confidence, communion, and obedience, answering to, and expressing, the enjoyment of the complacent love of God the Father. The two expressions together indicate the love and intelligent trust of the child.

8:16 The Spirit Himself—The A.V. "itself" is inaccurate. The Holy Spirit is a person in the Godhead and has just been mentioned as "the Spirit of adoption." The misrendering "itself" is due to the fact that the pronoun is neuter in the original, in grammatical agreement with the word *pneuma* (spirit), which is neuter only as a matter of grammar.

beareth witness with our spirit,—This is not to be rendered by "to our spirit." This statement expands the latter part of verse 15. The cry "Abba, Father," while it is the utterance of our own spirit, is at the same time, produced in us by the Spirit of God. All that we are and experience as God's children is the work of the indwelling Holy Spirit.

that we are children of God:—*Teknon,* "child," is connected with the verb *tiktō,* "to

beget." Both *teknon,* and *huios* (see v. 14), are frequently used to describe the relationship between believers and God, effected in the new birth. This verse provides ground for the assurance of salvation on the part of believers. At the same time it bears testimony against the doctrine of pantheism, which confounds the human spirit with the Divine.

8:17 and if children, then heirs;—The word means one who receives by lot, and so one who receives an allotted possession by right of sonship. Believers, in virtue of the sonship bestowed upon them, are, as heirs, to share in all that belongs to Christ, and therefore in all that will be established at His return. This verse brings us to the issue of the argument, which follows from the statement "ye shall live," at the end of verse 13. Since we are the children of God, the inheritance our Father has for us is secured to us.

heirs of God, and joint-heirs with Christ;—This makes known the dignity of our position. All that the Father has belongs to the sons (John 17:10, R.V.). Whatever we have as children of God is shared with us by Christ. His is the inheritance in virtue of His eternal relationship with the Father, and through His death and resurrection He shares His inheritance with those who by grace are children of God.

There are marked differences between the conditions attaching to this inheritance and those relating to an earthly inheritance. A natural inheritance is most frequently possessed upon the death of the father. The inheritance to be enjoyed by believers is to be bestowed by and shared with one who never dies. Again, under Jewish law, the eldest son received the largest share, and the daughters were excluded, unless there were no sons. Under Roman law sons, daughters and adopted children shared an inheritance equally. All believers will share Christ's inheritance. Moreover, the inheritance has been won for them by His death, and will be received by them through grace.

If so be that we suffer with *Him,*—This is not to be taken into such close connection with the phrase "joint-heirs" as to make that position conditional upon our suffering with Him here. The word *eiper,* "if so be," indicates here that to suffer with Christ is characteristic of believers generally. True Christianity is, in one way or another, a suffering quantity in this world. What is in view here is not the rewards hereafter to be given for the endurance of sufferings in this life, but the eternal portion of those who are in Christ as distinct from those who walk after the flesh and do not belong to Him. The sufferings of Christians arise from the same cause as the sufferings of Christ in the days of His flesh, namely, the hatred of the world to God. Man hated Christ, not because of His good work, but because He revealed His deity. The world does not hate Christians because of their good works; it hates their confession of Christ and their testimony to their relationship with Him. Into the fellowship of His sufferings Paul desired to enter that He might thus become conformed to His death, and attain here and now to the ideal state of "the resurrection from the dead" (Phil. 3:10, 11).

that we may be also glorified with Him.—This is not to be rendered "glorified together," as in the A.V. God has designed that present suffering should issue in future glory, and that in association with Christ, an association which will be a recompense for participation in His sufferings; the joy which is to be ours at the revelation of His glory is given to us now as an incentive of our joy in partaking of Christ's sufferings.

This verse brings us again to the subject of the future glory at the coming of the Lord, as in verse 11. The threefold proof of the coming glory in this section is that, (1) believers are led by the Spirit of God, showing that they are sons of God; (2) they have received the Spirit of adoption leading them to cry "Abba, Father"; (3) they have the inward witness of the Spirit that they are the children of God, involving joint-heirship with Christ, and consequent glory after present suffering.

8:18 For I reckon—This is not an expression of opinion or a supposition, nor is it simply a calculation. It conveys a considered judgment and an assurance.

that the sufferings of this present time— The word is *kairos* "a season," a period marked by special features, in distinction from *chronos,* "a time," which simply indicates the length of a period.

are not worthy to be compared—Literally, "not worth in comparison with." The word *axios* was used originally of drawing down a scale; hence it had to do with weight, and so of that which is of value. The idea, here, then, is that sufferings are of no weight in comparison with glory; they are not to be balanced in the scale with it.

with the glory which shall be revealed to usward.—Literally, "with the glory about to be revealed to usward." The verb *mellō,* "shall (be)," is used, not to express mere futurity, but of that which is destined to certain accomplishment, and upon this the word lays stress here. The time of the consummation of God's plans is not definitely stated. Neither is it stated in a way which necessarily relegates it to a distant time. That the time is regarded by human beings as protracted is consequent upon the limited faculties of human calculation. What the Spirit of God would impress upon us is the certainty of the prospect. The glory is already existent and embodied in Christ. It is destined to be revealed to us at the return of Christ. The preposition *eis,* signifies not merely direction but the effects upon the subjects of revelation. We shall not only witness the glory (that would be expressed by the dative case of the pronoun), but it will come upon us and affect us, and this has already been stated at the end of verse 17.

8:19 For the earnest expectation of the creation—*Apokaradokia* is suggestive of the stretching forth of the head in expectation of something. The only other place where the word is found is Philippians 1:20, "according to my earnest expectation." The object of attention there is the magnifying of Christ in life and death, Christ Himself being the absorbing object. Here the object in view is the revealing of the sons of God.

waiteth for—*Apekdechomai* is an intensive word, stressing the thought of expectancy.

the revealing of the sons of God.—When the Lord returns in manifested glory, the saints will be in association with Him and thus will be revealed to the creation. They will come as those who manifest a likeness to their heavenly Father, hence the appropriateness of the title "sons" here. That event is here put as a beginning of a proof that present sufferings are not worthy to be compared with future glory.

8:20 For the creation was subjected to vanity—This is the first of three reasons why the creation waits for the revealing of the sons of God. For *hupotassō*, "to subject," see at verse 7. *Mataiotēs* signifies what is devoid of good results, and is used in three places in the New Testament. Here of frailty, failure to achieve the full design of its being; in Ephesians 4:17, of the depravity of the human mind, the perversion of the powers bestowed by God; in 2 Peter 2:18, of words devoid of truth and usefulness. For the creation this condition was consequent upon the entrance of sin into the world. Creation shares in the effects of the curse that fell on man for his disobedience. There is stress on the word "vanity."

not of its own will, but by reason of Him who subjected it,—This is the second reason why the creation waits for the event mentioned. The phrase "not of its own will" continues the personification of nature, and shows that the present condition of failure to fulfill the design of its being is contrary to those qualities and powers bestowed upon it.

8:21 in hope—This may be connected with the first part of verse 20, expressive of the condition upon which the creation was subjected to vanity, a condition consequent upon the overruling providence of God. Hope describes the happy anticipation of good. The hope of the creation, like that of the believer, contains no element of uncertainty fraught with the possibility of disappointment. It is sure of fulfillment. It has to do with what is yet unseen.

that the creation itself also shall be delivered—That is, in addition to the children of God. For the verb *eleutheroō* cp. 6:18, 22; 8:2, there rendered "made free." This hope gives the third reason why the creation waits for the expected event.

from the bondage of corruption,—*Phthora*, "corruption," which expresses the effect of the withdrawal of those powers by which life or activity is maintained, is used in the New Testament either of decay and death, in the physical sphere (as here and in 1 Cor. 15:42, 50; 2 Pet. 2:12), or of moral degener-

acy (as in Col. 2:22; Gal. 6:8). The phrase "bondage of corruption" is taken by some in an objective sense, as signifying bondage which produces corruption, by others subjectively, as the bondage which consists in corruption. The latter seems to be the meaning.

into the liberty of the glory of the children of God.—This expands the phrase at the end of verse 19, "the revealing of the Sons of God." Liberty will be the characteristic of the glory. Creation is to share in the liberty which will belong to the children of God in their glorified state. For creation, instead of failure to realize then the design of its being, will have full scope for the exercise of the powers imparted to it by God. Its new state will match the condition of redeemed man (see e.g., Is. 65:17; 2 Pet. 3:13; Rev. 21:1).

The change from "sons of God" (v. 19) to "children of God" is significant. The former was appropriate to the thought of manifestation in glory, for then the saints will, as sons of God, fully represent their Father's character and display His power. The phrase "children of God" recalls the thought of adoption and heirship in verses 15–17, and is appropriate to the mention of "the liberty of the glory."

8:22 For we know that the whole creation groaneth and travaileth in pain together until now.—Literally, "groaneth-together and travaileth-in-pain-together"; that is to say, creation, in all its parts together, unites in the groaning and travailing. This is contingent upon its being subjected to vanity. Here the suggestion is the travail out of which a new condition of creation is to be born, when the sons of God are revealed. The phrase rendered "until now" suggests the unintermittent character of the groans of creation from the time when it was subjected to vanity.

8:23 And not only so, but we ourselves also, which have the firstfruits of the Spirit,—The Holy Spirit, indwelling the believer, is the firstfruits of the full harvest of the Cross. In His whole person He is given to each believer at the new birth. The phrase "the firstfruits of the Spirit" does not mean that believers possess a part of the Holy Spirit now and will possess Him entirely hereafter. He Himself is the earnest of the liberty of the glory hereafter to be enjoyed both by the children of God and by creation. So Christ is spoken of in His resurrection in relation to all who have fallen asleep in Him (1 Cor. 15:20, 23). So, again, believers now are spoken of in relationship to the whole of the redeemed in James 1:18 and in an alternative reading in 2 Thessalonians 2:13, of the rendering "from the beginning," the well-supported rendering being "God chose you as firstfruits." See 11:16, and 16:5.

even we ourselves groan within ourselves waiting for our adoption, *to wit,* **the redemption of our body.**—Believers are already possessed of adoption in their relationship to God by grace and in the gift of the Holy Spirit; they still earnestly wait for the redemption of their body as the assured completion of this adoption.

The redemption spoken of is the future actual liberation of the body from its present condition of sinfulness, weakness, decay and death. That redemption is otherwise spoken of as our being "clothed upon with our habitation which is from heaven" (2 Cor. 5:2), not a temporary condition till the Resurrection and Rapture, but that which will then take place. The redemption of the body is not precisely identical with the adoption but is included in it.

8:24 For by hope we were saved:—This does not mean that hope was the instrument of our salvation, but that it was an essential feature associated with it. Hope is the joyous anticipation of good, in this passage the redemption of our body.

but hope that is seen is not hope:—The word "hope" stands for the thing hoped for, as in Acts 23:6; 26:6, 7; Galatians 5:5; Ephesians 1:18; 2:12; 4:4; Colossians 1:5, 23; 1 Timothy 1:1; Titus 2:13. Realization removes expectation.

for who hopeth for that which he seeth?—Since the Word of God presents certain things to the believer as the object of his hope, the assurance of their fulfillment brings present spiritual realization of them.

8:25 But if we hope for that which we see not, *then* **do we with patience wait for it.**—What is secured for us being yet future, the anticipation is to be characterized by patience. Patience suggests the existence of

adverse circumstances which demand its exercise.

8:26 And in like manner the Spirit also helpeth our infirmity:—Without the aid of the Holy Spirit our patience would fail and we should succumb to despair. The word *sunantilambanomai,* "to help," is found elsewhere in the New Testament only in Luke 10:40. It denotes, literally, to take hold of anything with another, and so means "to give assistance by sharing a burden." The most authentic MSS. read "infirmity," not "infirmities" as in the A.V. The singular indicates a general condition of weakness.

for we know not how to pray as we ought;—A more literal rendering would be, "what we are to pray according to our need we know not," i.e., we do not know how to express ourselves so that our prayers shall correspond to the need. Not a mode of prayer is here especially in view, but the subjects.

Proseuchomai, "to pray," is always used of requests addressed to God, whereas *deomai,* "to pray," may be used of requests addressed to man as well. *Proseuchomai* carries with it a notion of worship which is not present in the word *deomai.*

but the Spirit Himself maketh intercession for *us*—As the indwelling Holy Spirit alone knows how to interpret our needs, He makes His intercession within us, inspiring our yearnings, and thus fulfilling His gracious function as the other comforter (or advocate) whom the Lord Jesus promised, a comforter of like character with Himself. Since we know not what to pray for apart from His help, we are exhorted to pray "at all seasons in the Spirit" (Eph. 6:18).

with groanings which cannot be uttered;—Creation groans, we groan, and the Holy Spirit groans. But the Spirit groans within us, and in doing so strengthens us to bear our trials with confidence and courage, and at the same time directs our hearts to God. These groanings do not necessarily find expression in actual speech, but they are effective with God. Human language is, it would seem, not essential to Divine intercession.

8:27 and He that searcheth the hearts—God, in His omniscience, is entirely acquainted with these desires, even though they cannot be uttered. For this aspect of God's omniscience see Psalm 139:1-6; Jeremiah 17:10; Revelation 2:23.

knoweth what is the mind of the Spirit, because He maketh intercession for the saints according to *the will of* **God.**—The word *hoti*, rendered "because," may also mean "that" (see margin), and this is probably the meaning. God's knowledge of the mind of the Holy Spirit is not consequent upon the nature of His intercession in our hearts. The Holy Spirit is one in godhood with the Father and with the Son. Since the Spirit's groanings are in accordance with God's mind, His intercession in our groanings is consistent with God's dealings with us and the fulfillment of His purposes toward us.

The phrase "according to the will of God" is, literally, "according to God," and has the position of emphasis.

God the Justifier, the Pledge of Glory; the Love of Christ, the Power for Victory, 8:28–39

Introductory Note

Having shown that suffering is not incompatible with a life of hope, the apostle now extends this to make clear that suffering is part of the working out of God's all-wise purposes for us, and that neither affliction nor anything else can prevent this or thwart God's ultimate designs for us. Here, too, he confirms the doctrine of the justification of the believer and establishes that of his eternal security.

8:28 And we know that to them that love God—This is the only place in the Epistle where our love to God is mentioned. The phrase "them that love God" is descriptive of believers as a class, and at the same time suggests that only those who love God realize that all things work together for their good.

all things work together for good,—An alternative rendering is "He worketh all things together for good." The "all things," while applying to circumstances in general, has special reference to those of adversity, as indicated in the context. All things, however contrary to us, are under His control. The

statement carries the suggestion that God works all things, for those who love Him, with designs for their good (see margin). Troubles, therefore, do not hinder Christian progress, they serve but to further the designs of God's grace.

even **to them that are called**—The two descriptions, "them that are called" and "them that love God," are to one another as cause and effect. Those who love God are necessarily those who are called. The call (always in the Epistles an effectual call) produces the response of love to Him who calls.

according to *His* **purpose.**—The special significance of this clause is twofold: firstly, it shows that the fact that some men love God is attributable solely to His sovereign grace, and, secondly, it confirms the fact of their eternal security.

8:29 For whom He foreknew,—This and the next verse confirm verse 28, providing the ground of the certainty that God works all things together for good. While God foreknows all men, according to His attribute of prescience, yet obviously the word here refers to those who have been described as "them that love God." He foreknew them as the objects of His favor. All idea of human merit is absent from the passage, as what is being stressed is the absolute sovereignty of God in all His purposes and actions. Foreknowledge is not the same as predestination; the very sentence before us distinguishes the two. His foreknowledge marks out the persons, His predestination determines His purposes and acts on their behalf.

He also foreordained—The verb *proorizō* literally signifies "to mark out beforehand." It is used in the New Testament only of God, and, besides this verse and the next, is found only in Acts 4:28; 1 Corinthians 2:7; Ephesians 1:5, 11. It was not the fact of our faith as foreknown by God that moved Him to foreordain us. The blessings and mercies here recounted are the result of His eternal purpose in Christ.

to be **conformed to the image of His Son,**—The word *summorphos*, "conformed," conveys the thought, not merely of an external appearance, but of the expression of what constitutes the nature of anything. The word *ei-kōn,* "image," is more than a real resemblance. It conveys the idea of representation and manifestation. Believers are to be conformed not merely to something that is like Him but to what He is Himself both in His spiritual body and in His moral character. In the latter respect Christ is to be manifested in believers now. The conformity will be fully and permanently accomplished, spirit, soul and body, when the Lord comes to receive them to Himself. This, again, in its full fruition, is determined not by their self-effort, but by the foreknowledge and foreordaining grace of God.

that He might be the Firstborn among many brethren:—The Divine purpose has as its great object the glory of the Son of God. The word *prototokos,* used of Christ, does not refer to His birth. Its chief use, indeed, has no reference to natural generation but rather to priority, dignity and supremacy. Thus an Israelite was forbidden to make the son of a second wife the firstborn in place of the son of a first wife. There are six passages in the New Testament where the word is used of Christ. Taken in chronological order they are as follows: firstly, Colossians 1:15, where His eternal preexistence is referred to, and He is mentioned as the One who produced creation (an objective clause, not subjective, as if classing Him with creation). Secondly and thirdly, Colossians 1:18 and Revelation 1:5, which refer to His priority and supremacy in resurrection. Fourthly, the present passage, which speaks of the future day when Christ will be seen in His preeminence above the redeemed, who are spoken of as "the Church of the First-born Ones" (Heb. 12:23). Fifthly, Hebrews 1:6, which refers to His Second Advent, when God will again bring Him into the world. See the R.V., which rightly puts the "again" after the beginning of the clause, the "again" not introducing a new quotation, but referring to the bringing in of the firstborn a second time into the world, i.e., in manifested glory hereafter.

8:30 and whom He foreordained, them He also called:—The divine counsels in eternity find expression in the course of time. The call is not simply that of the Gospel, though the Gospel is the instrument (2 Thess. 2:14); the call is what is effected in the be-

stowment of life in Christ (cp. 1 Cor. 1:9, 24). The aorist tense is used in these verbs and those which follow, not to indicate past history, but to signify the completeness and decisiveness of each act.

and whom He called, them He also justified: and whom He justified, them He also glorified.—Though the glorifying is still future, it is stated as an accomplished fact, in keeping with the preceding aorist tenses, as marking definiteness and certainty. In this series the apostle omits the present experiences in connection with the bestowment of the Holy Spirit, about which he has been writing in this chapter, for the argument in that respect has been completed, and the gift and operation of the Spirit of God are so inseparable from the calling and justification that no further mention is required. The series of acts of divine grace stretches from the eternity of the past to the eternity of the future. This is the fourth reference in this chapter to the time of the Rapture. See the introductory note to the chapter.

8:31 What then shall we say to these things? if God *is* for us, who *is* against us?—The strength of the adversary sinks into insignificance in comparison with the strength of God. Moreover, the efforts of our adversary, being under His absolute control, serve but for the fulfillment of His all-wise purposes toward us.

8:32 He that spared not His own Son,— This presents the chief point in the proof that God is for us, the greatest exhibition of the love of God toward us. The reference to Abraham's offering of Isaac is evident. The word rendered "spared" is the same as in the Septuagint of Genesis 22:16. The phrase "His own Son" stands antithetically not only in its reference to Abraham but also to what has been said about "adopted sons" (v. 15).

But further, the intimation is evident that the Son of God was and is of one nature with the Father. The emphasis in the phrase marks, too, not merely a comparison with natural relationship, but a unique relationship which extends back into the eternally preincarnate existence of the Son with the Father. Cp. Galatians 4:4, where the expression "born of a woman" marks, in the original, the circumstance of the sending, thus making clear that the One who was sent forth in this way was already the Son of God prior to His birth.

but delivered Him up for us all,—See 4:25. This states the delivering up as the act of God the Father. In Galatians 2:20, where the same word is rendered "gave (Himself) up," the act is mentioned as that of the Son Himself. The simple form *didōmi* is used of the Son in Galatians 1:4, the two statements thus providing clear intimation of the oneness of the Son with the Father. The "delivering up" was to "the death of the Cross."

how shall He not also with Him freely give us all things?—The greatest gift ensures all the rest. There is a definite article before the word "all" in the original, which perhaps points to all that has been brought before us in the Epistle, as made good to us in Christ. Perhaps there is a direct reference to the same word in verse 28. In that case the "all things" recalls even those things which are recorded as opposed to us, but which in point of fact are made a blessing to us. In any case the word may be taken without limitations. The single verb rendered "freely give" is *charizomai,* which literally means "to bestow as a gift of grace."

8:33 Who shall lay anything to the charge of God's elect?—This and the next two verses contain metaphors from a court of justice. In the case of the prisoner at the bar there are, so far as this passage goes, (1) the accuser, (2) the accused, (3) the judge, (4) the executioner. These are indicated in the three rhetorical questions in these verses, and (1) and (4) are seen to have no place in the sight of God with regard to the believer. Thus the apostle is recalling in a vivid way the great statements of truth in the preceding part of the Epistle as to the way in which God justifies the sinner through faith.

The word "elect" gathers up the preceding terms "foreknew," "foreordained," "called," "glorified," "justified." See 9:11; 11:5 and cp. 1 Thessalonians 1:4; Ephesians 1:4. Election signifies that act of the mind by which we choose a portion or certain number out of a whole. The act involves freedom on his part who makes the choice. Whatever God does He does without being influenced by things external to Himself, for apart from Him there

is no good. The reason for His ways and acts lies entirely within the scope of His own attributes and purposes.

It is God that justifieth;—A more literal rendering is "God is the (One) justifying," i.e., the justifier, with stress upon the word "God."

8:34 who is he that shall condemn?—This may be taken closely with the preceding statement, as is indicated in the R.V. For if God justifies He is Himself the judge and so condemnation is impossible.

It is Christ Jesus that died,—Possibly the marginal reading is right, "Shall Christ Jesus who died, yea, rather . . . ?" He it is to whom all judgment is committed (John 5:22, 27). His death has secured our justification and in His resurrection life He is altogether for us. The best MSS. have the full title "Christ Jesus," which marks Him as the exalted One who humbled Himself.

yea rather, that was raised from the dead, who is at the right hand of God,—This marks the position as one of dignity, power and authority, a position which is His prerogative as the One who has perfectly fulfilled the will of God, and has met the claims of Divine righteousness.

who also maketh intercession for us.—This was said of the Holy Spirit in verse 27. The word is used elsewhere of the Lord Jesus in Hebrews 7:25 only. For examples of the Lord's intercession see Luke 22:32 and John 17, and for the unfolding of the subject see Hebrews 4:15; 9:24; cp. 1 John 2:1. The mention of His position of authority serves to stress the efficacy of His intercession.

8:35 Who shall separate us from the love of Christ?—That would be the work of the executioner (see v. 33). To be separated from the love of Christ is death. Death involves separation. The body apart from the spirit is dead. The believer, separated from the love of Christ would be spiritually dead. But this is impossible, according to His own statement in John 10:28, 29. There is stress on the word "us."

Earlier in the Epistle the apostle mentions the love of God (5:5, 8), as he does here again in verse 39, a proof that the love of God is the love of Christ and an intimation of the essential oneness of the Father and the Son and so of the deity of Christ. So believers are said to be beloved of God (1 Thess. 1:4) and beloved of the Lord (2 Thess. 2:13). See also 2 Corinthians 5:14 and Ephesians 3:19.

shall tribulation,—See 2:9; 5:3.

or anguish,—See 2:9.

or persecution, or famine, or nakedness, or peril, or sword?—These complete a sevenfold series of adversaries, all of which were experienced by the apostle, and which in one respect or another have been the common lot of believers. They are in various ways the instruments of devilish and human hatred, but cannot interrupt the love of Christ toward us.

8:36 Even as it is written, For Thy sake we are killed all the day long; we were accounted as sheep for the slaughter.— The quotation is from the Septuagint of Psalm 44:22. Here the note is one of triumph. Hence we have a striking example of the increased force and new character of many of the New Testament quotations from the Old. The difference is due to the death and resurrection of Christ. A new significance attaches to the words "for Thy sake." There is no discrepancy between the Old and the New, but what the apostle is about to say shows by what means the opposition of adversaries is turned to a means of triumph. To suffer for Christ's sake and so to enter into the fellowship of His sufferings, transmutes the affliction into joy and victory, enabling the suffering saint to glory in tribulation.

8:37 Nay, in all these things we are more than conquerors—The word *huperni-kaō*, literally, to be supervictorious, has no adequate English equivalent. It is used here only in the New Testament. Not only are our adversaries deprived of power to snap the tie of the love of Christ, but their opposition is turned to our account, enhancing the power of our victory through Christ. As Chrysostom says, "This is a new order of victory, to conquer by means of our adversary."

through Him that loved us.—The aorist tense, while referring specially to the great expression of His love in that He died for us

(see v. 34), also conveys the fact of His love as timeless and immutable.

8:38 For I am persuaded, that neither death, nor life,—Death was the last item in the list in verse 35. The word is to be taken in its most comprehensive sense. Life is more dangerous for the believer than death.

nor angels, nor principalities,—This is the only place where principalities are mentioned in this Epistle. The two terms are used in a general sense, though the context obviously points to beings of a hostile character. Principalities are first in the lists in Ephesians 6:12, there indicating their superior order as spirit beings.

nor things present, nor things to come, nor powers,—The word *dunamis* may here refer not merely to angelic powers but to human potentates, as in the case of its associated word *exousia* (see 13:1), though the latter also is used of angels. The difference between *dunamis* and *exousia* is that *dunamis* signifies power in general and *exousia* the ability to use it.

8:39 nor height, nor depth,—This refers to dimensions of space, just as "things present," "things to come," referred to matters of time. The words "height" and "depth" may here indicate heaven and earth (see also Is. 7:11).

nor any other creature,—The order in the R.V., which is undoubtedly correct, places the various objects in alternating groups, according as they are personal and impersonal, the word "creature" at the end comprehending all besides those mentioned. The arrangement accordingly is: (a) neither death nor life (impersonal); (b) nor angels nor principalities (personal); (a) nor things present nor things to come (impersonal); (b) nor powers (personal); (a) nor height nor depth (impersonal); (b) nor any other creature (personal).

shall be able to separate us from the love of God, which is in Christ Jesus our Lord.—This forms the crowning arch of the whole Epistle. The love of God has been brought before us, first in 5:5; and in its essential connection with Christ in 5:8; in 8:35 it was spoken of as the love of Christ. Here it is definitely stated to be resident in Him, with the suggestion that it operates through Him.

The whole of chapter eight contains the mention of particular details in chapters five and eight. They are as follows:

Peace with God (5:1 and 8:6); the hope of the glory of God (5:2 and 8:20, 21); patience (5:24 and 8:25); the love of God (5:5 and 8:28, 29); the death of Christ (5:6, 8, 10 and 8:32); righteousness in life in contrast to sin and death (5:12–21 and 8:24); walking in newness of life and walking after the Spirit (6:4 and 8:4); life unto God (6:6, 11, 13, 22 and 8:13); eternal life in Christ Jesus our Lord and the love of God in Christ Jesus our Lord (5:23 and 8:39).

ROMANS

· CHAPTER NINE ·

The Righteousness of God with Regard to Israel and the Gentiles, 9:1 to 11:36

Introductory Note

The apostle is still continuing his subjects of the vindication of God's character and ways. He has shown in the first eight chapters that God is righteous in the exercise both of His wrath and of His grace. He now proceeds to establish the righteousness of God in His dealings nationally with Jews and Gentiles. Chapters nine to eleven run parallel to chapters three to eight. We find a striking harmony between the development of the theme in the ninth chapter and the argument of the third chapter. The tenth follows on with the subject of faith, just as the fourth chapter did. In the eleventh chapter the subject of God's grace and mercy through Christ corresponds to those of chapters five to eight. The themes are the same, the setting different.

The chief subject of chapter nine is the sovereignty of God. That of chapter ten is the possibilities of faith. That of chapter eleven is God's grace and mercy.

This section shows that divine retribution is not merely arbitrary, but is consequent upon man's own hardness of heart. The sovereignty of God has not been exercised by way of predestinating men to sin, as if they were helpless machines forced on by a predetermined fate and compelled thereby to reap the consequences of an evil for which they were not primarily responsible. The present condition of the Jews is chargeable, not to God, but to themselves.

As to the parallelism between chapter nine and the first part of chapter three, in the third chapter three questions were asked which represent supposed Jewish objections raised against the teaching that Jew and Gentile were on the same ground before God in the matters of sin and justification by faith.

The first objection was that such an equalization would abrogate the distinctive privileges of the Jew. The question in 3:1 was answered in 3:2. So now chapter nine shows what are the distinctive privileges of the nation (vv. 4, 5).

The second objection in chapter three was that the validity of God's promises would be destroyed (3:3). That was answered in 3:4. Similarly chapter nine shows that the unbelief of Israel is no evidence that the Word of God is come to naught (vv. 6-13).

The third objection in chapter three was that God would be unrighteous (3:5). That was answered in 3:6 to 8. This is taken again in chapter nine, verse 14, where the question is asked, "Is there unrighteousness with God?" The answer is given in verses 14 to 33.

9:1 I say the truth in Christ, I lie not,— The strong character of this language indicates that the apostle's Jewish opponents had charged him with hostility to his nation and insincerity in his actions. He begins his reply by a statement the force of which is to show that his fellowship with Christ makes insincerity impossible.

my conscience bearing witness with me in the Holy Ghost.—Not "my conscience bearing me witness." His conscience bore witness in accordance with his word. Moreover it was a conscience enlightened and guided by the Holy Spirit.

9:2 that I have great sorrow and unceasing pain in my heart.—There is stress upon the words "great" and "heart." The heart stands here for "hidden springs of the personal life."

9:3 For I could wish—The ellipsis to be supplied is not "but I may not" but "were it possible." He means that his love for Israel is such that he could desire what he expresses were it not for certain reasons which prevent it.

that I myself were anathema from Christ—The Greek word *anathema,* frequently translates, in the Septuagint, the Hebrew *cherem,* which signified a thing devoted to God, whether for His service, as in the case of the sacrifice (Lev. 27:28), or for its own destruction, e.g., an idol (Deut. 7:26), Jericho (Josh. 6:17). The term acquired the more general meaning of the disfavor of God, as in Isaiah 34:5; Malachi 4:6. This is its meaning here, as also in Acts 23:14; 1 Corinthians 12:3; 16:22; Galatians 1:8, 9. Perhaps the love of Paul for his fellow countrymen can be fully apprehended only by those with love as great as his. But whatever he might find in his heart to wish, in order that they might be saved, two things are plain, that the wish was impossible of accomplishment, and that had it been possible it could not have availed to secure the end he desired.

for my brethren's sake, my kinsmen according to the flesh:—The word "flesh" is here used of natural relationship; cp. 1 Corinthians 10:18; Galatians 4:23.

9:4 who are Israelites;—This is the national name, including all the descendants of Jacob, who from God obtained the name of Israel, "a prince with God" (Gen. 32:28). Cp. Hosea 12:3, and Galatians 6:16, where the phrase "Israel of God" suggests a contrast between a true and false Israel. The title Israel connotes the dignity and privileges attaching to those who come under the term.

whose is the adoption,—The reference is probably to Exodus 4:22 and Hosea 11:1. The relationship referred to is external, indicating that Israel was brought into a peculiar relation to God in contrast to other nations (cp. Ex. 4:22; Deut. 14:1; Jer. 31:9), a collective relationship rather than that of individuals.

and the glory,—That is, the special favor granted them of the manifestation of the presence of God in their midst. See especially Exodus 29:43, where God declared that the tabernacle would be sanctified by His glory, also Exodus 40:34; 2 Chronicles 5:14; Haggai 2:7.

and the covenants,—This refers to the promises made by God at various times to the patriarchs, that, e.g., originally given to Abraham (Gen. 12:1-3), and confirmed in a vision (Gen. 15:18), and again by the birth of Isaac (Gen. 21), and by Divine oath (Gen. 22:15-18). Cp. Ephesians 2:12.

Whereas the English word "covenant" signifies a mutual undertaking between two parties or more, who agree to discharge certain obligations, the word _diathēkē_ does not involve the idea of joint obligation, but signifies that which is undertaken by one person only. Hence it is frequently interchangeable with the word "promise," as in Galatians 3:16, 18. The covenants referred to here were of this character.

and the giving of the law, and the service _of God,_—The original has simply "the service," _latreai,_ a word specially used of the worship connected with the tabernacle and the temple and of the ordinances relating thereto. Cp. Hebrews 9:1.

and the promises;—The word here signifies those undertakings graciously given to Abraham and his seed (Gal. 3:16). The promise given to Abraham in Genesis 12:1-3 was purposely repeated. The first contained in itself all subsequent promises. Hence the plural involves all that God has undertaken to bestow upon Israel.

9:5 whose are the fathers, and of whom is Christ as concerning the flesh,—Literally, "from whom," not "whose," as in the preceding clause, as if Christ was the special property of the people of Israel, but signifying that He sprang from their race, being born of the Virgin Mary. That He thus sprang from the nation of Israel is the highest of all the privileges enumerated. The provision made in His person was universal.

who is over all, God blessed forever. Amen.—The words rendered "who is" consist, in the original, of the article with the present participle, literally, "the One being." This kind of phrase is not a statement of fact, though that is involved, but is descriptive of what is essential and characteristic. The same phrase is found in John 1:18, there showing that his Sonship is essential and unoriginated.

Alternative translations of the whole sentence are mentioned in the margin of the R.V. The rendering given in the text of both the A.V. and the R.V. is to be taken as right. It is a construction which would be unhesitatingly adopted by Greek scholars, apart from questions of doctrine. The preceding context, all the details of which speak of Christ, lead up to a climax concerning the deity of His being, rather than a detached doxology. The statement as to the deity of Christ puts the crowning arch upon the privileges and blessings enumerated concerning Israel. That the reference is to Christ is supported without exception by all the ante-Nicene fathers who refer to it. The statement is consistent with the doctrine of the deity of Christ, as set forth by Paul himself as well as by his fellow apostles. Lastly, as the apostle himself declares categorically that Christ is the creator of all things (see, e.g., Col. 1:16), that the reference is to Christ is consistent with what is said of the Creator in Romans 1:25.

God's Sovereign Right to Choose, 9:6–13

Introductory Note

In this section the apostle meets an objection that his teaching as to the rejection of the Jews would argue a failure on God's part to fulfill His promises. This is the first step toward his argument as to the righteousness of God in calling the Gentiles into blessing.

The following are the steps in the argument: (1) The subjects of the promise (v. 6); (2) The character of the promise (vv. 7–9); (3) The basis of the promise (vv. 10–13).

9:6 But *it is* **not as though the word of God hath come to nought.**—That is, the promise God made to Abraham.

For they are not all Israel, which are of Israel:—That is, the number of those who are of Israel is not determined by natural descent. One of the objects of the argument in the present chapter is to show that God had purposed to bring Gentiles into His favor. The phrase "which are of Israel" probably refers to the patriarch Jacob, and the meaning is that not all that are born of Jacob belong to the true Israel, the people of God. Israel as subjects of the promise does not consist simply of the natural descendants of Jacob.

9:7 neither, because they are Abraham's seed are they all children: but, In Isaac shall thy seed be called.—The promise was not conditional upon natural birth. The divine choice was made according to

God's own will. Ishmael was set aside. Accordingly not all the natural descendants of Abraham are spiritual children. Cp. Galatians 3:7, "they which be of faith the same are sons of Abraham." Zacchaeus (Luke 19:9) was not "a son of Abraham" because of his faith in Christ and the acknowledgment of His claims. Again, as God rejected Ishmael, so He would reject unbelieving Jews.

The word "called" is virtually the same as "to choose" (Is. 48:12; 49:1), which involves the bringing of the subjects of promise into its fulfillment.

9:8 That is, it is not the children of the flesh that are children of God;—The thought here is not quite the same as in Galatians 4:22–31. Here the immediate point in the argument is the sovereignty of God in His selection of one and rejection of another. At the same time there lies behind this what is set forth in the Galatians passage, that Abraham and Sarah planned according to the flesh and sought to hurry the fulfillment of God's promise, with disastrous consequences.

but the children of the promise are reckoned for a seed.—The choice made by God depended not upon the works of the flesh but on His own promise. The phrase "the children of the promise" signifies children who are such in virtue of the promise. Hence this verse is not exactly parallel to the phrase "the children of the flesh," for they are children of the flesh as such. As God discriminated in the case of Abraham's children so He is doing still. In this the ways of God, who is a law to Himself, are inscrutable.

9:9 For this is a word of promise,— There is stress on the word "promise," and the absence of the definite article lends emphasis to its character as a promise; that is to say, the fulfillment was conditioned solely upon the word of God and upon His power.

According to this season will I come, and Sarah shall have a son.—The season was that in Genesis 18:10. The quotation indicates more than the simple promise that Isaac should be born; that was to take place in consequence of God's giving, i.e., through the manifestation of His own power.

9:10 And not only so; but Rebecca also having conceived by one, *even* **by our father Isaac**—The same fact is illustrated in the case of Isaac's children. This provides a still more patent instance of the sovereignty of God's choice. So far a Jew might have replied that Ishmael and his descendants were reasonably rejected because he was a son of a bond-woman, but now even such an argument is rendered invalid in that Esau and Jacob were sons of the one mother.

9:11, 12 for *the children* **being not yet born,**—The selection of Isaac was only after Ishmael's birth, but the selection of Jacob was made before both he and his brother were born. The parenthesis which the A.V. inserts at the beginning of this verse interferes with the connection of the following verse. The form of the negative "not" in the original represents the circumstances not simply as a fact of history but as a part of the Divine plan, and so with the next clause.

neither having done anything good or bad,—Not only are claims of birth ruled out but claims of merit also. If this holds good in the case of Jacob and Esau it must also hold good in the case of Ishmael and Isaac.

that the purpose of God according to election might stand, not of works, but of Him that calleth, it was said unto her, The elder shall serve the younger.—This is quoted from the LXX of Genesis 25:23. The fulfillment of this lay, so far as the individual sons were concerned, in the circumstances of Esau and Jacob. What follows, however, shows that there was more than the individuals in view. In other words, the principles of God's dealings apply both to the individuals and to their descendants.

9:13 Even as it is written, Jacob I loved, but Esau I hated.—That the whole history of the nations of Edom and Israel is illustrative of the principles here laid down is confirmed by the quotation from Malachi 1:2, 3. The word "hated" is to be understood in the light of all that is said of God's rejection of Esau. It stands for the attitude which He adopted in acting consistently with His divine attributes, and presents the antithesis of the attitude adopted toward Jacob as expressed in the words "Jacob have I loved." These words

must therefore be distinguished from their use with reference to mere human emotion. God's love to Jacob was undeserved; His hatred of Esau had a moral ground and Esau deserved it.

God's Sovereignty Stated in the Old Testament and His Righteousness Established, 9:14–18

Introductory Note

The argument thus far has established God's sovereign right to exercise the privileges of the gospel to whomsoever and on whatever terms He please, natural conditions and human merit being ruled out. Accordingly, if the Jews refused the gospel God's decision to reject them and offer salvation to the Gentiles was unchallengeable. The Jew might object to this, that to make no distinction between Jew and Gentile in regard to merit or demerit would be inconsistent with Divine righteousness. To this Paul answers that God's sovereignty in these matters was (1) stated, (2) illustrated, in the Old Testament.

9:14 What shall we say then? Is there unrighteousness with God? God forbid.—That is, in choosing one and rejecting another.

9:15 For He saith to Moses,—This implies the assumption that the Scriptures are the Word of God, an assumption which his readers likewise took for granted. There is stress on the word "to Moses," and the mention of Moses would especially appeal to a Jew.

I will have mercy on whom I have mercy, and I will have compassion on whom I have compassion.—This was said to Moses in answer to his intercession for Israel after God's refusal to go up with them to the Land of Promise because of their sin in worshiping the golden calf. The quotation is from the Septuagint. The conclusion is that since God showed mercy to Israel after such a flagrant breach of the covenant into which they had entered with Him, surely He could show mercy to Gentiles who had not been guilty of such an act. But for the divine mercy and sovereignty none would be blessed. The point established is that the mercy and compassion shown by God are determined by nothing external to His attributes.

9:16 So then it is not of him that willeth, nor of him that runneth, but of God that hath mercy.—That is, the cause lies neither in human will nor in human effort ("runneth" is suggestive of the intense effort of a racer). Man cannot in any way boast of having been responsible for the blessing of salvation. The inference from what has been stated confirms the principle of God's sovereign right to exercise mercy.

9:17 For the Scripture saith unto Pharaoh,—This personification of Scripture intimates its permanent authority and living power, as well as its divine inspiration. This appeal to the Word of God is again a forceful argument in replying to a Jew who made his boast in the Law.

For this very purpose did I raise thee up, that I might shew in thee My power, and that My name might be published abroad in all the earth.—The special instance of Pharaoh and the hardening of his heart, serves to explain the hardened condition of the Jews, which is the particular subject of this chapter.

As a matter of fact, the narrative in Exodus, as correctly given in the R.V., states that to begin with Pharaoh persistently hardened his own heart. The whole record is deeply significant in this respect. Firstly, Exodus 3:19 establishes the prescience of God. Then 4:21 simply foretells what God will do as to Pharaoh's conduct. The effects of the first plagues were that Pharaoh was responsible for hardening his own heart. See 7:13, 22, 23; 8:15; 9:7, "Pharaoh's heart was stubborn." At 9:12 we find the statement of the Lord's intervention in this matter: "The Lord hardened the heart of Pharaoh." Yet again in 9:35 the hardening is ascribed to the monarch. After that in each case it is ascribed to God (10:1, 20; 11:10). Clearly, therefore, the hardening was retributive and not arbitrary. Yet, while God did not make Pharaoh wicked, and his punishment was nothing more than he deserved, the argument in Romans stresses the absolute sovereignty and righteousness of God. The recipient of pardoning mercy can never boast in

his priority of merit. He who is punished can never charge God with unrighteousness.

This idea, therefore, is not merely Pharaoh's exaltation to kingship but his being maintained in that position instead of being immediately cut off for his self-will. Not the creation of the man is in view but the object for which God permitted him so long to be kept in authority.

9:18 So then He hath mercy on whom He will, and whom He will He hardeneth.—There is stress on the phrase "whom He will." The reason for God's dealings is inscrutable. The secret, therefore, lies with God Himself. Man can never charge Him with injustice. His acts, and whatever significance He makes plain regarding them, are for man's recognition and instruction. They are neither capricious nor arbitrary. That he hardens a man or a people is not an uncalled-for procedure but a judicial act.

God's Sovereignty Unchallengeable; His Long-suffering and Mercy, 9:19–24

Introductory Note

The apostle now meets a possible objection arising from his statements in verses 7–18. This may be put as follows: If God hardens man, or if He has mercy on him, according to His own determination, and if man's wrongdoing subserves God's purposes, how can it be reasonable for Him to find fault with what simply accomplishes His irresistible will? The answer to this is twofold. Firstly, the objection reveals the ignorance of the relation between God and man, for man, being the creature, is not in a position to challenge his Creator (vv. 20, 21). Secondly, it reveals ignorance of both the character of God and the sinfulness of man. For He has used His sovereign will to exercise long-suffering (vv. 22, 24). Thus the apostle both establishes the sovereignty of God and shows in what a merciful way it has been directed. As regards the first, he argues, not from the fact of man's sinfulness, but from that of God's righteousness. In the second he enforces his argument from the facts of man's sinfulness and God's mercy. All men have forfeited any claim upon this, on account of sin. God has not made any man wicked. No one can therefore argue unrighteousness in His dealings nor can He be charged with partiality. The folly is urged of the creature's setting himself up against his Creator, and this is illustrated from the potter's art, but then again God has restrained His merited wrath. Then, too, the very fact of God's long-suffering implies the exercise of man's free will, and this was actually the case with Pharaoh. Again, He makes known the riches of His glory by displaying His mercy and this is seen in that Gentiles are included as well as Jews, consistently both with the prerogatives of God and with the principles of His righteous dealing.

9:19 Thou wilt say then unto me, Why doth He still find fault?—That is to say, why does He blame anyone for hardness of heart?

For who withstandeth His will?—The word rendered "will" is *boulēma,* which signifies a deliberate purpose and is to be distinguished from the more frequent and general word *thelēma,* which, while it may sometimes have much the same meaning as *boulēma,* frequently has the meaning simply of a desire, or spontaneous will. Here the apostle speaks of the determinate counsel of God which overrules human action. Man is able to resist the will, the *thelēma,* of God, but whatever takes place God's determinate counsel, *boulēma,* is never prevented from fulfillment.

9:20 Nay but, O man, who art thou that repliest against God?—The objection raised in verse 19 is repelled rather than refuted, as it is shown to be a case of ignorance of the relation existing between the creature and God the Creator.

Shall the thing formed say to him that formed it, Why didst thou make me thus?—See Isaiah 29:16; 45:9. While the apostle's argument is not precisely the same as that of Isaiah, yet he has the nation of Israel and its condition also in view.

9:21 Or hath not the potter a right over the clay, from the same lump to make one part of a vessel unto honor, and another unto dishonor?—The "Or" suggests the alternatives, that either there must be a

recognition of the absoluteness of God, or there must be a denial that the potter has power over the clay. To what use a particular part of the clay is to be put depends not upon its quality but upon the will of the potter. This verse stresses the unqualified sovereignty of God as Creator in contrast to the creature. For the removal of any possible objection to this that it argues the complete helpfulness of man, see next verse.

9:22 What if God,—Literally, "but if God." The "But" marks a change to a consummating reply in the argument, and introduces a sentence which the apostle does not finish, nor was there any need to finish it, as the actual fact, though introduced by a hypothetic "if," is unanswerable. The contending Jew might have been ready with what he would consider to be a cogent reply. But now that the apostle stresses the long-suffering and patience of God, there is more force in the unfinished sentence than if it had been completed. The "But," then, marks the contrast between what God had a perfect right to do and what He has actually done.

willing to shew His wrath,—This seems best understood in the sense of "having the will to show His wrath." The apostle is not suggesting that this is a reason for His action or that His showing mercy is carried out in spite of His wrath. The word "willing" recalls the implication, at the end of verse 19, of God's irresistible power to will, the stress being upon the fact of God's sovereignty.

and to make His power known,—By so doing He would manifest His character.

endured with much long-suffering vessels of wrath—There is no definite article, as what is being referred to now is not simply the special example of Pharaoh but a general principle with an including reference to the rejection of Israel. The phrase is not subjective as in Jeremiah 50:25, where the meaning is that they are instruments by which God executes His wrath, but objective, "vessels doomed to wrath."

fitted unto destruction:—The "fitting" is not imputed to God, as if God had prepared these vessels for wrath in contrast to those He had prepared for mercy. God has not created men with a view to their destruction. As a matter of fact, although the metaphor of the potter's vessel has been used, in which the material itself is helpless, yet that must not be pressed in the matter of the application to persons. The form of the word rendered "fitted" may be regarded as in the middle voice, which implies action done by oneself with a view to one's own aims and interests. There is a suggestion, therefore, that the persons referred to as "vessels of wrath" have fitted themselves for destruction, and this was actually the case with Pharaoh, as we have seen from Exodus. The apostle could have used a form of expression stating clearly that they had been fitted by an outward agency unto destruction. That form, however, is set aside in order to use one which throws the responsibility upon man for the hardness of his heart. God, then, has restrained His merited wrath. The objector might have had some reason if he had said "What if God, willing to show His wrath and to make His power known, executed His judgment upon the vessels of wrath." What he says instead is that God has endured with much long-suffering vessels of wrath who have fitted themselves unto destruction.

The word *apōleia*, "destruction" (here only in this Epistle) like its synonyms, means "not the destruction of being but of well-being, not annihilation, but its ruin so far as the purpose of its existence is concerned.

9:23 and that He might make known the riches of His glory—The glory here refers to the actings of God's grace toward believers, as mentioned in 8:18, 21.

upon vessels of mercy,—Mercy is the manifestation of pity; it assumes need on the part of him who receives it, and resources adequate to meet the need on the part of him that shows it.

While God has provided salvation for all men (Titus 3:5), the vessels of mercy are those who actually receive it. But the idea underlying the present phrase is that, according to the foreknowledge of God, they are destined to mercy.

which He afore prepared unto glory,—This is in striking contrast with what is said of the vessels of wrath. See note on "fitted." The apostle does not simply say, as might be

expected, "(vessels) prepared unto glory," but "which He afore prepared unto glory." While stress is laid on the gracious actings of God, there is a plain intimation that those who enjoy the glory of heaven are prepared on earth. There can be no entrance there without that preparation by which they are born of God and receive the forgiveness of sins and eternal life in Christ.

9:24 *even* us, whom He also called, not from the Jews only, but also from the Gentiles?—This brings the special point in the argument to a head, stressing the fact that Gentiles are included among the vessels of mercy as well as Jews, and that this is in accordance not only with the prerogatives of God (vv. 20, 21), but with the principles of His righteous dealing (v. 14).

God's Sovereignty in Relation to Israel and the Gentiles Foretold in the Old Testament, 9:25–29

9:25 As He saith also in Hosea, I will call that My people, which was not My people: and her beloved, which was not beloved.—The quotation is from the Septuagint of Hosea 2:23 with variations, the order of the statements being inverted. The Hebrew is, literally, "and I will have pity on the not-pitied-one (the gender being feminine), and I will say to not-My-people My people art thou." The word "pity," or "mercy," in the LXX is changed to the more tender word "beloved," love taking the place of mercy.

9:26 And it shall be, *that* in the place where it was said unto them, Ye are not My people, there shall they be called sons of the living God.—This quotation is from Hosea 1:10, almost word for word from the Septuagint. Thus the two passages in Hosea are connected, and are quoted in the opposite order.

The apostle shows that in the mind of the Spirit the promise embraces Gentiles, who would be brought into God's favor through the instrumentality of the gospel, this being in accordance with the principles set forth in Hosea's prophecy. Since Israel had placed themselves on a level with the Gentiles by their departure from God it was both reasonable and compatible with God's mercy that in recalling a remnant of Israel from their alienated state He should call in others also who are, as Israel had become, not His people.

9:27 And Isaiah crieth concerning Israel, If the number of the children of Israel be as the sand of the sea, it is the remnant that shall be saved:—This quotation is chiefly from the Septuagint version of Isaiah 10:22, 23; with a modification recalling Hosea 1:10, especially with regard to the word "number." Salvation was to be limited to a remnant of the people of Israel. That is the point in this phase of the argument concerning the exclusion of Jews.

9:28 for the Lord will execute *His* word upon the earth, finishing it and cutting it short.—This amplifies the thought in the preceding quotation. The word "work" in the A.V. is not the meaning of the word *logos*. Hence the necessary change in the R.V., where "the word" is that which the Lord fulfills in the execution of His judgments upon the nation, the mass being rejected and the remnant saved. That God finishes His word means that He brings it to an end; that He cuts it short would seem to indicate the summary and decisive character of the divine action. The rest of the quotation as given in the A.V. is not in the best texts.

9:29 And, as Isaiah hath said before, Except the Lord of Sabaoth had left us a seed, we had become as Sodom, and been like unto Gomorrah.—This quotation agrees with the Septuagint, where the word "a seed" replaces the Hebrew word for a small remnant. The word "Sabaoth" is a transliteration of a Hebrew word meaning "hosts."

While Paul laments the condition of his nation, he shows the righteousness of God in dealing retributively with His people. If the reduction of the nation to a small remnant was based upon God's righteousness, the Jew could not complain of the gospel; for in the matter of salvation, in reducing the number of the people to those only who believe, God was acting with perfect consistency. The gospel was, after all, doing only what Isaiah had prophesied. Isaiah foretold of a remnant yet future; Paul speaks of a remnant in the present day.

The Problem Explained; Faith the Key, 9:30–33

Introductory Note

The apostle now shows the ground upon which God has dealt both with Jew and Gentile: This recalls the teaching of the earlier part of the Epistle, that God reckons righteousness on the ground of faith.

9:30 What shall we say then? That the Gentiles, which followed not after righteousness, attained to righteousness, even the righteousness which is of faith:—The reference here to attainment does not suggest the result of human effort but the reception of the blessing granted to faith. Righteousness here signifies the justifying act of God's grace by which righteousness is reckoned to a person consistently with God's own attribute of righteousness, and in response to faith at the time of conversion.

9:31 but Israel, following after a law of righteousness, did not arrive at *that* law.—The phrase "law of righteousness" may be taken to indicate a general principle, presenting righteousness as the outcome of keeping a law, the Law of Moses being especially in view. The Israelite, being possessed of such a Law, looked upon righteousness as a possible outcome of keeping it. Their efforts found righteousness beyond their reach.

9:32 Wherefore? Because *they sought it* not by faith, but as it were by works.—the phrase "as it were" is literally, simply "as," that is, in the belief that righteousness could be so obtained. The responsibility of the choice is here seen to lie with man, and this gives the other side relative to the subject of God's sovereignty as mentioned in the preceding part of the chapter. Man has only himself to blame for his failure.

They stumbled at the stone of stumbling;—An alternative reading, making this one sentence with what precedes, is given in the margin: "because doing it, they stumbled at the stone of stumbling." Christ is definitely introduced as the one object of faith, and the definite article indicates Him as well-known in this respect. Salvation by faith in a once crucified Messiah, was utterly opposed to all their ideas. Yet both the plan of salvation and the way in which it would be rejected were foretold in the Old Testament.

9:33 even as it is written, Behold, I lay in Zion a stone of stumbling, and a rock of offense: and he that believeth on Him shall not be put to shame.—Two passages from Isaiah are combined, one from 8:14 and the other from 28:16, and the two are put together, that from 8:14 closely following the Hebrew, that from 28:6 giving a free rendering of the LXX. The passage in 28 was a warning against false confidence and the desire of the people of Israel for a league with Ephraim

against the Syrians. That in the eighth chapter was an exhortation not to fear the alliance between Syria and Ephraim (see 7:2). There was a better ground of confidence for God's people, in their true Messiah; He would be a stumbling-stone to the many but a reliable ground of confidence to believers. As in other quotations the application goes far beyond those immediate circumstances.

The word rendered "offense" is *skandalon,* originally the name of that part of a trap to which the bait was attached and hence the trap or snare itself. It became metaphorical of anything that arouses prejudice or becomes a hindrance to others, causing them to fall, the hindrance being good in itself as here, of Christ, and those who stumbled being unbelievers, or the hindrance being evil.

ROMANS

The Righteousness of Faith as Being in Accordance with the Old Testament, 10:1–21

Introductory Note

This chapter, in the series of chapters nine to eleven, runs parallel to the fourth chapter in the series three to eight. See the introduction to chapters nine to eleven. Here in chapter ten the argument is continued that the gospel is in perfect harmony with the teaching of the Old Testament (cp. 9:25–29). The apostle also confirms, what he has pointed out at the end of chapter nine, that the present rejection of Israel finds its explanation in their persistent rejection of God's way of salvation, in spite of the witness of the Law and the Prophets, and in their efforts to obtain righteousness by their own works; further, that the terms upon which salvation is offered were to be open alike to the Gentiles or Jews, faith not being the exclusive possession of believing Jews. This chapter expands 9:24–33.

10:1 Brethren, my heart's desire and my supplication to God is for them, that they may be saved.—Literally, "the good pleasure of my heart and my supplication toward God is unto salvation." The word *eudokia*, "desire," is, literally, "good pleasure." It is used of believers elsewhere only at Philippians 1:15. It is frequently used of God. It expresses not merely a benevolent attitude but an active pleasure, and, when used of something not yet realized, indicates a fervent desire. Spiritual desires should always be turned into prayer.

10:2 For I bear them witness that they have a zeal for God, but not according to knowledge.—Their religious zeal, in which in former days Paul had shared (Acts 22:3; 1 Tim. 1:13), was the reason for his heart's desire and supplication. This is implied in the connecting word "For." Zeal not regulated by knowledge leads to the substitution of error, and inspires a persecuting spirit. Paul's atti-

tude is an example to us to pray for such as have a mistaken zeal for God.

10:3 For being ignorant of God's righteousness, and seeking to establish their own,—"God's righteousness" stands for both His own character and His counsels and acts by which He reckons righteousness to the believing sinner. The substitution of human effort for God's way of salvation in Christ shows a complete misunderstanding of God's attitude toward man.

they did not subject themselves to the righteousness of God.—The verb rendered "subject themselves" is in the middle voice, and implies an intelligent interest in the subjection which in their case they refused (cp. 8:7). Subjection to God's righteousness, with all that that means, involves the laying aside of self-effort.

10:4 For Christ is the end of the law unto righteousness to everyone that believeth.—For the word *telos*, "end," see at 6:21, 22. This statement expands precisely and succinctly how the Jews were mistaken. That Christ is the end of the Law as stated is best explained by Galatians 3:23–26; where the meaning is, that we were kept in ward under the Law . . . with the coming of Christ in view, until that took place. There was no way of escape from the domination of the Law. The condemnatory power of the Law was not an end in itself. Its restraints were necessary that Christ might be welcomed when He came.

10:5 For Moses writeth that the man that doeth the righteousness which is of the Law shall live thereby.—The quotation is from Leviticus 18:5. Literally it is "the man that hath done these things," the whole past life being under review. The doing is to be lifelong and is never for a moment to fall below the divine standard. A Jew thus perfectly meeting the requirement of God would thereby find life. No one, save Christ, has ever acted so.

0:6 But the righteousness which is of iith saith thus,—The means by which a elieving sinner is reckoned righteous is virtuly personified and so is said to speak in the nguage of Scripture.

ay not in thy heart, Who shall ascend ito heaven? (that is, to bring Christ own:)—The quotation, which is used to 1ow that the book of the Law taught the very rinciples of the gospel concerning justification y faith, is from Deuteronomy 30:11-14. It is iken from the Septuagint, with certain modifiations and with some parenthetic explanaons, so as to apply the details of the passage ie more pointedly. Thus, "Who shall ascend ito heaven?" is explained by the statement, that is, to bring Christ down"; in other vords, to bring about His reincarnation.

0:7 or, Who shall descend into the byss? (that is, to bring Christ up from he dead.)—The Deuteronomy passage has, Neither is it beyond the sea that thou shouldst say, Who shall go over the sea for us?" In he quotation the thought of going across the ea is changed to descending into the abyss. he word "abyss" is found in the New Testaient elsewhere only in Luke 8:31 and seven imes in the Apocalypse. In the Old Testament was sometimes applied to the sea as fathom:ss, e.g., Genesis 1:2, 7:11 (Septuagint). It ; often set in contrast to heaven, cp. Genesis 9:25 (Septuagint). It stood frequently for the egion in which are fallen spirits and lost souls. n the present passage it stands, as in the)ld Testament, for Sheol, or the region of the lead, into which Christ went at His death. To hink of a repetition of the death and resurrecion of Christ would be to impute incom·leteness to that which was accomplished ·nce for all and stands eternally in its absolute fficacy.

10:8 But what saith it? The word is iigh thee, in thy mouth, and in thy heart: that is, the word of faith which ve preach:—The explanation shows that in he mind of the Spirit these words of Moses, hough used by him of the Law, were intended o bear also an interpretation with reference o the gospel, and that, in certain respects, vhat was true of the Law was applicable to the gospel. That changes are made from the literal neaning to the spiritual, and that the passage

is thus applied to the gospel, is accounted for by the fact that Christ had accomplished His redemptive work on the Cross and had ascended to heaven. The Spirit of God prepared, through Moses, the way for the apostle to apply the words to the subject of justification.

While presenting a contrast between the righteousness which is of the Law, and the righteousness which is of faith, he shows that there is this point of similarity, in that both the Law and the gospel were not inaccessible, but were "in the heart and in the mouth." He shows, too, that the essential difference between the Law and the gospel lies in the facts of the advent, death, resurrection and ascension of Christ, events which could never have been brought about by human effort. Man could neither bring Christ down from heaven nor raise Him from the dead. Works are ruled out. Man can do nothing. God has done all. The facts must be accepted by faith.

10:9 because if thou shalt confess with thy mouth Jesus *as* Lord,—The stress in the divine titles is upon "Lord." The confession is the acknowledgment, as a testimony to others, of the supreme and absolute authority of Jesus Christ; that is, the One who, having been despised and rejected of men, was afterward glorified as the exalted One to whom all authority is given, who has been invested with all His mediatorial prerogatives and power.

and shalt believe in thine heart that God raised Him from the dead, thou shalt be saved:—This exercise of faith is more than the acceptance of the historic fact of the resurrection of Christ. It is a matter of the heart, not simply of the mind. It therefore involves the appreciation of the promises of God as fulfilled in the death and resurrection of Christ and an appropriation of His person. The confession and faith are, then, the response to "the word of faith" (v. 8). Confession is put first for the following reasons: (1) as being appropriate to the order, mouth and heart, as in verse 8; (2) because the order of the Lordship of Christ and His resurrection from the dead are in agreement with the order in verses 6 and 7, verse 6 speaking of His present position in heaven, verse 7 of His resurrection from the dead; (3) because confession of the Christ as Lord is the evidence of faith; (4) because this confession provides the distinctive difference between those who have been justified by faith and those who are seeking righteousness by their own works (cp. 1 Cor. 12:3).

10:10 for with the heart man believeth unto righteousness; and with the mouth confession is made unto salvation.—The actual order of experience is now given: faith first, then confession. In order to be saved righteousness must be reckoned, and this depends upon faith, but faith necessarily leads to confession. Absence of confession betokens lack of faith.

10:11 For the Scripture saith, Whosoever believeth on Him shall not be put to shame.—This repeats the quotation in 9:33. There the object was to show that Israel's failure was due to unbelief; here the point is that faith is open to Jew and Gentile, and this is stressed by an alteration in the quotation. Isaiah says "he that believeth." Paul says "everyone that believeth," showing that even Isaiah's words were not confined to the Jewish nation. The subject of confession is dropped, for the argument has to do especially with faith, and faith alone is here dealt with.

10:12 For there is no distinction between Jew and Greek:—Compare and contrast 3:22. There the apostle said "There is no exception, for all have sinned"; here he says, "there is no distinction, all may be saved."

for the same _Lord_ is Lord of all,—In 3:29 the apostle showed that God was the same God for both Jew and Gentile; here he states that the same Lord is Lord of both.

and is rich unto all that call upon Him:—The argument passes from the universal provision of salvation to the bounty of the provider, stressing at the same time the fact that He has absolute authority. The reference here is to Christ. In Scripture calling upon God is always a habit, not a single act. Cp. Genesis 4:26; Zechariah 13:9; Acts 2:21; 9:14; 1 Corinthians 1:2; 2 Timothy 2:22; 1 Peter 1:17.

10:13 for, Whosoever shall call upon the name of the Lord shall be saved.—This confirms verses 11 and 12 by a quotation from the LXX of Joel 2:32. The prophet foretold that salvation would be granted, not on the ground of nationality, but on that of calling

upon the Name of the Lord. In the words "all flesh," in Joel 2:28, there was an intimation of the obliteration of national distinctions. In the passage in Joel "the Lord" is Jehovah. This quotation, applied to Christ as Lord in the matter of man's salvation, gives a clear testimony to the deity of Christ.

10:14 How then shall they call on him in whom they have not believed?—Here the apostle turns from the "whosoever" aspect of faith to the means of its production. The four questions asked in verses 14 and 15 strengthen the argument as to the universality of the gospel. Each question tacitly assumes this universality. He is vindicating the offer of salvation to Jew and Gentile alike.

and how shall they believe in him whom they have not heard? and how shall they hear without a preacher?—This is the accurate rendering, in contrast to the A.V., which inserts the word "of" before "whom." The voice of Christ is heard through His messengers; the quotation intimates that the voice of the preacher is the instrument of the voice of Christ.

10:15 and how shall they preach, except they be sent?—There would have been no sending if Jewish prejudice had its way. The Holy Spirit had come, His will had overridden the antagonism of this prejudice, and, in fulfillment of Old Testament prophecy, He had Himself sent forth heralds of the Gospel to proclaim the glad tidings. It was the Holy Spirit who said, in the church at Antioch, "Separate Me Barnabas and Saul for the work whereunto I have called them" (Acts 13:2). This prerogative and power of the Holy Spirit should not have been replaced by human devices. He still calls, equips and sends His messengers of peace, where churches seek to obey the revealed will of the Lord instead of following human tradition.

even as it is written, How beautiful are the feet of them that bring glad tidings of good things?—This is quoted freely from Isaiah 52:7; the words "upon the mountains" are omitted, the symbolic giving place to the actual.

10:16 But they did not all hearken to the glad tidings. For Isaiah saith, Lord, who hath believed our report?—This confirms what has just been said, that the unbelief of the Jews was foretold by the prophets.

10:17 So belief *cometh* **of hearing, and hearing by the word of Christ.**—Though Isaiah's words were immediately applicable to Israel, they suggest by implication the universality of the glad tidings. The main point here, however, is, that there must be a report to be believed, that is to say, there must be a proclamation of the gospel, if it is to be believed. As faith is demanded from all men, the proclamation of the gospel, which is prerequisite, must be universal.

The phrase "the word of Christ," which is supported by the majority of MSS., signifies "the word concerning Christ."

The subject of faith in verses 1-17 may be taken under the following headings, with a suggestion of chronological order: (1) The word of faith (v. 8); (2) The object of faith (vv. 4, 9); (3) The hearing of faith (v. 17); (4) The righteousness of faith (vv. 6, 10); (5) The saving power of faith (v. 9); (6) The confidence of faith (v. 11); (7) The universality of faith (vv. 12, 13).

10:18 But I say,—This introduces two rhetorical questions to meet the two possible excuses which might be advanced on behalf of Jewish unbelief, namely, (1) that all had not an opportunity of receiving the good tidings and (2) that the information was not given.

Did they not hear?—This question implies that the first excuse is invalid.

Yea, verily, Their sound went out into all the earth, and their words unto the ends of the world.—The answer to the first excuse is from Psalm 19:4, which, while primarily referring to the universal testimony to God in nature, is here shown to have contained a foreshadowing of the universal proclamation of the gospel. The Psalm itself couples together the voice of creation and that of the written word.

10:19 But I say, Did Israel not know?—There are two ways of understanding this question: (1) Did Israel not know the gospel? (2) Did Israel not know that God would save Gentiles? The latter is perhaps more in keeping with the context, and is indicated by the quotations which follow.

First Moses saith, I will provoke you to jealousy with that which is no nation, with a nation void of understanding will I anger you.—In this, from Deuteronomy 32:21 (see also Hos. 1:9; 2:23), the only difference in the wording from that in the Deuteronomy passage is that "you" is substituted for "them," making the reference to Israel more pointed. Moses, then, had foretold not only that God would show favor to Gentiles, but that, as Israel had moved God to wrath by their rebellion and rejection of His word, He would, by means of the favor shown to Gentiles, move Israel to jealousy. The word "nation" stands for gentile people in general.

10:20 And Isaiah is very bold,—He prophesied at the risk of his life. He goes further, too, than Moses.

and saith, I was found of them that sought Me not; I became manifest unto them that asked not of Me.—This is quoted almost verbatim from the LXX of Isaiah 65:1, save that the two clauses are inverted, perhaps to give immediate prominence to the first, and to express the more pointedly the fact of the reception of the gospel by Gentiles.

10:21 But as to Israel—The rendering should not be "to Israel," as in the A.V., but "with reference to Israel."

He saith, All the day long did I spread out my hands—This gives the suggestion of a gracious attitude of entreaty and invitation.

unto a disobedient and gainsaying people.—This quotation is from the LXX of Isaiah 65:2, with a slight change in the order of phrases. The word "disobedient" translates the verb *apeitheo,* the same word as in 2:8. It literally means "to refuse to be persuaded," and so signifies either to refuse compliance or to refuse belief.

This final quotation in the series lays to the charge of Israel the cause of their condition. In spite of God's long-suffering and patient invitation, they had persisted in guilt both in act ("disobedient") and word ("gainsaying"). They were not without knowledge nor without understanding of the will of God. The ignorance referred to in verse 3 was the result of stubbornness and pride. With the Gentiles it was different.

ROMANS

· CHAPTER ELEVEN ·

God's Sovereignty Shown in His Grace and Mercy, 11:1–36

Introductory Note

The subject of this chapter is the exhibition of God's sovereignty in grace and mercy, in the case both of Israel and of the Gentiles, individually at the present time, and nationally in the future.

In regard to Israel, though they have not attained to righteousness, owing to their unbelief (ch. 9), and have brought divine retribution upon them by their disobedience and gainsaying (ch. 10), yet their rejection is to be neither (1) total nor (2) final. That it is not total the apostle proves from present facts; that it is not final is established, he says, upon divine election, and upon the gifts and calling of God. Consistent with the fact that the rejection is not total, is the bringing of individual Gentiles onto the same ground of grace as the believing Jews, who form a present spiritual remnant; and, owing to the fact that the rejection is not final, the restoration of the nation will involve the blessing of all the gentile nations. Grace is shown toward the Jews in that there is a present spiritual remnant (v. 5), and toward Gentiles in that salvation has come to them (v. 11). Mercy is to be shown nationally first toward Israel (v. 20) and so toward Gentiles as nations (v. 32).

This chapter gives a beautiful illustration of the interweaving of God's providential arrangements. The circumstances under consideration are seen to be to one another as cause and effect: (1) Israel's downfall has resulted in the carrying of the gospel to the Gentiles (vv. 11, 12, 15, 30); (2) but this present mercy to Gentiles will lead to the obtaining of mercy by Israel (vv. 26, 31); (3) the mercy thus shown in the restoration of Israel will result in universal blessing (v. 15).

To the opening question, "Did God cast off His people?" there are three replies, which cover the ground of the whole chapter. Israel is not utterly given up, for (1) Paul himself is an Israelite, and therefore a spiritual remnant exists (vv. 1–10); (2) one of the reasons why God is calling Gentiles into His favor is in order that He may show mercy to Israel; so He could not have rejected His people (vv. 11–24); (3) God will fulfill His promise to the nation on the coming of their deliverer (vv. 25 to the end).

11:1 I say then, did God cast off His people? God forbid. For I also am an Israelite,—The meaning is not that, being an Israelite, he could not believe that God had cast off His people, but rather that his own experience of God's salvation is a proof that God had not thrust away the nation, and that the apostle himself had not taught such a thing.

of the seed of Abraham,—A descendant of the one to whom God gave the promises.

of the tribe of Benjamin,—This tribe was preserved from destruction (Judges 21) and with Judah remained faithful to God after the return from exile (Ezra 4:1; 10:9).

11:2 God did not cast off His people which He foreknew. Or know ye not what the Scripture saith of Elijah,—The words "of Elijah" are, literally, "in Elijah"; that is to say, that part of the Hebrew Scriptures relating to Elijah. The Scriptures were frequently so designated in Jewish writings.

how he pleadeth with God against Israel,—The word *entugchanō*, which signifies to plead either on behalf of others or against them, is used in the former sense in 8:27, 34, and in the latter sense here.

11:3 Lord, they have killed Thy prophets, they have digged down Thine altars and I am left alone and they seek my life.—Elijah did not mean that he was the only prophet left in the nation, but that he was the only faithful one remaining.

11:4 But what saith the answer of God unto him? I have left for Myself seven thousand men, who have not bowed the

knee to Baal.—This is taken from the Hebrew of 1 Kings 19:18, with the addition of the words "for Myself" by which stress is laid upon the electing prerogative and power of God (see the following verses).

11:5 Even so then at this present time also there is a remnant according to the election of grace.—That is to say, there is a spiritual remnant as a result of the gospel. This fact is a pledge that the nation is not completely and permanently forsaken.

11:6 But if it is by grace, it is no more of works: otherwise grace is no more grace.—As to the additional statement in this verse in the A.V., the weight of MS. evidence is in favor of its omission.

11:7 What then? That which Israel seeketh for, that he obtained not;—This recalls 9:31, 32 and 10:3. The aorist tense, rightly rendered "obtained not," regards the attitude of the nation of Israel as definite and as a crisis.

but the election obtained it, and the rest were hardened:—The election is the same as the remnant (v. 5). The hardening has been a matter of definite retribution. Cp. the case of Pharaoh, 9:18.

11:8 according as it is written, God gave them a spirit of stupor, eyes that they should not see, and ears that they should not hear, this very day.—The phrase "a spirit of stupor" is taken from Isaiah 29:4. The words "unto this day" form part of the latter quotation; accordingly, there is no reason for the brackets in the A.V.

11:9 And David saith,—This introduces a quotation from Psalm 69:22, the first part being an explanation of the Hebrew, the second almost verbatim from the Septuagint.

let their table be made a snare, and a trap, and a stumblingblock, and a recompense unto them:—The table stands by metathesis for that which is associated with it. It is here symbolical of the special privileges granted to Israel and centering in Christ.

11:10 Let their eyes be darkened, that they may not see, And bow Thou down their back alway.—This part, from the Septuagint, differs from the Hebrew, which reads

"make their loins continually to shake." Weakness, fear and dejection are indicated in both. The bowing down of the back is a figure of the decrepitude of age, in contrast to that youthful activity which is indicative of the favor of the Lord. Such a state is so grievous that, though it called forth the apostle's prayer at the opening of the chapter, at the same time it is a solemn warning to all against the neglect of God's mercies, the rejection of His revealed will and the refusal of His claims.

11:11 I say then, Did they stumble that they might fall?—This is again a rhetorical question, not calling for an answer but proving a point. The Jews stumbled over Christ, but not so as to fall irretrievably. The idea conveyed by falling is here suggestive of what is impossible of recovery.

God forbid but by their fall salvation *is come* **unto the Gentiles,**—The word rendered "fall," *paraptōma*, is different from that in the question preceding. It denotes a moral trespass, as in 5:15. Neither is the rejection of Israel total nor is it final; more still, their present condition has been overruled for blessing to the Gentiles.

for to provoke them to jealousy.—The conversion of Gentiles was intended to react upon the Jews, not to stir them to jealousy in the ordinary sense of the word, but to arouse them to emulation, and to a desire for a recovery of divine favor. Cp. 10:19.

11:12 Now if their fall is the riches of the world, and their loss the riches of the Gentiles;—That is, if their fall, with their consequent temporary rejection by God, has meant that the spiritual riches of the gospel have come to all men. The thought here is perhaps an actual diminution of the nation, but there is the additional suggestion of spiritual loss.

how much more their fullness?—That is, what still greater blessings will accrue from their ultimate national restoration? The Divine riches will then be bestowed not merely on individuals as now but upon the nations of the world as a whole. The word *plērōma*, here applied to Israel, indicates the time when as a nation they will all be converted, in contrast to the present existence of a remnant. Here again the significance is full and national prosperity. Verse 12 sums up the whole subject as regards the Divine dealings with nations.

11:13 But I speak to you that are Gentiles.—This is not addressed to a new set of readers but immediately to those believers who were nationally Gentiles. Those were probably considerably in the majority in Rome.

Inasmuch then as I am an apostle of Gentiles, I glorify my ministry:—This is expressive both of his appreciative recognition that the ministry of the gospel to the Gentiles was especially entrusted to him and of his zeal in the faithful discharge of his ministry, the object ever being before him that the salvation of Gentiles might lead also to that of Jews.

11:14 If by any means I may provoke to jealousy _them that are_ my flesh, and may save some of them.—This explains both the statement "I glorify my ministry," and that at the close of verse 11. The same word is used here as there. The apostle's aim is indicative of the close connection between the present and the future, the testimony of the believer and the work of the gospel in the present age and its future effect both individually and nationally. The purpose both intimates that conversions take place one by one and makes clear the necessity of denoting one's utmost effort to win souls.

11:15 For if the casting away of them is the reconciling of the world,—The word _apobolē_, "casting away," differs from that in verses 1 and 2. It here refers to the exclusion of the nation from its position of favor. The reconciling of the world does not mean that all men will be reconciled, but that all who will may be reconciled. The scope of reconciliation is the whole world and the instrument is the gospel.

what _shall_ the receiving _of them be,_ but life from the dead—Life from the dead does not here signify physical resurrection but a state of the worldwide enjoyment of the favor and blessing of God instead of the present condition of alienation from Him. In this verse the four dispensational events intimated in verse 12 are recalled, but in a different way: (a) the fall of Israel is now spoken of with reference to their "casting away"; (b) "the

riches" of the world is now called "the reconciling"; (c) "the fullness" of Israel is here spoken of as "the receiving of them" into God's favor, i.e., in millennial blessing.

11:16 And if the firstfruit is holy, so is the lump:—The reference is apparently to Numbers 15:21, where the command to Israel was to give to the Lord the first of their dough as a heave offering. Cp. Nehemiah 10:37; Jeremiah 2:3. Here only is the word _aparchē_ rendered in the singular. Elsewhere it is in the plural, "firstfruits." See at 8:23. Two Hebrew words are thus translated, one meaning the principal part, Numbers 18:12, Proverbs 3:9, etc.; the other the earliest ripe of the crop or of the tree, Exodus 23:16; Nehemiah 10:35, etc.; they are found together in Exodus 23:19, etc., "the first of the firstfruits."

and if the root is holy, so are the branches:—This second metaphor is that of the olive tree. The reference in both the firstfruit and the root is specially to Abraham, the progenitor of Israel. To him the promise was made regarding his descendants. Since he, as the firstfruit and the root, is holy, that is, belongs to God, then the nation which is sprung from him, the lump and the branches, must also belong to God.

11:17 But if some of the branches were broken off,—This speaks of unbelieving Jews. They were the more numerous, but the character of the subject now makes the delicate reference to them as "some of the branches" appropriate. The description of them as branches makes clear that they are not the root. They were broken off by their rejection of Christ.

and thou, being a wild olive,—That is, the Gentile who, though now a believer, is, naturally, a member of those nations which God had suffered to walk in their own ways (Acts 14:16), and who therefore remained unfaithful to God. The wild olive being a tree of comparatively little value, this part of the metaphor sets in contrast the glorious position of relationship into which God had brought Israel on the ground of covenant promise.

wast grafted in among them,—That is, admitted into the privileges of God's favor, which some of His own people have forfeited.

and didst become partaker with them of the root of the fatness of the olive tree;—The gentile believer had become a spiritual descendant of Abraham, partaking of the spiritual life and blessing which belonged to him and his descendants by divine covenant, and so of "the root of the fatness of the olive tree."

The process of grafting is almost invariably that of putting the good shoot into the inferior stock. Whenever the reverse process was adopted it was to invigorate the fruitful stock and not to fertilize the wild shoot. What is set forth here, therefore, does not correspond actually to either method, but is selected in order to suit the subject, namely, the enrichment of individual Gentiles by their admission to the blessings forfeited by some of God's ancient people through their unbelief.

11:18 glory not over the branches:— This warning is against any tendency on the part of a gentile believer to regard himself as being either better in himself or in a better position than Jews who were broken off. There is never any ground for a believer from among the Gentiles to hold a Jew as such in any measure of contempt or inferiority.

but if thou gloriest, it is not thou that bearest the root, but the root thee.—Salvation was from the Jews (John 4:22). Converted Gentiles, then, had no reason for glorying over Jews who became subjects of divine disfavor through unbelief. It is through Abraham and his offering that God's mercy has come to Gentiles.

11:19 Thou wilt say then, Branches were broken off, that I might be grafted in.—The fact that the rejection of Israel occasioned the advantage of Gentiles, afforded no ground for glorying.

11:20 Well; by their unbelief they were broken off, and thou standest by thy faith.—Granted that Jews were rejected because of their unbelief, there was no personal merit in Gentiles by which they became recipients of the divine favor. That favor was bestowed on the condition of faith, and faith excludes boasting (3:27). Accordingly the real cause of their rejection is sufficient to correct a false inference.

Be not highminded, but fear:—Highmindedness is the forerunner of stumbling. A privilege granted affords no room for self-glorying. On the contrary there is room for fear of the danger of stumbling, as Israel had done.

11:21 for if God spared not the natural branches, neither will He spare thee.—If the natural descendants of Abraham, and partakers of the blessings of the covenant, were deprived of their privileges through unbelief, verily the Gentile has reason to beware of the danger that God will not spare him, who by nature was a stranger from the covenant of promise (Eph. 2:5).

11:22 Behold then the goodness and severity of God toward them that fell, severity; but toward thee, God's goodness,—The severity lies in the present, temporary, retributive dealings of God with the unbelieving nation. His goodness lies in showing mercy to the Gentiles through the gospel.

if thou continue in His goodness otherwise thou also shalt be cut off.—The warning here does not signify that a believer can lose his salvation. Paul is not now dealing with the subject of individual union with Christ. That he had shown in chapter eight to be inseparable (8:1 and 30–39). He is here speaking of the principles upon which God has acted toward Jew and Gentile. The Gentile needs to be warned of the danger of an evil heart of unbelief as much as a Jew, and of coming under the disciplinary severity of God.

11:23 And they also, if they continue not in their unbelief, shall be grafted in:—The reference here is not to the restoration of the Jewish nation, the point is that the rejection of Jews is not irrevocable.

for God is able to graft them in again.—The obstacle lies in unbelieving Jews themselves, as long as they continue in their unbelief. There is no difficulty with God. On the contrary the next verse shows that, from the point of view of the illustration, it is more to be expected that God would restore the Jews to His favor than that He should bring Gentiles into it.

11:24 For if thou wast cut out of that which is by nature a wild olive tree, and wast grafted contrary to nature into a

good olive tree:—That is, if a Gentile, who was a stranger to the covenants of promise, was taken from his natural condition and brought through the gospel into the spiritual blessings contained in God's promise to Abraham.

how much more shall these, which are the natural _branches,_ **be grafted into their own olive tree?**—That is, it is still more probable that Jews, the natural descendants of Abraham, should be brought into the spiritual privileges contained in the promise given to their own ancestor, for nationally they have a covenant relationship with God already, which is not the case with Gentiles.

This illustration of the olive tree views the kingdom of God as essentially one in two different phases. The tree is the same tree with two stages of growth. The change brought in by the gospel was a new development of the one kingdom, in which latter phase unbelieving Jews were excluded from the kingdom and believing Jews brought in.

11:25 For I would not, brethren, have you ignorant of this mystery,—A mystery in Scripture is always a subject of Divine revelation, something which God intends His people to know. This is confirmed here by the desire that the readers should not be ignorant of the mystery about to be mentioned. At the same time a mystery is something beyond the ability of the natural mind to discover. It could be made known only to those who are enlightened by the Spirit of God.

lest ye be wise in your own conceits,—The knowledge of the mystery was to be a preventative against an assumption of superior wisdom on the part of believing Gentiles, as if it was due to them that what Israel had refused they had received.

that a hardening in part has befallen Israel, until the fullness of the Gentiles be come in;—There are thus two limitations to the "hardening," (a) extent; (b) duration. That it is (a) not universal, has just been stated; now it is shown (b) not to be final. The time limit is the coming in of "the fullness of the Gentiles." This phase cannot mean the blessing of the Gentiles as a whole, for that is to be consequent upon Israel's restoration, and not preliminary to it. Nor, again, does it

denote the consummation of the times of the Gentiles, the period during which world dominion is granted to gentile powers. Nor can it mean the consummation of gentile iniquity. The reference seems to be to the whole number of Gentiles who partake of the blessings of salvation in the present age. The phrase does not stand for quite the same thing as the Church, for Jews who have accepted Christ have become part of the Church, and those are distinct here from Gentiles. Paul is speaking of God's dispensational dealings with Jew and Gentile.

11:26 and so all Israel shall be saved:—That is, nationally; not all Israelites in the past, but the nation as such at the time of Christ's Second Advent, and the inauguration of His Millennial reign.

even as it is written,—The restoration is, then, a subject of divine revelation. The quotations are especially from the Septuagint of Isaiah 59:20, 21 and 27:9.

There shall come out of Zion the Deliverer;—The Septuagint puts "out of Zion," instead of "to (or for) Zion" as in the Hebrew. Both are true. See Psalm 14:7; 53:6; 110:2; Joel 2:32; 3:16; Zechariah 14:4, etc.

The title "the Deliverer" consists, in the original, of the definite article with the present participle, literally, "the delivering (One)." The same construction is found in 1 Thessalonians 1:10, where instead of "which delivereth us," we might accurately render "our Deliverer" (The A.V. "delivered" is wrong). The construction is virtually equivalent to a noun. In the Hebrew the word is "Goel," The Kinsman—Redeemer—Avenger (a threefold combination).

He shall turn away ungodliness from Jacob:—The plural is used in the original, "ungodlinesses," "impieties." The Hebrew, literally, is, "There shall come a Redeemer for Zion, and for them that turn from transgression in Jacob, saith the Lord."

11:27 And this is My covenant unto them, when I shall take away their sins.—The sentence "this is My covenant" is found in Isaiah 59:21. The next clause is from the LXX of Isaiah 27:9. For this new covenant, a fulfillment of the pristine promise to Abraham, see Jeremiah 31:31–34; Hebrews 8:8–12; 10:16.

11:28 As touching the gospel,—In the preceding section, verses 25–27, it was pointed out that the present state and future restoration were matters of divine revelation. Now in verses 28–32 they are shown to be consistent with God's character, and this in three respects, His wisdom (v. 28), His immutability (v. 29), His mercy (vv. 30–32).

they are enemies for your sake:—The phrase "for your sake" is, literally, "on account of you." This would be a more accurate rendering. The meaning is that God is judicially opposed to the Jews because of their disobedience, and owing to this He is bringing Gentiles into the mercy from which Israel as a nation has been temporarily excluded.

but as touching the election,—The reference is to the remnant, as in verse 7.

they are beloved for the father's sake.—They are the objects of God's love because of the unalterable covenants made to the fathers (Gen. 15:18; Deut. 9:5; 10:15; 16:3, etc.). The phrase "for the father's sake" signifies "on account of God's promises to the fathers."

11:29 For the gifts and the calling of God are without repentance.—This expresses His immutability. Having been chosen as His people, the nation is assured of future restoration. God changes His attitude toward men consistently with His own character, owing to their change of attitude toward Him, but this does not alter His promises. The immutability of His own character ensures the fulfillment of His covenant. God's various dealings with men are the actings of His eternal, unchanging counsel, and are in accordance with His foreknowledge of the ways and doings of men. The "gifts" are those privileges which have been enumerated in chapter nine, verses 4, 5. The "calling" is the divine relationship into which Israel has been brought as a nation.

11:30 For as ye in time past were disobedient to God, but now have obtained mercy by their disobedience,—While this begins a confirmation of verse 29, it also introduces three statements showing how God's plans in regard to Jew and Gentile have worked out and will work out in the exercise of His mercy.

11:31 even so have these also now been disobedient, that by the mercy shown to you they also may now obtain mercy.—Verses 30 and 31 present God's providential arrangements in two parallels, which may be set out as follows:—(a) The Gentiles were disobedient; (b) but now through the disobedience of the Jews (c) the Gentiles have obtained mercy. (a) The Jews are now disobedient; (b) but by the mercy to the Gentiles (c) the Jews will obtain mercy.

11:32 For God hath shut up all unto disobedience, that He might have mercy upon all.—This verse brings the argument to its climax and gives a final proof that God will yet show mercy to Israel and so to the world. The statement recalls chapter 3:19–24. The passage again demonstrates how all the world has been brought under the judgment of God, and how, whereas all have sinned, God's grace is extended toward all. It shows the interweaving of God's plans with a view to His worldwide mercy. God has so ordered that the disobedience of the Gentiles and of the Jews may be brought home to them, and that they should all of them stand convicted in His sight as sinners. The statement is similar to that of Galatians 3:22. There the apostle's point was that the impossibility of keeping the Law of God was the evidence of the sinful condition of mankind, and that God shut up all under sin that the promise of life and righteousness through faith in Christ might be given to all who believe, whether Jew or Gentile; there was no possibility of escape from the effects of sin by human effort. Here the point is that God has so ordered in His providence that all men should be convicted of disobedience, without possibility of escape from the position by human merit, in order that He might display His mercy. Jew and Gentile must receive mercy on the same footing, namely, sovereign grace.

There is no intimation in this verse of universal salvation; the plain meaning is that God has had mercy on the human race in the present age by offering the gospel to Jew and Gentile alike, without any distinction of nationality, and that when Israel as a nation is restored to Divine favor and privilege in the earth, He will show His mercy to all nations, i.e., in the Millennium. The word "all," in reference to Israel, is to be viewed in the light of verse 26, and, as to the Gentiles, in the light of what is said in verses 12–25. In whatever way man enjoys salvation he will never be able to attribute it to anything but the pure mercy of God.

Verse 32 falls in line with the two preceding verses in the following way: Verse 30, (a) disobedience (Jew and Gentile), (b) mercy (Gentile); Verse 31, (a) disobedience (Jew), (b) mercy (Jew and Gentile); Verse 32, (a) disobedience (Jew and Gentile), (b) mercy (Jew and Gentile).

11:33–36

Introductory Note

This stanza of ten lines consists of three parts: (1) verse 33, the incomprehensibility of God's wisdom and knowledge and ways, (2) verses 34–35, His independence of all creatures, (3) verse 36, His relation to creation, and the glory due to Him.

The five couplets may be set out antithetically, in chiasmic, or crosswise, order, as follows: (a) O the depth (b) of the riches, (c) both of the wisdom (d) and the knowledge of God! (e) How unsearchable are His judgments, (e) and His ways past finding out! (d) For who hath known the mind of the Lord? (c) Or who hath been His counselor? (b) Or who hath first given to Him and it shall be recompensed to Him again? (a) For of Him, and through Him, and unto Him are all things. To Him be the glory forever. Amen. The innermost pair, (e) (e), correspond in the expressions "unsearchable" and "past tracing out"; the next, (d) (d) in "knowledge" and "mind"; the next, (c) (c), in "wisdom" and "counselor"; (b) and (b) in God's "riches" and the impossibility of enriching Him. In (a) and (a) the exclamation, as to the depth of God's riches, wisdom and knowledge, finds its counterpart in the closing statement as to His infinitude.

11:33 O the depth of the riches both of the wisdom and the knowledge of God!—

From the point of view of translation this may either be rendered as in the English texts, in which the word "riches" describes both the wisdom and the knowledge of God; or the word "depth" may describe the three things, namely, the riches and the wisdom and the knowledge of God. This may be confirmed here by the fact that the latter part of verses 33 and 34 speaks of the wisdom and knowledge of God, while verse 35 refers separately to His riches. Moreover 10:12 contains a separate statement that "the Lord is rich unto all that call upon Him," and the apostle may have had that in mind. On the other hand the phrase "the riches both of the wisdom and the knowledge" is paralleled by the similar phraseology in 2:4, the riches of His goodness and forbearance and long-suffering.

With regard to wisdom and knowledge, speaking generally, knowledge relates to the apprehension of facts, wisdom to matters connected with them, their relations one to another, to details of cause and effect and arrangement and the way in which facts may receive a practical application.

how unsearchable are His judgments, and His ways past tracing out!—"His judgments" are here all His providential dispensations, His decisions, and decrees. The phrase "past tracing out" represents the single word *anexichniastos,* which is found elsewhere in the New Testament only in Ephesians 3:8, where it is rendered "unsearchable." The ways of the Lord are the outworkings of His judgments. See Deuteronomy 32:4.

11:34 For who hath known the mind of the Lord? or who hath been His counselor?—This verse confirms verse 33. The first question seems to have special reference to the judgments of God, the second to His ways. This is a quotation from Isaiah 40:13. Cp. Jeremiah 23:18. The verbs are in the aorist tense, and while no particular time is in view, yet the tense in each case indicates a decisive question.

11:35 or who hath first given to Him, and it shall be recompensed unto Him again?—This recalls the earlier arguments which ruled out all human merit and works in the matter of justification, both in the first eight chapters and again in the section chapters 9–11.

11:36 For of Him,—Literally, "from Him." God is the personal source, the first cause of all things. See also 1 Corinthians 8:6. This lends no support to the pantheistic doctrine that everything is an expression or phase of the Deity. On the contrary, all things owe their existence to Him.

and through Him, and unto Him, are all things. To Him be the glory forever. Amen.—He is the ultimate object, and all things are for His glory. In Colossians 1:15, the same facts are expressed in regard to Christ. There, however, the first of the three prepositions is *en,* in (an instrumental use). In Him as the architect, by Him as the Creator, and for His glory, were all things created.

ROMANS

· CHAPTER TWELVE ·

Practical Exhortations, 12:1 to 15:13

The Believer's Response to the Righteousness of God in Showing Mercy, 12:1–21

Introductory Note

The various exhortations which follow, issue from, and are dependent upon, the doctrine already given, and show what is to be the effect of the gospel on the believer, his mind, his body, and his various relationships. Doctrine determines duty. Christian practice is inseparably related to Christian truth The purpose of truth is holiness.

Chapter twelve may be viewed under the following headings: (1) verses 1, 2, conformity to God's will; (2) verses 3–13, communion with saints; (3) verses 14–21, conduct toward fellowmen. Again: (1) verses 1, 2, individual life; (2) verses 38, church life; (3) verses 9–21, social life.

The apostle first mentions the natural body, the individual, which is to be presented to God (v. 1); then the spiritual body, the corporate (v. 5).

12:1 I beseech you therefore, brethren, by the mercies of God,—This verse and the next present (1) the outward activity of the body in service to God, (2) the inward impulses of the mind in proving the will of God. These verses give the basic exhortations which govern all the duties subsequently mentioned. A life regulated toward God results in a life regulated toward man.

to present your bodies—The word *paristēmi* is here used in the aorist, or point, tense as in 6:19. The body stands here practically for the complete man, the part being put for the whole by a figure of speech called synecdoche. Cp. 5:9; James 3:6; Revelation 18:13. While the man is sometimes identified with his body (see Acts 9:37; 13:36), yet, as indicated by the metaphorical use, a man can exist apart from his body (2 Cor. 12:2, 4; Rev. 6:9; 20:4).

a living sacrifice,—That it is to be a sacrifice intimates that it is to be realized as the outcome of the sacrifice of Christ on the cross. That it is to be living sets it in contrast with animal sacrifices, whether those appointed by God for the Jews, or those offered in idolatrous worship by Gentiles. Secondly, it suggests that the sacrifice is to be constant.

holy, acceptable to God,—For the word *hagios,* "holy," see 1:7; 7:12; 11:16; it signifies that which is set apart to God. As the burnt, or ascending, offering under the Law caused a sweet-smelling savor to ascend to God, so does the believer's presentation of himself.

which is **your reasonable service.**—For the word *latreia,* "service," see at 9:4 and cp. the corresponding verb in 1:9. The presentation of the body is an act of worship. The word *logikos,* "reasonable," indicates that which appertains to the mind, the reasoning faculty. The sacrifice is therefore to be intelligent, and the idea suggested is by way of contrast to the sacrifices offered under the Law by ritual and by compulsion. The presentation is to be in accordance with the spiritual intelligence of those who are new creatures in Christ.

12:2 And be not fashioned—The word *suschēmatizomai,* elsewhere only at 1 Peter 1:14, lays stress on that which is external. The prefix *su,* which stands for *sun,* "together with," intimates an association involved in the conformity. This is represented in the word "according" in the next verse.

according to this world:—*Aiōn,* "world," or "age," here signifies the condition of humanity, which, since the Fall, is in spiritual darkness, with a nature, tendencies, and influences controlled by the powers of darkness in opposition to God, and now under the prince of this world.

but be ye transformed—The word *meta-morphoomai* is rendered "transfigured" in Matthew 17:2; Mark 9:2, and "transformed" in 2 Corinthians 3:18. While the word *schēma* (see the verb in the preceding clause) stresses what is outward, the word *morphē* lays stress upon that which is essential and inward, and which finds expression in outward manifestation. Both words represent what is real and not merely apparent, the difference being in the prominence given to what is outward and inward respectively.

by the renewing of your mind,—This renewal of the mind means the adjustment of our moral and spiritual vision to the mind of God. It is designed to have a transforming effect upon the whole life.

that ye may prove,—For *dokimazō,* "to prove," with the effect of approving. See 1:28 and 2:18. It is here used in the present continuous tense, indicating that the proving is to be a habit.

what is the good and acceptable and perfect will of God.—This clause may alternatively be taken as in the margin of the R.V., "the will of God, even the thing which is good and acceptable and perfect." It is good, i.e., beneficial in its effect. It is acceptable as being well pleasing in God's sight. It is perfect, *teleios,* as being not only complete but conditioned by maturity in divine things. To prove, and approve of, the will of God in these respects is impossible without the presentation to God of ourselves as a living sacrifice, abstention from conformity to the world, and the transforming power of the Spirit of God in the constant renewal of our mind.

Church Life, 12:3–13

12:3 For I say, through the grace that was given me, to every man that is among you, not to think of himself more highly than he ought to think; but so to think as to think soberly, according as God hath dealt to each man a measure of faith.—The corresponding verb is found once, in Titus 2:4. The phrase may be rendered more literally as follows, "not to be highminded above what is necessary, but so to be minded as to be sober-minded." A right estimate of oneself will always be a humble estimate, and will be confirmed in the realization of the fact that, whatever we are and whatever we do that is pleasing to God, comes from God. There is stress on "to each" which is appropriate to the thought of the diversity of gifts. That everything is derived from God is a corrective against self-complacency and pride. What room for glorying is there in that which we have received?

12:4 For even as we have many members in one body,—Cp. 1 Corinthians 12:12; Ephesians 4:15. The illustration suggests not only vital unity but harmony in operation.

and all the members have not the same office:—With the unity there is diversity; both are essential to the effectivity of the body. The word *praxis,* "office," is the same as that rendered "deeds" in 8:13. It represents not a position but a function discharged.

12:5 so we, who are many, are one body in Christ, and severally members one of another.—This unity is due not to external organization, but to a common and vital union in Christ, common because of our being in Christ, vital because we are members one of another. Corporate unity involves mutual responsibility.

12:6 And having gifts differing according to the grace that was given to us, whether prophecy,—Prophecy, literally, "forth-telling," signifies the telling forth of the mind of the Lord. Predictive prophecy is only one kind of prophecy. With the completion of the canon of Scripture prophecy passes away, 1 Corinthians 13:8, 9. In his measure the teacher has taken the place of the prophet; cp. the significant change in 2 Peter 2:1. The message of the prophet was a direct revelation of the mind of God for the occasion; the message of the teacher is gathered from the completed revelation contained in the Scriptures.

let us prophesy **according to the proportion of our faith;**—This recalls verse 3. It is a warning against going beyond what God has given and faith receives. This meaning, rather than the other rendering, "according to the analogy of the faith," is in keeping with the context. "Proportion" here represents its true meaning. That there is a definite article before "faith" in the original does not necessarily afford an intimation that the faith, the body of Christian doctrine, is here in view. The presence of the definite article is due to the fact that faith is an abstract noun. The meaning "the faith" is not relevant to the context.

12:7 or ministry, *let us give ourselves* **to our ministry; or he that teacheth, to his teaching;**—*Diakonia,* ministry, represents service of whatever character, and specially voluntary service, in contrast to bondservice.

12:8 or he that exhorteth, to his exhorting:—Exhortation is often coupled with teaching (cp. 1 Tim. 4:13; 6:2), and is addressed to the conscience and to the heart.

he that giveth, *let him do it* **with liberality;**—As applied to giving, the word *haplotēs,* rendered "liberality," suggests singleness of heart, freedom from selfishness of aim, and where this is the case liberality is inevitable. Mixed motives wither liberality.

he that ruleth, with diligence;—*Proistēmi* means "to take the lead." It is rendered "to be over" in 1 Thessalonians 5:12, "to rule" in 1 Timothy 3:4, 5, 12, where it is used of the family, and in 1 Timothy 5:17 of elders and their care of the church, as here.

he that showeth mercy, with cheerfulness.—Showing mercy here especially refers to relieving distress, and such actions are to be done in a spirit of cheerfulness, indicating joy and gladness in the service and its results.

12:9 Let love be without hypocrisy.—This is said of love again in 2 Corinthians 6:6 and 1 Peter 1:22; of faith in 1 Timothy 1:5 and 2 Timothy 1:5; and of wisdom in James 3:17. The hypocrite was originally a stage player, one who acted a part other than that of his true character. The love spoken of here is probably that shown by the fulfillment to be shown to all men. Its genuineness is to be expressed by the fulfillment of the exhortations which follow.

Abhor that which is evil; cleave to that which is good.—The original gives these clauses and those which follow as descriptions of the way in which the previous injunction is to be fulfilled; with it they are grammatically

connected; we should render as follows: "Let love be without hypocrisy, abhorring that which is evil, cleaving to that which is good." They are accordingly explanatory clauses. Love that makes no discrimination between good and evil is merely sentimental and worthless. To hate what is bad without cleaving to that which is good begets censoriousness.

12:10 In love of the brethren be tenderly affectioned one to another; in honor preferring one another;—The phrase "love of the brethren" represents the single word *philadelphia,* "brotherly love," the mutual affection of those who are children of God.

12:11 in diligence not slothful; fervent in spirit; serving the Lord;—These three exhortations are to be connected closely. The first might be rendered "not flagging in zeal." The fervency is in the realm of the spirit, as that which is guided by the Holy Spirit. If constant zeal and fervency of spirit are to characterize service for the Lord, zeal must be controlled by prudence and exercised not for self-interest but for Christ. Devotion to the Lord, then, is the inspiring motive.

12:12 rejoicing in hope; patient in tribulation; continuing steadfastly in prayer,—These three exhortations are likewise closely associated. Perseverance in prayer produces joy in hope and patience in tribulation. Communion with God is essential as a controlling influence in our joy and in our patience under trial. Otherwise joy may be mere ebullition of feeling and patience mere stoicism.

12:13 communicating to the necessities of the saints;—In this verse there is a return to relationships with other believers, as in verse 10. The verb *koinōneō* signifies to take part with another in anything, and especially to have in common; not simply to communicate, but to share.

given to hospitality.—The verb rendered "given to" is *diōkō,* "to pursue." We are earnestly to seek opportunities of hospitality rather than to wait for an occasion to rise. Cp. Hebrews 13:1, 16.

Duty Toward All Men, 12:14–21

12:14 Bless them that persecute you, bless, and curse not.—It is not sufficient to abstain from retaliation against those who do us injury; we must take pains to seek their welfare. The exhortations in this section are to some extent parallel to those in the Sermon on the Mount, which was designed by the Lord to be applicable in the present age as well as in the time when He was on earth. See Matthew 5:44 and cp. 6:28.

12:15 Rejoice with them that rejoice; weep with them that weep.—Here the exhortations pass from returning kindness for unkindness, to the call of sympathy both in joy and sorrow: not merely absence of selfish interest or disinterestedness, but a spirit of sharing in the feelings of others. While it is in one sense easier to weep with those that weep than to rejoice with those that rejoice, yea, as Chrysostom observed, it is natural to sympathize with sorrow, but it requires a noble soul to rejoice in the joy of others.

12:16 Be of the same mind one toward another.—In the original this goes closely with what precedes and is, literally, "minding the same thing one toward another." Thus it extends the thought of rejoicing with those who rejoice and weeping with those who weep. This one-mindedness results from realizing that we have a common nature; it is likewise a manifestation of the spirit of Christ. His first miracle was performed in rejoicing with them that rejoice and His greatest miracle while weeping with those that wept. The pride and ambition which cause us to set our mind on high things is a hindrance to the unanimity which expresses itself in practical sympathy.

Set not your mind on high things, but condescend to things that are lowly.—Here again the sentence is connected, in the original, with the preceding injunction, which it expands; hence we should render by "not minding high things, but condescending to things that are lowly." The high things are those upon which pride sets itself. They are not the spiritually high things which are above, but those things which foster selfishness and self-esteem.

"Condescend" is not the most suitable rendering of the word *sunapagomai*, which rather denotes to let oneself be carried along with. The most helpful influences over us come from things that are lowly, and the effect of such is harmony and peace.

Be not wise in your own conceits.—This injunction forms the climax to the preceding exhortations. Being wise in our own conceits is one of the great hindrances to concord among the saints.

12:17 Render to no man evil for evil.—This is not an exhortation simply concerning one's enemies. It has to do with anyone who may act with animosity upon any occasion. In no case is the believer to retaliate. The teaching is identical with that of Matthew 5:43–48. There is stress on the words "no man."

Take thought for things honorable in the sight of all men.—The last word "all men" bears stress. This injunction is closely connected with the preceding one, though it is of general application. In taking thought for things honorable in the sight of all men we not only abstain from retaliation against evil, but therein we avoid justifiable suspicion and criticism.

12:18 If it be possible, as much as in you lieth, be at peace with all men.—This again is closely connected with what precedes, for the verb rendered "be" is in the present participle, "being," in the original.

The exhortation is necessarily conditional. The word "you" bears emphasis, and this indicates that the believer is to see that he himself is not responsible for breaking the peace. Peace is a mutual relation possible of breach by either party. The preservation of it does not always lie within the believer's control. Faithfulness to God must never be sacrificed for the sake of peace. On the other hand, we are to see to it that we do not cherish feelings of bitterness and retaliation. The responsibility for discord must never lie at our door.

12:19 Avenge not yourselves, beloved, but give place unto wrath: for it is written, Vengeance belongeth unto Me, I will recompense, saith the Lord.—Here again the verb "avenge" is in the present participle, showing the close connection with the preceding exhortations. In other words, this indicates one way of living, as much as in us lieth, at peace with all men. The command is plain, and forbids any mode of retaliation.

The exhortation to give place unto wrath has been understood in various ways. We may notice three: (1) that the wrath is that of the injured person; (2) that it is that of the person who injures; (3) that the wrath is God's.

The first of these would mean that the injured person, instead of indulging his wrath, is to abstain from exercising it and so to let it pass. But the original will hardly bear that meaning.

The second would mean that the injured person is to allow the wrath of his enemy to be expended upon him, and so to make room for its action. This is a possible meaning of the original. But this explanation does not fit with the context. For, as to what has preceded, the evil inflicted is not necessarily a matter of wrath. Nor does this interpretation find support from the succeeding context.

The third explanation seems to be the right one. For the apostle assigns as a reason why the believer is to give place unto wrath instead of avenging himself that "It is written, Vengeance belongeth unto Me; I will recompense, saith the Lord." Moreover the apostle has constantly spoken of the wrath of God in the preceding part of the Epistle (see 1:18; 2:5, 8; 3:5; 4:15; 5:9; 9:22), and nowhere hitherto has it been mentioned in any other way. Both retrospectively and prospectively, therefore, the word points to that which it is God's prerogative to exercise. The believer is not to usurp God's authority. Nor does the injunction suggest that he is to desire that the wrath of God shall be inflicted upon his injurer. In giving place to God's wrath he simply leaves the matter to Him who will deal with it according to His perfect wisdom. Compare the proverb, "Say not thou, I will recompense evil: wait on the Lord, and He shall save thee" (Prov. 20:22, and see 24:29).

12:20 But if thine enemy hunger, feed him; if he thirst, give him to drink:—The "But" sets what follows in contrast to the self-avenging mentioned in the preceding exhortation, and continues the precept in verse 18.

for in so doing thou shalt heap coals of fire upon his head.—The meaning which suits the context best seems to be, that by repaying hostility by kindness the hard heart of one's enemy will be subdued to repentance, with resulting manifestation of friendliness.

12:21 Be not overcome of evil, but overcome evil with good.—The evil refers to what the evildoer does. The good is that which the one who suffers it is to show. The evil done is not to gain the mastery over the believer; it is to be the very means of the display of the opposite.

If we act in a spirit of vengeance, the grace which should work in our hearts is subdued. That gives a twofold victory to the wrong. If we return good for evil we subdue the antagonism of our foe, and bring him to a better mind. There are, of course, cases where kindness only hardens, but these are exceptional, and are not in view here.

ROMANS

CHAPTER THIRTEEN

The Duty of Exhibiting Christ to the World, 13:1–14

Introductory Note

The injunction to be in subjection to the higher powers, while important in every country, would have a special force in Rome, where the government would rigorously repress any religion which tended to run counter to that of the state, and especially Christianity, for Christians were largely regarded as a Jewish sect, and propaganda considered in any sense to be Jewish would be suspected as being of a revolutionary tendency. There was also a danger, no doubt, that Christians might entertain wrong notions of the kingdom of Christ and its present relation to the kingdoms of this world. To Jews, conscious of the covenant relationship of their nation to God, there was a natural repugnance to submit to heathen rulers.

13:1 Let every soul be in subjection to the high powers:—The word *exousia,* "power," denotes, firstly, freedom to do anything, and then authority to carry it out. Rulers hold, from God, freedom to act, however much they may abuse their authority.

for there is no power but of God; and the *powers* that be are ordained of God.—These are the two great reasons for being subject to rulers. Civil authority is derived from God, and is arranged by divine appointment. The first stresses the absolute supremacy of God, a supremacy which no adverse power can hinder or thwart. The second stresses the fact of God's power to exercise His authority in setting up and removing rulers. Whatever may be the form of government by the persons who exercise it, it is determined by divine providence. See the book of Daniel passim, and especially 4:25, 34, 35.

13:2 Therefore he that resisteth the power, withstandeth the ordinance of God:—Since civil government is God's design, and those who exercise it derive their authority from Him, resistance to that authority is disobedience to God.

and they that withstand shall receive to themselves judgment.—Whether the judgment is Divine or human is not specified. What seems to be referred to is the punishment inflicted by rulers as ministers of God. Circumstances in which rulers overstep their authority, and in which it becomes necessary for servants of God to say, "We must obey God rather than man," are not in view in this passage.

13:3 For rulers are not a terror to the good work, but to the evil—Though Nero was ruling when this was written, the unrighteousness of his tyranny and his acts of persecution are not in view in this statement. What is enforced here is the duty of the civil authority in the discharge of its regular functions, which punishes wrongdoing and favors right, and after all even the persecution of Christians was aroused by motives which, though mistaken, had in view the preservation of civil order.

It is in this respect that the good work and the evil (literally, "good works and evil," both being in the plural) are to be understood, inasmuch as the discharge of the function of rulers has regard to man's actions only.

And wouldst thou have no fear of the power?—This negative question does not suggest an exhortation, as in the A.V., but rather is by way of an appeal to the reasonable desires of the subject to live so as to have no fear of punishment by civil authority.

do that which is good, and thou shalt have praise from the same:—The Divine design of government is again here in view, and not the abuse of authority by tyrants. The believer is called, not to resist, but simply to do good. Thereby also he wins the praise of those who discharge civil functions, and experiences God's goodness in providing such authority.

13:4 for he is a minister of God to thee for good.—This means that the service he renders is for the welfare of the subjects under him. His rightful exercise of authority, under God, has in view its beneficial effect upon society in general.

But if thou do that which is evil, be afraid; for he bareth not the sword in vain:—A sword was actually worn by emperors and magistrates, as an emblem of their power of life and death; hence the metaphorical use of the phrase here. There is an intimation of the rights of capital punishment, though what is in view is the carrying out of any form of judicial sentence.

for he is a minister of God, an avenger for wrath to him that does evil.—The word *ekdikos* denotes one who deals justice. It is used of God in 1 Thessalonians 4:6. The wrath, *orgē*, here referred to is the wrath of a human ruler.

13:5 Wherefore *ye* must needs be in subjection, not only because of the wrath, but also for conscience sake.—The former is external, the execution of judgment on the part of the ruler; the latter is internal, a matter of conscience toward God and the recognition of the ruler's right. We are ever directed to view earthly relationships and circumstances in the light of our relationships with God.

13:6 For this cause ye pay tribute also;—*Phoros,* "tribute," was especially the yearly tax levied on persons or real property. It was frequently used of the tribute laid upon a subject nation, Nehemiah 5:4; Luke 20:22. Here it is used in a general way, of any kind of tax levied by a government for the exercise of its power.

for they are ministers of God's service,—Conscience is to be in exercise in this respect, in that rulers are God's appointed agents for the maintenance of civil authority. By being in subjection to them, and paying tribute, we recognize the ordinance of God, and so do honor to Him. The word *leitourgoi,* rendered "ministers of (God's) service," differs from that in verse 4, where *diakonos* was used. The *leitourgos* among the Greeks was a public servant appointed for any work, civil or religious. This word stresses here the fact that the service is rendered to God on behalf of the people. Rulers do not, of course, all serve God consciously. But whether or no, they discharge functions which are the ordinance of God.

attending continually upon this very thing.—This has been taken by some to refer to the exacting of tribute, by others to the service of God. Probably both are in view, for they are regarded as definitely connected.

13:7 Render to all their dues:—This summarizes the preceding exhortations, and includes all who in any way exercise civil authority.

tribute to whom tribute *is due;* **custom to whom custom;**—The *telos,* "custom," was an indirect tax on goods. Both kinds of tax were paid to the Roman government through the *publicani,* the agents who collected them, and who were bitterly hated. It was a constant practice to stir up plots against them, and revolutions against the whole system. Abuses on the part of the tax-collectors were so great that a little later than the date of this Epistle Nero laid proposals before the Roman senate for stringent reforms.

fear to whom fear; honor to whom honor.—This latter, while immediately referring to what is due to those in authority, perhaps also suggests what is inculcated elsewhere, namely, the duty of other individuals one toward another.

13:8 Owe no man anything, save to love one another:—This follows on from the beginning of verse 7, "render to all their due," but the exhortation widens out to the subject of love, which in all ways seeks the best interests of others. Here, while the interests of the creditor are in view, the precept is not limited to that; all obligations are to be discharged, including those mentioned in verse 7. The debt of love, however, is always owing. Any payment made in this respect does not release us from continued indebtedness. Do what we may for our neighbor, we are to love him. This is now enforced by two considerations: (1) that love fulfills the law of God (vv. 9, 10); (2) that the time is short (vv. 11–14).

for he that loveth his neighbor hath fulfilled the law.—Among Israel "neighbor" stood for a fellow-Israelite. The Lord widened its scope. See the parable of the good Samaritan. What constitutes the claim of the Law of God goes beyond the needs of fellow-nationals to needs of anyone of whatever race.

13:9 For this, Thou shalt not commit adultery, Thou shalt not kill, Thou shalt not steal, Thou shalt not covet, and if there be any other commandment, it is summed up in this word, namely, Thou shalt love thy neighbor as thyself.—The Mosaic Law is viewed here as expressing the general principle of right and wrong. The commandments mentioned are given as specimens of the whole Law. He who loves his neighbor has fulfilled all the commandments contained therein, and has carried out in action the whole principle of law. Paul and James express the same thing concerning the Law, but in different ways (see James 2:9-11). The former says that in keeping the one commandment we are keeping all, the latter that in breaking one we break all. Each therefore stresses the unity of the Law. James argues that the unity of the Law is the effect of the oneness of the Lawgiver, being the expression of a single will (v. 11, and 4:12).

There is an apparent difference between the Lord's treatment of the subject and that here. For Christ declares that the whole Law and the prophets hang upon both love to God and love to one's neighbor. Here, as in Galatians 5:14, the apostle sums up all in that of love to one's neighbor. There is no real distinction, however, for love to God finds its expression in love to one's neighbor. Moreover, Christ was answering a question as to the right interpretation of the Law, whereas the apostle is dealing with the responsibilities of believers toward all men.

13:10 Love worketh no ill to his neighbor: love therefore is the fulfillment of the law.—This verse runs parallel to verse 8, but puts the first part negatively. Love is personified, as in 1 Corinthians 13. Moving us to do good to others, it likewise keeps us from doing them harm. Again the article is absent, in the original, before the word "Law," stressing the principles in the Law.

13:11 And this, knowing the season,—This signifies being fully aware of the significance of the present time.

that now—The word *ēdē* denotes "already"; that is, there must be no delay, no neglect in the matter of the command to love one another. This word goes with "to awake."

it is high time for you to awake—The verb is in the aorist tense, and has the significance "to awake at once."

out of sleep:—this is the only place in the New Testament where *hupnos* is used of spiritual lethargy. In the five other places where it is found, it is used of natural sleep. In 1 Thessalonians 5:6, where the verb *katheudō* is used, believers are warned against falling into soul slumber; here they are exhorted to awake out of it. This is the only kind of sleep of the soul referred to in Scripture. Cp. Matthew 24:42, 43; Ephesians 5:14.

for now—The word is *nun*, "at this time"; contrast *ēdē* in the first part of the verse. There is a progressive narrowing in the passage, of the expressions of time to a climax; (a) "the season" (the whole era); (b) "high time," literally, "hour" (the present hour); (c) "now" (the immediate moment).

is salvation nearer to us than when we *first* **believed**—This salvation is deliverance from present conditions and from the coming wrath, at the return of the Lord to receive us to Himself. Cp. 1 Thessalonians 1:10 (R.V.); 5:9; 1 Peter 1:5, 13.

The apostles were ever consistent in their instruction concerning the Lord's return as an event to be regarded as imminent. Discussions as to whether any of them changed their view as to its imminence, or whether they were mistaken, are entirely beside the mark. The exhortations they gave were designed for the saints throughout the present era. To wait for the Son of God from heaven not only was the actual attitude of the church of the Thessalonians, their example was to be followed by all believers in each generation till the event takes place.

13:12 The night is far spent, and the day is at hand;—This represents in another form what has been said in the latter part of verse 11, and continues the metaphor of the first part of that verse. "The night" signifies the whole period of man's alienation from God; cp. 1 Thessalonians 5:5, 7. The verb rendered "is far spent," is not to be pressed into its literal translation "was far spent," as if it referred to the first Advent; the tense is equivalent to a perfect. "The day" is "the day of Christ," to be introduced when the Lord comes to receive His saints to Himself.

let us therefore cast off the works of darkness—The verb *apotithēmi*, "to put off," or "put away," is used in the New Testament only once of material things, in Acts 7:58, with reference to clothes. In the seven other passages, as in the present one, it is used metaphorically. The verb is in the aorist tense, suggesting immediate decision and completeness. To hate one's brother is to walk in darkness (1 John 2:9, 11), and with such a condition fellowship with God is incompatible (1 John 1:6). Again, the believer is to have "no fellowship with darkness" (2 Cor. 6:14; Eph. 5:11).

and let us put on the armor of light.—As the believer is now in the night season, he is involved in conflict with the spiritual forces of darkness, and victory can be gained only by putting on the armor of light. The word rendered armor is plural, literally, "weapons" *(hopla).*

The verb *enduō* rendered "put on" is again in the aorist tense, suggesting a decisive and complete act. It is used elsewhere, in this metaphorical sense of putting on spiritual armor, in Ephesians 6:11, 14 and 1 Thessalonians 5:8. The figure is appropriate to the description of the believer as a soldier (2 Tim. 2:4). As spiritual light can be received only by those who are born of God, so alone by such can righteousness in character and conduct, of which the armor of light consists, be worn. For they alone are "sons of light."

13:13 Let us walk honestly,—The word *euschēmonōs* denotes "becomingly," decently, which was the primary meaning of "honest." It is used of the believer's walk also in 1 Thessalonians 4:12, where it is said of conduct toward unbelievers. Here it is set in contrast to the world's evil social conditions.

as in the day;—That is, as one walks in the day, and so, as those who spiritually belong to the day, when we shall be like Christ and shall see Him as He is (1 John 3:2). Cp. "as children of light" (Eph. 5:18).

not in reveling and drunkenness, not in chambering and wantonness, not in strife and jealousy.—The word *kōmos,* "reveling," is in the plural, as in the two other places where it is found in the New Testament (Gal. 5:21, and 1 Pet. 4:3). It is always associated with drunkenness. The exhortation shows that the sins which characterize the world, in which believers once had their manner of life, remain as dangers against the ingress of which they are to be on their guard, and resistance to which can only be successful by the power of Christ.

13:14 But put ye on the Lord Jesus Christ,—This is contrasted with the conduct described in the preceding verse; it also recalls verse 12. The believer is so to apprehend the true meaning of the union with Christ into which he entered when he put on Christ (Gal. 3:27, cf. Rom. 6:3), that Christ becomes the element in which he lives, the moral raiment which displays His character.

and make not provision for the flesh, to *fulfill* **the lusts** *thereof*—The word *pronoia,* "provision," is, literally, forethought, hence we may render by "take no forethought." This negative command corresponds to the positive exhortation to "mortify the deed of the body," 8:13. Expressed as it is here it suggests the self-will with which sin is premeditated. The flesh is, here, the seat of sin in man.

ROMANS

CHAPTER FOURTEEN

Mutual Obligations, 14:1 to 15:13

Mutual Forebearance, and Christ as Lord, 14:1–12

Introductory Note

In verses 1-12 the apostle deals with the moral responsibilities of the strong brother toward the weak, and of the weak toward the strong. The strong are not to set at nought the weak; the weak are not to judge the strong. The mutual relations are to be viewed in the light of the authority of Christ over each, and of His Judgment Seat.

There is a connection with what has preceded. In the preceding chapters the need of mutual love has been stressed (e.g., 12:9, 10; 13:8-10). This is now made to govern the particular subject of the relations between the weak and the strong. At the end of the preceding chapter attention has been drawn to the imminence of the day of Christ. Accordingly the strong and the weak are to remember that all have to appear before the Judgment Seat. The apostle has been given injunctions against the indulgence of the flesh. This is now applied to the need of abstaining, on the one hand, from the abuse of liberty, and, on the other hand, from the indulgence of a critical and censorious spirit, in things morally indifferent. The injunction to put on the Lord Jesus Christ (13:14) influences the new subject in a twofold way: firstly in the emphasis placed on the authority of Christ (14:6-9), secondly, in the presentation of Christ as the pattern for believers (15:14).

14:1 But him that is weak in faith—The "But" shows that there is a definite connection with what has preceded. The weakness is "in faith," not "in the faith," as in the A.V. Though the article is present in the original, it does not here signify the faith, the body of Christian doctrine.

As to whether the definite article is to be translated or not the context is usually a guide, and here it decides the meaning, for the next verse speaks of faith and so verse 23 says, "He that eateth is condemned if he eat, because he eateth not of faith; and whatsoever is not of faith is sin."

The form of the word rendered "weak" (the present continuous tense of the verb) suggests that the trouble is not an inherent characteristic, but a condition into which a brother has been brought by outward influence.

As to the significance of the terms "weak" and "strong," he who is weak in faith is so through lack of an apprehension of the liberty into which one is brought who, trusting in Christ alone, is delivered from all bondage and finds freedom in serving the will of Christ as Lord of the life. The weakness is the effect of scruples about details that lie outside the scope of those things which the Christian faith demands. His danger lies in judging the brother who is strong, and in a liability to take offense. The "strong" is one who, while acting conscientiously toward God, is not fettered by scruples of that sort. His danger is twofold, namely, of despising the weak brother, and of setting a stumbling block before him.

receive ye,—The verb rendered "receive" is again in the present continuous tense, which indicates that the attitude adopted in receiving is to be continued.

yet **not to doubtful disputations.**—Literally, "not to judgments of reasonings," or, as the margin reads, "not for divisions of doubts." The brother who is weak, is not to be received with the purpose of judging his reasonings; the reception is to be unreserved. There is to be no setting up of oneself as a judge of the weak brother's scruples.

14:2 One man hath faith to eat all things: but he that is weak eateth herbs.—With regard to those now mentioned, in the case of the former his faith enables him to eat anything without fear of defilement (cp. Mark 7:15). The latter has scruples which impose abstinence from all meat or wine. Reference is not merely to abstention from unclean animals, or from meats offered to idols, as in 1 Corinthians 8, but from all meat. The apostle expresses no disapproval in either case. The right or wrong of the matter is left an open question. He is concerned with the feelings involved.

14:3 Let not him that eateth set at nought him that eateth not;—The strong are not to adopt this attitude toward the weak, imputing superstition and narrow-mindedness to them.

and let not him that eateth not judge him that eateth:—He who for religious reasons lived on a vegetarian diet was not to adopt a censorious attitude toward the one who ate meat, regarding him as unscrupulous. The warnings given in each case are against the dangers of unbrotherliness, against the tendency to criticize one another upon matters concerning regulations and precepts not given in the Word of God.

for God hath received him—The tense is aorist, referring to the time of conversion, when God received him, on the ground of faith and confession of Christ as Lord. That the strong brother partakes of meat does not argue, then, against his acceptance with God.

14:4 Who art thou that judgest the servant of another?—This provides a second ground of appeal to the one who is weak, against condemning one who is strong, namely, that he is the servant of the Lord. The word for "servant" is *oiketēs,* which signifies a household servant, in distinction from an ordinary slave (see Acts 10:7).

to his own lord he standeth or falleth.—It is presumption to pass sentence of condemnation upon a liberty which God has not condemned. The terms "stand" or "fall" might be understood (1) of acquittal or condemnation or (2) standing upright or falling into sin in using liberty, and that is to be judged by the Lord and not by the weak brother. This second meaning would seem to be the one intended.

Yea, he shall be made to stand;—The "Yea" is really "But," as suggesting a contrast to falling. Since what he does is a matter of faith (v. 2), he shall be maintained in his integ-

rity through the power of his Lord. What Paul opposes here, then, is not scrupulousness itself, but scrupulousness which produces Pharisaism; on the other hand he clearly intimates that the enjoyment of liberty is morally successful only through the grace and power of Christ as the Lord of His servants.

for the Lord hath power to make him stand.—The word rendered "stand" is in the aorist, or point, tense, signifying the decisive character of the act. The believer stands, not in his own strength, but in that which Christ imparts to him. What is in view here is, not that the strong man will fall and be restored, but that Christ is able to maintain him in spite of what his liberty may involve.

14:5 One man esteemeth one day above another: another man esteemeth every day *alike.*—The observance of days has reference to the Jewish sabbath, and other days, as mentioned in Colossians 2:16; cp. Galatians 4:10. It is the weak brother who esteems these as necessary to be regarded with strict observance. The strong brother esteems every day. The word "alike" is not part of the original and should be omitted. It does not help the sense of the statement. There is no suggestion, of course, that the strong brother is one who regards every day as a day upon which he can act as he likes, but rather that he is one who regards every day as consecrated to the Lord, and to be spent for Him; just as he regards meat as legitimate for consumption.

Let each man be fully assured in his own mind.—One's convictions are to be one's own, through an apprehension of responsibility to the Lord and to His revealed will. The believer's action should not be determined simply by another man's opinion. The mind is the seat of moral consciousness, and this, when enlightened by the Spirit of God, enables the believer to do His will and prevents the demoralizing experience of doing something merely because others think it right.

14:6 He that regardeth the day, regardeth it unto the Lord:—The word "regardeth" represents the verb *phroneō,* for which see at 8:5; it signifies the setting of one's mind upon a thing.

The second statement in the A.V., "and he that regardeth not the day, to the Lord doth he not regard it," does not rest on good manuscript evidence, and does not suit the apostle's argument. He has no intention of suggesting that any day should not be observed as set apart to God.

and he that eateth, eateth unto the Lord, for he giveth God thanks; and he that eateth not, unto the Lord he eateth not, and giveth God thanks.—Here, in contrast to the observance of days the insistence is made that both in eating and in abstaining, the course adopted is to the Lord. There is stress on "unto the Lord" in each statement, and the reference in the title is to Christ.

Just as the weak brother, who regards one day above others, may meet criticism by saying that he observes the day to the Lord, so may the brother who eats all things maintain that what he partakes of begets gratitude to God on his part; he could not give thanks for what he knew God had forbidden. Again, just as he who eats evinces his devotion to the Lord by giving thanks, so he who refrains evinces the same thing by his thankfulness for his simpler fare. Each regards himself as acting in responsibility to the Lord and in accordance with His will.

14:7 For none of us liveth to himself, and none dieth to himself.—The subject passes from the particular cases of those who regard special days, and those who eat flesh and those who abstain, to the case of every believer and his relationship with Christ as Lord. The reference now is to the daily Christian experience. The significance of the statement "none of us liveth to himself," is not as to how a believer's conduct affects others, but as to what is his attitude toward the Lord.

14:8 For whether we live, we live unto the Lord; or whether we die, we die unto the Lord: whether we live therefore, or die, we are the Lord's.—A believer's end in life is not his own will and interest but the Lord's. So with his death, he chooses neither the time nor the manner of it, nor does death itself alter the relationship. He still remains the Lord's possession, and lives to Him. Time and circumstance are determined by the Lord's will. Believers may differ in their opin-

ions as to what the Lord requires of them individually in certain matters, but the deciding principle in every case and every condition is that Christ is Lord.

Death, then, does not bring a cessation of service for Him; His authority as Lord continues over us in the spirit state. Not simply the fact of death is in view; the present continuous tense suggests also what follows that.

14:9 For to this end Christ died, and lived *again*, that He might be Lord of both the dead and the living.—The death and resurrection of Christ are the facts on which His possession of, and authority over, His people, are founded, both here and hereafter.

14:10 But thou, why dost thou judge thy brother?—Such judgment is both a usurpation of the prerogative of Christ and inconsistent with the relationship of believers to one another.

or thou again, why dost thou set at nought thy brother?—This is again addressed to the strong brother, as the preceding remonstrance was to the weak.

for we shall all stand before the judgment seat of God.—"God" is undoubtedly the right reading here. The Judgment Seat of Christ (2 Cor. 5:10) is thereby that of God. The *bēma*, or judgment seat, was originally a raised place mounted by steps, and so a platform. Hence the word signifies the official seat of a judge (Matt. 27:19; John 19:13; Acts 18:12, etc.). At the *bēma*, the Judgment Seat, of God and of Christ, believers are to be made manifest, that they may each one "receive the things done in (or through) the body, according to what they have done, whether it be good or bad" (2 Cor. 5:10). At that Judgment Seat in the "Parousia" of our Lord Jesus (i.e., His presence with His saints after His return to receive them to Himself), the saints will receive rewards for their faithfulness to the Lord, and will there see the effects of the service rendered to Him in accordance with the will of God as revealed in His Word. See 1 Thessalonians 2:19; 3:13; 5:23; 1 Peter 5:4; 1 John 2:28. For all that has been contrary to His will they will suffer loss; they will themselves be saved, "yet so as through fire" (1 Cor. 3:15).

14:11 For it is written, As I live, saith the Lord, to Me every knee shall bow, and every tongue shall confess to God.—This is a free quotation from the Septuagint of Isaiah 45:23. Both the Hebrew and the Septuagint have "By Myself have I sworn," a Divine oath also uttered in the case of Abraham, Genesis 22:16. The apostle gives the equivalent expression "as I live" (cp. Num. 14:21, 28; Deut. 32:40, R.V.), a form of oath expressive of Divine power and authority. The bowing of the knee is expressive of the recognition of, and subjection to, the Lord's authority; the confession of the tongue indicates the acknowledgment of the inerrancy and rightfulness of His judgment.

14:12 So then each one of us shall give account of himself to God.—In the original the two phrases "each one of us" and "of himself" are put together, with stress on the latter, thus giving emphasis to the argument against judging one another and introducing verse 13.

Mutual Forbearance and Edification, 14:13–23

14:13 Let us not therefore judge one another any more: but judge ye this rather, that no man put a stumbling block in his brother's way, or an occasion of falling.—This is addressed to the strong. There is a slight change in the use of the word *krinō,* "judge," amounting almost to a play on the word. It now signifies "let this be your decision," or "determination." Decisions thus made, in the exercise of our judgment in our service here below, will determine the nature of our reward at the Judgment Seat of Christ.

14:14 I know, and am persuaded in the Lord Jesus,—That is to say, not as a result of his own reasoning, but in virtue of his union with the Lord and the instruction received from Him.

that nothing is unclean of itself:—This statement reasserts the principle of liberty, but with a view to urging upon the strong brother the necessity for a loving consideration of the weak brother. The phrase "of itself" signifies "of its own nature" in distinction from what conscientious scruples estimate it to be.

save that to him that counteth anything to be unclean, to him it is unclean.—The argument here is that the weak brother must not be stumbled, for, as far as his conscience alone is concerned, his scruples are valid, and everything must be done to prevent his violating them. Conscience alone is not an infallible guide as to the right or wrong of a thing in itself, but to act against one's conscience, even when it is misguided, is always wrong.

The apostle is not speaking here of what is morally impure, but simply of what is ceremonially so. To apply the statement that nothing is unclean of itself to what is morally impure, is to pervert the meaning of this Scripture.

14:15 For if because of meat thy brother is grieved,—That is to say, if on account of what is eaten by the strong brother the weak brother is distressed.

thou walkest no longer in love.—The one who thus causes grief to the weak brother, departs from the path of love in which he has been walking as a believer.

Destroy not with thy meat him for whom Christ died.—The word *apollumi,* "to destroy," denotes to deprive of the possibility of fulfilling the object of one's existence. It is found elsewhere in the Epistle only at 2:12, where see note. Here the tense is the present continuous, indicating a process involving spiritual disaster. In giving way to what is to him sinful, the weak brother is liable by that step to be led into a path of departure from the will of God, with consequent ruin to his present spiritual life.

It is not a case merely of being pained at seeing what the strong brother does, and perhaps hardened against him in censoriousness of spirit; what is here in view is that the weak brother has been caused to stumble by acting against his conscience.

The mention of the death of Christ forms the climax of the appeal. The divine love displayed at the Cross is put in striking contrast to the selfishness which sets more value upon one's own desires and enjoyment than upon the spiritual welfare of a brother, and even runs the risk of bringing disaster upon him.

14:16 Let not then your good be evil spoken of:—The "good" is that which can be enjoyed or used with advantage; here it refers apparently to the stronger faith and greater liberty which are not to be exercised detrimentally to the weak brother, and prejudicially to the cause of Christ, through evil report on the part of unbelievers; cp. 2:24. Possibly there is a reference to what the weak brother esteems to be good, namely, abstaining from meat and from wine.

14:17 for the kingdom of God is not eating and drinking—The kingdom of God is the sphere of God's rule. In view, however, of the rebellion that has been raised against Him, the phrase most frequently signifies the sphere in which at any given time His rule is acknowledged. The evidence that a man has entered into the kingdom of God, and that its powers work in him, is seen, not in adherence to principles which have to do with outward things, such as eating and drinking, or refraining therefrom, but with inward, spiritual and essential matters, namely, righteousness, peace and joy in the Holy Spirit.

but righteousness and peace and joy in the Holy Ghost.—These three subjects, *righteousness, peace and joy,* have been already taken up in the first part of the Epistle in the same order. Righteousness forms the main subject of the first four chapters, and the three are brought together at the beginning of the fifth, *righteousness and peace* in verse 1, *joy* in verse 11. The same themes are resumed in a different connection later in the Epistle, *righteousness* in chapter 10:3-13, *peace* in 10:15, *joy* in 12:12, 15. While in the first part of the Epistle the three have to do with the provision made by God in the matter of justification and reconciliation with resulting joy, the present passage has especially in view the practical effects in the life of believers, namely, right moral relations one with the other, the peace that results from unity of heart and purpose, and joy in one another kindled by the Holy Spirit. The phrase "joy in the Holy Ghost" signifies, not only that the Holy Spirit is the Minister of joy, but that the joy can be experienced only in the fellowship of the Holy Spirit.

14:18 For he that herein serveth Christ is well pleasing to God, and approved of men.—The powers of the kingdom of God which are expressed in righteousness, peace and joy in the Holy Spirit, work by way of service to Christ. He who feels free to eat meat may be serving Christ as much as the one who abstains, but neither one nor the other can serve Him if righteousness, peace and joy in the Holy Spirit are lacking. On the other hand, where these things are in exercise he who manifests them can be assured of being pleasing to God and approved of men. God judges the inward motives. Man sees the outward effects.

14:19 So then let us follow after things which make for peace, and things thereby we may edify one another.—A more literal rendering is "the things of peace and the things of edification toward one another." The things of peace include righteousness and joy in the Holy Spirit (v. 7). Mutual upbuilding in the faith can proceed effectively only under conditions of peace.

14:20 Overthrow not for meat's sake the work of God.—The verb *kataluō,* "to overthrow," literally means "to loosen down." Here it is used of the marring of spiritual well-being, the pulling down of the work of God in a brother's life, and is set in contrast to building up (v. 19). The phrase "the work of God" suggests both the individual believer as constituting a part of God's spiritual building, and the effects in him of the spiritual teaching by which the building proceeds. Cp. 1 Corinthians 3:17.

All things indeed are clean; howbeit it is evil for that man who eateth with offense.—This has been taken in two ways: (1) as referring to the strong brother, who, by his eating, causes the weak brother to stumble; (2) as referring to the weak brother who, by his eating, stumbles through acting against his own conscience. It is true that the strong are here addressed, but that is not a sufficient indication to guide us, for the evil is not necessarily predicated of the action of the party addressed. Verse 23, to which the argument is leading, indicates that Paul is speaking of the weak brother and of the condemnation into which he falls through eating against the dictates of his own conscience; he thereby lapses from spiritual integrity.

14:21 It is good not to eat flesh, nor to drink wine, nor *to do anything* **whereby thy brother stumbleth.**—This statement broadens the principle already set forth, so as to include abstinence from everything on the part of the strong which would be prejudicial to the weak.

14:22 The faith which thou hast, have thou to thyself before God.—This recalls verse 2. The appeal is still to the strong and provides a further reason for abstinence. The faith spoken of is that by which he who is strong regards it as lawful to partake of all kinds of meat. He is not called upon to renounce a principle or to think that anything was wrong which was not actually so, but rather to exercise his liberty with a view to the welfare of the weak brother. Faith is necessary indeed, but it is not to be displayed, as if to show one's superiority to those who have scruples about things. The responsibility is to act before God, that is, in the secrecy of communion with Him.

Happy is he that judgeth not himself in that which he approveth.—This follows closely with the preceding sentence and shows the value of faith so exercised. It also recalls the closing statement of verse 5, "Let each man be fully assured in his own mind." The happiness consists, not so much in being free from scruples about doing anything, but in being free from having to judge himself for running the risk of stumbling his brother. He may approve of eating meat, but if he abstains in order not to stumble the weak brother, he will be saved from having to pass sentence upon himself for his action.

14:23 But he that doubteth is condemned if he eat, because *he eateth* **not of faith;**—The strong brother is reminded that the weak brother who is influenced to act contrary to his conscience, and consequently is troubled about his act, is condemned; not that he comes under the condemnation referred to in chapter 8:1, but that he is proved to be guilty of having acted apart from faith, and therefore of displeasing the Lord. This, though addressed to the strong, is intended as a warning also to the weak.

and whatsoever is not of faith is sin,—Faith is the basis of the believer's relation to Christ, and should be the guiding principle of all his actions, leading him to do whatever he does because he belongs to Christ, whom it is his aim to please, and because he must give account at His Judgment Seat. If a believer acts from any other motive than that of faith, if he acts, for instance, through simple compliance with the opinion of another person, his act is sin. Right motives never justify wrong actions. What is evil cannot be excused on the ground of good intentions.

ROMANS

CHAPTER FIFTEEN

Glorifying God by Living in Harmony, 15:1–7

Introductory Note

In this section the support of the weak is urged, and the subject develops into the broader view of seeking one another's best interests. The whole is set in the light of the example of Christ.

15:1 Now we that are strong ought to bear the infirmities of the weak.—The word "ought" is in the position of emphasis. While this injunction is based upon those in chapter fourteen, it has especially in view what is about to be said of the example of Christ. So far the exhortations have been to avoid stumbling the weak, and to follow things which make for peace and edification. There is something more to be done. The strong must actually support the burdens of the weak by submitting to self-restraint. They must regard their self-denial not merely as so much virtuous abstinence but as a means of bearing the infirmities of the weak (cp. Gal. 6:2). The infirmities are those scruples which arise through weakness of faith.

and not to please ourselves.—A Christian can claim liberty as a believer, but he is never to use it as a means of self-pleasing. Refusal to bear the burdens of others is mere selfishness.

15:2 Let each one of us please his neighbor for that which is good, unto edifying.—Whatever makes for the edification of a fellow-believer is good. If I consult for the good of another I consult for his edification. To please my neighbor, in the sense of this verse, is not weakly to comply with his desires, but to act with a view to his lasting benefit.

15:3 For Christ also pleased not Himself; but, as it is written, The reproaches of them that reproached Thee fell upon Me.—We might have expected that the apostle would show how Christ acted for our good in accomplishing our salvation. Instead of this he gives the higher motive which filled the heart of Christ, that of the accomplishment of the Father's will, with the suffering involved therein, and quotes from the Septuagint of Psalm 69:9.

The force of the quotation lies in this, that if Christ, instead of acting in self-gratification, voluntarily endured the effects of man's hostility to God, and that with a view to saving us from the consequences of our sin, what an obligation have we to abstain from self-gratification, submitting to the restraint involved therein in order to advance the welfare of others! How insignificant is any inconvenience or suffering caused to us in comparison with the sufferings which Christ endured!

15:4 For whatsoever things were written aforetime were written for our learning,—The quotation in verse 3 is thus made the basis of a most important principle, namely, that all the Old Testament Scriptures are of permanent and binding value, as given to instruct us. Thus the particular quotation just recorded, while directly speaking of Christ, was written for our sakes, that we might receive and carry out the instruction and derive the comfort. The character of Christ in Psalm 69:9 was described that we might have the mind that was in Him.

That through patience and comfort of the Scriptures—The definite article is used in the original before both "patience" and "comfort," and here there is an advantage perhaps in translating by "the patience and the comfort of the Scriptures," that is to say, the patience and the comfort which they effect.

Both the patience which persistently endures and the comfort which animates and empowers are required in the fulfillment of the injunctions given to the weak and the strong. The strong, who exercise patience, and the weak, who are supported by the comfort, both derive it from the Scriptures.

we might have hope.—The patience and comfort imparted by the Scriptures inspire those who subject themselves to them with hope of the glory of God. While the definite article also occurs before hope, it is not necessarily to be rendered in this case.

15:5 Now the God of patience and of comfort—We may translate the definite articles, which are used here again, and render by "the God of the patience and the comfort," that is, those just mentioned in verse 5. From the Scripture as the source of patience and comfort we are pointed to God as the author of these qualities and this is made the basis of a desire for like-mindedness.

grant you to be of the same mind one with another—The fulfillment of this would banish all bitterness, harsh judgment, recrimination, and petty controversies.

according to Christ Jesus:—This recalls verse 3. In not pleasing Himself, but acting for our good, Christ manifested that patience which it is necessary for us to imitate if we are to fulfill the will of God in our attitude one toward another. The example as set by Christ is designed to manifest in us both patience and comfort and harmony. But this has a still higher object in view, as mentioned in the next verse.

15:6 that with one accord ye may with one mouth glorify the God and Father of our Lord Jesus Christ.—Unity of mind and harmony of testimony are essential if God is to be glorified by believers. Where such unity exists, the difficulties with which the apostle has been dealing in chapter fourteen vanish, and God will be glorified.

15:7 Wherefore receive ye one another, even as Christ also received you,—Cp. 14:3; what was there said of God is here said of Christ. The R.V. "you" is right.

to the glory of God.—This is to be taken with the immediately preceding statement "as Christ received you." The glory of God was the object in view in the reception of each by Christ, and the same object is to govern the attitude of believers one toward another; it is to be kindly and considerate, not a mere toleration, but a hearty reception.

Glorifying God—Gentile and Jew Alike, 15:8–13

15:8 For I say that Christ hath been made a minister of the circumcision for the truth of God,—The connection with the preceding verse might be put in this way: "Christ has received you to the glory of God, and this became possible because of His grace on behalf of the weak and the strong, for He became a servant of the Jews, for the sake of the truth of God, in order to confirm by this fulfillment the promises made to the fathers, and that by this means Gentiles might be brought into the blessings of salvation." Jews and Gentiles, weak and strong, both have then a common interest in this ministration of Christ, and so this becomes an additional motive for Christian forbearance.

that He might confirm the promises *given* **unto the fathers,**—Christ came to minister primarily to the Jewish people. He Himself said, "I was not sent but unto the lost sheep of the house of Israel" (Matt. 15:24. Cp. 10:6).

15:9 and that the Gentiles might glorify God for His mercy;—That Christ was a minister of the circumcision in the days of His flesh was but preliminary to the carrying out of the ministry of the gospel to all nations. Therefore Jewish believers should not pass censorious judgment upon gentile believers who claim liberty from certain religious scruples.

as it is written, Therefore will I give praise unto Thee among the Gentiles, and sing unto Thy Name.—This is from the Septuagint of Psalm 18:49. The language of David in celebrating his conquests over the nations is seen to be prophetically the language of Christ expressed through Gentile believers in giving thanks to God for their salvation. Ultimately also the prophecy will be fulfilled in the Millennial Day.

15:10 And again He saith, Rejoice, ye Gentiles, with His people.—This is taken from the close of the Song of Moses (Deut. 32:43), which gives a history of the nation of Israel from its earliest times till the overthrow of Antichrist and the gentile nations gathered together under him, and the setting up of Messiah's Millennial Kingdom. The sword of Jehovah will destroy "the head of the leaders of the enemy" (v. 42, R.V.), that is to say, the Antichrist himself. In view of the overthrow of the great persecutor and his associates, and the deliverance of the Jews, the joyful summons goes forth to the world, "Rejoice, O ye nations, with His people." The national blessing of gentile peoples is dependent upon the deliverance of the Jewish nation. The same principle has held good in things spiritual, and hence the apostle applies such passages to the Gospel.

15:11 And again, Praise the Lord, all ye Gentiles; and let all the people praise Him.—This is from the Septuagint of Psalm 117:1.

15:12 And again, Isaiah saith, There shall be the root of Jesse, and He that ariseth to rule over the Gentiles; on Him shall the Gentiles hope.—This closing quotation goes further than those preceding, and specifically mentions Christ as the subject of Old Testament predictions concerning the blessing designed for Jews and Gentiles. In Isaiah, again, the scope is millennial, and while the apostle's application is to the gospel, in this case it necessarily includes the future period as well. The reference to Christ as the root of Jesse intimates (1) His incarnation as a descendant of the father of David, and (2) His fruitfulness as the source of all divinely appointed prosperity for the nation.

The four quotations are taken from all three parts of the Old Testament, the Law (v. 10), the Psalms (vv. 9, 11), and the prophets (v. 12). Accordingly, the truth of the inclusion of Jew and Gentile in Christ through the gospel is shown to extend through the whole range of Old Testament prophecy. This adds point to the preceding exhortations as to mutual forbearance.

15:13 Now the God of hope—Literally, "the God of the hope," because He is the author of that hope and therein His grace is set before both Jew and Gentile in Christ. The hope is not mere expectancy; it carries with it the assurance of faith.

fill you with joy and peace in believing, that ye may abound in hope, in the power of the Holy Ghost.—This verse not only brings to a close the main part of the

Epistle but affords a final reason for concord among brethren, in view of the unifying character of the hope set before us. We shall be dwelling in harmony in the future, why not in the present?

Personal Explanations, Etc., 15:14 to 16:27

15:14 And I myself also am persuaded of you, my brethren, that ye yourselves are full of goodness,—*Agathosunē*, "goodness," signifies, not moral excellence of itself, but a disposition to do good, to show a kindly activity toward others.

filled with all knowledge, able also to admonish one another.—*Noutheteō*, "to admonish," is used of both instruction and admonition. The combination of goodness with knowledge is requisite for effective ministry in instructing and admonishing.

15:15 But I write more boldly toward you in some measure, as putting you again in remembrance, because of the grace that was given me of God,—This is a beautiful combination of humility with authority. He has a divinely imparted authority for writing, but the bestowal of it was an act of God's favor. He instructs them, not from the lofty pinnacle of an ecclesiastical authority, but as one who, whilst divinely commissioned, is a sharer with them of grace. Cp. 12:3.

15:16 that I should be a minister of Christ Jesus unto the Gentiles, ministering the gospel of God,—The verb *hierourgea*, "to minister," is again a term of priestly service; see the next note. It is used only here in the New Testament.

that the offering up of the Gentiles—The word *prosphora*, "an offering," is used here of the presentation of believers themselves to God.

might be made acceptable, being sanctified by the Holy Ghost.—Literally, "having been sanctified." This completes the references to the Levitical sacrificial offerings. (1) The apostle is, figuratively speaking, the priest, not by natural descent but by divine call; (2) the gentile believers are the offerers and the offering, presenting themselves as living sacrifices (12:1); (3) as the sacrifices of old were to be free from physical defect and must be cleansed with water, so the offering of believers themselves must be sanctified by the Holy Spirit, that all may be acceptable to God, in contrast to those sacrifices in which God had "no pleasure" (Heb. 10:6, 9).

The Holy Spirit is said to be the agent in sanctification in 2 Thessalonians 2:13; 1 Peter 1:2, and here only. Cp. also 1 Corinthians 6:11. In all these the sanctification is associated with the electing grace of God, and is a divine act preceding the acceptance of the gospel by the individual. This is indicated here by the use of the perfect participle "having been."

15:17 I have therefore my glorying in Christ Jesus in things pertaining to God.—There are two further reasons which justify his glorying: (1) it is "in Christ Jesus" and not in himself (2) it is "in things pertaining to God," *i.e.,* not pertaining to his own advantage and interests, but to the service of the gospel and its effects, which he has just described as an offering to God.

15:18 For I will not dare to speak of any things save those which Christ wrought through me, for the obedience of the Gentiles, by word and deed,—It is plain from verse 20 that he had in mind the fact that others were engaged in gospel work besides himself.

15:19 in the power of signs and wonders,—*Sēmeion,* "a sign," is "a token or indication, whether given by man to man, 2 Thessalonians 3:17; Matthew 26:48; or appointed by God to be observed by man, as circumcision was, Romans 4:11; or whether given by God in natural phenomena, Luke 21:25; or in the trend of human affairs, Matthew 16:3; or through His Son, John 2:11; 20:30; or His servants, Acts 5:12; 7:36; or whether given by Satan through his agents, Matthew 24:24; 2 Thessalonians 2:9; Revelation 16:14."

A wonder is "something strange, exceptional, causing the beholder to marvel. 'Power' declares the source to be supernatural; 'sign' expresses the purpose and appeals to the understanding; 'wonder' describes the effect upon the observer and appeals to the imagination."

in the power of the Holy Ghost;—Cp. verse 13, and see note there. Cp. also 1 Corinthians 2:4. This clause probably applies both to what was stated in verse 18 and to what has just preceded. The Holy Spirit was the agent not only in the preaching but also in the signs and wonders. The effectivity of gospel ministry depends, then, not upon human power of eloquence, but upon the Lord, who works all by the Holy Spirit.

so that from Jerusalem, and round about even unto Illyricum, I have fully preached the gospel of Christ;—Literally, "I have fulfilled," *plēroō.* Cp. 8:4; 13:8. The word is suggestive of both the geographical extent of his evangelical ministry, as in the context, and the accomplishment of his ministry itself.

15:20 Yea, making it my aim so to preach the Gospel, not where Christ was *already* named, that I might not build upon another man's foundation,—The motive for this no doubt lay considerably in the realization of the tremendous needs of regions unreached by the gospel but also from the determination to avoid "glorying in other men's labors" (see 2 Cor. 10:13–18).

15:21 but, as it is written, They shall see, to whom no tidings of Him came, and they who have not heard shall understand.—This quotation, from the Septuagint of Isaiah 52:15, confirms the statement as to the scope of the apostle's ministry.

Paul's Purpose to Visit Rome, and to Go Further, 15:22–33

15:22 Wherefore also I was hindered these many times from coming to you:— What prevented him from coming had been his effort to visit places where Christ had not been proclaimed, though the demands made upon him in this respect were not the only reasons.

15:23 but now, having no more any place in these regions, and having these many years a longing to come unto you,—To have the assurance that any particular service committed to us has been completed, is necessarily the outcome of the habit of walking with God and of our having received the guidance and help of the Holy Spirit.

15:24 whensoever I go unto Spain—Spain passed under Roman rule in 133 B.C., and became a "province," though the conquest of the whole country was not complete till 19 B.C. By the apostle's time it contained large numbers of Jews, and this would probably strengthen his desire to preach Christ there. There is some evidence that he did so. In an epistle to the Corinthians written by Clement of Rome, a follower of the apostle, it is stated that Paul "went to the end of the west."

(for I hope to see you in my journey, and to be brought on my way thitherward by you, if first in some measure I shall have been satisfied with your company)—The fact that, in our path of service for the Lord, circumstances take place very differently from our expectations and desires, affords no necessary indication that we are not being guided of God. On the contrary, our very disappointments issue in the accomplishment of far greater things than we anticipate, and always in the fulfillment of God's all-wise purposes. So it was with the character of Paul's actual stay in Rome. As an outcome of his imprisonments there the churches have had all his later epistles.

15:25, 26 but now, *I say,* I go unto Jerusalem, ministering unto the saints. For it hath been the good pleasure of Macedonia and Achaia—The districts stand for the churches in them. The two provinces comprise the whole of Greece.

to make a certain contribution for the poor among the saints that are at Jerusalem.—There was evidently a large number of poor amongst the saints. The arrangement referred to in Acts 2:45, for a community of goods, had left an aftermath of poverty. It could be in any case only a temporary expedient. The statement in this verse plays an important part in enabling us to fix the date of this Epistle. It must have been written soon after 2 Corinthians, and just before Paul's visit to Jerusalem, mentioned in Acts 20:21, that is, about the year A.D. 57.

15:27 Yea, it hath been their good pleasure; and their debtors they are. For if the Gentiles have been made partakers of their spiritual things,—That is, those blessings which primarily, in the providence of God, belonged to Israel, but which also appertain to the Gospel.

they owe it *to them* also to minister unto them in carnal things:—The verb *leitourgeō,* "to minister," is used here only in this Epistle. For the noun see 13:6.

15:28 When, therefore, I have accomplished this, and have sealed to them this fruit, I will go on by you unto Spain.—This phraseology indicates the sacredness in God's sight of ministering material assistance to the saints.

The material help was the fruit of his spiritual ministry to the saints in Greece. But this spiritual blessing to Gentiles emanated in the first place from the Jewish nation. Hence, in meeting the needs of the saints in Jerusalem, the churches of the Gentiles were but bringing forth the fruits of their having shared with them in spiritual things.

15:29 And I know that, when I come unto you, I shall come in the fullness of the blessing of Christ.—*Eulogia,* "blessing," here expresses the sum of the favor shown by God to man in Christ. The addition of the words "of the gospel" in the A.V. does not rest on good MS. authority.

"Would a forger, writing under the name of the apostle in the second century, have drawn a picture of the future so opposite to the way in which things really came to pass?" *(Godet).*

15:30 Now I beseech you, brethren, by our Lord Jesus Christ, and by the love of the Spirit,—This second ground of appeal might mean either the love which the Spirit of God shows, or the love which is exercised by believers as the outcome of the Spirit's work in their hearts; this latter is probably the meaning here.

that ye strive together with me in your prayers—The request is suggestive of the spiritual foes whose efforts are directed against the prayers of God's people. Cp. Daniel 10:12, 13; Ephesians 6:12, and Colossians 2:1.

to God for me;—The order in the original is "on my behalf toward God." which throws emphasis upon the latter words. Paul's personal trust in God, and the divine assurance given to him, did not make him independent of the prayers of the saints. Prayer is never rendered superfluous by any circumstances, not even by the knowledge of God's will and purpose. On the contrary, the revelation of that will is an incentive to prayer. See Ezekiel 36:37.

15:31 that I may be delivered from them that are disobedient in Judaea,—Unbelief is disobedience; faith is an act of obedience. See at 1:5; 16:26.

and *that* **my ministration which** *I have* **for Jerusalem, may be acceptable to the saints;**—Suggesting that, in addition to the opposition of unbelieving Jews, there was a likelihood of misunderstanding and prejudice on the part of Jewish Christians, especially those who had inclinations toward Judaism.

15:32 that I may come unto you in joy through the will of God, and together with you find rest.—God hears prayer, but the manner of the answer often differs from that which the suppliant anticipates.

15:33 Now the God of peace be with you all. Amen.—His request for prayer on their part leads him to offer prayer for them. The title, "the God of peace," frequent in the apostle's writings, was sometimes suggested by way of contrast with troubles amongst his readers, as in 1 Thessalonians 5:23; sometimes by the sufferings and distractions which his readers were experiencing, as in 2 Corinthians 13:11, cp. Hebrews 13:20; sometimes in anticipation of the fulfillment of his exhortations, as in Philippians 4:9. Here it seems to be set in contrast with the circumstances of danger to which he has just been referring.

ROMANS

CHAPTER SIXTEEN

16:1–27

16:1 I commend unto you—This is more than a mere mode of introduction; *sunistēmi* suggests the praise which our word "commendation" carries with it. Letters of commendation of a more formal character are referred to by him in 2 Corinthians 3:1, and became general in the intercourse of the churches, in order to provide safeguards against imposture. The commendation here given was not of this character.

Phoebe our sister, who is a servant of the church that is at Cenchrea:—This is the only instance in the New Testament of the use of the word *diakonos* of a woman. It denotes one who renders service of any character to another. There is no ground for assuming that Phoebe was a "deaconess."

16:2 that ye receive her in the Lord, worthily of the saints,—That is, in such a manner as befits those who bear the name of saints.

and that ye assist her in whatsoever matter she may have need of you: for she herself also hath been a succorer of many, and of mine own self.—*Prostatis,* "succorer," is a feminine of *prostatēs,* and is a word of dignity, evidently chosen instead of another which might have easily been used. It indicates the high, not to say honorable, position which perhaps she occupied.

16:3 Salute Prisca and Aquila my fellow workers in Christ Jesus,—Priscilla (see Acts 18:2) is the diminutive form of Prisca. Here and in Acts 18:18, and 2 Timothy 4:19, the wife's name comes first, perhaps suggesting that she was the more distinguished in Christian service. In 1 Corinthians 16:19, where they send salutations, the husband's name naturally comes first.

16:4 who for my life laid down their own necks;—The original has the singular, "neck," indicating that the phrase is figurative.

The actual character of the danger is not known, but his life was frequently in peril of one sort or another.

unto whom not only I give thanks, but also all the churches of the Gentiles:—This makes clear that the circumstance referred to was widely known, and suggests that it was not of very recent occurrence, sufficient time having elapsed for the news to spread among the churches. Paul was indeed grateful to them for their devotion to him; his statement about the gratitude of the churches not only is indicative of the deep-rooted affection which the churches entertained for him, it expresses what he realized, without any self-congratulation, that his love and service for God among them was valuable to them. The phrase "the churches of the Gentiles" signifies the churches which had been formed in the various gentile nations.

16:5 and *salute* **the church that is in their house.**—In Ephesus their house was a meetingplace for the saints (v. 5 with 1 Cor. 16:19). The character of their occupation enabled them to put a room at the disposal of the Lord's people for the purpose. Cp. Colossians 4:15; Philemon 2. There is no clear example of a separate building set apart for Christian worship within the Roman Empire before the third century.

Salute Epaenetus, my beloved, who is the firstfruits of Asia unto Christ.—That Epaenetus was the first saved as a result of the apostle's testimony would make him very dear to Paul.

16:6 Salute Mary, who bestowed much labor on you.—Two forms of the name Mary are found in the Greek text: Mariam, which represents the Hebrew Miriam, and thus is Jewish, denoting bitterness, and Maria(n), a gentile name. In the former case it is the only Hebrew name in the chapter. The latter is the more probable reading.

16:7 Salute Andronicus and Junias, my kinsmen, and my fellow prisoners, who are of note among the apostles,—That the apostle speaks of them as his kinsmen indicates: (1) that they were Jews; if so, his mention of them in this way is consistent with what he had said about his fellow-nationals already in this Epistle (cp. 9:3), or (2) that they were his blood relations; this seems not unlikely from the emphatic way in which he speaks of them.

who also have been in Christ before me.—Literally, "they have become in Christ before me." They were evidently among the very early disciples. If, then, they were Paul's relatives, he had family relations in Christ while he himself was persecuting the saints.

16:8 Salute Ampliatus my beloved in the Lord.—Ampliatus was a Roman slave name, and is frequently found so in inscriptions.

16:9 Salute Urbanus our fellow worker in Christ,—Urbanus is a name also found in a list of imperial freed men, which suggests that he may have obtained his liberty.

and Stachys my beloved.—Stachys is a Greek name, of masculine gender, and comparatively rare.

16:10 Salute Apelles the approved in Christ.—This suggests that he had in some way been tested, had stood the test, and had gained the approval and esteem of his brethren.

Salute them which are of the *household* **of Aristobulus.**—This refers to his slaves rather than his kinsmen.

16:11 Salute Herodian my kinsman.—He was probably therefore a Jew.

Salute them of the *household* **of Narcissus, which are in the Lord.**—Narcissus was probably another slave owner. The addition "which are in the Lord" makes clear that only some of this household were converted.

16:12 Salute Tryphena and Tryphosa, who labor in the Lord.—These were almost certainly sisters by natural relationship.

Salute Persis the beloved, which labored much in the Lord.—As her service is spoken of as in the past (contrast what is said of the two preceding sisters), she may have been in advanced years at this time.

16:13 Salute Rufus the chosen in the Lord, and his mother and mine.—Rufus is a Latin name. Possibly the person referred to is the same as that in Mark 15:21, whose father bore the cross of Christ. If so, it may be that the father was dead and his widow and Rufus were living at Ephesus. Rufus was "chosen in the Lord." This would scarcely refer to the election of grace, which is common to all believers, but indicates some special approval by which he was distinguished for his excellence or his usefulness in service to Christ.

16:14 Salute Asyncritus, Phlegon, Hermes, Patrobas, Hermas, and the brethren that are with them.—In places like Rome, where Christians came from various lands, meetings were held in different houses, there being no public building where large meetings of believers were possible, even had they been permissible. This seems to be indicated in the present phrase.

16:15 Salute Philologus and Julia, Nereus and his sister, and Olympas, and all the saints that are with them.—Julia was probably the wife of Philologus. Possibly Nereus and his sister were their children, and Olympas was of the same family or household.

16:16 Salute one another with a holy kiss.—*Philēma,* "a kiss," was an ordinary mode of greeting between those of the same sex. The kiss was to be "holy," *hagios,* i.e., free from everything unworthy of their calling as saints *(hagioi).*

Moreover there was to be freedom from prejudice arising from social distinctions, and from partiality toward those who were well-to-do. In the assembly, masters and servants would thus salute one another with freedom from an attitude of condescension on the one part, and from disrespect on the other.

All the churches of Christ salute you.—The phrase "the churches of Christ" is found here only in the New Testament. It marks them in their relationship to Christ, as His possession.

16:17 Now I beseech you, brethren, mark them which are causing the divisions and occasions of stumbling,—It has been suggested that those of whom he is now speaking promulgated the errors of Antinomianism, with which he had dealt in chapter six, or belonged to the party referred to in chapter fourteen. Possibly the opposition was that arising from Judaistic teachings, with which Paul and his fellow-laborers were continually confronted.

contrary to the doctrine which ye learned and turn away from them.—The "ye" bears emphasis, which serves forcibly to distinguish their true teachings from the false. In exhorting them to turn away from the false teachers, the apostle is not speaking of excommunication, but of personal dissociation from the offenders.

16:18 For they that are such serve not our Lord Christ,—There is a certain stress on the negative, which practically conveys the thought of refusing to serve.

but their own belly;—A phrase indicative of any base interest, not necessarily gross, sensual indulgence, as in Philippians 3:19, though this is possibly also intended.

and by their smooth and fair speech—The word *chrēstologia* is suggestive of an insinuating mode of speech, and one which simulates goodness. *Eulogia,* which usually signifies "blessing," here indicates a fine style of utterance with the appearance of reasonableness.

they beguile the hearts of the innocent.—He who adopts an attitude of never expecting evil is liable to be deceived. To those who are not instructed in the ways of God as revealed in Scripture, the smooth and fair speech of those who propagate false teaching is especially dangerous. Safety lies in a knowledge of, and adherence to, the Word of God.

16:19 For your obedience is come abroad unto all men. I rejoice therefore over you: but I would have you wise unto that which is good, and simple unto that which is evil.—They were to be wise in the acceptance and pursuit of that which is according to the will of God, and so beneficial in its effects. Their attitude, therefore, was to be

one which would keep them free from taint. The word *akeraios,* "simple," and, in the only other two places where it occurs, "harmless" (Matt. 10:16; Phil. 2:15), means, literally, "without admixture." It was used of wine unmingled with water, of unalloyed metal, etc. Hence it means "without admixture of evil." Here, then, it would mean that his desire for them was that they might be untainted by the influences of evil teachers and the divisions and stumbling blocks caused thereby. Thus would they be wise in adherence to the truth. If we are to be kept from admixture of what is baneful we must be steadfast in the faith, abiding in the truth.

16:20 And the God of peace shall bruise Satan under your feet shortly.—This promise would seem to have immediate reference to the efforts of those who were antagonistic to the peace and harmony of the saints. Such efforts are put forth by Satan unremittingly and are continued till the promise is fulfilled by God. Cp. what is said about the Judaizing opponents in 2 Corinthians 11:12-15, where they are spoken of as ministers of Satan. There is also doubtless a reference to the promise in Genesis 3:15. The phrase *en tachei,* "shortly," may mean "quickly," "with speed." This is the meaning in Luke 18:8; Acts 12:7; 22:18; and perhaps in Revelation 1:1; 22:6. It also means "soon," at a time not far distant, as in Acts 25:4.

The grace of our Lord Jesus Christ be with you.—There is no real indication that the apostle primarily intended his Epistle to end here. Probably this is to be taken in immediate connection with the preceding context, in view of what is intimated about the opposition of Satan.

16:21 Timothy my fellow-worker saluteth you;—From 2 Corinthians 1:1, we learn that Timothy was with Paul in Macedonia when he wrote that Epistle (that was in the latter part of A.D. 57). Possibly the apostle came on to Corinth alone. He was with him just before setting out from Corinth for Jerusalem (Acts 20:4).

and Lucius and Jason and Sosipater, my kinsmen.—The first of these may have been

Lucius of Cyrene (Acts 13:1); the second the Jason mentioned in Acts 17:5; the third name is a longer form of Sopater, as in Acts 20:4.

16:22 I Tertius, who write the epistle, salute you in the Lord.—That the apostle's amanuensis should insert this salutation is, firstly, a mark of the genuineness of the Epistle, as no forger would have mentioned his doing so; secondly, an instance of Paul's characteristic courtesy, it would not have been like him to dictate such a salutation in the third person; thirdly, of the sympathetic spirit and wholehearted cooperation of this brother in the work in which the apostle was engaged. His spiritual joy therein is likewise intimated by his mode of salutation "in the Lord."

16:23 Gaius my host, and of the whole church, saluteth you.—If Gaius was one of the elders of the church at Corinth, he certainly fulfilled the qualification of an elder or bishop, as mentioned in 1 Timothy 3:2.

This Gaius is almost certainly the one of 1 Corinthians 1:14 and probably the Titus Justus of Acts 18:1–8, his full name being Gaius Titus Justus, with whom Paul lodged on his first visit to Corinth after he stayed with Aquila.

Erastus the treasurer of the city saluteth you—This was possibly the same Erastus whom Paul sent with Timothy into Macedonia before leaving Ephesus (Acts 19:22), and to whom he refers in 2 Timothy 4:20, as having remained at Corinth. The fact that the one here mentioned held a position of considerable importance in the city is not sufficient in itself to make the identification unlikely, as he may have relinquished his position after the time of the writing of the present Epistle.

and Quartus, the brother.—The article does not imply that he was related to Erastus naturally, or any of those who had been mentioned; it suggests rather that he was known both to writer and readers as a brother in the Lord.

16:25 Now to Him that is able to stablish you according to my gospel—The spiritual confirmation of the saints is in keeping with the teaching of the gospel, which not only proclaims remission of sins and justification through faith (3:21—5, end), but a new

life in Christ, which is maintained by the power of the indwelling Spirit (chh. 6—8), and effects the fulfillment of all righteousness (12:15).

and the preaching of Jesus Christ, according to the revelation of the mystery—That is, the gospel and the preaching of Jesus Christ, were in accordance with the revelation of the mystery, or, rather, "a mystery"; the absence of the article indicates that the mystery referred to is one among others. In speaking of the revelation of the mystery, he does not here imply that a special revelation had been given to him; he is merely stating in a general way that what had been hidden before by God had now been revealed. It was of another mystery that he wrote in 11:25.

which hath been kept in silence through times eternal,—There had been no Divine pronouncement on the subject. God's providential dealings with man are varied though continuous. His plans have unfolded gradually, each detail having its own divinely predetermined time for its disclosure, each being given not only as a self-revelation of His nature, His attributes and counsels, but also appropriately to the conditions and needs of the particular period allotted to it.

16:26 but now is manifested, and by the scriptures of the prophets,—Literally, "by prophetic writings." The apostle is referring to the means by which the manifestation of the mystery was being given, and for this purpose his own inspired writings were being used. He is pointing, therefore, not to Old Testament Scriptures, for this relevation had not been given through them, but to those parts of the New Testament which had already been, and were in process of being, written. This Epistle which he had now completed formed part of those prophetic writings. It is true that the Old Testament Scriptures were prophetic writings, and that the apostles made use of them in unfolding the truth of the mystery but that in itself would not adequately interpret his words here.

according to the commandment of the eternal God, is made known unto all the nations unto obedience of faith;—That is, faith which is characterized by obedience; for faith is an act of submission to God, a fulfillment of His command (John 6:29, and 1 John 3:23).

16:27 to the only wise God,—Or, rather, "to God only wise." These last two words bear emphasis, and the description is appropriate to all that the apostle has now stated about the Divine purpose. The title is also an appropriate close to the whole Epistle.

through Jesus Christ, to whom be glory forever. Amen.—This ascription of praise is undoubtedly to God the Father, but the apostle has framed the order of his words that Christ may likewise, at least by implication, be the subject of the praise and adoration by which the being, character and attributes of God are recognized by His people.